A Heron Books Collection

HISTORY OF ENGLAND

LORD MACAULAY

HISTORY
OF ENGLAND

To the Death of William III

VOL. III

HERON BOOKS

CONTENTS

OF

THE THIRD VOLUME.

CHAPTER XIII.

CHAPTER XIV.

CHAPTER XV.

CHAPTER XVI.

CHAPTER XVII.

CHAPTER XVIII.

CHAPTER XIX.

LIST OF ILLUSTRATIONS

HISTORY OF ENGLAND.

CHAPTER XIII.

THE violence of revolutions is generally proportioned to the degree of the maladministration which has produced them. It is therefore not strange that the government of Scotland, having been during many years far more oppressive and corrupt than the government of England, should have fallen with a far heavier ruin. The movement against the last king of the House of Stuart was in England conservative, in Scotland destructive. The English complained, not of the law, but of the violation of the law. They rose up against the first magistrate merely in order to assert the supremacy of the law. They were for the most part strongly attached to the Church established by law. Even in applying that extraordinary remedy to which an extraordinary emergency compelled them to have recourse, they deviated as little as possible from the ordinary methods prescribed by the law. The Convention which met at Westminster, though summoned by irregular writs, was constituted on the exact model of a regular Great Council of the Realm. No man was invited to the Upper House whose right to sit there was not clear. The knights and burgesses of the Lower House were chosen by those electors who would have been entitled to send members to a Parliament called under the great seal. The franchises of the forty shilling freeholder, of the householder paying scot and lot, of the burgage tenant, of the liveryman of London, of the Master of Arts of Oxford, were respected. The sense of the constituent bodies was taken with as little violence on the part of mobs, with as little trickery on the part of returning officers, as at any general election of that age. When at length the Estates met, their

The Revolution more violent in Scotland than in England.

deliberations were carried on with perfect freedom and in strict accordance with ancient forms. There was indeed, after the first flight of James, an alarming anarchy in London and in some parts of the country. But that anarchy nowhere lasted longer than forty-eight hours. From the day on which William reached Saint James's, not even the most unpopular agents of the fallen government, not even the ministers of the Roman Catholic Church, had anything to fear from the fury of the populace.

In Scotland the course of events was very different. There the law itself was a grievance; and James had perhaps incurred more unpopularity by enforcing it than by violating it. The Church established by law was the most odious institution in the realm. The tribunals had pronounced some sentences so flagitious, the Parliament had passed some Acts so oppressive, that, unless those sentences and those Acts were treated as nullities, it would be impossible to bring together a Convention commanding the public respect and expressing the public opinion. It was hardly to be expected, for example, that the Whigs, in this day of their power, would endure to see their hereditary leader, the son of a martyr, the grandson of a martyr, excluded from the Parliament House in which nine of his ancestors had sate as Earls of Argyle, and excluded by a judgment on which the whole kingdom cried shame. Still less was it to be expected that they would suffer the election of members for counties and towns to be conducted according to the provisions of the existing law. For under the existing law no elector could vote without swearing that he renounced the Covenant, and that he acknowledged the Royal supremacy in matters ecclesiastical.* Such an oath no rigid Presbyterian could take. If such an oath had been exacted, the constituent bodies would have been merely small knots of prelatists: the business of devising securities against oppression would have been left to the oppressors; and the great party which had been most active in effecting the Revolution would, in an assembly sprung from the Revolution, have had not a single representative.†

William saw that he must not think of paying to the laws of Scotland that scrupulous respect which he had wisely and righteously paid to the laws of England. It was absolutely necessary that he should determine by his own authority

---

* Act. Parl. Scot., Aug. 31. 1681.
† Balcarras's Memoirs; Short History of the Revolution in Scotland in a letter from a Scotch gentleman in Amsterdam to his friend in London, 1712.

how that Convention which was to meet at Edinburgh should be chosen, and that he should assume the power of annulling some judgments and some statutes. He accordingly summoned to the Parliament House several Lords who had been deprived of their honours by sentences which the general voice loudly condemned as unjust; and he took on himself to dispense with the Act which deprived Presbyterians of the elective franchise.

The consequence was that the choice of almost all the shires and burghs fell on Whig candidates. The defeated party complained loudly of foul play, of the rudeness of the populace, and of the partiality of the presiding magistrates; and these complaints were in many cases well founded. It is not under such rulers as Lauderdale and Dundee that nations learn justice and moderation.* Elections for the Convention.

Nor was it only at the elections that the popular feeling, so long and so severely compressed, exploded with violence. The heads and the hands of the martyred Whigs were taken down from the gates of Edinburgh, carried in procession by great multitudes to the cemeteries, and laid in the earth with solemn respect.† It would have been well if the public enthusiasm had manifested itself in no less praiseworthy form. Unhappily throughout a large part of Scotland the clergy of the Established Church were, to use the phrase then common, rabbled. The morning of Christmas day was fixed for the commencement of these outrages. For nothing disgusted the rigid Covenanter more than the reverence paid by the prelatist to the ancient holidays of the Church. That such reverence may be carried to an absurd extreme is true. But a philosopher may perhaps be inclined to think the opposite extreme not less absurd, and may ask why religion should reject the aid of associations which exist in every nation sufficiently civilised to have a calendar, and which are found by experience to have a powerful and often a salutary effect. The Puritan, who was, in general, but too ready to follow precedents and analogies drawn from the history and jurisprudence of the Jews might have found in the Old Testament quite as clear warrant for keeping festivals in honour of great events as for assassinating bishops and refusing quarter to captives. He certainly did not learn from his master, Calvin, to hold such festivals in abhorrence; for it was in consequence Rabbling of the Episcopal Clergy.

* Balcarras's Memoirs; Life of James, ii. 341.
† A Memorial for His Highness the Prince of Orange in relation to the Affairs of Scotland, by two Persons of Quality, 1689.

of the strenuous exertions of Calvin that Christmas was, after
an interval of some years, again observed by the citizens of
Geneva.* But there had arisen in Scotland Calvinists who
were to Calvin what Calvin was to Laud. To these austere
fanatics a holiday was an object of positive disgust and
hatred. They long continued in their solemn manifestoes
to reckon it among the sins which would one day bring down
some fearful judgment on the land that the Court of Session
took a vacation in the last week of December.†

On Christmas day, therefore, the Covenanters held armed
musters by concert in many parts of the western shires. Each
band marched to the nearest manse, and sacked the cellar
and larder of the minister, which at that season were probably better stocked than usual. The priest of Baal was reviled and insulted, sometimes beaten, sometimes ducked. His
furniture was thrown out of the windows; his wife and
children turned out of doors in the snow. He was then
carried to the marketplace, and exposed during some time
as a malefactor. His gown was torn to shreds over his head;
if he had a prayer book in his pocket it was burned; and he
was dismissed with a charge, never, as he valued his life, to
officiate in the parish again. The work of reformation having been thus completed, the reformers locked up the church
and departed with the keys. In fairness to these men it must
be owned that they had suffered such oppression as may excuse, though it cannot justify, their violence; and that, though
they were rude even to brutality, they do not appear to have
been guilty of any intentional injury to life or limb.‡

The disorder spread fast. In Ayrshire, Clydesdale, Nithis-
dale, Annandale, every parish was visited by these turbulent
zealots. About two hundred curates,—so the episcopal parish

* See Calvin's letter to Haller, iv.
Non. Jan. 1551: "Priusquam urbem un-
quam ingrederer, nullæ prorsus erant
feriæ præter diem Dominicum. Ex quo
sum revocatus hoc temperamentum quæ-
sivi, ut Christi natalis celebraretur."

† In the Act, Declaration, and Testimony of the Seceders, dated in December 1736, it is said that countenance is
given by authority of Parliament to the
observation of Holidays in Scotland, by
the vacation of our most considerable
Courts of Justice in the latter end of
December." This is declared to be a
national sin, and a ground of the Lord's
indignation. In March, 1758, the Associate Synod addressed a Solemn Warning
to the nation, in which the same com-

plaint was repeated. A poor crazy creature, whose nonsense has been thought
worthy of being reprinted even in our
own time, says: "I leave my testimony
against the abominable Act of the pretended Queen Anne and her pretended
British, really Brutish Parliament, for
enacting the observance of that which is
called the Yule Vacance."—The Dying
Testimony of William Wilson, sometime
Schoolmaster in Park, in the Parish of
Douglas, aged 68, who died in 1757.

‡ An Account of the Present Persecu-
tion of the Church in Scotland, in several
Letters, 1690; The Case of the afflicted
Clergy in Scotland, truly represented,
1690; Faithful Contendings Displayed ·
Burnet, i. 805.

priests were called,—were expelled. The graver Covenanters, while they applauded the fervour of their riotous brethren, were apprehensive that proceedings so irregular might give scandal, and learned, with especial concern, that here and there an Achan had disgraced the good cause by stooping to plunder the Canaanites whom he ought only to have smitten. A general meeting of ministers and elders was called for the purpose of preventing such discreditable excesses. In this meeting it was determined that, for the future, the ejection of the established clergy should be performed in a more ceremonious manner. A form of notice was drawn up and served on every curate in the Western Lowlands who had not yet been rabbled. This notice was simply a threatening letter, commanding him to quit his parish peaceably, on pain of being turned out by force.*

The Scottish Bishops, in great dismay, sent the Dean of Glasgow to plead the cause of their persecuted Church at Westminster. The outrages committed by the Covenanters were in the highest degree offensive to William, who had, in the south of the island, protected even Benedictines and Franciscans from insult and spoliation. But, though he had, at the request of a large number of the noblemen and gentlemen of Scotland, taken on himself provisionally the executive administration of that kingdom, the means of maintaining order there were not at his command. He had not a single regiment north of the Tweed, or indeed within many miles of that river. It was vain to hope that mere words would quiet a nation which had not, in any age, been very amenable to control, and which was now agitated by hopes and resentments, such as great revolutions, following great oppressions, naturally engender. A proclamation was however put forth, directing that all people should lay down their arms, and that, till the Convention should have settled the government, the clergy of the Established Church should be suffered to reside on their cures without molestation. But this proclamation, not being supported by troops, was little regarded. On the very day after it was published at Glasgow, the venerable Cathedral of that city, almost the only fine church of the middle ages which stands uninjured in Scotland, was attacked by a crowd of Presbyterians from the meeting houses, with whom were mingled many of their fiercer brethren from the hills. It was a Sunday: but to rabble a congregation of

---

* The form of notice will be found in the book entitled Faithful Contendings Displayed.

prelatists was held to be a work of necessity and mercy. The worshippers were dispersed, beaten, and pelted with snowballs. It was indeed asserted that some wounds were inflicted with much more formidable weapons.*

State of Edinburgh.

Edinburgh, the seat of government, was in a state of anarchy. The Castle, which commanded the whole city, was still held for James by the Duke of Gordon. The common people were generally Whigs. The College of Justice, a great forensic society composed of judges, advocates, writers to the signet, and solicitors, was the stronghold of Toryism: for a rigid test had during some years excluded Presbyterians from all the departments of the legal profession. The lawyers, some hundreds in number, formed themselves into a battalion of infantry, and for a time effectually kept down the multitude. They paid, however, so much respect to William's authority as to disband themselves when his proclamation was published. But the example of obedience which they had set was not imitated. Scarcely had they laid down their weapons when Covenanters from the west, who had done all that was to be done in the way of pelting and hustling the curates of their own neighbourhood, came dropping into Edinburgh, by tens and twenties, for the purpose of protecting, or, if need should be, of overawing the Convention. Glasgow alone sent four hundred of these men. It could hardly be doubted that they were directed by some leader of great weight. They showed themselves little in any public place: but it was known that every cellar was filled with them; and it might well be apprehended that, at the first signal, they would pour forth from their caverns, and appear armed round the Parliament House.†

The question of an Union between England and Scotland raised.

It might have been expected that every patriotic and enlightened Scotchman would have earnestly desired to see the agitation appeased, and some government established which might be able to protect property and to enforce the law. An imperfect settlement which could be speedily made might well appear to such a man preferable to a perfect settlement which must be the work of time. Just at this moment, however, a party, strong both in numbers and in abilities, raised a new and most important question, which seemed not unlikely to prolong the interregnum till the autumn. This

---

* Account of the Present Persecution, 1690; Case of the afflicted Clergy, 1690; A true Account of that Interruption that was made of the Service of God on Sunday last, being the 17th of February,

1689, signed by James Gibson, acting for the Lord Provost of Glasgow.

† Balcarras's Memoirs Mackay's Memoirs.

party maintained that the Estates ought not immediately to declare William and Mary King and Queen, but to propose to England a treaty of union, and to keep the throne vacant till such a treaty should be concluded on terms advantageous to Scotland.*

It may seem strange that a large portion of a people, whose patriotism, exhibited, often in a heroic, and sometimes in a comic form, has long been proverbial, should have been willing, nay impatient, to surrender an independence which had been, through many ages, dearly prized and manfully defended. The truth is that the stubborn spirit which the arms of the Plantagenets and Tudors had been unable to subdue had begun to yield to a very different kind of force. Customhouses and tariffs were rapidly doing what the carnage of Falkirk and Halidon, of Flodden and Pinkie, had failed to do. Scotland had some experience of the effects of an union. She had, near forty years before, been united to England on such terms as England, flushed with conquest, chose to dictate. That union was inseparably associated in the minds of the vanquished people with defeat and humiliation. And yet even that union, cruelly as it had wounded the pride of the Scots, had promoted their prosperity. Cromwell, with wisdom and liberality rare in his age, had established the most complete freedom of trade between the dominant and the subject country. While he governed, no prohibition, no duty, impeded the transit of commodities from any part of the island to any other. His navigation laws imposed no restraint on the trade of Scotland. A Scotch vessel was at liberty to carry a Scotch cargo to Barbadoes, and to bring the sugars of Barbadoes into the port of London.† The rule of the Protector therefore had been propitious to the industry and to the physical wellbeing of the Scottish people. Hating him and cursing him, they could not help thriving under him, and often, during the administration of their legitimate princes, looked back with regret to the golden days of the usurper.‡

* Burnet, ii. 21.

† Scobell, 1654, cap. 9.; and Oliver's Ordinance in Council of the 12th of April in the same year.

‡ Burnet and Fletcher of Saltoun mention the prosperity of Scotland under the Protector, but ascribe it to a cause quite inadequate to the production of such an effect. "There was," says Burnet, "a considerable force of about seven or eight thousand men kept in Scotland. The pay of the army brought so much money into the kingdom that it continued all that while in a very flourishing state. . . . . . . We always reckon those eight years of usurpation a time of great peace and prosperity." "During the time of the usurper Cromwell," says Fletcher, "we imagined ourselves to be in a tolerable condition with respect to the last particular (trade and money) by reason of that expense which was made in the realm by those forces that kept us in subjection." The true explanation of

The Restoration came, and changed everything. The Scots regained their independence, and soon began to find that independence had its discomfort as well as its dignity. The English Parliament treated them as aliens and as rivals. A new Navigation Act put them on almost the same footing with the Dutch. High duties, and in some case prohibitory duties, were imposed on the products of Scottish industry. It is not wonderful that a nation eminently industrious, shrewd, and enterprising, a nation which, having been long kept back by a sterile soil and a severe climate, was just beginning to prosper in spite of these disadvantages, and which found its progress suddenly stopped, should think itself cruelly treated. Yet there was no help. Complaint was vain. Retaliation was impossible. The Sovereign, even if he had the wish, had not the power, to bear himself evenly between his large and his small kingdom, between the kingdom from which he drew an annual revenue of a million and a half and the kingdom from which he drew an annual revenue of little more than sixty thousand pounds. He dared neither to refuse his assent to any English law injurious to the trade of Scotland, nor to give his assent to any Scotch law injurious to the trade of England.

The complaints of the Scotch, however, were so loud that Charles, in 1667, appointed Commissioners to arrange the terms of a commercial treaty between the two British kingdoms. The conferences were soon broken off; and all that passed while they continued proved that there was only one way in which Scotland could obtain a share of the commercial prosperity which England at that time enjoyed.* The Scotch must become one people with the English. The Parliament which had hitherto sate at Edinburgh must be incorporated with the Parliament which sate at Westminster. The sacrifice could not but be painfully felt by a brave and haughty people, who had, during twelve generations, regarded the southern domination with deadly aversion, and whose hearts still swelled at the thought of the death of Wallace and of the triumphs of Bruce. There were doubtless many punctilious patriots who would have strenuously opposed an

the phænomena about which Burnet and Fletcher blundered so grossly will be found in a pamphlet entitled, "Some seasonable and modest Thoughts partly occasioned by and partly concerning the Scotch East India Company," Edinburgh, 1696. See the proceedings of the Wednesday Club in Friday Street upon the

subject of an Union with Scotland, Dececember 1705. See also the seventh Chapter of Mr. Burton's valuable History of Scotland.

* See the paper in which the demands of the Scotch Commissioners are set forth. It will be found in the Appendix to De Foe's History of the Union, No. 13.

union even if they could have foreseen that the effect of an union would be to make Glasgow a greater city than Amsterdam, and to cover the dreary Lothians with harvests and woods, neat farmhouses and stately mansions. But there was also a large class which was not disposed to throw away great and substantial advantages in order to preserve mere names and ceremonies; and the influence of this class was such that, in the year 1670, the Scotch Parliament made direct overtures to England.* The King undertook the office of mediator; and negotiators were named on both sides: but nothing was concluded.

The question, having slept during eighteen years, was suddenly revived by the Revolution. Different classes, impelled by different motives, concurred on this point. With merchants, eager to share in the advantages of the West Indian Trade, were joined active and aspiring politicians who wished to exhibit their abilities in a more conspicuous theatre than the Scottish Parliament House, and to collect riches from a more copious source than the Scottish treasury. The cry for union was swelled by the voices of some artful Jacobites, who merely wished to cause discord and delay, and who hoped to attain this end by mixing up with the difficult question which it was the especial business of the Convention to settle another question more difficult still. It is probable that some who disliked the ascetic habits and rigid discipline of the Presbyterians wished for an union as the only mode of maintaining prelacy in the northern part of the island. In an united Parliament the English members must greatly preponderate; and in England the Bishops were held in high honour by the great majority of the population. The Episcopal Church of Scotland, it was plain, rested on a narrow basis, and would fall before the first attack. The Episcopal Church of Great Britain might have a foundation broad and solid enough to withstand all assaults.

Whether, in 1689, it would have been possible to effect a civil union without a religious union may well be doubted. But there can be no doubt that a religious union would have been one of the greatest calamities that could have befallen either kingdom. The union accomplished in 1707 has indeed been a great blessing both to England and to Scotland. But it has been a blessing because, in constituting one State, it left two Churches. The political interest of the contracting parties was the same: but the ecclesiastical dispute

* Act. Parl. Scot., July 30. 1670.

between them was one which admitted of no compromise.
They could therefore preserve harmony only by agreeing to
differ. Had there been an amalgamation of the hierarchies,
there never would have been an amalgamation of the nations.
Successive Mitchells would have fired at successive Sharpes.
Five generations of Claverhouses would have butchered five
generations of Camerons. Those marvellous improvements
which have changed the face of Scotland would never have
been effected. Plains now rich with harvests would have
remained barren moors. Waterfalls which now turn the
wheels of immense factories would have resounded in a
wilderness. New Lanark would still have been a sheepwalk,
and Greenock a fishing hamlet. What little strength Scotland could, under such a system, have possessed must, in an
estimate of the resources of Great Britain, have been, not
added, but deducted. So encumbered, our country never
could have held, either in peace or in war, a place in the
first rank of nations. We are unfortunately not without the
means of judging of the effect which may be produced on
the moral and physical state of a people by establishing, in
the exclusive enjoyment of riches and dignity, a Church
loved and reverenced only by the few, and regarded by the
many with religious and national aversion. One such Church
is quite burden enough for the energies of one empire.

Wish of the
English
Low
Church-
men to
preserve
Episcopacy
in Scotland

But these things, which to us, who have been taught by
a bitter experience, seem clear, were by no means clear in
1689, even to very tolerant and enlightened politicians. In
truth the English Low Churchmen were, if possible, more
anxious than the English High Churchmen to preserve Episcopacy in Scotland. It is a remarkable fact that Burnet,
who was always accused of wishing to establish the Calvinistic discipline in the south of the island, incurred great
unpopularity among his own countrymen by his efforts to
uphold prelacy in the north. He was doubtless in error :
but his error is to be attributed to a cause which does him no
discredit. His favourite object, an object unattainable indeed,
yet such as might well fascinate a large intellect and a benevolent heart, had long been an honourable treaty between the
Anglican Church and the Nonconformists. He thought it
most unfortunate that one opportunity of concluding such a
treaty should have been lost at the time of the Restoration.
It seemed to him that another opportunity was afforded by
the Revolution. He and his friends were eagerly pushing
forward Nottingham's Comprehension Bill, and were flatter-

ing themselves with vain hopes of success. But they felt that there could hardly be a Comprehension in one of the two British kingdoms, unless there were also a Comprehension in the other. Concession must be purchased by concession. If the Presbyterian pertinaciously refused to listen to any terms of compromise where he was strong, it would be almost impossible to obtain for him liberal terms of compromise where he was weak. Bishops must therefore be allowed to keep their sees in Scotland, in order that divines not ordained by Bishops might be allowed to hold rectories and canonries in England.

Thus the cause of the Episcopalians in the north and the cause of the Presbyterians in the south were bound up together in a manner which might well perplex even a skilful statesman. It was happy for our country that the momentous question which excited so many strong passions, and which presented itself in so many different points of view, was to be decided by such a man as William. He listened to Episcopalians, to Latitudinarians, to Presbyterians, to the Dean of Glasgow who pleaded for the apostolical succession, to Burnet who represented the danger of alienating the Anglican clergy, to Carstairs who hated prelacy with the hatred of a man whose thumbs were deeply marked by the screws of prelatists. Surrounded by these eager advocates, William remained calm and impartial. He was indeed eminently qualified by his situation as well as by his personal qualities to be the umpire in that great contention. He was the King of a prelatical kingdom. He was the Prime Minister of a presbyterian republic. His unwillingness to offend the Anglican Church of which he was the head, and his unwillingness to offend the reformed Churches of the Continent which regarded him as a champion divinely sent to protect them against the French tyranny, balanced each other, and kept him from leaning unduly to either side. His conscience was perfectly neutral. For it was his deliberate opinion that no form of ecclesiastical polity was of divine institution. He dissented equally from the school of Laud and from the school of Cameron, from the men who held there could not be a Christian Church without Bishops, and from the men who held that there could not be a Christian Church without synods. Which form of government should be adopted was in his judgment a question of mere expediency. He would probably have preferred a temper between the two rival systems, a hierarchy in which the chief spiritual functionaries should have been something more than moderators

Opinions of William about Church government in Scotland.

and something less than prelates.   But he was far too wise a
man to think of settling such a matter according to his own personal tastes. He determined therefore that, if there was on both
sides a disposition to compromise, he would act as mediator.
But, if it should appear that the public mind of England and
the public mind of Scotland had taken the ply strongly in opposite directions, he would not attempt to force either nation into
conformity with the opinion of the other. He would suffer each
to have its own church, and would content himself with re-
straining both churches from persecuting nonconformists, and
from encroaching on the functions of the civil magistrate.

The language which he held to those Scottish Episcopalians
who complained to him of their sufferings and implored his
protection was well weighed and well guarded, but clear and
ingenuous. He wished, he said, to preserve, if possible, the
institution to which they were so much attached, and to grant,
at the same time, entire liberty of conscience to that party
which could not be reconciled to any deviation from the Presbyterian model.   But the Bishops must take care that they did
not, by their own rashness and obstinacy, put it out of his
power to be of any use to them.   They must also distinctly
understand that he was resolved not to force on Scotland by
the sword a form of ecclesiastical government which she
detested. If, therefore, it should be found that prelacy could
be maintained only by arms, he should yield to the general
sentiment, and should merely do his best to obtain for the
Episcopalian minority permission to worship God in freedom
and safety.*

Com-
parative
strength of
religious
parties in
Scotland.

It is not likely that, even if the Scottish Bishops had, as
William recommended, done all that meekness and prudence
could do to conciliate their countrymen, episcopacy could, under any modification, have been maintained.   It was indeed
asserted by writers of that generation, and has been repeated
by writers of our generation, that the Presbyterians were not,
before the Revolution, the majority of the people of Scotland.†
But in this assertion there is an obvious fallacy.   The effective strength of sects is not to be ascertained merely by counting heads.   An established church, a dominant church, a
church which has the exclusive possession of civil honours and

* Burnet, ii. 23.
† See, for example, a pamphlet entitled "Some questions resolved concerning
episcopal and presbyterian government
in Scotland, 1690." One of the questions
is, whether Scottish presbytery be agreeable to the general inclinations of that
people.   The author answers the question in the negative, on the ground that
the upper and middle classes had generally conformed to the episcopal Church
before the Revolution.

emoluments, will always rank among its nominal members multitudes who have no religion at all; multitudes who, though not destitute of religion, attend little to theological disputes, and have no scruple about conforming to the mode of worship which happens to be established; and multitudes who have scruples about conforming, but whose scruples have yielded to worldly motives. On the other hand, every member of an oppressed church is a man who has a very decided preference for that church. Every person who, in the time of Diocletian, joined in celebrating the Christian mysteries might reasonably be supposed to be a firm believer in Christ. But it may well be doubted whether one single Pontiff or Augur in the Roman Senate was a firm believer in Jupiter. In Mary's reign, everybody who attended the secret meetings of the Protestants was a real Protestant: but hundreds of thousands went to mass, who, as appeared before she had been dead a month, were not real Roman Catholics. If, under the Kings of the House of Stuart, when a Presbyterian was excluded from political power and from the learned professions, was daily annoyed by informers, by tyrannical magistrates, by licentious dragoons, and was in danger of being hanged if he heard a sermon in the open air, the population of Scotland was not very unequally divided between Episcopalians and Presbyterians, the rational inference is that more than nineteen twentieths of those Scotchmen whose conscience was interested in the matter were Presbyterians, and that the Scotchmen, who were decidedly and on conviction Episcopalians, were a small minority. Against such odds the Bishops had but little chance; and whatever chance they had they made haste to throw away; some of them because they sincerely believed that their allegiance was still due to James; others probably because they apprehended that William would not have the power, even if he had the will, to serve them, and that nothing but a counterrevolution in the State could avert a revolution in the Church.

As the new King of England could not be at Edinburgh during the sitting of the Scottish Convention, a letter from him to the Estates was prepared with great skill. In this document he professed warm attachment to the Protestant religion, but gave no opinion touching those questions about which Protestants were divided. He had observed, he said, with great satisfaction that many of the Scottish nobility and gentry with whom he had conferred in London were inclined to an union of the two British kingdoms. He was sensible how much such an union would conduce to the

Letter from William to the Scotch Convention.

happiness of both ; and he would do all in his power towards the accomplishing of so good a work.

William's instructions to his agents in Scotland. It was necessary that he should allow a large discretion to his confidential agents at Edinburgh. The private instructions with which he furnished those persons could not be minute, but were highly judicious. He charged them to ascertain to the best of their power the real sense of the Convention, and to be guided by it. They must remember that the first object was to settle the government. To that object every other object, even the union, must be postponed. A treaty between two independent legislatures, distant from each other several days' journey, must necessarily be a work of time ; and the throne could not safely remain vacant while the negotiations were pending. It was therefore important that His Majesty's agents should be on their guard against the arts of persons who, under pretence of promoting the union, might really be contriving only to prolong the interregnum. If the Convention should be bent on establishing the Presbyterian form of church government, William desired that his friends would do all in their power to prevent the triumphant sect from retaliating what it had suffered.*

The Dalrymples. The person by whose advice William appears to have been at this time chiefly guided as to Scotch politics was a Scotchman of great abilities and attainments, Sir James Dalrymple of Stair, the founder of a family eminently distinguished at the bar, on the bench, in the senate, in diplomacy, in arms, and in letters, but distinguished also by misfortunes and misdeeds which have furnished poets and novelists with materials for the darkest and most heartrending tales. Already Sir James had been in mourning for more than one strange and terrible death. One of his sons had died by poison. One of his daughters had poniarded her bridegroom on the wedding night. One of his grandsons had in boyish sport been slain by another. Savage libellers asserted, and some of the superstitious vulgar believed, that calamities so portentous were the consequences of some connection between the unhappy race and the powers of darkness. Sir James had a wry neck; and he was reproached with this misfortune as if it had been a crime, and was told that it marked him out as a man doomed to the gallows. His wife, a woman of great ability,

* The instructions are in the Leven and Melville Papers. They bear date March 7. 168⅚. On the first occasion on which I quote this most valuable collection, I cannot refrain from acknowledging the obligations under which I, and all who take an interest in the history of our island, lie to the gentleman who has performed so well the duty of an editor.

art, and spirit, was popularly nicknamed the Witch of Endor. It was gravely said that she had cast fearful spells on those whom she hated, and that she had been seen in the likeness of a cat seated on the cloth of state by the side of the Lord High Commissioner. The man, however, over whose roof so many curses appeared to hang, did not, as far as we can now judge, fall short of that very low standard of morality which was generally attained by politicians of his age and nation. In force of mind and extent of knowledge he was superior to them all. In his youth he had borne arms: he had then been a professor of philosophy: he had then studied law, and had become, by general acknowledgment, the greatest jurist that his country had produced. In the days of the Protectorate, he had been a judge. After the Restoration, he had made his peace with the royal family, had sate in the Privy Council, and had presided with unrivalled ability in the Court of Session. He had doubtless borne a share in many unjustifiable acts; but there were limits which he never passed. He had a wonderful power of giving to any proposition which it suited him to maintain a plausible aspect of legality and even of justice; and this power he frequently abused. But he was not, like many of those among whom he lived, impudently and unscrupulously servile. Shame and conscience generally restrained him from committing any bad action for which his rare ingenuity could not frame a specious defence; and he was seldom in his place at the council board when anything outrageously unjust or cruel was to be done. His moderation at length gave offence to the Court. He was deprived of his high office, and found himself in so disagreeable a situation that he retired to Holland. There he employed himself in correcting the great work on jurisprudence which has preserved his memory fresh down to our own time. In his banishment he tried to gain the favour of his fellow exiles, who naturally regarded him with suspicion. He protested, and perhaps with truth, that his hands were pure from the blood of the persecuted Covenanters. He made a high profession of religion, prayed much, and observed weekly days of fasting and humiliation. He even consented, after much hesitation, to assist with his advice and his credit the unfortunate enterprise of Argyle. When that enterprise had failed, a prosecution was instituted at Edinburgh against Dalrymple; and his estates would doubtless have been confiscated, had they not been saved by an artifice which subsequently became common among the politicians of Scotland

His eldest son and heir apparent, John, took the side of the government, supported the dispensing power, declared against the Test, and accepted the place of Lord Advocate, when Sir George Mackenzie, after holding out through ten years of foul drudgery, at length showed signs of flagging. The services of the younger Dalrymple were rewarded by a remission of the forfeiture which the offences of the elder had incurred. Those services indeed were not to be despised. For Sir John, though inferior to his father in depth and extent of legal learning, was no common man. His knowledge was great and various : his parts were quick; and his eloquence was singularly ready and graceful. To sanctity he made no pretensions. Indeed Episcopalians and Presbyterians agreed in regarding him as little better than an atheist. During some months Sir John at Edinburgh affected to condemn the disloyalty of his unhappy parent Sir James ; and Sir James at Leyden told his Puritan friends how deeply he lamented the wicked compliances of his unhappy child Sir John.

The Revolution came, and brought a large increase of wealth and honours to the House of Stair. The son promptly changed sides, and cooperated ably and zealously with the father. Sir James established himself in London for the purpose of giving advice to William on Scotch affairs. Sir John's post was in the Parliament House at Edinburgh. He was not likely to find any equal among the debaters there, and was prepared to exert all his powers against the dynasty which he had lately served.*

By the large party which was zealous for the Calvinistic church government John Dalrymple was regarded with incurable distrust and dislike. It was therefore necessary that another agent should be employed to manage that party. Melville. Such an agent was George Melville, Lord Melville, a nobleman connected by affinity with the unfortunate Monmouth, and with that Leslie who had, in 1640, invaded England at the head of a Scottish army. Melville had always been accounted a Whig and a Presbyterian. Those who speak of him most favourably have not ventured to ascribe to him eminent intellectual endowments or exalted public spirit.

* As to the Dalrymples, see the Lord President's own writings, and among them his Vindication of the Divine Perfections ; Wodrow's Analecta ; Douglas's Peerage ; Lockhart's Memoirs ; the Satyre on the Familie of Stairs ; the Satyric Lines upon the long wished for and timely Death of the Right Honourable Lady Stairs; Law's Memorials; and the Hyndford Papers, written in 170⅘ and printed with the Letters of Carstairs. Lockhart, though a mortal enemy of John Dalrymple, says, "There was none in the parliament capable to take up the cudgels with him."

But he appears from his letters to have been by no means deficient in that homely prudence the want of which has often been fatal to men of brighter genius and of purer virtue. That prudence had restrained him from going very far in opposition to the tyranny of the Stuarts: but he had listened while his friends talked about resistance, and therefore, when the Rye House plot was discovered, thought it expedient to retire to the Continent. In his absence he was accused of treason, and was convicted on evidence which would not have satisfied any impartial tribunal. He was condemned to death: his honours and lands were declared forfeit: his arms were torn with contumely out of the Heralds' Book; and his domains swelled the estate of the cruel and rapacious Perth. The fugitive meanwhile, with characteristic wariness, lived quietly on the Continent, and discountenanced the unhappy projects of his kinsman Monmouth, but cordially approved of the enterprise of the Prince of Orange.

Illness had prevented Melville from sailing with the Dutch expedition: but he arrived in London a few hours after the new Sovereigns had been proclaimed there. William instantly sent him down to Edinburgh, in the hope, as it should seem, that the Presbyterians would be disposed to listen to moderate counsels proceeding from a man who was attached to their cause, and who had suffered for it. Melville's second son, David, who had inherited, through his mother, the title of Earl of Leven, and who had acquired some military experience in the service of the Elector of Brandenburgh, had the honour of being the bearer of a letter from the new King of England to the Scottish Convention.*

James had entrusted the conduct of his affairs in Scotland to John Graham, Viscount Dundee, and Colin Lindsay, Earl of Balcarras. Dundee had commanded a body of Scottish troops which had marched into England to oppose the Dutch: but he had found, in the inglorious campaign which had been fatal to the dynasty of Stuart, no opportunity of displaying the courage and military skill which those who most detest his merciless nature allow him to have possessed. He lay with his forces not far from Watford, when he was informed that James had fled from Whitehall, and that Feversham had ordered all the royal army to disband. The Scottish regiments were thus left, without pay or provisions, in the midst

James's agents in Scotland: Dundee: Balcarras.

* As to Melville, see the Leven and Melville Papers, *passim*, and the preface; the Act. Parl. Scot., June 16. 1685; and the Appendix, June 13.; Burnet, ii. 24.; and the Burnet MS. Harl. 6584.

of a foreign and indeed a hostile nation. Dundee, it is said,
wept with grief and rage. Soon, however, more cheering
intelligence arrived from various quarters. William wrote a
few lines to say that, if the Scots would remain quiet, he would
pledge his honour for their safety; and, some hours later,
it was known that James had returned to his capital. Dundee
repaired instantly to London.* There he met his friend Balcarras, who had just arrived from Edinburgh. Balcarras, a
man distinguished by his handsome person and by his accomplishments, had, in his youth, affected the character of a
patriot, but had deserted the popular cause, had accepted a
seat in the Privy Council, had become a tool of Perth and
Melfort, and had been one of the Commissioners who were
appointed to execute the office of Treasurer when Queensberry
was disgraced for refusing to betray the interests of the Protestant religion.†

Dundee and Balcarras went together to Whitehall, and
had the honour of accompanying James in his last walk up
and down the Mall. He told them that he intended to put
his affairs in Scotland under their management. "You, my
Lord Balcarras, must undertake the civil business: and you,
my Lord Dundee, shall have a commission from me to command the troops." The two noblemen vowed that they would
prove themselves deserving of his confidence, and disclaimed
all thought of making their peace with the Prince of Orange.‡

On the following day James left Whitehall for ever; and
the Prince of Orange arrived at Saint James's. Both Dundee
and Balcarras swelled the crowd which thronged to greet the
deliverer, and were not ungraciously received. Both were well
known to him. Dundee had served under him on the Con-
tinent§; and the first wife of Balcarras had been a lady of the

---

* Creichton's Memoirs.
† Mackay's Memoirs.
‡ Memoirs of the Lindsays.
§ About the early relation between
William and Dundee, some Jacobite,
many years after they were both dead,
invented a story which by successive
embellishments was at last improved
into a romance such as it seems strange
that even a child should believe to be
true. The last edition runs thus. William's horse was killed under him at
Seneff, and his life was in imminent
danger. Dundee, then Captain Graham,
mounted His Highness again. William
promised to reward this service with promotion, but broke his word, and gave to

another the commission which Graham
had been led to expect. The injured
hero went to Loo. There he met his
successful competitor and gave him a box
on the ear. The punishment for striking
in the palace was the loss of the offending
right hand; but this punishment the
Prince of Orange ungraciously remitted.
"You," he said, "saved my life: I spare
your right hand; and now we are quits."

Those who, down to our own time,
have repeated this nonsense seem to have
thought, first, that the Act of Henry the
Eighth "for punishment of murder and
malicious bloodshed within the King's
Court" (Stat. 33 Hen. VIII. c. 2.) was
law in Guelders; and, secondly, that, in

House of Orange, and had worn, on her wedding day, a superb pair of emerald earrings, the gift of her cousin the Prince.*

The Scottish Whigs, then assembled in great numbers at Westminster, earnestly pressed William to proscribe by name four or five men who had, during the evil times, borne a conspicuous part in the proceedings of the Privy Council at Edinburgh. Dundee and Balcarras were particularly mentioned. But the Prince had determined that, as far as his power extended, all the past should be covered with a general amnesty, and absolutely refused to make any declaration which could drive to despair even the most guilty of his uncle's servants.

Balcarras went repeatedly to Saint James's, had several audiences of William, professed deep respect for His Highness, and owned that King James had committed great errors, but would not promise to concur in a vote of deposition. William gave no signs of displeasure, but said at parting; "Take care, my Lord, that you keep within the law; for, if you break it, you must expect to be left to it."†

Dundee seems to have been less ingenuous. He employed the mediation of Burnet, opened a negotiation with Saint James's, declared himself willing to acquiesce in the new order of things, obtained from William a promise of protection, and promised in return to live peaceably. Such credit was given to his professions, that he was suffered to travel down to Scotland under the escort of a troop of cavalry. Without such an escort the man of blood, whose name was never mentioned but with a shudder at the hearth of any Presbyterian family, would, at that conjuncture, have had but a perilous journey through Berwickshire and the Lothians.‡

February was drawing to a close when Dundee and Balcarras reached Edinburgh. They had some hope that they might be at the head of a majority in the Convention. They therefore exerted themselves vigorously to consolidate and animate their party. They assured the rigid royalists, who had a scruple about sitting in an assembly convoked by an usurper, that the rightful King particularly wished no friend

---

1674, William was a King, and his house a King's Court. They were also not aware that he did not purchase Loo till long after Dundee had left the Netherlands. See Harris's Description of Loo. 1699.

This legend, of which I have not been able to discover the slightest trace in the voluminous Jacobite literature of William's reign, seems to have originated about a quarter of a century after Dundee's death, and to have attained its full absurdity in another quarter of a century.

* Memoirs of the Lindsays.

† Ibid.

‡ Burnet, ii. 22.; Memoirs of the Lindsays.

of hereditary monarchy to be absent. More than one waverer was kept steady by being assured, in confident terms, that a speedy restoration was inevitable. Gordon had determined to surrender the Castle, and had begun to remove his furniture : but Dundee and Balcarras prevailed on him to hold out some time longer. They informed him that they had received from Saint Germains full powers to adjourn the Convention to Stirling, and that, if things went ill at Edinburgh, those powers would be used.*

Meeting of the Convention. At length the fourteenth of March, the day fixed for the meeting of the Estates, arrived, and the Parliament House was crowded. Nine prelates were in their places. When Argyle presented himself, a single lord protested against the admission of a person whom a legal sentence, passed in due form, and still unreversed, had deprived of the honours of the peerage. But this objection was overruled by the general sense of the assembly. When Melville appeared, no voice was raised against his admission. The Bishop of Edinburgh officiated as chaplain, and made it one of his petitions that God would help and restore King James.† It soon appeared that the general feeling of the Convention was by no means in harmony with this prayer. The first matter to be decided was the choice of a president. The Duke of Hamilton was supported by the Whigs, the Marquess of Athol by the Jacobites. Neither candidate possessed, and neither deserved, the entire confidence of his supporters. Hamilton had been a Privy Councillor of James, had borne a part in many unjustifiable acts, and had offered but a very cautious and languid opposition to the most daring attacks on the laws and religion of Scotland. Not till the Dutch guards were at Whitehall had he ventured to speak out. Then he had joined the victorious party, and had assured the Whigs that he had pretended to be their enemy, only in order that he might, without incurring suspicion, act as their friend. Athol was still less to be trusted. His abilities were mean, his temper false, pusillanimous, and cruel. In the late reign he had gained a dishonourable notoriety by the barbarous actions of which he had been guilty in Argyleshire. He had turned with the turn of fortune, and had paid servile court to the Prince of Orange, but had been coldly received, and had now, from mere mortification, come back to the party

---

* Balcarras's Memoirs.
† Act. Parl. Scot., Mar. 14. 1689; History of the late Revolution in Scotland, 1690; An Account of the Proceedings of the Estates of Scotland, fol. Lond. 1689.

which he had deserted.* Neither of the rival noblemen had chosen to stake the dignities and lands of his house on the issue of the contention between the rival Kings. The eldest son of Hamilton had declared for James, and the eldest son of Athol for William, so that, in any event, both coronets and both estates were safe.

But in Scotland the fashionable notions touching political morality were lax; and the aristocratical sentiment was strong. The Whigs were therefore willing to forget that Hamilton had lately sate in the council of James. The Jacobites were equally willing to forget that Athol had lately fawned on William. In political inconsistency those two great lords were far indeed from standing by themselves; but in dignity and power they had scarcely an equal in the assembly. Their descent was eminently illustrious: their influence was immense: one of them could raise the Western Lowlands; the other could bring into the field an army of northern mountaineers. Round these chiefs therefore the hostile factions gathered.

The votes were counted; and it appeared that Hamilton had a majority of forty. The consequence was that about twenty of the defeated party instantly passed over to the victors.† At Westminster such a defection would have been thought strange: but it seems to have caused little surprise at Edinburgh. It is a remarkable circumstance that the same country should have produced in the same age the most wonderful specimens of both extremes of human nature. No class of men mentioned in history has ever adhered to a principle with more inflexible pertinacity than was found among the Scotch Puritans. Fine and imprisonment, the shears and the branding iron, the boot, the thumbscrew, and the gallows could not extort from the stubborn Covenanter one evasive word on which it was possible to put a sense inconsistent with his theological system. Even in things indifferent he would hear of no compromise; and he was but too ready to consider all who recommended prudence and charity as traitors to the cause of truth. On the other hand, the Scotchmen of that generation who made a figure in the Parliament House and in the Council Chamber were the most dishonest and unblushing timeservers that the world has ever

Hamilton elected President.

---

* Balcarras's narrative exhibits both Hamilton and Athol in a most unfavourable light. See also the Life of James, ii. 338, 339

† Act. Parl. Scot., March 14. 168⅝; Balcarras's Memoirs; History of the late Revolution in Scotland; Life of James, ii. 342.

seen. The English marvelled alike at both classes. There were indeed many stouthearted nonconformists in the South; but scarcely any who in obstinacy, pugnacity, and hardihood could bear a comparison with the men of the school of Cameron. There were many knavish politicians in the South; but few so utterly destitute of morality, and still fewer so utterly destitute of shame, as the men of the school of Lauderdale. Perhaps it is natural that the most callous and impudent vice should be found in the near neighbourhood of unreasonable and impracticable virtue. Where enthusiasts are ready to destroy or to be destroyed for trifles magnified into importance by a squeamish conscience, it is not strange that the very name of conscience should become a byword of contempt to cool and shrewd men of business.

Committee of Elections.

The majority, reinforced by the crowd of deserters from the minority, proceeded to name a Committee of Elections. Fifteen persons were chosen, and it soon appeared that twelve of these were not disposed to examine severely into the regularity of any proceeding of which the result had been to send up a Whig to the Parliament House. The Duke of Hamilton is said to have been disgusted by the gross partiality of his own followers, and to have exerted himself, with but little success, to restrain their violence.*

Edinburgh Castle summoned

Before the Estates proceeded to deliberate on the business for which they had met, they thought it necessary to provide for their own security. They could not be perfectly at ease while the roof under which they sate was commanded by the batteries of the Castle. A deputation was therefore sent to inform Gordon that the Convention required him to evacuate the fortress within twenty-four hours, and that if he complied, his past conduct should not be remembered against him. He asked a night for consideration. During that night his wavering mind was confirmed by the exhortations of Dundee and Balcarras. On the morrow he sent an answer drawn in respectful but evasive terms. He was very far, he declared, from meditating harm to the City of Edinburgh. Least of all could he harbour any thought of molesting an august assembly which he regarded with profound reverence. He would willingly give bond for his good behaviour to the amount of twenty thousand pounds sterling. But he was in communication with the government now established in England. He was in hourly expectation of important des-

---

* Balcarras's Memoirs; History of the late Revolution in Scotland, 1690.

patches from that government; and, till they arrived, he should not feel himself justified in resigning his command. These excuses were not admitted. Heralds and trumpeters were sent to summon the Castle in form, and to denounce the penalties of high treason against those who should continue to occupy that fortress in defiance of the authority of the Estates. Guards were at the same time posted to intercept all communication between the garrison and the city.*

Two days had been spent in these preludes, and it was expected that on the third morning the great contest would begin. Meanwhile the population of Edinburgh was in an excited state. It had been discovered that Dundee had paid visits to the Castle; and it was believed that his exhortations had induced the garrison to hold out. His own soldiers were known to be gathering round him; and it might well be apprehended that he would make some desperate attempt. He, on the other hand, had been informed that the Western Covenanters who filled the cellars of the city, had vowed vengeance on him: and, in truth, when we consider that their temper was singularly savage and implacable, that they had been taught to regard the slaying of a persecutor as a duty, that no examples furnished by Holy Writ had been more frequently held up to their admiration than Ehud stabbing Eglon and Samuel hewing Agag limb from limb, that they had never heard any achievement in the history of their own country more warmly praised by their favourite teachers than the butchery of Cardinal Beatoun and of Archbishop Sharpe, we may well wonder that a man who had shed the blood of the saints like water should have been able to walk the High Street in safety during a single day. The enemy whom Dundee had most reason to fear was a youth of distinguished courage and abilities named William Cleland. Cleland had, when little more than sixteen years old, borne arms in that insurrection which had been put down at Bothwell Bridge. He had since disgusted some virulent fanatics by his humanity and moderation. But with the great body of Presbyterians his name stood high. For with the strict morality and ardent zeal of a Puritan he united some accomplishments of which few Puritans could boast. His manners were polished, and his literary and scientific attainments respectable. He was a linguist, a mathema-

Dundee threatened by the Covenanters.

* Act. Parl. Scot., March 14. and 15. 1689; Balcarras's Memoirs; London Gaz. March 25.; History of the late Revolution in Scotland, 1690; Account of the Proceedings of the Estates of Scotland, 1689.

tician, and a poet. It is true that his hymns, odes, ballads, and Hudibrastic satires are of very little intrinsic value; but, when it is considered that he was a mere boy when most of them were written, it must be admitted that they show considerable vigour of mind. He was now at Edinburgh: his influence among the West Country Whigs assembled there was great: he hated Dundee with deadly hatred, and was believed to be meditating some act of violence.*

On the fifteenth of March Dundee received information that some of the Covenanters had bound themselves together to slay him and Sir George Mackenzie, whose eloquence and learning, long prostituted to the service of tyranny, had made him more odious to the Presbyterians than any other man of the gown. Dundee applied to Hamilton for protection; and Hamilton advised him to bring the matter under the consideration of the Convention at the next sitting.†

Letter
from
James to
the Convention.

Before that sitting a person named Crane arrived from France, with a letter addressed by the fugitive King to the Estates. The letter was sealed: the bearer, strange to say, was not furnished with a copy for the information of the heads of the Jacobite party; nor did he bring any message, written or verbal, to either of James's agents. Balcarras and Dundee were mortified by finding that so little confidence was reposed in them, and were harassed by painful doubts touching the contents of the document on which so much depended. They were willing, however, to hope for the best. King James could not, situated as he was, be so ill advised as to act in direct opposition to the counsel and entreaties of his friends. His letter, when opened, must be found to contain such gracious assurances as would animate the royalists

* See Cleland's Poems, and the commendatory poems contained in the same volume, Edinburgh, 1697. It has been repeatedly asserted that this William Cleland was the father of William Cleland, the Commissioner of Taxes, who was well known twenty years later in the literary society of London, who rendered some not very reputable services to Pope, and whose son John was the author of an infamous book but too widely celebrated. This is an entire mistake. William Cleland, who fought at Bothwell Bridge, was not twenty-eight when he was killed in August 1689; and William Cleland, the Commissioner of Taxes, died at sixty-seven in September 1741. The former therefore cannot have been the father of the latter. See the

Exact Narrative of the battle of Dunkeld; the Gentleman's Magazine for 1740; and Warburton's note on the Letter to the Publisher of the Dunciad, a letter signed W. Cleland, but really written by Pope. In a paper drawn up by Sir Robert Hamilton, the oracle of the extreme Covenanters, and a bloodthirsty ruffian, Cleland is mentioned as having been once leagued with those fanatics, but afterwards a great opposer of their testimony. Cleland probably did not agree with Hamilton in thinking it a sacred duty to cut the throats of prisoners of war who had been received to quarter. See Hamilton's Letter to the Societies, Dec. 7. 1685.

† Balcarras's Memoirs.

and conciliate the moderate Whigs. His adherents, therefore, determined that it should be produced.

When the Convention reassembled on the morning of Saturday the sixteenth of March, it was proposed that measures should be taken for the personal security of the members. It was alleged that the life of Dundee had been threatened ; that two men of sinister appearance had been watching the house where he lodged, and had been heard to say that they would use the dog as he had used them. Mackenzie complained that he too was in danger, and, with his usual copiousness and force of language, demanded the protection of the Estates. But the matter was lightly treated by the majority: and the Convention passed on to other business.*

It was then announced that Crane was at the door of the Parliament House. He was admitted. The paper of which he was in charge was laid on the table. Hamilton remarked that there was, in the hands of the Earl of Leven, a communication from the Prince by whose authority the Estates had been convoked. That communication seemed to be entitled to precedence. The Convention was of the same opinion; and the well weighed and prudent letter of William was read.

It was then moved that the letter of James should be opened. The Whigs objected that it might possibly contain a mandate dissolving the Convention. They therefore proposed that, before the seal was broken, the Estates should resolve to continue sitting, notwithstanding any such mandate. The Jacobites, who knew no more than the Whigs what was in the letter, and were impatient to have it read, eagerly assented. A vote was passed by which the members bound themselves to consider any order which should command them to separate as a nullity, and to remain assembled till they should have accomplished the work of securing the liberty and religion of Scotland. This vote was signed by almost all the lords and gentlemen who were present. Seven out of nine bishops subscribed it. The names of Dundee and Balcarras, written by their own hands, may still be seen on the original roll. Balcarras afterwards excused what, on his principles, was, beyond all dispute, a flagrant act of treason,

---

* Balcarras's Memoirs. But the fullest account of these proceedings is furnished by some manuscript notes which are in the library of the Faculty of Advocates. Balcarras's dates are not quite exact. He probably trusted to his memory for them. I have corrected them from the parliamentary records.

by saying that he and his friends had, from zeal for their
master's interest, concurred in a declaration of rebellion
against their master's authority; that they had anticipated
the most salutary effects from the letter; and that, if they
had not made some concession to the majority, the letter
would not have been opened.

Effect of
James's
letter.

In a few minutes the hopes of Balcarras were grievously
disappointed. The letter from which so much had been
hoped and feared was read with all the honours which Scottish Parliaments were in the habit of paying to royal communications: but every word carried despair to the hearts of
the Jacobites. It was plain that adversity had taught James
neither wisdom nor mercy. All was obstinacy, cruelty, insolence. A pardon was promised to those traitors who should
return to their allegiance within a fortnight. Against all
others unsparing vengeance was denounced. Not only was
no sorrow expressed for past offences: but the letter was itself a new offence: for it was written and countersigned by
the apostate Melfort, who was, by the statutes of the realm,
incapable of holding the office of Secretary, and who was not
less abhorred by the Protestant Tories than by the Whigs.
The hall was in a tumult. The enemies of James were loud
and vehement. His friends, angry with him, and ashamed
of him, saw that it was vain to think of continuing the
struggle in the Convention. Every vote which had been
doubtful when his letter was unsealed was now irrecoverably
lost. The sitting closed in great agitation.*

It was Saturday afternoon. There was to be no other
meeting till Monday morning. The Jacobite leaders held a
consultation, and came to the conclusion that it was necessary
to take a decided step. Dundee and Balcarras must use the
powers with which they had been entrusted. The minority
must forthwith leave Edinburgh and assemble at Stirling.
Athol assented, and undertook to bring a great body of his
clansmen from the Highlands to protect the deliberations of
the Royalist Convention. Everything was arranged for the
secession; but, in a few hours, the tardiness of one man and
the haste of another ruined the whole plan.

Flight of
Dundee.

The Monday came. The Jacobite lords and gentlemen
were actually taking horse for Stirling, when Athol asked for

* Act. Parl. Scot., March 16. 168⅞;
Balcarras's Memoirs; History of the
late Revolution in Scotland, 1690; Account of the Proceedings of the Estates
of Scotland, 1689; London Gaz., March
25. 1689; Life of James, ii. 342. Burnet
blunders strangely about these transactions.

a delay of twenty-four hours. He had no personal reason to be in haste. By staying he ran no risk of being assassinated. By going he incurred the risks inseparable from civil war. The members of his party, unwilling to separate from him, consented to the postponement which he requested, and repaired once more to the Parliament House. Dundee alone refused to stay a moment longer. His life was in danger. The Convention had refused to protect him. He would not remain to be a mark for the pistols and daggers of murderers. Balcarras expostulated to no purpose. "By departing alone," he said, "you will give the alarm and break up the whole scheme." But Dundee was obstinate. Brave as he undoubtedly was, he seems, like many other brave men, to have been less proof against the danger of assassination than against any other form of danger. He knew what the hatred of the Covenanters was: he knew how well he had earned their hatred; and he was haunted by that consciousness of inexpiable guilt, and by that dread of a terrible retribution, which the ancient polytheists personified under the awful name of the Furies. His old troopers, the Satans and Beelzebubs who had shared his crimes, and who now shared his perils, were ready to be the companions of his flight.

Meanwhile the Convention had assembled. Mackenzie was on his legs, and was pathetically lamenting the hard condition of the Estates, at once commanded by the guns of a fortress and menaced by a fanatical rabble, when he was interrupted by some sentinels who came running from the posts near the Castle. They had seen Dundee at the head of fifty horse on the Stirling road. That road ran close under the huge rock on which the citadel is built. Gordon had appeared on the ramparts, and had made a sign that he had something to say. Dundee had climbed high enough to hear and to be heard, and was then actually conferring with the Duke. Up to that moment the hatred with which the Presbyterian members of the assembly regarded the merciless persecutor of their brethren in the faith had been restrained by the decorous forms of parliamentary deliberation. But now the explosion was terrible. Hamilton himself, who, by the acknowledgment of his opponents, had hitherto performed the duties of President with gravity and impartiality, was the loudest and fiercest man in the hall. "It is high time," he cried, "that we should look to ourselves. The enemies of our religion and of our civil freedom are mustering all around us; and we may well suspect that they have accomplices even

Tumultuous sitting of the Convention.

here. Lock the doors. Lay the keys on the table. Let nobody go out but those lords and gentlemen whom we shall
appoint to call the citizens to arms. There are some good
men from the West in Edinburgh, men for whom I can answer." The assembly raised a general cry of assent. Several
members of the majority boasted that they too had brought
with them trusty retainers who would turn out at a moment's
notice against Claverhouse and his dragoons. All that Hamilton proposed was instantly done. The Jacobites, silent and
unresisting, became prisoners. Leven went forth and ordered the drums to beat. The Covenanters of Lanarkshire
and Ayrshire promptly obeyed the signal. The force thus
assembled had indeed no very military appearance, but was
amply sufficient to overawe the adherents of the House of
Stuart. From Dundee nothing was to be hoped or feared.
He had already scrambled down the Castle hill, rejoined his
troopers, and galloped westward. Hamilton now ordered the
doors to be opened. The suspected members were at liberty
to depart. Humbled and brokenspirited, yet glad that they
had come off so well, they stole forth through the crowd of
stern fanatics which filled the High Street. All thought of
secession was at an end.*

On the following day it was resolved that the kingdom
should be put into a posture of defence. The preamble of
this resolution contained a severe reflection on the perfidy
of the traitor who, within a few hours after he had, by an
engagement subscribed with his own hand, bound himself
not to quit his post in the Convention, had set the example
of desertion, and given the signal of civil war. All Protestants, from sixteen to sixty, were ordered to hold themselves in readiness to assemble in arms at the first summons ;
and, that none might pretend ignorance, it was directed that
the edict should be proclaimed at all the market crosses
throughout the realm.†

The Estates then proceeded to send a letter of thanks to
William. To this letter were attached the signatures of
many noblemen and gentlemen who were in the interest of
the banished King. The Bishops however unanimously refused to subscribe their names.

It had long been the custom of the Parliaments of Scotland
to entrust the preparation of Acts to a select number of

---

* Balcarras's Memoirs; MS. in the   History of the late Revolution in Scot-
Library of the Faculty of Advocates.   land, 1690.
  † Act. Parl. Scot., March 19. 168$\frac{8}{9}$;

members who were designated as the Lords of Articles. In conformity with this usage, the business of framing a plan for the settling of the government was now confided to a Committee of twenty-four. Of the twenty-four eight were peers, eight representatives of counties, and eight representatives of towns. The majority of the Committee were Whigs ; and not a single prelate had a seat.

A Committee appointed to frame a plan of government.

The spirit of the Jacobites, broken by a succession of disasters, was, about this time, for a moment revived by the arrival of the Duke of Queensberry from London. His rank was high : his influence was great : his character, by comparison with the characters of those who surrounded him, was fair. When Popery was in the ascendent, he had been true to the cause of the Protestant Church ; and, since Whiggism had been in the ascendent, he had been true to the cause of hereditary monarchy. Some thought that, if he had been earlier in his place he might have been able to render important service to the House of Stuart.* Even now the stimulants which he applied to his torpid and feeble party produced some faint symptoms of returning animation. Means were found of communicating with Gordon ; and he was earnestly solicited to fire on the city. The Jacobites hoped that, as soon as the cannon balls had beaten down a few chimneys, the Estates would adjourn to Glasgow. Time would thus be gained ; and the royalists might be able to execute their old project of meeting in a separate convention. Gordon however positively refused to take on himself so grave a responsibility on no better warrant than the request of a small cabal.†

By this time the Estates had a guard on which they could rely more firmly than on the undisciplined and turbulent Covenanters of the West. A squadron of English men of war from the Thames had arrived in the Frith of Forth. On board were the three Scottish regiments which had accompanied William from Holland. He had, with great judgment, selected them to protect the assembly which was to settle the government of their country ; and, that no cause of jealousy might be given to a people exquisitely sensitive on points of national honour, he had purged the ranks of all Dutch soldiers, and had thus reduced the number of men to about eleven hundred. This little force was commanded by Hugh Mackay, a Highlander of noble descent, who had long served on the Continent, and who was distinguished **by**

* Balcarras. † Ibid.

courage of the truest temper, and by a piety such as is seldom
found in soldiers of fortune. The Convention passed a resolution appointing Mackay general of their forces. When
the question was put on this resolution, the Archbishop of
Glasgow, unwilling doubtless to be a party to such an usurpation of powers which belonged to the King alone, begged
that the prelates might be excused from voting. Divines, he
said, had nothing to do with military arrangements. " The
Fathers of the Church," answered a member very keenly,
" have been lately favoured with a new light. I have myself
seen military orders signed by the Most Reverend person who
has suddenly become so scrupulous. There was indeed one
difference : those orders were for dragooning Protestants; and
the resolution before us is meant to protect us from Papists."*

The arrival of Mackay's troops, and the determination of
Gordon to remain inactive, quelled the spirit of the Jacobites. They had indeed one chance left. They might possibly, by joining with those Whigs who were bent on an
union with England, have postponed during a considerable
time the settlement of the government. A negotiation was
actually opened with this view, but was speedily broken off.
For it soon appeared that the party which was for James was
really hostile to the union, and that the party which was for
the union was really hostile to James. As these two parties
had no object in common, the only effect of a coalition
between them must have been that one of them would have
become the tool of the other. The question of the union
therefore was not raised.† Some Jacobites retired to their
country seats : others, though they remained at Edinburgh,
ceased to show themselves in the Parliament House : many
passed over to the winning side ; and, when at length the
resolutions prepared by the Twenty Four were submitted to
the Convention, it appeared that the great body which on
the first day of the session had rallied round Athol had
dwindled away to nothing.

Resolu-
tions pro-
posed by
the Com-
mittee.

The resolutions had been framed, as far as possible, in conformity with the example recently set at Westminster. In
one important point, however, it was absolutely necessary
that the copy should deviate from the original. The Estates
of England had brought two charges against James, his misgovernment and his flight, and had, by using the soft word
" Abdication," evaded, with some sacrifice of verbal precision,

---

* Act. Parl. Scot.; History of the late Revolution, 1690 ; Memoirs of North
Britain, 1715.   † Balcarras.

the question whether subjects may lawfully depose a bad prince. That question the Estates of Scotland could not evade. They could not pretend that James had deserted his post. For he had never, since he came to the throne, resided in Scotland. During many years that kingdom had been ruled by sovereigns who dwelt in another land. The whole machinery of the administration had been constructed on the supposition that the King would be absent, and was therefore not necessarily deranged by that flight which had, in the south of the island, dissolved all government, and suspended the ordinary course of justice. It was only by letter that the King could, when he was at Whitehall, communicate with the Council and the Parliament at Edinburgh; and by letter he could communicate with them when he was at Saint Germains or at Dublin. The Twenty Four were therefore forced to propose to the Estates a resolution distinctly declaring that James the Seventh had by his misconduct forfeited the crown. Many writers have inferred from the language of this resolution that sound political principles had made a greater progress in Scotland than in England. But the whole history of the two countries from the Restoration to the Union proves this inference to be erroneous. The Scottish Estates used plain language, simply because it was impossible for them, situated as they were, to use evasive language.

The person who bore the chief part in framing the resolution, and in defending it, was Sir John Dalrymple, who had recently held the high office of Lord Advocate, and had been an accomplice in some of the misdeeds which he now arraigned with great force of reasoning and eloquence. He was strenuously supported by Sir James Montgomery, member for Ayrshire, a man of considerable abilities, but of loose principles, turbulent temper, insatiable cupidity, and implacable malevolence. The Archbishop of Glasgow and Sir George Mackenzie spoke on the other side : but the only effect of their oratory was to deprive their party of the advantage of being able to allege that the Estates were under duress, and that liberty of speech had been denied to the defenders of hereditary monarchy.

When the question was put, Athol, Queensberry, and some of their friends withdrew. Only five members voted against the resolution which pronounced that James had forfeited his right to the allegiance of his subjects. When it was moved that the Crown of Scotland should be settled as the Crown of

England had been settled, Athol and Queensberry reappeared in the hall. They had doubted, they said, whether they could justifiably declare the throne vacant. But, since it had been declared vacant, they felt no doubt that William and Mary were the persons who ought to fill it.

William and Mary proclaimed.

The Convention then went forth in procession to the High Street. Several great nobles, attended by the Lord Provost of the capital and by the heralds, ascended the octagon tower from which rose the city cross surmounted by the unicorn of Scotland.* Hamilton read the vote of the Convention; and a King at Arms proclaimed the new Sovereigns with sound of trumpet. On the same day the Estates issued an order that the parochial clergy should, on pain of deprivation, publish from their pulpits the proclamation which had just been read at the city cross, and should pray for King William and Queen Mary.

The Claim of Right.

Still the interregnum was not at an end. Though the new Sovereigns had been proclaimed, they had not yet been put into possession of the royal authority by a formal tender and a formal acceptance. At Edinburgh, as at Westminster, it was thought necessary that the instrument which settled the government should clearly define and solemnly assert those privileges of the people which the Stuarts had illegally infringed. A Claim of Right was therefore drawn up by the Twenty Four, and adopted by the Convention. To this claim, which purported to be merely declaratory of the law as it stood, was added a supplementary paper containing a list of grievances which could be remedied only by new laws. One most important article which we should naturally expect to find at the head of such a list, the Convention, with great practical prudence, but in defiance of notorious facts and of unanswerable arguments, placed in the Claim of Right. Nobody could deny that prelacy was established by Act of Parliament. The power exercised by the Bishops might be pernicious, unscriptural, antichristian: but illegal it certainly was not ; and to pronounce it illegal was to outrage common sense. The Whig leaders however were much more desirous to get rid of episcopacy than to prove themselves consummate publicists and logicians. If they made the abolition of episcopacy an article of the contract by which William was to hold the crown, they attained their end, though doubtless in

Abolition of Episcopacy.

---

* Every reader will remember the malediction which Sir Walter Scott, in the Fifth Canto of Marmion, pronounced on the dunces who removed this interesting monument.

a manner open to much criticism. If, on the other hand, they contented themselves with resolving that episcopacy was a noxious institution which at some future time the legislature would do well to abolish, they might find that their resolution, though unobjectionable in form, was barren of consequences. They knew that William by no means sympathised with their dislike of Bishops, and that, even had he been much more zealous for the Calvinistic model than he was, the relation in which he stood to the Anglican Church would make it difficult and dangerous for him to declare himself hostile to a fundamental part of the constitution of that Church. If he should become King of Scotland without being fettered by any pledge on this subject, it might well be apprehended that he would hesitate about passing an Act which would be regarded with abhorrence by a large body of his subjects in the south of the island. It was therefore most desirable that the question should be settled while the throne was still vacant. In this opinion many politicians concurred, who had no dislike to rochets and mitres, but who wished that William might have a quiet and prosperous reign. The Scottish people,—so these men reasoned,—hated episcopacy. The English loved it. To leave William any voice in the matter was to put him under the necessity of deeply wounding the strongest feelings of one of the nations which he governed. It was therefore plainly for his own interest that the question, which he could not settle in any manner without incurring a fearful amount of obloquy, should be settled for him by others who were exposed to no such danger. He was not yet Sovereign of Scotland. While the interregnum lasted, the supreme power belonged to the Estates; and for what the Estates might do the prelatists of his southern kingdom could not hold him responsible. The elder Dalrymple wrote strongly from London to this effect; and there can be little doubt that he expressed the sentiments of his master. William would have sincerely rejoiced if the Scots could have been reconciled to a modified episcopacy. But, since that could not be, it was manifestly desirable that they should themselves, while there was yet no King over them, pronounce the irrevocable doom of the institution which they abhorred.*

The Convention, therefore, with little debate as it should

* "It will be neither secuir nor kynd to the King to expect it be (by) Act of Parliament after the setlement, which will lay it at his door."—Dalrymple to Melville, 5 April, 1689; Leven and Melville Papers.

seem, inserted in the Claim of Right a clause declaring that prelacy was an insupportable burden to the kingdom, that it had been long odious to the body of the people, and that it ought to be abolished.

Torture.　　Nothing in the proceedings at Edinburgh astonishes an Englishman more than the manner in which the Estates dealt with the practice of torture. In England torture had always been illegal. In the most servile times the judges had unanimously pronounced it so. Those rulers who had occasionally resorted to it had, as far as was possible, used it in secret, had never pretended that they had acted in conformity with either statute law or common law, and had excused themselves by saying that the extraordinary peril to which the state was exposed had forced them to take on themselves the responsibility of employing extraordinary means of defence. It had therefore never been thought necessary by any English Parliament to pass any Act or resolution touching this matter. The torture was not mentioned in the Petition of Right, or in any of the statutes framed by the Long Parliament. No member of the Convention of 1689 dreamed of proposing that the instrument which called the Prince and Princess of Orange to the throne should contain a declaration against the using of racks and thumbscrews for the purpose of forcing prisoners to accuse themselves. Such a declaration would have been justly regarded as weakening rather than strengthening a rule which, as far back as the days of the Plantagenets, had been proudly declared by the most illustrious sages of Westminster Hall to be a distinguishing feature of the English jurisprudence.* In the Scottish Claim of Right, the use of torture, without evidence, or in ordinary cases, was declared to be contrary to law. The use of torture, therefore, where there was strong evidence, and where the crime was extraordinary, was, by the plainest implication, declared to be according to law; nor did the Estates mention the use of torture among the grievances which required a legislative remedy. In truth, they could not condemn the use of torture without condemning themselves. It had chanced that, while they were employed in settling the government, the eloquent and learned Lord President Lockhart had been foully murdered in a public street through which he was returning from church on a Sunday. The murderer was seized, and proved to be a wretch who, having treated his wife barbarously and turned her out of doors, had

---

* There is a striking passage on this subject in Fortescue.

been compelled by a decree of the Court of Session to provide for her. A savage hatred of the Judges by whom she had been protected had taken possession of his mind, and had goaded him to a horrible crime and a horrible fate. It was natural that an assassination attended by so many circumstances of aggravation should move the indignation of the members of the Convention. Yet they should have considered the gravity of the conjuncture and the importance of their own mission. They unfortunately, in the heat of passion, directed the magistrates of Edinburgh to strike the prisoner in the boots, and named a Committee to superintend the operation. But for this unhappy event, it is probable that the law of Scotland concerning torture would have been immediately assimilated to the law of England.*

Having settled the Claim of Right, the Convention proceeded to revise the Coronation oath. When this had been done, three members were appointed to carry the Instrument of Government to London. Argyle, though not, in strictness of law, a Peer, was chosen to represent the Peers: Sir James Montgomery represented the Commissioners of Shires, and Sir John Dalrymple the Commissioners of Towns.

The Estates then adjourned for a few weeks, having first passed a vote which empowered Hamilton to take such measures as might be necessary for the preservation of the public peace till the end of the interregnum.

The ceremony of the inauguration was distinguished from ordinary pageants by some highly interesting circumstances. On the eleventh of May the three Commissioners came to the Council Chamber at Whitehall, and thence, attended by almost all the Scotchmen of note who were then in London, proceeded to the Banqueting House. There William and Mary appeared seated under a canopy. A splendid circle of English nobles and statesmen stood round the throne: but the sword of state was committed to a Scotch lord; and the oath of office was administered after the Scotch fashion. Argyle recited the words slowly. The royal pair, holding up their hands towards heaven, repeated after him till they came to the last clause. There William paused. That clause contained a promise that he would root out all heretics and all enemies of the true worship of God; and it was notorious that, in the opinion of many Scotchmen, not only all Roman Catholics, but all Protestant Episcopalians, all Independents,

William and Mary accept the crown of Scotland.

* Act. Parl. Scot., April 1. 1689; Orders of Committee of Estates, May 16. 1689; London Gazette, April 11.

Baptists, and Quakers, all Lutherans, nay all British Presbyterians who did not hold themselves bound by the Solemn League and Covenant, were enemies of the true worship of God.* The King had apprised the Commissioners that he could not take this part of the oath without a distinct and public explanation; and they had been authorised by the Convention to give such an explanation as would satisfy him. "I will not," he now said, "lay myself under any obligation to be a persecutor." "Neither the words of this oath," said one of the Commissioners, "nor the laws of Scotland, lay any such obligation on Your Majesty." "In that sense, then, I swear," said William; "and I desire you all, my lords and gentlemen, to witness that I do so." Even his detractors have generally admitted that on this great occasion he acted with uprightness, dignity, and wisdom.†

Discontent of the Covenanters.

As King of Scotland, he soon found himself embarrassed at every step by all the difficulties which had embarrassed him as King of England, and by other difficulties which in England were happily unknown. In the north of the island, no class was more dissatisfied with the Revolution than the class which owed most to the Revolution. The manner in which the Convention had decided the question of ecclesiastical polity had not been more offensive to the Bishops themselves than to those fiery Covenanters who had long, in defiance of sword and carbine, boot and gibbet, worshipped their Maker after their own fashion in caverns and on mountain tops. Was there ever, these zealots exclaimed, such a halting between two opinions, such a compromise between the

* As it has lately been denied that the extreme Presbyterians entertained an unfavourable opinion of the Lutherans, I will give two decisive proofs of the truth of what I have asserted in the text. In the book entitled Faithful Contendings Displayed is a report of what passed at the General Meeting of the United Societies of Covenanters on the 24th of October 1688. The question was propounded whether there should be an association with the Dutch. "It was concluded unanimously," says the Clerk of the Societies, "that we could not have an association with the Dutch in one body, nor come formally under their conduct, being such a promiscuous conjunction of reformed Lutheran malignants and sectaries, to join with whom were repugnant to the testimony of the Church of Scotland." In the Protestation and Testimony drawn up on the 2nd of Octo-

ber 1707, the United Societies complain that the crown has been settled on "tne Prince of Hanover, who has been bred and brought up in the Lutheran religion, which is not only different from, but even in many things contrary unto that purity in doctrine, reformation, and religion, we in these nations had attained unto, as is very well known." They add: "The admitting such a person to reign over us is not only contrary to our Solemn League and Covenant, but to the very Word of God itself, Deut. xvii."

† History of the late Revolution in Scotland; London Gazette, May 16. 1689. The official account of what passed was evidently drawn up with great care. See also the Royal Diary, 1702. The writer of this work professes to have derived his information from a divine who was present.

Lord and Baal? The Estates ought to have said that episcopacy was an abomination in God's sight, and that, in obedience to his word, and from fear of his righteous judgment, they were determined to deal with this great national sin and scandal after the fashion of those saintly rulers who of old cut down the groves and demolished the altars of Chemosh and Astarte. Unhappily, Scotland was ruled, not by pious Josiahs, but by careless Gallios. The antichristian hierarchy was to be abolished, not because it was an insult to heaven, but because it was felt as a burden on earth; not because it was hateful to the great Head of the Church, but because it was hateful to the people. Was public opinion, then, the test of right and wrong in religion? Was not the order which Christ had established in his own house to be held equally sacred in all countries and through all ages? And was there no reason for following that order in Scotland, except a reason which might be urged with equal force for maintaining Prelacy in England, Popery in Spain, and Mahometanism in Turkey? Why, too, was nothing said of those Covenants which the nation had so generally subscribed and so generally violated? Why was it not distinctly affirmed that the promises set down in those rolls were still binding, and would to the end of time be binding, on the kingdom? Were these truths to be suppressed from regard for the feelings and interests of a prince who was all things to all men, an ally of the idolatrous Spaniard and of the Lutheran Dane, a presbyterian at the Hague and a prelatist at Whitehall? He, like Jehu in ancient times, had doubtless so far done well that he had been the scourge of the idolatrous House of Ahab. But he, like Jehu, had not taken heed to walk in the divine law with his whole heart, but had tolerated and practised impieties differing only in degree from those of which he had declared himself the enemy. It would have better become godly senators to remonstrate with him on the sin which he was committing by conforming to the Anglican ritual, and by maintaining the Anglican Church government, than to flatter him by using a phraseology which seemed to indicate that they were as deeply tainted with Erastianism as himself. Many of those who held this language refused to do any act which could be construed into a recognition of the new Sovereigns, and would rather have been fired upon by files of musketeers, or tied to stakes within low water mark, than have uttered a prayer that God would bless William and Mary.

Yet the King had less to fear from the pertinacious adherence of these men to their absurd principles than from the ambition and avarice of another set of men who had no principles at all. It was necessary that he should immediately name ministers to conduct the government of Scotland; and, name whom he might, he could not fail to disappoint and irritate a multitude of expectants. Scotland was one of the least wealthy countries in Europe : yet no country in Europe contained a greater number of clever and selfish politicians. The places in the gift of the Crown were not enough to satisfy one twentieth part of the placehunters, every one of whom thought that his own services had been preeminent, and that, whoever might be passed by, he ought to be remembered. William did his best to satisfy these innumerable and insatiable claimants by putting many offices into commission. There were however a few great posts which it was impossible to divide. Hamilton was declared Lord High Commissioner, in the hope that immense pecuniary allowances, a residence in Holyrood Palace, and a pomp and dignity little less than regal, would content him. The Earl of Crawford was appointed President of the Parliament; and it was supposed that this appointment would conciliate the rigid Presbyterians : for Crawford was what they called a professor. His letters and speeches are, to use his own phraseology, exceeding savoury. Alone, or almost alone, among the prominent politicians of that time, he retained the style which had been fashionable in the preceding generation. He had a text from the Pentateuch or the Prophets ready for every occasion. He filled his despatches with allusions to Ishmael and Hagar, Hannah and Eli, Elijah, Nehemiah, and Zerubbabel, and adorned his oratory with quotations from Ezra and Haggai. It is a circumstance strikingly characteristic of the man, and of the school in which he had been trained, that, in all the mass of his writing which has come down to us, there is not a single word indicating that he had ever in his life heard of the New Testament. Even in our own time some persons of a peculiar taste have been so much delighted by the rich unction of his eloquence, that they have confidently pronounced him a saint. To those whose habit is to judge of a man rather by his actions than by his words, Crawford will appear to have been a selfish, cruel, politician, who was not at all the dupe of his own cant, and whose zeal against episcopal government was not a little whetted by his desire to obtain a grant of Episcopal domains. In excuse for his

Ministerial
arrangements in
Scotland.

Hamilton.

Crawford.

greediness, it ought to be said that he was the poorest noble of a poor nobility, and that before the Revolution he was sometimes at a loss for a meal and a suit of clothes.*

The ablest of Scottish politicians and debaters, Sir John Dalrymple, was appointed Lord Advocate. His father, Sir James, the greatest of Scottish jurists, was placed at the head of the Court of Session. Sir William Lockhart, a man whose letters prove him to have possessed considerable ability, became Solicitor General.

The Dalrymples.

Lockhart.

Sir James Montgomery had flattered himself that he should be the chief minister. He had distinguished himself highly in the Convention. He had been one of the Commissioners who had tendered the Crown and administered the oath to the new Sovereigns. In parliamentary ability and eloquence he had no superior among his countrymen, except the new Lord Advocate. The Secretaryship was, not indeed in dignity, but in real power, the highest office in the Scottish government; and this office was the reward to which Montgomery thought himself entitled. But the Episcopalians and the moderate Presbyterians dreaded him as a man of extreme opinions and of bitter spirit. He had been a chief of the Covenanters: he had been prosecuted at one time for holding conventicles, and at another time for harbouring rebels: he had been fined: he had been imprisoned: he had been almost driven to take refuge from his enemies beyond the Atlantic in the infant settlement of New Jersey. It was apprehended that, if he were now armed with the whole power of the Crown he would exact a terrible retribution for what he had suffered.† William therefore preferred Melville, who, though not a man of eminent talents, was regarded by the Presbyterians as a thoroughgoing friend, and yet not re-

Montgomery.

Melville.

---

* See Crawford's Letters and Speeches, *passim.* His style of begging for a place was peculiar. After owning, not without reason, that his heart was deceitful and desperately wicked, he proceeded thus: " The same Omnipotent Being who hath said, when the poor and needy seek water and there is none, and their tongue faileth for thirst, he will not forsake them, notwithstanding of my present low condition, can build me a house if He think fit."—Letter to Melville, of May 28. 1689. As to Crawford's poverty and his passion for Bishops' lands, see his letter to Melville of the 4th of December 1690. As to his humanity, see his letter to Melville, Dec. 11. 1690. All these

letters are among the Leven and Melville Papers. The author of An Account of the Late Establishment of Presbyterian Government says of a person who had taken a bribe of ten or twelve pounds, " Had he been as poor as my Lord Crawford, perhaps he had been the more excusable." See also the dedication of the celebrated tract entitled Scotch Presbyterian Eloquence Displayed.

† Burnet, ii. 23, 24.; Fountainhall Papers, 13. Aug. 1684, 14. and 15. Oct. 1684, 3. May 1685; Montgomery to Melville. June 23. 1689, in the Leven and Melville Papers; Pretences of the French Invasion Examined, licensed May 25. 1692.

garded by the Episcopalians as an implacable enemy. Melville fixed his residence at the English Court, and became the regular organ of communication between Kensington and the authorities at Edinburgh.

William had, however, one Scottish adviser who deserved and possessed more influence than any of the ostensible Carstairs. ministers. This was Carstairs, one of the most remarkable men of that age. He united great scholastic attainments with great aptitude for civil business, and the firm faith and ardent zeal of a martyr with the shrewdness and suppleness of a consummate politician. In courage and fidelity he resembled Burnet; but he had, what Burnet wanted, judgment, selfcommand, and a singular power of keeping secrets. There was no post to which he might not have aspired if he had been a layman, or a priest of the Church of England. But a Presbyterian clergyman could not hope to attain any high dignity either in the north or in the south of the island. Carstairs was forced to content himself with the substance of power, and to leave the semblance to others. He was named Chaplain to Their Majesties for Scotland: but wherever the King was, in England, in Ireland, in the Netherlands, there was this most trusty and most prudent of courtiers. He obtained from the royal bounty a modest competence; and he desired no more. But it was well known that he could be as useful a friend and as formidable an enemy as any member of the cabinet; and he was designated at the public offices and in the antechambers of the palace by the significant nickname of the Cardinal.*

The Club formed: Annandale; Ross. To Montgomery was offered the place of Lord Justice Clerk. But that place, though high and honourable, he thought below his merits and his capacity; and he returned from London to Scotland with a heart ulcerated by hatred of his ungrateful master and of his successful rivals. At Edinburgh a knot of Whigs, as severely disappointed as himself by the new arrangements, readily submitted to the guidance of so bold and able a leader. Under his direction these men, among whom the Earl of Annandale and Lord Ross were the most conspicuous, formed themselves into a society called the Club, appointed a clerk, and met daily at a tavern to concert plans of opposition. Round this nucleus soon gathered a

---

* See the life and correspondence of Carstairs, and the interesting memorials of him in the Caldwell Papers, printed in 1854. See also Mackay's character of him, and Swift's note. Swift's word is not to be taken against a Scotchman and a Presbyterian. I believe, however, that Carstairs, though an honest and pious man in essentials, had his full share of the wisdom of the serpent.

great body of greedy and angry politicians.* With these dishonest malecontents, whose object was merely to annoy the government and to get places, were leagued other malecontents, who, in the course of a long resistance to tyranny, had become so perverse and irritable that they were unable to live contentedly even under the mildest and most constitutional rule. Such a man was Sir Patrick Hume. He had returned from exile, as litigious, as impracticable, as morbidly jealous of all superior authority, and as fond of haranguing, as he had been four years before, and was as much bent on making a merely nominal sovereign of William as he had formerly been bent on making a merely nominal general of Argyle.† A man far superior morally and intellectually to Hume, Fletcher of Saltoun, belonged to the same party. Though not a member of the Convention, he was a most active member of the Club.‡ He hated monarchy: he hated democracy: his favourite project was to make Scotland an oligarchical republic. The King, if there must be a King, was to be a mere pageant. The lowest class of the people were to be bondsmen. The whole power, legislative and executive, was to be in the hands of the Parliament. In other words, the country was to be absolutely governed by a hereditary aristocracy, the most needy, the most haughty, and the most quarrelsome in Europe. Under such a polity there could have been neither freedom nor tranquillity. Trade, industry, science, would have languished; and Scotland would have been a smaller Poland, with a puppet sovereign, a turbulent diet, and an enslaved people. With unsuccessful candidates for office, and with honest but wrongheaded republicans, were mingled politicians whose course was determined merely by fear. Many sycophants, who were conscious that they had, in the evil time, done what deserved punishment, were desirous to make their peace with the powerful and vindictive Club, and were glad to be permitted to atone for their servility to James by their opposition to William.§ The great body of Jacobites meanwhile stood

Margin note: Hume.

Margin note: Fletcher of Saltoun.

---

* Sir John Dalrymple to Lord Melville, June 18. 20. 25. 1689; Leven and Melville Papers.

† There is an amusing description of Sir Patrick in the Hyndford MS. written about 1704, and printed among the Carstairs Papers. "He is a lover of set speeches, and can hardly give audience to private friends without them."

‡ "No man, though not a member,

busier than Saltoun."—Lockhart to Melville, July 11. 1689; Leven and Melville Papers. See Fletcher's own works, and the descriptions of him in Lockhart's and Mackay's Memoirs.

§ Dalrymple says, in a letter of the 5th of June, "All the malignants, for fear, are come into the Club; and they all vote alike."

aloof, saw with delight the enemies of the House of Stuart divided against one another, and indulged the hope that the confusion would end in the restoration of the banished king.*

War breaks out in the Highlands.
While Montgomery was labouring to form out of various materials a party which might, when the Convention should reassemble, be powerful enough to dictate to the throne, an enemy still more formidable than Montgomery had set up the standard of civil war in a region about which the politicians of Westminster, and indeed most of the politicians of Edinburgh, knew no more than about Abyssinia or Japan.

State of the Highlands.
It is not easy for a modern Englishman, who can pass in a day from his club in Saint James's Street to his shooting box among the Grampians, and who finds in his shooting box all the comforts and luxuries of his club, to believe that, in the time of his greatgrandfathers, Saint James's Street had as little connection with the Grampians as with the Andes. Yet so it was. In the south of our island scarcely any thing was known about the Celtic part of Scotland; and what was known excited no feeling but contempt and loathing. The crags and the glens, the woods and the waters, were indeed the same that now swarm every autumn with admiring gazers and sketchers. The Trosachs wound as now between gigantic walls of rock tapestried with broom and wild roses : Foyers came headlong down through the birchwood with the same leap and the same roar with which he still rushes to Loch Ness; and, in defiance of the sun of June, the snowy scalp of Ben Cruachan rose, as it still rises, over the willowy islets of Loch Awe. Yet none of these sights had power, till a recent period, to attract a single poet or painter from more opulent and more tranquil regions. Indeed, law and police, trade and industry, have done far more than people of romantic dispositions will readily admit, to develope in our minds a sense of the wilder beauties of nature. A traveller must be freed from all apprehension of being murdered or starved before he can be charmed by the bold outlines and rich tints of the hills. He is not likely to be thrown into ecstasies by the abruptness of a precipice from which he is in imminent danger of falling two thousand feet perpendicular; by the boiling waves of a torrent which suddenly whirls away his baggage and forces him to run for his life; by the gloomy grandeur of a pass where he finds a corpse which marauders have just stripped and mangled; or by the screams of those

* Balcarras.

eagles whose next meal may probably be on his own eyes. About the year 1730, Captain Burt, one of the first Englishmen who caught a glimpse of the spots which now allure tourists from every part of the civilised world, wrote an account of his wanderings. He was evidently a man of a quick, an observant, and a cultivated mind, and would doubtless, had he lived in our age, have looked with mingled awe and delight on the mountains of Invernessshire. But, writing with the feeling which was universal in his own age, he pronounced those mountains monstrous excrescences. Their deformity, he said, was such that the most sterile plains seemed lovely by comparison. Fine weather, he complained, only made bad worse; for, the clearer the day, the more disagreeably did those misshapen masses of gloomy brown and dirty purple affect the eye. What a contrast, he exclaimed, between these horrible prospects and the beauties of Richmond Hill!* Some persons may think that Burt was a man of vulgar and prosaical mind: but they will scarcely venture to pass a similar judgment on Oliver Goldsmith. Goldsmith was one of the very few Saxons who, more than a century ago, ventured to explore the Highlands. He was disgusted by the hideous wilderness, and declared that he greatly preferred the charming country round Leyden, the vast expanse of verdant meadow, and the villas with their statues and grottoes, trim flower beds, and rectilinear avenues. Yet it is difficult to believe that the author of the Traveller and of the Deserted Village was naturally inferior in taste and sensibility to the thousands of clerks and milliners who are now thrown into raptures by the sight of Loch Katrine and Loch Lomond.† His feelings may easily be explained. It was

* Captain Burt's Letters from Scotland.

† "Shall I tire you with a description of this unfruitful country, where I must lead you over their hills all brown with heath, or their valleys scarce able to feed a rabbit? . . . Every part of the country presents the same dismal landscape. No grove or brook lend their music to cheer the stranger."—Goldsmith to Bryanton, Edinburgh, Sept. 26. 1753. In a letter written soon after from Leyden to the Reverend Thomas Contarine, Goldsmith says, "I was wholly taken up in observing the face of the country. Nothing can equal its beauty. Wherever I turned my eye, fine houses, elegant gardens, statues, grottos, vistas presented themselves. Scotland and this country bear the highest contrast: there, hills and rocks intercept every prospect; here it is all a continued plain." See Appendix C. to the First Volume of Mr. Forster's Life of Goldsmith. I will cite the testimony of another man of genius in support of the doctrine propounded in the text. No human being has ever had a finer sense of the beauties of nature than Gray. No prospect surpasses in grandeur and loveliness the first view of Italy from Mount Cenis. Had Gray enjoyed that view from the magnificent road constructed in this century, he would undoubtedly have been in raptures. But in his time the descent was performed with extreme inconvenience and with not a little peril. He therefore, instead of breaking forth into ejacula-

not till roads had been cut out of the rocks, till bridges had been flung over the courses of the rivulets, till inns had succeeded to dens of robbers, till there was as little danger of being slain or plundered in the wildest defile of Badenoch or Lochaber as in Cornhill, that strangers could be enchanted by the blue dimples of the lakes and by the rainbows which overhung the waterfalls, and could derive a solemn pleasure even from the clouds and tempests which lowered on the mountain tops.

The change in the feeling with which the Lowlanders regarded the Highland scenery was closely connected with a change not less remarkable in the feeling with which they regarded the Highland race. It is not strange that the Wild Scotch, as they were sometimes called, should, in the seventeenth century, have been considered by the Saxons as mere savages. But it is surely strange that, considered as savages, they should not have been objects of interest and curiosity. The English were then abundantly inquisitive about the manners of rude nations separated from our island by great continents and oceans. Numerous books were printed describing the laws, the superstitions, the cabins, the repasts, the dresses, the marriages, the funerals of Laplanders and Hottentots, Mohawks and Malays. The plays and poems of that age are full of allusions to the usages of the black men of Africa and of the red men of America. The only barbarian about whom there was no wish to have any information was the Highlander. Five or six years after the Revolution, an indefatigable angler published an account of Scotland. He boasted that, in the course of his rambles from lake to lake, and from brook to brook, he had left scarcely a nook of the kingdom unexplored. But, when we examine his narrative, we find that he had never ventured beyond the extreme skirts of the Celtic region. He tells us that even from the people who lived close to the passes he could learn little or nothing about the Gaelic population. Few Englishmen, he says, had ever seen Inverary. All beyond Inverary was chaos.* In the reign of George the First, a work was

tions of admiration and delight, says most unpoetically, "Mount Cenis, I confess, carries the permission mountains have of being frightful rather too far; and its horrors were accompanied with too much danger to give one time to reflect upon their beauties."—Gray to West, Nov. 16. 1739.

* Northern Memoirs, by R. Franck

Philanthropus, 1694. The author had caught a few glimpses of Highland scenery, and speaks of it much as Burt spoke in the following generation: "It is a part of the creation left undressed; rubbish thrown aside when the magnificent fabric of the world was created; as void of form as the natives are indigent of morals and good manners."

published which professed to give a most exact account of Scotland; and in this work, consisting of more than three hundred pages, two contemptuous paragraphs were thought sufficient for the Highlands and the Highlanders.* We may well doubt whether, in 1689, one in twenty of the well read gentlemen who assembled at Will's coffeehouse knew that, within the four seas, and at the distance of less than five hundred miles from London, were many miniature courts, in each of which a petty prince, attended by guards, by armour bearers, by musicians, by a hereditary orator, by a hereditary poet laureate, kept a rude state, dispensed a rude justice, waged wars, and concluded treaties. While the old Gaelic institutions were in full vigour, no account of them was given by any observer, qualified to judge of them fairly. Had such an observer studied the character of the Highlanders, he would doubtless have found in it closely intermingled the good and the bad qualities of an uncivilised nation. He would have found that the people had no love for their country or for their king; that they had no attachment to any commonwealth larger than the clan, or to any magistrate superior to the chief. He would have found that life was governed by a code of morality and honour widely different from that which is established in peaceful and prosperous societies. He would have learned that a stab in the back, or a shot from behind a fragment of rock, were approved modes of taking satisfaction for insults. He would have heard men relate boastfully how they or their fathers had wreaked on hereditary enemies in a neighbouring valley such vengeance as would have made old soldiers of the Thirty Years' War shudder. He would have found that robbery was held to be a calling, not merely innocent, but honourable. He would have seen, wherever he turned, that dislike of steady industry, and that disposition to throw on the weaker sex the heaviest part of manual labour, which are characteristic of savages. He would have been struck by the spectacle of athletic men basking in the sun, angling for salmon, or taking aim at grouse, while their aged mothers, their pregnant wives, their tender daughters, were reaping the scanty harvest of oats. Nor did the women repine at their hard lot. In their view it was quite fit that a man, especially if he assumed the aristocratic title of Duinhe Wassel and adorned his bonnet with the eagle's feather, should take his ease, except when he was fighting, hunting, or marauding.

* Journey through Scotland, by the author of the Journey through England, 1723.

To mention the name of such a man in connection with commerce or with any mechanical art was an insult. Agriculture
was indeed less despised. Yet a highborn warrior was much
more becomingly employed in plundering the land of others
than in tilling his own. The religion of the greater part of
the Highlands was a rude mixture of Popery and Paganism.
The symbol of redemption was associated with heathen sacrifices and incantations. Baptised men poured libations of ale
to one Dæmon, and set out drink offerings of milk for another. Seers wrapped themselves up in bulls' hides, and
awaited, in that vesture, the inspiration which was to reveal
the future. Even among those ministrels and genealogists
whose hereditary vocation was to preserve the memory of
past events, an enquirer would have found very few who could
read. In truth, he might easily have journeyed from sea to
sea without discovering a page of Gaelic printed or written.
The price which he would have had to pay for his knowledge of
the country would have been heavy. He would have had to
endure hardships as great as if he had sojourned among the
Esquimaux or the Samoyeds. Here and there, indeed, at the
castle of some great lord who had a seat in the Parliament and
Privy Council, and who was accustomed to pass a large part
of his life in the cities of the South, might have been found
wigs and embroidered coats, plate and fine linen, lace and
jewels, French dishes and French wines. But, in general,
the traveller would have been forced to content himself with
very different quarters. In many dwellings the furniture,
the food, the clothing, nay the very hair and skin of his hosts,
would have put his philosophy to the proof. His lodging
would sometimes have been in a hut of which every nook
would have swarmed with vermin. He would have inhaled
an atmosphere thick with peat smoke, and foul with a
hundred noisome exhalations. At supper grain fit only for
horses would have been set before him, accompanied by a
cake of blood drawn from living cows. Some of the company
with which he would have feasted would have been covered
with cutaneous eruptions, and others would have been smeared
with tar like sheep. His couch would have been the bare
earth, dry or wet as the weather might be; and from that
couch he would have risen half poisoned with stench, half
blind with the reek of turf, and half mad with the itch.*

---

* Almost all these circumstances are
taken from Burt's Letters. For the
tar, I am indebted to Cleland's poetry.
In his verses on the "Highland Host"
he says :

"The reason is, they're smeared with tar,
Which doth defend their head and neck,
Just as it doth their sheep protect."

This is not an attractive picture. And yet an enlightened and dispassionate observer would have found in the character and manners of this rude people something which might well excite admiration and a good hope. Their courage was what great exploits achieved in all the four quarters of the globe have since proved it to be. Their intense attachment to their own tribe and to their own patriarch, though politically a great evil, partook of the nature of virtue. The sentiment was misdirected and ill regulated; but still it was heroic. There must be some elevation of soul in a man who loves the society of which he is a member and the leader whom he follows with a love stronger than the love of life. It was true that the Highlander had few scruples about shedding the blood of an enemy: but it was not less true that he had high notions of the duty of observing faith to allies and hospitality to guests. It was true that his predatory habits were most pernicious to the commonwealth. Yet those erred greatly who imagined that he bore any resemblance to villains who, in rich and well governed communities, live by stealing. When he drove before him the herds of Lowland farmers up the pass which led to his native glen, he no more considered himself as a thief than the Raleighs and Drakes considered themselves as thieves when they divided the cargoes of Spanish galleons. He was a warrior seizing lawful prize of war, of war never once intermitted during the thirty-five generations which had passed away since the Teutonic invaders had driven the children of the soil to the mountains. That, if he was caught robbing on such principles, he should, for the protection of peaceful industry, be punished with the utmost rigour of the law was perfectly just. But it was not just to class him morally with the pickpockets who infested Drury Lane Theatre, or the highwayman who stopped coaches on Blackheath. His inordinate pride of birth and his contempt for labour and trade were indeed great weaknesses, and had done far more than the inclemency of the air and the sterility of the soil to keep his country poor and rude. Yet even here there was some compensation. It must in fairness be acknowledged that the patrician virtues were not less widely diffused among the population of the Highlands than the patrician vices. As there was no other part of the island where men, sordidly clothed, lodged, and fed, indulged themselves to such a degree in the idle sauntering habits of an aristocracy, so there was no other part of the island where such men had in such a degree the better qualities of an aristocracy, grace and dignity of manner, selfrespect, and that noble sensibility which makes dishonour more terrible than death. A gentleman of Sky or Lochaber, whose clothes were begrimed with the accumulated filth of years, and whose hovel smelt worse than an English hogstye, would often do the honours of that hovel with a lofty courtesy worthy of the splendid circle of Versailles. Though he had as little booklearning as the most stupid ploughboys of England, it would have been a great error to put him in the same intellectual rank with such ploughboys. It is indeed only by reading that men can become profoundly acquainted with any science. But the arts of poetry and rhetoric may be carried near to absolute perfection, and may exercise a mighty influence on the public mind, in an age in which books are wholly or almost wholly unknown. The first great painter of life and manners has described with a vivacity which makes it impossible to doubt that he was copying from nature, the effect produced by eloquence and song on audiences ignorant of the alphabet. It is probable that, in the Highland councils, men who would not have been qualified for the duty of parish clerk sometimes argued questions of peace and war, of tribute and homage, with ability worthy of Halifax and Caermarthen, and that, at the Highland banquets, minstrels who did not know their letters sometimes poured forth rhapsodies in which a discerning critic might have found passages such as would have reminded him of the tenderness of Otway or of the vigour of Dryden.

There was therefore even then evidence sufficient to justify the belief that no natural inferiority had kept the Celt far behind the Saxon. It might safely have been predicted that, if ever an efficient police should make it impossible for the Highlander to avenge his wrongs by violence and to supply his wants by rapine, if ever his faculties should be developed by the civilising influence of the Protestant religion and of the English language, if ever he should transfer to his country and to her lawful magistrates the affection and respect with which he had been taught to regard his own petty community and his own petty prince, the kingdom would obtain an immense accession of strength for all the purposes both of peace and of war.

Such would doubtless have been the decision of a well informed and impartial judge. But no such judge was then to be found. The Saxons who dwelt far from the Gaelic provinces could not be well informed. The Saxons who dwelt near those provinces could not be impartial. National enmities have always been fiercest among borderers; and the enmity between the Highland borderer and the Lowland borderer along the whole frontier was the growth of ages, and was kept fresh by constant injuries. One day many square miles of pasture land were swept bare by armed plunderers from the hills. Another day a score of plaids dangled in a row on the gallows of Crieff or Stirling. Fairs were indeed held on the debatable land for the necessary interchange of commodities. But to those fairs both parties came prepared for battle; and the day often ended in bloodshed. Thus the Highlander was an object of hatred to his Saxon neighbours; and from his Saxon neighbours those Saxons who dwelt far from him learned the very little that they cared to know about his habits. When the English condescended to think of him at all,—and it was seldom that they did so,—they considered him as a filthy abject savage, a slave, a Papist, a cutthroat, and a thief.*

This contemptuous loathing lasted till the year 1745, and was then for a moment succeeded by intense fear and rage. England, thoroughly alarmed, put forth her whole strength. The Highlands were subjugated rapidly, completely, and for ever. During a short time the English nation, still heated by the recent conflict, breathed nothing but vengeance. The slaughter on the field of battle and on the scaffold was not sufficient to slake the public thirst for blood. The sight of the tartan inflamed the populace of London with hatred, which showed itself by unmanly outrages to defenceless captives. A

---

* A striking illustration of the opinion which was entertained of the Highlander by his Lowland neighbours, and which was by them communicated to the English, will be found in a volume of Miscellanies published by Afra Behn in 1685. One of the most curious pieces in the collection is a coarse and profane Scotch poem entitled, "How the first Hielandman was made." How and of what materials he was made I shall not venture to relate. The dialogue which immediately follows his creation may be quoted, I hope, without much offence.

" Says God to the Hielandman, 'Quhair wilt thou now?'
  'I will dcwn to the Lowlands, Lord, and there steal a cow.'
  'Ffy,' quod St. Peter, 'thou wilt never do weel,
  'An thou, but new made, so sone gais to steal.'
  'Umff,' quod the Hielandman, and swore by yon kirk,
  'So long as I may geir get to steal, will I nevir work.' "

An eminent Lowland Scot, the brave

Colonel Cleland, about the same time, described the Highlander in the same manner:

" For a misobliging word
  She'll dirk her neighbour o'er the board.
  If any ask her of her drift,
  Forsooth, her nainself lives by theft."

Much to the same effect are the very few words which Franck Philanthropus (1694) spares to the Highlanders: "They live like lairds and die like loons, hating to work and no credit to borrow: they make depredations and rob their neighbours." In the History of the Revolution in Scotland, printed at Edinburgh in 1690, is the following passage: "The Highlanders of Scotland are a sort of wretches that have no other consideration of honour, friendship, obedience, or government, than as, by any alteration of affairs or revolution in the government, they can improve to themselves an opportunity of robbing or plundering their bordering neighbours."

political and social revolution took place through the whole
Celtic region. The power of the chiefs was destroyed : the
people were disarmed : the use of the old national garb was
interdicted : the old predatory habits were effectually broken ;
and scarcely had this change been accomplished when a
strange reflux of public feeling began. Pity succeeded to
aversion. The nation execrated the cruelties which had been
committed on the Highlanders, and forgot that for those cruelties it was itself answerable. Those very Londoners, who,
while the memory of the march to Derby was still fresh, had
thronged to hoot and pelt the rebel prisoners, now fastened on
the prince who had put down the rebellion the nickname of
Butcher. Those barbarous institutions and usages, which,
while they were in full force, no Saxon had thought worthy
of serious examination, or had mentioned except with contempt, had no sooner ceased to exist than they became objects
of curiosity, of interest, even of admiration. Scarcely had the
chiefs been turned into mere landlords, when it became the
fashion to draw invidious comparisons between the rapacity of
the landlord and the indulgence of the chief. Men seemed to
have forgotten that the ancient Gaelic polity had been found
to be incompatible with the authority of law, had obstructed
the progress of civilisation, had more than once brought on the
empire the curse of civil war. As they had formerly seen only
the odious side of that polity, they could now see only the
pleasing side. The old tie, they said, had been parental : the
new tie was purely commercial. What could be more lamentable than that the head of a tribe should eject, for a paltry
arrear of rent, tenants who were his own flesh and blood,
tenants whose forefathers had often with their bodies covered
his forefathers on the field of battle ? As long as there were
Gaelic marauders, they had been regarded by the Saxon population as hateful vermin who ought to be exterminated without
mercy. As soon as the extermination had been accomplished,
as soon as cattle were as safe in the Perthshire passes as in
Smithfield market, the freebooter was exalted into a hero of
romance. As long as the Gaelic dress was worn, the Saxons
had pronounced it hideous, ridiculous, nay, grossly indecent.
Soon after it had been prohibited, they discovered that it was
the most graceful drapery in Europe. The Gaelic monuments,
the Gaelic usages, the Gaelic superstitions, the Gaelic verses,
disdainfully neglected during many ages, began to attract the
attention of the learned from the moment at which the peculiarities of the Gaelic race began to disappear. So strong was

this impulse that, where the Highlands were concerned, men of sense gave ready credence to stories without evidence, and men of taste gave rapturous applause to compositions without merit. Epic poems, which any skilful and dispassionate critic would at a glance have perceived to be almost entirely modern, and which, if they had been published as modern, would have instantly found their proper place in company with Blackmore's Alfred and Wilkie's Epigoniad, were pronounced to be fifteen hundred years old, and were gravely classed with the Iliad. Writers of a very different order from the impostor who fabricated these forgeries saw how striking an effect might be produced by skilful pictures of the old Highland life. Whatever was repulsive was softened down: whatever was graceful and noble was brought prominently forward. Some of these works were executed with such admirable art that, like the historical plays of Shakspeare, they superseded history. The visions of the poet were realities to his readers. The places which he described became holy ground, and were visited by thousands of pilgrims. Soon the vulgar imagination was so completely occupied by plaids, targets, and claymores, that, by most Englishmen, Scotchman and Highlander were regarded as synonymous words. Few people seemed to be aware that, at no remote period, a Macdonald or a Macgregor in his tartan was to a citizen of Edinburgh or Glasgow what an Indian hunter in his war paint is to an inhabitant of Philadelphia or Boston. Artists and actors represented Bruce and Douglas in striped petticoats. They might as well have represented Washington brandishing a tomahawk, and girt with a string of scalps. At length this fashion reached a point beyond which it was not easy to proceed. The last British King who held a court in Holyrood thought that he could not give a more striking proof of his respect for the usages which had prevailed in Scotland before the Union, than by disguising himself in what, before the Union, was considered by nine Scotchmen out of ten as the dress of a thief.

Thus it has chanced that the old Gaelic institutions and manners have never been exhibited in the simple light of truth. Up to the middle of the last century, they were seen through one false medium: they have since been seen through another. Once they loomed dimly through an obscuring and distorting haze of prejudice; and no sooner had that fog dispersed than they appeared bright with all the richest tints of poetry. The time when a perfectly fair picture could have been painted has now passed away. The

original has long disappeared: no authentic effigy exists:
and all that is possible is to produce an imperfect likeness by
the help of two portraits, of which one is a coarse caricature
and the other a masterpiece of flattery.

Peculiar
nature of
Jacobitism
in the
Highlands.

Among the erroneous notions which have been commonly
received concerning the history and character of the Highlanders is one which it is especially necessary to correct.
During the century which commenced with the campaign of
Montrose, and terminated with the campaign of the young
Pretender, every great military exploit which was achieved on
British ground in the cause of the House of Stuart was
achieved by the valour of Gaelic tribes. The English have
therefore very naturally ascribed to those tribes the feelings
of English cavaliers, profound reverence for the royal office,
and enthusiastic attachment to the royal family. A close
enquiry however will show that the strength of these feelings
among the Celtic clans has been greatly exaggerated.

In studying the history of our civil contentions, we must
never forget that the same names, badges, and warcries had
very different meanings in different parts of the British isles.
We have already seen how little there was in common between the Jacobitism of Ireland and the Jacobitism of England. The Jacobitism of the Scotch Highlander was, at least
in the seventeenth century, a third variety, quite distinct
from the other two. The Gaelic population was far indeed
from holding the doctrines of passive obedience and nonresistance. In fact disobedience and resistance made up the
ordinary life of that population. Some of those very clans
which it has been the fashion to describe as so enthusiastically loyal that they were prepared to stand by James
to the death, even when he was in the wrong, had never,
while he was on the throne, paid the smallest respect to his
authority, even when he was clearly in the right. Their
practice, their calling, had been to disobey and to defy him.
Some of them had actually been proscribed by sound of horn
for the crime of withstanding his lawful commands, and would
have torn to pieces without scruple any of his officers who
had dared to venture beyond the passes for the purpose of
executing his warrant. The English Whigs were accused by
their opponents of holding doctrines dangerously lax touching the obedience due to the chief magistrate. Yet no
respectable English Whig ever defended rebellion, except as
a rare and extreme remedy for rare and extreme evils. But
among those Celtic chiefs whose loyalty has been the theme

of so much warm eulogy were some whose whole existence from boyhood upwards had been one long rebellion. Such men, it is evident, were not likely to see the Revolution in the light in which it appeared to an Oxonian nonjuror. On the other hand they were not, like the aboriginal Irish, urged to take arms by impatience of Saxon domination. To such domination the Scottish Celt had never been subjected. He occupied his own wild and sterile region, and followed his own national usages. In his dealings with the Saxons, he was rather the oppressor than the oppressed. He exacted black mail from them : he drove away their flocks and herds; and they seldom dared to pursue him to his native wilderness. They had never portioned out among themselves his dreary region of moor and shingle. He had never seen the tower of his hereditary chieftains occupied by an usurper who could not speak Gaelic, and who looked on all who spoke it as brutes and slaves ; nor had his national and religious feelings ever been outraged by the power and splendour of a church which he regarded as at once foreign and heretical.

The real explanation of the readiness with which a large part of the population of the Highlands, twice in the seventeenth century, drew the sword for the Stuarts is to be found in the internal quarrels which divided the commonwealth of clans. For there was a commonwealth of clans, the image, on a reduced scale, of the great commonwealth of European nations. In the smaller of these two commonwealths, as in the larger, there were wars, treaties, alliances, disputes about territory and precedence, a system of public law, a balance of power. There was one inexhaustible source of discontents and quarrels. The feudal system had, some centuries before, been introduced into the hill country, but had neither destroyed the patriarchal system nor amalgamated completely with it. In general he who was lord in the Norman polity was also chief in the Celtic polity ; and, when this was the case, there was no conflict. But, when the two characters were separated, all the willing and loyal obedience was reserved for the chief. The lord had only what he could get and hold by force. If he was able, by the help of his own tribe, to keep in subjection tenants who were not of his own tribe, there was a tyranny of clan over clan, the most galling, perhaps, of all forms of tyranny. At different times different races had risen to an authority which had produced general fear and envy. The Macdonalds had once possessed, in the Hebrides and throughout the mountain country of Argyleshire and Invernessshire, an ascendency similar to that which the House of Austria had once possessed in Christendom. But the ascendency of the Macdonalds had, like the ascendency of the House of Austria, passed away ; and the Campbells, the children of Diarmid, had become in the Highlands what the Bourbons had become in Europe.* The parallel might be carried far. Imputations similar to those which it was the fashion to throw on the French government were thrown on the Campbells. A peculiar dexterity, a peculiar plausibility of address, a peculiar contempt for the obligations of plighted faith, were ascribed, with or without reason, to the dreaded race. " Fair and false like a Campbell," became a proverb. It was said that Mac Callum More after Mac Callum More had, with unwearied, unscrupulous, and unrelenting ambition, annexed mountain after mountain and island after island to the original domains of his House. Some tribes had been expelled from their territory, some compelled to pay tribute, some incorporated with the conquerors. At length the number of fighting men who bore the name of Campbell was sufficient to meet in the field of battle the combined forces of all the other western clans. It was during those civil troubles which commenced in 1638 that the power of this aspiring family reached the zenith. The Marquess of Argyle was the head of a party as well as the head of a tribe. Possessed of two different kinds of authority, he used each of them in such a way as to extend and fortify the other. The knowledge that he could bring into the field the claymores of five thousand half heathen mountaineers added to his influence among the austere Presbyterians who filled the Privy Council and the General Assembly at Edinburgh. His influence at Edinburgh added to the terror which he inspired among the mountains. Of all the Highland Princes whose history is well known to us he was the greatest and most dreaded. It was while his neighbours were watching the increase of his power with hatred which fear could scarcely keep down that Montrose called them to arms. The call was promptly obeyed. A powerful coalition of clans waged war, nominally for King Charles, but really against Mac Callum More   It is not easy for any person who has

Jealousy
of the
ascendency
of the
Campbells.

* Since this passage was written I was much pleased by finding that Lord Fountainhall used, in July 1676, exactly the same illustration which had occurred to me. He says that " Argyle's ambitious grasping at the mastery of the Highlands and Western Islands of Mull, Ila, &c., stirred up other clans to enter into a combination for bearing him downe, like the confederat forces of Germanie, Spain, Holland, &c., against the growth of the French."

studied the history of that contest to doubt that, if Argyle had supported the cause of monarchy, his neighbours would have declared against it. Grave writers tell of the victory gained at Inverlochy by the royalists over the rebels. But the peasants who dwell near the spot speak more accurately. They talk of the great battle won there by the Macdonalds over the Campbells.

The feelings which had produced the coalition against the Marquess of Argyle retained their force long after his death. His son, Earl Archibald, though a man of many eminent virtues, inherited, with the ascendency of his ancestors, the unpopularity which such ascendency could scarcely fail to produce. In 1675, several warlike tribes formed a confederacy against him, but were compelled to submit to the superior force which was at his command. There was therefore great joy from sea to sea when, in 1681, he was arraigned on a futile charge, condemned to death, driven into exile, and deprived of his dignities : there was great alarm when, in 1685, he returned from banishment, and sent forth the fiery cross to summon his kinsmen to his standard; and there was again great joy when his enterprise had failed, when his army had melted away, when his head had been fixed on the Tolbooth of Edinburgh, and when those chiefs who had regarded him as an oppressor had obtained from the Crown, on easy terms, remissions of old debts and grants of new titles. While England and Scotland generally were execrating the tyranny of James, he was honoured as a deliverer in Appin and Lochaber, in Glenroy and Glenmore.* The hatred excited by the power and ambition of the House of Argyle was not satisfied even when the head of that House had perished, when his children were fugitives, when strangers garrisoned the castle of Inverary, and when the whole shore of Loch Fyne had been laid waste by fire and sword. It was said that the terrible precedent which had been set in the case of the Macgregors ought to be followed, and that it ought to be made a crime to bear the odious name of Campbell.

On a sudden all was changed. The Revolution came. The heir of Argyle returned in triumph. He was, as his prede-

---

* In the introduction to the Memoirs of Sir Ewan Cameron is a very sensible remark : "It may appear paradoxical : but the editor cannot help hazarding the conjecture that the motives which prompted the Highlanders to support King James were substantially the same as those by which the promoters of the Revolution were actuated." The whole introduction, indeed, well deserves to be read.

cessors had been, the head, not only of a tribe, but of a party. The sentence which had deprived him of his estate and of his honours was treated by the majority of the Convention as a nullity. The doors of the Parliament House were thrown open to him : he was selected from the whole body of Scottish nobles to administer the oath of office to the new Sovereigns ; and he was authorised to raise an army on his domains for the service of the Crown. He would now, doubtless, be as powerful as the most powerful of his ancestors. Backed by the strength of the Government, he would demand all the long and heavy arrears of rent and tribute which were due to him from his neighbours, and would exact revenge for all the injuries and insults which his family had suffered. There was terror and agitation in the castles of twenty petty kings. The uneasiness was great among the Stewarts of Appin, whose territory was close pressed by the sea on one side, and by the race of Diarmid on the other. The Macnaghtens were still more alarmed. Once they had been the masters of those beautiful valleys through which the Ara and the Shira flow into Loch Fyne. But the Campbells had prevailed. The Macnaghtens had been reduced to subjection, and had, generation after generation, looked up with awe and detestation to the neighbouring Castle of Inverary. They had recently been promised a complete emancipation. A grant, by virtue of which their chief would have held his estate immediately from the Crown, had been prepared and was about to pass the seals, when the Revolution suddenly extinguished a hope which amounted almost to certainty.*

The Macleans remembered that, only fourteen years before, their lands had been invaded and the seat of their chief taken and garrisoned by the Campbells.† Even before William and Mary had been proclaimed at Edinburgh, a Maclean, deputed doubtless by the head of his tribe, had crossed the sea to Dublin, and had assured James that, if

The Stewarts and Macnaghtens.

The Macleans.

* Skene's Highlanders of Scotland ; Douglas's Baronage of Scotland.

† See the Memoirs of the Life of Sir Ewan Cameron, and the Historical and Genealogical Account of the Clan Maclean, by a Senachie. Though this last work was published so late as 1838, the writer seems to have been inflamed by animosity as fierce as that with which the Macleans of the seventeenth century regarded the Campbells. In the short compass of one page the Marquess of Argyle is designated as "the diabolical Scotch Cromwell," "the vile vindictive persecutor," "the base traitor," and "the Argyle impostor." In another page he is "the insidious Campbell, fertile in villany," "the avaricious slave," "the coward of Argyle," and "the Scotch traitor." In the next page he is "the base and vindictive enemy of the House of Maclean," "the hypocritical Covenanter," "the incorrigible traitor," "the cowardly and malignant enemy." It is a happy thing that passions so violent can now vent themselves only in scolding.

two or three battalions from Ireland landed in Argyleshire, they would be immediately joined by four thousand four hundred claymores.*

A similar spirit animated the Camerons. Their ruler, Sir Ewan Cameron, of Lochiel, surnamed the Black, was in personal qualities unrivalled among the Celtic princes. He was a gracious master, a trusty ally, a terrible enemy. His countenance and bearing were singularly noble. Some persons who had been at Versailles, and among them the shrewd and observant Simon Lord Lovat, said that there was, in person and manner, a most striking resemblance between Lewis the Fourteenth and Lochiel; and whoever compares the portraits of the two will perceive that there really was some likeness. In stature the difference was great. Lewis, in spite of highheeled shoes and a towering wig, hardly reached the middle size. Lochiel was tall and strongly built. In agility and skill at his weapons he had few equals among the inhabitants of the hills. He had repeatedly been victorious in single combat. He was a hunter of great fame. He made vigorous war on the wolves which, down to his time, preyed on the red deer of the Grampians; and by his hand perished the last of the ferocious breed which is known to have wandered at large in our island. Nor was Lochiel less distinguished by intellectual than by bodily vigour. He might indeed have seemed ignorant to educated and travelled Englishmen, who had studied the classics under Busby at Westminster and under Aldrich at Oxford, who had learned something about the sciences among Fellows of the Royal Society, and something about the fine arts in the galleries of Florence and Rome. But though Lochiel had very little knowledge of books, he was eminently wise in council, eloquent in debate, ready in devising expedients, and skilful in managing the minds of men. His understanding preserved him from those follies into which pride and anger frequently hurried his brother chieftains. Many, therefore, who regarded his brother chieftains as mere barbarians, mentioned him with respect. Even at the Dutch Embassy in Saint James's Square he was spoken of as a man of such capacity and courage that it would not be easy to find his equal. As a patron of literature, he ranks with the magnificent Dorset. If Dorset out of his own purse allowed Dryden a pension equal to the profits of the Laureateship, Lochiel is said to

The Camerons; Lochiel.

* Letter of Avaux to Louvois, April $\frac{6}{16}$. 1689, enclosing a paper entitled Mémoire du Chevalier Macklean.

have bestowed on a celebrated bard, who had been plundered
by marauders, and who implored alms in a pathetic Gaelic
ode, three cows, and the almost incredible sum of fifteen
pounds sterling. In truth, the character of this great chief
was depicted two thousand five hundred years before his
birth, and depicted,—such is the power of genius,—in
colours which will be fresh as many years after his death.
He was the Ulysses of the Highlands.*

He held a large territory peopled by a race which reverenced no lord, no king but himself. For that territory, however, he owed homage to the House of Argyle ; and he was
deeply in debt to his feudal superiors for rent. This vassalage
he had doubtless been early taught to consider as degrading
and unjust. In his minority he had been the ward in chivalry
of the politic Marquess, and had been educated at the Castle
of Inverary. But at eighteen the boy broke loose from the
authority of his guardian, and fought bravely both for
Charles the First and for Charles the Second. He was therefore considered by the English as a Cavalier, was well received at Whitehall after the Restoration, and was knighted
by the hand of James. The compliment, however, which
was paid to him, on one of his appearances at the English
Court, would not have seemed very flattering to a Saxon.
" Take care of your pockets, my lords," cried His Majesty ;
" here comes the king of the thieves." The loyalty of
Lochiel is almost proverbial : but it was very unlike what was
called loyalty in England. In the records of the Scottish
Parliament he was, in the days of Charles the Second, described as a lawless and rebellious man, who held lands
masterfully and in high contempt of the royal authority.*
On one occasion the Sheriff of Invernessshire was directed
by King James to hold a court in Lochaber. Lochiel,
jealous of this interference with his own patriarchal despotism, came to the tribunal at the head of four hundred armed
Camerons. He affected great reverence for the royal commis-

---

* See the singularly interesting Memoirs of Sir Ewan Cameron of Lochiel,
printed at Edinburgh for the Abbotsford
Club in 1842. The MS. must have been
at least a century older. See also in the
same volume the account of Sir Ewan's
death, copied from the Balhadie papers.
I ought to say that the author of the
Memoirs of Sir Ewan, though evidently
well informed about the affairs of the
Highlands and the characters of the

most distinguished chiefs, was grossly
ignorant of English politics and history.
I will quote what Van Citters wrote to
the States General about Lochiel, [Nov. 26.
Dec. 6.]
1689: " Sir Evan Cameron, Lord Loch-
eale, een man,—soo ik hoor van die hem
lange gekent en dagelyk hebben mede
omgegaan,—van so groot verstant, courage, en beleyt, als weyniges syns ge-
lycke syn."
† Act. Parl., July 5. 1661.

sion, but he dropped three or four words which were perfectly understood by the pages and armourbearers who watched every turn of his eye. "Is none of my lads so clever as to send this judge packing? I have seen them get up a quarrel when there was less need of one." In a moment a brawl began in the crowd, none could say how or where. Hundreds of dirks were out: cries of "Help" and "Murder" were raised on all sides: many wounds were inflicted: two men were killed: the sitting broke up in tumult; and the terrified Sheriff was forced to put himself under the protection of the chief, who, with a plausible show of respect and concern, escorted him safe home. It is amusing to think that the man who performed this feat is constantly extolled as the most faithful and dutiful of subjects by writers who blame Somers and Burnet as contemners of the legitimate authority of Sovereigns. Lochiel would undoubtedly have laughed the doctrine of nonresistance to scorn. But scarcely any chief in Invernessshire had gained more than he by the downfall of the House of Argyle, or had more reason than he to dread the restoration of that House. Scarcely any chief in Invernessshire, therefore, was more alarmed and disgusted by the proceedings of the Convention.

But of all those Highlanders who looked on the recent turn of fortune with painful apprehension the fiercest and the most powerful were the Macdonalds. More than one of the magnates who bore that widespread name laid claim to the honour of being the rightful successor of those Lords of the Isles, who, as late as the fifteenth century, disputed the preeminence of the Kings of Scotland. This genealogical controversy, which has lasted down to our own time, caused much bickering among the competitors. But they all agreed in regretting the past splendour of their dynasty, and in detesting the upstart race of Campbell. The old feud had never slumbered. It was still constantly repeated, in verse and prose, that the finest part of the domain belonging to the ancient heads of the Gaelic nation, Islay, where they had lived with the pomp of royalty, Iona, where they had been interred with the pomp of religion, the paps of Jura, the rich peninsula of Kintyre, had been transferred from the legitimate possessors to the insatiable Mac Callum More. Since the downfall of the House of Argyle, the Macdonalds, if they had not regained their ancient superiority, might at least boast that they had now no superior. Relieved from the fear of their mighty enemy in the West, they had turned their arms against weaker

The Macdonalds.

enemies in the East, against the clan of Mackintosh and against the town of Inverness.

Feud between the Macdonalds and Mackintoshes. The clan of Mackintosh, a branch of an ancient and renowned tribe which took its name and badge from the wild cat of the forests, had a dispute with the Macdonalds, which originated, if tradition may be believed, in those dark times when the Danish pirates wasted the coasts of Scotland. **Inverness.** Inverness was a Saxon colony among the Celts, a hive of traders and artisans in the midst of a population of loungers and plunderers, a solitary outpost of civilisation in a region of barbarians. Though the buildings covered but a small part of the space over which they now extend; though the arrival of a brig in the port was a rare event; though the Exchange was the middle of a miry street, in which stood a market cross much resembling a broken milestone; though the sittings of the municipal council were held in a filthy den with a roughcast wall; though the best houses were such as would now be called hovels; though the best roofs were of thatch: though the best ceilings were of bare rafters; though the best windows were, in bad weather, closed with shutters for want of glass; though the humbler dwellings were mere heaps of turf, in which barrels with the bottoms knocked out served the purpose of chimneys; yet to the mountaineer of the Grampians this city was as Babylon or as Tyre. Nowhere else had he seen four or five hundred houses, two churches, twelve maltkilns, crowded close together. Nowhere else had he been dazzled by the splendour of rows of booths, where knives, horn spoons, tin kettles, and gaudy ribands were exposed to sale. Nowhere else had he been on board of one of those huge ships which brought sugar and wine over the sea from countries far beyond the limits of his geography.* It is not strange that the haughty and warlike Macdonalds despising peaceful industry, yet envying the fruits of that industry, should have fastened a succession of quarrels on the people of Inverness. In the reign of Charles the Second, it had been apprehended that the town would be stormed and plundered by those rude neighbours. The terms of peace which they offered showed how little they regarded the authority of the prince and of the law. Their demand was that

---

* See Burt's Third and Fourth Letters. In the early editions is an engraving of the market cross of Inverness, and of that part of the street where the merchants congregated.

I ought here to acknowledge my obligations to Mr. Robert Carruthers, who kindly furnished me with much curious information about Inverness, and with some extracts from the municipal records.

a heavy tribute should be paid to them, that the municipal magistrates should bind themselves by an oath to deliver up to the vengeance of the clan every burgher who should shed the blood of a Macdonald, and that every burgher who should anywhere meet a person wearing the Macdonald tartan should ground arms in token of submission. Never did Lewis the Fourteenth, not even when he was encamped between Utrecht and Amsterdam, treat the States General with such despotic insolence.* By the intervention of the Privy Council of Scotland, a compromise was effected : but the old animosity was undiminished.

Common enmities and common apprehensions produced a good understanding between the town and the clan of Mackintosh. The foe most hated and dreaded by both was Colin Macdonald of Keppoch, an excellent specimen of the genuine Highland Jacobite. Keppoch's whole life had been passed in insulting and resisting the authority of the Crown. He had been repeatedly charged on his allegiance to desist from his lawless practices, but had treated every admonition with contempt. The government, however, was not willing to resort to extremities against him ; and he long continued to rule undisturbed the stormy peaks of Coryarrick, and the gigantic terraces which still mark the limits of what was once the Lake of Glenroy. He was famed for his knowledge of all the ravines and caverns of that dreary region ; and such was the skill with which he could track a herd of cattle to the most secret hidingplace that he was known by the nickname of Coll of the Cows.† At length his outrageous violations of all law compelled the Privy Council to take decided steps. He was proclaimed a rebel: letters of fire and sword were issued against him under the seal of James ; and a few weeks before the Revolution, a body of royal troops, supported by the whole strength of the Mackintoshes, marched into Keppoch's territories. Keppoch gave battle to the invaders, and was victorious. The King's forces were put to flight; the King's captain was slain ; and this by a hero whose loyalty to the King many writers have very complacently contrasted with the factious turbulence of the Whigs.‡

If Keppoch had ever stood in any awe of the government, he was completely relieved from that feeling by the general

Inverness threatened by Macdonald of Keppoch.

---

* I am indebted to Mr. Carruthers for a copy of the demands of the Macdonalds, and of the answer of the Town Council.

† Colt's Deposition, Appendix to the Act. Parl. of July 14. 1690.

‡ See the Life of Sir Ewan Cameron.

anarchy which followed the revolution. He wasted the lands
of the Mackintoshes, advanced to Inverness, and threatened
the town with destruction. The danger was extreme. The
houses were surrounded only by a wall which time and weather had so loosened that it shook in every storm. Yet the
inhabitants showed a bold front; and their courage was stimulated by their preachers. Sunday the twenty-eighth of
April was a day of alarm and confusion. The savages went
round and round the small colony of Saxons like a troop of
famished wolves round a sheepfold. Keppoch threatened and
blustered. He would come in with all his men. He would
sack the place. The burghers meanwhile mustered in arms
round the market cross to listen to the oratory of their ministers. The day closed without an assault: the Monday and
the Tuesday passed away in intense anxiety; and then an
unexpected mediator made his appearance.

Dundee
appears in
Keppoch's
camp.

Dundee, after his flight from Edinburgh, had retired to his
country seat in that valley through which the Glamis descends
to the ancient castle of Macbeth. Here he remained quiet
during some time. He protested that he had no intention of
opposing the new government. He declared himself ready to
return to Edinburgh, if only he could be assured that he
should be protected against lawless violence; and he offered
to give his word of honour, or, if that were not sufficient, to
give bail, that he would keep the peace. Some of his old soldiers had accompanied him, and formed a garrison sufficient
to protect his house against the Presbyterians of the neighbourhood. Here he might possibly have remained unharmed
and harmless, had not an event for which he was not answerable made his enemies implacable, and made him desperate.*

An emissary of James had crossed from Ireland to Scotland
with letters addressed to Dundee and Balcarras. Suspicion
was excited. The messenger was arrested, interrogated, and
searched; and the letters were found. Some of them proved
to be from Melfort and were worthy of him. Every line indicated those qualities which had made him the abhorrence of
his country, and the favourite of his master. He announced
with delight the near approach of the day of vengeance and
rapine, of the day when the estates of the seditious would be
divided among the loyal, and when many who had been great
and prosperous would be exiles and beggars. The king,
Melfort said, was determined to be severe. Experience had
at length convinced His Majesty that mercy would be weak-

* Balcarras's Memoirs; History of the late Revolution in Scotland.

ness. Even the Jacobites were disgusted by learning that a restoration would be immediately followed by a confiscation and a proscription. Some of them pretended to suspect a forgery. Others did not hesitate to say that Melfort was a villain, that he wished to ruin Dundee and Balcarras, and that, for that end, he had written these odious despatches, and had employed a messenger who had very dexterously managed to be caught. It is however quite certain that Melfort never disavowed these papers, and that, after they were published, he continued to stand as high as ever in the favour of James. It can therefore hardly be doubted that in those passages which shocked even the zealous supporters of hereditary right, the Secretary merely expressed with fidelity the feelings and intentions of his master.* Hamilton, by virtue of the powers which the Estates had, before their adjournment, confided to him, ordered Balcarras and Dundee to be arrested. Balcarras was taken, and was confined, first in his own house, and then in the Tolbooth of Edinburgh. But to seize Dundee was not so easy an enterprise. As soon as he heard that warrants were out against him, he crossed the Dee with his followers, and remained a short time in the wild domains of the House of Gordon. There he held some communication with the Macdonalds and Camerons about a rising. But he seems at this time to have known little and cared little about the Highlanders. For their national character he probably felt the dislike of a Saxon, for their military character the contempt of a professional soldier. He soon returned to the Lowlands, and stayed there till he learned that a considerable body of troops had been sent to apprehend him.† He then betook himself to the hill country as his last refuge, pushed northward through Strathdon and Strathbogie, crossed the Spey, and, on the morning of the first of May, arrived with a small band of horsemen at the camp of Keppoch before Inverness.

The new situation in which Dundee was now placed, the new view of society which was presented to him, naturally suggested new projects to his inventive and enterprising spirit.

---

* There is among the Nairne Papers in the Bodleian Library a curious MS. entitled "Journal de ce qui s'est passé en Irlande depuis l'arrivée de Sa Majesté." In this journal there are notes and corrections in English and French; the English in the handwriting of James, the French in the handwriting of Melfort. The letters intercepted by Hamilton are mentioned, and mentioned in a way which plainly shows that they were genuine; nor is there the least sign that James disapproved of them.

† "Nor did ever," says Balcarras, addressing James, "the Viscount of Dundee think of going to the Highlands without further orders from you, till a party was sent to apprehend him."

The hundreds of athletic Celts whom he saw in their national order of battle were evidently not allies to be despised. If he could form a great coalition of clans, if he could muster under one banner ten or twelve thousand of those hardy warriors, if he could induce them to submit to the restraints of discipline, what a career might be before him!

A commission from King James, even when King James was securely seated on the throne, had never been regarded with much respect by Coll of the Cows. That chief, however, hated the Campbells with all the hatred of a Macdonald, and promptly gave in his adhesion to the cause of the House of Stuart. Dundee undertook to settle the dispute between Keppoch and Inverness. The town agreed to pay two thousand dollars, a sum which, small as it might be in the estimation of the goldsmiths of Lombard Street, probably exceeded any treasure that had ever been carried into the wilds of Coryarrick. Half the sum was raised, not without difficulty, by the inhabitants; and Dundee is said to have passed his word for the remainder.*

He next tried to reconcile the Macdonalds with the Mackintoshes, and flattered himself that the two warlike tribes, lately arrayed against each other, might be willing to fight side by side under his command. But he soon found that it was no light matter to take up a Highland feud. About the rights of the contending Kings neither clan knew anything or cared anything. The conduct of both is to be ascribed to local passions and interests. What Argyle was to Keppoch, Keppoch was to the Mackintoshes. The Mackintoshes therefore remained neutral; and their example was followed by the Macphersons, another branch of the race of the wild cat. This was not Dundee's only disappointment. The Mackenzies, the Frasers, the Grants, the Munros, the Mackays, the Macleods, dwelt at a great distance from the territory of Mac Callum More. They had no dispute with him; they owed no debt to him; and they had no reason to dread the increase of his power. They therefore did not sympathise with his alarmed and exasperated neighbours, and could not be induced to join the confederacy against him.† Those chiefs, on the other hand, who lived nearer to Inverary, and to whom the name of Campbell had long been terrible and hateful, greeted

Insurrection of the clans hostile to the Campbells.

* See the narrative sent to James in Ireland and received by him July 7. 1689. It is among the Nairne Papers. See also the Memoirs of Dundee, 1714; Memoirs of Sir Ewan Cameron; Balcarras's Memoirs; Mackay's Memoirs.

These narratives do not perfectly agree with each other, or with the information which I obtained from Inverness.

† Memoirs of Dundee; Tarbet to Melville, 1st June 1689, in the Leven and Melville Papers.

Dundee eagerly, and promised to meet him at the head of their followers on the eighteenth of May. During the fortnight which preceded that day, he traversed Badenoch and Athol, and exhorted the inhabitants of those districts to rise in arms. He dashed into the Lowlands with his horsemen, surprised Perth, and carried off some Whig gentlemen prisoners to the mountains. Meanwhile the fiery crosses had been wandering from hamlet to hamlet over all the heaths and mountains thirty miles round Ben Nevis; and when he reached the trysting place in Lochaber he found that the gathering had begun. The head quarters were fixed close to Lochiel's house, a large pile built entirely of fir wood, and considered in the Highlands as a superb palace. Lochiel, surrounded by more than six hundred broadswords, was there to receive his guests. Macnaghten of Macnaghten and Stewart of Appin were at the muster with their little clans. Macdonald of Keppoch led the warriors who had, a few months before, under his command, put to flight the musketeers of King James. Macdonald of Clanronald was of tender years: but he was brought to the camp by his uncle, who acted as Regent during the minority. The youth was attended by a picked body guard composed of his own cousins, all comely in appearance, and good men of their hands. Macdonald of Glengarry, conspicuous by his dark brow and his lofty stature, came from that great valley where a chain of lakes, then unknown to fame, and scarcely set down in maps, is now the daily highway of steam vessels passing and repassing between the Atlantic and the German Ocean. None of the rulers of the mountains had a higher sense of his personal dignity, or was more frequently engaged in disputes with other chiefs. He generally affected in his manners and in his housekeeping a rudeness beyond that of his rude neighbours, and professed to regard the very few luxuries which had then found their way from the civilised parts of the world into the Highlands as signs of the effeminacy and degeneracy of the Gaelic race. But on this occasion he chose to imitate the splendour of Saxon warriors, and rode on horseback before his four hundred plaided clansmen in a steel cuirass and a coat embroidered with gold lace. Another Macdonald, destined to a lamentable and horrible end, led a band of hardy freebooters from the dreary pass of Glencoe. Somewhat later came the great Hebridean potentates. Macdonald of Sleat, the most opulent and powerful of all the grandees who laid claim to the lofty title of Lord of the Isles, arrived at the head of seven hundred fighting men from Sky. A fleet of long boats brought five hundred Macleans from Mull under the command of their chief, Sir John of Duart. A far more formidable array had in old times followed his forefathers to battle. But the power, though not the spirit, of the clan had been broken by the arts and arms of the Campbells. Another band of Macleans arrived under a valiant leader, who took his title from Lochbuy, which is, being interpreted, the Yellow Lake.*

Tarbet's advice to the government.

It does not appear that a single chief who had not some special cause to dread and detest the House of Argyle obeyed Dundee's summons. There is indeed strong reason to believe that the chiefs who came would have remained quietly at home if the government had understood the politics of the Highlands. Those politics were thoroughly understood by one able and experienced statesman, sprung from the great Highland family of Mackenzie, the Viscount Tarbet. He at this conjuncture pointed out to Melville by letter, and to Mackay in conversation, both the cause and the remedy of the distempers which seemed likely to bring on Scotland the calamities of civil war. There was, Tarbet said, no general disposition to insurrection among the Gael. Little was to be apprehended even from those popish clans which were under no apprehension of being subjected to the yoke of the Campbells. It was notorious that the ablest and most active of the discontented chiefs troubled themselves not at all about the questions which were in dispute between the Whigs and the Tories. Lochiel in particular, whose eminent personal qualities made him the most important man among the mountaineers, cared no more for James than for William. If the Camerons, the Macdonalds, and the Macleans could be convinced that, under the new government, their estates and their dignities would be safe, if Mac Callum More would make some concessions, if Their Majesties would take on themselves the payment of some arrears of rent, Dundee might call the clans to arms : but he would call to little purpose. Five thousand pounds, Tarbet

* Narrative in the Nairne Papers; Depositions of Colt, Osburne, Malcolm, and Stewart of Ballachan in the Appendix to the Act. Parl. of July 14. 1690 ; Memoirs of Sir Ewan Cameron. A few touches I have taken from an English translation of some passages in a lost epic poem written in Latin, and called the Grameis. The writer was a zealous Jacobite named Phillipps. I have seldom made use of the Memoirs of Dundee, printed in 1714, and never without some misgiving. The writer was certainly not, as he pretends. one of Dundee's officers, but a stupid and ignorant Grub Street garreteer. He is utterly wrong both as to the place and as to the time of the most important of all the events which he relates, the battle of Killiecrankie. He says that it was fought on the banks of the Tummell, and on the 13th of June. It was fought on the banks of the Garry, and on the 27th of July. After giving such a specimen of inaccuracy as this, it would be idle to point out minor blunders.

thought, would be sufficient to quiet all the Celtic magnates; and in truth, though that sum might seem ludicrously small to the politicians of Westminster, though it was not larger than the annual gains of the Groom of the Stole, or of the Paymaster of the Forces, it might well be thought immense by a barbarous potentate who, while he ruled hundreds of square miles, and could bring hundreds of warriors into the field, had perhaps never had fifty guineas at once in his coffers.*

Though Tarbet was considered by the Scottish ministers of the new Sovereigns as a very doubtful friend, his advice was not altogether neglected. It was resolved that overtures such as he recommended should be made to the malecontents. Much depended on the choice of an agent; and unfortunately the choice showed how little the prejudices of the wild tribes of the hills were understood at Edinburgh. A Campbell was selected for the office of gaining over to the cause of King William men whose only quarrel to King William was that he countenanced the Campbells. Offers made through such a channel were naturally regarded as at once snares and insults. After this it was to no purpose that Tarbet wrote to Lochiel and Mackay to Glengarry. Lochiel returned no answer to Tarbet; and Glengarry returned to Mackay a coldly civil answer, in which the general was advised to imitate the example of Monk.†

Mackay, meanwhile, wasted some weeks in marching, in countermarching, and in indecisive skirmishing. He afterwards honestly admitted that the knowledge which he had acquired, during thirty years of military service on the Continent, was, in the new situation in which he was placed, useless to him. It was difficult in such a country to track the enemy. It was impossible to drive him to bay. Food for an invading army was not to be found in the wilderness of heath and shingle; nor could supplies for many days be transported far over quaking bogs and up precipitous ascents. The general found that he had tired his men and their horses almost to death, and yet had effected nothing. Highland auxiliaries might have been of the greatest use to him: but he had few such auxiliaries. The chief of the Grants,

Indecisive campaign in the Highlands.

---

* From a letter of Archibald Earl of Argyle to Lauderdale, which bears date the 25th of June 1664, it appears that a hundred thousand marks Scots, little more than five thousand pounds sterling, would, at that time, have very nearly satisfied all the claims of Mac Callum More on his neighbours.

† Mackay's Memoirs; Tarbet to Melville, June 1. 1689, in the Leven and Melville Papers; Dundee to Melfort, June 27, in the Nairne Papers.

indeed, who had been persecuted by the late government, and had been accused of conspiring with the unfortunate Earl of Argyle, was zealous on the side of the Revolution. Two hundred Mackays, animated probably by family feeling, came from the northern extremity of our island, where at midsummer there is no night, to fight under a commander of their own name: but in general the clans which took no part in the insurrection awaited the event with cold indifference, and pleased themselves with the hope that they should easily make their peace with the conquerors, and be permitted to assist in plundering the conquered.

An experience of little more than a month satisfied Mackay that there was only one way in which the Highlands could be subdued. It was idle to run after the mountaineers up and down their mountains. A chain of fortresses must be built in the most important situations, and must be well garrisoned. The place with which the general proposed to begin was Inverlochy, where the huge remains of an ancient castle stood and still stand. This post was close to an arm of the sea, and was in the heart of the country occupied by the discontented clans. A strong force stationed there, and supported, if necessary, by ships of war, would effectually overawe at once the Macdonalds, the Camerons, and the Macleans.*

While Mackay was representing in his letters to the council at Edinburgh the necessity of adopting this plan, Dundee was contending with difficulties which all his energy and dexterity could not completely overcome.

Military character of the Highlanders.

The Highlanders, while they continued to be a nation living under a peculiar polity, were in one sense better and in another sense worse fitted for military purposes than any other nation in Europe. The individual Celt was morally and physically well qualified for war, and especially for war in so wild and rugged a country as his own. He was intrepid, strong, fleet, patient of cold, of hunger, and of fatigue. Up steep crags, and over treacherous morasses, he moved as easily as the French household troops paced along the great road from Versailles to Marli. He was accustomed to the use of weapons and to the sight of blood: he was a fencer: he was a marksman; and before he had ever stood in the ranks, he was already more than half a soldier.

As the individual Celt was easily turned into a soldier, so a tribe of Celts was easily turned into a battalion of soldiers.

See Mackay's Memoirs, and his letter to Hamilton of the 14th of June 1689.

All that was necessary was that the military organisation should be conformed to the patriarchal organisation. The Chief must be Colonel: his uncle or his brother must be Major: the tacksmen, who formed what may be called the peerage of the little community, must be the Captains: the company of each Captain must consist of those peasants who lived on his land, and whose names, faces, connections, and characters were perfectly known to him: the subaltern officers must be selected among the Duinhe Wassels, proud of the eagle's feather: the henchman was an excellent orderly: the hereditary piper and his sons formed the band; and the clan became at once a regiment. In such a regiment was found from the first moment that exact order and prompt obedience in which the strength of regular armies consists. Every man, from the highest to the lowest, was in his proper place, and knew that place perfectly. It was not necessary to impress by threats or by punishment on the newly enlisted troops the duty of regarding as their head him whom they had regarded as their head ever since they could remember anything. Every private had, from infancy, respected his corporal much and his Captain more, and had almost adored his Colonel. There was therefore no danger of mutiny. There was as little danger of desertion. Indeed the very feelings which most powerfully impel other soldiers to desert kept the Highlander to his standard. If he left it, whither was he to go? All his kinsmen, all his friends, were arrayed round it. To separate himself from it was to separate himself for ever from his family, and to incur all the misery of that very homesickness which, in regular armies, drives so many recruits to abscond at the risk of stripes and of death. When these things are fairly considered, it will not be thought strange that the Highland clans should have occasionally achieved great martial exploits.

But those very institutions which made a tribe of Highlanders, all bearing the same name, and all subject to the same ruler, so formidable in battle, disqualified the nation for war on a large scale. Nothing was easier than to turn clans into efficient regiments; but nothing was more difficult than to combine these regiments in such a manner as to form an efficient army. From the shepherds and herdsmen who fought in the ranks up to the chiefs, all was harmony and order. Every man looked up to his immediate superior; and all looked up to the common head. But with the chief this chain of subordination ended. He knew only how to govern, and had never learned to obey. Even to royal proclamations, even to Acts of Parliament, he was accustomed to yield obedience only when they were in perfect accordance with his own inclinations. It was not to be expected that he would pay to any delegated authority a respect which he was in the habit of refusing to the supreme authority. He thought himself entitled to judge of the propriety of every order which he received. Of his brother chiefs, some were his enemies, and some his rivals. It was hardly possible to keep him from affronting them, or to convince him that they were not affronting him. All his followers sympathised with all his animosities, considered his honour as their own, and were ready at his whistle to array themselves round him in arms against the commander in chief. There was therefore very little chance that by any contrivance any five clans could be induced to cooperate heartily with one another during a long campaign. The best chance, however, was when they were led by a Saxon. It is remarkable that none of the great actions performed by the Highlanders during our civil wars was performed under the command of a Highlander. Some writers have mentioned it as a proof of the extraordinary genius of Montrose and Dundee that those captains, though not themselves of Gaelic race or speech, should have been able to form and direct confederacies of Gaelic tribes. But in truth it was precisely because Montrose and Dundee were not Highlanders that they were able to lead armies composed of Highland clans. Had Montrose been chief of the Camerons, the Macdonalds would never have submitted to his authority. Had Dundee been chief of Clanronald, he would never have been obeyed by Glengarry. Haughty and punctilious men, who scarcely acknowledged the King to be their superior, would not have endured the superiority of a neighbour, an equal, a competitor. They could far more easily bear the preeminence of a distinguished stranger. Yet even to such a stranger they would allow only a very limited and a very precarious authority. To bring a chief before a court martial, to shoot him, to cashier him, to degrade him, to reprimand him publicly was impossible. Macdonald of Keppoch or Maclean of Duart would have struck dead any officer who had demanded his sword, and told him to consider himself as under arrest; and hundreds of claymores would instantly have been drawn to protect the murderer. All that was left to the commander under whom these potentates condescended to serve was to argue with them, to supplicate them, to flatter them, to bribe them; and it was only during a short time that any human skill could preserve harmony by these means. For every chief thought himself entitled to peculiar observance; and it was therefore impossible to pay marked court to any one without disobliging the rest. The general found himself merely the president of a congress of petty kings. He was perpetually called upon to hear and to compose disputes about pedigrees, about precedence, about the division of spoil. His decision, be it what it might, must offend somebody. At any moment he might hear that his right wing had fired on his centre in pursuance of some quarrel two hundred years old, or that a whole battalion had marched back to its native glen, because another battalion had been put in the post of honour. A Highland bard might easily have found in the history of the year 1689 subjects very similar to those with which the war of Troy furnished the great poets of antiquity. One day Achilles is sullen, keeps his tent, and announces his intention to depart with all his men. The next day Ajax is storming about the camp, and threatening to cut the throat of Ulysses.

Hence it was that, though the Highlanders achieved some great exploits in the civil wars of the seventeenth century, those exploits left no trace which could be discerned after the lapse of a few weeks. Victories of strange and almost portentous splendour produced all the consequences of defeat. Veteran soldiers and statesmen were bewildered by those sudden turns of fortune. It was incredible that undisciplined men should have performed such feats of arms. It was incredible that such feats of arms, having been performed, should be immediately followed by the triumph of the conquered and the submission of the conquerors. Montrose, having passed rapidly from victory to victory, was, in the full career of success, suddenly abandoned by his followers. Local jealousies and local interests had brought his army together. Local jealousies and local interests dissolved it. The Gordons left him because they fancied that he neglected them for the Macdonalds. The Macdonalds left him because they wanted to plunder the Campbells. The force which had once seemed sufficient to decide the fate of a kingdom melted away in a few days: and the victories of Tippermuir and Kilsyth were followed by the disaster of Philiphaugh. Dundee did not live long enough to experience a similar reverse of fortune; but there is every reason to believe that, had his life been prolonged one fortnight, his history would have been the history of Montrose retold.

Dundee made one attempt, soon after the gathering of the clans in Lochaber, to induce them to submit to the discipline of a regular army. He called a council of war to consider this subject. His opinion was supported by all the officers who had joined him from the low country. Distinguished among them were James Seton, Earl of Dunfermline, and James Galloway, Lord Dunkeld. The Celtic chiefs took the other side. Lochiel, the ablest among them, was their spokesman, and argued the point with much ingenuity and natural eloquence. " Our system,"—such was the substance of his reasoning,—" may not be the best: but we were bred to it from childhood : we understand it perfectly : it is suited to our peculiar institutions, feelings, and manners. Making war after our own fashion, we have the expertness and cool-ness of veterans. Making war in any other way, we shall be raw and awkward recruits. To turn us into soldiers like those of Cromwell and Turenne would be the business of years : and we have not even weeks to spare. We have time enough to unlearn our own discipline, but not time enough to learn yours." Dundee, with high compliments to Lochiel, declared himself convinced, and perhaps was convinced : for the reasonings of the wise old chief were by no means with-out weight.*

Quarrels in the High'and army.

Yet some Celtic usages of war were such as Dundee could not tolerate. Cruel as he was, his cruelty always had a method and a purpose. He still hoped that he might be able to win some chiefs who remained neutral; and he carefully avoided every act which could goad them into open hostility. This was undoubtedly a policy likely to promote the interest of James ; but the interest of James was nothing to the wild marauders who used his name and rallied round his banner merely for the purpose of making profitable forays and wreaking old grudges. Keppoch especially, who hated the Mackintoshes much more than he loved the Stuarts, not only plundered the territory of his enemies, but burned whatever he could not carry away. Dundee was moved to great wrath by the sight of the blazing dwellings. " I would rather," he said, " carry a musket in a respectable regiment than be captain of such a gang of thieves." Punishment was of course out of the question. Indeed it may be considered as a remark-

* Memoirs of Sir Ewan Cameron.

able proof of the general's influence that Coll of the Cows deigned to apologise for conduct for which, in a well governed army, he would have been shot.*

As the Grants were in arms for King William, their property was considered as fair prize. Their territory was invaded by a party of Camerons : a skirmish took place : some blood was shed; and many cattle were carried off to Dundee's camp, where provisions were greatly needed. This raid produced a quarrel, the history of which illustrates in the most striking manner the character of a Highland army. Among those who were slain in resisting the Camerons was a Macdonald of the Glengarry branch, who had long resided among the Grants, had become in feelings and opinions a Grant, and had absented himself from the muster of his tribe. Though he had been guilty of a high offence against the Gaelic code of honour and morality, his kinsmen remembered the sacred tie which he had forgotten. Good or bad, he was bone of their bone : he was flesh of their flesh; and he should have been reserved for their justice. The name which he bore, the blood of the Lords of the Isles, should have been his protection. Glengarry in a rage went to Dundee and demanded vengeance on Lochiel and the whole race of Cameron. Dundee replied that the unfortunate gentleman who had fallen was a traitor to the clan as well as to the King. Was it ever heard of in war that the person of an enemy, a combatant in arms, was to be held inviolable on account of his name and descent? And, even if wrong had been done, how was it to be redressed? Half the army must slaughter the other half before a finger could be laid on Lochiel. Glengarry went away raging like a madman. Since his complaints were disregarded by those who ought to right him, he would right himself: he would draw out his men, and fall sword in hand on the murderers of his cousin. During some time he would listen to no expostulation. When he was reminded that Lochiel's followers were in number nearly double of the Glengarry men, "No matter," he cried, "one Macdonald is worth two Camerons." Had Lochiel been equally irritable and boastful, it is probable that the Highland insurrection would have given little more trouble to the government, and that the rebels would have perished obscurely in the wilderness by one another's claymores. But nature had bestowed on him in large measure the qualities of a statesman, though fortune had hidden those qualities in an obscure corner of the

* Memoirs of Sir Ewan Cameron.

world. He saw that this was not a time for brawling; his own character for courage had long been established; and his temper was under strict government. The fury of Glengarry, not being inflamed by any fresh provocation, rapidly abated. Indeed there were some who suspected that he had never been quite so pugnacious as he had affected to be, and that his bluster was meant only to keep up his own dignity in the eyes of his retainers. However this might be, the quarrel was composed; and the two chiefs met with the outward show of civility at the general's table.*

Dundee applies to James for assistance.

What Dundee saw of his Celtic allies must have made him desirous to have in his army some troops on whose obedience he could depend, and who would not, at a signal from their colonel, turn their arms against their general and their king. He accordingly, during the months of May and June, sent to Dublin a succession of letters earnestly imploring assistance. If six thousand, four thousand, three thousand, regular soldiers were now sent to Lochaber, he trusted that His Majesty would soon hold a court in Holyrood. That such a force might be spared hardly admitted of a doubt. The authority of James was at that time acknowledged in every part of Ireland, except on the shores of Lough Erne and behind the ramparts of Londonderry. He had in that kingdom an army of forty thousand men. An eighth part of such an army would scarcely be missed there, and might, united with the clans which were in insurrection, effect great things in Scotland.

Dundee received such answers to his applications as encouraged him to hope that a large and well appointed force would soon be sent from Ulster to join him. He did not wish to try the chance of battle before these succours arrived.† Mackay, on the other hand, was weary of marching to and fro in a desert. His men were exhausted and out of heart. He thought it desirable that they should withdraw from the hill country; and William was of the same opinion.

The war in the Highlands suspended.

In June therefore the civil war was, as if by concert between the generals, completely suspended. Dundee remained in Lochaber, impatiently awaiting the arrival of troops and supplies from Ireland. It was impossible for him to keep his Highlanders together in a state of inactivity. A vast extent of moor and mountain was required to furnish food for so many mouths. The clans therefore went back to their own glens, having promised to reassemble on the first summons.

* Memoirs of Sir Ewan Cameron.   † Dundee to Melfort, June 27. 1689.

Meanwhile Mackay's soldiers, exhausted by severe exertions and privations, were taking their ease in quarters scattered over the low country from Aberdeen to Stirling. Mackay himself was at Edinburgh, and was urging the ministers there to furnish him with the means of constructing a chain of fortifications among the Grampians. The ministers had, it should seem, miscalculated their military resources. It had been expected that the Campbells would take the field in such force as would balance the whole strength of the clans which marched under Dundee. It had also been expected that the Covenanters of the West would hasten to swell the ranks of the army of King William. Both expectations were disappointed. Argyle had found his principality devastated, and his tribe disarmed and disorganised. A considerable time must elapse before his standard would be surrounded by an array such as his forefathers had led to battle. The Covenanters of the West were in general unwilling to enlist. They were assuredly not wanting in courage; and they hated Dundee with deadly hatred. In their part of the country the memory of his cruelty was still fresh. Every village had its own tale of blood. The greyheaded father was missed in one dwelling, the hopeful stripling in another. It was remembered but too well how the dragoons had stalked into the peasant's cottage, cursing and damning him, themselves, and each other at every second word, pushing from the ingle nook his grandmother of eighty, and thrusting their hands into the bosom of his daughter of sixteen; how the abjuration had been tendered to him; how he had folded his arms and said " God's will be done "; how the Colonel had called for a file with loaded muskets; and how in three minutes the good man of the house had been wallowing in a pool of blood at his own door. The seat of the martyr was still vacant at the fireside; and every child could point out his grave still green amidst the heath. When the people of this region called their oppressor a servant of the devil, they were not speaking figuratively. They believed that between the bad man and the bad angel there was a close alliance on definite terms; that Dundee had bound himself to do the work of hell on earth, and that, for high purposes, hell was permitted to protect its slave till the measure of his guilt should be full. But, intensely as these men abhorred Dundee, most of them had a scruple about drawing the sword for William. A great meeting was held in the parish church of Douglas: and the question was propounded, whether, at a time when war was

Scruples of the Covenanters about taking arms for King William.

in the land, and when an Irish invasion was expected, it were
not a duty to take arms.   The debate was sharp and tumultuous.   The orators on one side adjured their brethren not to
incur the curse denounced against the inhabitants of Meroz,
who came not to the help of the Lord against the mighty.
The orators on the other side thundered against sinful associations. There were malignants in William's army: Mackay's
own orthodoxy was problematical : to take military service
with such comrades, and under such a general, would be a sinful association.   At length after much wrangling, and amidst
great confusion, a vote was taken ; and the majority pronounced that to take military service would be a sinful association. There was however a large minority ; and, from among
the members of this minority, the Earl of Angus was able to
raise a body of infantry, which is still, after the lapse of more
than a hundred and sixty years, known by the name of the
The Came- Cameronian Regiment.   The first Lieutenant Colonel was
ronian
regiment
raised.
Cleland, that implacable avenger of blood who had driven
Dundee from the Convention.   There was no small difficulty
in filling the ranks ; for many West country Whigs, who did
not think it absolutely sinful to enlist, stood out for terms
subversive of all military discipline.   Some would not serve
under any colonel, major, captain, serjeant, or corporal, who
was not ready to sign the Covenant.   Others insisted that, if
it should be found absolutely necessary to appoint any officer
who had taken the tests imposed in the late reign, he should
at least qualify himself for command by publicly confessing
his sin at the head of the regiment.   Most of the enthusiasts
who had proposed these conditions were induced by dexterous
management to abate much of their demands.   Yet the new
regiment had a very peculiar character.   The soldiers were all
rigid Puritans.   One of their first acts was to petition the
Parliament that all drunkenness, licentiousness, and profaneness might be severely punished.   Their own conduct must
have been exemplary : for the worst crime which the most
austere bigotry could impute to them was that of huzzaing on
the King's birthday.   It was originally intended that with
the military organisation of the corps should be interwoven
the organisation of a Presbyterian congregation.   Each company was to furnish an elder ; and the elders were, with the
chaplain, to form an ecclesiastical court for the suppression
of immorality and heresy.   Elders, however, were not appointed : but a noted hill preacher, Alexander Shields, was
called to the office of chaplain.   It is not easy to conceive

Costumes of the Time of William and Mary

that fanaticism can be heated to a higher temperature than that which is indicated by the writings of Shields. According to him, it should seem to be the first duty of a Christian ruler to persecute to the death every heterodox subject, and the first duty of a Christian subject to poniard a heterodox ruler. Yet there was then in Scotland an enthusiasm compared with which the enthusiasm even of this man was lukewarm. The extreme Covenanters protested against his defection as vehemently as he had protested against the Black Indulgence and the oath of supremacy, and pronounced every man who entered Angus's regiment guilty of a wicked confederacy with malignants.*

Meanwhile Edinburgh Castle had fallen, after holding out more than two months. Both the defence and the attack had been languidly conducted. The Duke of Gordon, unwilling to incur the mortal hatred of those at whose mercy his lands and life might soon be, did not choose to batter the city. The assailants, on the other hand, carried on their operations with so little energy and so little vigilance that a constant communication was kept up between the Jacobites within the citadel and the Jacobites without. Strange stories were told of the polite and facetious messages which passed between the besieged and the besiegers. On one occasion Gordon sent to inform the magistrates that he was going to fire a salute on account of some news which he had received from Ireland, but that the good town need not be alarmed, for that his guns would not be loaded with ball. On another occasion, his drums beat a parley; the white flag was hung out: a conference took place; and he gravely informed the enemy that all his cards had been thumbed to pieces, and begged to have a few more packs. His friends established a telegraph by means of which they conversed with him across the lines of sentinels. From a window in the top story of one of the loftiest of those gigantic houses, a few of which still darken the High Street, a white cloth was hung out when all was well, and a black cloth when things went ill. If it was necessary to give more detailed information, a board

---

* See Faithful Contendings Displayed, particularly the proceedings of April 29. and 30. and of May 13. and 14. 1689; the petition to Parliament drawn up by the regiment, on July 18. 1689; the protestation of Sir Robert Hamilton of November 6. 1689; and the admonitory Epistle to the Regiment, dated March 27. 1690. The Society people, as they called themselves, seem to have been especially shocked by the way in which the King's birthday had been kept. "We hope," they wrote, "ye are against observing anniversary days as well as we, and that ye will mourn for what ye have done." As to the opinions and temper of Alexander Shields, see his Hind Let Loose.

was held up inscribed with capital letters so large that they could, by the help of a telescope, be read on the ramparts of the castle. Agents laden with letters and fresh provisions managed, in various disguises and by various shifts, to cross the sheet of water which then lay on the north of the fortress and to clamber up the precipitous ascent. The peal of a musket from a particular half moon was the signal which announced to the friends of the House of Stuart that another of their emissaries had got safe up the rock. But at length the supplies were exhausted; and it was necessary to capitulate. Favourable terms were readily granted: the garrison marched out; and the keys were delivered up amidst the acclamations of a great multitude of burghers.*

Session of Parliament at Edinburgh.

But the government had far more acrimonious and more pertinacious enemies in the Parliament House than in the Castle. When the Estates reassembled after their adjournment, the crown and sceptre of Scotland were displayed with the wonted pomp in the hall as types of the absent sovereign. Hamilton rode in state from Holyrood up the High Street as Lord High Commissioner; and Crawford took the chair as President. Two Acts, one turning the Convention into a Parliament, the other recognising William and Mary as King and Queen, were rapidly passed and touched with the sceptre; and then the conflict of factions began.†

Ascendency of the Club.

It speedily appeared that the opposition which Montgomery had organised was irresistibly strong. Though made up of many conflicting elements, Republicans, Whigs, Tories, zealous Presbyterians, bigoted Prelatists, it acted for a time as one man, and drew to itself a multitude of those mean and timid politicians who naturally gravitate towards the stronger party. The friends of the government were few and disunited. Hamilton brought but half a heart to the discharge of his duties. He had always been unstable; and he was now discontented. He held indeed the highest place to which a subject could aspire. But he imagined that he had only the show of power while others enjoyed the substance, and was not sorry to see those of whom he was jealous thwarted and annoyed. He did not absolutely betray the prince whom he represented: but he sometimes tampered with the chiefs of the Club, and sometimes did sly ill turns to those who were joined with him in the service of the Crown.

* Siege of the Castle of Edinburgh,   † Act. Parl. Scot., June 5., June 17. printed for the Bannatyne Club; Lond. 1689.
Gaz., June $\frac{10}{20}$. 1689.

His instructions directed him to give the royal assent to laws for the mitigating or removing of numerous grievances, and particularly to a law restricting the power and reforming the constitution of the Committee of Articles, and to a law establishing the Presbyterian Church Government.* But it mattered not what his instructions were. The chiefs of the Club were bent on finding a cause of quarrel. The propositions of the Government touching the Lords of the Articles were contemptuously rejected. Hamilton wrote to London for fresh directions; and soon a second plan, which left little more than the name of the once despotic Committee, was sent back. But the second plan, though such as would have contented judicious and temperate reformers, shared the fate of the first. Meanwhile the chiefs of the Club laid on the table a law which interdicted the King from ever employing in any public office any person who had ever borne any part in any proceeding inconsistent with the Claim of Right, or who had ever obstructed or retarded any good design of the Estates. This law, uniting, within a very short compass, almost all the faults which a law can have, was well known to be aimed at the Lord President of the Court of Session, and at his son the Lord Advocate. Their prosperity and power made them objects of envy to every disappointed candidate for office. That they were new men, the first of their race who had risen to distinction, and that nevertheless they had, by the mere force of ability, become as important in the state as the Duke of Hamilton or the Earl of Argyle, was a thought which galled the hearts of many needy and haughty patricians. To the Whigs of Scotland the Dalrymples were what Halifax and Caermarthen were to the Whigs of England. Neither the exile of Sir James, nor the zeal with which Sir John had promoted the Revolution, was received as an atonement for old delinquency. They had both served the bloody and idolatrous House. They had both oppressed the people of God. Their late repentance might perhaps give them a fair claim to pardon, but surely gave them no right to honours and rewards.

The friends of the government in vain attempted to divert the attention of the Parliament from the business of persecuting the Dalrymple family to the important and pressing question of Church Government. They said that the old system had been abolished; that no other system had been substituted; that it was impossible to say what was the estab-

* The instructions will be found among the Somers Tracts.

lished religion of the kingdom ; and that the first duty of the
legislature was to put an end to an anarchy which was daily
producing disasters and crimes.   The leaders of the Club
were not to be so drawn away from their object.   It was
moved and resolved that the consideration of ecclesiastical
affairs should be postponed till secular affairs had been
settled.   The unjust and absurd Act of Incapacitation was
carried by seventy-four voices to twenty-four.   Another vote
still more obviously aimed at the House of Stair speedily followed.   The Parliament laid claim to a Veto on the nomi-
nation of the Judges, and assumed the power of stopping the
signet, in other words, of suspending the whole administration of justice, till this claim should be allowed.   It was plain
from what passed in debate, that though the chiefs of the
Club had begun with the Court of Session, they did not mean
to end there.   The arguments used by Sir Patrick Hume
and others led directly to the conclusion that the King ought
not to have the appointment of any great public functionary.
Sir Patrick indeed avowed, both in speech and in writing, his
opinion that the whole patronage of the realm ought to be
transferred from the Crown to the Estates.   When the place
of Treasurer, of Chancellor, of Secretary, was vacant, the
Parliament ought to submit two or three names to His Majesty ; and one of those names His Majesty ought to be bound
to select.*

All this time the Estates obstinately refused to grant any
supply till their Acts should have been touched with the
sceptre.   The Lord High Commissioner was at length so
much provoked by their perverseness that, after long tempo-
rising, he refused to touch even Acts which were in themselves unobjectionable, and to which his instructions empowered him to consent.   This state of things would have
ended in some great convulsion, if the King of Scotland had
not been also King of a much greater and more opulent
kingdom.   Charles the First had never found any parliament
at Westminster more unmanageable than William, during
this session, found the parliament at Edinburgh.   But it was
not in the power of the parliament at Edinburgh to put on
William such a pressure as the parliament at Westminster
had put on Charles.   A refusal of supplies at Westminster
was a serious thing, and left the Sovereign no choice except
to yield, or to raise money by unconstitutional means.   But

---

* As to Sir Patrick's views, see his   letter of the 11th of July, in the Leven
letter of the 7th of June, and Lockhart's   and Melville Papers.

a refusal of supplies at Edinburgh reduced him to no such dilemma. The largest sum that he could hope to receive from Scotland in a year was less than what he received from England every fortnight. He had therefore only to entrench himself within the limits of his undoubted prerogative, and there to remain on the defensive, till some favourable conjuncture should arrive.*

While these things were passing in the Parliament House, the civil war in the Highlands, having been during a few weeks suspended, broke forth again more violently than before. Since the splendour of the House of Argyle had been eclipsed, no Gaelic chief could vie in power with the Marquess of Athol. The district from which he took his title, and of which he might almost be called the sovereign, was in extent larger than an ordinary county, and was more fertile, more diligently cultivated, and more thickly peopled than the greater part of the Highlands. The men who followed his banner were supposed to be not less numerous than all the Macdonalds and Macleans united, and were, in strength and courage, inferior to no tribe in the mountains. But the clan had been made insignificant by the insignificance of the chief. The Marquess was the falsest, the most fickle, the most pusillanimous, of mankind. Already, in the short space of six months, he had been several times a Jacobite, and several times a Williamite. Both Jacobites and Williamites regarded him with contempt and distrust, which respect for his immense power prevented them from fully expressing. After repeatedly vowing fidelity to both parties, and repeatedly betraying both, he began to think that he should best provide for his safety by abdicating the functions both of a peer and of a chieftain, by absenting himself both from the Parliament House at Edinburgh and from his castle in the mountains, and by quitting the country to which he was bound by every tie of duty and honour at the very crisis of her fate. While all Scotland was waiting with impatience and anxiety to see in which army his numerous retainers would be arrayed, he stole away to England, settled himself at Bath, and pretended to drink the waters.† His principality, left without a head, was divided

Troubles in Athol.

* My chief materials for the history of this session have been the Acts, the Minutes, and the Leven and Melville Papers.

† "Athol," says Dundee contemptuously, "is gone to England, who did not know what to do."—Dundee to Melfort, June 27. 1689. See Athol's letters to Melville of the 21st of May and the 8th of June, in the Leven and Melville Papers.

against itself. The general leaning of the Athol men
was towards King James. For they had been employed
by him, only four years before, as the ministers of his
vengeance against the House of Argyle. They had garrisoned Inverary : they had ravaged Lorn : they had demolished houses, cut down fruit trees, burned fishing boats,
broken millstones, hanged Campbells, and were therefore not
likely to be pleased by the prospect of Mac Callum More's
restoration. One word from the Marquess would have sent
two thousand claymores to the Jacobite side. But that word he
would not speak ; and the consequence was, that the conduct
of his followers was as irresolute and inconsistent as his own.

While they were waiting for some indication of his wishes,
they were called to arms at once by two leaders, either of
whom might, with some show of reason, claim to be considered as the representative of the absent chief. Lord
Murray, the Marquess's eldest son, who was married to a
daughter of the Duke of Hamilton, declared for King
William. Stewart of Ballenach, the Marquess's confidential
agent, declared for King James. The people knew not which
summons to obey. He whose authority would have been
held in profound reverence had plighted faith to both sides,
and had then run away for fear of being under the necessity
of joining either ; nor was it very easy to say whether the
place which he had left vacant belonged to his steward or to
his heir apparent.

The most important military post in Athol was Blair
Castle. The house which now bears that name is not distinguished by any striking peculiarity from other country
seats of the aristocracy. The old building was a lofty tower
of rude architecture which commanded a vale watered by
the Garry. The walls would have offered very little resistance to a battering train, but were quite strong enough
to keep the herdsmen of the Grampians in awe. About
five miles south of this stronghold, the valley of the Garry
contracts itself into the celebrated glen of Killiecrankie.
At present a highway as smooth as any road in Middlesex
ascends gently from the low country to the summit of the
defile. White villas peep from the birch forest ; and, on
a fine summer day, there is scarcely a turn of the pass at
which may not be seen some angler casting his fly on the
foam of the river, some artist sketching a pinnacle of rock,
or some party of pleasure banqueting on the turf in the fret-
work of shade and sunshine. But, in the days of William

the Third, Killiecrankie was mentioned with horror by the peaceful and industrious inhabitants of the Perthshire lowlands. It was deemed the most perilous of all those dark ravines through which the marauders of the hills were wont to sally forth. The sound, so musical to modern ears, of the river brawling round the mossy rocks and among the smooth pebbles, the masses of grey crag and dark verdure worthy of the pencil of Wilson, the fantastic peaks bathed, at sunrise and sunset, with light rich as that which glows on the canvass of Claude, suggested to our ancestors thoughts of murderous ambuscades, and of bodies stripped, gashed, and abandoned to the birds of prey. The only path was narrow and rugged : a horse could with difficulty be led up : two men could hardly walk abreast ; and, in some places, the way ran so close by the precipice that the traveller had great need of a steady eye and foot. Many years later, the first Duke of Athol constructed a road up which it was just possible to drag his coach. But even that road was so steep and so strait that a handful of resolute men might have defended it against an army* ; nor did any Saxon consider a visit to Killiecrankie as a pleasure, till experience had taught the English Government that the weapons by which the Celtic clans could be most effectually subdued were the pickaxe and the spade.

The country which lay just above this pass was now the theatre of a war such as the Highlands had not often witnessed. Men wearing the same tartan, and attached to the same lord, were arrayed against each other. The name of the absent chief was used, with some show of reason, on both sides. Ballenach, at the head of a body of vassals who considered him as the representative of the Marquess, occupied Blair Castle. Murray, with twelve hundred followers, appeared before the walls, and demanded to be admitted into the mansion of his family, the mansion which would one day be his own. The garrison refused to open the gates. Messengers were sent off by the besiegers to Edinburgh, and by the besieged to Lochaber.† In both places the tidings produced great agitation. Mackay and Dundee agreed in thinking that the crisis required prompt and strenuous exertion. On the fate of Blair Castle probably depended the fate of all Athol. On the fate of Athol might depend the fate of Scotland. Mackay hastened northward, and ordered his troops to assemble in the low country of Perthshire. Some of them were quartered at such a distance that they did not arrive in

The war breaks out again in the Highlands.

---

* Memoirs of Sir Ewan Cameron.   † Mackay's Memoirs.

time. He soon, however, had with him the three Scotch
regiments which had served in Holland, and which bore the
names of their colonels, Mackay himself, Balfour, and Ramsay. There was also a gallant regiment of infantry from
England, then called Hastings's, but now known as the
thirteenth of the line. With these old troops were joined
two regiments newly levied in the Lowlands. One of them
was commanded by Lord Kenmore ; the other, which had
been raised on the Border, and which is still styled the King's
Own Borderers, by Lord Leven. Two troops of horse, Lord
Annandale's and Lord Belhaven's, probably made up the
army to the number of above three thousand men. Belhaven
rode at the head of his troop : but Annandale, the most factious of all Montgomery's followers, preferred the Club and
the Parliament House to the field.*

Dundee, meanwhile, had summoned all the clans which
acknowledged his commission to assemble for an expedition
into Athol. His exertions were strenuously seconded by
Lochiel. The fiery crosses were sent again in all haste
through Appin and Ardnamurchan, up Glenmore, and along
Loch Leven. But the call was so unexpected, and the time
allowed was so short, that the muster was not a very full one.
The whole number of broadswords seems to have been under
three thousand. With this force, such as it was, Dundee set
forth. On his march he was joined by succours which had
just arrived from Ulster. They consisted of little more than
three hundred Irish foot, ill armed, ill clothed, and ill disciplined. Their commander was an officer named Cannon,
who had seen service in the Netherlands, and who might
perhaps have acquitted himself well in a subordinate post
and in a regular army, but who was altogether unequal to
the part now assigned to him.† He had already loitered
among the Hebrides so long that some ships which had been
sent with him, and which were laden with stores, had been
taken by English cruisers. He and his soldiers had with
difficulty escaped the same fate. Incompetent as he was, he
bore a commission which gave him military rank in Scotland
next to Dundee.

The disappointment was severe. In truth James would
have done better to withhold all assistance from the Highlanders than to mock them by sending them, instead of the
well appointed army which they had asked and expected, a

* Mackay's Memoirs.
† Van Odyck to the Greffier of the States General, Aug. $\frac{2}{12}$. 1689.

rabble contemptible in numbers and appearance. It was now evident that whatever was done for his cause in Scotland must be done by Scottish hands.*

While Mackay from one side, and Dundee from the other, were advancing towards Blair Castle, important events had taken place there. Murray's adherents soon began to waver in their fidelity to him. They had an old antipathy to Whigs; for they considered the name of Whig as synonymous with the name of Campbell. They saw arrayed against them a large number of their kinsmen, commanded by a gentleman who was supposed to possess the confidence of the Marquess. The besieging army therefore melted rapidly away. Many returned home on the plea that, as their neighbourhood was about to be the seat of war, they must place their families and cattle in security. Others more ingenuously declared that they would not fight in such a quarrel. One large body went to a brook, filled their bonnets with water, drank a health to King James, and then dispersed.† Their zeal for King James, however, did not induce them to join the standard of his general. They lurked among the rocks and thickets which overhang the Garry, in the hope that there would soon be a battle, and that, whatever might be the event, there would be fugitives and corpses to plunder.

Murray was in a strait. His force had dwindled to three or four hundred men: even in those men he could put little trust; and the Macdonalds and Camerons were advancing fast. He therefore raised the siege of Blair Castle, and retired with a few followers into the defile of Killiecrankie. There he was soon joined by a detachment of two hundred fusileers whom Mackay had sent forward to secure the pass. The main body of the Lowland army speedily followed.‡

Early in the morning of Saturday the twenty-seventh of July, Dundee arrived at Blair Castle. There he learned that Mackay's troops were already in the ravine of Killiecrankie. It was necessary to come to a prompt decision. A council of war was held. The Saxon officers were generally against hazarding a battle. The Celtic chiefs were of a different opinion. Glengarry and Lochiel were now both of a mind. "Fight, my Lord," said Lochiel with his usual energy: "fight immediately: fight, if you have only one to three. Our men are in heart. Their only fear is that the enemy should escape. Give them their way; and be assured that they will either

* Memoirs of Sir Ewan Cameron.   ‡ Mackay's Short Relation, dated
† Balcarras's Memoirs.   Aug. 17. 1689.

perish or gain a complete victory.   But if you restrain them,
if you force them to remain on the defensive, I answer for
nothing.   If we do not fight, we had better break up and
retire to our mountains."*

Dundee's countenance brightened.   "You hear, gentlemen," he said to his Lowland officers, " you hear the opinion
of one who understands Highland war better than any of us."
No voice was raised on the other side.   It was determined to
fight; and the confederated clans in high spirits set forward
to encounter the enemy.

The enemy meanwhile had made his way up the pass.
The ascent had been long and toilsome: for even the foot had
to climb by twos and threes; and the baggage horses, twelve
hundred in number, could mount only one at a time.   No
wheeled carriage had ever been tugged up that arduous path.
The head of the column had emerged and was on the table
land, while the rearguard was still in the plain below.   At
length the passage was effected; and the troops found themselves in a valley of no great extent.   Their right was flanked
by a rising ground, their left by the Garry.   Wearied with
their morning's work, they threw themselves on the grass to
take some rest and refreshment.

Early in the afternoon they were roused by an alarm that
the Highlanders were approaching.   Regiment after regiment
started up and got into order.   In a little while the summit
of an ascent which was about a musket shot before them
was covered with bonnets and plaids.   Dundee rode forward
for the purpose of surveying the force with which he was to
contend, and then drew up his own men with as much skill
as their peculiar character permitted him to exert.   It was
desirable to keep the clans distinct.   Each tribe, large or
small, formed a column separated from the next column by a
wide interval.   One of these battalions might contain seven
hundred men, while another consisted of only a hundred and
twenty.   Lochiel had represented that it was impossible to
mix men of different tribes without destroying all that constituted the peculiar strength of a Highland army.†

On the right, close to the Garry, were the Macleans.
Nearest to them were Cannon and his Irish foot.   Next
stood the Macdonalds of Clanronald, commanded by the
guardian of their young prince.   On their left were other
bands of Macdonalds.   At the head of one large battalion

---

*. Memoirs of Sir Ewan Cameron.   † Ibid.; Mackay's Memoirs.

towered the stately form of Glengarry, who bore in his hand
the royal standard of King James the Seventh.* Still further
to the left were the cavalry, a small squadron, consisting of
some Jacobite gentlemen who had fled from the Lowlands to
the mountains, and of about forty of Dundee's old troopers.
The horses had been ill fed and ill tended among the Grampians, and looked miserably lean and feeble. Beyond them
was Lochiel with his Camerons. On the extreme left, the
men of Sky were marshalled by Macdonald of Sleat.†

In the Highlands, as in all countries where war has not
become a science, men thought it the most important duty
of a commander to set an example of personal courage and
of bodily exertion. Lochiel was especially renowned for his
physical prowess. His clansmen looked big with pride when
they related how he had himself broken hostile ranks and
hewn down tall warriors. He probably owed quite as much
of his influence to these achievements as to the high qualities
which, if fortune had placed him in the English Parliament
or at the French court, would have made him one of the
foremost men of his age. He had the sense however to perceive how erroneous was the notion which his countrymen
had formed. He knew that to give and to take blows was
not the business of a general. He knew with how much
difficulty Dundee had been able to keep together, during a
few days, an army composed of several clans; and he knew
that what Dundee had effected with difficulty Cannon would
not be able to effect at all. The life on which so much depended must not be sacrificed to a barbarous prejudice.
Lochiel therefore adjured Dundee not to run into any unnecessary danger. " Your Lordship's business," he said, " is
to overlook everything, and to issue your commands. Our
business is to execute those commands bravely and promptly."
Dundee answered with calm magnanimity that there was
much weight in what his friend Sir Ewan had urged, but
that no general could effect anything great without possessing
the confidence of his men. " I must establish my character
for courage. Your people expect to see their leaders in the
thickest of the battle; and to-day they shall see me there. I
promise you, on my honour, that in future fights I will take
more care of myself.

Meanwhile a fire of musketry was kept up on both sides,
but more skilfully and more steadily by the regular soldiers
than by the mountaineers. The space between the armies

* Douglas's Baronage of Scotland.   † Memoirs of Sir Ewan Cameron.

was one cloud of smoke. Not a few Highlanders dropped;
and the clans grew impatient. The sun however was low in
the west before Dundee gave the order to prepare for action.
His men raised a great shout. The enemy, probably exhausted by the toil of the day, returned a feeble and wavering cheer. "We shall do it now," said Lochiel: "that is
not the cry of men who are going to win." He had walked
through all his ranks, had addressed a few words to every
Cameron, and had taken from every Cameron a promise to
conquer or die.*

It was past seven o'clock. Dundee gave the word. The
Highlanders dropped their plaids. The few who were so
luxurious as to wear rude socks of untanned hide spurned
them away. It was long remembered in Lochaber that
Lochiel took off what probably was the only pair of shoes in
his clan, and charged barefoot at the head of his men. The
whole line advanced firing. The enemy returned the fire and
did much execution. When only a small space was left
between the armies, the Highlanders suddenly flung away
their firelocks, drew their broadswords, and rushed forward
with a fearful yell. The Lowlanders prepared to receive the
shock: but this was then a long and awkward process; and
the soldiers were still fumbling with the muzzles of their
guns and the handles of their bayonets when the whole flood
of Macleans, Macdonalds, and Camerons came down. In two
minutes the battle was lost and won. The ranks of Balfour's
regiment broke. He was cloven down while struggling in
the press. Ramsay's men turned their backs and dropped
their arms. Mackay's own foot were swept away by the
furious onset of the Camerons. His brother and nephew
exerted themselves in vain to rally the men. The former was
laid dead on the ground by a stroke from a claymore. The
latter, with eight wounds on his body, made his way through
the tumult and carnage to his uncle's side. Even in that
extremity Mackay retained all his selfpossession. He had
still one hope. A charge of horse might recover the day;
for of horse the bravest Highlanders were supposed to stand
in awe. But he called on the horse in vain. Belhaven indeed
behaved like a gallant gentleman; but his troopers, appalled by
the rout of the infantry, galloped off in disorder: Annandale's
men followed: all was over; and the mingled torrent of red-
coats and tartans went raving down the valley to the gorge
of Killiecrankie.

* Memoirs of Sir Ewan Cameron.

Mackay, accompanied by one trusty servant, spurred bravely through the thickest of the claymores and targets, and reached a point from which he had a view of the field. His whole army had disappeared, with the exception of some Borderers whom Leven had kept together, and of the English regiment, which had poured a murderous fire into the Celtic ranks, and which still kept unbroken order. All the men that could be collected were only a few hundreds. The general made haste to lead them across the Garry, and, having put that river between them and the enemy, paused for a moment to meditate on his situation.

He could hardly understand how the conquerors could be so unwise as to allow him even that moment for deliberation. They might with ease have killed or taken all who were with him before the night closed in. But the energy of the Celtic warriors had spent itself in one furious rush and one short struggle. The pass was choked by the twelve hundred beasts of burden which carried the provisions and baggage of the vanquished army. Such a booty was irresistibly tempting to men who were impelled to war quite as much by the desire of rapine as by the desire of glory. It is probable that few even of the chiefs were disposed to leave so rich a prize for the sake of King James. Dundee himself might at that moment have been unable to persuade his followers to quit the heaps of spoil, and to complete the great work of the day; and Dundee was no more.

At the beginning of the action he had taken his place in front of his little band of cavalry. He bade them follow him, and rode forward. But it seemed to be decreed that, on that day, the Lowland Scotch should in both armies appear to disadvantage. The horse hesitated. Dundee turned round, stood up in his stirrups, and, waving his hat, invited them to come on. As he lifted his arm, his cuirass rose, and exposed the lower part of his left side. A musket ball struck him: his horse sprang forward and plunged into a cloud of smoke and dust, which hid from both armies the fall of the victorious general. A person named Johnstone was near him, and caught him as he sank down from the saddle. "How goes the day?" said Dundee. "Well for King James;" answered Johnstone: "but I am sorry for Your Lordship." "If it is well for him," answered the dying man, "it matters the less for me." He never spoke again: but when, half an hour later, Lord Dunfermline and some other friends came to the spot, they thought that they could still discern some faint

Death of Dundee.

remains of life. The body, wrapped in two plaids, was carried
to the Castle of Blair.*

Retreat of
Mackay. Mackay, who was ignorant of Dundee's fate, and well
acquainted with Dundee's skill and activity, expected to be
instantly and hotly pursued, and had very little expectation
of being able to save the scanty remains of the vanquished
army. He could not retreat by the pass: for the Highlanders
were already there. He therefore resolved to push across the
mountains towards the valley of the Tay. He soon overtook
two or three hundred of his runaways who had taken the
same road. Most of them belonged to Ramsay's regiment,
and must have seen service. But they were unarmed: they
were utterly bewildered by the recent disaster; and the
general could find among them no remains either of martial
discipline or of martial spirit. His situation was one which
must have severely tried the firmest nerves. Night had set
in: he was in a desert: he had no guide: a victorious enemy
was, in all human probability, on his track; and he had to
provide for the safety of a crowd of men who had lost both
head and heart. He had just suffered a defeat of all defeats
the most painful and humiliating. His domestic feelings had
been not less severely wounded than his professional feelings.
One dear kinsman had just been struck dead before his eyes.
Another, bleeding from many wounds, moved feebly at his
side. But the unfortunate general's courage was sustained
by a firm faith in God, and a high sense of duty to the state.
In the midst of misery and disgrace, he still held his head
nobly erect, and found fortitude, not only for himself, but for
all around him. His first care was to be sure of his road. A
solitary light which twinkled through the darkness guided
him to a small hovel. The inmates spoke no tongue but the
Gaelic, and were at first scared by the appearance of uniforms
and arms. But Mackay's gentle manner removed their apprehension: their language had been familiar to him in childhood; and he retained enough of it to communicate with
them. By their directions, and by the help of a pocket map,

---

* As to the battle, see Mackay's
Memoirs, Letters, and Short Relation;
the Memoirs of Dundee; Memoirs of
Sir Ewan Cameron; Nisbet's and Osburne's depositions in the Appendix to
the Act. Parl. of July 14. 1690. See
also the account of the battle in one of
Burt's Letters. Macpherson printed a
letter from Dundee to James dated the
day after the battle. I need not say
that it is as impudent a forgery as
Fingal. The author of the Memoirs of
Dundee says that Lord Leven was
scared by the sight of the Highland
weapons, and set the example of flight.
This is a spiteful falsehood. That
Leven behaved remarkably well is
proved by Mackay's Letters, Memoirs,
and Short Relation.

in which the routes through that wild country were roughly laid down, he was able to find his way. He marched all night. When day broke his task was more difficult than ever. Light increased the terror of his companions. Hastings's men and Leven's men indeed still behaved themselves like soldiers. But the fugitives from Ramsay's were a mere rabble. They had flung away their muskets. The broadswords from which they had fled were ever in their eyes. Every fresh object caused a fresh panic. A company of herdsmen in plaids driving cattle was magnified by imagination into a host of Celtic warriors. Some of the runaways left the main body and fled to the hills, where their cowardice met with a proper punishment. They were killed for their coats and shoes; and their naked carcasses were left for a prey to the eagles of Ben Lawers. The desertion would have been much greater, had not Mackay and his officers, pistol in hand, threatened to blow out the brains of any man whom they caught attempting to steal off.

At length the weary fugitives came in sight of Weem Castle. The proprietor of the mansion was a friend to the new government, and extended to them such hospitality as was in his power. His stores of oatmeal were brought out: kine were slaughtered; and a rude and hasty meal was set before the numerous guests. Thus refreshed, they again set forth, and marched all day over bog, moor, and mountain. Thinly inhabited as the country was, they could plainly see that the report of their disaster had already spread far, and that the population was everywhere in a state of great excitement. Late at night they reached Castle Drummond, which was held for King William by a small garrison; and, on the following day, they proceeded with less difficulty to Stirling.[*]

The tidings of their defeat had outrun them. All Scotland was in a ferment. The disaster had indeed been great: but it was exaggerated by the wild hopes of one party and by the wild fears of the other. It was at first believed that the whole army of King William had perished; that Mackay himself had fallen; that Dundee, at the head of a great host of barbarians, flushed with victory and impatient for spoil, had already descended from the hills; that he was master of the whole country beyond the Forth; that Fife was up to join him; that in three days he would be at Stirling; that in a week he would be at Holyrood. Messengers were sent to

Effect of the battle of Killiecrankie.

---

[*] Mackay's Memoirs; Life of General Hugh Mackay by J. Mackay of Rockfield.

urge a regiment which lay in Northumberland to hasten across the border. Others carried to London earnest entreaties that His Majesty would instantly send every soldier that could be spared, nay, that he would come himself to save his northern kingdom. The factions of the Parliament House, awestruck by the common danger, forgot to wrangle. Courtiers and malecontents with one voice implored the Lord High Commissioner to close the session, and to dismiss them from a place where their deliberations might soon be interrupted by the mountaineers. It was seriously considered whether it might not be expedient to abandon Edinburgh, to send the numerous state prisoners who were in the Castle and the Tolbooth on board of a man of war which lay off Leith, and to transfer the seat of government to Glasgow.

The Scottish Parliament adjourned.

The news of Dundee's victory was everywhere speedily followed by the news of his death; and it is a strong proof of the extent and vigour of his faculties that his death seems everywhere to have been regarded as a complete set off against his victory. Hamilton, before he adjourned the Estates, informed them that he had good tidings for them, that Dundee was certainly dead, and that therefore the rebels had on the whole sustained a defeat. In several letters written at that conjuncture by able and experienced politicians a similar opinion is expressed. The messenger who rode with the news of the battle to the English capital was fast followed by another who carried a despatch for the King, and, not finding His Majesty at St. James's, galloped to Hampton Court. Nobody in the capital ventured to break the seal: but fortunately, after the letter had been closed, some friendly hand had hastily written on the outside a few words of comfort: "Dundee is killed. Mackay has got to Stirling:" and these words seem to have quieted the minds of the Londoners.[*]

From the pass of Killiecrankie the Highlanders had retired, proud of their victory, and laden with spoil, to the Castle of Blair. They boasted that the field of battle was covered with heaps of Saxon soldiers, and that the appearance of the corpses bore ample testimony to the power of a good Gaelic broadsword in a good Gaelic right hand. Heads were found cloven down to the throat, and skulls struck clean off just above the ears. The conquerors however had bought their

[*] Letter of the Extraordinary Ambassadors to the Greffier of the States General, August $\frac{2}{12}$. 1689; and a letter of the same date from Van Odyck, who was at Hampton Court.

victory dear. While they were advancing they had been much galled by the musketry of the enemy : and, even after the decisive charge, Hastings's Englishmen and some of Leven's Borderers had continued to keep up a steady fire. A hundred and twenty Camerons had been slain : the loss of the Macdonalds had been still greater; and several gentlemen of birth and note had fallen.*

Dundee was buried in the church of Blair Athol : but no monument was erected over his grave; and the church itself has long disappeared. A rude stone on the field of battle marks, if local tradition can be trusted, the place where he fell.† During the last three months of his life he had approved himself a great warrior and politician; and his name is therefore mentioned with respect by that large class of persons who think that there is no excess of wickedness for which courage and ability do not atone.

It is curious that the two most remarkable battles that perhaps were ever gained by irregular over regular troops should have been fought in the same week; the battle of Killiecrankie and the battle of Newton Butler. In both battles the success of the irregular troops was singularly rapid and complete. In both battles the panic of the regular troops, in spite of the conspicuous example of courage set by their generals, was singularly disgraceful. It ought also to be noted, that, of these extraordinary victories, one was gained by Celts over Saxons, and the other by Saxons over Celts. The victory of Killiecrankie indeed, though neither more splendid nor more important than the victory of Newton Butler, is far more widely renowned; and the reason is evident. The Anglosaxon and the Celt have been reconciled in Scotland, and have never been reconciled in Ireland. In Scotland all the great actions of both races are thrown into a common stock, and are considered as making up the glory which belongs to the whole country. So completely has the old antipathy been extinguished that nothing is more usual than to hear a Lowlander talk with complacency and even with pride of the most humiliating defeat that his ancestors ever underwent. It would be difficult to name any eminent man in whom national feeling and clannish feeling were stronger than in Sir Walter Scott. Yet when Sir Walter Scott mentioned Killiecrankie he seemed utterly to forget that he was a

---

* Memoirs of Sir Ewan Cameron; Memoirs of Dundee.
† The tradition is certainly much more than a hundred and twenty years old. The stone was pointed out to Burt.

Saxon, that he was of the same blood and of the same speech with Ramsay's foot and Annandale's horse. His heart swelled with triumph when he related how his own kindred had fled like hares before a smaller number of warriors of a different breed and of a different tongue.

In Ireland the feud remains unhealed. The name of Newton Butler, insultingly repeated by a minority, is hateful to the great majority of the population. If a monument were set up on the field of battle, it would probably be defaced; if a festival were held in Cork or Waterford on the anniversary of the battle, it would probably be interrupted by violence. The most illustrious Irish poet of our time would have thought it treason to his country to sing the praises of the conquerors. One of the most learned and diligent Irish archæologists of our time has laboured, not indeed very successfully, to prove that the event of the day was decided by a mere accident from which the Englishry could derive no glory. We cannot wonder that the victory of the Highlanders should be more celebrated than the victory of the Enniskilleners when we consider that the victory of the Highlanders is matter of boast to all Scotland, and that the victory of the Enniskilleners is matter of shame to three fourths of Ireland.

As far as the great interests of the state were concerned, it mattered not at all whether the battle of Killiecrankie were lost or won. It is very improbable that even Dundee, if he had survived the most glorious day of his life, could have surmounted those difficulties which sprang from the peculiar nature of his army, and which would have increased tenfold as soon as the war was transferred to the Lowlands. It is certain that his successor was altogether unequal to the task. During a day or two, indeed, the new general might flatter himself that all would go well. His army was rapidly swollen to near double the number of claymores that Dundee had commanded. The Stewarts of Appin, who, though full of zeal, had not been able to come up in time for the battle, were among the first who arrived. Several clans who had hitherto waited to see which side was the stronger, were now eager to descend on the Lowlands under the standard of King James the Seventh. The Grants indeed continued to bear true allegiance to William and Mary; and the Mackintoshes were kept neutral by unconquerable aversion to Keppoch. But Macphersons, Farquharsons, and Frasers came in crowds to the camp at Blair. The hesitation of the Athol men was at an end. Many of them had lurked, during the fight, among

The High-
land army
reinforced.

the crags and birch trees of Killiecrankie, and, as soon as the event of the day was decided, had emerged from those hiding places to strip and butcher the fugitives who tried to escape by the pass. The Robertsons, a Gaelic race, though bearing a Saxon name, gave in at this conjuncture their adhesion to the cause of the exiled King. Their chief Alexander, who took his appellation from his lordship of Struan, was a very young man and a student at the University of St. Andrew's. He had there acquired a smattering of letters, and had been initiated much more deeply into Tory politics. He now joined the Highland army, and continued, through a long life, to be constant to the Jacobite cause. His part, however, in public affairs was so insignificant that his name would not now be remembered, if he had not left a volume of poems, always very stupid and often very profligate. Had this book been manufactured in Grub Street, it would scarcely have been honoured with a quarter of a line in the Dunciad. But it attracted some notice on account of the situation of the writer. For, a hundred and twenty years ago, an eclogue or a lampoon written by a Highland chief was a literary portent.*

But, though the numerical strength of Cannon's forces was increasing, their efficiency was diminishing. Every new tribe which joined the camp brought with it some new cause of dissension. In the hour of peril, the most arrogant and mutinous spirits will often submit to the guidance of superior genius. Yet, even in the hour of peril, and even to the genius of Dundee, the Celtic chiefs had yielded but a precarious and imperfect obedience. To restrain them, when intoxicated with success and confident of their strength, would probably have been too hard a task even for him, as it had been, in the preceding generation, too hard a task for Montrose. The new general did nothing but hesitate and blunder. One of his first acts was to send a large body of men, chiefly Robertsons, down into the low country for the purpose of collecting provisions. He seems to have supposed that this detachment would without difficulty occupy Perth. But Mackay had already restored order among the remains of his army: he had assembled round him some troops which had not shared in the disgrace of the late defeat; and he was again ready for

* See the History prefixed to the poems of Alexander Robertson. In this history he is represented as having joined before the battle of Killiecrankie. But it appears from the evidence which is in the Appendix to the Act. Parl. Scot. of July 14. 1690, that he came in on the following day.

action. Cruel as his sufferings had been, he had wisely and magnanimously resolved not to punish what was past. To distinguish between degrees of guilt was not easy. To decimate the guilty would have been to commit a frightful massacre. His habitual piety too led him to consider the unexampled panic which had seized his soldiers as a proof rather of the divine displeasure than of their cowardice. He acknowledged with heroic humility that the singular firmness which he had himself displayed in the midst of the confusion and havoc was not his own, and that he might well, but for the support of a higher power, have behaved as pusillanimously as any of the wretched runaways who had thrown away their weapons and implored quarter in vain from the barbarous marauders of Athol. His dependence on heaven did not, however, prevent him from applying himself vigorously to the work of providing, as far as human prudence could provide, against the recurrence of such a calamity as that which he had just experienced. The immediate cause of the late defeat was the difficulty of fixing bayonets. The firelock of the Highlander was quite distinct from the weapon which he used in close fight. He discharged his shot, threw away his gun, and fell on with his sword. This was the work of a moment. It took the regular musketeer two or three minutes to alter his missile weapon into a weapon with which he could encounter an enemy hand to hand ; and during these two or three minutes the event of the battle of Killiecrankie had been decided. Mackay therefore ordered all his bayonets to be so formed that they might be screwed upon the barrel, without stopping it up, and that his men might be able to receive a charge the very instant after firing.*

Skirmish at Saint Johnston's.

As soon as he learned that a detachment of the Gaelic army was advancing towards Perth, he hastened to meet them at the head of a body of dragoons who had not been in the battle, and whose spirit was therefore unbroken. On Wednesday the thirty-first of July, only four days after his defeat, he fell in with the Robertsons, attacked them, routed them, killed a hundred and twenty of them, and took thirty prisoners, with the loss of only a single soldier.† This skirmish produced an effect quite out of proportion to the number of the combatants or of the slain. The reputation of the Celtic arms went down almost as fast as it had risen. During

* Mackay's Memoirs.   † Ibid ; Memoirs of Sir Ewan Cameron.

two or three days it had been everywhere imagined that those arms were invincible. There was now a reaction. It was perceived that what had happened at Killiecrankie was an exception to ordinary rules, and that the Highlanders were not, except in very peculiar circumstances, a match for good regular troops.

Meanwhile the disorders of Cannon's camp went on increasing. He called a council of war to consider what course it would be advisable to take. But, as soon as the council had met, a preliminary question was raised. Who were entitled to be consulted? The army was almost exclusively a Highland army. The recent victory had been won exclusively by Highland warriors. Great chiefs, who had brought six or seven hundred fighting men into the field, did not think it fair that they should be outvoted by gentlemen from Ireland and from the low country, who bore indeed King James's commission, and were called Colonels and Captains, but who were Colonels without regiments and Captains without companies. Lochiel spoke strongly in behalf of the class to which he belonged : but Cannon decided that the votes of the Saxon officers should be reckoned.* *Disorders in the Highland army.*

It was next considered what was to be the plan of the campaign. Lochiel was for advancing, for marching towards Mackay wherever Mackay might be, and for giving battle again. It can hardly be supposed that success had so turned the head of the wise chief of the Camerons as to make him insensible of the danger of the course which he recommended. But he probably conceived that nothing but a choice between dangers was left to him. His notion was that vigorous action was necessary to the very being of a Highland army, and that the coalition of clans would last only while they were impatiently pushing forward from battlefield to battlefield. He was again overruled. All his hopes of success were now at an end. His pride was severely wounded. He had submitted to the ascendency of a great captain : but he cared as little as any Whig for a royal commission. He had been willing to be the right hand of Dundee : but he would not be ordered about by Cannon. He quitted the camp, and retired to Lochaber. He indeed directed his clan to remain. But the clan, deprived of the leader whom it adored, and aware that he had withdrawn himself in ill humour, was no longer the same terrible column which had a few days before kept so well the vow to perish or to conquer. Macdonald of

* Memoirs of Sir Ewan Cameron.

Sleat, whose forces exceeded in number those of any other
of the confederate chiefs, followed Lochiel's example and returned to Sky.*

Mackay's
advice dis-
regarded
by the
Scotch mi-
nisters.

Mackay's arrangements were by this time complete; and
he had little doubt that, if the rebels came down to attack
him, the regular army would retrieve the honour which had
been lost at Killiecrankie. His chief difficulties arose from
the unwise interference of the ministers of the Crown at
Edinburgh with matters which ought to have been left to his
direction. The truth seems to be that they, after the
ordinary fashion of men who, having no military experience,
sit in judgment on military operations, considered success as
the only test of the ability of a commander. Whoever wins
a battle is, in the estimation of such persons, a great general:
whoever is beaten is a bad general; and no general had ever
been more completely beaten than Mackay. William, on
the other hand, continued to place entire confidence in his
unfortunate lieutenant. To the disparaging remarks of
critics who had never seen a skirmish, Portland replied, by
his master's orders, that Mackay was perfectly trustworthy,
that he was brave, that he understood war better than any
other officer in Scotland, and that it was much to be regretted
that any prejudice should exist against so good a man and so
good a soldier.†

The Came-
ronians
stationed
at Dun-
keld.

The unjust contempt with which the Scotch Privy Councillors regarded Mackay led them into a great error which
might well have caused a great disaster. The Cameronian
regiment was sent to garrison Dunkeld. Of this arrangement Mackay altogether disapproved. He knew that at
Dunkeld these troops would be near the enemy; that they
would be far from all assistance; that they would be in an open
town; that they would be surrounded by a hostile population;
that they were very imperfectly disciplined, though doubtless brave and zealous; that they were regarded by the whole
Jacobite party throughout Scotland with peculiar malevolence; and that in all probability some great effort would be
made to disgrace and destroy them.‡

The General's opinion was disregarded; and the Cameronians occupied the post assigned to them. It soon appeared that his forebodings were just. The inhabitants of
the country round Dunkeld furnished Cannon with intelli-

* Memoirs of Sir Ewan Cameron.   Leven and Melville Papers.
† See Portland's Letters to Melville   ‡ Mackay's Memoirs; Memoirs of Sir
of April 22 and May 15. 1690, in the   Ewan Cameron.

gence, and urged him to make a bold push. The peasantry of Athol, impatient for spoil, came in great numbers to swell his army. The regiment hourly expected to be attacked, and became discontented and turbulent. The men, intrepid, indeed, both from constitution and from enthusiasm, but not yet broken to habits of military submission, expostulated with Cleland, who commanded them. They had, they imagined, been recklessly, if not perfidiously, sent to certain destruction. They were protected by no ramparts : they had a very scanty stock of ammunition : they were hemmed in by enemies. An officer might mount and gallop beyond reach of danger in an hour : but the private soldier must stay and be butchered. "Neither I," said Cleland, "nor any of my officers will, in any extremity, abandon you. Bring out my horse, all our horses : they shall be shot dead." These words produced a complete change of feeling. The men answered that the horses should not be shot, that they wanted no pledge from their brave Colonel except his word, and that they would run the last hazard with him. They kept their promise well. The Puritan blood was now thoroughly up ; and what that blood was when it was up had been proved on many fields of battle.

That night the regiment passed under arms. On the morning of the following day, the twenty-first of August, all the hills round Dunkeld were alive with bonnets and plaids. Cannon's army was much larger than that which Dundee had commanded, and was accompanied by more than a thousand horses laden with baggage. Both the horses and baggage were probably part of the booty of Killiecrankie. The whole number of Highlanders was estimated by those who saw them at from four to five thousand men. They came furiously on. The outposts of the Cameronians were speedily driven in. The assailants came pouring on every side into the streets. The church, however, held out obstinately. But the greater part of the regiment made its stand behind a wall which surrounded a house belonging to the Marquess of Athol. This wall, which had two or three days before been hastily repaired with timber and loose stones, the soldiers defended desperately with musket, pike, and halbert. Their bullets were soon spent ; but some of the men were employed in cutting lead from the roof of the Marquess's house and shaping it into slugs. Meanwhile all the neighbouring houses were crowded from top to bottom with Highlanders, who kept up a galling fire from the windows. Cleland, while

The Highlanders attack the Cameronians and are repulsed.

encouraging his men, was shot dead. The command de-
volved on Major Henderson. In another minute Henderson
fell pierced with three mortal wounds. His place was supplied by Captain Munro, and the contest went on with
undiminished fury. A party of the Cameronians sallied
forth, set fire to the houses from which the fatal shots had
come, and turned the keys in the doors. In one single dwelling sixteen of the enemy were burnt alive. Those who were
in the fight described it as a terrible initiation for recruits.
Half the town was blazing; and with the incessant roar of
the guns were mingled the piercing shrieks of wretches
perishing in the flames. The struggle lasted four hours.
By that time the Cameronians were reduced nearly to their
last flask of powder: but their spirit never flagged. "The
enemy will soon carry the wall. Be it so. We will retreat
into the house: we will defend it to the last; and, if they
force their way into it, we will burn it over their heads and
our own." But, while they were revolving these desperate
projects, they observed that the fury of the assault slackened.
Soon the Highlanders began to fall back: disorder visibly
spread among them; and whole bands began to march off
to the hills. It was in vain that their general ordered them
to return to the attack. Perseverance was not one of their
military virtues. The Cameronians meanwhile, with shouts
of defiance, invited Amalek and Moab to come back and to try
another chance with the chosen people. But these exhortations had as little effect as those of Cannon. In a short time
the whole Gaelic army was in full retreat towards Blair.
Then the drums struck up: the victorious Puritans threw
their caps into the air, raised, with one voice, a psalm of
triumph and thanksgiving, and waved their colours, colours
which were on that day unfurled for the first time in the face
of an enemy, but which have since been proudly borne in
every quarter of the world, and which are now embellished
with the Sphinx and the Dragon, emblems of brave actions
achieved in Egypt and in China.*

Dissolu-
tion of the
Highland
army.

The Cameronians had good reason to be joyful and thankful; for they had finished the war. In the rebel camp all
was discord and dejection. The Highlanders blamed Cannon:

---

* Exact Narrative of the Conflict at
Dunkeld between the Earl of Angus's
Regiment and the Rebels, collected from
several Officers of that Regiment who
were Actors in or Eye-witnesses of all
that's here narrated in Reference to those
Actions; Letter of Lieutenant Blackader
to his brother, dated Dunkeld, Aug. 21.
1689; Faithful Contendings Displayed;
Minute of the Scotch Privy Council of
August 28., quoted by Mr. Burton.

Cannon blamed the Highlanders; and the host which had been the terror of Scotland melted fast away. The confederate chiefs signed an association by which they declared themselves faithful subjects of King James, and bound themselves to meet again at a future time. Having gone through this form,—for it was no more,—they departed, each to his home. Cannon and his Irishmen retired to the Isle of Mull. The Lowlanders who had followed Dundee to the mountains shifted for themselves as they best could. On the twenty-fourth of August, exactly four weeks after the Gaelic army had won the battle of Killiecrankie, that army ceased to exist. It ceased to exist, as the army of Montrose had, more than forty years earlier, ceased to exist, not in consequence of any great blow from without, but by a natural dissolution, the effect of internal malformation. All the fruits of victory were gathered by the vanquished. The Castle of Blair, which had been the immediate object of the contest, opened its gates to Mackay; and a chain of military posts, extending northward as far as Inverness, protected the cultivators of the plains against the predatory inroads of the mountaineers.

During the autumn the government was much more an- noyed by the Whigs of the low country than by the Jacobites of the hills. The Club, which had, in the late session of Par- liament, attempted to turn the kingdom into an oligarchical republic, and which had induced the Estates to refuse supplies and to stop the administration of justice, continued to sit during the recess, and harassed the ministers of the Crown by systematic agitation. The organisation of this body, con- temptible as it may appear to the generation which has seen the Roman Catholic Association and the League against the Corn Laws, was then thought marvellous and formidable. The leaders of the confederacy boasted that they would force the King to do them right. They got up petitions and ad- dresses, tried to inflame the populace by means of the press and the pulpit, employed emissaries among the soldiers, and talked of bringing up a large body of Covenanters from the west to overawe the Privy Council. In spite of every artifice, however, the ferment of the public mind gradually subsided. The government, after some hesitation, ventured to open the Courts of Justice which the Estates had closed. The Lords of Session appointed by the King took their seats; and Sir James Dalrymple presided. The Club attempted to induce the advocates to absent themselves from the bar, and enter- tained some hope that the mob would pull the judges from

Intrigues of the Club: state of the Lowlands.

the bench. But it speedily became clear that there was much more likely to be a scarcity of fees than of lawyers to take them : the common people of Edinburgh were well pleased to see again a tribunal associated in their imagination with the dignity and prosperity of their city ; and by many signs it appeared that the false and greedy faction which had commanded a majority of the legislature did not command a majority of the nation.*

* The History of Scotland during this autumn will be best studied in the Leven and Melville Papers.

CHAPTER XIV.

TWENTY-FOUR hours before the war in Scotland was brought to a close by the discomfiture of the Celtic army at Dunkeld, the Parliament broke up at Westminster. The Houses had sate ever since January without a recess. The Commons, who were cooped up in a narrow space, had suffered severely from heat and discomfort; and the health of many members had given way. The fruit, however, had not been proportioned to the toil. The last three months of the session had been almost entirely wasted in disputes, which have left no trace in the Statute Book. The progress of salutary laws had been impeded, sometimes by bickerings between the Whigs and the Tories, and sometimes by bickerings between the Lords and the Commons.

Disputes in the English Parliament.

The Revolution had scarcely been accomplished when it appeared that the supporters of the Exclusion Bill had not forgotten what they had suffered during the ascendency of their enemies, and were bent on obtaining both reparation and revenge. Even before the throne was filled, the Lords appointed a committee to examine into the truth of the frightful stories which had been circulated concerning the death of Essex. The Committee, which consisted of zealous Whigs, continued its inquiries till all reasonable men were convinced that he had fallen by his own hand, and till his wife, his brother, and his most intimate friends were desirous that the investigation should be carried no further.* Atonement was made, without any opposition on the part of the Tories, to the memory and the families of some victims, who were themselves beyond the reach of human power. Soon after the Convention had been turned into a Parliament, a bill for reversing the attainder of Lord Russell was presented to the Peers, was speedily passed by them, was sent down to

The attainder of Russell reversed.

---

* See the Lords' Journals of Feb. 5. 168⅝, and of many subsequent days; Braddon's pamphlet, entitled the Earl of Essex's Memory and Honour Vindicated, 1690; and the London Gazettes of July 31. and August 4. and 7. 1690, in which Lady Essex and Burnet publicly contradicted Braddon.

the Lower House, and was welcomed there with no common signs of emotion. Many of the members had sate in that very chamber with Russell. He had long exercised there an influence resembling the influence which, within the memory of this generation, belonged to the upright and benevolent Althorpe; an influence derived, not from superior skill in debate or in declamation, but from spotless integrity, from plain good sense, and from that frankness, that simplicity, that good nature, which are singularly graceful and winning in a man raised by birth and fortune high above his fellows. By the Whigs Russell had been honoured as a chief; and his political adversaries had admitted that, when he was not misled by associates less respectable and more artful than himself, he was as honest and kindhearted a gentleman as any in England. The manly firmness and Christian meekness with which he had met death, the desolation of his noble house, the misery of the bereaved father, the blighted prospects of the orphan children*, above all, the union of womanly tenderness and angelic patience in her who had been dearest to the brave sufferer, who had sate, with the pen in her hand, by his side at the bar, who had cheered the gloom of his cell, and who, on his last day, had shared with him the memorials of the great sacrifice, had softened the hearts of many who were little in the habit of pitying an opponent. That Russell had many good qualities, that he had meant well, that he had been hardly used, was now admitted even by courtly lawyers who had assisted in shedding his blood, and by courtly divines who had done their worst to blacken his reputation. When, therefore, the parchment which annulled his sentence was laid on the table of that assembly in which, eight years before, his face and his voice had been so well known, the excitement was great. One old Whig member tried to speak, but was overcome by his feelings. "I cannot," he faltered out, "name my Lord Russell without disorder. It is enough to name him. I am not able to say more." Many eyes were directed towards that part of the house where Finch sate. The highly honourable manner in which he had quitted a lucrative office, as soon as he had found that he could not keep it

---

* Whether the attainder of Lord Russell would, if unreversed, have prevented his son from succeeding to the earldom of Bedford, is a difficult question. The old Earl collected the opinions of the greatest lawyers of the age, which may still be seen among the archives at Woburn. It is remarkable that one of these opinions is signed by Pemberton, who had presided at the trial. This circumstance seems to prove that the family did not impute to him any injustice or cruelty; and in truth he had behaved as well as any judge, before the Revolution, ever behaved on a similar occasion.

without supporting the dispensing power, and the conspicuous part which he had borne in the defence of the Bishops, had done much to atone for his faults. Yet, on this day, it could not be forgotten that he had strenuously exerted himself, as counsel for the Crown, to obtain that judgment which was now to be solemnly revoked. He rose, and attempted to defend his conduct: but neither his legal acuteness, nor that fluent and sonorous elocution which was in his family a hereditary gift, and of which none of his family had a larger share than himself, availed him on this occasion. The House was in no humour to hear him, and repeatedly interrupted him by cries of " Order." He had been treated, he was told, with great indulgence. No accusation had been brought against him. Why then should he, under pretence of vindicating himself, attempt to throw dishonourable imputations on an illustrious name, and to apologise for a judicial murder? He was forced to sit down, after declaring that he meant only to clear himself from the charge of having exceeded the limits of his professional duty, that he disclaimed all intention of attacking the memory of Lord Russell, and that he should sincerely rejoice at the reversing of the attainder. Before the House rose the bill was read a second time, and would have been instantly read a third time and passed, had not some additions and omissions been proposed, which would, it was thought, make the reparation more complete. The amendments were prepared with great expedition: the Lords agreed to them; and the King gladly gave his assent.*

This bill was soon followed by three other bills which annulled three wicked and infamous judgments, the judgment against Sidney, the judgment against Cornish, and the judgment against Alice Lisle.† Other attainders reversed.

Some living Whigs obtained without difficulty redress for injuries which they had suffered in the late reign. The sentence of Samuel Johnson was taken into consideration by the House of Commons. It was resolved that the scourging which he had undergone was cruel, and that his degradation was of no legal effect. The latter proposition admitted of no dispute: for he had been degraded by the prelates who had been appointed to govern the diocese of London during Case of Samuel Johnson.

---

* Grey's Debates, March 168⅝.

† The Acts which reversed the attainders of Russell, Sidney, Cornish, and Alice Lisle were private Acts. Only the titles therefore are printed in the Statute Book: but the Acts will be found in Howell's Collection of State Trials.

Compton's suspension.   Compton had been suspended by a
decree of the High Commission; and the decrees of the High
Commission were universally acknowledged to be nullities.
Johnson had therefore been stripped of his robe by persons
who had no jurisdiction over him.   The Commons requested
the King to compensate the sufferer by some ecclesiastical
preferment.*   William, however, found that he could not,
without great inconvenience, grant this request.   For Johnson, though brave, honest, and religious, had always been
rash, mutinous, and quarrelsome; and, since he had endured
for his opinions a martyrdom more terrible than death, the
infirmities of his temper and understanding had increased to
such a degree that he was as offensive to Low Churchmen as
to High Churchmen.   Like too many other men, who are not
to be turned from the path of right by pleasure, by lucre, or by
danger, he mistook the impulses of his pride and resentment
for the monitions of conscience, and deceived himself into a
belief that, in treating friends and foes with indiscriminate
insolence and asperity, he was merely showing his Christian
faithfulness and courage.   Burnet, by exhorting him to
patience and forgiveness of injuries, made him a mortal
enemy.   " Tell his Lordship," said the inflexible priest, " to
mind his own business, and to let me look after mine."†   It
soon began to be whispered that Johnson was mad.   He accused Burnet of being the author of the report, and avenged
himself by writing libels so violent that they strongly confirmed the imputation which they were meant to refute.   The
King thought it better to give out of his own revenue a liberal
compensation for the wrongs which the Commons had brought
to his notice than to place an eccentric and irritable man in
a situation of dignity and public trust.   Johnson was gratified with a present of a thousand pounds, and a pension of
three hundred a year for two lives.   His son was also provided for in the public service.‡

Case of   While the Commons were considering the case of Johnson,
Devon-   the Lords were scrutinising with severity the proceedings
shire.   which had, in the late reign, been instituted against one of
their own order, the Earl of Devonshire.   The judges who
had passed sentence on him were strictly interrogated; and a
resolution was passed declaring that in his case the privileges

---

* Commons' Journals, June 24. 1689.   Letter, 1694.
  † Johnson tells this story himself in   ‡ Some Memorials of the Reverend
his strange pamphlet entitled, Notes   Samuel Johnson, prefixed to the folio
upon the Phœnix Edition of the Pastoral   edition of his works, 1710.

Titus Oates before the Privy Council

of the peerage had been infringed, and that the Court of King's Bench, in punishing a hasty blow by a fine of thirty thousand pounds, had violated common justice and the Great Charter.*

In the cases which have been mentioned, all parties seem to have agreed in thinking that some public reparation was due. But the fiercest passions both of Whigs and Tories were soon roused by the noisy claims of a wretch whose sufferings, great as they might seem, had been trifling when compared with his crimes. Oates had come back, like a ghost from the place of punishment, to haunt the spots which had been polluted by his guilt. The three years and a half which followed his scourging he had passed in one of the cells of Newgate, except when on certain days, the anniversaries of his perjuries, he had been brought forth and set on the pillory. He was still, however, regarded by many fanatics as a martyr; and it was said that they were able so far to corrupt his keepers that, in spite of positive orders from the government, his sufferings were mitigated by many indulgences. While offenders, who, compared with him, were innocent, grew lean on the prison allowance, his cheer was mended by turkeys and chines, capons and sucking pigs, venison pasties and hampers of claret, the offerings of zealous Protestants.† When James had fled from Whitehall, and when London was in confusion, it was moved, in the Council of Lords which had provisionally assumed the direction of affairs, that Oates should be set at liberty. The motion was rejected ‡ : but the gaolers, not knowing whom to obey in that time of anarchy, and desiring to conciliate a man who had once been, and might perhaps again be, a terrible enemy, allowed their prisoner to go freely about the town.§ His uneven legs and his hideous face, made more hideous by the shearing which his ears had undergone, were now again seen every day in Westminster Hall and the Court of Requests.|| He fastened himself on his old patrons, and, in that drawl which he affected as a mark of gentility, gave them the history of his wrongs and of his hopes. It was impossible, he said, that now, when the good

Margin: Case of Oates.

---

* Lords' Journals, May 15. 1689.

† North's Examen, 224. North's evidence is confirmed by several contemporary squibs in prose and verse. See also the εἰκὼν βροτολοίγου, 1697.

‡ Halifax MS. in the British Museum.

§ Epistle Dedicatory to Oates's εἰκὼν Βασιλικὴ.

|| In a ballad of the time are the following lines :

"Come listen, ye Whigs, to my pitiful moan,
All you that have ears, when the Doctor has none."

These lines must have been in Mason's head when he wrote the couplet—

"Witness, ye Hills, ye Johnsons, Scots, Shebbeares;
Hark to my call : for some of you have ears."

cause was triumphant, the discoverer of the plot could be overlooked. " Charles gave me nine hundred pounds a year. Sure William will give me more."*

In a few weeks he brought his sentence before the House of Lords by a writ of error. This is a species of appeal which raises no question of fact. The Lords, while sitting judi-cially on the writ of error, were not competent to examine whether the verdict which pronounced Oates guilty was or was not according to the evidence. All that they had to con-sider was whether, the verdict being supposed to be according to the evidence, the judgment was legal. But it would have been difficult even for a tribunal composed of veteran magis-trates, and was almost impossible for an assembly of noble-men who were all strongly biassed on one side or on the other, and among whom there was at that time not a single person whose mind had been disciplined by the study of jurispru-dence, to look steadily at the mere point of law, abstracted from the special circumstances of the case. In the view of one party, a party which even among the Whig peers was probably a small minority, the appellant was a man who had rendered inestimable services to the cause of liberty and re-ligion, and who had been requited by long confinement, by degrading exposure, and by torture not to be thought of without a shudder. The majority of the House more justly regarded him as the falsest, the most malignant, and the most impudent being that had ever disgraced the human form. The sight of that brazen forehead, the accents of that lying tongue, deprived them of all mastery over themselves. Many of them doubtless remembered with shame and remorse that they had been his dupes, and that, on the very last occa-sion on which he had stood before them, he had by perjury induced them to shed the blood of one of their own illustrious order. It was not to be expected that a crowd of gentlemen under the influence of feelings like these would act with the cold impartiality of a court of justice. Before they came to any decision on the legal question which Titus had brought before them, they picked a succession of quarrels with him. He had published a paper magnifying his merits and his suf-ferings. The Lords found out some pretence for calling this publication a breach of privilege, and sent him to the Mar-shalsea. He petitioned to be released : but an objection was

* North's Examen, 224. 254. North says " six hundred a year." But I have taken the larger sum from the impudent petition which Oates addressed to the Commons, July 25. 1689. See the Jour-nals.

raised to his petition. He had described himself as a Doctor of Divinity; and their lordships refused to acknowledge him as such. He was brought to their bar, and asked where he had graduated. He answered, "At the university of Salamanca." This was no new instance of his mendacity and effrontery. His Salamanca degree had been, during many years, a favourite theme of all the Tory satirists from Dryden downwards; and even on the Continent the Salamanca Doctor was a nickname in ordinary use.* The Lords, in their hatred of Oates, so far forgot their own dignity as to treat this ridiculous matter seriously. They ordered him to efface from his petition the words "Doctor of Divinity." He replied that he could not in conscience do it; and he was accordingly sent back to gaol.†

These preliminary proceedings indicated, not obscurely, what the fate of the writ of error would be. The counsel for Oates had been heard. No counsel appeared against him. The Judges were required to give their opinions. Nine of them were in attendance; and among the nine were the Chiefs of the three Courts of Common Law. The unanimous answer of these grave, learned, and upright magistrates was that the Court of King's Bench was not competent to degrade a priest from his sacred office, or to pass a sentence of perpetual imprisonment; and that therefore the judgment against Oates was contrary to law, and ought to be reversed. The Lords should undoubtedly have considered themselves as bound by this opinion. That they knew Oates to be the worst of men was nothing to the purpose. To them, sitting as a court of justice, he ought to have been merely a John of Styles, or a John of Nokes. But their indignation was violently excited. Their habits were not those which fit men for the discharge of judicial duties. The debate turned almost entirely on matters to which no allusion ought to have been made. Not a single peer ventured to affirm that the judgment was legal: but much was said about the odious character of the appellant, about the impudent accusation which he had brought against Catharine of Braganza, and about the evil consequences which might follow if so bad a man were capable of being a witness. "There is only one way," said the Lord President, "in which I can consent to reverse the fellow's sentence. He has been whipped from Aldgate to Tyburn. He ought to be whipped from Tyburn

* Van Cittters, in his despatches to the States General, uses this nickname quite gravely.

† Lords' Journals, May 30. 1689.

back to Aldgate." The question was put. Twenty-three peers voted for reversing the judgment; thirty-five for affirming it.[*]

This decision produced a great sensation, and not without reason. A question was now raised which might justly excite the anxiety of every man in the kingdom. That question was whether the highest tribunal, the tribunal on which, in the last resort, depended the most precious interests of every English subject, was at liberty to decide judicial questions on other than judicial grounds, and to withhold from a suitor what was admitted to be his legal right, on account of the depravity of his moral character. That the supreme Court of Appeal ought not to be suffered to exercise arbitrary power under the forms of ordinary justice, was strongly felt by the ablest men in the House of Commons, and by none more strongly than by Somers. With him, and with those who reasoned like him, were, on this occasion, allied all the weak and hotheaded zealots who still regarded Oates as a public benefactor, and who imagined that to question the existence of the Popish plot was to question the truth of the Protestant religion. On the very morning after the decision of the Peers had been pronounced, keen reflections were thrown, in the House of Commons, on the justice of their lordships. Three days later, the subject was brought forward by a Whig Privy Councillor, Sir Robert Howard, member for Castle Rising. He was one of the Berkshire branch of his noble family, a branch which enjoyed, in that age, the unenviable distinction of being wonderfully fertile of bad rhymers. The poetry of the Berkshire Howards was the jest of three generations of satirists. The mirth began with the first representation of the Rehearsal, and continued down to the last edition of the Dunciad.[†] But Sir Robert, in spite of his bad verses, and of some foibles and vanities which had caused him to be brought on the stage under the name of Sir Positive Atall, had in Parliament the weight which a stanch party man, of ample fortune, of illustrious name, of ready utterance, and of resolute spirit, can scarcely fail to possess.[‡] When he rose to call

---

[*] Lords' Journals, May 31. 1689; Commons' Journals, Aug. 2.; North's Examen, 234.; Luttrell's Diary.

[†] Sir Robert was the original hero of the Rehearsal, and was called Bilboa. In the remodelled Dunciad, Pope inserted the lines—

"And highborn Howard, more majestic sire,
With Fool of Quality completes the quire."

Pope's highborn Howard was Edward Howard, the author of the British Princes. Dorset ridiculed Edward Howard's poetry in a short satire, in which thought and wit are packed as close as in the finest passages of Hudibras.

[‡] Key to the Rehearsal; Shadwell's Sullen Lovers; Pepys, May 5. 8. 1668; Evelyn, Feb. 16. 168½.

the attention of the Commons to the case of Oates, some Tories, animated by the same passions which had prevailed in the other House, received him with loud hisses. In spite of this most unparliamentary insult, he persevered; and it soon appeared that the majority was with him. Some orators extolled the patriotism and courage of Oates : others dwelt much on a prevailing rumour, that the solicitors who were employed against him on behalf of the Crown had distributed large sums of money among the jurymen. These were topics on which there was much difference of opinion. But that the sentence was illegal was a proposition which admitted of no dispute. The most eminent lawyers in the House of Commons declared that, on this point, they entirely concurred in the opinion given by the Judges in the House of Lords. Those who had hissed when the subject was introduced were so effectually cowed that they did not venture to demand a division; and a bill annulling the sentence was brought in, without any opposition.*

The Lords were in an embarrassing situation. To retract was not pleasant. To engage in a contest with the Lower House, on a question on which that House was clearly in the right, and was backed at once by the opinions of the sages of the law, and by the passions of the populace, might be dangerous. It was thought expedient to take a middle course. An address was presented to the King, requesting him to pardon Oates.† But this concession only made bad worse. Titus had, like every other human being, a right to justice : but he was not a proper object of mercy. If the judgment against him was illegal, it ought to have been reversed. If it was legal, there was no ground for remitting any portion of it. The Commons, very properly, persisted, passed their bill, and sent it up to the Peers. Of this bill the only objectionable part was the preamble, which asserted, not only that the judgment was illegal, a proposition which appeared on the face of the record to be true, but also that the verdict was corrupt, a proposition which, whether true or false, was certainly not proved.

The Lords were in a great strait. They knew that they were in the wrong. Yet they were determined not to proclaim, in their legislative capacity, that they had, in their judicial capacity, been guilty of injustice. They again tried a middle course. The preamble was softened down : a clause was added

---

* Grey's Debates and Commons' Journals, June 4. and 11. 1689.
† Lords' Journals, June 6. 1689.

which provided that Oates should still remain incapable of
being a witness; and the bill thus altered was returned to the
Commons.

The Commons were not satisfied. They rejected the amendments, and demanded a free conference. Two eminent Tories,
Rochester and Nottingham, took their seats in the Painted
Chamber as managers for the Lords. With them was joined
Burnet, whose well known hatred of Popery was likely to
give weight to what he might say on such an occasion.
Somers was the chief orator on the other side : and to his
pen we owe a singularly lucid and interesting abstract of the
debate.

The Lords frankly owned that the judgment of the Court
of King's Bench could not be defended. They knew it to be
illegal, and had known it to be so even when they affirmed it.
But they had acted for the best. They accused Oates of
bringing an impudently false accusation against Queen Catharine ; they mentioned other instances of his villany ; and they
asked whether such a man ought still to be capable of giving
testimony in a court of justice. The only excuse which in
their opinion could be made for him was, that he was insane;
and in truth, the incredible insolence and absurdity of his behaviour when he was last before them seemed to warrant the
belief that his brain had been turned, and that he was not to
be trusted with the lives of other men. The Lords could not
therefore degrade themselves by expressly rescinding what
they had done; nor could they consent to pronounce the verdict corrupt on no better evidence than common report.

The reply was complete and triumphant. " Oates is now the
smallest part of the question. He has, Your Lordships say,
falsely accused the Queen Dowager and other innocent persons. Be it so. This bill gives him no indemnity. We are
quite willing, that, if he is guilty, he shall be punished. But
for him, and for all Englishmen, we demand that punishment
shall be regulated by law, and not by the arbitrary discretion
of any tribunal. We demand that when a writ of error is
before Your Lordships, you shall give judgment on it according to the known customs and statutes of the realm. We
deny that you have any right, on such an occasion, to take
into consideration the moral character of a plaintiff or the
political effect of a decision. It is acknowledged by yourselves
that you have, merely because you thought ill of this man,
affirmed a judgment which you knew to be illegal. Against
this assumption of arbitrary power the Commons protest ; and

they hope that you will now redeem what you must feel to be an error. Your Lordships intimate a suspicion that Oates is mad. That a man is mad may be a very good reason for not punishing him at all. But how it can be a reason for inflicting on him a punishment which would be illegal even if he were sane, the Commons do not comprehend. Your Lordships think that you should not be justified in calling a verdict corrupt which has not been legally proved to be so. Suffer us to remind you that you have two distinct functions to perform. You are judges, and you are legislators. When you judge, your duty is strictly to follow the law. When you legislate, you may properly take facts from common fame. You invert this rule. You are lax in the wrong place, and scrupulous in the wrong place. As judges you break through the law for the sake of a supposed convenience. As legislators, you will not admit any fact without such technical proof as it is rarely possible for legislators to obtain." *

This reasoning was not and could not be answered. The Commons were evidently flushed with their victory in the argument, and proud of the appearance which Somers had made in the Painted Chamber. They particularly charged him to see that the report which he had made of the conference was accurately entered in the journals. The Lords very wisely abstained from inserting in their records an account of a debate in which they had been so signally discomfited. But, though conscious of their fault and ashamed of it, they could not be brought to do public penance by owning in the preamble of the Act, that they had been guilty of injustice. The minority was, however, strong. The resolution to adhere was carried by only twelve votes, of which ten were proxies.† Twenty-one Peers protested. The bill dropped. Two Masters in Chancery were sent to announce to the Commons the final resolution of the Peers. The Commons thought this proceeding unjustifiable in substance and uncourteous in form. They determined to remonstrate; and Somers drew up an excellent manifesto, in which the vile name of Oates was scarcely mentioned, and in which the Upper House was with great earnestness and gravity exhorted to treat judicial questions judicially, and not, under pretence of administering law, to make law.‡ The wretched man, who had now a

---

* Commons' Journals, Aug. 2. 1689; Dutch Ambassadors Extraordinary to the States General, $\frac{\text{July 30.}}{\text{Aug. 9.}}$

† Lords' Journals, July 30. 1689;

Luttrell's Diary; Clarendon's Diary, July 31. 1689.

‡ See the Commons' Journals of July 31. and August 13. 1689.

second time thrown the political world into confusion, received a pardon, and was set at liberty. His friends in the Lower House moved an address to the Throne, requesting that a pension sufficient for his support might be granted to him.* He was consequently allowed about three hundred a year, a sum which he thought unworthy of his acceptance, and which he took with the savage snarl of disappointed greediness.

Bill of Rights. From the dispute about Oates sprang another dispute, which might have produced very serious consequences. The instrument which had declared William and Mary King and Queen was a revolutionary instrument. It had been drawn up by an assembly unknown to the ordinary law, and had never received the royal sanction. It was evidently desirable that this great contract between the governors and the governed, this titledeed by which the King held his throne and the people their liberties, should be put into a strictly regular form. The Declaration of Rights was therefore turned into a Bill of Rights; and the Bill of Rights speedily passed the Commons: but in the Lords difficulties arose.

The Declaration had settled the crown, first on William and Mary jointly, then on the survivor of the two, then on Mary's posterity, then on Anne and her posterity, and, lastly, on the posterity of William by any other wife than Mary. The Bill had been drawn in exact conformity with the Declaration. Who was to succeed if Mary, Anne, and William should all die without posterity, was left in uncertainty. Yet the event for which no provision was made was far from improbable. Indeed it really came to pass. William had never had a child. Anne had repeatedly been a mother, but had no child living. It would not be very strange if, in a few months, disease, war, or treason should remove all those who stood in the entail. In what state would the country then be left? To whom would allegiance be due? The bill indeed contained a clause which excluded Papists from the throne. But would such a clause supply the place of a clause designating the successor by name? What if the next heir should be a prince of the House of Savoy not three months old? It would be absurd to call such an infant a Papist. Was he then to be proclaimed King? Or was the crown to be in abeyance till he came to an age at which he might be capable of choosing a religion? Might not the most honest and the most intelligent men be in doubt whether they ought to regard him as their Sovereign? And to whom could they look for

* Commons' Journals, Aug. 20.

a solution of this doubt? Parliament there would be none: for the Parliament would expire with the prince who had convoked it. There would be mere anarchy, anarchy which might end in the destruction of the monarchy, or in the destruction of public liberty. For these weighty reasons, Burnet, at William's suggestion, proposed in the House of Lords that the crown should, failing heirs of His Majesty's body, be entailed on an undoubted Protestant, Sophia, Duchess of Brunswick Lunenburg, granddaughter of James the First, and daughter of Elizabeth, Queen of Bohemia.

The Lords unanimously assented to this amendment: but the Commons unanimously rejected it. The cause of the rejection no contemporary writer has satisfactorily explained. One Whig historian talks of the machinations of the republicans, another of the machinations of the Jacobites. But it is quite certain that four fifths of the representatives of the people were neither Jacobites nor republicans. Yet not a single voice was raised in the Lower House in favour of the clause which in the Upper House had been carried by acclamation.* The most probable explanation seems to be that the gross injustice which had been committed in the case of Oates had irritated the Commons to such a degree that they were glad of an opportunity to quarrel with the Peers. A conference was held. Neither assembly would give way. While the dispute was hottest, an event took place which, it might have been thought, would have restored harmony. Anne gave birth to a son. The child was baptised at Hampton Court with great pomp, and with many signs of public joy. William was one of the sponsors. The other was the accomplished Dorset, whose roof had given shelter to the Princess in her distress. The King bestowed his own name on his godson, and announced to the splendid circle assembled round the font that the little William was henceforth to be called Duke of Gloucester.†

The birth of this child had greatly diminished the risk against which the Lords had thought it necessary to guard. They might therefore have retracted with a good grace. But their pride had been wounded by the severity with which

---

* Oldmixon accuses the Jacobites, Burnet the republicans. Though Burnet took a prominent part in the discussion of this question, his account of what passed is grossly inaccurate. He says that the clause was warmly debated in the Commons, and that Hampden spoke strongly for it. But we learn from the Journals (June 19. 1689) that it was rejected *nemine contradicente*. The Dutch Ambassadors describe it as "een propositie 'twelck geen ingressie schÿnt te sullen vinden."

† London Gazette, Aug. 1. 1689; Luttrell's Diary.

their decision on Oates's writ of error had been censured in the Painted Chamber. They had been plainly told across the table that they were unjust judges; and the imputation was not the less irritating because they were conscious that it was deserved. They refused to make any concession; and the Bill of Rights was suffered to drop.*

Disputes about a Bill of Indemnity.

But the most exciting question of this long and stormy session was, what punishment should be inflicted on those men who had, during the interval between the dissolution of the Oxford Parliament and the Revolution, been the advisers or the tools of Charles and James. It was happy for England that, at this crisis, a prince who belonged to neither of her factions, who loved neither, who hated neither, and who, for the accomplishment of a great design, wished to make use of both, was the moderator between them.

The two parties were now in a position closely resembling that in which they had been twenty-eight years before. The party indeed which had then been undermost was now uppermost: but the analogy between the situations is one of the most perfect that can be found in history. Both the Restoration and the Revolution were accomplished by coalitions. At the Restoration, those politicians who were peculiarly zealous for liberty assisted to reestablish monarchy: at the Revolution those politicians who were peculiarly zealous for monarchy assisted to vindicate liberty. The Cavalier would, at the former conjuncture, have been able to effect nothing without the help of Puritans who had fought for the Covenant; nor would the Whig, at the latter conjuncture, have offered a successful resistance to arbitrary power, had he not been backed by men who had a very short time before condemned resistance to arbitrary power as a deadly sin. Conspicuous among those by whom, in 1660, the royal family was brought back, were Hollis, who had, in the days of the tyranny of Charles the First, held down the Speaker in the chair by main force, while Black Rod knocked for admission in vain; Ingoldsby, whose name was subscribed to the memorable death warrant; and Prynne, whose ears Laud had cut off, and who, in return, had borne the chief part in cutting off Laud's head. Among the seven who, in 1688, signed the invitation to William were Compton, who had long enforced the duty of obeying Nero; Danby, who had been impeached for endeavouring to establish mili-

* The history of this Bill may be traced in the Journals of the two Houses, and in Grey's Debates.

tary despotism; and Lumley, whose bloodhounds had tracked Monmouth to that last sad hidingplace among the fern. Both in 1660 and in 1688, while the fate of the nation still hung in the balance, forgiveness was exchanged between the hostile factions. On both occasions the reconciliation, which had seemed to be cordial in the hour of danger, proved false and hollow in the hour of triumph. As soon as Charles the Second was at Whitehall, the Cavalier forgot the good service recently done by the Presbyterians, and remembered only their old offences. As soon as William was King, too many of the Whigs began to demand vengeance for all that they had, in the days of the Rye House plot, suffered at the hands of the Tories. On both occasions the Sovereign found it difficult to save the vanquished party from the fury of his triumphant supporters; and on both occasions those whom he had disappointed of their revenge murmured bitterly against the government which had been so weak and ungrateful as to protect its foes against its friends.

So early as the twenty-fifth of March, William called the attention of the Commons to the expediency of quieting the public mind by an amnesty. He expressed his hope that a bill of general pardon and oblivion would be as speedily as possible presented for his sanction, and that no exceptions would be made, except such as were absolutely necessary for the vindication of public justice and for the safety of the state. The Commons unanimously agreed to thank him for this instance of his paternal kindness: but they suffered many weeks to pass without taking any step towards the accomplishment of his wish. When at length the subject was resumed, it was resumed in such a manner as plainly showed that the majority had no real intention of putting an end to the suspense which embittered the lives of all those Tories who were conscious that, in their zeal for prerogative, they had sometimes overstepped the exact line traced by law. Twelve categories were framed, some of which were so extensive as to include tens of thousands of delinquents; and the House resolved that, under every one of these categories, some exceptions should be made. Then came the examination into the cases of individuals. Numerous culprits and witnesses were summoned to the bar; the debates were long and sharp; and it soon became evident that the work was interminable. The summer glided away: the autumn was approaching: the session could not last much longer; and of the twelve distinct inquisitions, which the Commons

had resolved to institute, only three had been brought to a
close.   It was necessary to let the bill drop for that year.*

Last days   Among the many offenders whose names were mentioned
of Jeffreys. in the course of these enquiries, was one who stood alone and
unapproached in guilt and infamy, and whom Whigs and
Tories were equally willing to leave to the extreme rigour of
the law.   On that terrible day which was succeeded by the
Irish Night, the roar of a great city disappointed of its revenge had followed Jeffreys to the drawbridge of the Tower.
His imprisonment was not strictly legal : but he at first accepted with thanks and blessings the protection which those
dark walls, made famous by so many crimes and sorrows,
afforded him against the fury of the multitude.†   Soon, however, he became sensible that his life was still in imminent
peril.   For a time he flattered himself with the hope that a
writ of Habeas Corpus would liberate him from his confinement, and that he should be able to steal away to some
foreign country, and to hide himself with part of his ill
gotten wealth from the detestation of mankind : but, till the
government was settled, there was no Court competent to
grant a writ of Habeas Corpus; and, as soon as the government had been settled, the Habeas Corpus Act was suspended.‡   Whether the legal guilt of murder could be brought
home to Jeffreys may be doubted.   But he was morally guilty
of so many murders that, if there had been no other way of
reaching his life, a retrospective Act of Attainder would have
been clamorously demanded by the whole nation.   A disposition to triumph over the fallen has never been one of the
besetting sins of Englishmen : but the hatred of which
Jeffreys was the object was without a parallel in our history,
and partook but too largely of the savageness of his own
nature.   The people, where he was concerned, were as cruel
as himself, and exulted in his misery as he had been accustomed to exult in the misery of convicts listening to the
sentence of death, and of families clad in mourning.   The
rabble congregated before his deserted mansion in Duke
Street, and read on the door, with shouts of laughter, the
bills which announced the sale of his property.   Even delicate women, who had tears for highwaymen and housebreakers, breathed nothing but vengeance against him.   The

* See Grey's debates, and the Com-   † Halifax MS. in the British Museum.
mons' Journals from March to July.   ‡ The Life and Death of George Lord
The twelve categories will be found in   Jeffreys; Finch's speech in Grey's De-
the Journals of the 23rd and 29th of   bates, March 1. 168⅚.
May and of the 8th of June.

lampoons on him which were hawked about the town were distinguished by an atrocity rare even in those days.* Hanging would be too mild a death for him: a grave under the gibbet would be too respectable a resting place: he ought to be whipped to death at the cart's tail: he ought to be tortured like an Indian: he ought to be devoured alive. The street poets portioned out all his joints with cannibal ferocity, and computed how many pounds of steaks might be cut from his well fattened carcass. Nay, the rage of his enemies was such that, in language seldom heard in England, they proclaimed their wish that he might go to the place of wailing and gnashing of teeth, to the worm that never dies, to the fire that is never quenched. They exhorted him to hang himself in his garters, and to cut his throat with his razor. They put up horrible prayers that he might not be able to repent, that he might die the same hard-hearted, wicked Jeffreys that he had lived. His spirit, as mean in adversity as insolent and inhuman in prosperity, sank down under the load of public abhorrence. His constitution, originally bad, and much impaired by intemperance, was completely broken by distress and anxiety. He was tormented by a cruel internal disease, which the most skilful surgeons of that age were seldom able to relieve. One solace was left to him, brandy. Even when he had causes to try and councils to attend, he had seldom gone to bed sober. Now, when he had nothing to occupy his mind save terrible recollections and terrible forebodings, he abandoned himself without reserve to his favourite vice. Many believed him to be bent on shortening his life by excess. He thought it better, they said, to go off in a drunken fit than to be hacked by Ketch, or torn limb from limb by the populace.

Once he was roused from a state of abject despondency by an agreeable sensation, speedily followed by a mortifying disappointment. A parcel had been left for him at the Tower. It appeared to be a barrel of Colchester oysters, his favourite dainties. He was greatly moved: for there are moments when those who least deserve affection are pleased to think that they inspire it. "Thank God," he exclaimed, "I have

---

* See among many other pieces, Jeffreys's Elegy, the Letter to the Lord Chancellor exposing to him the sentiments of the people, the Elegy on Dangerfield, Dangerfield's Ghost to Jeffreys, the Humble Petition of Widows and fatherless Children in the West, the Lord Chancellor's Discovery and Confession made in the Time of his Sickness in the Tower; Hickeringill's Ceremonymonger; a broadside entitled "O rare show! O rare sight! O strange monster! The like not in Europe! To be seen near Tower Hill, a few doors beyond the Lion's den."

still some friends left." He opened the barrel; and from among a heap of shells out tumbled a stout halter.*

It does not appear that one of the flatterers or buffoons whom he had enriched out of the plunder of his victims came to comfort him in the day of trouble. But he was not left in utter solitude. John Tutchin, whom he had sentenced to be flogged every fortnight for seven years, made his way into the Tower, and presented himself before the fallen oppressor. Poor Jeffreys, humbled to the dust, behaved with abject civility, and called for wine. "I am glad, sir," he said, "to see you." "And I am glad," answered the resentful Whig, "to see Your Lordship in this place." "I served my master," said Jeffreys: "I was bound in conscience to do so." "Where was your conscience," said Tutchin, "when you passed that sentence on me at Dorchester?" "It was set down in my instructions," answered Jeffreys, fawningly, "that I was to show no mercy to men like you, men of parts and courage. When I went back to court I was reprimanded for my lenity."† Even Tutchin, acrimonious as was his nature, and great as were his wrongs, seems to have been a little mollified by the pitiable spectacle which he had at first contemplated with vindictive pleasure. He always denied the truth of the report that he was the person who sent the Colchester barrel to the Tower.

A more benevolent man, John Sharp, the excellent Dean of Norwich, forced himself to visit the prisoner. It was a painful task: but Sharp had been treated by Jeffreys, in old times, as kindly as it was in the nature of Jeffreys to treat anybody, and had once or twice been able, by patiently waiting till the storm of curses and invectives had spent itself, and by dexterously seizing the moment of good humour, to obtain for unhappy families some mitigation of their sufferings. The prisoner was surprised and pleased. "What," he said, "dare you own me now?" It was in vain, however, that the amiable divine tried to give salutary pain to that seared conscience. Jeffreys, instead of acknowledging his guilt, exclaimed vehemently against the injustice of mankind. "People call me a murderer for doing what at the time was applauded by some who are now high in public favour. They call me a drunkard because I take punch to relieve me in my agony." He would not admit that, as President of the High Commission, he had done anything

---

* Life and Death of George Lord Jeffreys.   † Tutchin himself gives this narrative in the Bloody Assizes.

that deserved reproach. His colleagues, he said, were the real criminals; and now they threw all the blame on him. He spoke with peculiar asperity of Sprat, who had undoubtedly been the most humane and moderate member of the board.

It soon became clear that the wicked judge was fast sinking under the weight of bodily and mental suffering. Doctor John Scott, prebendary of Saint Paul's, a clergyman of great sanctity, and author of the Christian Life, a treatise once widely renowned, was summoned, probably on the recommendation of his intimate friend Sharp, to the bedside of the dying man. It was in vain, however, that Scott spoke, as Sharp had already spoken, of the hideous butcheries of Dorchester and Taunton. To the last Jeffreys continued to repeat that those who thought him cruel did not know what his orders were, that he deserved praise instead of blame, and that his clemency had drawn on him the extreme displeasure of his master.*

Disease, assisted by strong drink and by misery, did its work fast. The patient's stomach rejected all nourishment. He dwindled in a few weeks from a portly and even corpulent man to a skeleton. On the eighteenth of April he died, in the forty-first year of his age. He had been Chief Justice of the King's Bench at thirty-five, and Lord Chancellor at thirty-seven. In the whole history of the English bar there is no other instance of so rapid an elevation, or of so terrible a fall. The emaciated corpse was laid, with all privacy, next to the corpse of Monmouth in the chapel of the Tower.†

* See the Life of Archbishop Sharp by his son. What passed between Scott and Jeffreys was related by Scott to Sir Joseph Jekyl. See Tindall's History; Eachard, iii. 932. Eachard's informant, who is not named, but who seems to have had good opportunities of knowing the truth, said that Jeffreys died, not, as the vulgar believed, of drink, but of the stone. The distinction is of little importance. It is certain that Jeffreys was grossly intemperate; and his malady was one which intemperance notoriously tends to aggravate.

† See a Full and True Account of the Death of George Lord Jeffreys, licensed on the day of his death. The wretched Le Noble was never weary of repeating that Jeffreys was poisoned by the usurper. I will give a short passage as a specimen of the calumnies of which William was the object. "Il envoya," says Pasquin, "ce fin ragoût de champignons au Chancelier Jeffreys, prisonnier dans la Tour, qui les trouva du même goust, et du même assaisonnement que furent les derniers dont Agrippine regala le bonhomme Claudius son époux, et que Neron appella depuis la viande de Dieux." Marforio asks: "Le Chancelier est donc mort dans la Tour?" Pasquin answers: "Il estoit trop fidèle à son Roi légitime, et trop habile dans les loix du royaume, pour échapper à l'Usurpateur qu'il ne vouloit point reconnoistre. Guillemot prit soin de faire publier que ce malheureux prisonnier estoit attaqué d'une fièvre maligne: mais, à parler franchement, il vivroit peut-estre encore, s'il n'avoit rien mangé que de la main de ses anciens cuisiniers."—Le Festin de Guillemot, 1689. Dangeau (May 7.) mentions a report that Jeffreys had poisoned himself. In 1693 the corpse of Jeffreys was, by the royal permission, removed from the chapel of the Tower, and laid in the church of St. Mary Aldermanbury

The fall of this man, once so great and so much dreaded, the horror with which he was regarded by all the respectable members of his own party, the manner in which the least respectable members of that party renounced fellowship with him in his distress, and threw on him the whole blame of crimes which they had encouraged him to commit, ought to have been a lesson to those intemperate friends of liberty who were clamouring for a new proscription. But it was a lesson which too many of them disregarded. The King had, at the very commencement of his reign, displeased them by appointing a few Tories and Trimmers to high offices; and the discontent excited by these appointments had been inflamed by his attempt to obtain a general amnesty for the vanquished. He was in truth not a man to be popular with the vindictive zealots of any faction. For among his peculiarities was a certain ungracious humanity which rarely conciliated his foes, which often provoked his adherents, but in which he doggedly persisted, without troubling himself either about the thanklessness of those whom he had saved from destruction, or about the rage of those whom he had disappointed of their revenge. Some of the Whigs now spoke of him as bitterly as they had ever spoken of either of his uncles. He was a Stuart after all, and was not a Stuart for nothing. Like the rest of the race, he loved arbitrary power. In Holland, he had succeeded in making himself, under the forms of a republican polity, scarcely less absolute than the old hereditary Counts had been. In consequence of a strange combination of circumstances, his interest had, during a short time, coincided with the interest of the English people: but, though he had been a deliverer by accident, he was a despot by nature. He had no sympathy with the just resentments of the Whigs. He had objects in view which the Whigs would not willingly suffer any Sovereign to attain. He knew that the Tories were the only tools for his purpose. He had, therefore, from the moment at which he took his seat on the throne, favoured them unduly. He was now trying to procure an indemnity for those very delinquents whom he had, a few months before, described in his Declaration as deserving of exemplary punishment. In November he had told the world that the crimes in which these men had borne a part had made it the duty of subjects to violate their oath of allegiance, of soldiers to desert their standards, of children to make war on their parents. With what consistency then could he recommend that such crimes should be covered by a general oblivion? And was there not too much reason to fear that he wished to save the agents of tyranny from the fate which they merited, in the hope that, at some future time, they might serve him as unscrupulously as they had served his father in law ? *

Of the members of the House of Commons who were animated by these feelings, the fiercest and most audacious was Howe. He went so far on one occasion as to move that an enquiry should be instituted into the proceedings of the Parliament of 1685, and that some note of infamy should be put on all who, in that Parliament, had voted with the Court. This absurd and mischievous motion was discountenanced by all the most respectable Whigs, and strongly opposed by Birch and Maynard.† Howe was forced to give way : but he was a man whom no check could abash : and he was encouraged by the applause of many hotheaded members of his party, who were far from foreseeing that he would, after having been the most rancorous and unprincipled of Whigs, become. at no distant time, the most rancorous and unprincipled of Tories.

Intemperance of Howe.

This quickwitted, restless, and malignant politician, though himself occupying a lucrative place in the royal household, declaimed, day after day, against the manner in which the great offices of state were filled ; and his declamations were echoed in tones somewhat less sharp and vehement, by other orators. No man, they said, who had been a minister of Charles or of James ought to be a minister of William. The first attack was directed against the Lord President Caermarthen. Howe moved that an address should be presented to the King, requesting that all persons who had ever been impeached by the Commons might be dismissed from His Majesty's counsels and presence. The debate on this motion was repeatedly adjourned. While the event was doubtful, William sent Dykvelt to expostulate with Howe. Howe was obdurate. He was what is vulgarly called a disinterested man ; that is to say, he valued money less than the pleasure of venting his spleen and of making a sensation. " I am doing the King a service," he said : " I am rescuing him from false friends ; and, as to my place, that shall never be a gag to prevent me from speaking my mind." The motion was made,

Attack on Caermarthen.

* Among the numerous pieces in which the malecontent Whigs vented their anger, none is more curious than the poem entitled the Ghost of Charles the Second. Charles addresses William thus :

" Hail, my blest Nephew, whom the fates ordain
To fill the measure of the Stuarts' reign,

That all the ills by our whole race designed
In thee their full accomplishment might find :
'Tis thou that art decreed this point to clear,
Which we have laboured for these four-score year."

† Grey's Debates, June 12. 1689.

but completely failed. In truth the proposition, that mere accusation, never prosecuted to conviction, ought to be considered as a decisive proof of guilt, was shocking to natural justice. The faults of Caermarthen had doubtless been great; but they had been exaggerated by party spirit, had been expiated by severe suffering, and had been redeemed by recent and eminent services. At the time when he raised the great county of York in arms against Popery and tyranny, he had been assured by some of the most eminent Whigs that all old quarrels were forgotten. Howe indeed maintained that the civilities which had passed in the moment of peril signified nothing. "When a viper is on my hand," he said, "I am very tender of him: but as soon as I have him on the ground, I set my foot on him and crush him." The Lord President, however, was so strongly supported that, after a discussion which lasted three days, his enemies did not venture to take the sense of the House on the motion against him. In the course of the debate a grave constitutional question was incidentally raised. This question was whether a pardon could be pleaded in bar of a parliamentary impeachment. The Commons resolved, without a division, that a pardon could not be so pleaded.*

Attack on Halifax.

The next attack was made on Halifax. He was in a much more invidious position than Caermarthen, who had, under pretence of ill health, withdrawn himself almost entirely from business. Halifax was generally regarded as the chief adviser of the Crown, and was in an especial manner held responsible for all the faults which had been committed with respect to Ireland. The evils which had brought that kingdom to ruin might, it was said, have been averted by timely precaution, or remedied by vigorous exertion. But the government had foreseen nothing: it had done little; and that little had been done neither at the right time nor in the right way. Negotiation had been employed instead of troops, when a few troops might have sufficed. A few troops had been sent when many were needed. The troops that had been sent had been ill equipped and ill commanded. Such, the vehement Whigs exclaimed, were the natural fruits of that great error which King William had committed on the first day of his reign. He had placed in Tories and Trimmers a confidence which they did not deserve. He had, in a peculiar manner, entrusted the direction of Irish affairs to the Trimmer of Trimmers, to a man whose

* See Commons' Journals, and Grey's Debates, June 1. 3. and 4. 1689; Life of William, 1704.

ability nobody disputed, but who was not firmly attached to the new government, who, indeed, was incapable of being firmly attached to any government, who had always halted between two opinions, and who, till the moment of the flight of James, had not given up the hope that the discontents of the nation might be quieted without a change of dynasty. Howe, on twenty occasions, designated Halifax as the cause of all the calamities of the country. Monmouth held similar language in the House of Peers. Though First Lord of the Treasury, he paid no attention to financial business, for which he was altogether unfit, and of which he had very soon become weary. His whole heart was in the work of persecuting the Tories. He plainly told the King that nobody who was not a Whig ought to be employed in the public service. William's answer was cool and determined. "I have done as much for your friends as I can do without danger to the state; and I will do no more."* The only effect of this reprimand was to make Monmouth more factious than ever. Against Halifax especially he intrigued and harangued with indefatigable animosity. The other Whig Lords of the Treasury, Delamere and Capel, were scarcely less eager to drive the Lord Privy Seal from office; and personal jealousy and antipathy impelled the Lord President to conspire with his own accusers against his rival.

What foundation there may have been for the imputations thrown at this time on Halifax cannot now be fully ascertained. His enemies, though they interrogated numerous witnesses, and though they obtained William's reluctant permission to inspect the minutes of the Privy Council, could find no evidence which would support a definite charge.† But it was undeniable that the Lord Privy Seal had acted as minister for Ireland, and that Ireland was all but lost. It is unnecessary, and indeed absurd, to suppose, as many Whigs supposed, that his administration was unsuccessful because he did not wish it to be successful. The truth seems to be that the difficulties of the situation were great, and that he, with all his ingenuity and eloquence, was ill qualified to cope with those difficulties. The whole machinery of government was out of joint; and he was not the man to set it right. What was wanted was not what he had in large measure, wit, taste, amplitude of comprehension, subtlety in drawing distinctions; but what he had not, prompt decision, indefatigable energy, and stubborn

* Burnet MS. Harl. 6584.; Avaux to De Croissy, June 16/26. 1689.
† As to the minutes of the Privy Council, see the Commons' Journals of June 22. and 28., and of July 3. 5. 13. and 16.

resolution. His mind was at best of too soft a temper for such
work as he had now to do, and had been recently made softer
by severe affliction. He had lost two sons in less than twelve
months. A letter is still extant, in which he at this time
complained to his honoured friend Lady Russell of the desolation of his hearth and of the cruel ingratitude of the Whigs.
We possess, also, the answer, in which she gently exhorted
him to seek for consolation where she had found it under trials
not less severe than his.*

The first attack on him was made in the Upper House.
Some Whig Peers, among whom the wayward and petulant
First Lord of the Treasury was conspicuous, proposed that the
King should be requested to appoint a new Speaker. The
friends of Halifax moved and carried the previous question.†
About three weeks later his persecutors brought forward, in a
Committee of the whole House of Commons, a resolution
which imputed to him no particular crime either of omission
or of commission, but which simply declared it to be advisable
that he should be dismissed from the service of the Crown.
The debate was warm. Moderate politicians of both parties
were unwilling to put a stigma on a man, not indeed faultless,
but distinguished both by his abilities and by his amiable
qualities. His accusers saw that they could not carry their
point, and tried to escape from a decision which was certain
to be adverse to them, by proposing that the Chairman should
report progress. But their tactics were disconcerted by the
judicious and spirited conduct of Lord Eland, now the Marquess's only son. "My father has not deserved, said the
young nobleman, "to be thus trifled with. If you think him
culpable, say so. He will at once submit to your verdict.
Dismission from Court has no terrors for him. He is raised,
by the goodness of God, above the necessity of looking to office
for the means of supporting his rank." The Committee
divided, and Halifax was absolved by a majority of fourteen.‡

* The letter of Halifax to Lady Russell is dated on the 23d of July 1689,
about a fortnight after the attack on him
in the Lords, and about a week before
the attack on him in the Commons.

† See the Lords' Journals of July 10.
1689, and a letter from London dated
July $\frac{11}{21}$., and transmitted by Croissy to
Avaux. Don Pedro de Ronquillo men-
tions this attack of the Whig Lords on
Halifax in a despatch of which I cannot
make out the date.

‡ This was on Saturday the 3d of
August. As the division was in Com-

mittee, the numbers do not appear in
the Journals. Clarendon, in his Diary,
says that the majority was eleven. But
Narcissus Luttrell, Oldmixon, and Tindal agree in putting it at fourteen. Most
of the little information which I have
been able to find about the debate is
contained in a despatch of Don Pedro de
Ronquillo, " Se resolvio," he says, " que
el sabado, en comity de toda la casa, se
tratasse del estado de la nacion para
representarle al Rey. Empezose por
acusar al Marques de Olifax; y recono-
ciendo sus emulos que no tenian partido

Had the division been postponed a few hours, the majority would probably have been much greater. The Commons voted under the impression that Londonderry had fallen, and that all Ireland was lost. Scarcely had the House risen when a courier arrived with news that the boom on the Foyle had been broken. He was speedily followed by a second, who announced the raising of the siege, and by a third who brought the tidings of the battle of Newton Butler. Hope and exultation succeeded to discontent and dismay.* Ulster was safe; and it was confidently expected that Schomberg would speedily reconquer Leinster, Connaught, and Munster. He was now ready to set out. The port of Chester was the place from which he was to take his departure. The army which he was to command had assembled there; and the Dee was crowded with men of war and transports. Unfortunately almost all those English soldiers who had seen war had been sent to Flanders. The bulk of the force destined for Ireland consisted of men just taken from the plough and the threshing floor. There was, however, an excellent brigade of Dutch troops under the command of an experienced officer, the Count of Solmes. Four regiments, one of cavalry and three of infantry, had been formed out of the French refugees, many of whom had borne arms with credit. No person did more to promote the raising of these regiments than the Marquess of Ruvigny. He had been during many years an eminently faithful and useful servant of the French government. So highly was his merit appreciated at Versailles that he had been solicited to accept indulgences which scarcely any other heretic could by any solicitation obtain. Had he chosen to remain in his native country, he and his household would have been permitted to worship God privately according to their own forms. But Ruvigny rejected all offers, cast in his lot with his brethren, and, at upwards of eighty years of age, quitted Versailles, where he might still have been a favourite, for a modest dwelling at Greenwich. That dwelling was, during the last months of his life, the resort of all that was most distinguished

Preparations for a campaign in Ireland.

bastante, quisieron remitir para otro dia esta mocion: pero el Conde de Elan, primogenito del Marques de Olifax, miembro de la casa, les dijo que su padre no era hombre para andar peloteando con el, y que se tubiesse culpa lo acabasen de castigar, que el no havia menester estar en la corte para portarse conforme á su estado, pues Dios le havia dado abundamente para poderlo hazer; con que por pluralidad de voces vencio su partido." I suspect that Lord Eland meant to sneer at the poverty of some of his father's persecutors, and at the greediness of others.

* This change of feeling, immediately following the debate on the motion for removing Halifax, is noticed by Ronquillo.

among his fellow exiles. His abilities, his experience, and his munificent kindness, made him the undisputed chief of the refugees. He was at the same time half an Englishman: for his sister had been Countess of Southampton, and he was uncle of Lady Russell. He was long past the time of action. But his two sons, both men of eminent courage, devoted their swords to the service of William. The younger son, who bore the name of Caillemot, was appointed colonel of one of the Huguenot regiments of foot. The two other regiments of foot were commanded by La Melloniere and Cambon, officers of high reputation. The regiment of horse was raised by Schomberg himself, and bore his name. Ruvigny lived just long enough to see these arrangements complete.*

Schomberg.

The general to whom the direction of the expedition against Ireland was confided had wonderfully succeeded in obtaining the affection and esteem of the English nation. He had been made a Duke, a Knight of the Garter, and Master of the Ordnance; he was now placed at the head of an army; and yet his elevation excited none of that jealousy which showed itself as often as any mark of royal favour was bestowed on Bentinck, on Zulestein, or on Auverquerque. Schomberg's military skill was universally acknowledged. He was regarded by all Protestants as a confessor who had endured everything short of martyrdom for the truth. For his religion he had resigned a splendid income, had laid down the truncheon of a Marshal of France, and had, at near eighty years of age, begun the world again as a needy soldier of fortune. As he had no connection with the United Provinces, and had never belonged to the little Court of the Hague, the preference given to him over English captains was justly ascribed, not to national or personal partiality, but to his virtues and his abilities. His deportment differed widely from that of the other foreigners who had just been created English peers. They, with many respectable qualities, were, in tastes, manners, and predilections, Dutchmen, and could not catch the tone of the society to which they had been transferred. He was a citizen of the world, had travelled over all Europe, had commanded armies on the Meuse, on the Ebro, and on the Tagus, had shone in the splendid circle of Versailles, and had been

---

* As to Ruvigny, see Saint Simon's Memoirs of the year 1697; Burnet, i. 366. There is some interesting information about Ruvigny and about the Huguenot regiments in a narrative written by a French refugee of the name of Dumont. This narrative, which is in manuscript, and which I shall occasionally quote as the Dumont MS., was kindly lent to me by Dr. Vignoles, Dean of Ossory.

in high favour at the court of Berlin. He had often been taken by French noblemen for a French nobleman. He had passed some time in England, spoke English remarkably well, accommodated himself easily to English manners, and was often seen walking in the park with English companions. In youth his habits had been temperate; and his temperance had its proper reward, a singularly green and vigorous old age. At fourscore he retained a strong relish for innocent pleasures: he conversed with great courtesy and sprightliness: nothing could be in better taste than his equipages and his table; and every cornet of cavalry envied the grace and dignity with which the veteran appeared in Hyde Park on his charger at the head of his regiment.* The House of Commons had, with general approbation, compensated his losses and rewarded his services by a grant of a hundred thousand pounds. Before he set out for Ireland, he requested permission to express his gratitude for this magnificent present. A chair was set for him within the bar. He took his seat there with the mace at his right hand, rose, and in a few graceful words returned his thanks and took his leave. The Speaker replied that the Commons could never forget the obligation under which they already lay to His Grace, that they saw him with pleasure at the head of an English army, that they felt entire confidence in his zeal and ability, and that, at whatever distance he might be, he would always be in a peculiar manner an object of their care. The precedent set on this interesting occasion was followed with the utmost minuteness, a hundred and twenty-five years later, on an occasion more interesting still. Exactly on the same spot on which, in July 1689, Schomberg had acknowledged the liberality of the nation, a chair was set, in July 1814, for a still more illustrious warrior, who came to return thanks for a still more splendid mark of public gratitude. Few things illustrate more strikingly the peculiar character of the English government and people than the circumstance that the House of Commons, a popular assembly, should, even in a moment of joyous enthusiasm, have adhered to ancient forms with the punctilious accuracy of a College of Heralds; that the sitting and rising, the covering and the uncovering, should have been regulated by exactly the same etiquette in the nineteenth century as in the seventeenth; and that the same mace which

* See the Abrégé de la Vie de Frederic Duc de Schomberg by Luzancy, 1690, the Memoirs of Count Dohna, and the note of Saint Simon on Dangeau's Journal, July 30. 1690.

had been held at the right hand of Schomberg should have been held in the same position at the right hand of Wellington.*

Recess of the Parliament.

On the twentieth of August the Parliament, having been constantly engaged in business during seven months, broke up, by the royal command, for a short recess. The same Gazette which announced that the Houses had ceased to sit announced that Schomberg had landed in Ireland.†

State of Ireland. Advice of Avaux.

During the three weeks which preceded his landing, the dismay and confusion at Dublin Castle had been extreme. Disaster had followed disaster so fast that the mind of James, never very firm, had been completely prostrated. He had learned first that Londonderry had been relieved; then that one of his armies had been beaten by the Enniskilleners; then that another of his armies was retreating, or rather flying, from Ulster, reduced in numbers and broken in spirit; then that Sligo, the key of Connaught, had been abandoned to the Englishry. He had found it impossible to subdue the colonists, even when they were left almost unaided. He might therefore well doubt whether it would be possible for him to contend against them when they were backed by an English army, under the command of the greatest general living. The unhappy prince seemed, during some days, to be sunk in despondency. On Avaux the danger produced a very different effect. Now, he thought, was the time to turn the war between the English and the Irish into a war of extirpation, and to make it impossible that the two nations could ever be united under one government. With this view, he coolly submitted to the King a proposition of almost incredible atrocity. There must be a Saint Bartholomew. A pretext would easily be found. No doubt, when Schomberg was known to be in Ireland, there would be some excitement in those southern towns of which the population was chiefly English. Any disturbance, wherever it might take place, would furnish an excuse for a general massacre of the Protestants of Leinster, Munster, and Connaught.‡ As the King did not at first express any horror at this suggestion,§ the Envoy, a few days later, returned to the subject, and pressed His Majesty to give

* See the Commons' Journals of July 16. 1689, and of July 1. 1814.

† Journals of the Lords and Commons, Aug. 20. 1689; London Gazette, Aug. 22.

‡ "J'estois d'avis qu', après que la descente seroit faite, si on apprenoit que des Protestans se fussent soulevez en quelques endroits du royaume, on fit main basse sur tous généralement."—Avaux, $\frac{\text{July 31.}}{\text{Aug. 10.}}$ 1689.

§ "Le Roy d'Angleterre m'avoit écouté assez paisiblement la première fois que je luy avois proposé ce qu'il y avoit à faire contre les Protestans."—Avaux, Aug. $\frac{4}{14}$.

the necessary orders. Then James, with a warmth which did
him honour, declared that nothing should induce him to commit such a crime. "These people are my subjects: and I
cannot be so cruel as to cut their throats while they live
peaceably under my government." "There is nothing cruel,"
answered the callous diplomatist, "in what I recommend.
Your Majesty ought to consider that mercy to Protestants is
cruelty to Catholics." James, however, was not to be moved;
and Avaux retired in very bad humour. His belief was that
the King's professions of humanity were hypocritical, and
that, if the orders for the butchery were not given, they were
not given only because His Majesty was confident that the
Catholics all over the country would fall on the Protestants
without waiting for orders.* But Avaux was entirely mistaken. That he should have supposed James to be as profoundly immoral as himself is not strange. But it is strange
that so able a man should have forgotten that James and
himself had quite different objects in view. The object of the
Ambassador's politics was to make the separation between
England and Ireland eternal. The object of the King's
politics was to unite England and Ireland under his own
sceptre; and he could not but be aware that, if there should
be a general massacre of the Protestants of three provinces,
and he should be suspected of having authorised it or of having
connived at it, there would in a fortnight be not a Jacobite
left even at Oxford.†

Just at this time the prospects of James, which had
seemed hopelessly dark, began to brighten. The danger
which had unnerved him had roused the Irish people. They
had, six months before, risen up as one man against the
Saxons. The army which Tyrconnel had formed was, in
proportion to the population from which it was taken, the
largest that Europe had ever seen. But that army had
sustained a long succession of defeats and disgraces, unre-
deemed by a single brilliant achievement. It was the
fashion, both in England and on the Continent, to ascribe

* Avaux, Aug. $\frac{4}{14}$. He says, "Je
m'imagine qu'il est persuadé que, quoiqu'il ne donne point d'ordre sur cela, la
plupart des Catholiques de la campagne
se jetteront sur les Protestans."

† Lewis, $\frac{\text{Aug. 27.}}{\text{Sept. 6.}}$, reprimanded Avaux,
though much too gently, for proposing to
butcher the whole Protestant population
of Leinster, Connaught, and Munster.
"Je n'approuve pas cependant la proposition que vous faites de faire main basse

sur tous les Protestans du royaume, du
moment qu', en quelque endroit que ce
soit, ils se seront soulevez: et, outre que
la punition d'une infinité d'innocens pour
peu de coupables ne seroit pas juste,
d'ailleurs les représailles contre les Catholiques seroient d'autant plus dange-
reuses, que les premiers se trouveront
mieux armez et soutenus de toutes les
forces d'Angleterre."

those defeats and disgraces to the pusillanimity of the Irish race.* That this was a great error is sufficiently proved by the history of every war which has been carried on in any part of Christendom during five generations. The raw material out of which a good army may be formed existed in great abundance among the Irish. Avaux informed his government that they were a remarkably handsome, tall, and well made race; that they were personally brave; that they were sincerely attached to the cause for which they were in arms; that they were violently exasperated against the colonists. After extolling their strength and spirit, he proceeded to explain why it was that, with all their strength and spirit, they were constantly beaten. It was vain, he said, to imagine that bodily prowess, animal courage, or patriotic enthusiasm would, in the day of battle, supply the place of discipline. The infantry were ill armed and ill trained. They were suffered to pillage wherever they went. They had contracted all the habits of banditti. There was among them scarcely one officer capable of showing them their duty. Their colonels were generally men of good family, but men who had never seen service. The captains were butchers, tailors, shoemakers. Hardly one of them troubled himself about the comforts, the accoutrements, or the drilling of those over whom he was placed. The dragoons were little better than the infantry. But the horse were, with some exceptions, excellent. Almost all the Irish gentlemen who had any military experience held commissions in the cavalry; and, by the exertions of these officers, some regiments had been raised and disciplined which Avaux pronounced equal to any that he had ever seen. It was therefore evident that the inefficiency of the foot and of the dragoons was to be ascribed to the vices, not of the Irish character but of the Irish administration.†

* Ronquillo, Aug. ⁹⁄₁₉., speaking of the Siege of Londonderry, expresses his astonishment "que una plaza sin fortificazion y sin gentes de guerra aya hecho una defensa tan gloriosa, y que los sitiadores al contrario ayan sido tan poltrones."

† This account of the Irish army is compiled from numerous letters written by Avaux to Lewis and to Lewis's ministers. I will quote a few of the most remarkable passages. "Les plus beaux hommes," Avaux says of the Irish, "qu'on peut voir. Il n'y en a presque point au dessous de cinq pieds cinq à six

pouces." It will be remembered that the French foot is longer than ours. "Ils sont très bien faits: mais ils ne sont ny disciplinez ny armez, et de surplus sont de grands voleurs." "La plupart de ces régimens sont levez par des gentilshommes qui n'ont jamais esté à l'armée. Ce sont des tailleurs, des bouchers, des cordonniers, qui ont formé les compagnies et qui en sont les Capitaines." "Jamais troupes n'ont marché comme font celles-cy. Ils vont comme des bandits, et pillent tout ce qu'ils trouvent en chemin." "Quoiqu'il soit vrai que les soldats paraissent fort résolus à bien faire, et qu'ils

The events which took place in the autumn of 1689 sufficiently proved that the ill fated race, which enemies and
allies generally agreed in regarding with unjust contempt,
had, together with the faults inseparable from poverty,
ignorance, and superstition, some fine qualities which have
not always been found in more prosperous and more enlightened communities. The evil tidings which terrified and
bewildered James stirred the whole population of the
southern provinces like the peal of a trumpet sounding to
battle. That Ulster was lost, that the English were coming,
that the death grapple between the two hostile nations was
at hand, was proclaimed from all the altars of three and
twenty counties. One last chance was left; and, if that
chance failed, nothing remained but the despotic, the merciless, rule of the Saxon colony and of the heretical church.
The Roman Catholic priest who had just taken possession
of the glebe house and the chancel, the Roman Catholic
squire who had just been carried back on the shoulders of
the shouting tenantry into the hall of his fathers, would be
driven forth to live on such alms as peasants, themselves
oppressed and miserable, could spare. A new confiscation
would complete the work of the Act of Settlement; and the
followers of William would seize whatever the followers of
Cromwell had spared. These apprehensions produced such
an outbreak of patriotic and religious enthusiasm as deferred
for a time the inevitable day of subjugation. Avaux was
amazed by the energy which, in circumstances so trying, the
Irish displayed. It was indeed the wild and unsteady energy
of a half barbarous people : it was transient: it was often
misdirected : but, though transient and misdirected, it did
wonders. The French Ambassador was forced to own that
those officers of whose incompetency and inactivity he had
so often complained had suddenly shaken off their lethargy.
Recruits came in by thousands. The ranks which had been
thinned under the walls of Londonderry were soon again full
to overflowing. Great efforts were made to arm and clothe

soient fort animez contre les rebelles,
néantmoins il ne suffit pas de cela pour
combattre. . . . . Les officiers subalternes
sont mauvais, et, à la reserve d'un très
petit nombre, il n'y en a point qui ayt
soin des soldats, des armes, et de la discipline." "On a beaucoup plus de confiance en la cavalerie, dont la plus grande
partie est assez bonne." Avaux men-

tions several regiments of horse with
particular praise. Of two of these he
says, "On ne peut voir de meilleur régi-
ment." The correctness of the opinion
which he had formed both of the infantry
and of the cavalry was, after his departure from Ireland, signally proved at the
Boyne.

the troops; and, in the short space of a fortnight, everything presented a new and cheering aspect.*

Dismission of Melfort.

The Irish required of the King, in return for their strenuous exertions in his cause, one concession which was by no means agreeable to him. The unpopularity of Melfort had become such that his person was scarcely safe. He had no friend to speak a word in his favour. The French hated him. In every letter which arrived at Dublin from England or from Scotland, he was described as the evil genius of the House of Stuart. It was necessary for his own sake to dismiss him. An honourable pretext was found. He was ordered to repair to Versailles, to represent there the state of affairs in Ireland, and to implore the French government to send over without delay six or seven thousand veteran infantry. He laid down the seals; and they were, to the great delight of the Irish, put into the hands of an Irishman, Sir Richard Nagle, who had made himself conspicuous as Attorney General and Speaker of the House of Commons. Melfort took his departure under cover of the night: for the rage of the populace against him was such that he could not without danger show himself in the streets of Dublin by day. On the following morning James left his capital in the opposite direction to encounter Schomberg.†

Schomberg lands in Ulster.

Schomberg had landed in the north of Ulster. The force which he had brought with him did not exceed ten thousand men. But he expected to be joined by the armed colonists and by the regiments which were under Kirke's command. The coffeehouse politicians of London fully expected that such a general with such an army would speedily reconquer the island. Unhappily it soon appeared that the means which had been furnished to him were altogether inadequate to the work which he had to perform: of the greater part of these means he was speedily deprived by a succession of unforeseen calamities; and the whole campaign was merely a long struggle maintained by his prudence and resolution against the utmost spite of fortune.

---

* I will quote a passage or two from the despatches written at this time by Avaux. On September $\frac{7}{17}$. he says: "De quelque costé qu'on se tournât, on ne pouvoit rien prevoir que de désagréable. Mais dans cette extrémité chacun s'est évertué. Les officiers ont fait leurs recrues avec beaucoup de diligence." Three days later he says: "Il y a quinze jours que nous n'espérions guère de pouvoir mettre les choses en si bon estat:

mais my Lord Tyrconnel et tous les Irlandais ont travaillé avec tant d'empressement qu'on s'est mis en estat de deffense."

† Avaux, Aug. $\frac{20}{30}$. $\frac{Aug.\ 25.}{Sept.\ 4.}$ $\frac{Aug.\ 26.}{Sept.\ 5.}$; Life of James, ii. 373.; Melfort's vindication of himself among the Nairne Papers. Avaux says: "Il pourra partir ce soir à la nuit: car je vois bien qu'il apprehende qu'il ne sera pas sur pour luy de partir en plein jour."

He marched first to Carrickfergus. That town was held for James by two regiments of infantry. Schomberg battered the walls; and the Irish, after holding out a week, capitulated. He promised that they should depart unharmed; but he found it no easy matter to keep his word. The people of the town and neighbourhood were generally Protestants of Scottish extraction. They had suffered much during the short ascendency of the native race; and what they had suffered they were now eager to retaliate. They assembled in great multitudes, exclaiming that the capitulation was nothing to them, and that they would be revenged, They soon proceeded from words to blows. The Irish disarmed, stripped, and hustled, clung for protection to the English officers and soldiers. Schomberg with difficulty prevented a massacre by spurring, pistol in hand, through the throng of enraged colonists.*

Carrick-fergus taken.

From Carrickfergus Schomberg proceeded to Lisburn, and thence, through towns left without an inhabitant, and over plains on which not a cow, nor a sheep, nor a stack of corn was to be seen, to Loughbrickland. Here he was joined by three regiments of Enniskilleners, whose dress, horses, and arms looked strange to eyes accustomed to the pomp of reviews, but who in natural courage were inferior to no troops in the world, and who had, during months of constant watching and skirmishing, acquired many of the essential qualities of soldiers.†

Schomberg continued to advance towards Dublin through a desert. The few Irish troops which remained in the south of Ulster retreated before him, destroying as they retreated. Newry, once a well built and thriving Protestant borough, he found a heap of smoking ashes. Carlingford too had perished. The spot where the town had once stood was marked only by the massy remains of the old Norman castle. Those who ventured to wander from the camp reported that the country, as far as they could explore it, was a wilderness. There were cabins, but no inmates: there was rich pasture, but neither flock nor herd: there were cornfields: but the harvest lay on the ground soaked with rain.‡

Schomberg advances into Leinster.

While Schomberg was advancing through a vast solitude, the Irish forces were rapidly assembling from every quarter.

---

* Story's Impartial History of the Wars of Ireland, 1693; Life of James, ii. 374.; Avaux, Sept. ⁷⁄₁₇. 1689; Nihell's Journal, printed in 1689, and reprinted by Macpherson.
† Story's Impartial History.
‡ Ibid.

On the tenth of September the royal standard of James was unfurled on the tower of Drogheda; and beneath it were soon collected twenty thousand fighting men, the infantry generally bad, the cavalry generally good, but both infantry and cavalry full of zeal for their country and their religion.* The troops were attended as usual by a great multitude of camp followers, armed with scythes, half pikes, and skeans. By this time Schomberg had reached Dundalk. The distance between the two armies was not more than a long day's march. It was therefore generally expected that the fate of the island would speedily be decided by a pitched battle.

The English and Irish armies encamp near each other.

In both camps, all who did not understand war were eager to fight; and, in both camps, the few who had a high reputation for military science were against fighting. Neither Rosen nor Schomberg wished to put everything on a cast. Each of them knew intimately the defects of his own army; and neither of them was fully aware of the defects of the other's army. Rosen was certain that the Irish infantry were worse equipped, worse officered, and worse drilled, than any infantry that he had ever seen from the Gulf of Bothnia to the Atlantic; and he supposed that the English troops were well trained, and were, as they doubtless ought to have been, amply provided with everything necessary to their efficiency. Numbers, he rightly judged, would avail little against a great superiority of arms and discipline. He therefore advised James to fall back, and even to abandon Dublin to the enemy rather than hazard a battle the loss of which would be the loss of all. Athlone was the best place in the kingdom for a determined stand. The passage of the Shannon might be defended till the succours which Melfort had been charged to solicit came from France; and those succours would change the whole character of the war. But the Irish, with Tyrconnel at their head, were unanimous against retreating. The blood of the whole nation was up. James was pleased with the enthusiasm of his subjects, and positively declared that he would not disgrace himself by leaving his capital to the invaders without a blow.†

Schomberg declines a battle.

In a few days it became clear that Schomberg had determined not to fight. His reasons were weighty. He had some good Dutch and French troops. The Enniskilleners who had

---

* Avaux, Sept. $\frac{10}{20}$. 1689; Story's Impartial History; Life of James, ii. 377, 378. Orig. Mem. Story and James agree in estimating the Irish army at about twenty thousand men. See also Dangeau, Oct. 28. 1689

† Life of James, ii. 377, 378. Orig. Mem.

joined him had served a military apprenticeship, though not in a very regular manner. But the bulk of his army consisted of English peasants who had just left their cottages. His musketeers had still to learn how to load their pieces: his dragoons had still to learn how to manage their horses; and these inexperienced recruits were for the most part commanded by officers as inexperienced as themselves. His troops were therefore not generally superior in discipline to the Irish, and were in number far inferior. Nay, he found that his men were almost as ill armed, as ill lodged, and as ill clad, as the Celts to whom they were opposed. The wealth of the English nation and the liberal votes of the English parliament had entitled him to expect that he should be abundantly supplied with all the munitions of war. But he was cruelly disappointed. The administration had, ever since the death of Oliver, been constantly becoming more and more imbecile, more and more corrupt; and now the Revolution reaped what the Restoration had sown. A crowd of negligent or ravenous functionaries, formed under Charles and James, plundered, starved, and poisoned the armies and fleets of William. Of these men the most important was Henry Shales, who, in the late reign, had been Commissary General to the camp at Hounslow. It is difficult to blame the new government for continuing to employ him: for, in his own department, his experience far surpassed that of any other Englishman. Unfortunately, in the same school in which he had acquired his experience, he had learned the whole art of peculation. The beef and brandy which he furnished were so bad that the soldiers turned from them with loathing: the tents were rotten: the clothing was scanty: the muskets broke in the handling. Great numbers of shoes were set down to the account of the government: but, two months after the Treasury had paid the bill, the shoes had not arrived in Ireland. The means of transporting baggage and artillery were almost entirely wanting. An ample number of horses had been purchased in England with the public money, and had been sent to the banks of the Dee. But Shales had let them out for harvest work to the farmers of Cheshire, had pocketed the hire, and had left the troops in Ulster to get on as they best might.[*] Schomberg thought that, if he should, with an ill trained and ill appointed army, risk a battle against a superior force, he might not improbably be defeated; and he knew that a de-

---

[*] See Grey's Debates, Nov. 26, 27, 28. 1689, and the Dialogue between a Lord Lieutenant and one of his Deputies, 1692.

feat might be followed by the loss of one kingdom, perhaps by the loss of three kingdoms. He therefore made up his mind to stand on the defensive till his men had been disciplined, and till reinforcements and supplies should arrive.

He entrenched himself near Dundalk in such a manner that he could not be forced to fight against his will. James, emboldened by the caution of his adversary, and disregarding the advice of Rosen, advanced to Ardee, appeared at the head of the whole Irish army before the English lines, drew up horse, foot, and artillery, in order of battle, and displayed his banner. The English were impatient to fall on. But their general had made up his mind, and was not to be moved by the bravadoes of the enemy or by the murmurs of his own soldiers. During some weeks he remained secure within his defences, while the Irish lay a few miles off. He set himself assiduously to drill those new levies which formed the greater part of his army. He ordered the musketeers to be constantly exercised in firing, sometimes at marks, and sometimes by platoons; and, from the way in which they at first acquitted themselves, it plainly appeared that he had judged wisely in not leading them out to battle. It was found that not one in four of the English soldiers could manage his piece at all; and whoever succeeded in discharging it, no matter in what direction, thought that he had performed a great feat.

Conspiracy among the French troops in the English service.

While the Duke was thus employed, the Irish eyed his camp without daring to attack it. But within that camp soon appeared two evils more terrible than the foe, treason and pestilence. Among the best troops under his command were the French exiles. And now a grave doubt arose touching their fidelity. The real Huguenot refugee indeed might safely be trusted. The dislike with which the most zealous English Protestant regarded the House of Bourbon and the Church of Rome was a lukewarm feeling when compared with that inextinguishable hatred which glowed in the bosom of the persecuted, dragooned, expatriated Calvinist of Languedoc. The Irish had already remarked that the French heretic neither gave nor took quarter.* Now, however, it was found that with those emigrants who had sacrificed everything for the reformed religion were intermingled emigrants of a very different sort, deserters who had run away from their standards in the Low Countries, and had coloured their crime by pre-

---

* Nihell's Journal. A French officer, in a letter to Avaux, written soon after Schomberg's landing, says, "Les Hugue-

nots font plus de mal que les Anglois, et tuent force Catholiques pour avoir fait résistance."

tending that they were Protestants, and that their conscience would not suffer them to fight for the persecutor of their Church. Some of these men, hoping that by a second treason they might obtain both pardon and reward, opened a correspondence with Avaux. The letters were intercepted; and a formidable plot was brought to light. It appeared that, if Schomberg had been weak enough to yield to the importunity of those who wished him to give battle, several French companies would, in the heat of the action, have fired on the English, and gone over to the enemy. Such a defection might well have produced a general panic in a better army than that which was encamped under Dundalk. It was necessary to be severe. Six of the conspirators were hanged. Two hundred of their accomplices were sent in irons to England. Even after this winnowing, the refugees were long regarded by the rest of the army with unjust but not unnatural suspicion. During some days indeed there was great reason to fear that the enemy would be entertained with a bloody fight between the English soldiers and their French allies.*

A few hours before the execution of the chief conspirators, a general muster of the army was held; and it was observed that the ranks of the English battalions looked thin. From the first day of the campaign, there had been much sickness among the recruits : but it was not till the time of the equinox that the mortality became alarming. The autumnal rains of Ireland are usually heavy; and this year they were heavier than usual. The whole country was deluged; and the Duke's camp became a marsh. The Enniskillen men were seasoned to the climate. The Dutch were accustomed to live in a country which, as a wit of that age said, draws fifty feet of water. They kept their huts dry and clean; and they had experienced and careful officers who did not suffer them to omit any precaution. But the peasants of Yorkshire and Derbyshire had neither constitutions prepared to resist the pernicious influence, nor skill to protect themselves against it. The bad provisions furnished by the Commissariat aggravated the maladies generated by the air. Remedies were almost entirely wanting. The surgeons were few. The medicine chests contained little more than lint and plasters for wounds. The English sickened and died by hundreds. Even those who

Pestilence in the English army.

* Story; Narrative transmitted by Avaux to Seignelay, $\frac{Nov. 26.}{Dec. 6.}$ 1689; London Gazette, Oct. 14. 1689. It is curious that, though Dumont was in the camp before Dundalk, there is in his MS. no mention of the conspiracy among the French

were not smitten by the pestilence were unnerved and dejected, and, instead of putting forth the energy which is the heritage of our race, awaited their fate with the helpless apathy of Asiatics. It was in vain that Schomberg tried to teach them to improve their habitations, and to cover the wet earth with a thick carpet of fern. Exertion had become more dreadful to them than death. It was not to be expected that men who would not help themselves should help each other. Nobody asked and nobody showed compassion. Familiarity with ghastly spectacles produced a hardheartedness and a desperate impiety of which an example will not easily be found even in the history of infectious diseases. The moans of the sick were drowned by the blasphemy and ribaldry of their comrades. Sometimes, seated on the body of a wretch who had died in the morning, might be seen a wretch destined to die before night, cursing, singing loose songs, and swallowing usquebaugh to the health of the devil. When the corpses were taken away to be buried the survivors grumbled. A dead man, they said, was a good screen and a good stool. Why, when there was so abundant a supply of such useful articles of furniture, were people to be exposed to the cold air and forced to crouch on the moist ground.*

Many of the sick were sent by the English vessels which lay off the coast to Belfast, where a great hospital had been prepared. But scarce half of them lived to the end of the voyage. More than one ship lay long in the bay of Carrickfergus, heaped with carcasses, and exhaling the stench of death, without a living man on board.†

The Irish army suffered much less. The kerne of Munster or Connaught was quite as well off in the camp as if he had been in his own mud cabin inhaling the vapours of his own quagmire. He naturally exulted in the distress of the Saxon heretics, and flattered himself that they would be destroyed without a blow. He heard with delight the guns pealing all day over the graves of the English officers, till at length the funerals became too numerous to be celebrated with military pomp, and the mournful sounds were succeeded by a silence more mournful still.

The superiority of force was now so decidedly on the side of James that he could safely venture to detach five regiments

---

* Story's Impartial History; Dumont MS. The profaneness and dissoluteness of the camp during the sickness are mentioned in many contemporary pamphlets both in verse and prose. See particularly a Satire entitled Reformation of Manners, part ii.

† Story's Impartial History.

from his army, and to send them into Connaught. Sarsfield commanded them. He did not, indeed, stand so high as he deserved in the royal estimation. The King, with an air of intellectual superiority which must have made Avaux and Rosen bite their lips, pronounced him a brave fellow, but very scantily supplied with brains. It was not without great difficulty that the Ambassador prevailed on His Majesty to raise the best officer in the Irish army to the rank of Brigadier. Sarsfield now fully vindicated the favourable opinion which his French patrons had formed of him. He dislodged the English from Sligo; and he effectually secured Galway, which had been in considerable danger.*

No attack, however, was made on the English entrenchments before Dundalk. In the midst of difficulties and disasters hourly multiplying, the great qualities of Schomberg appeared hourly more and more conspicuous. Not in the full tide of success, not on the field of Montes Claros, not under the walls of Maestricht, had he so well deserved the admiration of mankind. His resolution never gave way. His prudence never slept. His temper, in spite of manifold vexations and provocations, was always cheerful and serene. The effective men under his command, even if all were reckoned as effective who were not stretched on the earth by fever, did not now exceed five thousand. These were hardly equal to their ordinary duty; and yet it was necessary to harass them with double duty. Nevertheless so masterly were the old man's dispositions that with this small force he faced during several weeks twenty thousand troops who were accompanied by a multitude of armed banditti. At length early in November the Irish dispersed, and went to winter quarters. The Duke then broke up his camp and retired into Ulster. Just as the remains of his army were about to move, a rumour spread that the enemy was approaching in great force. Had this rumour been true, the danger would have been extreme. But the English regiments, though they had been reduced to a third part of their complement, and though the men who were in best health were hardly able to shoulder arms, showed a strange joy and alacrity at the prospect of battle, and swore that the Papists should pay for all the misery of the last month. "We English," Schomberg said, identifying himself goodhumouredly with the people of the country which had adopted him, "we English have stomach enough for fighting. It is a

The English and Irish armies go into winter quarters

---

* Avaux, Oct. $\frac{11}{21}$. Nov. $\frac{14}{24}$. 1689; James, ii. 382, 383. Orig. Mem.; Nihell's Story's Impartial History; Life of Journal.

pity, that we are not as fond of some other parts of a soldier's business."

The alarm proved false. The Duke's army departed unmolested: but the highway along which he retired presented a piteous and hideous spectacle. A long train of waggons laden with the sick jolted over the rugged pavement. At every jolt some wretched man gave up the ghost. The corpse was flung out and left unburied to the foxes and crows. The whole number of those who died, in the camp at Dundalk, in the hospital at Belfast, on the road, and on the sea, amounted to above six thousand. The survivors were quartered for the winter in the towns and villages of Ulster. The general fixed his head quarters at Lisburn.*

Various opinions about Schomberg's conduct.

His conduct was variously judged. Wise and candid men said that he had surpassed himself, and that there was no other captain in Europe who, with raw troops, with ignorant officers, with scanty stores, having to contend at once against a hostile army of greatly superior force, against a villanous commissariat, against a nest of traitors in his own camp, and against a disease more murderous than the sword, would have brought the campaign to a close without the loss of a flag or a gun. On the other hand, many of those newly commissioned majors and captains, whose helplessness had increased all his perplexities, and who had not one qualification for their post except personal courage, grumbled at the skill and patience which had saved them from destruction. Their complaints were echoed on the other side of Saint George's Channel. Some of the murmuring, though unjust, was excusable. The parents, who had sent a gallant lad, in his first uniform, to fight his way to glory, might be pardoned if, when they learned that he had died on a wisp of straw without medical attendance, and had been buried in a swamp without any Christian or military ceremony, their affliction made them hasty and unreasonable. But with the cry of bereaved families was mingled another cry much less respectable. All the hearers and tellers of news abused the general who furnished them with so little news to hear and to tell. For men of that sort are so greedy after excitement that they far more

* Story's Impartial History; Schomberg's Despatches; Nihell's Journal, and James's Life; Burnet, ii. 20.; Dangeau's journal during this autumn; the Narrative sent by Avaux to Seignelay, and the Dumont MS. The lying of the London Gazette is monstrous. Through the whole autumn the troops are constantly said to be in good condition. In the absurd drama entitled the Royal Voyage, which was acted for the amusement of the rabble of London in 1689, the Irish are represented as attacking some of the sick English. The English put the assailants to the rout, and then drop down dead.

readily forgive a commander who loses a battle than a commander who declines one. The politicians who delivered their oracles from the thickest cloud of tobacco smoke at Garroway's, confidently asked, without knowing anything, either of war in general, or of Irish war in particular, why Schomberg did not fight. They could not venture to say that he did not understand his calling. He had, in his day, they acknowledged, been an excellent officer: but he was very old. He seemed to bear his years well: but his faculties were not what they had been: his memory was failing; and it was well known that he sometimes forgot in the afternoon what he had done in the morning. It may be doubted whether there ever existed a human being whose mind was quite as firmly toned at eighty as at forty. But that Schomberg's intellectual powers had been little impaired by years is sufficiently proved by his despatches, which are still extant, and which are models of official writing, terse, perspicuous, full of important facts and weighty reasons, compressed into the smallest possible number of words. In those despatches he sometimes alluded, not angrily, but with calm disdain, to the censures thrown upon his conduct by shallow babblers, who, never having seen any military operation more important than the relieving of the guard at Whitehall, imagined that the easiest thing in the world was to gain great victories in any situation and against any odds, and by sturdy patriots who were convinced that one English carter or thresher, who had not yet learned how to load a gun or port a pike, was a match for any six musketeers of King Lewis's household.*

Unsatisfactory as had been the results of the campaign in Ireland, the results of the maritime operations of the year were more unsatisfactory still. It had been confidently expected that, on the sea, England, allied with Holland, would have been far more than a match for the power of Lewis: but everything went wrong. Herbert had, after the unimportant skirmish of Bantry Bay, returned with his squadron to Portsmouth. There he found that he had not lost the good opinion either of the public or of the government. The House of Commons thanked him for his services; and he received signal marks of the favour of the Crown. He had not been at the coronation, and had therefore missed his share of the rewards which, at the time of that solemnity, had been distributed among the chief agents in the Revolution. The omission was now repaired; and he was created Earl of Torrington.

Maritime affairs.

* See his despatches in the Appendix to Dalrymple's Memoirs.

The King went down to Portsmouth, dined on board of the Admiral's flag ship, expressed the fullest confidence in the valour and loyalty of the navy, knighted two gallant captains, Cloudesley Shovel and John Ashby, and ordered a donative to be divided among the seamen.*

Maladministration of Torrington.

We cannot justly blame William for having a high opinion of Torrington. For Torrington was generally regarded as one of the bravest and most skilful officers in the navy. He had been promoted to the rank of Rear Admiral of England by James, who, if he understood anything, understood maritime affairs. That place and other lucrative places Torrington had relinquished when he found that he could retain them only by submitting to be a tool of the Jesuitical cabal. No man had taken a more active, a more hazardous, or a more useful part in effecting the Revolution. It seemed, therefore, that no man had fairer pretensions to be put at the head of the naval administration. Yet no man could be more unfit for such a post. His morals had always been loose, so loose indeed that the firmness with which in the late reign he had adhered to his religion had excited much surprise. His glorious disgrace indeed seemed to have produced a salutary effect on his character. In poverty and exile he rose from a voluptuary into a hero. But, as soon as prosperity returned, the hero sank again into a voluptuary; and the relapse was deep and hopeless. The nerves of his mind, which had been during a short time braced to a high tone, were now so much relaxed by vice that he was utterly incapable of selfdenial or of strenuous exertion. The vulgar courage of a foremast man he still retained. But both as Admiral and as First Lord of the Admiralty he was utterly inefficient. Month after month the fleet which should have been the terror of the seas lay in harbour while he was diverting himself in London. The sailors, punning upon his new title, gave him the name of Lord Tarry-in-Town. When he came on shipboard he was accompanied by a bevy of courtesans. There was scarcely an hour of the day or of the night when he was not under the influence of claret. Being insatiable of pleasure, he necessarily became insatiable of wealth. Yet he loved flattery almost as much as either wealth or pleasure. He had long been in the habit of exacting the most abject homage from those who were under his command. His flag ship was a little Versailles. He expected his captains to attend him to his cabin when he went to bed, and to assemble every morning

* London Gazette, May 20. 1689.

at his levee. He even suffered them to dress him. One of them combed his flowing wig; another stood ready with the embroidered coat. Under such a chief there could be no discipline. His tars passed their time in rioting among the rabble of Portsmouth. Those officers who had won his favour by servility and adulation easily obtained leave of absence, and spent weeks in London, revelling in taverns, scouring the streets, or making love to the masked ladies in the pit of the theatre. The victuallers soon found out with whom they had to deal, and sent down to the fleet casks of meat which dogs would not touch, and barrels of beer which smelt worse than bilge water. Meanwhile the British Channel seemed to be abandoned to French rovers. Our merchantmen were boarded in sight of the ramparts of Plymouth. The sugar fleet from the West Indies lost seven ships. The whole value of the prizes taken by the cruisers of the enemy in the immediate neighbourhood of our island, while Torrington was engaged with his bottle and his haram, was estimated at six hundred thousand pounds. So difficult was it to obtain the convoy of a man of war, except by giving immense bribes, that our traders were forced to hire the services of Dutch privateers, and found these foreign mercenaries much more useful and much less greedy than the officers of our own royal navy.*

The only department with which no fault could be found was the department of Foreign Affairs. There William was his own minister; and, where he was his own minister, there were no delays, no blunders, no jobs, no treasons. The difficulties with which he had to contend were indeed great. Even at the Hague he had to encounter an opposition which all his wisdom and firmness could, with the strenuous support of Heinsius, scarcely overcome. The English were not aware that, while they were murmuring at their Sovereign's partiality for the land of his birth, a strong party in Holland was murmuring at his partiality for the land of his adoption. The Dutch ambassadors at Westminster complained that the terms of alliance which he proposed were derogatory to the dignity and prejudicial to the interests of the republic; that wherever the honour of the English flag was concerned, he was punctilious and obstinate; that he peremptorily insisted on an article which interdicted all trade with France, and

Continental affairs.

---

* Commons' Journals, Nov. 13. 23. 1689; Grey's Debates, Nov. 13, 14. 18. 23. 1689. See among numerous pasquinades, the Parable of the Bearbaiting, Reformation of Manners, a Satire, the Mock Mourners, a Satire. See also Pepys's Diary kept at Tangier, Oct. 15. 1683.

which could not but be grievously felt on the Exchange of
Amsterdam; that, when they expressed a hope that the
Navigation Act would be repealed, he burst out a laughing,
and told them that the thing was not to be thought of. He
carried all his points; and a solemn contract was made by
which England and the Batavian federation bound themselves
to stand firmly by each other against France, and not to
make peace except by mutual consent. But one of the Dutch
plenipotentiaries declared that he was afraid of being one day
held up to obloquy as a traitor for conceding so much; and
the signature of another plainly appeared to have been traced
by a hand shaking with emotion.*

Meanwhile under William's skilful management a treaty of
alliance had been concluded between the States General and
the Emperor. To that treaty Spain and England gave in
their adhesion; and thus the four great powers which had
long been bound together by a friendly understanding were
bound together by a formal contract.†

But before that formal contract had been signed and sealed,
all the contracting parties were in arms. Early in the year
1689 war was raging all over the Continent from the Hæmus
to the Pyrenees. France, attacked at once on every side,
made on every side a vigorous defence; and her Turkish
allies kept a great German force fully employed in Servia and
Bulgaria. On the whole, the results of the military operations of the summer were not unfavourable to the confederates. Beyond the Danube, the Christians, under Prince
Lewis of Baden, gained a succession of victories over the
Mussulmans. In the passes of Roussillon, the French troops
contended without any decisive advantage against the martial
peasantry of Catalonia. One German army, led by the
Elector of Bavaria, occupied the Archbishopric of Cologne.
Another was commanded by Charles, Duke of Lorraine, a
sovereign who, driven from his own dominions by the arms
of France, had turned soldier of fortune, and had, as such,
obtained both distinction and revenge. He marched against
the devastators of the Palatinate, forced them to retire behind the Rhine, and, after a long siege, took the important
and strongly fortified city of Mentz.

* The best account of these negotiations will be found in Wagenaar, lxi.
He had access to Witsen's papers, and
has quoted largely from them. It was
Witsen who signed in violent agitation,
"zo als," he says, " myne beevende hand
getuigen kan." The treaties will be
found in Dumont's Corps Diplomatique.
They were signed in August 1689.

† The treaty between the Emperor
and the States General is dated May 12.
1689. It will be found in Dumont's
Corps Diplomatique.

Between the Sambre and the Meuse the French, commanded by Marshal Humieres, were opposed to the Dutch, commanded by the Prince of Waldeck, an officer who had long served the States General with fidelity and ability, though not always with good fortune, and who stood high in the estimation of William. Under Waldeck's orders was Marlborough, to whom William had confided an English brigade consisting of the best regiments of the old army of James. Second to Marlborough in command, and second also in professional skill, was Thomas Talmash, a brave soldier, destined to a fate never to be mentioned without shame and indignation. Between the army of Waldeck and the army of Humieres no general action took place: but in a succession of combats the advantage was on the side of the confederates. Of these combats the most important took place at Walcourt on the fifth of August. The French attacked an outpost defended by the English brigade, were vigorously repulsed, and were forced to retreat in confusion, abandoning a few field pieces to the conquerors and leaving more than six hundred corpses on the ground. Marlborough, on this as on every similar occasion, acquitted himself like a valiant and skilful captain. The Coldstream Guards commanded by Talmash, and the regiment which is now called the sixteenth of the line, commanded by Colonel Robert Hodges, distinguished themselves highly. The Royal regiment too, which had a few months before set up the standard of rebellion at Ipswich, proved on this day that William, in freely pardoning that great fault, had acted not less wisely than generously. The testimony which Waldeck in his despatch bore to the gallant conduct of the islanders was read with delight by their countrymen. The fight indeed was no more than a skirmish: but it was a sharp and bloody skirmish. There had within living memory been no equally serious encounter between the English and French; and our ancestors were naturally elated by finding that many years of inaction and vassalage did not appear to have enervated the courage of the nation.*

The Jacobites however discovered in the events of the campaign abundant matter for invective. Marlborough was, not without reason, the object of their bitterest hatred. In his behaviour on a field of battle malice itself could find little to cen-

Marginal note: Skirmish at Walcourt

Marginal note: Imputations thrown on Marlborough.

* See the despatch of Waldeck in the London Gazette, Aug. 26. 1689; Historical Records of the First Regiment of Foot; Dangeau, Aug. 28.; Monthly Mercury, September 1689.

sure: but there were other parts of his conduct which presented
a fair mark for obloquy. Avarice is rarely the vice of a young
man: it is rarely the vice of a great man: but Marlborough
was one of the few who have, in the bloom of youth, loved
lucre more than wine or women, and who have, at the height
of greatness, loved lucre more than power or fame. All the
precious gifts which nature had lavished on him he valued
chiefly for what they would fetch. At twenty he made money
of his beauty and his vigour. At sixty he made money of his
genius and his glory. The applauses which were justly due
to his conduct at Walcourt could not altogether drown the
voices of those who muttered that, wherever a broad piece
was to be saved or got, this hero was a mere Euclio, a mere
Harpagon; that, though he drew a large allowance under
pretence of keeping a public table, he never asked an officer
to dinner; that his muster rolls were fraudulently made up;
that he pocketed pay in the names of men who had long been
dead, of men who had been killed in his own sight four years
before at Sedgemoor; that there were twenty such names in
one troop; that there were thirty-six in another. Nothing
but the union of dauntless courage and commanding powers
of mind with a bland temper and winning manners could
have enabled him to gain and keep, in spite of faults eminently unsoldierlike, the good will of his soldiers.*

Pope In-
nocent XI.
succeeded
by Alexan-
der VIII.

About the time at which the contending armies in every
part of Europe were going into winter quarters, a new Pontiff
ascended the chair of Saint Peter. Innocent the Eleventh
was no more. His fate had been strange indeed. His conscientious and fervent attachment to the Church of which he
was the head had induced him, at one of the most critical
conjunctures in her history, to ally himself with her mortal
enemies. The news of his decease was received with concern
and alarm by Protestant princes and commonwealths, and
with joy and hope at Versailles and Dublin. An extraordinary ambassador of high rank was instantly despatched by
Lewis to Rome. The French garrison which had been placed
in Avignon was withdrawn. When the votes of the Conclave
had been united in favour of Peter Ottobuoni, an ancient
Cardinal who assumed the appellation of Alexander the
Eighth, the representative of France assisted at the installa-
tion, bore up the cope of the new Pontiff, and put into the

* See the Dear Bargain, a Jacobite
pamphlet, clandestinely printed in 1690.
"I have not patience," says the writer,
"after this wretch (Marlborough) to
mention any other. All are innocent
comparatively, even Kirke himself."

hands of His Holiness a letter in which the Most Christian King declared that he renounced the odious privilege of protecting robbers and assassins. Alexander pressed the letter to his lips, embraced the bearer, and talked with rapture of the near prospect of reconciliation. Lewis began to entertain a hope that the influence of the Vatican might be exerted to dissolve the alliance between the House of Austria and the heretical usurper of the English throne. James was even more sanguine. He was foolish enough to expect that the new Pope would give him money, and ordered Melfort, who had now acquitted himself of his mission at Versailles, to hasten to Rome, and beg His Holiness to contribute something towards the good work of upholding pure religion in the British islands. But it soon appeared that Alexander, though he might hold language different from that of his predecessor, was determined to follow in essentials his predecessor's policy. The original cause of the quarrel between the Holy See and Lewis was not removed. The King continued to appoint prelates: the Pope continued to refuse them institution; and the consequence was that a fourth part of the dioceses of France had bishops who were incapable of performing any episcopal function.*

The Anglican Church was, at this time, not less distracted than the Gallican Church. The first of August had been fixed by Act of Parliament as the day before the close of which all beneficed clergymen and all persons holding academical offices must, on pain of suspension, swear allegiance to William and Mary. During the earlier part of the summer, the Jacobites had hoped that the number of nonjurors would be so considerable as seriously to alarm and embarrass the government. But this hope was disappointed. Few indeed of the clergy were Whigs. Few were Tories of that moderate school which acknowledged, reluctantly and with reserve, that extreme abuses might sometimes justify a nation in resorting to extreme remedies. The great majority of the profession still held the doctrine of passive obedience: but that majority was now divided into two sections. A question, which, before the Revolution, had been mere matter of speculation, and had therefore, though sometimes incidentally

The High Church clergy divided on the subject of the oaths

---

* See the Mercuries for September 1689, and the four following months. See also Welwood's Mercurius Reformatus of Sept. 18. Sept. 25. and Oct. 8. 1689. Melfort's Instructions, and his memorials to the Pope and the Cardinal of Este, are among the Nairne Papers; and some extracts have been printed by Macpherson.

raised, been, by most persons, very superficially considered, had now become practically most important. The doctrine of passive obedience being taken for granted, to whom was that obedience due? While the hereditary right and the possession were conjoined, there was no room for doubt: but the hereditary right and the possession were now separated. One prince raised by the Revolution, was reigning at Westminster, passing laws, appointing magistrates and prelates. sending forth armies and fleets. His Judges decided causes. His Sheriffs arrested debtors, and executed criminals. Justice, order, property, would cease to exist, and society would be resolved into chaos, but for his Great Seal. Another prince, deposed by the Revolution, was living abroad. He could exercise none of the powers and perform none of the duties of a ruler, and could, as it seemed, be restored only by means as violent as those by which he had been displaced. To which of these two princes did Christian men owe allegiance?

Arguments for taking the oaths. To a large part of the clergy it appeared that the plain letter of Scripture required them to submit to the Sovereign who was in possession, without troubling themselves about his title. The powers which the Apostle, in the text most familiar to the Anglican divines of that age, pronounces to be ordained of God, are not the powers that can be traced back to a legitimate origin, but the powers that be. When Jesus was asked whether the chosen people might lawfully give tribute to Cæsar, he replied by asking the questioners, not whether Cæsar could make out a pedigree derived from the old royal house of Judah, but whether the coin which they scrupled to pay into Cæsar's treasury came from Cæsar's mint, in other words, whether Cæsar actually possessed the authority and performed the functions of a ruler.

It is generally held, with much appearance of reason, that the most trustworthy comment on the text of the Gospels and Epistles is to be found in the practice of the primitive Christians, when that practice can be satisfactorily ascertained; and it so happened that the times during which the Church is universally acknowledged to have been in the highest state of purity were times of frequent and violent political change. One at least of the Apostles appears to have lived to see four Emperors pulled down in little more than a year. Of the martyrs of the third century a great proportion must have been able to remember ten or twelve revolutions. Those martyrs must have had occasion often to consider what was their duty towards a prince just raised to power by a successful insurrection. That they were, one and all, deterred by the fear of punishment from doing what they thought right, is an imputation which no candid infidel would throw on them. Yet, if there be any proposition which can with perfect confidence be affirmed touching the early Christians, it is this, that they never once refused obedience to any actual ruler on account of the illegitimacy of his title. At one time, indeed, the supreme power was claimed by twenty or thirty competitors. Every province from Britain to Egypt had its own Augustus. All these pretenders could not be rightful Emperors. Yet it does not appear that, in any place, the faithful had any scruple about submitting to the person who, in that place, exercised the imperial functions. While the Christian of Rome obeyed Aurelian, the Christian of Lyons obeyed Tetricus, and the Christian of Palmyra obeyed Zenobia. " Day and night,"—such were the words which the great Cyprian, Bishop of Carthage, addressed to the representative of Valerian and Gallienus,—" day and night do we Christians pray to the one true God for the safety of our Emperors." Yet those Emperors had a few months before pulled down their predecessor Æmilianus, who had pulled down his predecessor Gallus, who had climbed to power on the ruins of the house of his predecessor Decius, who had slain his predecessor Philip, who had slain his predecessor Gordian. Was it possible to believe that a saint, who had, in the short space of thirteen or fourteen years, borne true allegiance to this series of rebels and regicides, would have made a schism in the Christian body rather than acknowledge King William and Queen Mary? A hundred times those Anglican divines who had taken the oaths challenged their more scrupulous brethren to cite a single instance in which the primitive Church had refused obedience to a successful usurper; and a hundred times the challenge was evaded. The nonjurors had little to say on this head, except that precedents were of no force when opposed to principles, a proposition which came with but a bad grace from a school which had always professed an almost superstitious reverence for the authority of the Fathers.*

* See the Answer of a Nonjuror to the Bishop of Sarum's challenge in the Appendix to the Life of Kettlewell. Among the Tanner MSS. in the Bodleian Library is a paper which, as Sancroft thought it worth preserving, I venture to quote. The writer, a strong nonjuror, after trying to evade, by many pitiable shifts, the argument drawn by a more compliant divine from the practice of the primitive Church, proceeds thus : " Suppose the primitive Christians all along, from the time of the very Apostles, had been as regardless of their oaths by former princes as he suggests, will he therefore say that their practice

To precedents drawn from later and more corrupt times little respect was due. But, even in the history of later and more corrupt times, the nonjurors could not easily find any precedent that could serve their purpose. In our own country many Kings, who had not the hereditary right, had filled the throne: but it had never been thought inconsistent with the duty of a Christian to be a true liegeman to such Kings. The usurpation of Henry the Fourth, the more odious usurpation of Richard the Third, had produced no schism in the Church. As soon as the usurper was firm in his seat, Bishops had done homage to him for their domains: Convocations had presented addresses to him, and granted him supplies; nor had any casuist ever pronounced that such submission to a prince in possession was deadly sin.*

With the practice of the whole Christian world the authoritative teaching of the Church of England appeared to be in strict harmony. The Homily on Wilful Rebellion, a discourse which inculcates, in unmeasured terms, the duty of obeying rulers, speaks of none but actual rulers. Nay, the people are distinctly told in that Homily that they are bound to obey, not only their legitimate prince, but any usurper whom God shall in anger set over them for their sins. And surely it would be the height of absurdity to say that we must accept submissively such usurpers as God sends in anger, but must pertinaciously withhold our obedience from usurpers whom He sends in mercy. Grant that it was a crime to invite the Prince of Orange over, a crime to join him, a crime to make him King; yet what was the whole history of the Jewish nation and of the Christian Church but a record of cases in which Providence had brought good out of evil? And what theologian would assert that, in such

---

is to be a rule? Ill things have been done, and very generally abetted, by men of otherwise very orthodox principles." The argument from the practice of the primitive Christians is very strongly put in a tract entitled The Doctrine of Nonresistance or Passive Obedience No Way concerned in the Controversies now depending between the Williamites and the Jacobites, by a Lay Gentleman, of the Communion of the Church of England, as by Law establish'd, 1689. The author of this tract was Edmund Bohun, whom I shall have occasion to mention hereafter.

* One of the most adulatory addresses ever voted by a Convocation was to Richard the Third. It will be found in Wilkins's Concilia. Dryden, in his fine *rifacimento* of one of the finest passages in the Prologue to the Canterbury Tales, represents the Good Parson as choosing to resign his benefice rather than acknowledge the Duke of Lancaster to be King of England. For this representation no warrant can be found in Chaucer's Poem, or anywhere else. Dryden wished to write something that would gall the clergy who had taken the oaths, and therefore attributed to a Roman Catholic priest of the fourteenth century a superstition which originated among the Anglican priests of the seventeenth century.

cases, we ought, from abhorrence of the evil, to reject the good?

On these grounds a large body of divines, still asserting the doctrine that to resist the Sovereign must always be sinful, conceived that William was now the Sovereign whom it would be sinful to resist.

To these arguments the nonjurors replied that Saint Paul must have meant by the powers that be the rightful powers that be; and that to put any other interpretation on his words would be to outrage common sense, to dishonour religion, to give scandal to weak believers, to give an occasion of triumph to scoffers. The feelings of all mankind must be shocked by the proposition that, as soon as a King, however clear his title, however wise and good his administration, is expelled by traitors, all his servants are bound to abandon him, and to range themselves on the side of his enemies. In all ages and nations, fidelity to a good cause in adversity had been regarded as a virtue. In all ages and nations, the politician whose practice was always to be on the side which was uppermost had been despised. This new Toryism was worse than Whiggism. To break through the ties of allegiance because the Sovereign was a tyrant was doubtless a very great sin: but it was a sin for which specious names and pretexts might be found, and into which a brave and generous man, not instructed in divine truth and guarded by divine grace, might easily fall. But to break through the ties of allegiance merely because the Sovereign was unfortunate was not only wicked, but dirty. Could any unbeliever offer a greater insult to the Scriptures than by asserting that the Scriptures had enjoined on Christians as a sacred duty what the light of nature had taught heathens to regard as the last excess of baseness? In the Scriptures was to be found the history of a King of Israel, driven from his palace by an unnatural son, and compelled to fly beyond Jordan. David, like James, had the right: Absalom, like William, had the possession. Would any student of the sacred writings dare to affirm that the conduct of Shimei on that occasion was proposed as a pattern to be imitated, and that Barzillai, who loyally adhered to his fugitive master, was resisting the ordinance of God, and receiving to himself damnation? Would any true son of the Church of England seriously maintain that a man who was a strenuous royalist till after the battle of Naseby, who then went over to the Parliament, who, as soon as the Parliament had been purged,

Arguments against taking the oaths.

became an obsequious servant of the Rump, and who, as soon
as the Rump had been ejected, professed himself a faithful
subject of the Protector, was more deserving of the respect
of Christian men than the stout old Cavalier who bore true
fealty to Charles the First in prison and to Charles the
Second in exile, and who was ready to put lands, liberty, life,
in peril, rather than acknowledge, by word or act, the authority of any of the upstart governments which, during that
evil time, obtained possession of a power not legitimately
theirs? And what distinction was there between that case
and the case which had now arisen? That Cromwell had
actually enjoyed as much power as William, nay much more
power than William, was quite certain. That the power of
William, as well as the power of Cromwell, had an illegiti-
mate origin, every divine who held the doctrine of nonresistance would admit. How then was it possible for such a
divine to deny that obedience had been due to Cromwell, and
yet to affirm that it was due to William? To suppose that
there could be such inconsistency without dishonesty would
be, not charity, but weakness. Those who were determined
to comply with the Act of Parliament would do better to
speak out, and to say, what everybody knew, that they complied simply to save their benefices. The motive was no
doubt strong. That a clergyman who was a husband and a
father should look forward with dread to the first of August
and the first of February was natural. But he would do
well to remember that, however terrible might be the day of
suspension and the day of deprivation, there would assuredly
come two other days more terrible still, the day of death and
the day of judgment.*

The swearing clergy, as they were called, were not a little
perplexed by this reasoning. Nothing embarrassed them
more than the analogy which the nonjurors were never weary
of pointing out between the usurpation of Cromwell and the
usurpation of William. For there was in that age no High
Churchman who would not have thought himself reduced to
an absurdity, if he had been reduced to the necessity of saying that the Church had commanded her sons to obey Cromwell. And yet it was impossible to prove that William was
more fully in possession of supreme power than Cromwell
had been. The swearers therefore avoided coming to close

* See the Defence of the Profession   made upon his Deathbed concerning
which the Right Reverend Father in God   Passive Obedience and the New Oaths.
John Lake, Lord Bishop of Chichester,   1690.

quarters with the nonjurors on this point, as carefully as the nonjurors avoided coming to close quarters with the swearers on the question touching the practice of the primitive Church.

The truth is that the theory of government which had long been taught by the clergy was so absurd that it could lead to nothing but absurdity. Whether the priest who adhered to that theory swore or refused to swear, he was alike unable to give a rational explanation of his conduct. If he swore, he could vindicate his swearing only by laying down propositions against which every honest heart instinctively revolts, only by proclaiming that Christ had commanded the Church to desert the righteous cause as soon as that cause ceased to prosper, and to strengthen the hands of successful villany against afflicted virtue. And yet, strong as were the objections to this doctrine, the objections to the doctrine of the nonjuror were, if possible, stronger still. According to him, a Christian nation ought always to be in a state of slavery or in a state of anarchy. Something is to be said for the man who sacrifices liberty to preserve order. Something is to be said for the man who sacrifices order to preserve liberty. For liberty and order are two of the greatest blessings which a society can enjoy; and, when unfortunately they appear to be incompatible, much indulgence is due to those who take either side. But the nonjuror sacrificed, not liberty to order, not order to liberty, but both liberty and order to a superstition as stupid and degrading as the Egyptian worship of cats and onions. While a particular person, differing from other persons by the mere accident of birth, was on the throne, though he might be a Nero, there was to be no insubordination. When any other person was on the throne, though he might be an Alfred, there was to be no obedience. It mattered not how frantic and wicked might be the administration of the dynasty which had the hereditary title, or how wise and virtuous might be the administration of a government sprung from a revolution. Nor could any time of limitation be pleaded against the claim of the expelled family. The lapse of years, the lapse of ages, made no change. To the end of the world, Christians were to regulate their political conduct simply according to the pedigree of their ruler. The year 1800, the year 1900, might find princes who derived their title from the votes of the Convention reigning in peace and prosperity. No matter: they would still be usurpers; and, if, in the twentieth or twenty-first century, any person who could make out a better right by blood to the crown should call on a late posterity to acknowledge him as King, the call must be obeyed on peril of eternal perdition.

A Whig might well enjoy the thought that the controversies which had arisen among his adversaries had established the soundness of his own political creed. The disputants who had long agreed in accusing him of an impious error had now effectually vindicated him, and refuted one another. The High Churchman who took the oaths had shown by irrefragable arguments from the Gospels and the Epistles, from the uniform practice of the primitive Church, and from the explicit declarations of the Anglican Church, that Christians were not in all cases bound to pay obedience to the prince who had the hereditary title. The High Churchman who would not take the oaths had shown as satisfactorily that Christians were not in all cases bound to pay obedience to the prince who was actually reigning. It followed that, to entitle a government to the allegiance of subjects, something was necessary different from mere legitimacy, and different also from mere possession. What that something was the Whigs had no difficulty in pronouncing. In their view, the end for which all governments had been instituted was the happiness of society. While the magistrate was, on the whole, notwithstanding some faults, a minister for good, Reason taught mankind to obey him; and Religion, giving her solemn sanction to the teaching of Reason, commanded mankind to revere him as divinely commissioned. But if he proved to be a minister for evil, on what grounds was he to be considered as divinely commissioned? The Tories who swore had proved that he ought not to be so considered on account of the origin of his power: the Tories who would not swear had proved as clearly that he ought not to be so considered on account of the existence of his power.

Some violent and acrimonious Whigs triumphed ostentatiously and with merciless insolence over the perplexed and divided priesthood. The nonjuror they generally affected to regard with contemptuous pity as a dull and perverse, but sincere, bigot, whose absurd practice was in harmony with his absurd theory, and who might plead, in excuse for the infatuation which impelled him to ruin his country, that the same infatuation had impelled him to ruin himself. They reserved their sharpest taunts for those divines who, having, in the days of the Exclusion Bill and the Rye House plot, been distinguished by zeal for the divine and indefeasible right of the hereditary Sovereign, were now ready to swear fealty to an usurper. Was this then the real sense of all those sublime phrases which had resounded during twenty-nine years from innumerable pulpits? Had the thousands of clergymen, who had so loudly boasted of the unchangeable loyalty of their order, really meant only that their loyalty would remain unchangeable till the next change of fortune? It was idle, it was impudent in them to pretend that their present conduct was consistent with their former language. If any Reverend Doctor had at length been convinced that he had been in the wrong, he surely ought, by an open re-cantation, to make all the amends now possible to the per-secuted, the calumniated, the murdered defenders of liberty. If he was still convinced that his old opinions were sound, he ought manfully to cast in his lot with the nonjurors. Respect, it was said, is due to him who ingenuously confesses an error: respect is due to him who courageously suffers for an error: but it is difficult to respect a minister of religion, who, while asserting that he still adheres to the principles of the Tories, saves his benefice by taking an oath which can be honestly taken only on the principles of the Whigs.

These reproaches, though perhaps not altogether unjust, were unseasonable. The wiser and more moderate Whigs, sensible that the throne of William could not stand firm if it had not a wider basis than their own party, abstained at this conjuncture from sneers and invectives, and exerted them-selves to remove the scruples and to soothe the irritated feelings of the clergy. The collective power of the rectors and vicars of England was immense; and it was much better that they should swear for the most flimsy reason which could be devised by a sophist than that they should not swear at all.

It soon became clear that the arguments for swearing, backed as they were by some of the strongest motives which can influence the human mind, had prevailed. Above twenty-nine thirtieths of the profession submitted to the law. Most of the divines of the capital, who then formed a separate class, and who were as much distinguished from the rural clergy by liberality of sentiment as by eloquence and learn-ing, gave in their adhesion to the government early, and with every sign of cordial attachment. Eighty of them repaired together, in full term, to Westminster Hall, and were there sworn. The ceremony occupied so long a time that little else was done that day in the Courts of Chancery and King's

A great majority of the clergy take the oaths.

Bench.* But in general the compliance was tardy, sad, and
sullen. Many, no doubt, deliberately violated what they
believed to be their duty. Conscience told them that they
were committing a sin. But they had not fortitude to resign
the parsonage, the garden, the glebe, and to go forth without
knowing where to find a meal or a roof for themselves and
their little ones. Many swore with doubts and misgivings.†
Some declared, at the moment of taking the oath, that they
did not mean to promise that they would not submit to
James, if he should ever be in a condition to demand their
allegiance.‡ Some clergymen in the North were, on the first
of August, going in a company to swear, when they were met
on the road by the news of the battle which had been fought,
four days before, in the pass of Killiecrankie. They immediately turned back, and did not again leave their homes on
the same errand till it was clear that Dundee's victory had
made no change in the state of public affairs.§ Even of
those whose understandings were fully convinced that obedience was due to the existing government, very few kissed
the book with the heartiness with which they had formerly
plighted their faith to Charles and James. Still the thing
was done. Ten thousand clergymen had solemnly called
heaven to attest their promise that they would be true liege-
men to William; and this promise, though it by no means
warranted him in expecting that they would strenuously support him, had at least deprived them of a great part of their
power to injure him. They could not, without entirely forfeiting that public respect on which their influence depended,
attack, except in an indirect and timidly cautious manner,
the throne of one whom they had, in the presence of God,
vowed to obey as their King. Some of them, it is true,
affected to read the prayers for the new Sovereigns in a peculiar tone which could not be misunderstood.‖ Others were
guilty of still grosser indecency. Thus, one wretch, just
after praying for William and Mary in the most solemn office
of religion, took off a glass to their damnation. Another,
after performing divine service on a fast day appointed by
their authority, dined on a pigeon pie, and while he cut it

---

* London Gazette, June 30. 1689;
Luttrell's Diary. "The eminentest men,"
says Luttrell.

† See in Kettlewell's Life, iii. 72., the
retractation drawn by him for a clergyman who had taken the oaths, and who
afterwards repented of having done so.

‡ See the account of Dr. Dove's con-

duct in Clarendon's Diary, and the account of Dr. Marsh's conduct in the Life
of Kettlewell,

§ The Anatomy of a Jacobite Tory,
1690.

‖ Dialogue between a Whig and a
Tory.

up, uttered a wish that it was the usurper's heart. But such audacious wickedness was doubtless rare and was injurious rather to the Church than to the government.*

Those clergymen and members of the Universities who incurred the penalties of the law were about four hundred in number. Foremost in rank stood the Primate and six of his suffragans, Turner of Ely, Lloyd of Norwich, Frampton of Gloucester, Lake of Chichester, White of Peterborough, and Ken of Bath and Wells. Thomas of Worcester would have made a seventh : but he died three weeks before the day of suspension. On his deathbed he adjured his clergy to be true to the cause of hereditary right, and declared that those divines who tried to make out that the oaths might be taken without any departure from the loyal doctrines of the Church of England seemed to him to reason more Jesuitically than the Jesuits themselves.† *The nonjurors.*

Ken, who, both in intellectual and in moral qualities, ranked highest among the nonjuring prelates, hesitated long. There were few clergymen who could have submitted to the new government with a better grace. For, when nonresistance and passive obedience were the favourite themes of his brethren, he had scarcely ever alluded to politics in the pulpit. He owned that the arguments in favour of swearing were very strong. He went indeed so far as to say that his scruples would be completely removed, if he could be convinced that James had entered into engagements for ceding Ireland to the French King. It is evident therefore that the difference between Ken and the Whigs was not a difference of principle. He thought, with them, that misgovernment, carried to a certain point, justified a transfer of allegiance, and doubted only whether the misgovernment of James had been carried quite to that point. Nay, the good Bishop actually began to prepare a pastoral letter explaining his reasons for taking the oaths. But, before it was finished, he received information which convinced him that Ireland had not been made over to France : doubts came thick upon him : he threw his unfinished letter into the fire, and implored his less scrupulous friends not to urge him further. He was sure, he said, that they had acted uprightly : he was glad that they could do with a clear conscience what he shrank from doing : he felt the force of their reasoning : he was all but persuaded ; and he was afraid to listen longer lest he should be quite *Ken.*

* Luttrell's Diary, November 1691, February 1692.
† Life of Kettlewell, iii. 4.

persuaded: for, if he should comply, and his misgivings should afterwards return, he should be the most miserable of men. Not for wealth, not for a palace, not for a peerage, would he run the smallest risk of ever feeling the torments of remorse. It is a curious fact that, of the seven nonjuring prelates, the only one whose name carries with it much weight was on the point of swearing, and was prevented from doing so, as he himself acknowledged, not by the force of reason, but by a morbid scrupulosity which he did not advise others to imitate.*

Among the priests who refused the oaths were some men eminent in the learned world, as grammarians, chronologists, canonists, and antiquaries, and a very few who were distinguished by wit and eloquence; but scarcely one can be named who was qualified to discuss any large question of morals or politics, scarcely one whose writings do not indicate either extreme feebleness or extreme flightiness of mind. Those who distrust the judgment of a Whig on this point will probably allow some weight to the opinion which was expressed, many years after the Revolution, by a philosopher of whom the Tories are justly proud. Johnson, after passing in review the celebrated divines who had thought it sinful to swear allegiance to William the Third and George the First, pronounced that, in the whole body of nonjurors, there was one, and one only, who could reason.†

* See Turner's Letter to Sancroft, dated on Ascension Day, 1689. The original is among the Tanner MSS. in the Bodleian Library. But the letter will be found, with much other curious matter, in the Life of Ken by a Layman, lately published. See also the Life of Kettlewell, iii. 95.; and Ken's Letter to Burnet, dated Oct. 5. 1689, in Hawkins's Life of Ken. "I am sure," Lady Russell wrote to Dr. Fitzwilliam, "the Bishop of Bath and Wells excited others to comply, when he could not bring himself to do so, but rejoiced when others did." Ken declared that he had advised nobody to take the oaths, and that his practice had been to remit those who asked his advice to their own studies and prayers. Lady Russell's assertion and Ken's denial will be found to come nearly to the same thing, when we make those allowances which ought to be made for situation and feeling, even in weighing the testimony of the most veracious witnesses. Ken, having at last determined to cast in his lot with the nonjurors, naturally tried to vindicate his consistency as far as he honestly could. Lady Russell, wishing to induce her friend to take the oaths, naturally made as much of Ken's disposition to compliance as she honestly could. She went too far in using the word "excited." On the other hand, it is clear that Ken, by remitting those who consulted him to their own studies and prayers, gave them to understand that, in his opinion, the oath was lawful to those who, after a serious enquiry, thought it lawful. If people had asked him whether they might lawfully commit perjury or adultery, he would assuredly have told them, not to consider the point maturely and to implore the divine direction, but to abstain on peril of their souls.

† See the conversation of June 9. 1784, in Boswell's Life of Johnson, and the note. Boswell, with his usual absurdity, is sure that Johnson could not have recollected "that the seven bishops, so justly celebrated for their magnanimous resistance to arbitrary power, were yet nonjurors." Only five of the seven were nonjurors; and anybody but Bos-

The nonjuror in whose favour Johnson made this exception was Charles Leslie. Leslie had, before the Revolution, been Chancellor of the diocese of Connor in Ireland. He had been forward in opposition to Tyrconnel; had, as a justice of the peace for Monaghan, refused to acknowledge a papist as Sheriff of that county; and had been so courageous as to send some officers of the Irish army to prison for marauding. But the doctrine of nonresistance, such as it had been taught by Anglican divines in the days of the Rye House Plot, was immovably fixed in his mind. When the state of Ulster became such that a Protestant who remained there could hardly avoid being either a rebel or a martyr, Leslie fled to London. His abilities and his connections were such that he might easily have obtained high preferment in the Church of England. But he took his place in the front rank of the Jacobite body, and remained there steadfastly through all the dangers and vicissitudes of three and thirty troubled years. Though constantly engaged in theological controversy with Deists, Jews, Socinians, Presbyterians, Papists, and Quakers, he found time to be one of the most voluminous political writers of his age. Of all the nonjuring clergy he was the best qualified to discuss constitutional questions. For, before he had taken orders, he had resided long in the Temple, and had been studying English history and law, while most of the other chiefs of the schism had been poring over the Acts of Chalcedon, or seeking for wisdom in the Targum of Onkelos.*

In 1689, however, Leslie was almost unknown in England. Sherlock. Among the divines who incurred suspension on the first of August in that year, the highest in popular estimation was without dispute Doctor William Sherlock. Perhaps no simple presbyter of the Church of England has ever possessed a greater authority over his brethren than belonged

well would have known that a man may resist arbitrary power, and yet not be a good reasoner. Nay, the resistance which Sancroft and the other nonjuring bishops offered to arbitrary power, while they continued to hold the doctrine of nonresistance, is the most decisive proof that they were incapable of reasoning. It must be remembered that they were prepared to take the whole kingly power from James and to bestow it on William, with the title of Regent. Their scruple was merely about the word King.

I am surprised that Johnson should have pronounced William Law no reasoner. Law did indeed fall into great errors; but they were errors against which logic affords no security. In mere dialectical skill he had very few superiors. That he was more than once victorious over Hoadley no candid Whig will deny. But Law did not belong to the generation with which I have now to do.

* Ware's History of the Writers of Ireland, continued by Harris.

to Sherlock at the time of the Revolution. He was not of
the first rank among his contemporaries as a scholar, as a
preacher, as a writer on theology, or as a writer on politics :
but in all the four characters he had distinguished himself.
The perspicuity and liveliness of his style have been praised by
Prior and Addison. The facility and assiduity with which he
wrote are sufficiently proved by the bulk and the dates of his
works. There were indeed among the clergy men of brighter
genius and men of wider attainments : but during a long
period there was none who more completely represented the
order, none who, on all subjects, spoke more precisely the
sense of the Anglican priesthood, without any taint of Latitudinarianism, of Puritanism, or of Popery. He had, in the
days of the Exclusion Bill, when the power of the dissenters
was very great in Parliament and in the country, written
strongly against the sin of nonconformity. When the Rye
House Plot was detected, he had zealously defended by
tongue and pen the doctrine of nonresistance. His services
to the cause of episcopacy and monarchy were so highly valued
that he was made Master of the Temple. A pension was
also bestowed on him by Charles : but that pension James
soon took away : for Sherlock, though he held himself bound
to pay passive obedience to the civil power, held himself
equally bound to combat religious errors, and was the keenest and most laborious of that host of controversialists who,
in the day of peril, manfully defended the Protestant faith.
In little more than two years he published sixteen treatises,
some of them large books, against the high pretensions of
Rome. Not content with the easy victories which he gained
over such feeble antagonists as those who were quartered at
Clerkenwell and the Savoy, he had the courage to measure
his strength with no less a champion than Bossuet, and came
out of the conflict without discredit. Nevertheless Sherlock
still continued to maintain that no oppression could justify
Christians in resisting the kingly authority. When the Convention was about to meet, he strongly recommended, in a
tract which was considered as the manifesto of a large part
of the clergy, that James should be invited to return on such
conditions as might secure the laws and religion of the nation.* The vote which placed William and Mary on the
throne filled Sherlock with sorrow and anger. He is said
to have exclaimed that if the Convention was determined
on a revolution, the clergy would find forty thousand good

* Letter to a member of the Convention, 1689.

Churchmen to effect a restoration.* Against the new oaths he gave his opinion plainly and warmly. He professed himself at a loss to understand how any honest man could doubt that, by the powers that be, Saint Paul meant legitimate powers and no others. No name was in 1689 cited by the Jacobites more proudly or more fondly than that of Sherlock. Before the end of 1690 that name excited very different feelings.

A few other nonjurors ought to be particularly noticed. Hickes. High among them in rank was George Hickes, dean of Worcester. Of all the Englishmen of his time he was the most versed in the old Teutonic languages; and his knowledge of the early Christian literature was extensive. As to his capacity for political discussions, it may be sufficient to say that his favourite argument for passive obedience was drawn from the story of the Theban legion. He was the younger brother of that unfortunate John Hickes who had been found hidden in the malthouse of Alice Lisle. James had, in spite of all solicitation, put both John Hickes and Alice Lisle to death. Persons who did not know the strength of the Dean's principles thought that he might possibly feel some resentment on this account: for he was of no gentle or forgiving temper, and could retain during many years a bitter remembrance of small injuries. But he was strong in his religious and political faith: he reflected that the sufferers were dissenters; and he submitted to the will of the Lord's Anointed not only with patience but with complacency. He became indeed a more loving subject than ever from the time when his brother was hanged and his brother's benefactress beheaded. While almost all other clergymen, appalled by the Declaration of Indulgence and by the proceedings of the High Commission, were beginning to think that they had pushed the doctrine of nonresistance a little too far, he was writing a vindication of his darling legend, and trying to convince the troops at Hounslow that, if James should be pleased to massacre them all, as Maximian had massacred the Theban legion, for refusing to commit idolatry, it would be their duty to pile their arms, and meekly to receive the crown of martyrdom. To do Hickes justice, his whole conduct after the Revolution proved that his servility had sprung neither from fear nor from cupidity, but from mere bigotry.†

* Johnson's Notes on the Phœnix Edition of Burnet's Pastoral Letter, 1692.

† The best notion of Hickes's character will be formed from his numerous controversial writings, particularly his

Jeremy Collier, who was turned out of the preachership of the Rolls, was a man of a much higher order. He is well entitled to grateful and respectful mention : for to his eloquence and courage is to be chiefly ascribed the purification of our lighter literature from that foul taint which had been contracted during the Antipuritan reaction. He was, in the full force of the words, a good man. He was also a man of eminent abilities, a great master of sarcasm, a great master of rhetoric.* His reading too, though undigested, was of immense extent. But his mind was narrow : his reasoning, even when he was so fortunate as to have a good cause to defend, was singularly futile and inconclusive ; and his brain was almost turned by pride, not personal, but professional. In his view, a priest was the highest of human beings, except a bishop. Reverence and submission were due from the best and greatest of the laity to the least respectable of the clergy. However ridiculous a man in holy orders might make himself, it was impiety to laugh at him. So nervously sensitive indeed was Collier on this point that he thought it profane to throw any reflection even on the ministers of false religions. He laid it down as a rule that Muftis and Augurs ought always to be mentioned with respect. He blamed Dryden for sneering at the Hierophants of Apis. He praised Racine for giving dignity to the character of a priest of Baal. He praised Corneille for not bringing that learned and reverend divine Tiresias on the stage in the tragedy of Œdipus. The omission, Collier owned, spoiled the dramatic effect of the piece : but the holy function was much too solemn to be played with. Nay, incredible as it may seem, he thought it improper in the laity to sneer even at Presbyterian preachers. Indeed his Jacobitism was little more than one of the forms in which his zeal for the dignity of his profession manifested itself. He abhorred the Revolution less as a rising up of subjects against their King than as a rising up of the laity against the sacerdotal caste. The doctrines which had been proclaimed from the pulpit during thirty years had been treated with contempt by the Convention. A new government had been set up in opposition to the wishes of the spiritual peers in the House

Jovian, written in 1684, his Thebæan Legion no Fable, written in 1687, though not published till 1714, and his Discourses upon Dr. Burnet and Dr. Tillotson, 1695. His literary fame rests on works of a very different kind.

* Collier's Tracts on the Stage are, on the whole, his best pieces. But there is much that is striking in his political pamphlets. His "Persuasive to Consideration, tendered to the Royalists, particularly those of the Church of England," seems to me one of the best productions of the Jacobite press.

of Lords and of the priesthood throughout the country. A secular assembly had taken upon itself to pass a law requiring archbishops and bishops, rectors and vicars, to abjure, on pain of deprivation, what they had been teaching all their lives. Whatever meaner spirits might do, Collier was determined not to be led in triumph by the victorious enemies of his order. To the last he would confront, with the authoritative port of an ambassador of heaven, the anger of the powers and principalities of the earth.

In parts Collier was the first man among the nonjurors. In Dodwell. erudition the first place must be assigned to Henry Dodwell, who, for the unpardonable crime of having a small estate in Mayo, had been attainted by the Popish Parliament at Dublin. He was Camdenian Professor of Ancient History in the University of Oxford, and had already acquired considerable celebrity by chronological and geographical researches; but though he never could be persuaded to take orders, theology was his favourite study. He was doubtless a pious and sincere man. He had perused innumerable volumes in various languages, and had indeed acquired more learning than his slender faculties were able to bear. The small intellectual spark which he possessed was put out by the fuel. Some of his books seem to have been written in a madhouse, and, though filled with proofs of his immense reading, degrade him to the level of James Naylor and Ludowick Muggleton. He began a dissertation intended to prove that the law of nations was a divine revelation made to the family which was preserved in the ark. He published a treatise in which he maintained that a marriage between a member of the Church of England and a Dissenter was a nullity, and that the couple were in the sight of heaven guilty of adultery. He defended the use of instrumental music in public worship on the ground that the notes of the organ had a power to counteract the influence of devils on the spinal marrow of human beings. In his treatise on this subject he remarked that there was high authority for the opinion that the spinal marrow, when decomposed, became a serpent. Whether this opinion were or were not correct, he thought it unnecessary to decide. Perhaps, he said, the eminent men in whose works it was found had meant only to express figuratively the great truth, that the Old Serpent operates on us chiefly through the spinal marrow.*

* See Brokesby's Life of Dodwell. The Discourse against Marriages in different Communions is known to me, I ought to say, only from Brokesby's copious abstract. That Discourse is very rare. It was originally printed as an

Dodwell's speculations on the state of human beings after
death are, if possible, more extraordinary still. He tells us
that our souls are naturally mortal. Annihilation is the fate
of the greater part of mankind, of heathens, of Mahometans,
of unchristened babes. The gift of immortality is conveyed
in the sacrament of baptism: but to the efficacy of the sacrament it is absolutely necessary that the water be poured and
the words pronounced by a minister who has been ordained
by a bishop. In the natural course of things, therefore, all
Presbyterians, Independents, Baptists, and Quakers would,
like the inferior animals, cease to exist. But Dodwell was
far too good a churchman to let off dissenters so easily.
He informs them that, as they have had an opportunity of
hearing the Gospel preached, and might, but for their own
perverseness, have received episcopalian baptism, God will, by
a preternatural act of power, bestow immortality on them in
order that they may be tormented for ever and ever.*

No man abhorred the growing latitudinarianism of those
times more than Dodwell. Yet no man had more reason to
rejoice in it. For, in the earlier part of the seventeenth century, a speculator who had dared to affirm that the human
soul is by its nature mortal, and does, in the great majority
of cases, actually die with the body, would have been burned
alive in Smithfield. Even in days which Dodwell could well
remember, such heretics as himself would have been thought
fortunate if they escaped with life, their backs flayed, their
ears clipped, their noses slit, their tongues bored through
with red hot iron, and their eyes knocked out with brickbats.
With the nonjurors, however, the author of this theory was
still the great Mr. Dodwell; and some, who thought it culpable lenity to tolerate a Presbyterian meeting, thought it at
the same time gross illiberality to blame a learned and pious
Jacobite for denying a doctrine so utterly unimportant in a
religious point of view as that of the immortality of the soul.†

appendage to a sermon preached by
Leslie. When Leslie collected his works
he omitted the discourse, probably because he was ashamed of it. I have not
been able to find it in the Library of the
British Museum. The Treatise on the
Lawfulness of Instrumental Music I have
read: and incredibly absurd it is.

* Dodwell tells us that the title of
the work in which he first promulgated
this theory was framed with great care
and precision. I will therefore transcribe
the title-page. "An Epistolary Discourse
proving from Scripture and the First

Fathers that the Soul is naturally Mortal,
but Immortalized actually by the Pleasure of God to Punishment or to Reward,
by its Union with the Divine Baptismal
Spirit, wherein is proved that none have
the Power of giving this Divine Immor-
talizing Spirit since the Apostles but
only the Bishops. By H. Dodwell." Dr.
Clarke, in a Letter to Dodwell (1706),
says that this Epistolary Discourse is "a
book at which all good men are sorry,
and all profane men rejoice."

† See Leslie's Rehearsals, No. 286, 287.

Two other nonjurors deserve special mention, less on account of their abilities and learning, than on account of their rare integrity, and of their not less rare candour. These were John Kettlewell, Rector of Coleshill, and John Fitzwilliam, Canon of Windsor. It is remarkable that both these men had seen much of Lord Russell, and that both, though differing from him in political opinions, and strongly disapproving the part which he had taken in the Whig plot, had thought highly of his character, and had been sincere mourners for his death. He had sent to Kettlewell an affectionate message from the scaffold in Lincoln's Inn Fields. Lady Russell, to her latest day, loved, trusted, and revered Fitzwilliam, who, when she was a girl, had been the friend of her father, the virtuous Southampton. The two clergymen agreed in refusing to swear: but they, from that moment, took different paths. Kettlewell was one of the most active members of his party: he declined no drudgery in the common cause, provided only that it were such drudgery as did not misbecome an honest man; and he defended his opinions in several tracts, which give a much higher notion of his sincerity than of his judgment or acuteness.* Fitzwilliam thought that he had done enough in quitting his pleasant dwelling and garden under the shadow of Saint George's Chapel, and in betaking himself with his books to a small lodging in an attic. He could not with a safe conscience acknowledge William and Mary: but he did not conceive that he was bound to be always stirring up sedition against them; and he passed the last years of his life, under the powerful protection of the House of Bedford, in innocent and studious repose.†

Kettlewell. Fitzwilliam.

Among the less distinguished divines who forfeited their benefices, were doubtless many good men: but it is certain that the moral character of the nonjurors, as a class, did not stand high. It seems hard to impute laxity of principle to persons who undoubtedly made a great sacrifice to principle. And yet experience abundantly proves that many who are capable of making a great sacrifice, when their blood is heated by conflict, and when the public eye is fixed upon

General character of the nonjuring clergy.

* See his works, and the highly curious life of him which was compiled from the papers of his friends Hickes and Nelson.

† See Fitzwilliam's correspondence with Lady Russell, and his evidence on the trial of Ashton, in the State Trials. the only work which Fitzwilliam, as far as I have been able to discover, ever published was a sermon on the Rye House Plot, preached a few weeks after Russell's execution. There are some sentences in this sermon which I a little wonder that the widow and the family forgave.

them, are not capable of persevering long in the daily practice of obscure virtues. It is by no means improbable that zealots may have given their lives for a religion which had never effectually restrained their vindictive or their licentious passions. We learn indeed from fathers of the highest authority that, even in the purest ages of the Church, some confessors, who had manfully refused to save themselves from torments and death by throwing frankincense on the altar of Jupiter, afterwards brought scandal on the Christian name by gross fraud and debauchery.* For the nonjuring divines great allowance must in fairness be made. They were doubtless in a most trying situation. In general, a schism, which divides a religious community, divides the laity as well as the clergy. The seceding pastors therefore carry with them a large part of their flocks, and are consequently assured of a maintenance. But the schism of 1689 scarcely extended beyond the clergy. The law required the rector to take the oaths, or to quit his living : but no oath, no acknowledgment of the title of the new King and Queen, was required from the parishioner as a qualification for attending divine service, or for receiving the Eucharist. Not one in fifty, therefore, of those laymen who disapproved of the Revolution thought himself bound to quit his pew in the old church, where the old liturgy was still read, and where the old vestments were still worn, and to follow the ejected priest to a conventicle, a conventicle, too, which was not protected by the Toleration Act. Thus the new sect was a sect of preachers without hearers ; and such preachers could not make a livelihood by preaching. In London, indeed, and in some other large towns, those vehement Jacobites, whom nothing would satisfy but to hear King James and the Prince of Wales prayed for by name, were sufficiently numerous to make up a few small congregations, which met secretly, and under constant fear of the constables, in rooms so mean that the meeting houses of the Puritan dissenters might by comparison be called palaces. Even Collier, who had all the qualities which

---

* Cyprian, in one of his Epistles, addresses the confessors thus : " Quosdam audio inficere numerum vestrum, et laudem præcipui nominis prava sua conversatione destruere. . . Cum quanto nominis vestri pudore delinquitur quando aiius aliquis temulentus et lasciviens demoratur; alius in eam patriam unde extorris est regreditur, ut deprehensus non jam quasi Christianus, sed quasi nocens pereat." He uses still stronger language in the book de Unitate Ecclesiæ : "Neque enim confessio immunem facit ab insidiis diaboli, aut contra tentationes et pericula et incursus atque impetus sæculares adhuc in sæculo positum perpetua securitate defendit; cæterum nunquam in confessoribus fraudes et stupra et adulteria postmodum videremus, quæ nunc in quibusdam videntea ingemiscimus et dolemus."

attract large audiences, was reduced to be the minister of a little knot of malecontents, whose oratory was on a second floor in the city. But the nonjuring clergymen who were able to obtain even a pittance by officiating at such places were very few. Of the rest some had independent means: some lived by literature: one or two practised physic. Thomas Wagstaffe, for example, who had been Chancellor of Lichfield, had many patients, and made himself conspicuous by always visiting them in full canonicals.* But these were exceptions. Industrious poverty is a state by no means unfavourable to virtue: but it is dangerous to be at once poor and idle; and most of the clergymen who had refused to swear found themselves thrown on the world with nothing to eat and with nothing to do. They naturally became beggars and loungers. Considering themselves as martyrs suffering in a public cause, they were not ashamed to ask any good churchman for a guinea. Most of them passed their lives in running about from one Tory coffeehouse to another, abusing the Dutch, hearing and spreading reports that within a month His Majesty would certainly be on English ground, and wondering who would have Salisbury when Burnet was hanged. During the session of Parliament the lobbies and the Court of Requests were crowded with deprived parsons, asking who was up, and what the numbers were on the last division. Many of the ejected divines became domesticated, as chaplains, tutors, and spiritual directors, in the houses of opulent Jacobites. In a situation of this kind, a man of pure and exalted character, such a man as Ken was among the nonjurors, and Watts among the nonconformists, may preserve his dignity, and may much more than repay by his example and his instructions the benefits which he receives. But to a person whose virtue is not high toned this way of life is full of peril. If he is of a quiet disposition, he is in danger of sinking into a servile, sensual, drowsy parasite. If he is of an active and aspiring nature, it may be feared that he will become expert in those bad arts by which, more easily than by faithful service, retainers make themselves agreeable or formidable. To discover the weak side of every character, to flatter every passion and prejudice, to sow discord and jealousy where love and confidence ought to exist, to watch the moment of indiscreet openness for the purpose of ex-

* Much curious information about the nonjurors will be found in the Biographical Memoirs of William Bowyer, Printer, which forms the first volume of Nichols's Literary Anecdotes of the eighteenth century. A specimen of Wagstaffe's prescriptions is in the Bodleian Library.

tracting secrets important to the prosperity and honour of
families, such are the practices by which keen and restless
spirits have too often avenged themselves for the humiliation
of dependence. The public voice loudly accused many nonjurors of requiting the hospitality of their benefactors with
villany as black as that of the hypocrite depicted in the
masterpiece of Moliere. Indeed, when Cibber undertook to
adapt that noble comedy to the English stage, he made his
Tartuffe a nonjuror: and Johnson, who cannot be supposed
to have been prejudiced against the nonjurors, frankly owned
that Cibber had done them no wrong.*

There can be no doubt that the schism caused by the
oaths would have been far more formidable, if, at this crisis,
any extensive change had been made in the government or in
the ceremonial of the Established Church. It is a highly instructive fact that those enlightened and tolerant divines who
most ardently desired such a change saw reason, not long afterwards, to be thankful that their favourite project had failed.

The plan of Comprehension. Whigs and Tories had in the late Session combined to get
rid of Nottingham's Comprehension Bill by voting an address
which requested the King to refer the whole subject to the
Convocation. Burnet foresaw the effect of this vote. The
whole scheme, he said, was utterly ruined.† Many of his
friends however, thought differently; and among these was
Tillotson. Tillotson. Of all the members of the Low Church party
Tillotson stood highest in general estimation. As a preacher
he was thought by his contemporaries to have surpassed all
rivals living or dead. Posterity has reversed this judgment.

---

* Cibber's play, as Cibber wrote it,
ceased to be popular when the Jacobites
ceased to be formidable, and is now
known only to the curious. In 1768
Bickerstaffe altered it into the Hypocrite,
and substituted Dr. Cantwell, the Me-
thodist, for Dr. Wolf, the Nonjuror. "I
do not think," said Johnson, "the character of the Hypocrite justly applicable
to the Methodists; but it was very applicable to the nonjurors." Boswell
asked him if it were true that the nonjuring clergymen intrigued with the wives
of their patrons. "I am afraid," said
Johnson, "many of them did." This
conversation took place on the 27th of
March, 1775. It was not merely in
careless talk that Johnson expressed an
unfavourable opinion of the nonjurors.
In his Life of Fenton, who was a nonjuror, are these remarkable words: "It
must be remembered that he kept his
name unsullied, and never suffered him-

self to be reduced, like too many of the
same sect, to mean arts and dishonourable shifts." See the character of a
Jacobite, 1690. Even in Kettlewell's
Life, compiled from the papers of his
friends Hickes and Nelson, will be found
admissions which show that, very soon
after the schism, some of the nonjuring
clergy fell into habits of idleness, dependence, and mendicancy, which lowered the character of the whole party.
"Several undeserving persons, who are
always the most confident, by their going up and down, did much prejudice to
the truly deserving, whose modesty would
not suffer them to solicit for themselves.
. . . . . Mr. Kettlewell was also very
sensible that some of his brethren spent
too much of their time in places of concourse and news, by depending for their
subsistence upon those whom they there
got acquainted with."

† Reresby's Memoirs, 344.

Yet Tillotson still keeps his place as a legitimate English classic. His highest flights were indeed far below those of Taylor, of Barrow, and of South; but his oratory was more correct and equable than theirs. No quaint conceits, no pedantic quotations from Talmudists and scholiasts, no mean images, buffoon stories, scurrilous invectives, ever marred the effect of his grave and temperate discourses. His reasoning was just sufficiently profound and sufficiently refined to be followed by a popular audience with that slight degree of intellectual exertion which is a pleasure. His style is not brilliant; but it is pure, transparently clear, and equally free from the levity and from the stiffness which disfigure the sermons of some eminent divines of the seventeenth century. He is always serious: yet there is about his manner a certain graceful ease which marks him as a man who knows the world, who has lived in populous cities and in splendid courts, and who has conversed, not only with books, but with lawyers and merchants, wits and beauties, statesmen and princes. The greatest charm of his compositions, however, is derived from the benignity and candour which appear in every line, and which shone forth not less conspicuously in his life than in his writings.

As a theologian, Tillotson was certainly not less latitudinarian than Burnet. Yet many of those clergymen to whom Burnet was an object of implacable aversion, spoke of Tillotson with tenderness and respect. It is therefore not strange that the two friends should have formed different estimates of the temper of the priesthood, and should have expected different results from the meeting of the Convocation. Tillotson was not displeased with the vote of the Commons. He conceived that changes made in religious institutions by mere secular authority might disgust many churchmen, who would yet be perfectly willing to vote, in an ecclesiastical synod, for changes more extensive still; and his opinion had great weight with the King.* It was resolved that the Convocation should meet at the beginning of the next session of Parliament, and that in the meantime a commission should issue empowering some eminent divines to examine the Liturgy, the canons, and the whole system of jurisprudence administered by the Courts Christian, and to report on the alterations which it might be desirable to make.†

* Birch's Life of Tillotson.
† See the Discourse concerning the Ecclesiastical Commission, 1689.

An Ecclesiastical Commission issued.

Most of the Bishops who had taken the oaths were in this commission; and with them were joined twenty priests of great note. Of the twenty Tillotson was the most important: for he was known to speak the sense both of the King and of the Queen. Among those Commissioners who looked up to Tillotson as their chief were Stillingfleet, Dean of St. Paul's, Sharp, Dean of Norwich, Patrick, Dean of Peterborough, Tenison, Rector of Saint Martin's, and Fowler, to whose judicious firmness was chiefly to be ascribed the determination of the London clergy not to read the Declaration of Indulgence.

With such men as those who have been named were mingled some divines who belonged to the High Church party. Conspicuous among these were two of the rulers of Oxford, Aldrich and Jane. Aldrich had recently been appointed Dean of Christchurch, in the room of the Papist Massey, whom James had, in direct violation of the laws, placed at the head of that great college. The new Dean was a polite, though not a profound, scholar, and a jovial, hospitable gentleman. He was the author of some theological tracts which have long been forgotten, and of a compendium of logic which is still used: but the best works which he has bequeathed to posterity are his catches. Jane, the King's Professor of Divinity, was a graver but a less estimable man. He had borne the chief part in framing that decree by which his University ordered the works of Milton and Buchanan to be publicly burned in the Schools. A few years later, irritated and alarmed by the persecution of the Bishops and by the confiscation of the revenues of Magdalene College, he had renounced the doctrine of nonresistance, had repaired to the head quarters of the Prince of Orange, and had assured His Highness that Oxford would willingly coin her plate for the support of the war against her oppressor. During a short time Jane was generally considered as a Whig, and was sharply lampooned by some of his old allies. He was so unfortunate as to have a name which was an excellent mark for the learned punsters of his University. Several epigrams were written on the doublefaced Janus, who, having got a professorship by looking one way, now hoped to get a bishopric by looking another. That he hoped to get a bishopric was perfectly true. He demanded the see of Exeter as a reward due to his services. He was refused: the refusal convinced him that the Church had as much to apprehend from Latitudinarianism as from Popery; and he speedily became a Tory again.*

Early in October the Commissioners assembled in the Jerusalem Chamber. At their first meeting they determined to propose that, in the public services of the Church, lessons taken from the canonical books of Scripture should be substituted for the lessons taken from the Apocrypha.† At the second meeting a strange question was raised by the very last person who ought to have raised it. Sprat, Bishop of Rochester, had, without any scruple, sate, during two years, in the unconstitutional tribunal which had, in the late reign, oppressed and pillaged the Church of which he was a ruler. But he had now become scrupulous, and was not ashamed, after acting without hesitation under King James's commission, to express a doubt whether King William's commission were legal. To a plain understanding the doubt seems to be childish. King William's commission gave power neither to make laws nor to administer laws, but simply to enquire and to report. Even without a royal commission Tillotson, Patrick, and Stillingfleet might, with perfect propriety, have met to discuss the state and prospects of the Church, and to consider whether it would or would not be desirable to make some concession to the dissenters. And how could it be a crime for subjects to do at the request of their Sovereign that which it would have been innocent and laudable to do without any such request? Sprat, however, was seconded by Jane. There was a sharp altercation; and Lloyd, Bishop of Saint Asaph, who, with many good qualities, had an irritable temper, was provoked into saying something about spies. Sprat withdrew and came no more. His example was soon followed by Jane and Aldrich.‡ The Commissioners proceeded to take into consideration the question of the posture at the Eucharist. It was determined to recommend that a communicant, who, after conference with his minister, should declare that he could not conscientiously receive the bread and wine kneeling, might receive them sitting. Mew, Bishop of Winchester, an honest man, but illiterate, weak even in his best days, and now fast sinking into dotage, protested against this

---

* Birch's Life of Tillotson; Life of Prideaux; Gentleman's Magazine for June and July 1745.

† Diary of the Proceedings of the Commissioners, taken by Dr. Williams, afterwards Bishop of Chichester, one of the Commissioners, every night after he went home from the several meetings. This most curious Diary was printed by order of the House of Commons in 1854.

‡ Williams's Diary.

concession, and withdrew from the assembly. The other members continued to apply themselves vigorously to their task; and no more secessions took place, though there were great differences of opinion, and though the debates were sometimes warm. The highest churchmen who still remained were Doctor William Beveridge, Archdeacon of Colchester, who many years later became Bishop of Saint Asaph, and Doctor John Scott, the same who had prayed by the deathbed of Jeffreys. The most active among the Latitudinarians appear to have been Burnet, Fowler, and Tenison.

The baptismal service was repeatedly discussed. As to matter of form the Commissioners were disposed to be indulgent. They were generally willing to admit infants into the Church without sponsors and without the sign of the cross. But the majority, after much debate, steadily refused to soften down or explain away those words which, to all minds not sophisticated, appear to assert the regenerating virtue of the sacrament.*

As to the surplice, the Commissioners determined to recommend that a large discretion should be left to the Bishops. Expedients were devised by which a person who had received Presbyterian ordination might, without admitting, either expressly or by implication, the invalidity of that ordination, become a minister of the Church of England.†

The ecclesiastical calendar was carefully revised. The great festivals were retained. But it was not thought desirable that Saint Valentine, Saint Chad, Saint Swithin, Saint Edward King of the West Saxons, Saint Dunstan, and Saint Alphage, should share the honours of Saint John and Saint Paul; or that the Church should appear to class the ridiculous fable of the discovery of the cross with facts so awfully important as the Nativity, the Passion, the Resurrection, and the Ascension of her Lord.‡

The Athanasian Creed caused much perplexity. Most of the Commissioners were equally unwilling to give up the doctrinal clauses and to retain the damnatory clauses. Burnet, Fowler, and Tillotson were desirous to strike this famous symbol out of the Liturgy altogether. Burnet brought forward one argument, which to himself probably did not appear to have much weight, but which was admirably calculated to perplex his opponents, Beveridge and Scott. The

* Williams's Diary.   † Ibid.
‡ See the alterations in the Book of Common Prayer prepared by the Royal Commissioners for the revision of the Liturgy in 1689, and printed by order of the House of Commons in 1854.

Council of Ephesus had always been reverenced by Anglican divines as a synod which had truly represented the whole body of the faithful, and which had been divinely guided in the way of truth. The voice of that Council was the voice of the Holy Catholic and Apostolic Church, not yet corrupted by superstition, or rent asunder by schism. During more than twelve centuries the world had not seen an ecclesiastical assembly which had an equal claim to the respect of believers. The Council of Ephesus had, in the plainest terms, and under the most terrible penalties, forbidden Christians to frame or to impose on their brethren any creed other than the creed settled by the Nicene Fathers. It should seem therefore that, if the Council of Ephesus was really under the direction of the Holy Spirit, whoever uses the Athanasian Creed must, in the very act of uttering an anathema against his neighbours, bring down an anathema on his own head.* In spite of the authority of the Ephesian Fathers, the majority of the Commissioners determined to leave the Athanasian Creed in the Prayer Book : but they proposed to add a rubric drawn up by Stillingfleet, which declared that the damnatory clauses were to be understood to apply only to such as obstinately denied the substance of the Christian Faith. Obstinacy is of the nature of moral pravity, and is not imputable to a candid and modest enquirer who, from some defect or malformation of the intellect, is mistaken as to the comparative weight of opposite arguments or testimonies. Orthodox believers were therefore permitted to hope that the heretic who had honestly and humbly sought for truth would not be everlastingly punished for having failed to find it.†

Tenison was entrusted with the business of examining the Liturgy, and of collecting all those expressions to which objections had been made, either by theological or by literary critics. It was determined to remove some obvious blemishes. And it would have been wise in the Commissioners to stop here. Unfortunately they determined to rewrite a great part of the Prayer Book. It was a bold undertaking; for in

---

* It is difficult to conceive stronger or clearer language than that used by the Council. Τούτων τοίνυν ἀναγνωσθέντων, ὥρισεν ἡ ἁγία σύνοδος, ἑτέραν πίστιν μηδενὶ ἐξεῖναι προσφέρειν, ἤγουν συγγράφειν, ἢ συντιθέναι, παρὰ τὴν ὁρισθεῖσαν παρὰ τῶν ἁγίων πατέρων τῶν ἐν τῇ Νικαέων συνελθόντων σὺν ἁγίῳ πνεύματι· τοὺς δὲ τολμῶντας ἢ συντιθέναι πίστιν ἑτέραν, ἤγουν προκομίζειν, ἢ προσφέρειν τοῖς ἐθέλουσιν ἐπιστρέφειν εἰς ἐπίγνωσιν τῆς ἀληθείας, ἢ ἐξ Ἑλληνισμοῦ, ἢ ἐξ Ἰουδαϊσμοῦ, ἢ ἐξ αἱρέσεως οἱασδηποτοῦν, τούτους, εἰ μὲν εἶεν ἐπίσκοποι ἢ κληρικοὶ, ἀλλοτρίους εἶναι τοὺς ἐπισκόπους τῆς ἐπισκοπῆς, καὶ τοὺς κληρικοὺς τοῦ κλήρου, εἰ δὲ λαϊκοὶ εἶεν, ἀναθεματίζεσθαι.—Concil. Ephes. Actio VI.

† Williams's Diary ; Alterations in the Book of Common Prayer.

general the style of that volume is such as cannot be improved. The English Liturgy indeed gains by being compared even with those fine ancient Liturgies from which it is to a great extent taken. The essential qualities of devotional eloquence, conciseness, majestic simplicity, pathetic earnestness of supplication, sobered by a profound reverence, are common between the translations and the originals. But in the subordinate graces of diction the originals must be allowed to be far inferior to the translations. And the reason is obvious. The technical phraseology of Christianity did not become a part of the Latin language till that language had passed the age of maturity and was sinking into barbarism. But the technical phraseology of Christianity was found in the Anglosaxon and in the Norman French, long before the union of those two dialects had produced a third dialect superior to either. The Latin of the Roman Catholic services, therefore, is Latin in the last stage of decay. The English of our services is English in all the vigour and suppleness of early youth. To the great Latin writers, to Terence and Lucretius, to Cicero and Cæsar, to Tacitus and Quinctilian, the noblest compositions of Ambrose and Gregory would have seemed to be, not merely bad writing, but senseless gibberish.* The diction of our Book of Common Prayer, on the other hand, has directly or indirectly contributed to form the diction of almost every great English writer, and has extorted the admiration of the most accomplished infidels and of the most accomplished nonconformists, of such men as David Hume and Robert Hall.

The style of the Liturgy, however, did not satisfy the Doctors of the Jerusalem Chamber. They voted the Collects too short and too dry; and Patrick was entrusted with the duty of expanding and ornamenting them. In one respect, at least, the choice seems to have been unexceptionable; for, if we judge by the way in which Patrick paraphrased the most sublime Hebrew poetry, we shall probably be of opinion that, whether he was or was not qualified to make the collects better, no man that ever lived was more competent to make them longer.†

---

* It is curious to consider how those great masters of the Latin tongue who used to sup with Mæcenas and Pollio would have been perplexed by "Tibi Cherubim et Seraphim incessabili voce proclamant, Sanctus, Sanctus, Sanctus, Dominus Deus Sabaoth;" or by "Ideo cum angelis et archangelis, cum thronis et

dominationibus."

† I will give two specimens of Patrick's workmanship. "He maketh me," says David, "to lie down in green pastures: he leadeth me beside the still waters." Patrick's version is as follows: "For as a good shepherd leads his sheep in the violent heat to shady places,

It mattered little, however, whether the recommendations of the Commission were good or bad. They were all doomed before they were known. The writs summoning the Convocation of the Province of Canterbury had been issued; and the clergy were everywhere in a state of violent excitement. They had just taken the oaths, and were smarting from the earnest reproofs of nonjurors, from the insolent taunts of Whigs, and often undoubtedly from the stings of remorse. The announcement that a Convocation was to sit for the purpose of deliberating on a plan of comprehension roused all the strongest passions of the priest who had just complied with the law, and was ill satisfied or half satisfied with himself for complying. He had an opportunity of contributing to defeat a favourite scheme of that government which had exacted from him, under severe penalties, a submission not easily to be reconciled to his conscience or his pride. He had an opportunity of signalising his zeal for that Church whose characteristic doctrines he had been accused of deserting for lucre. She was now, he conceived, threatened by a danger as great as that of the preceding year. The Latitudinarians of 1689 were not less eager to humble and to ruin her than the Jesuits of 1688 had been. The Toleration Act had done for the Dissenters quite as much as was compatible with her dignity and security; and nothing more ought to be conceded, not the hem of one of her vestments, not an epithet from the beginning to the end of her Liturgy. All the reproaches which had been thrown on the ecclesiastical commission of James were transferred to the ecclesiastical commission of William. The two commissions indeed had nothing but the name in common. But the name was associated with illegality and oppression, with the violation of dwellings and the confiscation of freeholds, and was therefore assiduously sounded with no small effect by the tongues of the spiteful in the ears of the ignorant.

The King too, it was said, was not sound. He conformed

The Convocation of the Province of Canterbury summoned. Temper of the clergy.

where they may lie down and feed (not in parched, but) in fresh and green pastures, and in the evening leads them (not to muddy and troubled waters, but) to pure and quiet streams; so hath he already made a fair and plentiful provision for me, which I enjoy in peace without any disturbance."

In the Song of Solomon is an exquisitely beautiful verse. "I charge you, O daughters of Jerusalem, if ye find my beloved, that ve tell him that I am sick

of love." Patrick's version runs thus: "So I turned myself to those of my neighbours and familiar acquaintance who were awakened by my cries to come and see what the matter was; and conjured them, as they would answer it to God, that, if they met with my beloved, they would let him know—What shall I say?—What shall I desire you to tell him but that I do not enjoy myself now that I want his company, nor can be well till I recover his love again?"

indeed to the established worship; but his was a local and occasional conformity. For some ceremonies to which High Churchmen were attached he had a distaste which he was at no pains to conceal. One of his first acts had been to give orders that in his private chapel the service should be said instead of being sung; and this arrangement, though warranted by the rubric, caused much murmuring.* It was known that he was so profane as to sneer at a practice which had been sanctioned by high ecclesiastical authority, the practice of touching for the scrofula. This ceremony had come down almost unaltered from the darkest of the dark ages to the time of Newton and Locke. The Stuarts frequently dispensed the healing influences in the Banqueting House. The days on which this miracle was to be wrought were fixed at sittings of the Privy Council, and were solemnly notified by the clergy in all the parish churches of the realm.† When the appointed time came, several divines in full canonicals stood round the canopy of state. The surgeon of the royal household introduced the sick. A passage from the sixteenth chapter of the Gospel of Saint Mark was read. When the words, "They shall lay their hands on the sick, and they shall recover," had been pronounced, there was a pause; and one of the sick was brought up to the King. His Majesty stroked the ulcers and swellings, and hung round the patient's neck a white riband to which was fastened a gold coin. The other sufferers were then led up in succession; and, as each was touched, the chaplain repeated the incantation, "They shall lay their hands on the sick, and they shall recover." Then came the epistle, prayers, antiphonies, and a benediction. The service may still be found in the prayer books of the reign of Anne. Indeed it was not till some time after the accession of George the First that the University of Oxford ceased to reprint the Office of Healing together with the Liturgy. Theologians of eminent learning, ability, and virtue gave the sanction of their authority to this mummery‡; and, what is stranger still, medical men of high note

The clergy ill affected towards the King. (margin note)

---

* William's dislike of the Cathedral service is sarcastically noticed by Leslie in the Rehearsal, No 7. See also a Letter from a Member of the House of Commons to his Friend in the Country, 1689, and Bisset's Modern Fanatic, 1710.

† See the Order in Council of Jan. 9. 1683.

‡ See Collier's Desertion discussed, 1689. Thomas Carte, who was a disciple, and, at one time, an assistant, of Collier, inserted, so late as the year 1747, in a bulky History of England, an exquisitely absurd note, in which he assured the world that, to his certain knowledge, the Pretender had cured the scrofula, and very gravely inferred that the healing virtue was transmitted by inheritance, and was quite independent of any unction. See Carte's History of England, vol. i. page 291.

believed, or affected to believe, in the balsamic virtues of the royal hand. We must suppose that every surgeon who attended Charles the Second was a man of high repute for skill; and more than one of the surgeons who attended Charles the Second has left us a solemn profession of faith in the King's miraculous power. One of them is not ashamed to tell us that the gift was communicated by the unction administered at the coronation; that the cures were so numerous and sometimes so rapid that they could not be attributed to any natural cause; that the failures were to be ascribed to want of faith on the part of the patients; that Charles once handled a scrofulous Quaker and made him a healthy man and a sound Churchman in a moment; that, if those who had been healed lost or sold the piece of gold which had been hung round their necks, the ulcers broke forth again, and could be removed only by a second touch and a second talisman. We cannot wonder that, when men of science gravely repeated such nonsense, the vulgar should have believed it. Still less can we wonder that wretches tortured by a disease over which natural remedies had no power should have eagerly drunk in tales of preternatural cures: for nothing is so credulous as misery. The crowds which repaired to the palace on the days of healing were immense. Charles the Second, in the course of his reign, touched near a hundred thousand persons. The number seems to have increased or diminished as the king's popularity rose or fell. During that Tory reaction which followed the dissolution of the Oxford Parliament, the press to get near him was terrific. In 1682, he performed the rite eight thousand five hundred times. In 1684, the throng was such that six or seven of the sick were trampled to death. James, in one of his progresses, touched eight hundred persons in the choir of the Cathedral of Chester. The expense of the ceremony was little less than ten thousand pounds a year, and would have been much greater but·for the vigilance of the royal surgeons, whose business it was to examine the applicants, and to distinguish those who came for the cure from those who came for the gold.*

* See the Preface to a Treatise on Wounds, by Richard Wiseman, Sergeant Chirurgeon to His Majesty, 1676. But the fullest information on this curious subject will be found in the Charisma Basilicon, by John Browne. Chirurgeon in ordinary to His Majesty, 1684. See also the Ceremonies used in the Time of King Henry VII. for the Healing of them that·beDiseased with the King's Evil, published by His Majesty's Command, 1686; Evelyn's Diary, March 28. 1684; and Bishop Cartwright's Diary, August 28, 29, and 30. 1687. It is incredible that so large a proportion of the population should have been really scrofulous. No

William had too much sense to be duped, and too much honesty to bear a part in what he knew to be an imposture. "It is a silly superstition," he exclaimed, when he heard that, at the close of Lent, his palace was besieged by a crowd of the sick: "Give the poor creatures some money, and send them away."* On one single occasion he was importuned into laying his hand on a patient. "God give you better health," he said, "and more sense." The parents of scrofulous children cried out against his cruelty: bigots lifted up their hands and eyes in horror at his impiety: Jacobites sarcastically praised him for not presuming to arrogate to himself a power which belonged only to legitimate sovereigns; and even some Whigs thought that he acted unwisely in treating with such marked contempt a superstition which had a strong hold on the vulgar mind: but William was not to be moved, and was accordingly set down by many High Churchmen as either an infidel or a puritan.*

The chief cause, however, which at this time made even the most moderate plan of comprehension hateful to the priesthood still remains to be mentioned. What Burnet had foreseen and foretold had come to pass. There was through out the clerical profession a strong disposition to retaliate on the Presbyterians of England the wrongs of the Episcopalians of Scotland. It could not be denied that even the highest churchmen had, in the summer of 1688, generally declared themselves willing to give up many things for the sake of union. But it was said, and not without plausibility, that what was passing on the other side of the Border proved union on any reasonable terms to be impossible. With what face, it was asked, can those who will make no concession to us where we are weak, blame us for refusing to make any concession to them where we are strong? We cannot judge correctly of the principles and feelings of a sect from the professions which it makes in a time of feebleness and suffering. If we would know what the Puritan spirit really is, we must observe the Puritan when he is dominant. He was dominant here in the last generation; and his little finger was thicker than the loins of the prelates. He drove hun-

The clergy exasperated against the Dissenters by the proceedings of the Scotch Presbyterians.

---

doubt many persons who had slight and transient maladies were brought to the king; and the recovery of these persons kept up the vulgar belief in the efficacy of his touch.

* Paris Gazette, April 23. 1689.
† See Whiston's Life of himself. Poor

Whiston, who believed in everything but the Trinity, tells us gravely that the single person whom William touched was cured, notwithstanding His Majesty's want of faith. See also the Athenian Mercury of January 16. 1691.

dreds of quiet students from their cloisters, and thousands of respectable divines from their parsonages, for the crime of refusing to sign his Covenant. No tenderness was shown to learning, to genius, or to sanctity. Such men as Hall and Sanderson, Chillingworth and Hammond, were not only plundered but flung into prisons, and exposed to all the rudeness of brutal gaolers. It was made a crime to read fine psalms and prayers bequeathed to the faithful by Ambrose and Chrysostom. At length the nation became weary of the reign of the saints. The fallen dynasty and the fallen hierarchy were restored. The Puritan was in his turn subjected to disabilities and penalties; and he immediately found out that it was barbarous to punish men for entertaining conscientious scruples about a garb, about a ceremony, about the functions of ecclesiastical officers. His piteous complaints and his arguments in favour of toleration had at length imposed on many well meaning persons. Even zealous churchmen had begun to entertain a hope that the severe discipline which he had undergone had made him candid, moderate, charitable. Had this been really so, it would doubtless have been our duty to treat his scruples with extreme tenderness. But, while we were considering what we could do to meet his wishes in England, he had obtained ascendency in Scotland; and, in an instant, he was all himself again, bigoted, insolent, and cruel. Manses had been sacked; churches shut up; prayer books burned; sacred garments torn; congregations dispersed by violence; priests hustled, pelted, pilloried, driven forth, with their wives and babes, to beg or die of hunger. That these outrages were to be imputed, not to a few lawless marauders, but to the great body of the Presbyterians of Scotland, was evident from the fact that the government had not dared either to inflict punishment on the offenders or to grant relief to the sufferers. Was it not fit then that the Church of England should take warning? Was it reasonable to ask her to mutilate her apostolical polity and her beautiful ritual for the purpose of conciliating those who wanted nothing but power to rabble her as they had rabbled her sister? Already these men had obtained a boon which they ill deserved, and which they never would have granted. They worshipped God in perfect security. Their meeting houses were as effectually protected as the choirs of our cathedrals. While no episcopal minister could, without putting his life in jeopardy, officiate in Ayrshire or Renfrewshire, a hundred Presbyterian ministers preached unmolested every Sunday in

Middlesex. The legislature had, with a generosity perhaps imprudent, granted toleration to the most intolerant of men; and with toleration it behoved them to be content.

Constitution of the Convocation.

Thus several causes conspired to inflame the parochial clergy against the scheme of comprehension. Their temper was such that, if the plan framed in the Jerusalem Chamber had been directly submitted to them, it would have been rejected by a majority of twenty to one. But in the Convocation their weight bore no proportion to their number. The Convocation has, happily for our country, been so long utterly insignificant that, till a recent period, none but curious students cared to enquire how it was constituted; and even now many persons, not generally ill informed, imagine it to be a council representing the Church of England. In truth the Convocation so often mentioned in our ecclesiastical history is merely the synod of the Province of Canterbury, and never had a right to speak in the name of the whole clerical body. The Province of York has also its Convocation: but, till the eighteenth century was far advanced, the Province of York was generally so poor, so rude, and so thinly peopled, that, in political importance, it could hardly be considered as more than a tenth part of the kingdom. The sense of the Southern clergy was therefore popularly considered as the sense of the whole profession. When the formal concurrence of the Northern clergy was required, it seems to have been given as a matter of course. Indeed the canons passed by the Convocation of Canterbury in 1604 were ratified by James the First, and were ordered to be strictly observed in every part of the kingdom two years before the Convocation of York went through the form of approving them. Since these ecclesiastical councils became mere names, a great change has taken place in the relative position of the two Archbishoprics. In all the elements of power, the region beyond Trent is now at least a third part of England. When in our own time the representative system was adjusted to the altered state of the country, almost all the small boroughs which it was necessary to disfranchise were in the south. Two thirds of the new members given to great provincial towns were given to the north. If therefore any English government should suffer the Convocations, as now constituted, to meet for the despatch of business, two independent synods would be legislating at the same time for one Church. It is by no means impossible that one assembly might adopt canons which the other might reject, that one assembly might condemn as heretical propositions which the other might hold to be orthodox.* In the seventeenth century no such danger was apprehended. So little indeed was the Convocation of York then considered, that the two Houses of Parliament had, in their address to William, spoken only of one Convocation, which they called the Convocation of the Clergy of the Kingdom.

The body which they thus not very accurately designated is divided into two Houses. The Upper House is composed of the Bishops of the Province of Canterbury. The Lower House consisted, in 1689, of a hundred and forty-four members. Twenty-two Deans and fifty-four Archdeacons sate there in virtue of their offices. Twenty-four divines sate as proctors for twenty-four chapters. Only forty-four proctors were elected by the eight thousand parish priests of the twenty-two dioceses. These forty-four proctors, however, were almost all of one mind. The elections had in former times been conducted in the most quiet and decorous manner. But on this occasion the canvassing was eager: the contests were sharp: Clarendon, who had refused to take the oaths, and his brother Rochester, the leader of the party which in the House of Lords had opposed the Comprehension Bill, had gone to Oxford, the head quarters of that party, for the purpose of animating and organising the opposition.† The representatives of the parochial clergy must have been men whose chief distinction was their zeal: for in the whole list can be found not a single illustrious name, and very few names which are now known even to persons well read in ecclesiastical history.‡ The official members of the Lower House, among whom were many distinguished scholars and preachers, seem to have been not very unequally divided.

During the summer of 1689 several high spiritual dignities became vacant, and were bestowed on divines who were sitting in the Jerusalem Chamber. It has already been men-

Election of members of Convocation.

Ecclesiastical preferments bestowed.

---

* In several recent publications the apprehension that differences might arise between the Convocation of York and the Convocation of Canterbury has been contemptuously pronounced chimerical. But it is not easy to understand why two independent Convocations should be less likely to differ than two Houses of the same Convocation; and it is matter of notoriety that, in the reigns of William the Third and Anne, the two Houses of the Convocation of Canterbury scarcely ever agreed.

† Birch's Life of Tillotson; Life of Prideaux. From Clarendon's Diary, it appears that he and Rochester were at Oxford on the 23rd of September.

‡ See the Roll in the Historical Account of the present Convocation, appended to the second edition of Vox Cleri, 1690. The most considerable name that I perceive in the list of proctors chosen by the parochial clergy is that of Dr. John Mill, the editor of the Greek Testament.

tioned that Thomas, Bishop of Worcester, died just before
the day fixed for taking the oaths, Lake, Bishop of Chichester, lived just long enough to refuse them, and with his last
breath declared that he would maintain even at the stake the
doctrine of indefeasible hereditary right. The see of Chichester was filled by Patrick, and that of Worcester by Stillingfleet; and the deanery of Saint Paul's which Stillingfleet
quitted was given to Tillotson. That Tillotson was not raised
to the episcopal bench excited some surprise. But in truth it
was because the government held his services in the highest
estimation that he was suffered to remain a little longer a
simple presbyter. The most important office in the Convocation was that of Prolocutor of the Lower House : the Prolocutor was to be chosen by the members; and it was hoped
at Court that they would choose Tillotson. It had in fact
been already determined that he should be the next Archbishop of Canterbury. When he went to kiss hands for his
new deanery he warmly thanked the King. " Your Majesty
has now set me at ease for the remainder of my life." " No
such thing, Doctor, I assure you," said William. He then
plainly intimated that, whenever Sancroft should cease to fill
the highest ecclesiastical station, Tillotson would succeed to
it. Tillotson stood aghast: for his nature was quiet and un-
ambitious : he was beginning to feel the infirmities of old
age; he cared little for rank or money: the worldly advantages which he most valued were an honest fame and the
general good will of mankind: those advantages he already
possessed; and he could not but be aware that, if he became
primate, he should incur the bitterest hatred of a powerful
party, and should become a mark for obloquy, from which his
gentle and sensitive nature shrank as from the rack or the
wheel. William was earnest and resolute. " It is necessary,"
he said, " for my service ; and I must lay on your conscience
the responsibility of refusing me your help." Here the conversation ended. It was, indeed, not necessary that the point
should be immediately decided; for several months were still
to elapse before the Archbishopric would be vacant.

Tillotson bemoaned himself with unfeigned anxiety and
sorrow to Lady Russell, whom, of all human beings, he most
honoured and trusted.* He hoped, he said, that he was not

* The letter in which Tillotson informed Lady Russell of the King's intentions is printed in Birch's book : but the
date is clearly erroneous. Indeed I feel
assured that parts of two distinct letters
have been by some blunder joined together. In one passage Tillotson informs
his correspondent that Stillingfleet ·

inclined to shrink from the service of the Church: but he was convinced that his present line of service was that in which he could be most useful. If he should be forced to accept so high and so invidious a post as the primacy, he should soon sink under the load of duties and anxieties too heavy for his strength. His spirits, and with his spirits his abilities, would fail him. He gently complained of Burnet, who loved and admired him with a truly generous heartiness, and who had laboured to persuade both the King and Queen that there was in England only one man fit for the highest ecclesiastical dignity. "The Bishop of Salisbury," said Tillotson, "is one of the best and worst friends that I know."

Nothing that was not a secret to Burnet was likely to be long a secret to anybody. It soon began to be whispered about that the King had fixed on Tillotson to fill the place of Sancroft. The news caused cruel mortification to Compton, who, not unnaturally, conceived that his own claims were unrivalled. He had educated the Queen and her sister; and to the instruction which they had received from him might fairly be ascribed, at least in part, the firmness with which, in spite of the influence of their father, they had adhered to the established religion. Compton was, moreover, the only prelate who, during the late reign, had raised his voice in Parliament against the dispensing power, the only prelate who had been suspended by the High Commission, the only prelate who had signed the invitation to the Prince of Orange, the only prelate who had actually taken arms against Popery and arbitrary power, the only prelate, save one, who had voted against a Regency. Among the ecclesiastics of the Province of Canterbury who had taken the oaths, he was highest in rank. He had therefore held, during some months, a vicarious primacy; he had crowned the new Sovereigns; he had consecrated the new Bishops: he was about to preside in the Convocation. It may be added, that he was the son of an Earl, and that no person of equally high birth then sate, or had ever sate, since the Reformation, on the episcopal bench. That the government should put over his head a priest of his own diocese, who was the son of a Yorkshire clothier, and who was distinguished only by abilities and virtues, was provoking; and Compton, though by no means a badhearted man, was much provoked. Perhaps his vexation was in-

Compton discontented.

made Bishop of Worcester, and in another that Walker is made Bishop of Derry. Now Stillingfleet was consecrated Bishop of Worcester on the 13th of October 1689, and Walker was not made Bishop of Derry till June 1690.

creased by the reflection that he had, for the sake of those by
whom he was thus slighted, done some things which had
strained his conscience and sullied his reputation, that he had
at one time practised the disingenuous arts of a diplomatist,
and at another time given scandal to his brethren by wearing
the buffcoat and jackboots of a trooper. He could not accuse
Tillotson of inordinate ambition. But, though Tillotson was
most unwilling to accept the Archbishopric himself, he did
not use his influence in favour of Compton, but earnestly recommended Stillingfleet as the man fittest to preside over the
Church of England. The consequence was that, on the eve
of the meeting of Convocation, the Bishop who was to be at
the head of the Upper House became the personal enemy of
the presbyter whom the government wished to see at the head
of the Lower House. This quarrel added new difficulties to
difficulties which little needed any addition.*

The Con-
vocation
meets.

It was not till the twentieth of November that the
Convocation met for the despatch of business. The place of
meeting had, in former times, been Saint Paul's Cathedral.
But Saint Paul's Cathedral was slowly rising from its ruins;
and, though the dome already towered high above the hundred steeples of the City, the choir had not yet been opened
for public worship. The assembly therefore sate at Westminster.† A table was placed in the beautiful chapel of
Henry the Seventh. Compton was in the chair. On his
right and left those suffragans of Canterbury who had taken
the oaths were ranged in gorgeous vestments of scarlet and
miniver. Below the table was assembled the crowd of presbyters. Beveridge preached a Latin sermon, in which he
warmly eulogised the existing system, and yet declared himself favourable to a moderate reform. Ecclesiastical laws
were, he said, of two kinds. Some laws were fundamental
and eternal: they derived their authority from God; nor
could any religious community abrogate them without ceasing to form a part of the universal Church. Other laws were
local and temporary. They had been framed by human wisdom, and might be altered by human wisdom. They ought
not indeed to be altered without grave reasons. But surely,
at that moment, such reasons were not wanting. To unite a
scattered flock in one fold under one shepherd, to remove

* Birch's Life of Tillotson. The Account there given of the coldness between
Compton and Tillotson was taken by
Birch from the MSS. of Henry Wharton,
and is confirmed by many circumstances
which are known from other sources of
intelligence.

† Chamberlayne's State of England,
18th edition.

stumblingblocks from the path of the weak, to reconcile
hearts long estranged, to restore spiritual discipline to its
primitive vigour, to place the best and purest of Christian
societies on a base broad enough to stand against all the
attacks of earth and hell, these were objects which might well
justify some modification, not of Catholic institutions, but of
national or provincial usages.*

The Lower House, having heard this discourse, proceeded
to appoint a Prolocutor. Sharp, who was probably put
forward by the members favourable to a comprehension as
one of the highest churchmen among them, proposed Tillotson. Jane, who had refused to act under the Royal Commission, was proposed on the other side. After some
animated discussion, Jane was elected by fifty-five votes to
twenty-eight.†

The High Churchmen a majority of the Lower House of Convocation.

The Prolocutor was formally presented to the Bishop of
London, and made, according to ancient usage, a Latin
oration. In this oration the Anglican Church was extolled
as the most perfect of all institutions. There was a very intelligible intimation that no change whatever in her doctrine,
her discipline, or her ritual was required; and the discourse
concluded with a most significant sentence. Compton, when
a few months before he exhibited himself in the somewhat
unclerical character of a colonel of horse, had ordered the
colours of his regiment to be embroidered with the well-
known words " Nolumus leges Angliæ mutari "; and with
these words Jane closed his peroration.‡

Still the Low Churchmen did not relinquish all hope.
They very wisely determined to begin by proposing to sub-
stitute lessons taken from the canonical books for the lessons
taken from the Apocrypha. It should seem that this was a
suggestion which, even if there had not been a single dissenter in the kingdom, might well have been received with
favour. For the Church had, in her sixth Article, declared
that the canonical books were, and that the Apocryphal
books were not, entitled to be called Holy Scriptures, and to
be regarded as the rule of faith. Even this reform, however,
the High Churchmen were determined to oppose. They
asked, in pamphlets which covered the counters of Paternoster Row and Little Britain, why country congregations
should be deprived of the pleasure of hearing about the ball

* Concio ad Synodum per Gulielmum
Beveregium, 1689.
  † Luttrell's Diary; Historical Ac-
count of the Present Convocation.
  ‡ Kennet's History, iii. 552.

of pitch with which Daniel choked the dragon, and about the
fish whose liver gave forth such a fume as sent the devil flying from Ecbatana to Egypt. And were there not chapters
of the wisdom of the Son of Sirach far more interesting and
edifying than the genealogies and muster rolls which made
up a large part of the Chronicles of the Jewish Kings, and
of the narrative of Nehemiah? No grave divine however
would have liked to maintain, in Henry the Seventh's Chapel,
that it was impossible to find, in many hundreds of pages
dictated by the Holy Spirit, fifty or sixty chapters more
edifying than anything which could be extracted from the
works of the most respectable uninspired moralist or historian. The leaders of the majority therefore determined to
shun a debate in which they must have been reduced to a
disagreeable dilemma. Their plan was, not to reject the
recommendations of the Commissioners, but to prevent those
recommendations from being discussed; and with this view
a system of tactics was adopted which proved successful.

The law, as it had been interpreted during a long course of
years, prohibited the Convocation from even deliberating on
any ecclesiastical ordinance without a previous warrant from
the Crown. Such a warrant, sealed with the great seal, was
brought in form to Henry the Seventh's Chapel by Nottingham. He at the same time delivered a message from the
King. His Majesty exhorted the assembly to consider
calmly and without prejudice the recommendations of the
Commission, and declared that he had nothing in view but
the honour and advantage of the Protestant religion in
general, and of the Church of England in particular.*

Difference
between
the two
Houses of
Convoca-
tion.

The Bishops speedily agreed on an address of thanks for
the royal message, and requested the concurrence of the
Lower House. Jane and his adherents raised objection after
objection. First they claimed the privilege of presenting
a separate address. When they were forced to waive this
claim, they refused to agree to any expression which imported
that the Church of England had any fellowship with any
other Protestant community. Amendments and reasons
were sent backward and forward. Conferences were held at
which Burnet on one side and Jane on the other were the
chief speakers. At last, with great difficulty, a compromise
was made; and an address, cold and ungracious compared
with that which the Bishops had framed, was presented to
the King in the Banqueting House. He dissembled his

* Historical Account of the Present Convocation, 1689.

vexation, returned a kind answer, and intimated a hope that the assembly would now at length proceed to consider the great question of Comprehension.*

Such however was not the intention of the leaders of the Lower House. As soon as they were again in Henry the Seventh's Chapel, one of them raised a debate about the nonjuring Bishops. In spite of the unfortunate scruple which those prelates entertained, they were learned and holy men. Their advice might, at this conjuncture, be of the greatest service to the Church. The Upper House was hardly an Upper House in the absence of the Primate and of many of his most respectable suffragans. Could nothing be done to remedy this evil? † Another member complained of some pamphlets which had lately appeared, and in which the Convocation was not treated with proper deference. The assembly took fire. Was it not monstrous that this heretical and schismatical trash should be cried by the hawkers about the streets, and should be exposed to sale in the booths of Westminster Hall, within a hundred yards of the Prolocutor's chair? The work of mutilating the Liturgy and of turning cathedrals into conventicles might surely be postponed till the Synod had taken measures to protect its own freedom and dignity. It was then debated how the printing of such scandalous books should be prevented. Some were for indictments, some for ecclesiastical censures.‡ In such deliberations as these week after week passed away. Not a single proposition tending to a Comprehension had been even discussed. Christmas was approaching. At Christmas there was to be a recess. The Bishops were desirous that, during the recess, a committee should sit to prepare business. The Lower House refused to consent.§ That House, it was now evident, was fully determined not even to enter on the consideration of any part of the plan which had been framed by the Royal Commissioners. The proctors of the dioceses were in a worse humour than when they first came up to Westminster. Many of them had probably never before passed a week in the capital, and had not been aware how great the difference was between a town divine and a country divine. The sight of the luxuries and comforts enjoyed by the popular preachers of the city raised, not unnaturally, some sore feel-

The Lower House of Convocation proves unmanageable.

* Historical Account of the Present Convocation; Burnet, ii. 58.; Kennet's History of the Reign of William and Mary.

† Historical Account of the Present Convocation; Kennet's History.

‡ Historical Account of the Present Convocation; Kennet.

§ Historical Account of the Present Convocation.

ing in a Lincolnshire or Caernarvonshire vicar who was
accustomed to live as hardly as a small farmer. The very
circumstance that the London clergy were generally for a
comprehension made the representatives of the rural clergy
obstinate on the other side.* The prelates were, as a body,
sincerely desirous that some concession might be made to the
nonconformists. But the prelates were utterly unable to
curb the mutinous democracy. They were few in number.
Some of them were objects of extreme dislike to the parochial
clergy. The President had not the full authority of a
primate ; nor was he sorry to see those who had, as he
conceived, used him ill, thwarted and mortified. It was
necessary to yield. The Convocation was prorogued for six
weeks. When those six weeks had expired, it was prorogued
again ; and many years elapsed before it was permitted to
transact business.

The Convocation prorogued.

So ended, and for ever, the hope that the Church of England might be induced to make some concession to the
scruples of the nonconformists. A learned and respectable
minority of the clerical order relinquished that hope with
deep regret. Yet in a very short time even Burnet and
Tillotson found reason to believe that their defeat was really
an escape, and that victory would have been a disaster. A
reform, such as, in the days of Elizabeth, would have united
the great body of English Protestants, would, in the days of
William, have alienated more hearts than it would have conciliated. The schism which the oaths had produced was, as
yet, insignificant. Innovations such as those proposed by
the Royal Commissioners would have given it a terrible importance. As yet a layman, though he might think the proceedings of the Convention unjustifiable, and though he
might applaud the virtue of the nonjuring clergy, still continued to sit under the accustomed pulpit, and to kneel at
the accustomed altar. But if, just at this conjuncture, while
his mind was irritated by what he thought the wrong done
to his favourite divines, and while he was perhaps doubting

---

* That there was such a jealousy as I
have described is admitted in the pamphlet entitled Vox Cleri. " Some country
ministers, now of the Convocation, do
now see in what great ease and plenty
the City ministers live, who have their
readers and lecturers, and frequent supplies, and sometimes tarry in the vestry
till prayers be ended, and have great
dignities in the Church, besides their
rich parishes in the City." The author
of this tract, once widely celebrated, was
Thomas Long, proctor for the clergy of
the diocese of Exeter. In another pamphlet, published at this time, the rural
clergymen are said to have seen with an
evil eye their London brethren refresh-
ing themselves with sack after preaching.
Several satirical allusions to the fable of
the Town Mouse and the Country Mouse
will be found in the pamphlets of that
winter.

whether he ought not to follow them, his ears and eyes had
been shocked by changes in the worship to which he was
fondly attached, if the compositions of the doctors of the
Jerusalem Chamber had taken the place of the old collects, if
he had seen clergymen without surplices carrying the chalice
and the paten up and down the aisle to seated communicants,
the tie which bound him to the Established Church would
have been dissolved. He would have repaired to some nonjuring assembly, where the service which he loved was performed without mutilation. The new sect, which as yet
consisted almost exclusively of priests, would soon have been
swelled by numerous and large congregations; and in those
congregations would have been found a much greater proportion of the opulent, of the highly descended, and of the highly
educated, than any other body of dissenters could show.
The episcopal schismatics, thus reinforced, would probably
have been as formidable to the new King and his successors
as ever the Puritan schismatics had been to the princes of
the House of Stuart. It is an indisputable and a most
instructive fact, that we are, in a great measure, indebted for
the civil and religious liberty which we enjoy to the pertinacity with which the High Church party, in the Convocation
of 1689, refused even to deliberate on any plan of Comprehension.*

* Burnet, ii. 33, 34. The best narratives of what passed in this Convocation
are the Historical Account appended to
the second edition of Vox Cleri, and the
passage in Kennet's History to which I
have already referred the reader. The
former narrative is by a very high churchman, the latter by a very low churchman.
Those who are desirous of obtaining
fuller information must consult the contemporary pamphlets. Among them are
Vox Populi; Vox Laici; Vox Regis et
Regni; the Healing Attempt; the Letter
to a Friend, by Dean Prideaux; the Letter from a Minister in the Country to a
Member of the Convocation; the Answer
to the Merry Answer to Vox Cleri; the
Remarks from the Country upon two
Letters relating to the Convocation; the
Vindication of the Letters in answer to
Vox Cleri; the Answer to the Country
Minister's Letter. All these tracts ap-
peared late in 1689 or early in 1690.

CHAPTER XV.

WHILE the Convocation was wrangling on one side of Old Palace Yard, the Parliament was wrangling even more fiercely on the other. The Houses, which had separated on the twentieth of August, had met again on the nineteenth of October. On the day of meeting an important change struck every eye. Halifax was no longer on the woolsack. He had reason to expect that the persecution, from which he had narrowly escaped in the summer, would be renewed. The events which had taken place during the recess, and especially the disasters of the campaign in Ireland, had furnished his enemies with fresh means of annoyance. His administration had not been successful; and, though his failure was partly to be ascribed to causes against which no human wisdom could have contended, it was also partly to be ascribed to the peculiarities of his temper and his intellect. It was certain that a large party in the Commons would attempt to remove him; and he could no longer depend on the protection of his master. It was natural that a prince who was emphatically a man of action should become weary of a minister who was a man of speculation. Charles, who went to Council as he went to the play, solely to be amused, was delighted with an adviser who had a hundred pleasant and ingenious things to say on both sides of every question. But William had no taste for disquisitions and disputations, however lively and subtle, which occupied much time and led to no conclusion. It was reported, and is not improbable, that on one occasion he could not refrain from expressing in sharp terms at the council board his impatience at what seemed to him a morbid habit of indecision.* Halifax, mortified by his mischances in public life, dejected by domestic calamities, disturbed by apprehensions of an impeachment, and no longer supported by

---

* "Halifax a eu une reprimande sévère publiquement dans le conseil par le Prince d'Orange pour avoir trop balancé."—Avaux to De Croissy, Dublin, June $\frac{18}{28}$. 1689. "His mercurial wit," says Burnet, ii. 4., "was not well suited with the King's phlegm."

royal favour, became sick of public life, and began to pine for the silence and solitude of his seat in Nottinghamshire, an old Cistercian Abbey buried deep among woods. Early in October it was known that he would no longer preside in the Upper House. It was at the same time whispered as a great secret that he meant to retire altogether from business, and that he retained the Privy Seal only till a successor should be named. Chief Baron Atkyns was appointed Speaker of the Lords.*

On some important points there appeared to be no difference of opinion in the legislature. The Commons unanimously resolved that they would stand by the King in the work of reconquering Ireland, and that they would enable him to prosecute with vigour the war against France.† With equal unanimity they voted an extraordinary supply of two millions.‡ It was determined that the greater part of this sum should be levied by an assessment on real property. The rest was to be raised partly by a poll tax, and partly by new duties on tea, coffee, and chocolate. It was proposed that a hundred thousand pounds should be exacted from the Jews; and this proposition was at first favourably received by the House: but difficulties arose. The Jews presented a petition in which they declared that they could not afford to pay such a sum, and that they would rather leave the kingdom than stay there to be ruined. Enlightened politicians could not but perceive that special taxation, laid on a small class which happens to be rich, unpopular, and defenceless, is really confiscation, and must ultimately impoverish rather than enrich the State. After some discussion, the Jew tax was abandoned.§

Supplies voted.

The Bill of Rights, which, in the last Session, had, after causing much altercation between the Houses, been suffered to drop, was again introduced, and was speedily passed. The peers no longer insisted that any person should be designated by name as successor to the crown, if Mary, Anne, and William should all die without posterity. During eleven years nothing more was heard of the claims of the House of Brunswick.

The Bill of Rights passed

The Bill of Rights contained some provisions which deserve

* Clarendon's Diary, Oct. 10. 1689: Lords' Journals, Oct. 19. 1689.
† Commons' Journals, Oct. 24. 1689.
‡ Commons' Journals, Nov. 2. 1689.
§ Commons' Journals, November 7. 19., Dec. 30. 1689. The rule of the House then was that no petition could be received against the imposition of a tax. This rule was, after a very hard fight, rescinded in 1842. The petition of the Jews was not received, and is not mentioned in the Journals. But something may be learned about it from Luttrell's Diary and from Grey's Debates, Nov. 19. 1689.

special mention. The Convention had resolved that it was contrary to the interest of the kingdom to be governed by a Papist, but had prescribed no test which could ascertain whether a prince was or was not a Papist. The defect was now supplied. It was enacted that every English Sovereign should, in full Parliament, and at the coronation, repeat and subscribe the Declaration against Transubstantiation.

It was also enacted that no person who should marry a Papist should be capable of reigning in England, and that, if the Sovereign should marry a Papist, the subject should be absolved from allegiance. Burnet boasts that this part of the Bill of Rights was his work. He had little reason to boast: for a more wretched specimen of legislative workmanship will not easily be found. In the first place, no test is prescribed. Whether the consort of a Sovereign has taken the oath of supremacy, has signed the declaration against transubstantiation, has communicated according to the ritual of the Church of England, are very simple issues of fact. But whether the consort of a Sovereign is or is not a Papist is a question about which people may argue for ever. What is a Papist? The word is not a word of definite signification either in law or in theology. It is merely a popular nickname, and means very different things in different mouths. Is every person a Papist who is willing to concede to the Bishop of Rome a primacy among Christian prelates? If so, James the First, Charles the First, Laud, Heylyn, were Papists.* Or is the appellation to be confined to persons who hold the ultramontane doctrines touching the authority of the Holy See? If so, neither Bossuet nor Pascal was a Papist.

What again is the legal effect of the words which absolve the subject from his allegiance? Is it meant that a person arraigned for high treason may tender evidence to prove that the Sovereign has married a Papist? Would Thistlewood, for example, have been entitled to an acquittal, if he could have proved that King George the Fourth had married Mrs. Fitzherbert, and that Mrs. Fitzherbert was a Papist? It is not easy to believe that any tribunal would have gone into

* James, in the very treatise in which he tried to prove the Pope to be Anti-Christ, says: "For myself, if that were yet the question, I would with all my heart give my consent that the Bishop of Rome should have the first seat." There is a remarkable letter on this subject written by James to Charles and Buckingham, when they were in Spain. Heylyn, speaking of Laud's negotiation with Rome, says: "So that upon the point the Pope was to content himself among us in England with a priority instead of a superiority over other Bishops, and with a primacy instead of a supremacy in these parts of Christendom, which I conceive no man of learning and sobriety would have grudged to grant him."

such a question. Yet to what purpose is it to enact that, in a certain case, the subject shall be absolved from his allegiance, if the tribunal before which he is tried for a violation of his allegiance is not to go into the question whether that case has arisen?

The question of the dispensing power was treated in a very different manner, was fully considered, and was finally settled in the only way in which it could be settled. The Declaration of Right had gone no further than to pronounce that the dispensing power, as of late exercised, was illegal. That a certain dispensing power belonged to the Crown was a proposition sanctioned by authorities and precedents of which even Whig lawyers could not speak without respect: but as to the precise extent of this power hardly any two jurists were agreed; and every attempt to frame a definition had failed. At length by the Bill of Rights the anomalous prerogative which had caused so many fierce disputes was absolutely and for ever taken away.*

In the House of Commons there was, as might have been expected, a series of sharp debates on the misfortunes of the autumn. The negligence or corruption of the Navy Board, the frauds of the contractors, the rapacity of the captains of the King's ships, the losses of the London merchants, were themes for many keen speeches. There was indeed reason for anger. A severe enquiry, conducted by William in person at the Treasury, had just elicited the fact that much of the salt with which the meat furnished to the fleet had been cured had been by accident mixed with galls such as are used for the purpose of making ink. The victuallers threw the blame on the rats, and maintained that the provisions thus seasoned, though certainly disagreeable to the palate, were not injurious to health.† The Commons were in no temper to listen to such excuses. Several persons who had been concerned in cheating the government and poisoning the seamen were taken into custody by the Serjeant.‡ But no censure was passed on the chief offender, Torrington; nor does it appear that a single voice was raised against him. He had personal friends in both parties. He had many popular qualities. Even his vices were not those which excite public hatred. The people readily forgave a courageous openhanded sailor for being too fond of his bottle, his boon companions, and his mistresses, and did not sufficiently con-

Enquiry into naval abuses.

---

* Stat. 1 W. & M. sess. 2. c. 2.
† Treasury Minute Book, Nov. 3. 1689.
‡ Commons' Journals and Grey's Debates, Nov. 13, 14. 18, 19. 23. 28. 1689.

sider how great must be the perils of a country of which the
safety depends on a man sunk in indolence, stupified by wine,
enervated by licentiousness, ruined by prodigality, and enslaved by sycophants and harlots.

Enquiry
into the
conduct of
the Irish
war.

The sufferings of the army in Ireland called forth strong
expressions of sympathy and indignation. The Commons did
justice to the firmness and wisdom with which Schomberg had
conducted the most arduous of all campaigns. That he had
not achieved more was attributed chiefly to the villany of the
Commissariat. The pestilence itself, it was said, would have
been no serious calamity if it had not been aggravated by the
wickedness of man. The disease had generally spared those
who had warm garments and bedding, and had swept away by
thousands those who were thinly clad and who slept on the
wet ground. Immense sums had been drawn out of the Treasury: yet the pay of the troops was in arrear. Hundreds of
horses, tens of thousands of shoes, had been paid for by the
public: yet the baggage was left behind for want of beasts to
draw it; and the soldiers were marching barefoot through the
mire. Seventeen hundred pounds had been charged to the
government for medicines: yet the common drugs with which
every apothecary in the smallest market town was provided
were not to be found in the plaguestricken camp. The cry
against Shales was loud. An address was carried to the
throne, requesting that he might be sent for to England, and
that his accounts and papers might be secured. With this
request the King readily complied: but the Whig majority was
not satisfied. By whom had Shales been recommended for so
important a place as that of Commissary General? He had
been a favourite at Whitehall in the worst times. He had
been zealous for the Declaration of Indulgence. Why had
this creature of James been entrusted with the business of
catering for the army of William? It was proposed by some
of those who were bent on driving all Tories and Trimmers
from office to ask His Majesty by whose advice a man so undeserving of the royal confidence had been employed. The
most moderate and judicious Whigs pointed out the indecency
and impolicy of interrogating the King, and of forcing him
either to accuse his ministers or to quarrel with the representatives of his people. "Advise His Majesty, if you will," said
Somers, "to withdraw his confidence from the counsellors who
recommended this unfortunate appointment. Such advice,
given, as we should probably give it, unanimously, must have
great weight with him. But do not put to him a question

such as no private gentleman would willingly answer. Do not force him, in defence of his own personal dignity, to protect the very men whom you wish him to discard." After a hard fight of two days, and several divisions, the address was carried by a hundred and ninety-five votes to a hundred and forty-six.* The King, as might have been foreseen, coldly refused to turn informer; and the House did not press him further.† To another address, which requested that a Commission might be sent to examine into the state of things in Ireland, William returned a very gracious answer, and desired the Commons to name the Commissioners. The Commons, not to be outdone in courtesy, excused themselves, and left it to His Majesty's wisdom to select the fittest persons.‡

In the midst of the angry debates on the Irish war a pleasing incident produced for a moment goodhumour and unanimity. Walker had arrived in London, and had been received there with boundless enthusiasm. His face was in every print shop. Newsletters describing his person and his demeanour were sent to every corner of the kingdom. Broadsides of prose and verse written in his praise were cried in every street. The Companies of London feasted him splendidly in their halls. The common people crowded to gaze on him wherever he moved, and almost stifled him with rough caresses. Both the Universities offered him the degree of Doctor of Divinity. Some of his admirers advised him to present himself at the palace in that military garb in which he had repeatedly headed the sallies of his fellow townsmen. But, with a better judgment than he sometimes showed, he made his appearance at Hampton Court in the peaceful robe of his profession, was most graciously received, and was presented with an order for five thousand pounds. "And do not think, Doctor," William said, with great benignity, "that I offer you this sum as payment for your services. I assure you that I consider your claims on me as not at all diminished."§

It is true that amidst the general applause the voice of detraction made itself heard. The defenders of Londonderry were men of two nations and of two religions. During the siege, hatred of the Irishry had held together all Saxons; and

Marginal note: Reception of Walker in England.

* Commons' Journals and Grey's Debates, Nov. 26. and 27. 1689.
† Commons' Journals, November 28. December 2. 1689.
‡ Commons' Journals and Grey's Debates, November 30., December 2. 1689.
§ London Gazette, September 2. 1689;

Observations upon Mr. Walker's Account of the Siege of Londonderry, licensed October 4. 1689; Luttrell's Diary; Mr. J. Mackenzie's Narrative a False Libel, a Defence of Mr. G. Walker written by his Friend in his Absence, 1690.

hatred of Popery had held together all Protestants. But, when the danger was over, the Englishman and the Scotchman, the Episcopalian and the Presbyterian, began to wrangle about the distribution of praises and awards. The dissenting preachers, who had zealously assisted Walker in the hour of peril, complained that, in the account which he had published of the siege, he had, though acknowledging that they had done good service, omitted to mention their names. The complaint was just, and, had it been made in a manner becoming Christians and gentlemen, would probably have produced a considerable effect on the public mind. But Walker's accusers in their resentment disregarded truth and decency, used scurrilous language, brought calumnious accusations which were triumphantly refuted, and thus threw away the advantage which they had possessed. Walker defended himself with moderation and candour. His friends fought his battle with vigour, and retaliated keenly on his assailants. At Edinburgh perhaps the public opinion might have been against him. But in London the controversy seems only to have raised his character. He was regarded as an Anglican divine of eminent merit, who, after having heroically defended his religion against an army of Irish Rapparees, was rabbled by a mob of Scotch Covenanters.*

He presented to the Commons a petition setting forth the destitute condition to which the widows and orphans of some brave men who had fallen during the siege were now reduced. The Commons instantly passed a vote of thanks to him, and resolved to present to the King an address requesting that ten thousand pounds might be distributed among the families whose sufferings had been so touchingly described. The next day it was rumoured about the benches that Walker was in the lobby. He was called in. The Speaker, with great dignity and grace, informed him that the House had made haste to comply with his request, commended him in high terms for having taken on himself to govern and defend a city betrayed by its proper governors and defenders, and charged him to tell those who had fought under him that their fidelity and valour

* Walker's True Account, 1689; An Apology for the Failures charged on the True Account, 1689; Reflections on the Apology, 1689; A Vindication of the True Account by Walker, 1689; Mackenzie's Narrative, 1690; Mr. Mackenzie's Narrative a False Libel, 1690; Dr. Walker's Invisible Champion foyled by Mackenzie, 1690; Welwood's Mercurius Reformatus, Dec. 4. and 11. 1689. The Oxford editor of Burnet's History expresses his surprise at the silence which the Bishop observes about Walker. In the Burnet MS. Harl. 6584. there is an animated panegyric on Walker. Why that panegyric does not appear in the History, I am at a loss to explain.

would always be held in grateful remembrance by the Commons of England.*

About the same time the course of parliamentary business was diversified by another curious and interesting episode, which, like the former, sprang out of the events of the Irish war. In the preceding spring, when every messenger from Ireland brought evil tidings, and when the authority of James was acknowledged in every part of that kingdom, except behind the ramparts of Londonderry and on the banks of Lough Erne, it was natural that Englishmen should remember with how terrible an energy the great Puritan warriors of the preceding generation had crushed the insurrection of the Celtic race. The names of Cromwell, of Ireton, and of the other chiefs of the conquering army, were in many mouths. One of those chiefs, Edmund Ludlow, was still living. At twenty-two he had served as a volunteer in the parliamentary army: at thirty he had risen to the rank of Lieutenant General. He was now old: but the vigour of his mind was unimpaired. His courage was of the truest temper; his understanding strong, but narrow. What he saw he saw clearly: but he saw not much at a glance. In an age of perfidy and levity, he had, amidst manifold temptations and dangers, adhered firmly to the principles of his youth. His enemies could not deny that his life had been consistent, and that with the same spirit with which he had stood up against the Stuarts he had stood up against the Cromwells. There was but a single blemish on his fame: but that blemish, in the opinion of the great majority of his countrymen, was one for which no merit could compensate and which no time could efface. His name and seal were on the death warrant of Charles the First.

After the Restoration, Ludlow found a refuge on the shores of the Lake of Geneva. He was accompanied thither by another member of the High Court of Justice, John Lisle, the husband of that Alice Lisle whose death has left a lasting stain on the memory of James the Second. But even in Switzerland the regicides were not safe. A large price was set on their heads; and a succession of Irish adventurers, inflamed by national and religious animosity, attempted to earn the bribe. Lisle fell by the hand of one of these assassins. But Ludlow escaped unhurt from all the machinations of his enemies. A small knot of vehement and determined Whigs regarded him with a veneration, which increased as years rolled away, and left him almost the only survivor, certainly the most illustrious

Edmund Ludlow.

* Commons' Journals. November 18. and 19. 1689; and Grey's Debates.

survivor, of a mighty race of men, the conquerors in a terrible
civil war, the judges of a king, the founders of a republic.
More than once he had been invited by the enemies of the
House of Stuart to leave his asylum, to become their captain,
and to give the signal for rebellion : but he had wisely refused
to take any part in the desperate enterprises which the
Wildmans and Fergusons were never weary of planning.*

The Revolution opened a new prospect to him.   The right
of the people to resist oppression, a right which, during many
years, no man could assert without exposing himself to ecclesiastical anathemas and to civil penalties, had been solemnly
recognised by the Estates of the realm, and had been proclaimed by Garter King at Arms on the very spot where the
memorable scaffold had been set up forty years before.   James
had not, indeed, like Charles, died the death of a traitor.
Yet the punishment of the son might seem to differ from the
punishment of the father rather in degree than in principle.
Those who had recently waged war on a tyrant, who had
turned him out of his palace, who had frightened him out of
his country, who had deprived him of his crown, might perhaps think that the crime of going one step further had been
sufficiently expiated by thirty years of banishment.   Ludlow's
admirers, some of whom appear to have been in high public
situations, assured him that he might safely venture over,
nay, that he might expect to be sent in high command to
Ireland, where his name was still cherished by his old soldiers
and by their children.†   He came ; and early in September
it was known that he was in London.‡   But it soon appeared
that he and his friends had misunderstood the temper of the
English people.   By all, except a small extreme section of the
Whig party, the act, in which he had borne a part never to
be forgotten, was regarded, not merely with the disapprobation due to a great violation of law and justice, but with
horror such as even the Gunpowder Plot had not excited.   The
absurd and almost impious service which is still read in our
churches on the thirtieth of January had produced in the
minds of the vulgar a strange association of ideas.   The
sufferings of Charles were confounded with the sufferings of
the Redeemer of mankind ; and every regicide was a Judas,
a Caiaphas, or a Herod.   It was true that, when Ludlow sate

* Wade's Confession, Harl. MS. 6845.
† See the Preface to the First Edition
of his Memoirs, Vevay, 1698.
‡ " Colonel Ludlow, an old Oliverian,

and one of King Charles the First his
Judges, is arrived lately in this kingdom
from Switzerland."   Luttrell's Diary,
September 1689.

on the tribunal in Westminster Hall, he was an ardent enthusiast of twenty-eight, and that he now returned from exile a greyheaded and wrinkled man in his seventieth year. Perhaps, therefore, if he had been content to live in close retirement, and to shun places of public resort, even zealous Royalists might not have grudged the old Republican a grave in his native soil. But he had no thought of hiding himself. It was soon rumoured that one of those murderers, who had brought on England guilt, for which she annually, in sackcloth and ashes, implored God not to enter into judgment with her, was strutting about the streets of her capital and boasting that he should ere long command her armies. His lodgings, it was said, were the head quarters of the most noted enemies of monarchy and episcopacy.* The subject was brought before the House of Commons. The Tory members called loudly for justice on the traitor. None of the Whigs ventured to say a word in his defence. One or two faintly expressed a doubt whether the fact of his return had been proved by evidence such as would warrant a parliamentary proceeding. This objection was disregarded. It was resolved, without a division, that the King should be requested to issue a proclamation for the apprehending of Ludlow. Seymour presented the address; and the King promised to do what was asked. Some days however elapsed before the proclamation appeared.† Ludlow had time to make his escape, and hid himself in his Alpine retreat, never again to emerge. English travellers are still taken to see his house close to the lake, and his tomb in a church among the vineyards which overlook the little town of Vevay. On the house was formerly legible an inscription purporting that to him to whom God is a father every land is a fatherland ‡; and the epitaph on the tomb still attests the feelings with which the stern old Puritan to the last regarded the people of Ireland and the House of Stuart.

Tories and Whigs had concurred, or had affected to concur, in paying honour to Walker and in putting a brand on Ludlow. But the feud between the two parties was more bitter than ever. The King had entertained a hope that, during the recess, the animosities which had in the preceding session

Violence of the Whigs,

---

* Third Caveat against the Whigs, 1712.

† Commons' Journals, November 6. and 8. 1689; Grey's Debates; London Gazette, November 18.

‡ "Omne solum forti patria, quia patris." See Addison's Travels. It is a remarkable circumstance that Addison, though a Whig, speaks of Ludlow in language which would better have become a Tory, and sneers at the inscription as cant.

prevented an Act of Indemnity from passing would have been mitigated. On the day on which the Houses reassembled, he had pressed them earnestly to put an end to the fear and discord which could never cease to exist, while great numbers held their property and their liberty, and not a few even their lives, by an uncertain tenure. His exhortation proved of no effect. October, November, December passed away; and nothing was done. An Indemnity Bill indeed had been brought in, and read once : but it had ever since lain neglected on the table of the House.* Vindictive as had been the mood in which the Whigs had left Westminster, the mood in which they returned was more vindictive still. Smarting from old sufferings, drunk with recent prosperity, burning with implacable resentment, confident of irresistible strength, they were not less rash and headstrong than in the days of the Exclusion Bill. Sixteen hundred and eighty was come again. Again all compromise was rejected. Again the voices of the wisest and most upright friends of liberty were drowned by the clamour of hotheaded and designing agitators. Again moderation was despised as cowardice, or execrated as treachery. All the lessons taught by a cruel experience were forgotten. The very same men who had expiated, by years of humiliation, of imprisonment, of penury, of exile, the folly with which they had misused the advantage given them by the Popish plot, now misused with equal folly the advantage given them by the Revolution. The second madness would, in all probability, like the first, have ended in their proscription, dispersion, decimation, but for the magnanimity and wisdom of that great prince, who, bent on fulfilling his mission, and insensible alike to flattery and to outrage, coldly and inflexibly saved them in their own despite.

Impeachments.

It seemed that nothing but blood would satisfy them. The aspect and the temper of the House of Commons reminded men of the time of the ascendency of Oates; and that nothing might be wanting to the resemblance, Oates himself was there. As a witness, indeed, he could now render no service : but he had caught the scent of carnage, and came to gloat on the butchery in which he could no longer take an active part. His loathsome features were again daily seen, and his well known " Ah Laard, ah Laard !" was again daily heard in the lobbies and in the gallery.† The House fell first on the renegades of the late reign. Of those renegades the Earls of Peterborough and Salisbury were the highest in

* Commons' Journals, Nov. 1. 7. 1689.   † Roger North's Life of Dudley North.

1ank, but were also the lowest in intellect : for Salisbury had always been an idiot; and Peterborough had long been a dotard. It was however resolved by the Commons that both had, by joining the Church of Rome, committed high treason, and that both should be impeached.* A message to that effect was sent to the Lords. Poor old Peterborough was instantly taken into custody, and was sent tottering on a crutch, and wrapped up in woollen stuffs, to the Tower. The next day Salisbury was brought to the bar of his peers. He muttered something about his youth and his foreign education, and was then sent to bear Peterborough company.† The Commons had meanwhile passed on to offenders of humbler station and better understanding. Sir Edward Hales was brought before them. He had doubtless, by holding office in defiance of the Test Act, incurred heavy penalties. But these penalties fell far short of what the revengeful spirit of the victorious party demanded; and he was committed as a traitor.‡ Then Obadiah Walker was led in. He behaved with a pusillanimity and disingenuousness which deprived him of all claim to respect or pity. He protested that he had never changed his religion, that his opinions had always been and still were those of some highly respectable divines of the Church of England, and that there were points on which he differed from the Papists. In spite of this quibbling, he was pronounced guilty of high treason, and sent to prison.§ Then Castelmaine was put to the bar, interrogated, and committed under a warrant which charged him with the capital crime of trying to reconcile the kingdom to the Church of Rome.‖

In the meantime the Lords had appointed a Committee to enquire who were answerable for the deaths of Russell, of Sidney, and of some other eminent Whigs. Of this Committee, which was popularly called the Murder Committee, the Earl of Stamford, a Whig who had been deeply concerned in the plots formed by his party against the Stuarts, was chairman.¶ The books of the Council were inspected: the clerks of the Council were examined: some facts disgraceful to the Judges, to the Solicitors of the Treasury, to the witnesses for the Crown, and to the keepers of the state prisons, were elicited: but about the packing of the juries no evidence

Committee of Murder.

---

* Commons' Journals, Oct. 26. 1689.
† Lords' Journals, October 26. and 27. 1689.
‡ Commons' Journals, Oct. 26. 1689.
§ Commons' Journals, Oct. 26. 1689; Wood's Athenæ Oxonienses; Dod's

Church History, VIII. ii. 3.
‖ Commons' Journals, October 28. 1689. The proceedings will be found in the collection of State Trials.
¶ Lords' Journals, Nov. 2. and 6. 1689.

could be obtained. The Sheriffs kept their own counsel. Sir Dudley North, in particular, underwent a most severe cross examination with characteristic clearness of head and firmness of temper, and steadily asserted that he had never troubled himself about the political opinions of the persons whom he put on any panel, but had merely enquired whether they were substantial citizens. He was undoubtedly lying; and so some of the Whig peers told him in very plain words and in very loud tones: but, though they were morally certain of his guilt, they could find no proofs which would support a criminal charge against him. The indelible stain however remains on his memory, and is still a subject of lamentation to those who, while loathing his dishonesty and cruelty, cannot forget that he was one of the most original, profound, and accurate thinkers of his age.*

Halifax, more fortunate than Dudley North, was completely cleared, not only from legal, but also from moral guilt. He was the chief object of attack; and yet a severe examination brought nothing to light that was not to his honour. Tillotson was called as a witness. He swore that he had been the channel of communication between Halifax and Russell when Russell was a prisoner in the Tower. "My Lord Halifax," said the Doctor, "showed a very compassionate concern for my Lord Russell; and my Lord Russell charged me with his last thanks for my Lord Halifax's humanity and kindness." It was proved that the unfortunate Duke of Monmouth had borne similar testimony to Halifax's good nature. One hostile witness indeed was produced, John Hampden, whose mean supplications and enormous bribes had saved his neck from the halter. He was now a powerful and prosperous man: he was a leader of the dominant party in the House of Commons; and yet he was one of the most unhappy beings on the face of the earth. The recollection of the pitiable figure which he had made at the bar of the Old Bailey embittered his temper and impelled him to avenge himself without mercy on those who had directly or indirectly contributed to his humiliation. Of all the Whigs he was the most intolerant and the most obstinately hostile to all plans of amnesty. The consciousness that he had disgraced himself made him jealous of his dignity and quick to take offence. He constantly paraded his services and his sufferings, as if he hoped that this ostentatious display would hide from others the stain which nothing could hide from himself. Having during

Malevolence of John Hampden.

---

* Lords' Journals, Dec. 20. 1689; Life of Dudley North.

John Hampden

many months harangued vehemently against Halifax in the House of Commons, he now came to swear against Halifax before the Lords. The scene was curious. The witness represented himself as having saved his country, as having planned the Revolution, as having placed Their Majesties on the throne. He then gave evidence intended to show that his life had been endangered by the machinations of the Lord Privy Seal: but that evidence missed the mark at which it was aimed, and recoiled on him from whom it proceeded. Hampden was forced to acknowledge that he had sent his wife to implore the intercession of the man whom he was now persecuting. "Is it not strange," asked Halifax, "that you should have requested the good offices of one whose arts had brought your head into peril?" "Not at all," said Hampden: "to whom was I to apply except to the men who were in power? I applied to Lord Jeffreys: I applied to Father Petre; and I paid them six thousand pounds for their services." "But did Lord Halifax take any money?" "No: I cannot say that he did." "And, Mr. Hampden, did not you afterwards send your wife to thank him for his kindness?" "Yes: I believe I did," answered Hampden: "but I know of no solid effects of that kindness. If there were any, I should be obliged to my Lord to tell me what they were." Disgraceful as had been the appearance which this degenerate heir of an illustrious name had made at the Old Bailey, the appearance which he made before the Committee of Murder was more disgraceful still.* It is pleasing to know that a person who had been far more cruelly wronged than he, but whose nature differed widely from his, the nobleminded Lady Russell, remonstrated against the injustice with which the extreme Whigs treated Halifax.†

The malice of John Hampden, however, was unwearied and unabashed. A few days later, in a committee of the whole House of Commons, on the state of the nation, he made a bitter speech, in which he ascribed all the disasters of the year to the influence of the men who had, in the days of the Exclusion Bill, been censured by Parliaments, of the men who had attempted to mediate between James and William. The King, he said, ought to dismiss from his counsels and presence all the three noblemen who had been sent to nego-

---

* The report is in the Lords' Journals, Dec. 20. 1689. Hampden's examination was on the 18th of November.

† This, I think, is clear from a letter of Lady Montague to Lady Russell, dated Dec. 23. 1689, three days after the Committee of Murder had reported.

tiate with him at Hungerford. He went on to speak of the
danger of employing men of republican principles. He doubtless alluded to the chief object of his implacable malignity.
For Halifax, though from temper averse to violent changes, was
well known to be in speculation a republican, and often talked,
with much ingenuity and pleasantry, against hereditary
monarchy. The only effect, however, of the reflection now
thrown on him was to call forth a roar of derision. That a
Hampden, that the grandson of the great leader of the Long
Parliament, that a man who boasted of having conspired with
Algernon Sidney against the royal House, should use the
word republican as a term of reproach! When the storm of
laughter had subsided, several members stood up to vindicate
the accused statesmen. Seymour declared that, much as he
disapproved of the manner in which the administration had
lately been conducted, he could not concur in the vote which
John Hampden had proposed. "Look where you will," he
said, " to Ireland, to Scotland, to the navy, to the army, you
will find abundant proofs of mismanagement. If the war is
still to be conducted by the same hands, we can expect nothing but a recurrence of the same disasters. But I am not
prepared to proscribe men for the best thing that they ever
did in their lives, to proscribe men for attempting to avert a
revolution by timely mediation." It was justly said by
another speaker that Halifax and Nottingham had been sent
to the Dutch camp because they possessed the confidence of
the nation, because they were universally known to be hostile
to the dispensing power, to the Popish religion, and to the
French ascendency. It was at length resolved that the King
should be requested in general terms to find out and to remove
the authors of the late miscarriages.* A committee was
appointed to prepare an address. John Hampden was chairman, and drew up a representation in terms so bitter that,
when it was reported to the House, his own father expressed
disapprobation, and one member exclaimed: "This an address! It is a libel." After a sharp debate, the Address was
recommitted, and was not again mentioned.†

Indeed, the animosity which a large part of the House had
felt against Halifax was beginning to abate. It was known
that, though he had not yet formally delivered up the Privy
Seal, he had ceased to be a confidential adviser of the Crown.
The power which he had enjoyed during the first months of

* Commons' Journals, Dec. 14. 1689;   † Commons' Journals, Dec. 21.; Grey's
Grey's Debates ; Boyer's Life of William. Debates ; Oldmixon.

the reign of William and Mary had passed to the more daring, more unscrupulous, and more practical Caermarthen, against whose influence Shrewsbury contended in vain. Personally Shrewsbury stood high in the royal favour: but he was a leader of the Whigs, and, like all leaders of parties, was frequently pushed forward against his will by those who seemed to follow him. He was himself inclined to a mild and moderate policy: but he had not sufficient firmness to withstand the clamorous importunity with which such politicians as John Howe and John Hampden demanded vengeance on their enemies. His advice had therefore, at this time, little weight with his master, who neither loved the Tories nor trusted them, but who was fully determined not to proscribe them.

Meanwhile the Whigs, conscious that they had lately sunk in the opinion both of the King and of the nation, resolved on making a bold and crafty attempt to become independent of both. A perfect account of that attempt cannot be constructed out of the scanty and widely dispersed materials which have come down to us. Yet the story, as it may still be put together, is both interesting and instructive.

A bill for restoring the rights of those corporations which had surrendered their charters to the Crown during the last two reigns had been brought into the House of Commons, had been received with general applause by men of all parties, had been read twice, and had been referred to a select committee, of which Somers was chairman. On the second of January Somers brought up the report. The attendance of Tories was scanty; for, as no important discussion was expected, many country gentlemen had left town, and were keeping a merry Christmas by the blazing chimneys of their manor houses. The muster of zealous Whigs was strong. As soon as the bill had been reported, Sacheverell, renowned in the stormy Parliaments of the reign of Charles the Second as one of the ablest and keenest of the Exclusionists, stood up and moved to add a clause providing that every municipal functionary who had in any manner been a party to the surrendering of the franchises of a borough should be incapable for seven years of holding any office in that borough. The constitution of almost every corporate town in England had been remodelled during that hot fit of loyalty which followed the detection of the Rye House Plot; and, in almost every corporate town, the voice of the Tories had been for delivering up the charter, and for trusting everything to the paternal

1690.
The Corporation Bill.

care of the Sovereign. The effect of Sacheverell's clause, therefore, was to make some thousands of the most opulent and highly considered men in the kingdom incapable, during seven years, of bearing any part in the government of the places in which they resided, and to secure to the Whig party, during seven years, an overwhelming influence in borough elections.

The minority exclaimed against the gross injustice of passing, rapidly and by surprise, at a season when London was empty, a law of the highest importance, a law which retrospectively inflicted a severe penalty on many hundreds of respectable gentlemen, a law which would call forth the strongest passions in every town from Berwick to Saint Ives, a law which must have a serious effect on the composition of the House itself. Common decency required at least an adjournment. An adjournment was moved: but the motion was rejected by a hundred and twenty-seven votes to eighty-nine. The question was then put that Sacheverell's clause should stand part of the bill, and was carried by a hundred and thirty-three to sixty-eight. Sir Robert Howard immediately moved that every person who, being under Sacheverell's clause disqualified for municipal office, should presume to take any such office, should forfeit five hundred pounds, and should be for life incapable of holding any public employment whatever. The Tories did not venture to divide.* The rules of the House put it in the power of a minority to obstruct the progress of a bill; and this was assuredly one of the very rare occasions on which that power would have been with great propriety exerted. It does not appear however that the parliamentary tacticians of the seventeenth century were aware of the extent to which a small number of members can, without violating any form, retard the course of business.

It was immediately resolved that the bill, enlarged by Sacheverell's and Howard's clauses, should be engrossed. The most vehement Whigs were bent on finally passing it within forty-eight hours. The Lords, indeed, were not likely to regard it very favourably. But it should seem that some desperate men were prepared to withhold the supplies till it should pass, nay, even to tack it to the bill of supply, and thus to place the Upper House under the necessity of either consenting to a vast proscription of the Tories or refusing to the govern-

* Commons' Journals, Jan. 2. 16$\frac{89}{90}$.

ment the means of carrying on the war.* There were Whigs, however, honest enough to wish that fair play should be given to the hostile party, and prudent enough to know that an advantage obtained by violence and cunning could not be permanent. These men insisted that at least a week should be suffered to elapse before the third reading, and carried their point. Their less scrupulous associates complained bitterly that the good cause was betrayed. What new laws of war were these? Why was chivalrous courtesy to be shown to foes who thought no stratagem immoral, and who had never given quarter? And what had been done that was not in strict accordance with the law of Parliament? That law knew nothing of short notices and long notices, of thin houses and full houses. It was the business of a representative of the people to be in his place. If he chose to shoot and guzzle at his country seat when important business was under consideration at Westminster, what right had he to murmur because more upright and laborious servants of the public passed, in his absence, a bill which appeared to them necessary to the public safety? As however a postponement of a few days appeared to be inevitable, those who had intended to gain the victory by stealing a march now disclaimed that intention. They solemnly assured the King, who could not help showing some displeasure at their conduct, and who felt much more displeasure than he showed, that they had owed nothing to surprise, and that they were quite certain of a majority in the fullest house. Sacheverell is said to have declared with great warmth that he would stake his seat on the issue, and that if he found himself mistaken he would never show his face in Parliament again. Indeed, the general opinion at first was that the Whigs would win the day. But it soon became clear that the fight would be a hard one. The mails had carried out along all the high roads the tidings that, on the second of January, the Commons had agreed to a retrospective penal law against the whole Tory party, and that, on the tenth, that law would be considered for the last time. The whole kingdom was moved from Northumberland to Cornwall. A hundred knights and squires left their halls hung with mistletoe and holly, and their boards groaning with brawn and plum porridge, and rode up post to town, cursing the

---

* Thus, I think, must be understood some remarkable words in a letter written by William to Portland, on the day after Sacheverell's bold and unexpected move. William calculates the amount of the supplies and then says: "S'ils n'y mettent des conditions que vous savez, c'est une bonne affaire: mais les Wigges sont si glorieux d'avoir vaincu qu'ils entreprendront tout."

short days, the cold weather, the miry roads, and the villanous Whigs. The Whigs, too, brought up reinforcements, but not to the same extent; for the clauses were generally unpopular, and not without good cause. Assuredly no reasonable man of any party will deny that the Tories, in surrendering to the Crown all the municipal franchises of the realm, and, with those franchises, the power of altering the constitution of the House of Commons, committed a great fault. But in that fault the nation itself had been an accomplice. If the Mayors and Aldermen whom it was now proposed to punish had, when the tide of loyal enthusiasm ran high, sturdily refused to comply with the wish of their Sovereign, they would have been pointed at in the street as Roundhead knaves, preached at by the Rector, lampooned in ballads, and probably burned in effigy before their own doors. That a community should be hurried into errors alternately by fear of tyranny and by fear of anarchy is doubtless a great evil. But the remedy for that evil is not to punish for such errors some persons who have merely erred with the rest, and who have since repented with the rest. Nor ought it to have been forgotten that the offenders against whom Sacheverell's clause was directed had, in 1688, made large atonement for the misconduct of which they had been guilty in 1683. They had, as a class, stood up firmly against the dispensing power; and most of them had actually been turned out of their municipal offices by James for refusing to support his policy. It is not strange therefore that the attempt to inflict on all these men without exception a degrading punishment should have raised such a storm of public indignation as many Whig members of parliament were unwilling to face.

As the decisive conflict drew near, and as the muster of the Tories became hourly stronger and stronger, the uneasiness of Sacheverell and of his confederates increased. They found that they could hardly hope for a complete victory. They must make some concession. They must propose to recommit the bill. They must declare themselves willing to consider whether any distinction could be made between the chief offenders and the multitudes who had been misled by evil example. But as the spirit of one party fell the spirit of the other rose. The Tories, glowing with resentment which was but too just, were resolved to listen to no terms of compromise.

The tenth of January came; and, before the late daybreak of that season, the House was crowded. More than a hun-

dred and sixty members had come up to town within a week.
From dawn till the candles had burned down to their sockets
the ranks kept unbroken order: and few members left their
seats except for a minute to take a crust of bread or a glass
of claret. Messengers were in waiting to carry the result to
Kensington, where William, though shaken by a violent
cough, sate up till midnight, anxiously expecting the news,
and writing to Portland, whom he had sent on an important
mission to the Hague.

The only remaining account of the debate is defective and
confused: but from that account it appears that the excitement was great. Sharp things were said. One young Whig
member used language so hot that he was in danger of being
called to the bar. Some reflections were thrown on the
Speaker for allowing too much licence to his own friends.
But in truth it mattered little whether he called transgressors
to order or not. The House had long been quite unmanageable: and veteran members bitterly regretted the old gravity
of debate and the old authority of the chair.* That Somers
disapproved of the violence of the party to which he belonged
may be inferred, both from the whole course of his public
life, and from the very significant fact that, though he had
charge of the Corporation Bill, he did not move the penal
clauses, but left that ungracious office to men more impetuous
and less sagacious than himself. He did not however abandon his allies in this emergency, but spoke for them, and tried
to make the best of a very bad case. The House divided
several times. On the first division a hundred and seventy-
four voted with Sacheverell, a hundred and seventy-nine
against him. Still the battle was stubbornly kept up; but
the majority increased from five to ten, from ten to twelve,
and from twelve to eighteen. Then at length, after a stormy
sitting of fourteen hours, the Whigs yielded. It was near
midnight when, to the unspeakable joy and triumph of the
Tories, the clerk tore away from the parchment on which the
bill had been engrossed the odious clauses of Sacheverell and
Howard.†

* "The authority of the chair, the
awe and reverence to order, and the
due method of debates being irrecoverably lost by the disorder and tumul-
tuousness of the House."—Sir J. Trevor
to the King, Appendix to Dalrymple's
Memoirs, Part ii. Book 4.

† Commons' Journals, Jan. 10. 16$\frac{89}{90}$.
I have done my best to frame an account

of this contest out of very defective
materials. Burnet's narrative contains
more blunders than lines. He evidently
trusted to his memory, and was completely deceived by it. My chief authorities are the Journals; Grey's Debates;
William's Letters to Portland; the Despatches of Van Citters; a Letter concerning the Disabling Clauses, lately

Debates
on the
Indemnity
Bill.

Emboldened by this great victory, the Tories made an attempt to push forward the Indemnity Bill which had lain many weeks neglected on the table.* But the Whigs, notwithstanding their recent defeat, were still the majority of the House; and many members, who had shrunk from the unpopularity which they would have incurred by supporting the Sacheverell clause and the Howard clause, were perfectly willing to assist in retarding the general pardon. They still propounded their favourite dilemma. How, they asked, was it possible to defend this project of amnesty without condemning the Revolution? Could it be contended that crimes which had been grave enough to justify rebellion had not been grave enough to deserve punishment? And, if those crimes were of such magnitude that they could justly be visited on the Sovereign whom the Constitution had exempted from responsibility, on what principle was immunity to be granted to his advisers and tools, who were beyond all doubt responsible? One facetious member put this argument in a singular form. He contrived to place in the Speaker's chair a paper which, when examined, appeared to be a Bill of Indemnity for King James, with a sneering preamble about the mercy which had, since the Revolution, been extended to more heinous offenders, and about the indulgence due to a King, who, in oppressing his people, had only acted after the fashion of all Kings.†

On the same day on which this mock Bill of Indemnity disturbed the gravity of the Commons, it was moved that the House should go into Committee on the real Bill. The Whigs threw the motion out by a hundred and ninety-three votes to a hundred and fifty-six. They then proceeded to

offered to the House of Commons, for regulating Corporations, 1690; The True Friends to Corporations vindicated, in an answer to a letter concerning the Disabling Clauses, 1690; and Some Queries concerning the Election of Members for the ensuing Parliament, 1690. To this last pamphlet is appended a list of those who voted for the Sacheverell clause. See also Clarendon's Diary, Jan. 10. 16$\frac{89}{90}$. and the Third Part of the Caveat against the Whigs, 1712. I will quote the last sentences of William's Letter of the 10th of January. The news of the first division only had reached Kensington. "Il est à présent onze eures de nuit, et à dix eures la Chambre Basse estoit encore ensemble. Ainsi je ne vous puis escrire par cette ordinaire l'issue de l'affaire. Les previos

questions les Tories l'ont emporté de cinq vois. Ainsi vous pouvez voir que la chose est bien disputée. J'ay si grand somiel, et mon toux m'incomode que je ne vous en saurez dire d'avantage. Jusques à mourir à vous."

On the same night Van Citters wrote to the States General. The debate, he said, had been very sharp. The design of the Whigs, whom he calls the Presbyterians, had been nothing less than to exclude their opponents from all offices, and to obtain for themselves the exclusive possession of power.

* Commons' Journals, January 11. 16$\frac{89}{90}$.

† Luttrell's Diary, Jan. 16. 1690; Van Citters to the States General, Jan. $\frac{21}{31}$.

resolve that a bill of pains and penalties against delinquents should be forthwith brought in, and engrafted on the Bill of Indemnity.*

A few hours later a vote passed which showed more clearly than anything that had yet taken place how little chance there was that the public mind would be speedily quieted by an amnesty. Few persons stood higher in the estimation of the Tory party than Sir Robert Sawyer. He was a man of ample fortune and aristocratical connections, of orthodox opinions and regular life, an able and experienced lawyer, a well read scholar, and, in spite of a little pomposity, a good speaker. He had been Attorney General at the time of the detection of the Rye House Plot: he had been employed for the Crown in the prosecutions which followed; and he had conducted those prosecutions with an eagerness which would, in our time, be called cruelty by all parties, but which, in his own time, and to his own party, seemed to be merely laudable zeal. His friends indeed asserted that he was conscientious even to scrupulosity in matters of life and death †: but this is an eulogy which persons who bring the feelings of the nineteenth century to the study of the State Trials of the seventeenth century will have some difficulty in understanding. The best excuse which can be made for this part of his life is that the stain of innocent blood was common to him with almost all the eminent public men of those evil days. When we blame him for prosecuting Russell, we must not forget that Russell had prosecuted Stafford.

Great as Sawyer's offences were, he had made great atonement for them. He had stood up manfully against Popery and despotism: he had, in the very presence chamber, positively refused to draw warrants in contravention of Acts of Parliament: he had resigned his lucrative office rather than appear in Westminster Hall as the champion of the dispensing power: he had been the leading counsel for the seven Bishops; and he had, on the day of their trial, done his duty ably, honestly, and fearlessly. He was therefore a favourite with High Churchmen, and might be thought to have fairly earned his pardon from the Whigs. But the Whigs were not in a pardoning mood; and Sawyer was now called to account for his conduct in the case of Sir Thomas Armstrong.

If Armstrong was not belied, he was deep in the worst secrets of the Rye House Plot, and was one of those who

Marginal note: Case of Sir Robert Sawyer.

* Commons' Journals, Jan. 16. 16⁸⁹⁄₉₀.   † Roger North's Life of Guildford.

undertook to slay the two royal brothers. When the conspiracy was discovered, he fled to the Continent and was outlawed. The magistrates of Leyden were induced by a bribe to deliver him up. He was hurried on board of an English ship, carried to London, and brought before the King's Bench. Sawyer moved the Court to award execution on the outlawry. Armstrong represented that a year had not yet elapsed since he had been outlawed, and that, by an Act passed in the reign of Edward the Sixth, an outlaw who yielded himself within the year was entitled to plead Not Guilty, and to put himself on his country. To this it was answered that Armstrong had not yielded himself, that he had been dragged to the bar a prisoner, and that he had no right to claim a privilege which was evidently meant to be given only to persons who voluntarily rendered themselves up to public justice. Jeffreys and the other judges unanimously overruled Armstrong's objection, and granted the award of execution. Then followed one of the most terrible of the many terrible scenes which, in those times, disgraced our Courts. The daughter of the unhappy man was at his side. "My Lord," she cried out, " you will not murder my father. This is murdering a man." "How now?" roared the Chief Justice. "Who is this woman? Take her, Marshal. Take her away." She was forced out, crying as she went, "God Almighty's judgments light on you!" "God Almighty's judgments," said Jeffreys, "will light on traitors. Thank God, I am clamour proof." When she was gone, her father again insisted on what he conceived to be his right. "I ask," he said, " only the benefit of the law." "And, by the grace of God, you shall have it," said the judge. "Mr. Sheriff, see that execution be done on Friday next. There is the benefit of the law for you." On the following Friday, Armstrong was hanged, drawn and quartered; and his head was placed over Westminster Hall.*

The insolence and cruelty of Jeffreys excite, even at the distance of so many years, an indignation which makes it difficult to be just to him. Yet a perfectly dispassionate enquirer may perhaps think it by no means clear that the award of execution was illegal. There was no precedent;

* See the account of the proceedings in the collection of State Trials. It has been asserted that I have committed an error here, and that Armstrong's head was placed on Temple Bar. The truth is that one of his quarters was placed on Temple Bar. His head was on Westminster Hall. See Luttrell's Diary, June 1684.

and the words of the Act of Edward the Sixth may, without
any straining, be construed as the Court construed them.
Indeed, had the penalty been only fine and imprisonment,
nobody would have seen anything reprehensible in the proceeding. But to send a man to the gallows as a traitor,
without confronting him with his accusers, without hearing
his defence, solely because a timidity which is perfectly compatible with innocence has impelled him to hide himself,
is surely a violation, if not of any written law, yet of
those great principles to which all laws ought to conform.
The case was brought before the House of Commons. The
orphan daughter of Armstrong came to the bar to demand
vengeance; and a warm debate followed. Sawyer was fiercely
attacked, and strenuously defended. The Tories declared
that he appeared to them to have done only what, as counsel
for the Crown, he was bound to do, and to have discharged
his duty to God, to the King, and to the prisoner. If the
award was legal, nobody was to blame; and if the award was
illegal, the blame lay, not with the Attorney General, but
with the Judges. There would be an end of all liberty of
speech at the bar, if an advocate was to be punished for
making a strictly regular application to a Court, and for
arguing that certain words in a statute were to be understood in a certain sense. The Whigs called Sawyer murderer,
bloodhound, hangman. If the liberty of speech claimed by
advocates meant the liberty of haranguing men to death, it
was high time that the nation should rise up and exterminate
the whole race of lawyers. "Things will never be well
done," said one orator, "till some of that profession be made
examples." "No crime to demand execution!" exclaimed
John Hampden. "We shall be told next that it was no
crime in the Jews to cry out, 'Crucify him.'" A wise and
just man would probably have been of opinion that this was
not a case for severity. Sawyer's conduct might have been,
to a certain extent, culpable: but, if an Act of Indemnity
was to be passed at all, it was to be passed for the benefit of
persons whose conduct had been culpable. The question was
not whether he was guiltless, but whether his guilt was of so
peculiarly black a dye that he ought, notwithstanding all his
sacrifices and services, to be excluded by name from the
mercy which was to be granted to many thousands of offenders. This question calm and impartial judges would probably
have decided in his favour. It was, however, resolved that

he should be excepted from the Indemnity and expelled from the House.*

On the morrow the Bill of Indemnity, now transformed into a Bill of Pains and Penalties, was again discussed. The Whigs consented to refer it to a Committee of the whole House, but proposed to instruct the Committee to begin its labours by making out a list of the offenders who were to be proscribed. The Tories moved the previous question. The House divided : and the Whigs carried their point by a hundred and ninety votes to a hundred and seventy-three.†

The King purposes to retire to Holland.

The King watched these events with painful anxiety. He was weary of his crown. He had tried to do justice to both the contending parties ; but justice would satisfy neither. The Tories hated him for protecting the Dissenters. The Whigs hated him for protecting the Tories. The amnesty seemed to be more remote than when, ten months before, he first recommended it from the throne. The last campaign in Ireland had been disastrous. It might well be that the next campaign would be more disastrous still. The malpractices, which had done more than the exhalations of the marshes of Dundalk to destroy the efficiency of the English troops, were likely to be as monstrous as ever. Every part of the administration was thoroughly disorganised ; and the people were surprised and angry because a foreigner, newly come among them, imperfectly acquainted with them, and constantly thwarted by them, had not, in a year, put the whole machine of government to rights. Most of his ministers, instead of assisting him, were trying to get up addresses and impeachments against each other. Yet if he employed his own countrymen, on whose fidelity and attachment he could rely, a general cry of rage was set up by all the English factions. The knavery of the English Commissariat had destroyed an army ; yet a rumour that he intended to employ an able, experienced, and trusty Commissary from Holland had excited general discontent. The King felt that he could not, while thus situated, render any service to that great cause to which

* Commons' Journals, Jan. 20. 16$\frac{89}{90}$; Grey's Debates, Jan. 18. and 20.
† Commons' Journals, Jan. 21. 16$\frac{89}{90}$. On the same day William wrote thus from Kensington to Portland: "C'est aujourd'hui le grand jour à l'égard du Bill of Indemnité. Selon tout ce que je puis aprendre, il y aura beaucoup de chaleur, et rien déterminer; et de la manière que la chose est entourré, il n'y a point d'aparence que cette affaire viene à aucune conclusion. Et ainsi il se pouroit que la cession fust fort courte ; n'ayant plus d'argent à espérer ; et les esprits s'aigrissent l'un contre l'autre de plus en plus." Three days later Van Citters informed the States General that the excitement about the Bill of Indemnity was extreme.

his whole soul was devoted. Already the glory which he had won by conducting to a successful issue the most important enterprise of that age was becoming dim. Even his friends had begun to doubt whether he really possessed all that sagacity and energy which had a few months before extorted the unwilling admiration of his enemies. But he would endure his splendid slavery no longer. He would return to his native country. He would content himself with being the first citizen of a commonwealth to which the name of Orange was dear. As such, he might still be foremost among those who were banded together in defence of the liberties of Europe. As for the turbulent and ungrateful islanders, who detested him because he would not let them tear each other in pieces, Mary must try what she could do with them. She was born on their soil. She spoke their language. She did not dislike some parts of their Liturgy, which they fancied to be essential, and which to him seemed at best harmless. If she had little knowledge of politics and war, she had what might be more useful, feminine grace and tact, a sweet temper, a smile and a kind word for everybody. She might be able to compose the disputes which distracted the State and the Church. Holland, under his government, and England under hers, might act cordially together against the common enemy.

He secretly ordered preparations to be made for his voyage. Having done this, he called together a few of his chief counsellors, and told them his purpose. A squadron, he said, was ready to convey him to his country. He had done with them. He hoped that the Queen would be more successful. The ministers were thunderstruck. For once all quarrels were suspended. The Tory Caermarthen on one side, the Whig Shrewsbury on the other, expostulated and implored with a pathetic vehemence rare in the conferences of statesmen. Many tears were shed. At length the King was induced to give up, at least for the present, his design of abdicating the government. But he announced another design which he was fully determined not to give up. Since he was still to remain at the head of the English administration, he would go himself to Ireland. He would try whether the whole royal authority, strenuously exerted on the spot where the fate of the empire was to be decided, would suffice to prevent peculation and to maintain discipline.*

He is induced to change his intention.

* Burnet, ii. 39.; MS. Memoir written by the first Lord Lonsdale among the Mackintosh Papers.

That he had seriously meditated a retreat to Holland long continued to be a secret, not only to the multitude, but even to the Queen.* That he had resolved to take the command of his army in Ireland was soon rumoured all over London. It was known that his camp furniture was making, and that Sir Christopher Wren was busied in constructing a house of wood which was to travel about, packed in two waggons, and to be set up wherever His Majesty might fix his quarters.† The Whigs raised a violent outcry against the whole scheme. Not knowing, or affecting not to know, that it had been formed by William, and by William alone, and that none of his ministers had dared to advise him to encounter the Irish swords and the Irish atmosphere, the whole party confidently affirmed that he had been misled by some traitor in the cabinet, by some Tory who hated the Revolution and all that had sprung from the Revolution. Would any true friend have advised His Majesty, infirm in health as he was, to expose himself, not only to the dangers of war, but to the malignity of a climate which had recently been fatal to thousands of men much stronger than himself? In private the King sneered bitterly at this anxiety for his safety. It was merely, in his judgment, the anxiety which a hard master feels lest his slaves should become unfit for their drudgery. The Whigs, he wrote to Portland, were afraid to lose their tool before they had done their work. "As to their friendship," he added, "you know what it is worth." His resolution, he told his friend, was unalterably fixed. Everything was at stake; and go he must, even though the Parliament should present an address imploring him to stay.‡

He soon learned that such an address would be immediately moved in both Houses and supported by the whole strength of the Whig party. This intelligence satisfied him that it was time to take a decisive step. He would not discard the Whigs: but he would give them a lesson of which they stood

---

* Burnet, ii. 40.

† Luttrell's Diary, January and February.

‡ William to Portland, Jan. $\frac{10}{20}$. 1690. "Les Wiges ont peur de me perdre trop tost, avant qu'ils n'ayent fait avec moy ce qu'ils veulent: car, pour leur amitié, vous savez ce qu'il y a à compter làdessus en ce pays icy."

Jan. $\frac{14}{24}$. "Me voilà le plus embarassé du monde, ne sachant quel parti prendre, estant toujours persuadé que, sans que j'aille en Irlande, l'on n'y faira rien qui vaille. Pour avoir du conseil en cette

affaire, je n'en ay point à attendre, personne n'ausant dire ses sentimens. Et l'on commence déjà à dire ouvertement que ce sont des traitres qui m'ont conseillé de prendre cette résolution."

Jan. $\frac{21}{31}$. "Je n'ay encore rien dit,"— he means to the Parliament,—"de mon voyage pour l'Irlande. Et je ne suis point encore déterminé si j'en parlerez: mais je crains que nonobstant j'aurez une adresse pour n'y point aller; ce qui m'embarassera beaucoup, puis que c'est une nécessité absolue que j'y aille."

much in need. He would break the chain in which they imagined that they had him fast. He would not let them have the exclusive possession of power. He would not let them persecute the vanquished party. In their despite, he would grant an amnesty to his people. In their despite, he would take the command of his army in Ireland. He arranged his plan with characteristic prudence, firmness, and secrecy. A single Englishman it was necessary to trust : for William was not sufficiently master of our language to address the Houses from the throne in his own words ; and on very important occasions, his practice was to write his speech in French, and to employ a translator. It is certain that to one person, and to one only, the King confided the momentous resolution which he had taken ; and it can hardly be doubted that this person was Caermarthen.

On the twenty-seventh of January, Black Rod knocked at the door of the Commons. The Speaker and the members repaired to the House of Lords. The King was on the throne. He gave his assent to the Supply Bill, thanked the Houses for it, announced his intention of going to Ireland, and prorogued the Parliament. None could doubt that a dissolution would speedily follow. As the concluding words, " I have thought it convenient now to put an end to this session," were uttered, the Tories, both above and below the bar, broke forth into a shout of joy. The King meanwhile surveyed his audience from the throne with that bright eagle eye which nothing escaped. He might be pardoned if he felt some little vindictive pleasure in annoying those who had cruelly annoyed him. " I saw," he wrote to Portland the next day, " faces an ell long. I saw some of those men change colour twenty times while I was speaking." *

A few hours after the prorogation, a hundred and fifty Tory members of Parliament had a parting dinner together at the Apollo Tavern in Fleet Street, before they set out for their counties. They were in better temper with William than they had been since his father in law had been turned out of Whitehall. They had scarcely recovered from the joyful surprise

Joy of the Tories.

---

* William to Portland, $\frac{\text{Jan. 28.}}{\text{Feb. 7.}}$ 1690; Van Citters to the States General, same date ; Evelyn's Diary ; Lords' Journals, Jan. 27. I will quote William's own words. "Vous vairez mon harangue imprimée : ainsi je ne vous en direz rien. Et pour les raisons qui m'y ont obligé, je les reserverez à vous les dire jusques à vostre retour. Il semble que les Toris en sont bien aise, mais point les Wiggs. Ils estoient tous fort surpris quand je leur parlois, n'ayant communiqué mon dessin qu'à une seule personne. Je vis des visages long comme un aune, changé de couleur vingt fois pendant que je parlois. Tous ces particularités jusques à vostre heureux retour."

with which they had heard it announced from the throne that the session was at an end. The recollection of their danger and the sense of their deliverance were still fresh. They talked of repairing to Court in a body to testify their gratitude; but they were induced to forego their intention; and not without cause: for a great crowd of squires, after a revel, at which doubtless neither October nor claret had been spared, might have caused some inconvenience in the presence chamber. Sir John Lowther, who in wealth and influence was inferior to no country gentleman of that age, was deputed to carry the thanks of the assembly to the palace. He spoke, he told the King, the sense of a great body of honest gentlemen. They begged His Majesty to be assured that they would in their counties do their best to serve him; and they cordially wished him a safe voyage to Ireland, a complete victory, a speedy return, and a long and happy reign. During the following week, many, who had never shown their faces in the circle at Saint James's since the Revolution, went to kiss the King's hand. So warmly indeed did those who had hitherto been regarded as half Jacobites express their approbation of the policy of the government that the thoroughgoing Jacobites were much disgusted, and complained bitterly of the strange blindness which seemed to have come on the sons of the Church of England.*

All the acts of William, at this time, indicated his determination to restrain, steadily though gently, the violence of the Whigs, and to conciliate, if possible, the good will of the Tories. Several persons whom the Commons had thrown into prison for treason were set at liberty on bail.† The prelates who held that their allegiance was still due to James were treated with a tenderness rare in the history of revolutions. Within a week after the prorogation, the first of February came, the day on which those ecclesiastics who refused to take the oaths were to be finally deprived. Several of the suspended clergy, after holding out till the last moment, swore just in time to save themselves from beggary. But the Primate and five of his suffragans were still inflexible. They consequently forfeited their bishoprics: but Sancroft was informed that the King had not yet relinquished the hope of being able to make some arrangement which might avert the necessity of appointing successors, and that the nonjuring

* Evelyn's Diary; Clarendon's Diary,   by Dalrymple.
Feb. 9. 1690; Van Citters to the States   † Narcissus Luttrell's Diary.
General, $\frac{\text{Jan. 31.}}{\text{Feb. 10.}}$; Lonsdale MS. quoted

prelates might continue for the present to reside in their palaces. Their receivers were appointed receivers for the Crown, and continued to collect the revenues of the vacant sees.* Similar indulgence was shown to some divines of lower rank. Sherlock, in particular, continued, after his deprivation, to live unmolested in his official mansion close to the Temple Church.

And now appeared a proclamation dissolving the Parliament. The writs for a general election went out; and soon every part of the kingdom was in a ferment. Van Citters, who had resided in England during many eventful years, declared that he had never seen London more violently agitated.† The excitement was kept up by compositions of all sorts, from sermons with sixteen heads down to jingling street ballads. Lists of divisions were, for the first time in our history, printed and dispersed for the information of constituent bodies. Two of these lists may still be seen in old libraries. One of the two, circulated by the Whigs, contained the names of those Tories who had voted against declaring the throne vacant. The other, circulated by the Tories, contained the names of those Whigs who had supported the Sacheverell clause.

Dissolution and general election.

It soon became clear that public feeling had undergone a great change during the year which had elapsed since the Convention had met: and it is impossible to deny that this change was, at least in part, the natural consequence and the just punishment of the intemperate and vindictive conduct of the Whigs. Of the City of London they thought themselves sure. The livery had in the preceding year returned four zealous Whigs without a contest. But all the four had voted for the Sacheverell clause; and by that clause many of the merchant princes of Lombard Street and Cornhill, men powerful in the twelve great companies, men whom the goldsmiths followed humbly, hat in hand, up and down the arcades of the Royal Exchange, would have been turned with all indignity out of the Court of Aldermen and out of the Common Council. The struggle was for life or death. No exertions, no artifices, were spared. William wrote to Portland that the Whigs of the City, in their despair, stuck at nothing, and that, as they went on, they would soon stand as much in need of an Act of Indemnity as the Tories. Four Tories however were returned, and that by so decisive a majority that the Tory who stood lowest polled four hundred votes more than the Whig who

* Clarendon's Diary, Feb. 11. 1690.
† Van Citters to the States General, February $\frac{14}{24}$. 1690; Evelyn s Diary.

stood highest.* The Sheriffs, desiring to defer as long as possible the triumph of their enemies, granted a scrutiny. But, though the majority was diminished, the result was not affected.† At Westminster, two opponents of the Sacheverell clause were elected without a contest.‡ But nothing indicated more strongly the disgust excited by the proceedings of the late House of Commons than what passed in the University of Cambridge. Newton retired to his quiet observatory over the gate of Trinity College. Two Tories were returned by an overwhelming majority. At the head of the poll was Sawyer, who had, but a few days before, been excepted from the Indemnity Bill and expelled from the House of Commons. The records of the University contain curious proofs that the unwise severity with which he had been treated had raised an enthusiastic feeling in his favour. Newton voted for Sawyer; and this remarkable fact justifies us in believing that the great philosopher, in whose genius and virtue the Whig party justly glories, had seen the headstrong and revengeful conduct of that party with concern and disapprobation.§

It was soon plain that the Tories would have a majority in the new House of Commons.‖ All the leading Whigs however obtained seats, with one exception. John Hampden was excluded, and was regretted only by the most intolerant and unreasonable members of his party.¶

Changes in the executive departments.

The King meanwhile was making, in almost every department of the executive government, a change corresponding to

* William to Portland, $\frac{\text{Feb. 28.}}{\text{March 10.}}$ 1690; Van Citters to the States General, March $\frac{4}{14}$; Narcissus Luttrell's Diary.

† Van Citters, March $\frac{11}{21}$ 1690; Narcissus Luttrell's Diary.

‡ Van Citters to the States General, March $\frac{11}{21}$ 1690.

§ The votes were for Sawyer 165, for Finch 141, for Bennet, whom I suppose to have been a Whig, 87. At the University every voter delivers his vote in writing. One of the votes given on this occasion is in the following words, "Henricus Jenkes, ex amore justitiæ, eligit virum consultissimum Robertum Sawyer."

‖ Van Citters to the States General, March $\frac{18}{28}$ 1690.

¶ It is amusing to see how absurdly foreign pamphleteers, ignorant of the real state of things in England, exaggerated the importance of John Hampden, whose name they could not spell. In a French Dialogue between William and the Ghost of Monmouth, William

says, "Entre ces membres de la Chambre Basse étoit un certain homme hardy, opiniâtre, et zélé à l'excès pour sa créance; on l'appelle Embden, également dangereux par son esprit et par son crédit. . . . Je ne trouvay point de chemin plus court pour me délivrer de cette traverse que de casser le parlement, en convoquer un autre, et empescher que cet homme, qui me faisoit tant d'ombrages, ne fust nommé pour un des deputez au nouvel parlement." "Ainsi," says the Ghost, "cette cassation de parlement qui a fait tant de bruit, et a produit tant de raisonnemens et de spéculations, n'estoit que pour exclure Embden. Mais s'il estoit si adroit et si zélé, comment as-tu pu trouver le moyen de le faire exclure du nombre des deputez?" To this sensible question the King replies, not very explicitly, "Il m'a fallu faire d'étranges manœuvres pour en venir à bout."—L'Ombre de Monmouth, 1690.

the change which the general election was making in the composition of the legislature. Still, however, he did not think of forming what is now called a ministry. He still reserved to himself more especially the direction of foreign affairs, and he superintended with minute attention all the preparations for the approaching campaign in Ireland. In his confidential letters he complained that he had to perform, with little or no assistance, the task of organising the disorganised military establishments of the kingdom. The work, he said, was heavy; but it must be done; for everything depended on it.* In general, the government was still a government by independent departments; and in almost every department Whigs and Tories were still mingled, though not exactly in the old proportions. The Whig element had decidedly predominated in 1689. The Tory element predominated though not very decidedly, in 1690.

Halifax had laid down the Privy Seal. It was offered to Chesterfield, a Tory who had voted in the Convention for a Regency. But Chesterfield refused to quit his country house and gardens in Derbyshire for the Court and the Council Chamber; and the Privy Seal was put into Commission.† Caermarthen was now the chief adviser of the crown on all matters relating to the internal administration and to the management of the two Houses of Parliament. The white staff, and the immense power which accompanied the white staff, William was still determined never to entrust to any subject. Caermarthen therefore continued to be Lord President; but he took possession of a suite of apartments in Saint James's Palace which was considered as peculiarly belonging to the Prime Minister.‡ He had, during the preceding year, pleaded ill health as an excuse for seldom appearing at the Council Board; and the plea was not without foundation: for his digestive organs had some morbid peculiarities which puzzled the whole College of Physicians: his complexion was livid: his frame was meagre; and his face, handsome and intellectual as it was, had a haggard look which indicated the

Caermarthen chief minister.

---

* "A présent tout dépendra d'un bon succès en Irlande; et à quoy il faut que je m'aplique entièrement pour régler le mieux que je puis toutte chose. . . . . Je vous asseure que je n'ay pas peu sur les bras, estant aussi mal assisté que je suis."—William to Portland, $\frac{Jan. 28.}{Feb. 7.}$ 1690.

† Van Citters, Feb. $\frac{14}{24}$. $16\frac{89}{90}$; Memoir of the Earl of Chesterfield, by himself; Halifax to Chesterfield, Feb. 6.; Chesterfield to Halifax, Feb. 8. The editor of the letters of the second Earl of Chesterfield, not allowing for the change of style, has misplaced this correspondence by a year.

‡ Van Citters to the States General, Feb. $\frac{11}{21}$. 1690.

restlessness of pain as well as the restlessness of ambition.*
As soon, however, as he was once more minister, he applied
himself strenuously to business, and toiled, every day, and all
day long, with an energy which amazed everybody who saw
his ghastly countenance and tottering gait.

Though he could not obtain for himself the office of Lord
Treasurer, his influence at the Treasury was great. Monmouth, the First Commissioner, and Delamere, the Chancellor
of the Exchequer, two of the most violent Whigs in England,
quitted their seats. On this, as on many other occasions, it
appeared that they had nothing but their Whiggism in
common. The volatile Monmouth, sensible that he had none
of the qualities of a financier, seems to have taken no personal
offence at being removed from a place which he never ought
to have occupied. He thankfully accepted a pension, which
his profuse habits made necessary to him, and still continued
to attend Councils, to frequent the Court, and to discharge the
duties of a Lord of the Bedchamber.† He also tried to make
himself useful in military business, which he understood, if
not well, yet better than most of his brother nobles : and he
professed, during a few months, a great regard for Caermarthen. Delamere was in a very different mood. It was in
vain that his services were overpaid with honours and riches.
He was created Earl of Warrington. He obtained a grant of
all the lands that could be discovered belonging to Jesuits in
five or six counties. A demand made by him on account of
expenses incurred at the time of the Revolution was allowed ;
and he carried with him into retirement as the reward of his
patriotic exertions a large sum which the State could ill
spare. But his anger was not to be so appeased ; and to the
end of his life he continued to complain bitterly of the ingratitude with which he and his party had been treated.‡

* A strange peculiarity of his constitution is mentioned in an account of
him which was published a few months
after his death. See the volume entitled "Lives and Characters of the
most Illustrious Persons, British and
Foreign, who died in the year 1712."
So early as the days of Charles the
Second, the leanness and ghastliness of
Caermarthen were among the favourite
topics of Whig satirists. In a ballad
entitled the Chequer Inn are these lines:

" He is as stiff as any stake,
  And leaner, Dick, than any rake :
    Envy is not so pale ;
  And though, by selling of us all,
  He has wrought himself into Whitehall,
    He looks like bird of gaol."

† Monmouth's pension and the good
understanding between him and the
Court are mentioned in a letter from a
Jacobite agent in England, which is in
the Archives of the French War Office.
The date is April $\frac{8}{18}$. 1690.

‡ The grants of land obtained by
Delamere are mentioned by Narcissus
Luttrell. It appears from the Treasury
Letter Book of 1690 that Delamere continued to dun the government for money
after his retirement. As to his general
character it would not be safe to trust
the representations of his enemies. But
his own writings, and the admissions of
the divine who preached his funeral
sermon, show that his temper was not

Sir John Lowther became first Lord of the Treasury, and was the person on whom Caermarthen chiefly relied for the conduct of the ostensible business of the House of Commons. Lowther was a man of ancient descent, ample estate, and great parliamentary interest. Though not an old man, he was an old senator : for he had, before he was of age, succeeded his father as knight of the shire for Westmoreland. In truth the representation of Westmoreland was almost as much one of the hereditaments of the Lowther family as Lowther Hall. Sir John's abilities were respectable: his manners, though sarcastically noticed in contemporary lampoons as too formal, were eminently courteous : his personal courage he was but too ready to prove : his morals were irreproachable : his time was divided between respectable labours and respectable pleasures : his chief business was to attend the House of Commons and to preside on the Bench of Justice : his favourite amusements were reading and gardening. In opinions he was a very moderate Tory. He was attached to hereditary monarchy and to the Established Church : but he had concurred in the Revolution: he had no misgivings touching the title of William and Mary : he had sworn allegiance to them without any mental reservation ; and he appears to have strictly kept his oath. Between him and Caermarthen there was a close connection. They had acted together cordially in the Northern insurrection ; and they agreed in their political views, as nearly as a very cunning statesman and a very honest country gentleman could be expected to agree.* By Caermarthen's influence Lowther was now raised to one of the most important places in the kingdom. Unfortunately it was a place requiring qualities very different from those which suffice to make a valuable county member and chairman of quarter sessions. The tongue of the new First Lord of the Treasury was not sufficiently ready, nor was his temper sufficiently callous for

Sir John Lowther.

the most gentle. Clarendon remarks (Dec. 17. 1688) that a little thing sufficed to put Lord Delamere into a passion. In the poem entitled the King of Hearts, Delamere is described as—

" A restless malecontent even when preferred."

His countenance furnished a subject for satire :

" His boding looks a mind distracted show ;
And envy sits engraved upon his brow."

* My notion of Lowther's character has been chiefly formed from two papers written by himself, one of which has

been printed, though I believe not published. A copy of the other is among the Mackintosh MSS. Something I have taken from contemporary satires. That Lowther was too ready to expose his life in private encounters is sufficiently proved by the fact that, when he was First Lord of the Treasury, he accepted a challenge from a custom house officer whom he had dismissed. There was a duel; and Lowther was severely wounded. This event is mentioned in Luttrell's Diary, April 1691.

his post. He had neither adroitness to parry, nor fortitude to endure, the gibes and reproaches to which, in his new character of courtier and placeman, he was exposed. There was also something to be done which he was too scrupulous to do; something which had never been done by Wolsey or Burleigh; something which has never been done by any English statesman of our generation; but which, from the time of Charles the Second to the time of George the Third, was one of the most important parts of the business of a minister.

Rise and progress of parliamentary corruption in England. The history of the rise, progress, and decline of parliamentary corruption in England still remains to be written. No subject has called forth a greater quantity of eloquent vituperation and stinging sarcasm. Three generations of serious and of sportive writers wept and laughed over the venality of the senate. That venality was denounced on the hustings, anathematised from the pulpit, and burlesqued on the stage; was attacked by Pope in brilliant verse, and by Bolingbroke in stately prose, by Swift with savage hatred, and by Gay with festive malice. The voices of Tories and Whigs, of Johnson and Akenside, of Smollett and Fielding, contributed to swell the cry. But none of those who railed or of those who jested took the trouble to verify the phænomena, or to trace them to the real causes.

Sometimes the evil was imputed to the depravity of a particular minister: but, when he had been driven from power, and when those who had most loudly accused him governed in his stead, it was found that the change of men had produced no change of system. Sometimes the evil was imputed to the degeneracy of the national character. Luxury and cupidity, it was said, had produced in our country the same effect which they had produced of old in the Roman republic. The modern Englishman was to the Englishman of the sixteenth century what Verres and Curio were to Dentatus and Fabricius. Those who held this language were as ignorant and shallow as people generally are who extol the past at the expense of the present. A man of sense would have perceived that, if the English of the time of George the Second had really been more sordid and dishonest than their forefathers, the deterioration would not have shown itself in one place alone. The progress of judicial venality and of official venality would have kept pace with the progress of parliamentary venality. But nothing is more certain than that, while the legislature was becoming more and more venal, the courts of law and the public offices were becoming purer and purer. The representatives of the people were undoubtedly more mercenary in the days of Hardwicke and Pelham than in the days of the Tudors. But the Chancellors of the Tudors took plate, jewels, and purses of broad pieces, from suitors without scruple or shame; and Hardwicke would have committed for contempt any suitor who had dared to bring him a present. The Treasurers of the Tudors raised princely fortunes by the sale of places, titles, and pardons; and Pelham would have ordered his servants to turn out of his house any man who had offered him money for a peerage or a commissionership of customs. It is evident, therefore that the prevalence of corruption in the Parliament cannot be ascribed to a general depravation of morals. The taint was local: we must look for some local cause; and such a cause will without difficulty be found.

Under our ancient sovereigns the House of Commons rarely interfered with the executive administration. The Speaker was charged not to let the members meddle with matters of State. If any gentleman was very troublesome, he was cited before the Privy Council, interrogated, reprimanded, and sent to meditate on his undutiful conduct in the Tower. The Commons did their best to protect themselves by keeping their deliberations secret, by excluding strangers, by making it a crime to repeat out of doors what had passed within doors. But these precautions were of small avail. In so large an assembly there were always talebearers, ready to carry the evil report of their brethren to the palace. To oppose the Court was therefore a service of serious danger. In those days, of course, there was little or no buying of votes. For an honest man was not to be bought, and it was much cheaper to intimidate or to coerce a knave than to buy him.

For a very different reason there has been no direct buying of votes within the memory of the present generation. The House of Commons is now supreme in the State, but is accountable to the nation. Even those members who are not chosen by large constituent bodies are kept in awe by public opinion. Everything is printed: everything is discussed: every material word uttered in debate is read by a million of people on the morrow. Within a few hours after an important division, the lists of the majority and the minority are scanned and analysed in every town from Plymouth to Inverness. If a name be found where it ought not to be, the apostate is certain to be reminded in sharp language of the promises which he has broken, and of the professions which he has belied. At present, therefore, the best way in which a government can secure the support of a majority of the representative body is by gaining the confidence of the nation.

But between the time when our Parliaments ceased to be controlled by royal prerogative and the time when they began to be constantly and effectually controlled by public opinion there was a long interval. After the restoration, no government ventured to return to those methods by which, before the civil war, the freedom of deliberation had been restrained. A member could no longer be called to account for his harangues or his votes. He might obstruct the passing of bills of supply : he might arraign the whole foreign policy of the country : he might lay on the table articles of impeachment against all the chief ministers ; and he ran not the smallest risk of being treated as Morrice had been treated by Elizabeth, or Eliot by Charles the First. The senator now stood in no awe of the Court. Nevertheless all the defences behind which the feeble Parliaments of the sixteenth century had entrenched themselves against the attacks of prerogative were not only still kept up, but were extended and strengthened. No politician seems to have been aware that these defences were no longer needed for their original purpose, and had begun to serve a purpose very different. The rules which had been originally designed to secure faithful representatives against the displeasure of the Sovereign, now operated to secure unfaithful representatives against the displeasure of the people, and proved much more effectual for the latter end than they had ever been for the former. It was natural, it was inevitable, that, in a legislative body emancipated from the restraints of the sixteenth century, and not yet subjected to the restraints of the nineteenth century, in a legislative body which feared neither the King nor the public, there should be corruption.

The plague spot began to be visible and palpable in the days of the Cabal. Clifford, the boldest and fiercest of the wicked Five, had the merit of discovering that a noisy patriot, whom it was no longer possible to send to prison, might be turned into a courtier by a goldsmith's note. Clifford's example was followed by his successors. It soon became a proverb that a Parliament resembled a pump. Often, the wits said, when a pump appears to be dry, if a very small quantity of water is poured in, a great quantity of water gushes out : and so, when a Parliament appears to be niggardly, ten thousand pounds judiciously given in bribes will often produce a million in supplies. The evil was not diminished, nay, it was aggravated, by that Revolution which freed our country from so many other evils. The House of Commons was now more powerful than ever as against the Crown, and yet was not more strictly responsible than formerly to the nation. The government had a new motive for buying the members; and the members had no new motive for refusing to sell themselves. William, indeed, had an aversion to bribery: he resolved to abstain from it; and during the first year of his reign, he kept his resolution. Unhappily the events of that year did not encourage him to persevere in his good intentions. As soon as Caermarthen was placed at the head of the internal administration of the realm, a complete change took place. He was in truth no novice in the art of purchasing votes. He had, sixteen years before, succeeded Clifford at the Treasury, had inherited Clifford's tactics, had improved upon them, and had employed them to an extent which would have amazed the inventor. From the day on which Caermarthen was called a second time to the chief direction of affairs, parliamentary corruption continued to be practised, with scarcely any intermission, by a long succession of statesmen, till the close of the American war. Neither of the great English parties can justly charge the other with any peculiar guilt on this account. The Tories were the first who introduced the system and the last who clung to it: but it attained its greatest vigour in the time of Whig ascendency. The extent to which parliamentary support was bartered for money cannot be with any precision ascertained. But it seems probable that the number of hirelings was greatly exaggerated by vulgar report, and was never large, though often sufficient to turn the scale on important divisions. An unprincipled minister eagerly accepted the services of these mercenaries. An honest minister reluctantly submitted, for the sake of the commonwealth, to what he considered as a shameful and odious extortion. But during many years every minister, whatever his personal character might be, consented, willingly or unwillingly, to manage the Parliament in the only way in which the Parliament could then be managed. It at length became as notorious that there was a market for votes at the Treasury as that there was a market for cattle in Smithfield. Numerous demagogues out of power declaimed against this vile traffic: but every one of those demagogues, as soon as he was in power, found himself driven by a kind of fatality to engage in that traffic, or at least to connive at it. Now and then perhaps a man who had romantic notions of public virtue refused to be himself the paymaster of the corrupt crew, and averted his eyes while his less scrupulous colleagues did that which he knew to be indispensable, and yet felt to be degrading. But the instances of this prudery were rare indeed. The doctrine generally received, even among upright and honourable politicians, was that it was shameful to receive bribes, but that it was necessary to distribute them. It is a remarkable fact that the evil reached the greatest height during the administration of Henry Pelham, a statesman of good intentions, of spotless morals in private life, and of exemplary disinterestedness. It is not difficult to guess by what arguments he and other well meaning men, who, like him, followed the fashion of their age, quieted their consciences. No casuist, however severe, has denied that it may be a duty to give what it is a crime to take. It was infamous in Jeffreys to demand money for the lives of the unhappy prisoners whom he tried at Dorchester and Taunton. But it was not infamous, nay, it was laudable, in the kinsmen and friends of a prisoner to contribute of their substance in order to make up a purse for Jeffreys. The Sallee rover, who threatened to bastinado a Christian captive to death unless a ransom was forthcoming, was an odious ruffian. But to ransom a Christian captive from a Sallee rover was, not merely an innocent, but a highly meritorious act. It is improper in such cases to use the word corruption. Those who receive the filthy lucre are corrupt already. He who bribes them does not make them wicked : he finds them so ; and he merely prevents their evil propensities from producing evil effects. And might not the same plea be urged in defence of a minister who, when no other expedient would avail, paid greedy and lowminded members of parliament not to ruin their country ?

It was by some such reasoning as this that the scruples of William were overcome. Honest Burnet, with the uncourtly courage which distinguished him, ventured to remonstrate with the King. "Nobody," William answered, "hates bribery more than I. But I have to do with a set of men who must be managed in this vile way or not at all. I must strain a point ; or the country is lost."*

Sir John Trevor.

It was necessary for the Lord President to have in the House of Commons an agent for the purchase of members ; and Lowther was both too awkward and too scrupulous to be

* Burnet, ii. 76

such an agent. But a man in whom craft and profligacy were united in a high degree was without difficulty found. This was the Master of the Rolls, Sir John Trevor, who had been Speaker in the single Parliament held by James. High as Trevor had risen in the world, there were people who could still remember him a strange looking clerk in the Inner Temple. Indeed, nobody who had ever seen him was likely to forget him. For his grotesque features and his hideous squint were far beyond the reach of caricature. His parts, which were quick and vigorous, had enabled him early to master the science of chicane. Gambling and betting were his amusements; and out of these amusements he contrived to extract much business in the way of his profession. For his opinion on a question arising out of a wager or a game at chance had as much authority as a judgment of any court in Westminster Hall. He soon rose to be one of the boon companions whom Jeffreys hugged in fits of maudlin friendship over the bottle at night, and cursed and reviled in court on the morrow. Under such a teacher, Trevor rapidly became a proficient in that peculiar kind of rhetoric which had enlivened the trials of Baxter and of Alice Lisle. Report indeed spoke of some scolding matches between the Chancellor and his friend, in which the disciple had been not less voluble and scurrilous than the master. These contests, however, did not take place till the younger adventurer had attained riches and dignities such that he no longer stood in need of the patronage which had raised him.* Among High Churchmen Trevor, in spite of his notorious want of principle, had at this time a certain popularity, which he seems to have owed chiefly to their conviction that, however insincere he might be in general, his hatred of the dissenters was genuine and hearty. There was little doubt that, in a House of Commons in which the Tories had a majority, he might easily, with the support of the Court, be chosen Speaker. He was impatient to be again in his old post, which he well knew how to make one of the most lucrative in the kingdom; and he willingly undertook that secret and shameful office for which Lowther was altogether unqualified.

Richard Hampden was appointed Chancellor of the Exchequer. This appointment was probably intended as a mark of royal gratitude for the moderation of his conduct,

* Roger North's Life of Guildford.

and for the attempts which he had made to curb the violence
of his Whig friends, and especially of his son.

Godolphin retires. Godolphin voluntarily left the Treasury; why, we are not
informed. We can scarcely doubt that the dissolution and
the result of the general election must have given him
pleasure. For his political opinions leaned towards Toryism;
and he had, in the late reign, done some things which,
though not very heinous, stood in need of an indemnity. It
is probable that he did not think it compatible with his
personal dignity to sit at the Board below Lowther, who was
in rank his inferior.*

Changes at the Admiralty. A new Commission of Admiralty was issued. At the head
of the naval administration was placed Thomas Herbert,
Earl of Pembroke, a high born and high bred man, who
had ranked among the Tories, who had voted for a Regency,
and who had married the daughter of Sawyer. That Pembroke's Toryism, however, was not of a narrow and illiberal
kind is sufficiently proved by the fact that, immediately after
the Revolution, the Essay on the Human Understanding was
dedicated to him by John Locke, in token of gratitude for
kind offices done in evil times.†

Nothing was omitted which could reconcile Torrington to
this change. For, though he had been found an incapable
administrator, he still stood so high in general estimation as
a seaman that the government was unwilling to lose his
services. He was assured that no slight was intended to
him. He could not serve his country at once on the ocean
and at Westminster; and it had been thought less difficult
to supply his place in his office than on the deck of his flag
ship. He was at first very angry, and actually laid down
his commission: but some concessions were made to his
pride: a pension of three thousand pounds a year and a grant
of ten thousand acres of crown land in the Peterborough
level were irresistible baits to his cupidity; and, in an evil
hour for England, he consented to remain at the head of
the naval force on which the safety of her coasts depended.‡

While these changes were making in the offices round

---

* Till some years after this time the
First Lord of the Treasury was always
the man of highest rank at the Board.
Thus Monmouth, Delamere, and Godolphin took their places according to
the order of precedence in which they
stood as peers.

† The dedication, however, was

thought too laudatory. "The only
thing, Mr. Pope used to say, he could
never forgive his philosophic master
was the dedication to the Essay."—
Ruffhead's Life of Pope.

‡ Van Citters to the States General,
$\frac{\text{April 25.}}{\text{May 5.}}$ 1690; Narcissus Luttrell's Diary;
Treasury Letter Book, Feb. 4. 16$\frac{89}{90}$.

Whitehall, the Commissions of Lieutenancy all over the kingdom were revised. The Tories had, during twelve months, been complaining that their share in the govern- Changes in the Commissions of Lieutenancy. ment of the districts in which they lived bore no proportion to their number, to their wealth, and to the consideration which they enjoyed in society. They now regained with great delight their former position in their shires. The Whigs raised a cry that the King was foully betrayed, and that he had been induced by evil counsellors to put the sword into the hands of men who, as soon as a favourable opportunity offered, would turn the edge against himself. In a dialogue which was believed to have been written by the newly created Earl of Warrington, and which had a wide circulation at the time, but has long been forgotten, the Lord Lieutenant of a county was introduced expressing his apprehensions that the majority of his deputies were traitors at heart.* But nowhere was the excitement produced by the new distribution of power so great as in the capital. By a Commission of Lieutenancy which had been issued immediately after the Revolution, the trainbands of London had been put under the command of stanch Whigs. Those powerful and opulent citizens whose names were omitted alleged that the list was filled with elders of Puritan congregations, with Shaftesbury's brisk boys, with Rye House plotters, and that it was scarcely possible to find, mingled with that multitude of fanatics and levellers, a single man sincerely attached to monarchy and to the Church. A new Commission now appeared framed by Caermarthen and Nottingham. They had taken counsel with Compton, the Bishop of the diocese; and Compton was not a very discreet adviser. He had originally been a High Churchman and a Tory. The severity with which he had been treated in the late reign had transformed him into a Latitudinarian and a rebel; and he had now, from jealousy of Tillotson, turned High Churchman and Tory again. The changes which were made by his recommendation raised a storm in the City. The Whigs complained that they were ungratefully proscribed by a government which owed its existence to them; that some of the best friends of King William had been dismissed with contumely to make room for some of his worst enemies, for men who were as unworthy of trust as

* The Dialogue between a Lord Lieutenant and one of his Deputies will not be found in the collection of Warrington's writings which was published in 1694, under the sanction, as it should seem, of his family.

any Irish Rapparee, for men who had delivered up to a
tyrant the charter and the immemorial privileges of London,
for men who had made themselves notorious by the cruelty
with which they had enforced the penal laws against
Protestant dissenters, nay, for men who had sate on those
juries which had found Russell and Cornish guilty.* The
discontent was so great that it seemed, during a short
time, likely to cause pecuniary embarrassment to the State.
The supplies voted by the late Parliament came in slowly.
The wants of the public service were pressing. In such
circumstances it was to the citizens of the capital that the
government always looked for help; and the government of
William had hitherto looked especially to those citizens who
professed Whig opinions. Things were now changed. A
few eminent Whigs, in their first anger, sullenly refused to
advance money. Nay, one or two unexpectedly withdrew
considerable sums from the Exchequer.† The financial difficulties might have been serious, had not some wealthy
Tories, who, if Sacheverell's clause had become law, would
have been excluded from all municipal honours, offered the
Treasury a hundred thousand pounds down, and promised to
raise a still larger sum.‡

While the City was thus agitated, came a day appointed
by royal proclamation for a general fast. The reasons assigned for this solemn act of devotion were the lamentable
state of Ireland and the appoaching departure of the King.
Prayers were offered up for the safety of His Majesty's person
and for the success of his arms. The churches of London
were crowded. The most eminent preachers of the capital,
who were, with scarcely an exception, either moderate Tories
or moderate Whigs, did their best to calm the public mind,
and earnestly exhorted their flocks not to withhold, at this
great conjuncture, a hearty support from the prince, with
whose fate was bound up the fate of the whole nation.
Burnet told a large congregation from the pulpit how the
Greeks, when the Great Turk was preparing to besiege
Constantinople, could not be persuaded to contribute any
part of their wealth for the common defence, and how

---

* Van Citters to the States General,
March $\frac{18}{28}$, April $\frac{4}{14}$. 1690 ; Narcissus
Luttrell's Diary ; Burnet, ii. 72. ; The
Triennial Mayor, or the Rapparees, a
Poem, 1691. The poet says of one of
the new civic functionaries :

" Soon his pretence to conscience we can rout,
  And in a bloody jury find him out,
  Where noble Publius worried was with
  rogues."

† Treasury Minute Book, Feb. 5. 16$\frac{89}{90}$.
‡ Van Citters, Feb. $\frac{11}{21}$., Mar. $\frac{14}{24}$.,
Mar. $\frac{18}{28}$. 1690.

bitterly they repented of their avarice when they were compelled to deliver up to the victorious infidels the treasures which had been refused to the supplications of the last Christian emperor.*

The Whigs, however, as a party, did not stand in need of such an admonition. Grieved and angry as they were, they were perfectly sensible that on the stability of the throne of William depended all that they most highly prized. What some of them might, at this conjuncture, have been tempted to do if they could have found another leader, if, for example, their Protestant Duke, their King Monmouth, had still been living, may be doubted. But their only choice was between the Sovereign whom they had set up and the Sovereign whom they had pulled down. It would have been strange indeed if they had taken part with James in order to punish William, when the worst fault which they imputed to William was that he did not participate in the vindictive feeling with which they remembered the tyranny of James. Much as they disliked the Bill of Indemnity, they had not forgotten the Bloody Circuit. They therefore, even in their ill humour, continued true to their own King, and, while grumbling at him, were ready to stand by him against his adversary with their lives and fortunes.†

There were indeed exceptions: but they were very few; and they were to be found almost exclusively in two classes, which, though widely differing from each other in social position, closely resembled each other in laxity of principle. All the Whigs who are known to have trafficked with Saint Germains, belonged, not to the main body of the party, but either to the head or to the tail. They were either patricians high in rank and office, or caitiffs who had long been employed in the foulest drudgery of faction. To the former class belonged Shrewsbury. Of the latter class the most remarkable specimen was Robert Ferguson. From the day on which the Convention Parliament was dissolved, Shrewsbury began to waver in his allegiance: but that he had ever wavered was not, till long after, suspected by the public. That Ferguson had, a few months after the Revolution, become a furious Jacobite, was no secret to anybody, and ought not to have been matter of surprise to anybody. For his apostasy he could not plead even the miserable excuse

Marginal note: Temper of the Whigs

Marginal note: Dealings of some Whigs with Saint Germains: Shrewsbury; Ferguson.

---

* Van Citters, March 14/24. 1690. But he is mistaken as to the preacher. The sermon is extant. It was preached at Bow Church before the Court of Aldermen.

† Welwood's Mercurius Reformatus, Feb. 12. 1690.

that he had been neglected. The ignominious services which he had formerly rendered to his party as a spy, a raiser of riots, a dispenser of bribes, a writer of libels, a prompter of false witnesses, had been rewarded only too prodigally for the honour of the new government. That he should hold any high office was of course impossible. But a sinecure place of five hundred a year had been created for him in the department of the Excise. He now had what to him was opulence: but opulence did not satisfy him. For money indeed he had never scrupled to be guilty of fraud aggravated by hypocrisy: yet the love of money was not his strongest passion. Long habit had developed in him a moral disease from which people who have made political agitation their calling are seldom wholly free. He could not be quiet. Sedition, from being his business, had become his pleasure. It was as impossible for him to live without doing mischief as for an old dram drinker or an old opium eater to live without the daily dose of poison. The very discomforts and hazards of a lawless life had a strange attraction for him. He could no more be turned into a peaceable and loyal subject than the fox can be turned into a shepherd's dog, or than the kite can be taught the habits of the barn door fowl. The Red Indian prefers his hunting ground to cultivated fields and stately cities: the gipsy, sheltered by a commodious roof, and provided with meat in due season, still pines for the ragged tent on the moor and the chance meal of carrion; and even so Ferguson became weary of plenty and security, of his salary, his house, his table, and his coach, and longed to be again the president of societies into which none could enter without a password, the director of secret presses, the distributor of inflammatory pamphlets; to see the walls placarded with descriptions of his person and offers of reward for his apprehension; to have six or seven names, with a different wig and cloak for each, and to change his lodgings thrice a week at dead of night. His hostility was not to Popery or to Protestantism, to monarchical government or to republican government, to the House of Stuart or to the House of Nassau, but to whatever was at the time established.

Hopes of the Jacobites.

By the Jacobites this new ally was eagerly welcomed. They were at that moment busied with schemes in which the help of a veteran plotter was much needed. There had been a great stir among them from the day on which it had been announced that William had determined to take the command in Ireland; and they were all looking forward with impatient hope to his departure. He was not one of those princes against whom men lightly venture to set up a standard of rebellion. His courage, his sagacity, the secrecy of his counsels, the success which had generally crowned his enterprises, overawed the vulgar. Even his most acrimonious enemies feared him at least as much as they hated him. While he was at Kensington, ready to take horse at a moment's notice, malecontents who prized their heads and their estates were generally content to vent their hatred by drinking confusion to his hooked nose, and by squeezing with significant energy the orange which was his emblem. But their courage rose when they reflected that the sea would soon roll between him and our island. In the military and political calculations of that age, thirty leagues of water were as important as three hundred leagues now are. The winds and waves frequently interrupted all communication between England and Ireland. It sometimes happened that, during a fortnight or three weeks, not a word of intelligence from London reached Dublin. Twenty English counties might be up in arms long before any rumour that an insurrection was even apprehended could reach Ulster. Early in the spring, therefore, the leading malecontents assembled in London for the purpose of concerting an extensive plan of action, and corresponded assiduously both with France and with Ireland.

Such was the temper of the English factions when, on the twentieth of March, the new Parliament met. The first duty which the Commons had to perform was that of choosing a Speaker. Trevor was proposed by Lowther, was elected without opposition, and was presented and approved with the ordinary ceremonial. The King then made a speech in which he especially recommended to the consideration of the Houses two important subjects, the settling of the revenue and the granting of an amnesty. He represented strongly the necessity of despatch. Every day was precious, the season for action was approaching. " Let not us," he said, " be engaged in debates while our enemies are in the field."*

Meeting of the new Parliament.

The first subject which the Commons took into consideration was the state of the revenue. A great part of the taxes had, since the accession of William and Mary, been collected under the authority of Acts passed for short terms, and it

Settlement of the revenue.

* Commons' Journals, March 20, 21, 22. 16$\frac{89}{90}$.

was now time to determine on a permanent arrangement. A list of the salaries and pensions for which provision was to be made was laid before the House; and the amount of the sums thus expended called forth very just complaints from the independent members, among whom Sir Charles Sedley distinguished himself by his sarcastic pleasantry. A clever speech which he made against the placemen stole into print and was widely circulated: it has since been often republished; and it proves, what his poems and plays might make us doubt, that his contemporaries were not mistaken in considering him as a man of parts and vivacity. Unfortunately the ill humour which the sight of the Civil List caused evaporated in jests and invectives without producing any reform.

The ordinary revenue by which the government had been supported before the Revolution had been partly hereditary, and had been partly drawn from taxes granted to each sovereign for life. The hereditary revenue had passed, with the crown, to William and Mary. It was derived from the rents of the royal domains, from fees, from fines, from wine licenses, from the first fruits and tenths of benefices, from the receipts of the Post Office, and from that part of the excise which had, immediately after the Restoration, been granted to Charles the Second and to his successors for ever in lieu of the feudal services due to our ancient kings. The income from all these sources was estimated at between four and five hundred thousand pounds.*

Those duties of excise and customs which had been granted to James for life had, at the close of his reign, yielded about nine hundred thousand pounds annually. William naturally wished to have this income on the same terms on which his uncle had enjoyed it; and his ministers did their best to gratify his wishes. Lowther moved that the grant should be to the King and Queen for their joint and separate lives, and spoke repeatedly and earnestly in defence of this motion. He set forth William's claims to public gratitude and confidence; the nation rescued from Popery and arbitrary power; the Church delivered from persecution; the constitution established on a firm basis. Would the Commons deal grudgingly with a prince who had done more for England than had ever been done for her by any of his predecessors in so short a time, with a prince who was now about to expose himself to hostile weapons and pestilential air in order to preserve the

* Commons' Journals, March 2?. 1690, and March 1. and March 20. 168⅞.

English colony in Ireland, with a prince who was prayed for in every corner of the world where a congregation of Protestants could meet for the worship of God?* But on this subject Lowther harangued in vain. Whigs and Tories were equally fixed in the opinion that the liberality of Parliaments had been the chief cause of the disasters of the last thirty years; that to the liberality of the Parliament of 1660 was to be ascribed the misgovernment of the Cabal, that to the liberality of the Parliament of 1685 was to be ascribed the Declaration of Indulgence, and that the Parliament of 1690 would be inexcusable if it did not profit by experience. After much dispute a compromise was made. That portion of the excise which had been settled for life on James, and which was estimated at three hundred thousand pounds a year, was settled on William and Mary for their joint and separate lives. It was supposed that, with the hereditary revenue, and with three hundred thousand a year more from the excise, Their Majesties would have, independent of parliamentary control, between seven and eight hundred thousand a year. Out of this income was to be defrayed the charge both of the royal household and of those civil offices of which a list had been laid before the House. This income was therefore called the Civil List. The expenses of the royal household are now entirely separated from the expenses of civil government: but, by a whimsical perversion, the name of Civil List has remained attached to that portion of the revenue which is appropriated to the expenses of the royal household. It is still more strange that several neighbouring nations should have thought this most unmeaning of all names worth borrowing. Those duties of customs which had been settled for life on Charles and James successively, and which, in the year before the Revolution, had yielded six hundred thousand pounds, were granted to the Crown for a term of only four years.†

William was by no means well pleased with this arrangement. He thought it unjust and ungrateful in a people whose liberties he had saved to bind him over to his good behaviour. "The gentlemen of England," he said to Burnet, "trusted King James who was an enemy of their religion and of their laws; and they will not trust me by whom their

---

* Grey's Debates, March 27. and 28. 1690.

† Commons' Journals, Mar. 28. 1690. A very clear and exact account of the way in which the revenue was settled was sent by Van Citters to the States General, April 7/17. 1690.

religion and their laws have been preserved." Burnet answered very properly that there was no mark of personal confidence which His Majesty was not entitled to demand, but that this question was not a question of personal confidence. The Estates of the Realm wished to establish a general principle. They wished to set a precedent which might secure a remote posterity against evils such as the indiscreet liberality of former Parliaments had produced. "From those evils Your Majesty has delivered this generation. By accepting the gift of the Commons on the terms on which it is offered Your Majesty will be also a deliverer of future generations." William was not convinced : but he had too much wisdom and self-command to give way to his ill humour; and he accepted graciously what he could not but consider as ungraciously given.*

Provision for the Princess of Denmark.

The Civil List was charged with an annuity of twenty thousand pounds to the Princess of Denmark, in addition to an annuity of thirty thousand pounds which had been settled on her at the time of her marriage. This arrangement was the result of a compromise which had been effected with much difficulty and after many irritating disputes. The King and Queen had never, since the commencement of their reign, been on very good terms with their sister. That William should have been disliked by a woman who had just sense enough to perceive that his temper was sour and his manners repulsive, and who was utterly incapable of appreciating his higher qualities, is not extraordinary. But Mary was made to be loved. So lively and intelligent a woman could not indeed derive much pleasure from the society of Anne, who, when in good humour, was meekly stupid, and, when in bad humour, was sulkily stupid. Yet the Queen, whose kindness had endeared her to her humblest attendants, would hardly have made an enemy of one whom it was her duty and her interest to make a friend, had not an interest strangely potent and strangely malignant been incessantly at work to divide the Royal House against itself. The fondness of the Princess for Lady Marlborough was such as, in a superstitious age, would have been ascribed to some talisman or potion. Not only had the friends, in their confidential intercourse with each other, dropped all ceremony and all titles, and become plain Mrs. Morley and plain Mrs. Freeman ; but even Prince George, who cared as much for the dignity of his birth as he was capable of caring for anything but claret and

* Burnet, ii. 43.

calvered salmon, submitted to be Mr. Morley. The Countess boasted that she had selected the name of Freeman because it was peculiarly suited to the frankness and boldness of her character; and, to do her justice, it was not by the ordinary arts of courtiers that she established and long maintained her despotic empire over the feeblest of minds. She had little of that tact which is the characteristic talent of her sex: she was far too violent to flatter or to dissemble: but, by a rare chance, she had fallen in with a nature on which dictation and contradiction acted as philtres. In this grotesque friendship all the loyalty, the patience, the selfdevotion, was on the side of the mistress. The whims, the haughty airs, the fits of ill temper, were on the side of the waiting woman.

Nothing is more curious than the relation in which the two ladies stood to Mr. Freeman, as they called Marlborough. In foreign countries people knew in general that Anne was governed by the Churchills. They knew also that the man who appeared to enjoy so large a share of her favour was not only a great soldier and politician, but also one of the finest gentlemen of his time, that his face and figure were eminently handsome, his temper at once bland and resolute, his manners at once engaging and noble. Nothing could be more natural than that graces and accomplishments like his should win a female heart. On the Continent therefore many persons imagined that he was Anne's favoured lover; and he was so described in contemporary French libels which have long been forgotten. In England this calumny never gained credit even with the vulgar, and is nowhere to be found even in the most ribald doggrel that was sung about our streets. In truth the Princess seems never to have been guilty of a thought inconsistent with her conjugal vows. To her, Marlborough, with all his genius and his valour, his beauty and his grace, was nothing but the husband of her friend. Direct power over Her Royal Highness he had none. He could influence her only by the instrumentality of his wife; and his wife was no passive instrument. Though it is impossible to discover, in anything that she ever did, said, or wrote, any indication of superior understanding, her fierce passions and strong will enabled her often to rule a husband who was born to rule grave senates and mighty armies. His courage, that courage which the most perilous emergencies of war only made cooler and more steady, failed him when he had to encounter his Sarah's ready tears and voluble reproaches, the poutings of her lip and the tossings of her head. History exhibits to us few spectacles more remarkable than that of a great and wise man, who, when he had contrived vast and profound schemes of policy, could carry them into effect only by inducing one foolish woman, who was often unmanageable, to manage another woman who was more foolish still.

In one point the Earl and the Countess were perfectly agreed. They were equally bent on getting money; though, when it was got, he loved to hoard it, and she was not unwilling to spend it.* The favour of the Princess they both regarded as a valuable estate. In her father's reign they had begun to grow rich by means of her bounty. She was naturally inclined to parsimony; and even when she was on the throne, her equipages and tables were by no means sumptuous.† It might have been thought, therefore, that, while she was a subject, thirty thousand a year, with a residence in the palace, would have been more than sufficient for all her wants. There were probably not in the kingdom two noblemen possessed of such an income. But no income would satisfy the greediness of those who governed her. She repeatedly contracted debts which James repeatedly discharged, not without expressing much surprise and displeasure.

The Revolution opened to the Churchills a new and boundless prospect of gain. The whole conduct of their mistress at the great crisis had proved that she had no will, no judgment, no conscience, but theirs. To them she had sacrificed affections, prejudices, habits, interests. In obedience to them, she had joined in the conspiracy against her father: she had fled from Whitehall in the depth of winter, through ice and mire, to a hackney coach: she had taken refuge in the rebel camp: she had consented to yield her place in the order of succession to the Prince of Orange. They saw with pleasure that she, over whom they possessed such boundless influence, possessed no common influence over others. Scarcely had the Revolution been accomplished when many Tories, disliking both the King who had been driven out and the King who had come in, and doubting whether their religion had more to fear from Jesuits or from Latitudinarians, showed a strong disposition to rally round Anne. Nature had made

* In a contemporary lampoon are these lines:

"Oh, happy couple! In their life
There does appear no sign of strife;
They do agree so in the main,
To sacrifice their souls for gain."—The Female Nine, 1690.

† Swift mentions the deficiency of hospitality and magnificence in her household. Journal to Stella, August 8. 1711.

her a bigot. Such was the constitution of her mind that to the religion of her nursery she could not but adhere, without examination and without doubt, till she was laid in her coffin. In the court of her father she had been deaf to all that could be urged in favour of transubstantiation and auricular confession. In the court of her brother in law she was equally deaf to all that could be urged in favour of a general union among Protestants. This slowness and obstinacy made her important. It was a great thing to be the only member of the Royal Family who regarded Papists and Presbyterians with impartial aversion. While a large party was disposed to make her an idol, she was regarded by her two artful servants merely as a puppet. They knew that she had it in her power to give serious annoyance to the government; and they determined to use this power in order to extort money, nominally for her, but really for themselves. While Marlborough was commanding the English forces in the Low Countries, the execution of the plan was necessarily left to his wife; and she acted, not as he would doubtless have acted, with prudence and temper, but, as is plain even from her own narrative, with odious violence and insolence. Indeed she had passions to gratify from which he was altogether free. He, though one of the most covetous was one of the least acrimonious of mankind: but malignity was in her a stronger passion than avarice. She hated easily: she hated heartily; and she hated implacably. Among the objects of her hatred were all who were related to her mistress either on the paternal or on the maternal side. No person who had a natural interest in the Princess could observe without uneasiness the strange infatuation which made her the slave of an imperious and reckless termagant. This the Countess well knew. In her view the Royal Family and the family of Hyde, however they might differ as to other matters, were leagued against her; and she detested them all, James and James's Queen, William and Mary, Clarendon and Rochester. Now was the time to wreak the accumulated spite of years. It was not enough to obtain a great, a regal, revenue for Anne. That revenue must be obtained by means which would wound and humble those whom the favourite abhorred. It must not be asked, it must not be accepted, as a mark of fraternal kindness, but demanded in hostile tones, and wrung by force from reluctant hands. No application was made to the King and Queen. But they learned with astonishment that Lady Marlborough was indefatigable in canvassing the Tory members of Parliament, that a Princess's party was forming, that the House of Commons would be moved to settle on Her Royal Highness a vast income independent of the Crown. Mary asked her sister what these proceedings meant. "I hear," said Anne, "that my friends have a mind to make me some settlement." It is said, that the Queen, greatly hurt by an expression which seemed to imply that she and her husband were not among her sister's friends, replied with unwonted sharpness, "Of what friends do you speak? What friends have you except the King and me?"* The subject was never again mentioned between the sisters. Mary was probably sensible that she had make a mistake, in addressing herself to one who was merely a passive instrument in the hands of others. An attempt was made to open a negotiation with the Countess. After some inferior agents had expostulated with her in vain, Shrewsbury waited on her. It might have been expected that his intervention would have been successful: for, if the scandalous chronicle of those times could be trusted, he had stood high, too high, in her favour.† He was authorised by the King to promise that, if the Princess would desist from soliciting the members of the House of Commons to support her cause, the income of Her Royal Highness should be increased from thirty thousand pounds to fifty thousand. The Countess flatly rejected this offer. The King's word, she had the insolence to hint, was not a sufficient security. "I am confident," said Shrewsbury, "that His Majesty will strictly fulfil his engagements. If he breaks them I will not serve him an hour longer." "That may be very honourable in you," answered the pertinacious vixen: "but it will be very poor comfort to the Princess." Shrewsbury after vainly attempting to move the servant, was at length admitted to an audience of the mistress. Anne, in language doubtless dictated by her friend Sarah, told him that the business had gone too far to be stopped, and must be left to the decision of the Commons.‡

The truth was that the Princess's prompters hoped to obtain from Parliament a much larger sum than was offered

---

* Duchess of Marlborough's Vindication. But the Duchess was so abandoned a liar that it is impossible to believe a word that she says, except when she accuses herself.

† See the Female Nine.

‡ The Duchess of Marlborough's Vindication. With that habitual inaccuracy, which, even when she has no motive for lying, makes it necessary to read every word written or dictated by her with suspicion, she creates Shrewsbury a Duke, and represents herself as calling him "Your Grace." He was not made a Duke till 1694.

by the King. Nothing less than seventy thousand a year would content them. But their cupidity overreached itself. The House of Commons showed a great disposition to gratify Her Royal Highness. But, when at length her too eager adherents ventured to name the sum which they wished to grant, the murmurs were loud. Seventy thousand a year at a time when the necessary expenses of the State were daily increasing, when the receipt of the customs was daily diminishing, when trade was low, when every gentleman, every merchant, was retrenching something from the charge of his table and his cellar! The general opinion was that the sum which the King was understood to be willing to give would be amply sufficient.* At last something was conceded on both sides. The Princess was forced to content herself with fifty thousand a year; and William agreed that this sum should be settled on her by Act of Parliament. She rewarded the services of Lady Marlborough with a pension of a thousand a year†; but this was in all probability a very small part of what the Churchills gained by the arrangement.

After these transactions the two royal sisters continued during many months to live on terms of civility and even of apparent friendship. But Mary, though she seems to have borne no malice to Anne, undoubtedly felt against Lady Marlborough as much resentment as a very gentle heart is capable of feeling. Marlborough had been out of England during a great part of the time which his wife had spent in canvassing among the Tories, and, though he had undoubtedly acted in concert with her, had acted, as usual, with temper and decorum. He therefore continued to receive from William many marks of favour which were unaccompanied by any indication of displeasure.

In the debates on the settling of the revenue, the distinction between Whigs and Tories does not appear to have been very clearly marked. In truth, if there was anything about which the two parties were agreed, it was the expediency of granting the customs to the Crown for a time not exceeding four years. But there were other questions which called forth the old animosity in all its strength. The Whigs were now a minority, but a minority formidable in numbers, and more formidable in ability. They carried on the parliamentary war, not less acrimoniously than when they were a

* Commons' Journals, December 17. and 18. 1689.   † Vindication of the Duchess of Marlborough.

majority, but somewhat more artfully. They brought forward
several motions, such as no High Churchman could well support, yet such as no servant of William and Mary could well
oppose. The Tory who voted for those motions would run a
great risk of being pointed at as a turncoat by the sturdy
Cavaliers of his county. The Tory who voted against those
motions would run a great risk of being frowned upon at
Kensington.

Bill de-
claring the
Acts of the
preceding
Parlia-
ment valid.
It was apparently in pursuance of this policy that the
Whigs laid on the table of the House of Lords a bill declaring
all the laws passed by the late Parliament to be valid laws.
No sooner had this bill been read than the controversy of the
preceding spring was renewed. The Whigs were joined on
this occasion by almost all those noblemen who were connected with the government. The rigid Tories, with Nottingham at their head, professed themselves willing to enact
that every statute passed in 1689 should have the same force
that it would have had if it had been passed by a parliament
convoked in a regular manner : but nothing would induce
them to acknowledge that an assembly of lords and gentle-
lemen, who had come together without authority from the
Great Seal, was constitutionally a Parliament. Few questions
seem to have excited stronger passions than the question,
practically altogether unimportant, whether the bill should
or should not be declaratory. Nottingham, always upright
and honourable, but a bigot and a formalist, was on this
subject singularly obstinate and unreasonable. In one debate
he lost his temper, forgot the decorum which in general he
strictly observed, and narrowly escaped being committed to
the custody of the Black Rod.* After much wrangling, the
Whigs carried their point by a majority of seven.† Many
peers signed a strong protest written by Nottingham. In
this protest the bill, which was indeed open to verbal criticism, was contemptuously described as being neither good
English nor good sense. The majority passed a resolution
that the protest should be expunged ; and against this resolution Nottingham and his followers again protested.‡ The
King was displeased by the pertinacity of his Secretary of
State ; so much displeased indeed that Nottingham declared
his intention of resigning the Seals : but the dispute was soon
accommodated. William was too wise not to know the value

* Van Citters, April $\frac{8}{18}$. 1690.   ‡ Lords' Journals, April 8. and 10.
† Van Citters, April $\frac{8}{18}$.; Luttrell's 1690; Burnet, ii 41.
Diary.

of an honest man in a dishonest age. The very scrupulosity which made Nottingham a mutineer was a security that he would never be a traitor.*

The Bill went down to the Lower House; and it was fully expected that the contest there would be long and fierce : but a single speech settled the question. Somers, with a force and eloquence which surprised even an audience accustomed to hear him with pleasure, exposed the absurdity of the doctrine held by the High Tories. " If the Convention,"— it was thus that he argued,—" was not a Parliament, how can we be a Parliament ? An Act of Elizabeth provides that no person shall sit or vote in this House till he has taken the old oath of supremacy. Not one of us has taken that oath. Instead of it, we have all taken the new oath of supremacy which the late Parliament substituted for the old oath. It is therefore a contradiction to say that the Acts of the late Parliament are not now valid, and yet to ask us to enact that they shall henceforth be valid. For either they already are so, or we never can make them so." This reasoning, which was in truth as unanswerable as that of Euclid, brought the debate to a speedy close. The bill passed the Commons within forty-eight hours after it had been read the first time.†

This was the only victory won by the Whigs during the whole session. They complained loudly in the Lower House of the change which had been made in the military government of the city of London. The Tories, conscious of their strength, and heated by resentment, not only refused to censure what had been done, but determined to express publicly and formally their gratitude to the King for having brought in so many churchmen and turned out so many schismatics. An address of thanks was moved by Clarges, member for Westminster, who was known to be attached to Caermarthen. "The alterations which have been made in the City," said Clarges, "show that His Majesty has a tender care of us. I hope that he will make similar alterations in every county of the realm." The minority struggled hard. " Will you thank the King," they said, " for putting the sword into the hands of his most dangerous enemies ? Some of those whom he has been advised to entrust with military command have not yet been able to bring themselves to take the oath of alle-

Marginal note: Debate on the changes in the Lieutenancy of London.

---

* Van Citters, $\frac{\text{April 25.}}{\text{May 5.}}$ 1690.

† Commons' Journals, April 8. and 9. 1690; Grey's Debates; Burnet, ii. 42.

Van Citters, writing on the 8th, mentions that a great struggle in the Lower House was expected.

giance to him.   Others were well known, in the evil days, as
stanch jurymen, who were sure to find an Exclusionist guilty
on any evidence or no evidence."   Nor did the Whig orators
refrain from using those topics on which all factions are
eloquent in the hour of distress, and which all factions are
but too ready to treat lightly in the hour of prosperity.
" Let us not," they said, "pass a vote which conveys a reflection on a large body of our countrymen, good subjects, good
Protestants.   The King ought to be the head of his whole
people.   Let us not make him the head of a party."   This
was excellent doctrine : but it scarcely became the lips of
men who, a few weeks before, had opposed the Indemnity
Bill and voted for the Sacheverell clause.   The address was
carried by a hundred and eighty-five votes to a hundred and
thirty-six.*

Abjuration
bill.

As soon as the numbers had been announced, the minority,
smarting from their defeat, brought forward a motion which
caused no little embarrassment to the Tory placemen.   The
oath of allegiance, the Whigs said, was drawn in terms far
too lax.   It might exclude from public employment a few
honest Jacobites who were generally too dull to be mischievous : but it was altogether inefficient as a means of binding
the supple and slippery consciences of cunning priests, who,
while affecting to hold the Jesuits in abhorrence, were pro-
ficients in that immoral casuistry which was the worst part
of Jesuitism.   Some grave divines had openly said, others
had even dared to write, that they had sworn fealty to
William in a sense altogether different from that in which
they had sworn fealty to James.   To James they had plighted
the entire faith which a loyal subject owes to a rightful sovereign : but, when they promised to bear true allegiance to
William, they meant only that they would not, whilst he
was able to hang them for rebelling or conspiring against
him, run any risk of being hanged.   None could wonder that
the precepts and example of the malecontent clergy should
have corrupted the malecontent laity.   When Prebendaries
and Rectors were not ashamed to avow that they had equi-
vocated in the very act of kissing the Gospels, it was hardly
to be expected that attorneys and taxgatherers would be more
scrupulous.   The consequence was that every department
swarmed with traitors ; that men who ate the King's bread,
men who were entrusted with the duty of collecting and dis-
bursing his revenues, of victualling his ships, of clothing his

* Commons' Journals, April 24. 1690 ; Grey's Debates.

soldiers, of making his artillery ready for the field, were in the habit of calling him an usurper, and of drinking to his speedy downfall. Could any government be safe which was hated and betrayed by its own servants? And was not the English government exposed to dangers which, even if all its servants were true, might well excite serious apprehensions? A disputed succession, war with France, war in Scotland, war in Ireland, was not all this enough without treachery in every arsenal and in every custom house? There must be an oath drawn in language too precise to be explained away, in language which no Jacobite could repeat without the consciousness that he was perjuring himself. Though the zealots of indefeasible hereditary right had in general no objection to swear allegiance to William, they would probably not choose to abjure James. On such grounds as these, an Abjuration Bill of extreme severity was brought into the House of Commons. It was proposed to enact that every person who held any office, civil, military, or spiritual, should, on pain of deprivation, solemnly abjure the exiled King; that the oath of abjuration might be tendered by any justice of the peace to any subject of Their Majesties; and that, if it were refused, the recusant should be sent to prison, and should lie there as long as he continued obstinate.

The severity of this last provision was generally and most justly blamed. To turn every ignorant meddling magistrate into a state inquisitor, to insist that a plain man, who lived peaceably, who obeyed the laws, who paid his taxes, who had never held and who did not expect ever to hold any office, and who had never troubled his head about problems of political philosophy, should declare, under the sanction of an oath, a decided opinion on a point about which the most learned doctors of the age had written whole libraries of controversial books, and to send him to rot in a gaol if he could not bring himself to swear, would surely have been the height of tyranny. The clause, which required public functionaries, on pain of deprivation, to abjure the deposed King, was not open to the same objections. Yet even against this clause some weighty arguments were urged. A man, it was said, who has an honest heart and a sound understanding, is sufficiently bound by the present oath. Every such man, when he swears to be faithful and to bear true allegiance to King William, does, by necessary implication, abjure King James. There may doubtless be among the servants of the State, and even among the ministers of the Church, some persons who have no sense of honour or religion, and who are ready to forswear themselves for lucre. There may be others who have contracted the pernicious habit of quibbling away the most sacred obligations, and who have convinced themselves that they can innocently make, with a mental reservation, a promise which it would be sinful to make without such a reservation. Against these two classes of Jacobites it is true that the present test affords no security. But will the new test, will any test, be more efficacious? Will a person who has no conscience, or a person whose conscience can be set at rest by immoral sophistry, hesitate to repeat any phrase that you can dictate? The former will kiss the book without any scruple at all. The scruples of the latter will be very easily removed. He now swears allegiance to one King with a mental reservation. He will then abjure the other King with a mental reservation. Do not flatter yourselves that the ingenuity of lawgivers will ever devise an oath which the ingenuity of casuists will not evade. What indeed is the value of any oath in such a matter? Among the many lessons which the troubles of the last generation have left us none is more plain than this, that no form of words, however precise, no imprecation, however awful, ever saved, or ever will save, a government from destruction. Was not the Solemn League and Covenant burned by the common hangman amidst the huzzas of tens of thousands who had themselves subscribed it? Among the statesmen and warriors who bore the chief part in restoring Charles the Second, how many were there who had not repeatedly abjured him? Nay, is it not well known that some of those persons boastfully declared that, if they had not abjured him, they never could have restored him?

The debates were sharp; and the issue during a short time seemed doubtful: for some of the Tories who were in office were unwilling to give a vote which might be thought to indicate that they were lukewarm in the cause of the King whom they served. William, however, took care to let it be understood that he had no wish to impose a new test on his subjects. A few words from him decided the event of the conflict. The bill was rejected thirty-six hours after it had been brought in by a hundred and ninety-two votes to a hundred and sixty-five.*

* Commons' Journals, April 24, 25, and 26; Grey's Debates; Narcissus Luttrell's Diary. Narcissus is unusually angry. He calls the bill "a perfect trick of the fanatics to turn out the Bishops and most of the Church of Eng-

Even after this defeat the Whigs pertinaciously returned to the attack. Having failed in one House they renewed the battle in the other. Five days after the Abjuration Bill had been thrown out in the Commons, another Abjuration Bill, somewhat milder, but still very severe, was laid on the table of the Lords.* What was now proposed was that no person should sit in either House of Parliament or hold any office, civil, military, or judicial, without making a declaration that he would stand by William and Mary against James and James's adherents. Every male in the kingdom who had attained the age of sixteen was to make the same declaration before a certain day. If he failed to do so he was to pay double taxes and to be incapable of exercising the elective franchise.

On the day fixed for the second reading, the King came down to the House of Peers. He gave his assent in form to several laws, unrobed, took his seat on a chair of state which had been placed for him, and listened with much interest to the debate. To the general surprise, two noblemen who had been eminently zealous for the Revolution spoke against the proposed test. Lord Wharton, a Puritan who had fought for the Long Parliament, said, with amusing simplicity, that he was a very old man, that he had lived through troubled times, that he had taken a great many oaths in his day, and that he was afraid that he had not kept them all. He prayed that the sin might not be laid to his charge; and he declared that he could not consent to lay any more snares for his own soul and for the souls of his neighbours. The Earl of Macclesfield, the captain of the English volunteers who had accompanied William from Helvoetsluys to Torbay, declared that he was much in the same case with Lord Wharton. Marlborough supported the bill. He wondered, he said, that it should be opposed by Macclesfield, who had borne so prominent a part in the Revolution. Macclesfield, irritated by the charge of inconsistency, retorted with terrible severity: "The noble Earl," he said, "exaggerates the share which I had in the deliverance of our country. I was ready, indeed, and always shall be ready, to venture my life in defence of her laws and liber-

land Clergy." In a Whig pasquinade entitled "A Speech intended to have been spoken on the Triennial Bill, on Jan. 28." 169⅔, the King is said to have "browbeaten the Abjuration Bill."

* Lords' Journals, May 1. 1690. This Bill is among the Archives of the House of Lords. Burnet confounds it with the bill which the Commons had rejected in the preceding week. Ralph, who saw that Burnet had committed a blunder, but did not see what the blunder was, has, in trying to correct it, added several blunders of his own; and the Oxford editor of Burnet has been misled by Ralph.

ties. But there are lengths to which, even for the sake of her laws and liberties, I could never go. I only rebelled against a bad King: there were those who did much more." Marlborough, though not easily discomposed, could not but feel the edge of this sarcasm: William looked displeased; and the aspect of the whole House was troubled and gloomy. It was resolved by fifty-one votes to forty that the bill should be committed; and it was committed, but never reported. After many hard struggles between the Whigs headed by Shrewsbury and the Tories headed by Caermarthen, it was so much mutilated that it retained little more than its name, and did not seem to those who had introduced it to be worth any further contest.*

Act of Grace.

The discomfiture of the Whigs was completed by a communication from the King. Caermarthen appeared in the House of Lords bearing in his hand a parchment signed by William. It was an Act of Grace for political offences.

Between an Act of Grace originating with the Sovereign and an Act of Indemnity originating with the Estates of the Realm there are some remarkable distinctions. An Act of Indemnity passes through all the stages through which other laws pass, and may, during its progress, be amended by either House. An Act of Grace is received with peculiar marks of respect, is read only once by the Lords and once by the Commons, and must be either rejected altogether or accepted as it stands.† William had not ventured to submit such an Act to the preceding Parliament. But in the new Parliament he was certain of a majority. The minority gave no trouble. The stubborn spirit which had, during two sessions, obstructed the progress of the Bill of Indemnity had been at length broken by defeats and humiliations. Both Houses stood up uncovered while the Act of Grace was read, and gave their sanction to it without one dissentient voice.

There would not have been this unanimity had not a few great criminals been excluded from the benefits of the amnesty. Foremost among them stood the surviving members of the High Court of Justice which had sate on Charles the First. With these ancient men were joined the two nameless executioners who had done their office, with masked faces, on the scaffold before the Banqueting House. None

* Lords' Journals, May 2. and 3. 1690; Van Citters, May 2.; Narcissus Luttrell's Diary; Burnet, ii. 44.; and Lord Dartmouth's note. The changes made by the Committee may be seen on the bill in the Archives of the House of Lords.

† These distinctions were much discussed at the time. Van Citters, May $\frac{20}{30}$. 1690.

knew who they were, or of what rank. It was probable that they had been long dead. Yet it was thought necessary to declare that, if even now, after the lapse of forty-one years, they should be discovered, they would still be liable to the punishment of their great crime. Perhaps it would hardly have been thought necessary to mention these men, if the animosities of the preceding generation had not been rekindled by the recent appearance of Ludlow in England. About thirty of the agents of the tyranny of James were left to the law. With these exceptions, all political offences, committed before the day on which the royal signature was affixed to the Act, were covered with a general oblivion.* Even the criminals who were by name excluded had little to fear. Many of them were in foreign countries; and those who were in England were well assured that, unless they committed some new fault, they would not be molested.

The Act of Grace the nation owed to William alone; and it is one of his noblest and purest titles to renown. From the commencement of the civil troubles of the seventeenth century down to the Revolution, every victory gained by either party had been followed by a sanguinary proscription. When the Roundheads triumphed over the Cavaliers, when the Cavaliers triumphed over the Roundheads, when the fable of the Popish plot gave the ascendency to the Whigs, when the detection of the Rye House Plot transferred the ascendency to the Tories, blood, and more blood, and still more blood, had flowed. Every great explosion and every great recoil of public feeling had been accompanied by severities which, at the time, the predominant faction loudly applauded, but which, on a calm review, history and posterity have condemned. No wise and humane man, whatever may be his political opinions, now mentions without reprehension the death either of Laud or of Vane, either of Stafford or of Russell. Of the alternate butcheries the last and the worst is that which is inseparably associated with the names of James and Jeffreys. But it assuredly would not have been the last, perhaps it might not have been the worst, if William had not had the virtue and the firmness resolutely to withstand the importunity of his most zealous adherents. These men were bent on exacting a terrible retribution for all they had undergone during seven disastrous years. The scaffold of Sidney, the gibbet of Cornish, the stake at which Elizabeth Gaunt had perished in the flames for the crime of harbouring a fugitive,

* Stat. 2 W. & M. sess. 1. c. 10.

the porches of the Somersetshire churches surmounted by the skulls and quarters of murdered peasants, the holds of those Jamaica ships from which every day the carcass of some prisoner dead of thirst and foul air had been flung to the sharks, all these things were fresh in the memory of the party which the Revolution had made, for a time, dominant in the State. Some chiefs of that party had redeemed their necks by paying heavy ransom. Others had languished long in Newgate. Others had starved and shivered, winter after winter, in the garrets of Amsterdam. It was natural that in the day of their power and prosperity they should wish to inflict some part of what they had suffered. During a whole year they pursued their scheme of revenge. They succeeded in defeating Indemnity Bill after Indemnity Bill. Nothing stood between them and their victims, but William's immutable resolution that the glory of the great deliverance which he had wrought should not be sullied by cruelty. His clemency was peculiar to himself. It was not the clemency of an ostentatious man, or of a sentimental man, or of an easy tempered man. It was cold, unconciliating, inflexible. It produced no fine stage effects. It drew on him the savage invectives of those whose malevolent passions he refused to satisfy. It won for him no gratitude from those who owed to him fortune, liberty, and life. While the violent Whigs railed at his lenity, the agents of the fallen tyranny, as soon as they found themselves safe, instead of acknowledging their obligations to him, reproached him in insulting language with the mercy which he had extended to them. His Act of Grace, they said, had completely refuted his Declaration. Was it possible to believe that, if there had been any truth in the charges which he had brought against the late government, he would have granted impunity to the guilty? It was now acknowledged by himself, under his own hand, that the stories by which he and his friends had deluded the nation and driven away the royal family were mere calumnies devised to serve a turn. The turn had been served; and the accusations by which he had inflamed the public mind to madness were coolly withdrawn.* But none of these things moved him. He had done well. He had risked his popularity with men who had been his warmest admirers, in order to give repose and security to men by whom his name was never mentioned without a curse. Nor had he conferred a less benefit on those whom he had dis-

---

* Roger North was one of the many malecontents who were never tired of harping on this string.

appointed of their revenge than on those whom he had protected. If he had saved one faction from a proscription, he had saved the other from the reaction which such a proscription would inevitably have produced. If his people did not justly appreciate his policy, so much the worse for them. He had discharged his duty by them. He feared no obloquy; and he wanted no thanks.

On the twentieth of May the Act of Grace was passed. The King then informed the Houses that his visit to Ireland could no longer be delayed, that he had therefore determined to prorogue them, and that, unless some unexpected emergency made their advice and assistance necessary to him, he should not call them again from their homes till the next winter. "Then," he said, "I hope, by the blessing of God, we shall have a happy meeting." *The Parliament prorogued.*

The Parliament had passed an Act providing that, whenever he should go out of England, it should be lawful for Mary to administer the government of the kingdom in his name and her own. It was added that he should neverthe less, during his absence, retain all his authority. Some ob jections were made to this arrangement. Here, it was said, were two supreme powers in one State. A public functionary might receive diametrically opposite orders from the King and the Queen, and might not know which to obey. The objection was, beyond all doubt, speculatively just; but there was such perfect confidence and affection between the royal pair that no practical inconvenience was to be apprehended.*

As far as Ireland was concerned, the prospects of William were much more cheering than they had been a few months earlier. The activity with which he had personally urged forward the preparations for the next campaign had produced an extraordinary effect. The nerves of the government were new strung. In every department of the military administration the influence of a vigorous mind was perceptible. Abundant supplies of food, clothing, and medicine, very different in quality from those which Shales had furnished, were sent across Saint George's Channel. A thousand baggage waggons had been made or collected with great expedition; and, during some weeks, the road between London and Chester was covered with them. Great numbers of recruits were sent to fill the chasms which pestilence had made in the English ranks. Fresh regiments from Scotland, Cheshire, Lancashire, and Cumberland had landed in the Bay of Belfast. *Preparations for the first war.*

* Stat. 2 W. & M. sess. 1. c. 6.; Grey's Debates, April 29., May 1. 5. 6, 7. 1690.

The uniforms and arms of the new comers clearly indicated the potent influence of the master's eye. With the British battalions were interspersed several hardy bands of German and Scandinavian mercenaries. Before the end of May the English force in Ulster amounted to thirty thousand fighting men. A few more troops and an immense quantity of military stores were on board of a fleet which lay in the estuary of the Dee, and which was ready to weigh anchor as soon as the King was on board.*

Administration of James at Dublin.

James ought to have made an equally good use of the time during which his army had been in winter quarters. Strict discipline and regular drilling might, in the interval between November and May, have turned the athletic and enthusiastic peasants who were assembled under his standard into good soldiers. But the opportunity was lost. The Court of Dublin was, during that season of inaction, busied with dice and claret, love letters and challenges. The aspect of the capital was indeed not very brilliant. The whole number of coaches which could be mustered there, those of the King and of the French legation included, did not amount to forty.† But though there was little splendour there was much dissoluteness. Grave Roman Catholics shook their heads and said that the Castle did not look like the palace of a King who gloried in being the champion of the Church.† The military administration was as deplorable as ever. The cavalry indeed was, by the exertions of some gallant officers, kept in a high state of efficiency. But a regiment of infantry differed in nothing but name from a large gang of Rapparees. Indeed a gang of Rapparees gave less annoyance to peaceable citizens, and more annoyance to the enemy, than a regiment of infantry. Avaux strongly represented, in a memorial which he delivered to James, the abuses which made the Irish foot a curse and a scandal to Ireland. Whole companies, said the ambassador, quit their colours on the line of march and wander to right and left pillaging and destroying : the soldier takes no care of his arms : the captain never troubles himself to ascertain whether the arms are in good order : the consequence is that one man in every three has lost his musket, and that

* Story's Impartial History; Narcissus Luttrell's Diary.

† Avaux, Jan. $\frac{15}{25}$. 1690.

‡ Macariæ Excidium. This most curious work has been recently edited with great care and diligence by Mr. O'Callaghan. I owe so much to his learning and industry that I most readily excuse the national partiality which sometimes, I cannot but think, perverts his judgment. When I quote the Macariæ Excidium, I always quote the Latin text. The English version is, I am convinced, merely a translation from the Latin, and a very careless and imperfect translation.

another man in every three has a musket that will not go off. Avaux adjured the King to prohibit marauding, to give orders that the troops should be regularly exercised, and to punish every officer who suffered his men to neglect their weapons and accoutrements. If these things were done, His Majesty might hope to have, in the approaching spring, an army with which the enemy would be unable to contend. This was good advice: but James was so far from taking it that he would hardly listen to it with patience. Before he had heard eight lines read he flew into a passion and accused the ambassador of exaggeration. "This paper, Sir," said Avaux, "is not written to be published. It is meant solely for Your Majesty's information; and, in a paper meant solely for Your Majesty's information, flattery and disguise would be out of place: but I will not persist in reading what is so disagreeable." "Go on," said James very angrily; "I will hear the whole." He gradually became calmer, took the memorial, and promised to adopt some of the suggestions which it contained. But his promise was soon forgotten.*

His financial administration was of a piece with his military administration. His one fiscal resource was robbery, direct or indirect. Every Protestant who had remained in any part of the three southern provinces of Ireland was robbed directly, by the simple process of taking money out of his strong box, drink out of his cellars, fuel from his turf stack, and clothes from his wardrobe. He was robbed indirectly by a new issue of counters, smaller in size and baser in material than any which had yet borne the image and superscription of James. Even brass had begun to be scarce at Dublin; and it was necessary to ask assistance from Lewis, who charitably bestowed on his ally an old cracked piece of cannon to be coined into crowns and shillings.†

But the French king had determined to send over succours of a very different kind. He proposed to take into his own service, and to form by the best discipline then known in the world, four Irish regiments. They were to be commanded by Macarthy, who had been severely wounded and taken prisoner at Newton Butler. His wounds had been healed; and he had regained his liberty by violating his parole. This disgraceful

An auxiliary force sent from France to Ireland.

---

* Avaux, Nov. $\frac{14}{24}$. 1689.

† Louvois writes to Avaux, $\frac{\text{Dec. 26.}}{\text{Jan. 5.}}$ 16$\frac{89}{90}$: "Comme le Roy a veu par vos lettres que le Roy d'Angleterre craignoit de manquer de cuivre pour faire de la monnoye, Sa Majesté a donné ordre que l'on mist sur le bastiment qui portera cette lettre une pièce de canon du calibre de deux qui est éventée, de laquelle ceux qui travaillent à la monnoye du Roy d'Angleterre pourront se servir pour continuer a faire de la monnoye."

breach of faith he had made more disgraceful by paltry tricks and sophistical excuses which would have become a Jesuit better than a gentleman and a soldier. Lewis was willing that the Irish regiments should be sent to him in rags and unarmed, and insisted only that the men should be stout, and that the officers should not be bankrupt traders and discarded lacqueys, but, if possible, men of good family who had seen service. In return for these troops, who were in number not quite four thousand, he undertook to send to Ireland between seven and eight thousand excellent French infantry, who were likely in a day of battle to be of more use than all the kernes of Leinster, Munster, and Connaught together.*

One great error he committed. The army which he was sending to assist James, though small indeed when compared with the army of Flanders or with the army of the Rhine, was destined for a service on which the fate of Europe might depend, and ought therefore to have been commanded by a general of eminent abilities. There was no want of such generals in the French service. But James and his Queen begged hard for Lauzun, and carried this point against the strong representations of Avaux, against the advice of Louvois, and against the judgment of Lewis himself.

When Lauzun went to the cabinet of Louvois to receive instructions, the wise minister held language which showed how little confidence he felt in the vain and eccentric knight errant. "Do not, for God's sake, suffer yourself to be hurried away by your desire of fighting. Put all your glory in tiring the English out; and, above all things, maintain strict discipline."†

Not only was the appointment of Lauzun in itself a bad appointment: but, in order that one man might fill a post for which he was unfit, it was necessary to remove two men from posts for which they were eminently fit. Immoral and hard-hearted as Rosen and Avaux were, Rosen was a skilful captain, and Avaux was a skilful politician. Though it is

---

* Louvois to Avaux, Nov. $\frac{1}{11}$. 1689. The force sent by Lewis to Ireland appears by the lists at the French War Office to have amounted to seven thousand two hundred and ninety-one men of all ranks. At the French War Office s a letter from Marshal d'Estrées who saw the four Irish regiments soon after they had landed at Brest. He describes them as "mal chaussés, mal vêtus, et n'ayant point d'uniforme dans leurs ha-

bits, si ce n'est qu'ils sont tous fort mauvais." A very exact account of Macarthy's breach of parole will be found in Mr. O'Callaghan's History of the Irish Brigades. I am sorry that a writer to whom I owe so much should try to vindicate conduct which, as described by himself, was in the highest degree dishonourable.

† Lauzun to Louvois, $\frac{May\ 28.}{June\ 7.}$ and June $\frac{16}{26}$. 1690, at the French War Office.

not probable that they would have been able to avert the doom of Ireland, it is probable that they might have been able to protract the contest; and it was evidently for the interest of France that the contest should be protracted. But it would have been an affront to the old general to put him under the orders of Lauzun; and between the ambassador and Lauzun there was such an enmity that they could not be expected to act cordially together. Both Rosen and Avaux, therefore, were, with many soothing assurances of royal approbation and favour, recalled to France. They sailed from Cork early in the spring by the fleet which had conveyed Lauzun thither.* Lauzun had no sooner landed than he found that, though he had been long expected, nothing had been prepared for his reception. No lodgings had been provided for his men, no place of security for his stores, no horses, no carriages.† His troops had to undergo the hardships of a long march through a desert before they arrived at Dublin. At Dublin, indeed, they found tolerable accommodation. They were billeted on Protestants, lived at free quarter, had plenty of bread, and threepence a day. Lauzun was appointed Commander in Chief of the Irish army, and took up his residence in the Castle.‡ His salary was the same with that of the Lord Lieutenant, eight thousand Jacobuses, equivalent to ten thousand pounds sterling, a year. This sum James offered to pay, not in the brass which bore his own effigy, but in French gold. But Lauzun, among whose faults avarice had no place, refused to fill his own coffers from an almost empty treasury.§

On him and on the Frenchmen who accompanied him the misery of the Irish people and the imbecility of the Irish administration produced an effect which they found it difficult to describe. Lauzun wrote to Louvois that the Court and the whole kingdom were in a state not to be imagined by a person who had always lived in happier countries. It was, he said, a chaos, such as he had read of in the book of Genesis. The whole business of all the public functionaries was to quarrel with each other, and to plunder the government and the people. After he had been about a month at the Castle, he declared that he would not go through such another month for all the world. His ablest

---

* See the later letters of Avaux.

† Avaux to Louvois, March $\frac{14}{24}$. 1690; Lauzun to Louvois, $\frac{\text{March 23.}}{\text{April 2.}}$

‡ Story's Impartial History; Lauzun to Louvois, May $\frac{20}{30}$. 1690.

§ Lauzun to Louvois, $\frac{\text{May 28.}}{\text{June 7.}}$ 1690.

officers confirmed his testimony.* One of them, indeed, was
so unjust as to represent the people of Ireland, not merely as
ignorant and idle, which they were, but as hopelessly stupid
and unfeeling, which they assuredly were not. The English
policy, he said, had so completely brutalised them that they
could hardly be called human beings. They were insensible
to praise and blame, to promises and threats. And yet it
was pity of them : for they were physically the finest race of
men in the world.†

By this time Schomberg had opened the campaign auspi-
ciously. He had with little difficulty taken Charlemont, the
last important fastness which the Irish occupied in Ulster.
But the great work of reconquering the three southern provinces of the island he deferred till William should arrive.
William meanwhile was busied in making arrangements for
the government and defence of England during his absence.
He well knew that the Jacobites were on the alert. They
had not till very lately been an united and organised faction.

Plan of the
English
Jacobites;
Clarendon,
Ailesbury,
Dart-
mouth.
There had been, to use Melfort's phrase, numerous gangs,
which were all in communication with James at Dublin
Castle, or with Mary of Modena at Saint Germains, but
which had no connection with each other and were unwilling
to trust each other.‡ But since it had been known that the
usurper was about to cross the sea, and that his sceptre
would be left in a female hand, these gangs had been drawing close together, and had begun to form one extensive
confederacy. Clarendon, who had refused the oaths, and
Ailesbury, who had dishonestly taken them, were among the
chief traitors. Dartmouth, though he had sworn allegiance
to the sovereigns who were in possession, was one of their
most active enemies, and undertook what may be called the
maritime department of the plot. His mind was constantly
occupied by schemes, disgraceful to an English seaman, for
the destruction of the English fleets and arsenals. He was
in close communication with some naval officers, who, though

* Lauzun to Louvois, April $\frac{9}{19}$., May
$\frac{19}{29}$. 1690. La Hoguette, who held the
rank of Maréchal de Camp, wrote to
Louvois to the same effect about the
same time.

† "La politique des Anglois a été de
tenir ces peuples cy comme des esclaves,
et si bas qu'il ne leur estoit pas permis
d'apprendre à lire et à écrire. Cela les
a rendu si bestes qu'ils n'ont presque
point d'humanité. Rien ne les esmeut.

Ils sont peu sensibles à l'honneur; et
les menaces ne les estonnent point. L'interest même ne les peut engager au tra-
vail. Ce sont pourtant les gens du
monde les mieux faits."—Desgrigny to
Louvois, $\frac{\text{May 27.}}{\text{June 6.}}$ 1690.

‡ See Melfort's Letters to James
written in October 1689. They are
among the Nairne Papers, and were
printed by Macpherson.

they served the new government, served it sullenly and with half a heart; and he flattered himself that by promising these men ample rewards, and by artfully inflaming the jealous animosity with which they regarded the Dutch flag, he should prevail on them to desert and to carry their ships into some French or Irish port.*

The conduct of Penn was scarcely less scandalous. He was a zealous and busy Jacobite; and his new way of life was even more unfavourable than his late way of life had been to moral purity. It was hardly possible to be at once a consistent Quaker and a courtier: but it was utterly impossible to be at once a consistent Quaker and a conspirator. It is melancholy to relate that Penn, while professing to consider even defensive war as sinful, did everything in his power to bring a foreign army into the heart of his own country. He wrote to inform James that the adherents of the Prince of Orange dreaded nothing so much as an appeal to the sword, and that, if England were now invaded from France or from Ireland, the number of Royalists would appear to be greater than ever. Avaux thought this letter so important, that he sent a translation of it to Lewis.† A good effect, the shrewd ambassador wrote, had been produced, by this and similar communications, on the mind of King James. His Majesty was at last convinced that he could recover his dominions only sword in hand. It is a curious fact that it should have been reserved for the great preacher of peace to produce this conviction in the mind of the old tyrant.‡ Penn's proceedings had not escaped the observation of the government. Warrants had been out against him; and he had been taken into custody; but the evidence

Penn.

---

* Life of James, ii. 443. 450.; and Trials of Ashton and Preston.

† Avaux wrote thus to Lewis on the 5th of June 1689: "Il nous est venu des nouvelles assez considérables d'Angleterre et d'Escosse. Je me donne l'honneur d'en envoyer des mémoires à vostre Majesté, tels que je les ay receus du Roy de la Grande Bretagne. Le commencement des nouvelles datées d'Angleterre est la copie d'une lettre de M. Pen, que j'ay veue en original." The Mémoire des Nouvelles d'Angleterre et d'Escosse, which was sent with this despatch, begins with the following sentences, which must therefore have been part of Penn's letter: "Le Prince d'Orange commence d'estre fort dégoutté de l'humeur des Anglois; et la face des

choses change bien viste, selon la nature des insulaires; et sa santé est fort mauvaise. Il y a un nuage qui commence à se former au nord des deux royaumes, où le Roy a beaucoup d'amis, ce qui donne beaucoup d'inquiétude aux principaux amis du Prince d'Orange, qui estant riches, commencent à estre persuadez que ce sera l'espée qui décidera de leur sort, ce qu'ils ont tant taché d'éviter. Ils appréhendent une invasion d'Irlande et de France; et en ce cas le Roy aura plus d'amis que jamais."

‡ "Le bon effet, Sire, que ces lettres d'Escosse et d'Angleterre ont produit, est qu'elles ont enfin persuadé le Roy d'Angleterre qu'il ne recouvrera ses estats que les armes à la main; et ce n'est pas peu de l'en avoir convaincu."

against him had not been such as would support a charge of high treason : he had, as, with all his faults, he deserved to have, many friends in every party : he therefore soon regained his liberty, and returned to his plots.*

Preston.

But the chief conspirator was Richard Graham, Viscount Preston, who had, in the late reign, been Secretary of State. Though a peer in Scotland, he was only a baronet in England. He had, indeed, received from Saint Germains an English patent of nobility, but the patent bore a date posterior to that flight which the Convention had pronounced an abdication. The Lords had, therefore, not only refused to admit him to a share of their privileges, but had sent him to prison for presuming to call himself one of their order. He had, however, by humbling himself, and by withdrawing his claim, obtained his liberty.† Though the submissive language which he had condescended to use on this occasion did not indicate a spirit prepared for martyrdom, he was regarded by his party, and by the world in general, as a man of courage and honour. He still retained the seals of his office, and was still considered by the adherents of indefeasible hereditary right as the real Secretary of State. He was in high favour with Lewis, at whose court he had formerly resided, and had, since the Revolution, been entrusted by the French government with considerable sums of money for political purposes.‡

While Preston was consulting in the capital with the other heads of the faction, the rustic Jacobites were laying in arms, holding musters, and forming themselves into companies, troops, and regiments. There were alarming symptoms in Worcestershire. In Lancashire many gentlemen had received commissions signed by James, called themselves colonels and captains, and made out long lists of noncommissioned officers and privates. Letters from Yorkshire brought news that large bodies of men, who seemed to have met for no good purpose, had been seen on the moors near Knaresborough. Letters from Newcastle gave an account of a great match at football which had been played in Northumberland, and was suspected to have been a pretext for a gathering of the disaffected. In the crowd, it was said, were a hun-

---

* Van Citters to the States General, March 1/11. 1689. Van Citters calls Penn "den bekenden Archquaker."

† See his trial in the Collection of State Trials, and the Lords' Journals of Nov. 11, 12. and 27. 1689.

‡ One remittance of two thousand pistoles is mentioned in a letter of Croissy to Avaux, Feb. 16/26. 1689. James, in a letter dated Jan. 26. 1689, directs Preston to consider himself as still Secretary, notwithstanding Melfort's appointment.

dred and fifty horsemen well mounted and armed, of whom many were Papists.*

Meantime packets of letters full of treason were constantly passing and repassing between Kent and Picardy, and between Wales and Ireland. Some of the messengers were honest fanatics: but others were mere mercenaries, and trafficked in the secrets of which they were the bearers.

Of these double traitors the most remarkable was William Fuller. This man has himself told us that, when he was very young, he fell in with a pamphlet which contained an account of the flagitious life and horrible death of Dangerfield. The boy's imagination was set on fire: he devoured the book: he almost got it by heart; and he was soon seized, and ever after haunted, by a strange presentiment that his fate would resemble that of the wretched adventurer whose history he had so eagerly read.† It might have been supposed that the prospect of dying in Newgate, with a back flayed and an eye knocked out, would not have seemed very attractive. But experience proves that there are some distempered minds for which notoriety, even when accompanied with pain and shame, has an irresistible fascination. Animated by this loathsome ambition, Fuller equalled, and perhaps surpassed, his model. He was bred a Roman Catholic, and was page to Lady Melfort, when Lady Melfort shone at Whitehall as one of the loveliest women in the train of Mary of Modena. After the Revolution, he followed his mistress to France, was repeatedly employed in delicate and perilous commissions, and was thought at Saint Germains to be a devoted servant of the House of Stuart. In truth, however, he had, in the course of one of his expeditions to London, sold himself to the new government, and had abjured the faith in which he had been brought up. The honour, if it is to be so called, of turning him from a worthless Papist into a worthless Protestant he ascribed, with characteristic impudence, to the lucid reasoning and blameless life of Tillotson.

In the spring of 1690, Mary of Modena wished to send to her correspondents in London some highly important des-

The Jacobites betrayed by Fuller.

---

* Narcissus Luttrell's Diary; Commons' Journals, May 14, 15. 20. 1690; Kingston's True History, 1697.

† The Whole Life of Mr. William Fuller, being an Impartial Account of his Birth, Education, Relations and Introduction into the service of the late King James and his Queen, together with a True Discovery of the Intrigues for which he lies now confined; as also of the Persons that employed and assisted him therein, with his Hearty Repentance for the Misdemeanours he did in the late Reign, and all others whom he hath injured; impartially writ by Himself during his Confinement in the Queen's Bench, 1703. Of course I shall use this narrative with caution.

patches. As these despatches were too bulky to be concealed in the clothes of a single messenger, it was necessary to employ two confidential persons. Fuller was one. The other was a zealous young Jacobite named Crone. Before they set out, they received full instructions from the Queen herself. Not a scrap of paper was to be detected about them by an ordinary search; but their buttons contained letters written in invisible ink.

The pair proceeded to Calais. The governor of that town furnished them with a boat, which, under cover of the night, set them on the low marshy coast of Kent, near the lighthouse of Dungeness. They walked to a farmhouse, procured horses, and took different roads to London. Fuller hastened to the palace at Kensington, and delivered the documents with which he was charged into the King's hand. The first letter which William unrolled seemed to contain only florid compliments: but a pan of charcoal was lighted: a liquor well known to the diplomatists of that age was applied to the paper: an unsavoury steam filled the closet; and lines full of grave meaning began to appear.

Crone arrested.

The first thing to be done was to secure Crone. He had unfortunately had time to deliver his letters before he was caught; but a snare was laid for him into which he easily fell. In truth the sincere Jacobites were generally wretched plotters. There was among them an unusually large proportion of sots, braggarts, and babblers; and Crone was one of these. Had he been wise, he would have shunned places of public resort, kept strict guard over his tongue, and stinted himself to one bottle at a meal. He was found by the messengers of the government at a tavern table in Gracechurch Street, swallowing bumpers to the health of King James, and ranting about the coming restoration, the French fleet, and the thousands of honest Englishmen who were awaiting the signal to rise in arms for their rightful Sovereign. He was carried to the Secretary's office at Whitehall. He at first seemed to be confident and at his ease; but when, among the bystanders, Fuller appeared at liberty, and in a fashionable garb, with a sword, the prisoner's courage fell; and he was scarcely able to articulate.*

The news that Fuller had turned king's evidence, that Crone had been arrested, and that important letters from Saint Germains were in the hands of William, flew fast through London, and spread dismay among all who were conscious of

* Fuller's Life of himself.

guilt.* It was true that the testimony of one witness, even if that witness had been more respectable than Fuller, was not legally sufficient to convict any person of high treason. But Fuller had so managed matters that several witnesses could be produced to corroborate his evidence against Crone; and, if Crone, under the strong terror of death, should imitate Fuller's example, the heads of all the chiefs of the conspiracy would be at the mercy of the government. The spirits of the Jacobites rose, however, when it was known that Crone, though repeatedly interrogated by those who had him in their power, and though assured that nothing but a frank confession could save his life, had resolutely continued silent. What effect a verdict of Guilty and the near prospect of the gallows might produce on him remained to be seen. His accomplices were by no means willing that his fortitude should be tried by so severe a test. They therefore employed numerous artifices, legal and illegal, to avert a conviction. A woman named Clifford, with whom he had lodged, and who was one of the most active and cunning agents of the Jacobite faction, was entrusted with the duty of keeping him steady to the cause, and of rendering to him services from which scrupulous or timid agents might have shrunk. When the dreaded day came, Fuller was too ill to appear in the witness box, and the trial was consequently postponed. He asserted that his malady was not natural, that a noxious drug had been administered to him in a dish of porridge, that his nails were discoloured, that his hair came off, and that able physicians pronounced him poisoned. But such stories, even when they rest on authority much better than his, ought to be received with very great distrust.

While Crone was awaiting his trial, another agent of the Court of Saint Germains, named Tempest, was seized on the road between Dover and London, and was found to be the bearer of numerous letters addressed to malecontents in England.† Every day it became more plain that the State was surrounded by dangers; and yet it was absolutely necessary that, at this conjuncture, the Chief of the State should quit his post.

William, with painful anxiety, such as he alone was able to conceal under an appearance of stoical serenity, prepared to take his departure. Mary was in agonies of grief; and her distress affected him more than was imagined by those

Difficulties
of William

---

* Clarendon's Diary, March 6. 1690 ; Narcissus Luttrell's Diary.
† Clarendon's Diary, May 10. 1690.

who judged of his heart by his demeanour.* He knew too that he was about to leave her surrounded by difficulties with which her habits had not qualified her to contend. She would be in constant need of wise and upright counsel; and where was such counsel to be found? There were indeed among his servants many able men, and a few virtuous men. But, even when he was present, their political and personal animosities had too often made both their abilities and their virtues useless to him. What chance was there that the gentle Mary would be able to restrain that party spirit and that emulation which had been but very imperfectly kept in order by her resolute and politic husband? If the interior cabinet which was to assist the Queen were composed exclusively either of Whigs or of Tories, half the nation would be disgusted. Yet, if Whigs and Tories were mixed, it was certain that there would be constant dissension. Such was William's situation that he had only a choice of evils.

Conduct of Shrewsbury.

All these difficulties were increased by the conduct of Shrewsbury. The character of this man is a curious study. He seemed to be the petted favourite both of nature and of fortune. Illustrious birth, exalted rank, ample possessions, fine parts, extensive acquirements, an agreeable person, manners singularly graceful and engaging, combined to make him an object of admiration and envy. But, with all these advantages, he had some moral and intellectual peculiarities which made him a torment to himself and to all connected with him. His conduct at the time of the Revolution had given the world a high opinion, not merely of his patriotism, but of his courage, energy, and decision. It should seem, however, that youthful enthusiasm and the exhilaration produced by public sympathy and applause had, on that occasion, raised him above himself. Scarcely any other part of his life was of a piece with that splendid commencement. He had hardly become Secretary of State when it appeared that his nerves were too weak for such a post. The daily toil, the heavy responsibility, the failures, the mortifications, the obloquy, which are inseparable from power, broke his spirit, soured his temper, and impaired his health. To such natures as his the sustaining power of high religious principle seems to be peculiarly necessary; and unfortunately Shrewsbury had, in the act of shaking off the yoke of that superstition in which he had been brought up, liberated himself also from more salutary bands which might perhaps

* He wrote to Portland, "Je plains la povre reine, qui est en des terribles afflictions."

have braced his too delicately constituted mind into stead-fastness and uprightness. Destitute of such support, he was, with great abilities, a weak man, and, though endowed with many amiable and attractive qualities, could not be called an honest man. For his own happiness, he should either have been much better or much worse. As it was, he never knew either that noble peace of mind which is the reward of rectitude, or that abject peace of mind which springs from impudence and insensibility. Few people who have had so little power to resist temptation have suffered so cruelly from remorse and shame.

To a man of this temper the situation of a minister of state during the year which followed the Revolution must have been constant torture. The difficulties by which the government was beset on all sides, the malignity of its enemies, the unreasonableness of its friends, the virulence with which the hostile factions fell on each other and on every mediator who attempted to part them, might indeed have discouraged a more resolute spirit. Before Shrewsbury had been six months in office, he had completely lost heart and head. He began to address to William letters which it is difficult to imagine that a prince so strongminded can have read without mingled compassion and contempt. " I am sensible,"—such was the constant burden of these epistles, —" that I am unfit for my place. I cannot exert myself. I am not the same man that I was half a year ago. My health is giving way. My mind is on the rack. My memory is failing. Nothing but quiet and retirement can restore me." William returned friendly and soothing answers; and for a time these answers calmed the troubled mind of his minister.* But at length the dissolution, the general election, the change in the Commissions of Peace and Lieu-tenancy, and finally the debates on the two Abjuration Bills, threw Shrewsbury into a state bordering on distraction. He was angry with the Whigs for using the King ill, and still more angry with the King for showing favour to the Tories. At what moment and by what influence the unhappy man was induced to commit a treason, the consciousness of which threw a dark shade over all his remaining years, is not accurately known. But it is highly probable that his mother, who, though the most abandoned of women, had great power over him, took a fatal advantage of some unguarded hour, when he was irritated by finding his advice slighted, and

* See the Letters of Shrewsbury in Coxe's Correspondence, Part I. chap. i.

that of Danby and Nottingham preferred. She was still a member of that Church which her son had quitted, and may have thought that, by reclaiming him from rebellion, she might make some atonement for the violation of her marriage vow and the murder of her lord.* What is certain is that, before the end of the spring of 1690, Shrewsbury had offered his services to James, and that James had accepted them. One proof of the sincerity of the convert was demanded. He must resign the seals which he had taken from the hand of the usurper.† It is probable that Shrewsbury had scarcely committed his fault when he began to repent of it. But he had not strength of mind to stop short in the path of evil. Loathing his own baseness, dreading a detection which must be fatal to his honour, afraid to go forward, afraid to go back, he underwent tortures of which it is impossible to think without commiseration. The true cause of his distress was as yet a profound secret: but his mental struggles and changes of purpose were generally known, and furnished the town, during some weeks, with topics of conversation. One night, when he was actually setting out in a state of great excitement for the palace, with the seals in his hand, he was induced by Burnet to defer his resignation for a few hours. Some days later the eloquence of Tillotson was employed for the same purpose.‡ Three or four times the Earl laid the ensigns of his office on the table of the royal closet, and was three or four times induced, by the kind expostulations of the master whom he was conscious of having wronged, to take them up and carry them away. Thus the resignation was deferred till the eve of the King's departure. By that time agitation had thrown Shrewsbury into a low fever. Bentinck, who made a last effort to persuade him to retain office, found him in bed and too ill for conversation.§ The resignation so often tendered was at length accepted, and during some months Nottingham was the only Secretary of State.

It was no small addition to William's trouble that, at

* That Lady Shrewsbury was a Jacobite, and did her best to make her son so, is certain from Lloyd's Paper of May 1694, which is among the Nairne MSS., and was printed by Macpherson.

† This is proved by a few words in a paper which James, in November 1692, laid before the French government. "Il y a," says he, "le Comte de Shrusbery, qui, étant Secrétaire d'Etat du Prince d'Orange, s'est défait de sa charge par mon ordre." One copy of this most valuable paper is in the Archives of the French Foreign Office. Another is among the Nairne MSS. in the Bodleian Library. A translation into English will be found in Macpherson's collection.

‡ Burnet, ii. 45.

§ Shrewsbury to Somers, Sept. 22. 1697.

such a moment, his government should be weakened by this defection. He tried, however, to do his best with the materials which remained to him, and finally selected nine privy councillors, by whose advice he enjoined Mary to be guided. Four of these, Devonshire, Dorset, Monmouth, and Edward Russell, were Whigs. The other five, Caermarthen, Pembroke, Nottingham, Marlborough, and Lowther, were Tories.*

The Council of Nine.

William ordered the nine to attend him at the office of the Secretary of State. When they were assembled, he came leading in the Queen, desired them to be seated, and addressed to them a few earnest and weighty words. "She wants experience," he said : but I hope that, by choosing you to be her counsellors, I have supplied that defect. I put my kingdom into your hands. Nothing foreign or domestic shall be kept secret from you. I implore you to be diligent and to be united."† In private he told his wife what he thought of the characters of the Nine ; and it should seem, from her letters to him, that there were few of the number for whom he expressed any high esteem. Marlborough was to be her guide in military affairs, and was to command the troops in England. Russell, who was Admiral of the Blue, and had been rewarded for the service which he had done at the time of the Revolution with the lucrative place of Treasurer of the Navy, was well fitted to be her adviser on all questions relating to the fleet. But Caermarthen was designated as the person on whom, in case of any difference of opinion in the council, she ought chiefly to rely. Caermarthen's sagacity and experience were unquestionable : his principles, indeed, were lax : but, if there was any person in existence to whom he was likely to be true, that person was Mary. He had long been in a peculiar manner her friend and servant : he had gained a high place in her favour by bringing about her marriage ; and he had, in the Convention, carried his zeal for her interests to a length which she had herself blamed as excessive. There was, therefore, every reason to hope that he would serve her at this critical conjuncture with sincere good will.‡

---

* Among the State Poems (vol. ii. p. 211.) will be found a piece which some ignorant editor has entitled, "A Satyr written when the K—— went to Flanders and left nine Lords Justices." I have a manuscript copy of this satire, evidently contemporary, and bearing the date 1690. It is indeed evident at a glance that the nine persons satirised are the nine members of the interior council which William appointed to assist Mary when he went to Ireland. Some of them never were Lords Justices.

† From a narrative written by Lowther, which is among the Mackintosh MSS.

‡ See Mary's Letters to William, published by Dalrymple.

One of her nearest kinsmen, on the other hand, was one of her bitterest enemies. The evidence which was in the possession of the government proved beyond dispute that Clarendon was deeply concerned in the Jacobite schemes of insurrection. But the Queen was most unwilling that her kindred should be harshly treated; and William, remembering through what ties she had broken, and what reproaches she had incurred, for his sake, readily gave her uncle's life and liberty to her intercession. But, before the King set out for Ireland, he spoke seriously to Rochester. " Your brother has been plotting against me. I am sure of it. I have the proofs under his own hand. T was urged to leave him out of the Act of Grace; but I would not do what would have given so much pain to the Queen. For her sake I forgive the past: but my Lord Clarendon will do well to be cautious for the future. If not, he will find that these are no jesting matters." Rochester communicated the admonition to Clarendon. Clarendon, who was in constant correspondence with Dublin and Saint Germains, protested that his only wish was to be quiet, and that, though he felt a scruple about the oaths, the existing government had not a more obedient subject than he purposed to be.*

Conduct of Clarendon.

Among the letters which the government had intercepted was one from James to Penn. That letter, indeed, was not legal evidence to prove that the person to whom it was addressed had been guilty of high treason: but it raised suspicions which are now known to have been well founded. Penn was brought before the Privy Council, and interrogated. He said very truly that he could not prevent people from writing to him, and that he was not accountable for what they might write to him. He acknowledged that he was bound to the late King by ties of gratitude and affection which no change of fortune could dissolve. " I should be glad to do him any service in his private affairs: but I owe a sacred duty to my country; and therefore I was never so wicked as even to think of endeavouring to bring him back." This was a falsehood; and William was probably aware that it was so. He was unwilling however to deal harshly with a man who had many titles to respect, and who was not likely to be a very formidable plotter. He therefore declared himself satisfied, and proposed to discharge the prisoner. Some of the Privy Councillors, however, remonstrated; and Penn was required to give bail.†

Penn held to bail.

* Clarendon's Diary, May 30. 1690.   † Gerard Croese

Bishop Burnet

On the day before William's departure, he called Burnet into his closet, and, in firm but mournful language, spoke of the dangers which on every side menaced the realm, of the fury of the contending factions, and of the evil spirit which seemed to possess too many of the clergy. "But my trust is in God. I will go through with my work or perish in it. Only I cannot help feeling for the poor Queen; and twice he repeated with unwonted tenderness, "the poor Queen." "If you love me," he added, "wait on her often, and give her what help you can. As for me, but for one thing, I should enjoy the prospect of being on horseback and under canvass again. For I am sure that I am fitter to direct a campaign than to manage your Houses of Lords and Commons. But, though I know that I am in the path of duty, it is hard on my wife that her father and I must be opposed to each other in the field. God send that no harm may happen to him. Let me have your prayers, Doctor." Burnet retired greatly moved, and doubtless put up, with no common fervour, those prayers for which his master had asked.* Interview between William and Burnet.

On the following day, the fourth of June, the King set out for Ireland. Prince George had offered his services, had equipped himself at great charge, and fully expected to be complimented with a seat in the royal coach. But William, who promised himself little pleasure or advantage from His Royal Highness's conversation, and who seldom stood on ceremony, took Portland for a travelling companion, and never once, during the whole of that eventful campaign, seemed to be aware of the Prince's existence.† George, if left to himself, would hardly have noticed the affront. But, though he was too dull to feel, his wife felt for him; and her resentment was studiously kept alive by mischiefmakers of no common dexterity. On this, as on many other occasions, the infirmities of William's temper proved seriously detrimental to the great interests of which he was the guardian. His reign would have been far more prosperous if, with his own courage, capacity, and elevation of mind, he had had a little of the easy good humour and politeness of his uncle Charles. William sets out for Ireland.

In four days the King arrived at Chester, where a fleet of transports was awaiting the signal for sailing. He embarked on the eleventh of June, and was convoyed across Saint

---

* Burnet, ii. 46.   † The Duchess of Marlborough's Vindication.

George's Channel by a squadron of men of war under the command of Sir Cloudesley Shovel.*

The month which followed William's departure from London was one of the most eventful and anxious months in the whole history of England. A few hours after he had set out, Crone was brought to the bar of the Old Bailey. A great array of judges was on the bench. Fuller had recovered sufficiently to make his appearance in court; and the trial proceeded. The Jacobites had been indefatigable in their efforts to ascertain the political opinions of the persons whose names were on the jury list. So many were challenged that there was some difficulty in making up the number of twelve; and among the twelve was one on whom the malecontents thought that they could depend. Nor were they altogether mistaken; for this man held out against his eleven companions all night and half the next day; and he would probably have starved them into submission had not Mrs. Clifford, who was in league with him, been caught throwing sweetmeats to him through the window. His supplies having been cut off, he yielded; and a verdict of Guilty, which, it was said, cost two of the jurymen their lives, was returned. A motion in arrest of judgment was instantly made, on the ground that a Latin word endorsed on the back of the indictment was incorrectly spelt. The objection was undoubtedly frivolous. Jeffreys would have at once overruled it with a torrent of curses, and would have proceeded to the most agreeable part of his duty, that of describing to the prisoner the whole process of half hanging, disembowelling, mutilating, and quartering. But Holt and his brethren remembered that they were now for the first time since the Revolution trying a culprit on a charge of high treason. It was therefore desirable to show, in a manner not to be misunderstood, that a new era had commenced, and that the tribunals would in future rather err on the side of humanity than imitate the cruel haste and levity with which Cornish had, when pleading for his life, been silenced by servile judges. The passing of the sentence was therefore deferred: a day was appointed for considering the point raised by Crone; and counsel were assigned to argue in his behalf. "This would not have been done, Mr. Crone," said the Lord Chief Justice significantly, "in either of the last two reigns." After a full hearing, the Bench unanimously pronounced the error to be immaterial;

* London Gazettes, June 5. 12. 16. Chester, June 9/19. Hop attended William to Ireland as envoy from the States. 1690; Hop to the States General from

and the prisoner was condemned to death. He owned that his trial had been fair, thanked the judges for their patience, and besought them to intercede for him with the Queen.*

He was soon informed that his fate was in his own hands. The government was willing to spare him if he would earn his pardon by a full confession. The struggle in his mind was terrible and doubtful. At one time Mrs. Clifford, who had access to his cell, reported to the Jacobite chiefs that he was in a great agony. He could not die, he said: he was too young to be a martyr.† The next morning she found him cheerful and resolute.‡ He held out till the eve of the day fixed for his execution. Then he sent to ask for an interview with the Secretary of State. Nottingham went to Newgate: but, before he arrived, Crone had changed his mind and was determined to say nothing. "Then," said Nottingham," I shall see you no more; for tomorrow will assuredly be your last day." But after Nottingham had departed, Monmouth repaired to the gaol, and flattered himself that he had shaken the prisoner's resolution. At a very late hour that night came a respite for a week.§ The week however passed away without any disclosure: the gallows and quartering block were ready at Tyburn: the sledge and axe were at the door of Newgate: the crowd was thick all up Holborn Hill and along the Oxford road; when a messenger brought another respite, and Crone, instead of being dragged to the place of execution, was conducted to the Council chamber at Whitehall. His fortitude had been at last overcome by the near prospect of death; and on this occasion he gave important information.‖

Such information as he had it in his power to give was indeed at that moment much needed. Both an invasion and an insurrection were hourly expected.¶ Scarcely had William set out from London when a great French fleet commanded by the Count of Tourville left the port of Brest and entered the British Channel. Tourville was the ablest maritime commander that his country then possessed. He had studied every part of his profession. It was said of him that he was competent to fill any place on shipboard from that of car-

Danger of invasion and insurrection.

Tourville's fleet in the Channel.

* Clarendon's Diary, June 7. and 12. 1690; Narcissus Luttrell's Diary; Baden, the Dutch Secretary of Legation, to Van Citters, June $\frac{19}{30}$.; Fuller's Life of himself; Welwood's Mercurius Reformatus, June 11. 1690.

† Clarendon's Diary, June 8. 1690.

‡ Clarendon's Diary, June 10.

§ Baden to Van Citters, June $\frac{22}{30}$. 1690; Clarendon's Diary, June 19.; Luttrell's Diary.

‖ Clarendon's Diary, June 25.

¶ Luttrell's Diary.

penter up to that of Admiral. It was said of him, also, that to the dauntless courage of a seaman he united the suavity and urbanity of an accomplished gentleman.* He now stood over to the English shore, and approached it so near that his ships could be plainly descried from the ramparts of Plymouth. From Plymouth he proceeded slowly along the coast of Devonshire and Dorsetshire. There was great reason to apprehend that his movements had been concerted with the English malecontents.†

The Queen and her Council hastened to take measures for the defence of the country against both foreign and domestic enemies. Torrington took the command of the English fleet which lay in the Downs, and sailed to Saint Helens. He was there joined by a Dutch squadron under the command of Evertsen. It seemed that the cliffs of the Isle of Wight would witness one of the greatest naval conflicts recorded in history. A hundred and fifty ships of the line could be counted at once from the watchtower of Saint Catharine. On the east of the huge precipice of Black Gang Chine, and in full view of the richly wooded rocks of Saint Lawrence and Ventnor, were collected the maritime forces of England and Holland. On the west, stretching to that white cape where the waves roar among the Needles, lay the armament of France.

Arrests of suspected persons.

It was on the twenty-sixth of June, less than a fortnight after William had sailed for Ireland, that the hostile fleets took up these positions. A few hours earlier, there had been an important and anxious sitting of the Privy Council at Whitehall. The malecontents who were leagued with France were alert and full of hope. Mary had remarked, while taking her airing, that Hyde Park was swarming with them, The whole board was of opinion that it was necessary to arrest some persons of whose guilt the government had proofs. When Clarendon was named, something was said in his behalf by his friend and relation Sir Henry Capel. The other councillors stared, but remained silent. It was no pleasant task to accuse the Queen's kinsman in the Queen's presence. Mary had scarcely ever opened her lips at Council: but now, being possessed of clear proofs of her uncle's treason in his own handwriting, and knowing that respect for her prevented her advisers from proposing what the public safety required, she broke silence. "Sir Henry," she said, "I know, and everybody here knows as well as I, that there is too

* Memoirs of Saint Simon.
† London Gazette, June 26. 1690; Baden to Van Citters, $\frac{\text{June 24.}}{\text{July 4.}}$

much against my Lord Clarendon to leave him out." The warrant was drawn up; and Capel signed it with the rest. "I am more sorry for Lord Clarendon," Mary wrote to her husband, "than, may be, will be believed." That evening Clarendon, and several other noted Jacobites, were lodged in the Tower.*

When the Privy Council had risen, the Queen and the interior Council of Nine had to consider a question of the gravest importance. What orders were to be sent to Torrington? The safety of the State might depend on his judgment and presence of mind; and some of Mary's advisers apprehended that he would not be found equal to the occasion. Their anxiety increased when news came that he had abandoned the coast of the Isle of Wight to the French, and was retreating before them towards the Straits of Dover. The sagacious Caermarthen and the enterprising Monmouth agreed in blaming these cautious tactics. It was true that Torrington had not so many vessels as Tourville: but Caermarthen thought that, at such a time, it was advisable to fight, although against odds; and Monmouth was, through life, for fighting at all times and against all odds. Russell, who was indisputably one of the best seamen of the age, held that the disparity of numbers was not such as ought to cause any uneasiness to an officer who commanded English and Dutch sailors. He therefore proposed to send to the Admiral a reprimand couched in terms so severe that the Queen did not like to sign it. The language was much softened: but, in the main, Russell's advice was followed. Torrington was positively ordered to retreat no further, and to give battle immediately. Devonshire, however, was still unsatisfied. "It is my duty, Madam," he said, to tell Your Majesty exactly what I think on a matter of this importance; and I think that my Lord Torrington is not a man to be trusted with the fate of three kingdoms." Devonshire was right: but his colleagues were unanimously of opinion that to supersede a commander in sight of the enemy, and on the eve of a general action, would be a course full of danger; and it is difficult to say that they were wrong. "You must either," said Russell, "leave him where he is, or send for him as a prisoner." Several expedients were suggested. Caermarthen proposed that Russell should be sent to assist Torrington. Monmouth passionately implored permission to join the fleet

Marginal note: Torrington ordered to give battle to Tourville.

* Mary to William, June 26. 1690; Clarendon's Diary of the same date; Luttrell's Diary.

in any capacity, as a captain, or as a volunteer. "Only let me be once on board; and I pledge my life that there shall be a battle." After much discussion and hesitation, it was resolved that both Russell and Monmouth should go down to the coast.* They set out, but too late. The despatch which ordered Torrington to fight had preceded them. It reached him when he was off Beachy Head. He read it, and was in a great strait. Not to give battle was to be guilty of direct disobedience. To give battle was, in his judgment, to incur serious risk of defeat. He probably suspected,—for he was of a captious and jealous temper,—that the instructions which placed him in so painful a dilemma had been framed by enemies and rivals with a design unfriendly to his fortune and his fame. He was exasperated by the thought that he was ordered about and overruled by Russell, who, though his inferior in professional rank, exercised, as one of the Council of Nine, a supreme control over all the departments of the public service. There seems to be no sufficient ground for charging Torrington with disaffection. Still less can it be suspected that an officer, whose whole life had been passed in confronting danger, and who had always borne himself bravely, wanted the personal courage which hundreds of sailors on board of every ship under his command possessed. But there is a higher courage of which Torrington was wholly destitute. He shrank from all responsibility, from the responsibility of fighting, and from the responsibility of not fighting; and he succeeded in finding out a middle way which united all the inconveniences which he wished to avoid. He would conform to the letter of his instructions: yet he would not put everything to hazard. Some of his ships should skirmish with the enemy: but the great body of his fleet should not be risked. It was evident that the vessels which engaged the French would be placed in a most dangerous situation, and would suffer much loss; and there is but too good reason to believe that Torrington was base enough to lay his plans in such a manner that the danger and loss might fall almost exclusively to the share of the Dutch. He bore them no love; and in England they were so unpopular that the destruction of their whole squadron was likely to cause fewer murmurs than the capture of one of our own frigates.

Battle of Beachy Head.   It was on the twenty-ninth of June that the Admiral received the order to fight. The next day, at four in the morning, he bore down on the French fleet and formed his

* Mary to William, June 28. and July 2. 1690.

vessels in order of battle. He had not sixty sail of the line, and the French had at least eighty; but his ships were more strongly manned than those of the enemy. He placed the Dutch in the van and gave them the signal to engage. That signal was promptly obeyed. Evertsen and his countrymen fought with a courage to which both their English allies and their French enemies, in spite of national prejudices, did full justice. In none of Van Tromp's or De Ruyter's battles had the honour of the Batavian flag been more gallantly upheld. During many hours the van maintained the unequal contest with very little assistance from any other part of the fleet. At length the Dutch Admiral drew off, leaving one shattered and dismasted hull to the enemy. His second in command and several officers of high rank had fallen. To keep the sea against the French after this disastrous and ignominious action was impossible. The Dutch ships which had come out of the fight were in lamentable condition. Torrington ordered some of them to be destroyed: the rest he took in tow: he then fled along the coast of Kent, and sought a refuge in the Thames. As soon as he was in the river, he ordered all the buoys to be pulled up, and thus made the navigation so dangerous, that the pursuers could not venture to follow him.*

It was, however, thought by many, and especially by the French ministers, that, if Tourville had been more enterprising, the allied fleet might have been destroyed. He seems to have borne, in one respect, too much resemblance to his vanquished opponent. Though a brave man, he was a timid commander. His life he exposed with careless gaiety: but it was said that he was nervously anxious and pusillanimously cautious when his professional reputation was in danger. He was so much annoyed by these censures that he soon became, unfortunately for his country, bold even to temerity.†

* Report of the Commissioners of the Admiralty to the Queen, dated Sheerness, July 18. 1690; Evidence of Captains Cornwall, Jones, Martin and Hubbard, and of Vice Admiral Delaval; Burnet, ii. 52., and Speaker Onslow's note; Mémoires du Maréchal de Tourville; Memoirs of Transactions at Sea by Josiah Burchett, Esq., Secretary to the Admiralty, 1703; London Gazette, July 3.; Historical and Political Mercury for July 1690; Mary to William, July 2.; Torrington to Caermarthen, July 1. The account of the battle in the Paris Gazette of July 15. 1690 is not to be read without shame: "On a sçeu que les Hollandois s'estoient très bien battus, et qu'ils s'estoient comportez en cette occasion en braves gens, mais que les Anglois n'en avoient pas agi de même." In the French official relation of the battle off Cape Bevézier,—an odd corruption of Pevensey,—are some passages to the same effect: "Les Hollandois combattirent avec beaucoup de courage et de fermeté; mais ils ne furent pas bien secondez par les Anglois." "Les Anglois se distinguèrent des vaisseaux de Hollande par le peu de valeur qu'ils montrèrent dans le combat."

† Life of James, ii. 409.; Burnet. i. 5.

Alarm in London.

There has scarcely ever been so sad a day in London as that on which the news of the Battle of Beachy Head arrived. The shame was insupportable : the peril was imminent. What if the victorious enemy should do what De Ruyter had done ? What if the dockyards of Chatham should again be destroyed ? What if the Tower itself should be bombarded ? What if the vast wood of masts and yardarms below London Bridge should be in a blaze ? Nor was this all. Evil tidings had just arrived from the Low Countries. The allied forces under Waldeck had, in the neighbourhood of Fleurus, encountered the French commanded by the Duke of Luxemburg. The day had been long and fiercely disputed. At length the skill of the French general and the impetuous valour of the French cavalry had prevailed.* Thus at the same moment the army of Lewis was victorious in Flanders, and his navy was in undisputed possession of the Channel. Marshal Humieres with a considerable force lay not far from the Straits of Dover. It had been given out that he was about to join Luxemburg. But the information which the English government received from able military men in the Netherlands and from spies who mixed with the Jacobites, and which to so great a master of the art of war as Marlborough seemed to deserve serious attention, was that the army of Humieres would instantly march to Dunkirk and would there be taken on board of the fleet of Tourville.† Between the coast of Artois and the Nore not a single ship bearing the red cross of Saint George could venture to show herself. The embarkation would be the business of a few hours. A few hours more might suffice for the voyage. At any moment London might be appalled by the news that twenty thousand French veterans were in Kent. It was notorious that, in every part of the kingdom, the Jacobites had been, during some months, making preparations for a rising. All the regular troops who could be assembled for the defence of the island did not amount to more than ten thousand men. It may be doubted whether our country has ever passed through a more alarming crisis than that of the first week of July 1690.

Battle of Fleurus.

Spirit of the nation.

But the evil brought with it its own remedy. Those little knew England who imagined that she could be in danger at once of rebellion and invasion : for in truth the danger of invasion was the best security against the danger of rebellion.

---

* London Gazette, June 30. 1690 ;   † Nottingham to William, July 15.
Historical and Political Mercury for July   1690.
1690.

The cause of James was the cause of France; and, though to superficial observers the French alliance seemed to be his chief support, it really was the obstacle which made his restoration impossible. In the patriotism, the too often unamiable and unsocial patriotism of our forefathers, lay the secret at once of William's weakness and of his strength. They were jealous of his love for Holland: but they cordially sympathised with his hatred of Lewis. To their strong sentiment of nationality are to be ascribed almost all those petty annoyances which made the throne of the Deliverer, from his accession to his death, so uneasy a seat. But to the same sentiment it is to be ascribed that his throne, constantly menaced and frequently shaken, was never subverted. For, much as his people detested his foreign favourites, they detested his foreign adversaries still more. The Dutch were Protestants; the French were Papists. The Dutch were regarded as selfseeking, grasping, overreaching allies: the French were mortal enemies. The worst that could be apprehended from the Dutch was that they might obtain too large a share of the patronage of the Crown, that they might throw on us too large a part of the burdens of the war, that they might obtain commercial advantages at our expense. But the French would conquer us: the French would enslave us: the French would inflict on us calamities such as those which had turned the fair fields and cities of the Palatinate into a desert. The hopgrounds of Kent would be as the vineyards of the Neckar. The High Street of Oxford and the close of Salisbury would be piled with ruins such as those which covered the spots where the palaces and churches of Heidelberg and Manheim had once stood. The parsonage overshadowed by the old steeple, the farmhouse peeping from among beehives and appleblossoms, the manorial hall embosomed in elms, would be given up to a soldiery which knew not what it was to pity old men or delicate women, or sucking children. The words, "The French are coming," like a spell, quelled at once all murmurs about taxes and abuses, about William's ungracious manners and Portland's lucrative places, and raised a spirit as high and unconquerable as had pervaded, a hundred years before, the ranks which Elizabeth reviewed at Tilbury. Had the army of Humieres landed, it would assuredly have been withstood by every male capable of bearing arms. Not only the muskets and pikes but the scythes and pitchforks would have been too few for the hundreds of thousands who, forgetting all distinction of sect

or faction, would have risen up like one man to defend the
English soil.

The immediate effect therefore of the disasters in the
Channel and in Flanders was to unite for a moment the great
body of the people. The national antipathy to the Dutch
seemed to be suspended. Their gallant conduct in the fight
off Beachy Head was loudly applauded. The inaction of
Torrington was loudly condemned. London set the example
of concert and of exertion. The irritation produced by the
late election at once subsided. All distinctions of party disappeared. The Lord Mayor was summoned to attend the
Queen. She requested him to ascertain as soon as possible
what the capital would undertake to do if the enemy should
venture to make a descent. He called together the representatives of the wards, conferred with them, and returned to
Whitehall to report that they had unanimously bound themselves to stand by the government with life and fortune; that
a hundred thousand pounds were ready to be paid into the
Exchequer; that ten thousand Londoners, well armed and
appointed, were prepared to march at an hour's notice; and
that an additional force, consisting of six regiments of foot,
a strong regiment of horse, and a thousand dragoons, should
be instantly raised without costing the Crown a farthing.
Of Her Majesty the City had nothing to ask, but that she
would be pleased to set over these troops officers in whom
she could confide. The same spirit was shown in every part
of the country. Though in the southern counties the harvest
was at hand, the rustics repaired with unusual cheerfulness
to the musters of the militia. The Jacobite country gentlemen, who had, during several months, been laying in swords
and carbines for the insurrection which was to take place as
soon as William was gone and as help arrived from France,
now that William was gone, now that a French invasion was
hourly expected, burned their commissions signed by James,
and hid their arms behind wainscots or in haystacks. The
malecontents in the towns were insulted wherever they appeared, and were forced to shut themselves up in their houses
from the exasperated populace.*

Conduct of
Shrews-
bury.

Nothing is more interesting to those who love to study the
intricacies of the human heart than the effect which the
public danger produced on Shrewsbury. For a moment he
was again the Shrewsbury of 1688. His nature, lamentably

* Burnet, ii. 53, 54.; Narcissus Luttrell's Diary, July 7. 11. 1690; London
Gazette, July 14. 1690.

unstable, was not ignoble; and the thought, that, by standing foremost in the defence of his country at so perilous a crisis, he might repair his great fault and regain his own esteem, gave new energy to his body and his mind. He had retired to Epsom, in the hope that repose and pure air would produce a salutary effect on his shattered frame and wounded spirit. But, a few hours after the news of the Battle of Beachy Head had arrived, he was at Whitehall, and had offered his purse and sword to the Queen. It had been in contemplation to put the fleet under the command of some great nobleman with two experienced naval officers to advise him. Shrewsbury begged that, if such an arrangement were made, he might be appointed. It concerned, he said, the interest and the honour of every man in the kingdom not to let the enemy ride victorious in the Channel; and he would gladly risk his life to retrieve the lost fame of the English flag.*

His offer was not accepted. Indeed, the plan of dividing the naval command between a man of quality who did not know the points of the compass, and two weatherbeaten old seamen who had risen from being cabin boys to be Admirals, was very wisely laid aside. Active exertions were made to prepare the allied squadrons for service. Nothing was omitted which could assuage the natural resentment of the Dutch. The Queen sent a Privy Councillor, charged with a special mission to the States General. He was the bearer of a letter to them in which she extolled the valour of Evertsen's gallant squadron. She assured them that their ships should be repaired in the English dockyards, and that the wounded Dutchmen should be as carefully tended as wounded Englishmen. It was announced that a strict inquiry would be instituted into the causes of the late disaster; and Torrington, who indeed could not at that moment have appeared in public without risk of being torn in pieces, was sent to the Tower.†

During the three days which followed the arrival of the disastrous tidings from Beachy Head the aspect of London was gloomy and agitated. But on the fourth day all was changed. Bells were pealing: flags were flying: candles were arranged in the windows for an illumination: men were eagerly shaking hands with each other in the streets. A courier had that morning arrived at Whitehall with great news from Ireland.

* Mary to William, July 3. 10. 1690; Shrewsbury to Caermarthen, July 15.
† Mary to the States General, July 12.: Burchett's Memoirs; An important Account of some remarkable Passages in the Life of Arthur, Earl of Torrington, 1691.

CHAPTER XVI.

William lands at Carrickfergus and proceeds to Belfast.

WILLIAM had been, during the whole spring, impatiently expected in Ulster. The Protestant settlements along the coast of that province had, in the course of the month of May, been repeatedly agitated by false reports of his arrival.

It was not, however, till the afternoon of the fourteenth of June that he landed at Carrickfergus. The inhabitants of the town crowded the main street and greeted him with loud acclamations: but they caught only a glimpse of him. As soon as he was on dry ground he mounted and set off for Belfast. On the road he was met by Schomberg. The meeting took place close to a white house, the only human dwelling then visible, in the space of many miles, on the dreary strand of the estuary of the Laggan. A village and a cotton mill now rise where the white house then stood alone: and all the shore is adorned by a gay succession of country houses, shrubberies, and flower beds. Belfast has become one of the greatest and most flourishing seats of industry in the British isles. A busy population of a hundred thousand souls is collected there. The duties annually paid at the Custom House exceed the duties annually paid at the Custom House of London in the most prosperous years of the reign of Charles the Second. Other Irish towns may present more picturesque forms to the eye. But Belfast is the only large Irish town in which the traveller is not disgusted by the loathsome aspect and odour of long lines of human dens far inferior in comfort and cleanliness to the dwellings which, in happier countries, are provided for cattle. No other large Irish town is so well cleaned, so well paved, so brilliantly lighted. The place of domes and spires is supplied by edifices, less pleasing to the taste, but not less indicative of prosperity, huge factories, towering many stories above the chimneys of the houses, and resounding with the roar of machinery. The Belfast which William entered was a small English settlement of about three hundred houses, commanded by a castle which has long disappeared, the seat of the noble family of Chichester. In this mansion, which is said to have borne some resemblance to the palace of White-hall, and which was celebrated for its terraces and orchards stretching down to the river side, preparations had been made for the King's reception. He was welcomed at the North Gate by the magistrates and burgesses in their robes of office. The multitude pressed on his carriage with shouts of " God save the Protestant King." For the town was one of the strongholds of the Reformed Faith ; and, when, two generations later, the inhabitants were, for the first time, numbered, it was found that the Roman Catholics were not more than one in fifteen.*

The night came : but the Protestant counties were awake and up. A royal salute had been fired from the castle of Belfast. It had been echoed and reechoed by guns which Schomberg had placed at wide intervals for the purpose of conveying signals from post to post. Wherever the peal was heard, it was known that King William was come. Before midnight all the heights of Antrim and Down were blazing with bonfires. The light was seen across the bays of Carling-ford and Dundalk, and gave notice to the outposts of the enemy that the decisive hour was at hand. Within forty-eight hours after William had landed, James set out from Dublin for the Irish camp, which was pitched near the northern frontier of Leinster.†

In Dublin the agitation was fearful. None could doubt that the decisive crisis was approaching ; and the agony of suspense stimulated to the highest point the passions of both the hostile castes. The majority could easily detect, in the looks and tones of the oppressed minority, signs which in-dicated the hope of a speedy deliverance and of a terrible revenge. Simon Luttrell, to whom the care of the capital was entrusted, hastened to take such precautions as fear and hatred dictated. A proclamation appeared, enjoining all Protestants to remain in their houses from nightfall to dawn, *State of Dublin.*

---

* London Gazette, June 19. 1690; History of the Wars in Ireland by an Officer in the Royal Army, 1690 ; Villare Hibernicum, 1690 ; Story's Impartial History, 1691 ; Historical Collections relating to the town of Belfast, 1817. This work contains curious extracts from MSS. of the seventeenth century. In the British Museum is a map of Belfast made in 1685, so exact that the houses may be counted.

† Lauzun to Louvois, June $\frac{16}{26}$. The messenger who brought the news to Lauzun had heard the guns and seen the bonfires. History of the Wars in Ireland by an Officer of the Royal Army, 1690 ; Life of James, ii. 392. Orig. Mem. ; Burnet, ii. 47. Burnet is strangely mistaken when he says that William had been six days in Ireland before his arrival was known to James.

and prohibiting them, on pain of death, from assembling in any place or for any purpose to the number of more than five. No indulgence was granted even to those divines of the Established Church who had never ceased to teach the doctrine of nonresistance. Doctor William King, who had, after long holding out, lately begun to waver in his political creed, was committed to custody. There was no gaol large enough to hold one half of those whom the governor suspected of evil designs. The College and several parish churches were used as prisons; and into those buildings men accused of no crime but their religion were crowded in such numbers that they could hardly breathe.*

William's military arrangements.

The two rival princes meanwhile were busied in collecting their forces. Loughbrickland was the place appointed by William for the rendezvous of the scattered divisions of his army. While his troops were assembling, he exerted himself indefatigably to improve their discipline and to provide for their subsistence. He had brought from England two hundred thousand pounds in money, and a great quantity of ammunition and provisions. Pillaging was prohibited under severe penalties. At the same time supplies were liberally dispensed; and all the paymasters of regiments were directed to send in their accounts without delay, in order that there might be no arrears.† Thomas Coningsby, Member of Parliament for Leominster, a busy and unscrupulous Whig, accompanied the King, and acted as Paymaster General. It deserves to be mentioned that William, at this time, authorised the Collector of Customs at Belfast to pay every year twelve hundred pounds into the hands of some of the principal dissenting ministers of Down and Antrim, who were to be trustees for their brethren. The King declared that he bestowed this sum on the nonconformist divines, partly as a reward for their eminent loyalty to him, and partly as a compensation for their recent losses. Such was the origin of that donation which is still annually bestowed by the government on the Presbyterian clergy of Ulster.‡

William was all himself again. His spirits, depressed by eighteen months passed in dull state, amidst factions and intrigues which he but half understood, rose high as soon as

---

* A True and Perfect Journal of the Affairs of Ireland by a Person of Quality, 1690; King, iii. 18. Luttrell's proclamation will be found in King's Appendix.

† Villare Hibernicum, 1690.

‡ The order addressed to the Collector of Customs will be found in Dr. Reid's History of the Presbyterian Church in Ireland.

he was surrounded by tents and standards.* It was strange to see how rapidly this man, so unpopular at Westminster, obtained a complete mastery over the hearts of his brethren in arms. They observed with delight that, infirm as he was, he took his share of every hardship which they underwent; that he thought more of their comfort than of his own; that he sharply reprimanded some officers, who were so anxious to procure luxuries for his table as to forget the wants of the common soldiers; that he never once, from the day on which he took the field, lodged in a house, but, even in the neighbourhood of cities and palaces, slept in his small travelling hut of wood; that no solicitations could induce him, on a hot day and in a high wind, to move out of the choking cloud of dust, which overhung the line of march, and which severely tried lungs less delicate than his. Every man under his command became familiar with his looks and with his voice; for there was not a regiment which he did not inspect with minute attention. His pleasant looks and sayings were long remembered. One brave soldier has recorded in his journal the kind and courteous manner in which a basket of the first cherries of the year was accepted from him by the King, and the sprightliness with which His Majesty conversed at supper with those who stood round the table.†

On the twenty-fourth of June, the tenth day after William's landing, he marched southward from Loughbrickland with all his forces. He was fully determined to take the first opportunity of fighting. Schomberg and several other officers recommended caution and delay. But the King answered that he had not come to Ireland to let the grass grow under his feet. The event seems to prove that he judged rightly as a general. That he judged rightly as a statesman cannot be doubted. He knew that the English nation was discontented with the way in which the war had hitherto been conducted, that nothing but rapid and splendid success could revive the enthusiasm of his friends and quell the spirit of his enemies, and that a defeat could scarcely be more injurious to his fame and to his interests than a languid and indecisive campaign.

The country through which he advanced had, during eighteen months, been fearfully wasted both by soldiers and by

William marches southward.

---

* "La gayeté peinte sur son visage," says Dumont, who saw him at Belfast, "nous fit tout espérer pour les heureux succès de la campagne."

† Story's Impartial Account; MS. Journal of Colonel Bellingham; The Royal Diary.

Rapparees. The cattle had been slaughtered : the plantations had been cut down : the fences and houses were in
ruins. Not a human being was to be found near the road,
except a few naked and meagre wretches who had no food
but the husks of oats, and who were seen picking those husks,
like chickens, from amidst dust and cinders.* Yet, even
under such disadvantages, the natural fertility of the country,
the rich green of the earth, the bays and rivers so admirably
fitted for trade, could not but strike the King's observant
eye. Perhaps he thought how different an aspect that unhappy region would have presented if it had been blessed
with such a government and such a religion as had made his
native Holland the wonder of the world ; how endless a
succession of pleasure houses, tulip gardens, and dairy farms
would have lined the road from Lisburn to Belfast; how
many hundreds of barges would have been constantly passing
up and down the Laggan ; what a forest of masts would
have bristled in the desolate port of Newry ; and what vast
warehouses and stately mansions would have covered the
space occupied by the noisome alleys of Dundalk. "The
country," he was heard to say, "is worth fighting for."

The Irish army retreats.

The original intention of James seems to have been to try
the chances of a pitched field on the border between Leinster
and Ulster. But this design was abandoned, in consequence,
apparently, of the representations of Lauzun, who, though
very little disposed and very little qualified to conduct a
campaign on the Fabian system, had the admonitions of
Louvois still in his ears.† James, though resolved not to
give up Dublin without a battle, consented to retreat till he
should reach some spot where he might have the vantage of
ground. When therefore William's advanced guard reached
Dundalk, nothing was to be seen of the Irish army, except
a great cloud of dust which was slowly rolling southward
towards Ardee. The English halted one night near the
ground on which Schomberg's camp had been pitched in the
preceding year ; and many sad recollections were awakened
by the sight of that dreary marsh, the sepulchre of thousands
of brave men.‡

Still William continued to push forward, and still the Irish
receded before him, till, on the morning of Monday, the
thirtieth of June, his army, marching in three columns,

---

* Story's Impartial Account.   ‡ Story's Impartial Account; Dumont
† Lauzun to Louvois, $\frac{June\ 25}{July\ 5}$ 1690; MS.
Life of James. ii. 393. Orig. Mem.

reached the summit of a rising ground near the southern frontier of the county of Louth. Beneath lay a valley, now so rich and so cheerful that the Englishman who gazes on it may imagine himself to be in one of the most highly favoured parts of his own highly favoured country. Fields of wheat, woodlands, meadows bright with daisies and clover, slope gently down to the edge of the Boyne. That bright and tranquil stream, the boundary of Louth and Meath, having flowed many miles between green banks crowned by modern palaces, and by the ruined keeps of old Norman barons of the pale, is here about to mingle with the sea. Five miles to the west of the place from which William looked down on the river, now stands, on a verdant bank, amidst noble woods, Slane Castle, the mansion of the Marquess of Conyngham. Two miles to the east, a cloud of smoke from factories and steam vessels overhangs the busy town and port of Drogheda. On the Meath side of the Boyne, the ground, still all corn, grass, flowers, and foliage, rises with a gentle swell to an eminence surmounted by a conspicuous tuft of ash trees which overshades the ruined church and desolate graveyard of Donore.*

In the seventeenth century the landscape presented a very different aspect. The traces of art and industry were few. Scarcely a vessel was on the river except those rude coracles of wickerwork covered with the skins of horses, in which the Celtic peasantry fished for trout and salmon. Drogheda, now peopled by twenty thousand industrious inhabitants, was a small knot of narrow, crooked, and filthy lanes, encircled by a ditch and a mound. The houses were built of wood with high gables and projecting upper stories. Without the walls of the town, scarcely a dwelling was to be seen except at a place called Oldbridge. At Oldbridge the river was fordable; and on the south of the ford were a few mud cabins, and a single house built of more solid materials.

When William caught sight of the valley of the Boyne, he could not suppress an exclamation and gesture of delight. He had been apprehensive that the enemy would avoid a decisive action, and would protract the war till the autumnal rains should return with pestilence in their train. He was now at ease. It was plain that the contest would be sharp and short. The pavilion of James was pitched on the eminence

The Irish make a stand at the Boyne.

---

* Much interesting information respecting the field of battle and the surrounding country will be found in Mr. Wilde's pleasing volume entitled "The Beauties of the Boyne and Blackwater."

of Donore. The flags of the House of Stuart and of the House of Bourbon waved together in defiance on the walls of Drogheda. All the southern bank of the river was lined by the camp and batteries of the hostile army. Thousands of armed men were moving about among the tents ; and every one, horse soldier or foot soldier, French or Irish, had a white badge in his hat. That colour had been chosen in compliment to the House of Bourbon. "I am glad to see you, gentlemen," said the King, as his keen eye surveyed the Irish lines. "If you escape me now the fault will be mine." *

The army of James.

Each of the contending princes had some advantages over his rival. James, standing on the defensive behind entrenchments, with a river before him, had the stronger position † : but his troops were inferior both in number and in quality to those which were opposed to him. He probably had thirty thousand men. About a third part of this force consisted of excellent French infantry and excellent Irish cavalry. But the rest of his army was the scoff of all Europe. The Irish dragoons were bad ; the Irish foot worse. It was said that their ordinary way of fighting was to discharge their pieces once, and then to run away bawling "Quarter" and "Murder." Their inefficiency was, in that age, commonly imputed, both by their enemies and by their allies, to natural poltroonery. How little ground there was for such an imputation has since been signally proved by many brave achievements in every part of the globe. It ought indeed, even in the seventeenth century, to have occurred to reasonable men, that a race which furnished some of the best horse soldiers in the world, would certainly, with judicious training, furnish good foot soldiers. But the Irish foot soldiers had not merely not been well trained : they had been elaborately ill trained. The greatest of our generals repeatedly and emphatically declared that even the admirable army which fought its way, under his command, from Torres Vedras to Toulouse, would, if he had suffered it to contract habits of pillage, have become, in a few weeks, unfit for all military

---

* Memorandum in the handwriting of Alexander, Earl of Marchmont. He derived his information from Lord Selkirk, who was in William's army.

† James says (Life, ii. 393. Orig. Mem.) that the country afforded no better position. King, in a thanksgiving sermon which he preached at Dublin after the close of the campaign, told his hearers that "the advantage of the post of the Irish was, by all intelligent men, reckoned above three to one." See King's Thanksgiving Sermon, preached on Nov. 16. 1690, before the Lords Justices. This is, no doubt, an absurd exaggeration. But M. de la Hoguette, one of the principal French officers who was present at the battle of the Boyne, informed Louvois that the Irish army occupied a good defensive position. Letter of La Hoguette from Limerick, $\frac{\text{July 31.}}{\text{Aug. 10.}}$ 1690.

purposes. What then was likely to be the character of troops who, from the day on which they enlisted, were not merely permitted, but invited, to supply the deficiencies of pay by marauding? They were, as might have been expected, a mere mob, furious indeed, and clamorous in their zeal for the cause which they had espoused, but incapable of opposing a steadfast resistance to a well ordered force. In truth, all that the discipline, if it is to be so called, of James's army had done for the Celtic kerne had been to debase and enervate him. After eighteen months of nominal soldiership, he was positively farther from being a soldier than on the day on which he quitted his hovel for the camp.

William had under his command near thirty-six thousand men, born in many lands, and speaking many tongues. Scarcely one Protestant Church, scarcely one Protestant nation, was unrepresented in the army which a strange series of events had brought to fight for the Protestant religion in the remotest island of the west. About half the troops were natives of England. Ormond was there with the Life Guards, and Oxford with the Blues. Sir John Lanier, an officer who had acquired military experience on the Continent, and whose prudence was held in high esteem, was at the head of the Queen's regiment of horse, now the First Dragoon Guards. There were Beaumont's foot, who had, in defiance of the mandate of James, refused to admit Irish Papists among them, and Hastings's foot, who had, on the disastrous day of Killiecrankie, maintained the military reputation of the Saxon race. There were the two Tangier battalions, hitherto known only by deeds of violence and rapine, but destined to begin on the following morning a long career of glory. Two fine English regiments, which had been in the service of the States General, and had often looked death in the face under William's leading, followed him in this campaign, not only as their general, but as their native King. They now rank as the fifth and sixth of the line. The former was led by an officer who had no skill in the higher parts of military science, but whom the whole army allowed to be the bravest of all the brave, John Cutts. The Scotch footguards marched under the command of their countryman James Douglas. Conspicuous among the Dutch troops were Portland's and Ginkell's Horse, and Solmes's Blue regiment, consisting of two thousand of the finest infantry in Europe. Germany had sent to the field some warriors sprung from her nobles' houses. Prince George of Hesse Darmstadt,

The army of William.

a gallant youth, who was serving his apprenticeship in the military art, rode near the King. A strong brigade of Danish mercenaries was commanded by Duke Charles Frederic of Wurtemberg. It was reported that of all the soldiers of William these were most dreaded by the Irish. For centuries of Saxon domination had not effaced the recollection of the violence and cruelty of the Scandinavian sea kings; and an ancient prophecy that the Danes would one day destroy the children of the soil was still repeated with superstitious horror.* Among the foreign auxiliaries were a Brandenburg regiment and a Finland regiment. But in that great array, so variously composed, were two bodies of men animated by a spirit peculiarly fierce and implacable, the Huguenots of France thirsting for the blood of the French, and the Englishry of Ireland impatient to trample down the Irish. The ranks of the refugees had been effectually purged of spies and traitors, and were now made up of men such as had contended in the preceding century against the power of the House of Valois and the genius of the House of Lorraine. All the boldest spirits of the unconquerable colony had repaired to William's camp. Mitchelburne was there with the stubborn defenders of Londonderry, and Wolseley with the warriors who had raised the unanimous shout of "Advance" on the day of Newton Butler. Sir Albert Conyngham, the ancestor of the noble family whose seat now overlooks the field of battle, had brought from the neighbourhood of Lough Erne a regiment of dragoons which still glories in the name of Enniskillen, and which has proved on the shores of the Euxine that it has not degenerated since the day of the Boyne.†

Walker, now Bishop of Derry, accompanies the army.

Walker, notwithstanding his advanced age and his peaceful profession, accompanied the men of Londonderry, and tried to animate their zeal by exhortation and by example. He was now a great prelate. Ezekiel Hopkins had taken refuge from Popish persecutors and Presbyterian rebels in the city of London, had brought himself to swear allegiance to the government, had obtained a cure, and had died in the performance of the humble duties of a parish priest.‡ William, on his march through Louth, learned that the rich see of Derry was at his disposal. He instantly made choice of

---

* Luttrell's Diary, March 1690.

† See the Historical records of the Regiments of the British army, and Story's list of the army of William as it passed in review at Finglass, a week after the battle.

‡ See his Funeral Sermon preached at the church of Saint Mary Aldermary on the 24th of June 1690.

Walker to be the new Bishop. The brave old man, during the few hours of life which remained to him, was overwhelmed with salutations and congratulations. Unhappily he had, during the siege in which he had so highly distinguished himself, contracted a passion for war; and he easily persuaded himself that, in indulging this passion, he was discharging a duty to his country and his religion. He ought to have remembered that the peculiar circumstances which had justified him in becoming a combatant had ceased to exist, and that, in a disciplined army led by generals of long experience and great fame, a fighting divine was likely to give less help than scandal. The Bishop elect was determined to be wherever danger was; and the way in which he exposed himself excited the extreme disgust of his royal patron, who hated a meddler almost as much as a coward. A soldier who ran away from a battle and a gownsman who pushed himself into a battle were the two objects which most strongly excited William's spleen.

It was still early in the day. The King rode slowly along the northern bank of the river, and closely examined the position of the Irish, from whom he was sometimes separated by an interval of little more than two hundred feet. He was accompanied by Schomberg, Ormond, Sidney, Solmes, Prince George of Hesse, Coningsby, and others. "Their army is but small:" said one of the Dutch officers. Indeed it did not appear to consist of more than sixteen thousand men. But it was well known, from the reports brought by deserters, that many regiments were concealed from view by the undulations of the ground. "They may be stronger than they look," said William; "but, weak or strong, I will soon know all about them."[*] William reconnoitres the Irish position.

At length he alighted at a spot nearly opposite to Oldbridge, sate down on the turf to rest himself, and called for breakfast. The sumpter horses were unloaded: the canteens were opened; and a tablecloth was spread on the grass. The place is marked by an obelisk, built while many veterans who could well remember the events of that day were still living.

While William was at his repast, a group of horsemen appeared close to the water on the opposite shore. Among them his attendants could discern some who had once been conspicuous at reviews in Hyde Park and at balls in the William is wounded.

[*] Story's Impartial History; History of the Wars in Ireland by an Officer of the Royal Army; Hop to the States General, $\frac{June\ 30.}{July\ 10.}$ 1690.

gallery of Whitehall, the youthful Berwick, the small, fair-haired Lauzun, Tyrconnel, once admired by maids of honour as the model of manly vigour and beauty, but now bent down by years and crippled by gout, and, overtopping all, the stately head of Sarsfield.

The chiefs of the Irish army soon discovered that the person who, surrounded by a splendid circle, was breakfasting on the opposite bank, was the Prince of Orange. They sent for artillery. Two field pieces, screened from view by a troop of cavalry, were brought down almost to the brink of the river, and placed behind a hedge. William, who had just risen from his meal, and was again in the saddle, was the mark of both guns. The first shot struck one of the holsters of Prince George of Hesse, and brought his horse to the ground. "Ah!" cried the King; "the poor Prince is killed." As the words passed his lips, he was himself hit by a second ball, a sixpounder. It merely tore his coat, grazed his shoulder, and drew two or three ounces of blood. Both armies saw that the shot had taken effect; for the King sank down for a moment on his horse's neck. A yell of exultation rose from the Irish camp. The English and their allies were in dismay. Solmes flung himself prostrate on the earth, and burst into tears. But William's deportment soon reassured his friends. "There is no harm done," he said: "but the bullet came quite near enough." Coningsby put his handkerchief to the wound: a surgeon was sent for: a plaster was applied; and the King, as soon as the dressing was finished, rode round all the posts of his army amidst loud acclamations. Such was the energy of his spirit that, in spite of his feeble health, in spite of his recent hurt, he was that day nineteen hours on horseback.*

A cannonade was kept up on both sides till the evening. William observed with especial attention the effect produced by the Irish shots on the English regiments which had never been in action, and declared himself satisfied with the result. "All is right," he said: "they stand fire well." Long after sunset he made a final inspection of his forces by torchlight, and gave orders that everything should be ready for forcing a passage across the river on the morrow. Every soldier was to put a green bough in his hat. The baggage and great

---

* London Gazette, July 7. 1690; Story's Impartial History; History of the Wars in Ireland by an Officer of the Royal Army; Narcissus Luttrell's Diary; Lord Marchmont's Memorandum; Burnet, ii. 50. and Thanksgiving Sermon; Dumont MS.

James entering Dublin after the Battle of the Boyne

coats were to be left under a guard. The word was West-minster.

The King's resolution to attack the Irish was not approved by all his lieutenants. Schomberg, in particular, pronounced the experiment too hazardous, and, when his opinion was overruled, retired to his tent in no very good humour. When the order of battle was delivered to him, he muttered that he had been more used to give such orders than to receive them. For this little fit of sullenness, very pardonable in a general who had won great victories when his master was still a child, the brave veteran made, on the following morning, a noble atonement.

The first of July dawned, a day which has never since returned without exciting strong emotions of very different kinds in the two populations which divide Ireland. The sun rose bright and cloudless. Soon after four both armies were in motion. William ordered his right wing, under the command of Meinhart Schomberg, one of the Duke's sons, to march to the bridge of Slane, some miles up the river, to cross there, and to turn the left flank of the Irish army. Meinhart Schomberg was assisted by Portland and Douglas. James, anticipating some such design, had already sent to the bridge a regiment of dragoons, commanded by Sir Neil O'Neil. O'Neil behaved himself like a brave gentleman: but he soon received a mortal wound: his men fled; and the English right wing passed the river.

Battle of the Boyne

This move made Lauzun uneasy. What if the English right wing should get into the rear of the army of James? About four miles south of the Boyne was a place called Duleek, where the road to Dublin was so narrow, that two cars could not pass each other, and where on both sides of the road lay a morass which afforded no firm footing. If Meinhart Schomberg should occupy this spot, it would be impossible for the Irish to retreat. They must either conquer, or be cut off to a man. Disturbed by this apprehension, the French general marched with his countrymen and with Sarsfield's horse in the direction of Slane Bridge. Thus the fords near Oldbridge were left to be defended by the Irish alone.

It was now near ten o'clock. William put himself at the head of his left wing, which was composed exclusively of cavalry, and prepared to pass the river not far above Drogheda. The centre of his army, which consisted almost exclusively of foot, was entrusted to the command of Schomberg, and was marshalled opposite to Oldbridge. At Oldbridge

had been collected the whole Irish army, foot, dragoons, and
horse, Sarsfield's regiment alone excepted. The Meath bank
bristled with pikes and bayonets. A fortification had been
made by French engineers out of the hedges and buildings;
and a breastwork had been thrown up close to the water
side.* Tyrconnel was there; and under him were Richard
Hamilton and Antrim.

Schomberg gave the word. Solmes's Blues were the first to
move. They marched gallantly, with drums beating, to the
brink of the Boyne. Then the drums stopped; and the men,
ten abreast, descended into the water. Next plunged Londonderry and Enniskillen. A little to the left of Londonderry
and Enniskillen, Caillemot crossed, at the head of a long
column of French refugees. A little to the left of Caillemot
and his refugees, the main body of the English infantry
struggled through the river, up to their armpits in water.
Still further down the stream the Danes found another ford.
In a few minutes the Boyne, for a quarter of a mile, was alive
with muskets and green boughs.

It was not till the assailants had reached the middle of the
channel that they became aware of the whole difficulty and
danger of the service in which they were engaged. They
had as yet seen little more than half the hostile army. Now
whole regiments of foot and horse seemed to start out of the
earth. A wild shout of defiance rose from the whole shore:
during one moment the event seemed doubtful: but the Protestants pressed resolutely forward; and in another moment
the whole Irish line gave way. Tyrconnel looked on in helpless despair. He did not want personal courage: but his
military skill was so small that he hardly ever reviewed his
regiment in the Phœnix Park without committing some
blunder; and to rally the ranks which were breaking all
round him was no task for a general who had survived the
energy of his body and of his mind, and yet had still the rudiments of his profession to learn. Several of his best officers
fell while vainly endeavouring to prevail on their soldiers to
look the Dutch Blues in the face. Richard Hamilton ordered
a body of foot to fall on the French refugees, who were still
deep in water. He led the way, and, accompanied by some
courageous gentlemen, advanced, sword in hand, into the
river. But neither his commands nor his example could in-
fuse valour into that mob of cowstealers. He was left almost
alone, and retired from the bank in despair. Further down

* La Hoguette to Louvois, $\frac{\text{July 31.}}{\text{Aug. 10.}}$ 1690.

the river, Antrim's division ran like sheep at the approach of the English column. Whole regiments flung away arms, colours, and cloaks, and scampered off to the hills without striking a blow or firing a shot.[*]

It required many years and many heroic exploits to take away the reproach which that ignominious rout left on the Irish name. Yet, even before the day closed, it was abundantly proved that the reproach was unjust. Richard Hamilton put himself at the head of the cavalry, and, under his command, they made a gallant, though an unsuccessful attempt to retrieve the day. They maintained a desperate fight in the bed of the river with Solmes's Blues. They drove the Danish brigade back into the stream. They fell impetuously on the Huguenot regiments, which, not being provided with pikes, then ordinarily used by foot to repel horse, began to give ground. Caillemot, while encouraging his fellow exiles, received a mortal wound in the thigh. Four of his men carried him back across the ford to his tent. As he passed, he continued to urge forward the rear ranks which were still up to the breast in the water. " On ; on ; my lads ! To glory ! To glory." Schomberg, who had remained on the northern bank, and who had thence watched the progress of his troops with the eye of a general, now thought that the emergency required from him the personal exertion of a soldier. Those who stood about him besought him in vain to put on his

[*] That I have done no injustice to the Irish infantry and dragoons will appear from the accounts which the French officers who were at the Boyne sent to their government and their families. La Hoguette, writing hastily to Louvois on the $\frac{4}{14}$th of July, says : " Je vous diray seulement, Monseigneur, que nous n'avons pas esté battus, mais que les ennemys ont chassés devant eux les trouppes Irlandoises comme des moutons, sans avoir essayé un seul coup de mousquet." Writing some weeks later more fully from Limerick, he says, " J'en meurs de honte." He admits that it would have been no easy matter to win the battle, at best. " Mais il est vray aussi," he adds, " que les Irlandois ne firent pas la moindre resistance, et plièrent sans tirer un seul coup." Zurlauben, Colonel of one of the finest regiments in the French service, wrote to the same effect, but did justice to the courage of the Irish horse, whom La Hoguette does not mention.

There is at the French War Office a letter hastily scrawled by Boisseleau,

Lauzun's second in command, to his wife after the battle. He wrote thus : " Je me porte bien, ma chère feme. Ne t'inquieste pas de moy. Nos Irlandois n'ont rien fait qui vaille. Ils ont tous laché le piè."

Desgrigny, writing on the $\frac{10}{20}$th of July, assigns several reasons for the defeat. " La première et la plus forte est la fuite des Irlandois qui sont en vérité des gens sur lesquels il ne faut pas compter du tout." In the same letter he says : " Il n'est pas naturel de croire qu'une armée de vingt cinq mille hommes qui paroissoit de la meilleure volonté du monde, et qui à la veue des ennemis faisoit des cris de joye, dût être entièrement défaite sans avoir tiré l'épée et un seul coup de mousquet. Il y a eu tel regiment tout entier qui a laissé ses habits, ses armes, et ses drapeaux sur le champ de bataille, et a gagné les montagnes avec ses officiers."

I looked in vain for the despatch in which Lauzun must have given Louvois a detailed account of the battle.

cuirass. Without defensive armour he rode through the river, and rallied the refugees whom the fall of Caillemot had dismayed. "Come on," he cried in French, pointing to the Popish squadrons : "come on, gentlemen : there are your persecutors." Those were his last words. As he spoke, a band of Irish horsemen rushed upon him and encircled him for a moment. When they retired, he was on the ground. His friends raised him : but he was already a corpse. Two sabre wounds were on his head ; and a bullet from a carbine was lodged in his neck. Almost at the same moment Walker, while exhorting the colonists of Ulster to play the men, was shot dead. During near half an hour the battle continued to rage along the southern shore of the river. All was smoke, dust, and din. Old soldiers were heard to say that they had seldom seen sharper work in the Low Countries. But, just at this conjuncture, William came up with the left wing. He had found much difficulty in crossing. The tide was running fast. His charger had been forced to swim, and had been almost lost in the mud. As soon as the King was on firm ground he took his sword in his left hand,—for his right arm was stiff with his wound and his bandage,—and led his men to the place where the fight was the hottest. His arrival decided the fate of the day. Yet the Irish horse retired fighting obstinately. It was long remembered among the Protestants of Ulster that, in the midst of the tumult, William rode to the head of the Enniskilleners. "What will you do for me?" he cried. He was not immediately recognised ; and one trooper, taking him for an enemy, was about to fire. William gently put aside the carbine. "What," said he, "do you not know your friends?" "It is His Majesty;" said the Colonel. The ranks of sturdy Protestant yeomen set up a shout of joy. "Gentlemen," said William, "you shall be my guards today. I have heard much of you. Let me see something of you." One of the most remarkable peculiarities of this man, ordinarily so saturnine and reserved, was that danger acted on him like wine, opened his heart, loosened his tongue, and took away all appearance of constraint from his manner. On this memorable day he was seen wherever the peril was greatest. One ball struck the cap of his pistol : another carried off the heel of his jackboot : but his lieutenants in vain implored him to retire to some station from which he could give his orders without exposing a life so valuable to Europe. His troops, animated by his example, gained ground fast. The Irish cavalry made their last stand at a house called Plottin Castle, about a mile and a half south of Oldbridge. There the Ennis-killeners were repelled with the loss of fifty men, and were hotly pursued, till William rallied them and turned the chase back. In this encounter Richard Hamilton, who had done all that could be done by valour to retrieve a reputation forfeited by perfidy,* was severely wounded, taken prisoner, and in-stantly brought, through the smoke and over the carnage, be-fore the prince whom he had foully wronged. On no occasion did the character of William show itself in a more striking manner. "Is this business over?" he said; "or will your horse make more fight?" "On my honour, Sir," answered Hamilton, "I believe that they will." "Your honour!" muttered William; "your honour!" That half suppressed exclamation was the only revenge which he condescended to take for an injury for which many sovereigns, far more affable and gracious in their ordinary deportment, would have ex-acted a terrible retribution. Then restraining himself, he ordered his own surgeon to look to the hurts of the captive.†

And now the battle was over. Hamilton was mistaken in thinking that his horse would continue to fight. Whole troops had been cut to pieces. One fine regiment had only thirty unwounded men left. It was enough that these gal-lant soldiers had disputed the field till they were left without support, or hope, or guidance, till their bravest leader was a captive, and till their King had fled.

Whether James had owed his early reputation for valour to accident and flattery, or whether, as he advanced in life, his character underwent a change, may be doubted. But it is certain that, in his youth, he was generally believed to pos-sess, not merely that average measure of fortitude which quali-fies a soldier to go through a campaign without disgrace, but

Flight of James.

---

* Lauzun wrote to Seignelay, July ¹⁶/₂₆, 1690, "Richard Amilton a été fait pri-sonnier, faisant fort bien son devoir."

† My chief materials for the history of this battle are Story's Impartial Ac-count and Continuation; the History of the War in Ireland by an Officer of the Royal Army; the despatches in the French War Office; The Life of James, Orig. Mem.; Burnet, ii. 50. 60.; Nar-cissus Luttrell's Diary; the London Ga-zette of July 10. 1690; the Despatches of Hop and Baden; a narrative probably drawn up by Portland, which William sent to the States General; Portland's private letter to Melville; Captain Rich-ardson's Narrative and map of the battle; the Dumont MS., and the Bel-lingham MS. I have also seen an account of the battle in a Diary kept in bad Latin and in an almost undecipher-able hand by one of the beaten army who seems to have been a hedge schoolmaster turned Captain. This Diary was kindly lent to me by Mr. Walker, to whom it belongs. The writer relates the misfor-tunes of his country in a style of which a short specimen may suffice: "1 July, 1690. O diem illum infandum, cum ini-mici potiti sunt pass apud Oldbridge et nos circumdederant et fregerunt prope Plottin. Hinc omnes fugimus Dublin versus. Ego mecum tuli Cap Moore et Georgium Ogle, et venimus hac nocte Dub."

that high and serene intrepidity which is the virtue of great commanders.* It is equally certain that, in his later years, he repeatedly, at conjunctures such as have often inspired timorous and delicate women with heroic courage, showed a pusillanimous anxiety about his personal safety. Of the most powerful motives which can induce human beings to en-counter peril, none was wanting to him on the day of the Boyne. The eyes of contending nations and churches, of friends devoted to his cause and of enemies eager to witness his humiliation, were fixed upon him. He had, in his own opinion, sacred rights to maintain and cruel wrongs to revenge. He was a King come to fight for three kingdoms. He was a father come to fight for the birthright of his child. He was a zealous Roman Catholic, come to fight in the holiest of crusades. If all this was not enough, he saw, from the secure position which he occupied on the height of Donore, a sight which, it might have been thought, would have roused the most torpid of mankind to emulation. He saw his rival, weak, sickly, wounded, swimming the river, struggling through the mud, leading the charge, stopping the flight, grasping the sword with the left hand, managing the bridle with a bandaged arm. But none of these things moved that sluggish and ignoble nature. He watched, from a safe distance, the beginning of the battle on which his fate and the fate of his race depended. When it became clear that the day was going against Ireland, he was seized with an apprehension that his flight might be intercepted, and galloped towards Dublin. He was escorted by a bodyguard under the command of Sarsfield, who had, on that day, had no opportunity of displaying the skill and courage which his enemies allowed that he possessed.† The French auxiliaries, who had been employed the whole morning in keeping William's right wing in check, covered the flight of the

* See Pepys's Diary, June 4. 1664. "He tells me above all of the Duke of York, that he is more himself, and more of judgment is at hand in him, in the middle of a desperate service than at other times." Clarendon repeatedly says the same. Swift wrote on the margin of his copy of Clarendon, in one place, "How old was he (James) when he turned Papist and a coward?"—in another, "He proved a cowardly Popish king."

† The Père Orléans mentions that Sarsfield accompanied James. The battle of the Boyne had scarcely been fought when it was made the subject of a drama, the Royal Flight, or the Conquest of Ireland, a Farce, 1690. Nothing more execrable was ever written, even for Bartholomew Fair. But it deserves to be remarked that, in this wretched piece, though the Irish generally are repre-sented as poltroons, an exception is made in favour of Sarsfield. "This fellow," says James, aside, "will make me valiant, I think, in spite of my teeth." "Curse of my stars!" says Sarsfield, after the battle. "That I must be de-tached! I would have wrested victory out of heretic Fortune's hands."

beaten army. They were indeed in some danger of being broken and swept away by the torrent of runaways, all pressing to get first to the pass of Duleek, and were forced to fire repeatedly on these despicable allies.* The retreat was, however, effected with less loss than might have been expected. For even the admirers of William owned that he did not show in the pursuit the energy which even his detractors acknowledged that he had shown in the battle. Perhaps his physical infirmities, his hurt, and the fatigue which he had undergone, had made him incapable of bodily or mental exertion. Of the last forty hours he had passed thirty-five on horseback. Schomberg, who might have supplied his place, was no more. It was said in the camp that the King could not do everything, and that what was not done by him was not done at all.

The slaughter had been less than on any battle field of equal importance and celebrity. Of the Irish only about fifteen hundred had fallen: but they were almost all cavalry, the flower of the army, brave and well disciplined men, whose place could not easily be supplied. William gave strict orders that there should be no unnecessary bloodshed, and enforced those orders by an act of laudable severity. One of his soldiers, after the fight was over, butchered three defenceless Irishmen who asked for quarter. The King ordered the murderer to be hanged on the spot.† Loss of the two armies.

The loss of the conquerors did not exceed five hundred men : but among them was the first captain in Europe. To his corpse every honour was paid. The only cemetery in which so illustrious a warrior, slain in arms for the liberties and religion of England, could properly be laid was that venerable Abbey, hallowed by the dust of many generations of princes, heroes, and poets. It was announced that the brave veteran would have a public funeral at Westminster. In the meantime his corpse was embalmed with such skill as could be found in the camp, and was deposited in a leaden coffin.†

Walker was treated less respectfully. William thought him a busybody who had been properly punished for running into danger without any call of duty, and expressed that feeling, with characteristic bluntness, on the field of battle. " Sir,"

* Both La Hoguette and Zurlauben informed their government that it had been necessary to fire on the Irish fugitives, who would otherwise have thrown the French ranks into confusion,
† Baden to Van Citters, July $\frac{9}{18}$. 1690.
‡ New and Perfect Journal, 1690 ; Luttrell's Diary.

said an attendant, " the Bishop of Derry has been killed by a shot at the ford." " What took him there ?" growled the King.

The victorious army advanced that day to Duleek, and passed the warm summer night there under the open sky. The tents and the baggage waggons were still on the north of the river. William's coach had been brought over; and he slept in it surrounded by his soldiers. On the following day, Drogheda surrendered without a blow, and the garrison, thirteen hundred strong, marched out unarmed.*

Fall of
Drogheda.

Meanwhile Dublin had been in violent commotion. On the thirtieth of June it was known that the armies were face to face with the Boyne between them, and that a battle was almost inevitable. The news that William had been wounded came that evening. The first report was that the wound was mortal. It was believed, and confidently repeated, that the usurper was no more ; and, before the truth was known, couriers started bearing the glad tidings of his death to the French ships which lay in the ports of Munster. From daybreak on the first of July the streets of Dublin were filled with persons eagerly asking and telling news. A thousand wild rumours wandered to and fro among the crowd. A fleet of men of war under the white flag had been seen from the hill of Howth. An army commanded by a Marshal of France had landed in Kent. There had been hard fighting at the Boyne: but the Irish had won the day : the English right wing had been routed : the Prince of Orange was a prisoner. While the Roman Catholics heard and repeated these stories in all the places of public resort, the few Protestants who were still out of prison, afraid of being torn to pieces, shut themselves up in their inner chambers. But, towards five in the afternoon, a few runaways on tired horses came straggling in with evil tidings. By six it was known that all was lost. Soon after sunset, James, escorted by two hundred cavalry, rode into the Castle. At the threshold he was met by the wife of Tyrconnel, once the gay and beautiful Fanny Jennings, the loveliest coquette in the brilliant Whitehall of the Restoration. To her the vanquished King had to announce the ruin of her fortunes and of his own. And now the tide of fugitives came in fast. Till midnight all the northern avenues of the capital were choked by trains of cars and by bands of dragoons, spent with running and riding, and begrimed with dust. Some had lost their fire arms, and some

State of
Dublin.

* Story; London Gazette, July 10, 1690.

their swords. Some were disfigured by recent wounds. At two in the morning Dublin was still: but, before the early dawn of midsummer, the sleepers were roused by the peal of trumpets; and the horse, who had, on the preceding day, so well supported the honour of their country, came pouring through the streets, with ranks fearfully thinned, yet preserving, even in that extremity, some show of military order. Two hours later Lauzun's drums were heard; and the French regiments, in unbroken array, marched into the city.* Many thought that, with such a force, a stand might still be made. But, before six o'clock, the Lord Mayor and some of the principal Roman Catholic citizens were summoned in haste to the Castle. James took leave of them with a speech which did him little honour. He had often, he said, been warned that Irishmen, however well they might look, would never acquit themselves well on a field of battle: and he had now found that the warning was but too true. He had been so unfortunate as to see himself in less than two years abandoned by two armies. His English troops had not wanted courage: but they had wanted loyalty. His Irish troops were, no doubt, attached to his cause, which was their own. But, as soon as they were brought front to front with an enemy, they ran away. The loss indeed had been little. More shame for those who had fled with so little loss. "I will never command an Irish army again. I must shift for myself; and so must you." After thus reviling his soldiers for being the rabble which his own mismanagement had made them, and for following the example of cowardice which he had himself set them, he uttered a few words more worthy of a King. He knew, he said, that some of his adherents had declared that they would burn Dublin down rather than suffer it to fall into the hands of the English. Such an act would disgrace him in the eyes of all mankind: for nobody would believe that his friends would venture so far without his sanction. Such an act would also draw on those who committed it severities which otherwise they had no cause to apprehend: for inhumanity to vanquished enemies was not among the faults of the Prince of Orange. For these reasons James charged his hearers on their allegiance neither to sack nor to destroy the city.† He then took his departure, crossed the Wicklow hills with all speed, and never stopped till he

* True and Perfect Journal; Villare Hibernicum; Story's Impartial History. London Gazette, July 10. 1690, Burnet, ii. 51.; Leslie's Answer to King.
† Story; True and Perfect Journal;

was fifty miles from Dublin. Scarcely had he alighted to take some refreshment when he was scared by an absurd report that the pursuers were close upon him. He started again, rode hard all night, and gave orders that the bridges should be pulled down behind him. At sunrise on the third of July he reached the harbour of Waterford. Thence he went by sea to Kinsale, where he embarked on board of a French frigate, and sailed for Brest.*

James flies to France.

After his departure the confusion in Dublin increased hourly. During the whole of the day which followed the battle, flying foot soldiers, weary and soiled with travel, were constantly coming in. Roman Catholic citizens, with their wives, their families and their household stuff, were constantly going out. In some parts of the capital there was still an appearance of martial order and preparedness. Guards were posted at the gates: the castle was occupied by a strong body of troops; and it was generally supposed that the enemy would not be admitted without a struggle. Indeed some swaggerers, who had, a few hours before, run from the breastwork at Oldbridge without drawing a trigger, now swore that they would lay the town in ashes rather than leave it to the Prince of Orange. But towards the evening Tyrconnel and Lauzun collected all their forces, and marched out of the city by the road leading to that vast sheepwalk which extends over the table land of Kildare. Instantly the face of things in Dublin was changed. The Protestants everywhere came forth from their hidingplaces. Some of them entered the houses of their persecutors and demanded arms. The doors of the prisons were opened. The Bishops of Meath and Limerick, Doctor King, and others, who had long held the doctrine of passive obedience, but who had at length been converted by oppression into moderate Whigs, formed themselves into a provisional government, and sent a messenger to William's camp, with the news that Dublin was prepared to welcome him. At eight that evening a troop of English dragoons arrived. They were met by the whole Protestant population on College Green, where the statue of the deliverer now stands. Hundreds embraced the soldiers, hung fondly about the necks of the horses, and ran wildly about, shaking hands with each other. On the morrow a large body of cavalry arrived; and soon from every side came news of the effects which the victory of the Boyne had produced. James had quitted the island. Wexford had

Dublin evacuated by the French and Irish troops.

* Life of James, ii. 404. Orig. Mem.; Monthly Mercury for August, 1690.

declared for King William. Within twenty-five miles of the capital there was not a Papist in arms. Almost all the baggage and stores of the defeated army had been seized by the conquerors. The Enniskilleners had taken not less than three hundred cars, and had found among the booty ten thousand pounds in money, much plate, many valuable trinkets, and all the rich camp equipage of Tyrconnel and Lauzun.*

William fixed his head quarters at Finglass, about two miles from Dublin. Thence on the morning of Sunday, the sixth of July, he rode in great state to the cathedral, and there, with the crown on his head, returned public thanks to God in the choir which is now hung with the banners of the Knights of Saint Patrick. There the remains of Schomberg were deposited, as it was then thought, only for a time ; and there they still remain. Doctor King preached, with all the fervour of a neophyte, on the great deliverance which God had wrought for the Church. The Protestant magistrates of the city appeared again, after a long interval, in the pomp of office. William could not be persuaded to repose himself at the Castle, but in the evening returned to his camp, and slept there in his wooden cabin.†

Entry of William into Dublin.

The fame of these great events flew fast, and excited strong emotions all over Europe. The news of William's wound everywhere preceded by a few hours the news of his victory. Paris was roused at dead of night by the arrival of a courier who brought the joyful intelligence that the heretic, the parricide, the mortal enemy of the greatness of France, had been struck dead by a cannon ball in the sight of the two armies. The commissaries of police ran about the city, knocked at the doors, and called the people up to illuminate. In an hour streets, quays, and bridges were in a blaze : drums

Effect produced in France by the news from Ireland.

---

* True and Perfect Journal; London Gazette, July 10. and 14. 1690 ; Narcissus Luttrell's Diary. In the Life of James Bonnell, Accountant General of Ireland (1703), is a remarkable religious meditation, from which I will quote a short passage. " How did we see the Protestants on the great day of our Revolution, Thursday the Third of July, a day ever to be remembered by us with the greatest thankfulness, congratulate and embrace one another as they met, like persons alive from the dead, like brothers and sisters meeting after a long absence, and going about from house to house to give each other joy of God's great mercy, enquiring of one another

how they past the late days of distress and terror, what apprehensions they had, what fears or dangers they were under; those that were prisoners, how they got their liberty, how they were treated, and what, from time to time, they thought of things."

† London Gazette, July 14. 1690; Story; True and Perfect Journal; Dumont MS. Dumont is the only person who mentions the crown. As he was present, he could not be mistaken. It was probably the crown which James had been in the habit of wearing when he appeared on the throne at the King's Inns.

were beating and trumpets sounding: the bells of Notre
Dame were ringing: peals of cannon were resounding from
the batteries of the Bastille. Tables were set out in the
streets; and wine was served to all who passed. A Prince
of Orange, made of straw, was trailed through the mud, and
at last committed to the flames. He was attended by a
hideous effigy of the devil, carrying a scroll, on which was
written, "I have been waiting for thee these two years."
The shops of several Huguenots, who had been dragooned
into calling themselves Catholics, but who were suspected of
being still heretics at heart, were sacked by the rabble. It
was hardly safe to question the truth of the report which had
been so eagerly welcomed by the multitude. Soon, however,
some coolheaded people ventured to remark that the fact of
the tyrant's death was not quite so certain as might be
wished. Then arose a vehement controversy about the effect
of such wounds: for the vulgar notion was that no person
struck by a cannon ball on the shoulder could recover. The
disputants appealed to medical authority; and the doors of
the great surgeons and physicians were thronged, it was
jocosely said, as if there had been a pestilence in Paris. The
question was soon settled by a letter from James, which announced his defeat and his arrival at Brest.[*]

Effect
produced
at Rome
by the
news from
Ireland.

At Rome the news from Ireland produced a sensation of
a very different kind. There too the report of William's
death was, during a short time, credited. At the French
embassy all was joy and triumph: but the Ambassadors of
the House of Austria were in despair; and the aspect of the
Pontifical Court by no means indicated exultation.[†] Melfort, in a transport of joy, sate down to write a letter of
congratulation to Mary of Modena. That letter is still
extant, and would alone suffice to explain why he was the
favourite of James. Herod,—so William was designated,—
was gone. There must be a restoration; and that restoration ought to be followed by a terrible revenge and by the
establishment of despotism. The power of the purse must be
taken away from the Commons. Political offenders must be
tried, not by juries, but by judges on whom the Crown
could depend. The Habeas Corpus Act must be rescinded.

* Monthly Mercury for August 1690;
Burnet, ii. 50.; Dangeau, Aug. 2. 1690,
and Saint Simon's note; The Follies of
France, or a true Relation of the extravagant Rejoicings, &c., dated Paris, Aug.
8. 1690.

† "Me tiene," the Marquis of Cogolludo, Spanish minister at Rome, says of
this report, "en sumo cuidado y descon-
suelo, pues esta seria la ultima ruina de
la causa comun."—Cogolludo to Ronquillo, Rome, Aug. 2. 1690.

The authors of the Revolution must be punished with merciless severity. "If," the cruel apostate wrote, "if the King is forced to pardon, let it be as few rogues as he can." [*] After the lapse of some anxious hours, a messenger bearing later and more authentic intelligence alighted at the palace occupied by the representative of the Catholic King. In a moment all was changed. The enemies of France,—and all the population, except Frenchmen and British Jacobites, were her enemies,—eagerly felicitated one another. All the clerks of the Spanish legation were too few to make transcripts of the despatches for the Cardinals and Bishops who were impatient to know the details of the victory. The first copy was sent to the Pope, and was doubtless welcome to him.[†]

The good news from Ireland reached London at a moment when good news was needed. The English flag had been disgraced in the English seas. A foreign enemy threatened the coast. Traitors were at work within the realm. Mary had exerted herself beyond her strength. Her gentle nature was unequal to the cruel anxieties of her position; and she complained that she could scarcely snatch a moment from business to calm herself by prayer. Her distress rose to the highest point when she learned that the camps of her father and her husband were pitched near to each other, and that tidings of a battle might be hourly expected. She stole time for a visit to Kensington, and had three hours of quiet in the garden, then a rural solitude.[‡] But the recollection of days passed there with him whom she might never see again overpowered her. "The place," she wrote to him, "made me think how happy I was there when I had your dear company. But now I will say no more; for I shall hurt my own eyes, which I want now more than ever. Adieu. Think of me and love me as much as I shall you, whom I love more than my life."[§]

Early on the morning after these tender lines had been despatched, Whitehall was roused by the arrival of a post from Ireland. Nottingham was called out of bed. The Queen, who was just going to the chapel where she daily

Marginal note: Effect produced in London by the news from Ireland.

---

[*] Original Letters published by Sir Henry Ellis.

[†] "Dell sucesso de Irlanda doy a v. Exca la enorabuena, y le aseguro no ha bastado casi la gente que tengo en la Secretaria para repartir copias dello, pues le he embiado a todo el lugar, y la primera al Papa."—Cogolludo to Ronquillo,

postscript to the letter of Aug. 2. Cogolludo, of course, uses the new style. The tidings of the battle, therefore, had been three weeks in getting to Rome.

[‡] Evelyn (Feb. 25. 16⁸⁹⁄₉₀) calls it "a sweet villa."

[§] Mary to William, July 5. 1690.

attended divine service, was informed that William had been
wounded. She had wept much : but till that moment she
had wept alone, and had constrained herself to show a
cheerful countenance to her Court and Council. But when
Nottingham put her husband's letter into her hands, she
burst into tears. She was still trembling with the violence
of her emotions, and had scarcely finished a letter to William
in which she poured out her love, her fears, and her thankfulness, with the sweet natural eloquence of her sex, when
another messenger arrived with the news that the English
army had forced a passage across the Boyne, that the Irish
were flying in confusion, and that the King was well. Yet
she was visibly uneasy till Nottingham had assured her that
James was safe. The grave Secretary, who seems to have
really esteemed and loved her, afterwards described with
much feeling that struggle of filial duty with conjugal affection. On the same day she wrote to adjure her husband to
see that no harm befell her father. "I know," she said, "I
need not beg you to let him be taken care of : for I am
confident you will for your own sake : yet add that to all
your kindness : and, for my sake, let people know you would
have no hurt happen to his person." * This solicitude,
though amiable, was superfluous. Her father was perfectly
competent to take care of himself. He had never, during
the battle, run the smallest risk of hurt ; and, while his
daughter was shuddering at the dangers to which she fancied
that he was exposed in Ireland, he was half way on his
voyage to France.

It chanced that the glad tidings arrived at Whitehall on
the day to which the Parliament stood prorogued. The
Speaker and several members of the House of Commons
who were in London met, according to form, at ten in the
morning, and were summoned by Black Rod to the bar of
the Peers. The Parliament was then again prorogued by
commission. As soon as this ceremony had been performed,
the Chancellor of the Exchequer put into the hands of the
Clerk the despatch which had just arrived from Ireland, and
the Clerk read it with a loud voice to the Lords and gentlemen present.† The good news spread rapidly from Westminster Hall to all the coffeehouses, and was received with
transports of joy. For those Englishmen who wished to see
an English army beaten and an English colony extirpated

---

* Mary to William, July 6. and 7. 1690 ; Burnet, ii. 55.
† Baden to Van Citters, July $\frac{8}{18}$. 1690.

by the French and Irish were a minority even of the Jacobite party.

On the ninth day after the battle of the Boyne James landed at Brest, with an excellent appetite, in high spirits, and in a talkative humour. He told the history of his defeat to everybody who would listen to him. But French officers who understood war, and who compared his story with other accounts, pronounced that, though His Majesty had witnessed the battle, he knew nothing about it, except that his army had been routed.* From Brest he proceeded to Saint Germains, where, a few hours after his arrival, he was visited by Lewis. The French King had too much delicacy and generosity to utter a word which could sound like reproach. Nothing, he declared, that could conduce to the comfort of the royal family of England should be wanting, as far as his power extended. But he was by no means disposed to listen to the political and military projects of his unlucky guest. James recommended an immediate descent on England. That kingdom, he said, had been drained of troops by the demands of Ireland. The seven or eight thousand regular soldiers who were left would be unable to withstand a great French army. The people were ashamed of their error and impatient to repair it. As soon as their rightful King showed himself, they would rally round him in multitudes.† Lewis was too polite and goodnatured to express what he must have felt. He contented himself with answering coldly that he could not decide upon any plan about the British islands till he had heard from his generals in Ireland. James was importunate, and seemed to think himself ill used, because, a fortnight after he had run away from one army, he was not entrusted with another. Lewis was not to be provoked into uttering an unkind or uncourteous word: but he was resolute; and in order to avoid solicitations which gave him pain, he pretended to be unwell. During some time, whenever James came to Versailles, he was respectfully informed that His Most Christian Majesty was not equal to the

---

* See two letters annexed to the Memoirs of the Intendant Foucault, and printed in the work of M. de Sirtema de Grovestins. In the archives of the War Office at Paris is a letter written from Brest by the Count of Bouridal on July $\frac{11}{21}$. 1690. The Count says: "Par la relation du combat que j'ay entendu faire au Roy d'Angleterre et à plusieurs de sa suite en particulier, il ne me paroit pas qu'il soit bien informé de tout ce qui s'est passé dans cette action, et qu'il ne sçait que la déroute de ses troupes."

† It was not only on this occasion that James held this language. From one of the letters quoted in the last note it appears that on his road from Brest to Paris he told everybody that the English were impatiently expecting him. "Ce pauvre prince croit que ses sujets l'aiment encore."

transaction of business. The highspirited and quickwitted
nobles who daily crowded the antechambers could not help
sneering while they bowed low to the royal visitor, whose
poltroonery and stupidity had a second time made him an
exile and a mendicant. They even whispered their sarcasms
loud enough to call up the haughty blood of Este in the
cheeks of Mary of Modena. But her husband stood among
the scoffers serene and well pleased with himself. Contempt,
says the fine Indian proverb, pierces through the shell of the
tortoise: but the insensibility of James was proof even against
contempt.*

Tourville
attempts a
descent on
England.

While he was enduring with ignominious fortitude the
polite scorn of the French aristocracy, and doing his best to
weary out his benefactor's patience and good breeding by
repeating that this was the very moment for an invasion of
England, and that the whole island was impatiently expecting
its foreign deliverers, events were passing which signally
proved how little the banished oppressor understood the
character of his countrymen.

Tourville had, since the battle of Beachy Head, ranged the
Channel unopposed. On the twenty-first of July his masts
were seen from the rocks of Portland. On the twenty-second
he anchored in the harbour of Torbay, under the same heights
which had, not many months before, sheltered the armament
of William. The French fleet, which now had a considerable number of troops on board, consisted of a hundred and
eleven sail. The galleys, which formed a large part of this
force, resembled rather those ships with which Alcibiades and
Lysander disputed the sovereignty of the Ægean than those
which contended at the Nile and at Trafalgar. The galley
was very long and very narrow, the deck not more than two
feet from the water edge. Each galley was propelled by fifty
or sixty huge oars, and each oar was tugged by five or six
slaves. The full complement of slaves to a vessel was three
hundred and thirty-six; the full complement of officers and
soldiers a hundred and fifty. Of the unhappy rowers some
were criminals who had been justly condemned to a life of
hardship and danger: a few had been guilty only of adhering
obstinately to the Huguenot worship: the great majority
were purchased bondsmen, generally Turks and Moors. They
were of course always forming plans for massacring their
tyrants and escaping from servitude, and could be kept in
order only by constant stripes, and by the frequent infliction

* Life of James, ii. 411, 412.; Burnet, ii. 57., and Dartmouth's note.

of death in horrible forms. An Englishman, who happened to fall in with about twelve hundred of these most miserable and most desperate of human beings on their road from Marseilles to join Tourville's squadron, heard them vowing that, if they came near a man of war bearing the cross of St. George, they would never again see a French dockyard.*

In the Mediterranean Sea galleys were in ordinary use: but none had ever before been tossed on the stormy ocean which roars round our island. The flatterers of Lewis said that the appearance of such a squadron on the Atlantic was one of those wonders which were reserved for his reign; and a medal was struck at Paris to commemorate this bold experiment in maritime war.† English sailors, with more reason, predicted that the first gale would send the whole of his fairweather armament to the bottom of the Channel. Indeed the galley, like the ancient trireme, generally kept close to the shore, and ventured out of sight of land only when the water was unruffled and the sky serene. But the qualities which made this sort of ship unfit to brave tempests and billows made it peculiarly fit for the purpose of landing soldiers. Tourville determined to try what effect would be produced by a disembarkation. The English Jacobites who had taken refuge in France were all confident that the whole population of the island was ready to rally round an invading army; and he probably gave them credit for understanding the temper of their countrymen.

Never was there a greater error. Indeed the French admiral is said by tradition to have received, while he was still out at sea, a lesson which might have taught him not to rely on the assurances of exiles. He picked up a fishing boat, and interrogated the owner, a plain Sussex man, about the sentiments of the nation. "Are you," Tourville asked, "for King James?" "I do not know much about such matters," answered the fisherman. "I have nothing to say against King James. He is a very worthy gentleman, I believe. God bless him!" "A good fellow!" said Tourville: "then I am sure you will have no objection to take service with us." "What!" cried the prisoner; "go with the French to fight against the English! Your honour must excuse me. I could not do it

* See the articles Galère and Galérien, in the Encyclopédie, with the plates; A True Relation of the Cruelties and Barbarities of the French upon the English

Prisoners of War, by R. Hutton, licensed June 27. 1690.

† See the Collection of Medals of Lewis the Fourteenth.

to save my life."* This poor fisherman, whether he was a real or an imaginary person, spoke the sense of the nation. The beacon on the ridge overlooking Teignmouth was kindled: the High Tor and Causland made answer; and soon all the hill tops of the West were on fire. Messengers were riding hard all night from Deputy Lieutenant to Deputy Lieutenant. Early the next morning, without chief, without summons, five hundred gentlemen and yeomen, armed and mounted, had assembled on the summit of Haldon Hill. In twenty-four hours all Devonshire was up. Every road in the county from sea to sea was covered by multitudes of fighting men, all with their faces set towards Torbay. The lords of a hundred manors, proud of their long pedigrees and old coats of arms, took the field at the head of their tenantry, Drakes, Prideauxes, and Rolles, Fowel of Fowelscombe and Fulford of Fulford, Sir Bourchier Wrey of Tawstock Park and Sir William Courtenay of Powderham Castle. Letters written by several of the Deputy Lieutenants who were most active during this anxious week are still preserved. All these letters agree in extolling the courage and enthusiasm of the people. But all agree also in expressing the most painful solicitude as to the result of an encounter between a raw militia and veterans who had served under Turenne and Luxemburg; and all call for the help of regular troops, in language very unlike that which, when the pressure of danger was not felt, country gentlemen were then in the habit of using about standing armies.

Teign-
mouth
destroyed.

Tourville, finding that the whole population was united as one man against him, contented himself with sending his galleys to ravage Teignmouth, an unfortified market town which had given no provocation and could make no defence. A short cannonade put the inhabitants to flight. Seventeen hundred men landed and marched into the deserted streets. More than a hundred houses were burned to the ground. The cattle were slaughtered. The barks and fishing smacks which lay in the river were destroyed. Two parish churches were sacked, the Bibles and Prayerbooks torn and scattered about the roads, the pulpits and communion tables demolished. By this time sixteen or seventeen thousand Devonshire men had encamped close to the shore; and all the neighbouring counties had risen. The tin mines of Cornwall had sent forth a great

* This anecdote, true or false, was current at the time, or soon after. In 1745 it was mentioned as a story which old people had heard in their youth. It is quoted in the Gentleman's Magazine of that year from another periodical work.

multitude of rude and hardy men mortally hostile to Popery. Ten thousand of them had just signed an address to the Queen, in which they had promised to stand by her against every enemy; and they now kept their word.* In truth, the whole nation was stirred. Two and twenty troops of cavalry, furnished by Suffolk, Essex, Hertfordshire and Buckinghamshire, were reviewed by Mary at Hounslow, and were complimented by Marlborough on their martial appearance. The militia of Kent and Surrey encamped on Blackheath.† Van Citters informed the States General that all England was up in arms, on foot or on horseback, that the disastrous event of the battle of Beachy Head had not cowed, but exasperated the people, and that every company of soldiers which he passed on the road was shouting with one voice, " God bless King William and Queen Mary."‡

Charles Granville, Lord Lansdowne, eldest son of the Earl of Bath, came with some troops from the garrison of Plymouth to take the command of the tumultuary army which had assembled round the basin of Torbay. Lansdowne was no novice. He had served several hard campaigns against the common enemy of Christendom, and had been created a Count of the Roman Empire in reward of the valour which he had displayed on that memorable day, sung by Filicaja and by Waller, when the infidels retired from the walls of Vienna. He made preparations for action; but the French did not choose to attack him, and were indeed impatient to depart. They found some difficulty in getting away. One day the wind was adverse to the sailing vessels. Another day the water was too rough for the galleys. At length the fleet stood out to sea. As the line of ships turned the lofty cape which overlooks Torquay, an incident happened which, though slight in itself, greatly interested the thousands who lined the coast. Two wretched slaves disengaged themselves from an oar, and sprang overboard. One of them perished. The other, after struggling more than an hour in the water, came safe to English ground, and was cordially welcomed by a population to which the discipline of the galleys was a thing strange and shocking.

---

* London Gazette, July 7. 1690.
† Narcissus Luttrell's Diary.
‡ I give this interesting passage in Van Citters's own words. " Door geheel het ryk alles te voet en te paarde in de wapenen op was; en 't gene een seer groote gerustheyt gaf was dat alle en een yder even seer tegen de Franse door de laatste voorgevallen bataille verbittert en geanimeert waren. Gelyk door de troupes, dewelke ik op de weg alomme gepasseert ben, niet anders heb konnen hooren als een eenpaarig en generaal geluydt van God bless King William en Queen Mary." July 25. Aug. 4. 1690.

He proved to be a Turk, and was humanely sent back to his own country.

Excitement of the English nation against the French. A pompous description of the expedition appeared in the Paris Gazette. But in truth Tourville's exploits had been inglorious, and yet less inglorious than impolitic. The injury which he had done bore no proportion to the resentment which he had roused. Hitherto the Jacobites, had tried to persuade the nation that the French would come as friends and deliverers, would observe strict discipline, would respect the temples and the ceremonies of the established religion, and would depart as soon as the Dutch oppressors had been expelled and the ancient constitution of the realm restored. The short visit of Tourville to our coast had shown how little reason there was to expect such moderation from the soldiers of Lewis. They had been in our island only a few hours, and had occupied only a few acres. But within a few hours and a few acres had been exhibited in miniature the devastation of the Palatinate. What had happened was communicated to the whole kingdom far more rapidly than by gazettes or newsletters. A brief for the relief of the people of Teignmouth was read in all the ten thousand parish churches of the land. No congretion could hear without emotion that the Popish marauders had made desolate the habitations of quiet fishermen and peasants, had outraged the altars of God, had torn to pieces the Gospels and the Liturgy. A street, built out of the contributions of the charitable, on the site of the dwellings which the invaders had destroyed, still retains the name of French Street.*

The outcry against those who were, with good reason, suspected of having invited the enemy to make a descent on our shores was vehement and general, and was swollen by many voices which had recently been loud in clamour against the government of William. The question had ceased to be a

---

* As to this expedition I have consulted the London Gazettes of July 24. 28. 31., Aug. 4. 1690; Narcissus Luttrell's Diary; Welwood's Mercurius Reformatus, Sept. 5.; the Gazette de Paris; a letter from Mr. Duke, a Deputy Lieutenant of Devonshire, to Hampden, dated July 25.; a letter from Mr. Fulford of Fulford to Lord Nottingham, dated July 26.; a letter of the same date from the Deputy Lieutenants of Devonshire to the Earl of Bath; a letter of the same date from Lord Lansdowne to the Earl of Bath. These four letters are among the MSS. of the Royal Irish Academy. Mr. Jordan of Teignmouth has kindly sent me a copy of the brief, which has enabled me to correct some errors of detail into which I had been led by documents less authentic. Dangeau inserted in his Journal, August 16., a series of extravagant lies. Tourville had routed the militia, taken their cannon and colours, burned men of war, captured richly laden merchantships, and was going to destroy Plymouth. This is a fair specimen of Dangeau's English news. Indeed he complains that it was hardly possible to get at true information about England.

question between two dynasties, and had become a question between England and France. So strong was the national sentiment that nonjurors and Papists shared or affected to share it. Dryden, not long after the burning of Teignmouth, laid a play at the feet of Halifax, with a dedication eminently ingenious, artful, and eloquent. The dramatist congratulated his patron on having taken shelter in a calm haven from the storms of public life, and, with great force and beauty of diction, magnified the felicity of the statesman who exchanges the bustle of office and the fame of oratory for philosophic studies and domestic endearments. England could not complain that she was defrauded of the service to which she had a right. Even the severe discipline of ancient Rome permitted a soldier, after many campaigns, to claim his dismission; and Halifax had surely done enough for his country to be entitled to the same privilege. But the poet added that there was one case in which the Roman veteran, even after his discharge, was required to resume his shield and his pilum; and that one case was a Gallic invasion. That a writer who had purchased the smiles of James by apostasy, who had been driven in disgrace from the court of William, and who had a deeper interest in the restoration of the exiled House than any man who made letters his calling, should have used such language as this, is a fact which may convince us that the determination never to be subjugated by foreigners was fixed in the hearts of the people.*

There was indeed a Jacobite literature in which no trace of this patriotic spirit can be detected, a literature the remains of which prove that there were Englishmen perfectly willing to see the English flag dishonoured, the English soil invaded, the English capital sacked, the English crown worn by a vassal of Lewis, if only they might avenge themselves on their enemies, and especially on William, whom they hated with a hatred half frightful, half ludicrous. But this literature was altogether a work of darkness. The law by which the Parliament of James had subjected the press to the control of censors was still in force; and, though the officers whose business it was to prevent the infraction of that law were not extreme to mark every irregularity committed by a bookseller who understood the art of conveying a guinea in a squeeze of the hand, they could not wink at the open vending of unlicensed pamphlets filled with ribald insults to the Sovereign, and with direct instigations to rebellion. But

The Jacobite Press.

* Dedication of Arthur.

there had long lurked in the garrets of London a class
of printers who worked steadily at their calling with precautions resembling those employed by coiners and forgers.
Women were on the watch to give the alarm by their screams
if an officer appeared near the workshop. The press was immediately pushed into a closet behind the bed: the types
were flung into the coalhole, and covered with cinders: the
compositor disappeared through a trapdoor in the roof, and
made off over the tiles of the neighbouring houses. In these
dens were manufactured treasonable works of all classes and
sizes, from halfpenny broadsides of doggrel verse up to massy
quartos filled with Hebrew quotations. It was not safe to
exhibit such publications openly on a counter. They were
sold only by trusty agents, and in secret places. Some tracts,
which were thought likely to produce a great effect, were
given away in immense numbers at the expense of wealthy
Jacobites. Sometimes a paper was thrust under a door,
sometimes dropped on the table of a coffeehouse. One day
a thousand copies of a scurrilous pamphlet went out by the
postbags. On another day, when the shopkeepers rose early
to take down their shutters, they found the whole of Fleet
Street and the Strand white with seditious handbills.*

The Jaco-
bite Form
of Prayer
and Humi-
liation.

Of the numerous performances which were ushered into
the world by such shifts as these, none produced a greater
sensation than a little book which purported to be a form of
prayer and humiliation for the use of the persecuted Church.
It was impossible to doubt that a considerable sum had been
expended on this work. Ten thousand copies were, by various
means, scattered over the kingdom. No more mendacious
more malignant, or more impious lampoon was ever penned.
Though the government had as yet treated its enemies with
a lenity unprecedented in the history of our country, though
not a single person had, since the Revolution, suffered death
for any political offence, the authors of this liturgy were not
ashamed to pray that God would assuage their enemy's insatiable thirst for blood, or would, if any more of them were
to be brought through the Red Sea to the Land of Promise,
prepare them for the passage.†   They complained that the

---

* See the accounts of Anderton's Trial,
1693; the Postman of March 12. 169⅚;
the Flying Post of March 7. 1700; Some
Discourses upon Dr. Burnet and Dr. Tillotson, by Hickes, 1695. The appendix
to these Discourses contains a curious
account of the inquisition into printing
offices under the Licensing Act.

† This was the ordinary cant of the
Jacobites. A Whig writer had justly said
in the preceding year, "They scurri-
lously call our David a man of blood,
though, to this day, he has not suffered
a drop to be spilt."—Mephibosheth and
Ziba, licensed Aug. 30. 1689.

Church of England, once the perfection of beauty, had become a scorn and derision, a heap of ruins, a vineyard of wild grapes; that her services had ceased to deserve the name of public worship; that the bread and wine which she dispensed had no longer any sacramental virtue; that her priests, in the act of swearing fealty to the usurper, had lost the sacred character which had been conferred on them by their ordination.* James was profanely described as the stone which foolish builders had rejected; and a fervent petition was put up that Providence would again make him the head of the corner. The blessings which were called down on our country were of a singular description. There was something very like a prayer for another Bloody Circuit; "Give the King the necks of his enemies:" there was something very like a prayer for a French invasion; "Raise him up friends abroad;" and there was a more mysterious prayer, the best comment on which was afterwards furnished by the Assassination Plot; "Do some great thing for him, which we in particular know not how to pray for."†

This liturgy was composed, circulated, and read, it is said, in some congregations of Jacobite schismatics, before William set out for Ireland, but did not attract general notice till the appearance of a foreign armament on our coast had roused the national spirit. Then rose a roar of indignation against the Englishmen who had dared, under the hypocritical pretence of devotion, to imprecate curses on England. The deprived Prelates were suspected, and not without some show of reason. For the nonjurors were, to a man, zealous Episcopalians. Their doctrine was that, in ecclesiastical matters of grave moment, nothing could be well done without the sanction of the Bishop. And could it be believed that any who held this doctrine would compose a service, print it, circulate it, and actually use it in public worship, without the approbation of Sancroft, whom the whole party revered, not only as the true Primate of all England, but also as a Saint and a Confessor? It was known that the Prelates who had refused the oaths had lately held several consultations at Lambeth. The subject of those consultations, it was now said, might easily be guessed. The holy fathers had been

Clamour against the nonjuring Bishops.

---

* "Restore unto us again the publick worship of thy name, the reverent administration of thy sacraments. Raise up the former government both in church and state, that we may be no longer without King, without priest, without God in the world."

† A Form of Prayer and Humiliation for God's Blessing upon His Majesty and his Dominions, and for Removing and Averting of God's Judgments from this Church and State, 1690.

engaged in framing prayers for the destruction of the Protestant colony in Ireland, for the defeat of the English fleet in the Channel, and for the speedy arrival of a French army in Kent. The extreme section of the Whig party pressed this accusation with vindictive eagerness. This then, said those implacable politicians, was the fruit of King William's merciful policy. Never had he committed a greater error than when he had conceived the hope that the hearts of the clergy were to be won by clemency and moderation. He had not chosen to give credit to men who had learned by a long and bitter experience that no kindness will tame the sullen ferocity of a priesthood. He had stroked and pampered when he should have tried the effect of chains and hunger. He had hazarded the good will of his best friends by protecting his worst enemies. Those Bishops who had publicly refused to acknowledge him as their Sovereign, and who, by that refusal, had forfeited their dignities and revenues, still continued to live unmolested in palaces which ought to be occupied by better men. And for his indulgence, an indulgence unexampled in the history of revolutions, what return had been made? Even this, that the men, whom he had, with so much tenderness, screened from just punishment, had the insolence to describe him in their prayers as a persecutor defiled with the blood of the righteous; that they asked for grace to endure with fortitude his sanguinary tyranny; that they cried to heaven for a foreign fleet and army to deliver them from his yoke; nay, that they hinted at a wish so odious that even they had not the front to speak it plainly. One writer, in a pamphlet which produced a great sensation, expressed his wonder that the people had not, when Tourville was riding victorious in the Channel, Dewitted the nonjuring Prelates. Excited as the public mind then was, there was some danger that this suggestion might bring a furious mob to Lambeth. At Norwich indeed the people actually rose, attacked the palace which the Bishop was still suffered to occupy, and would have pulled it down but for the timely arrival of the trainbands.* The government very properly instituted criminal proceedings against the publisher of the work which had produced this alarming breach of the peace.† The deprived Prelates meanwhile put forth a defence of their conduct. In this document they declared, with all solemnity, and as in the presence of God, that they

---

* Letter of Lloyd, Bishop of Norwich, to Sancroft, in the Tanner MSS.
† Luttrell's Diary.

had no hand in the new liturgy, that they knew not who had framed it, that they had never used it, that they had never held any correspondence directly or indirectly with the French court, that they were engaged in no plot against the existing government, and that they would willingly shed their blood rather than see England subjugated by a foreign prince, who had, in his own kingdom, cruelly persecuted their Protestant brethren. As to the writer who had marked them out to the public vengeance by a fearful word, but too well understood, they commended him to the Divine mercy, and heartily prayed that his great sin might be forgiven him. Most of those who signed this paper did so doubtless with sincerity: but there is good reason to believe that one at least of the subscribers added to the crime of betraying his country the crime of calling his God to witness a falsehood.*

The events which were passing in the Channel and on the Continent compelled William to make repeated changes in his plans. During the week which followed his triumphal entry into Dublin, messengers charged with evil tidings arrived from England in rapid succession. First came the account of Waldeck's defeat at Fleurus. The King was much disturbed. All the pleasure, he said, which his own victory had given him was at an end. Yet, with that generosity which was hidden under his austere aspect, he sate down, even in the moment of his first vexation, to write a kind and encouraging letter to the unfortunate general.† Three days later came intelligence more alarming still. The allied fleet had been ignominiously beaten. The sea from the Downs to the Land's End was in possession of the enemy. The next post might bring news that Kent was invaded. A French squadron might appear in Saint George's Channel, and might without difficulty burn all the transports which lay at anchor in the Bay of Dublin. William determined to return to England: but he wished to obtain, before

Military operations in Ireland Waterford taken.

---

* A Modest Inquiry into the Causes of the present Disasters in England, and who they are that brought the French into the English Channel described, 1690; Reflections upon a Form of Prayer lately set out for the Jacobites, 1690 ; A Midnight Touch at an Unlicensed Pamphlet, 1690. The paper signed by the nonjuring Bishops has often been reprinted.

Since the first edition of this part of my work appeared I have learned that the Jacobite Form of Prayer which produced so much excitement and controversy in 1690 was, to a great extent, copied from a Form of Prayer which had been composed and clandestinely printed, soon after the battle of Worcester, for the use of the Royalists. This curious fact, which seems to have been quite unknown both to the accused Bishops and to their accusers, was discovered by Mr. Lathbury, after the publication of his History of the Nonjurors, and was, in the most obliging manner, communicated by him to me.

† William to Heinsius, July $\frac{4}{14}$. 1690.

he went, the command of a safe haven on the eastern coast
of Ireland. Waterford was the best place suited to his purpose; and towards Waterford he immediately proceeded.
Clonmel and Kilkenny were abandoned by the Irish troops
as soon as it was known that he was approaching. At Kilkenny he was entertained, on the nineteenth of July, by the
Duke of Ormond, in the ancient castle of the Butlers, which
had not long before been occupied by Lauzun, and which
therefore, in the midst of the general devastation, still had
tables and chairs, hangings on the walls, and claret in the
cellars. On the twenty-first, two regiments which garrisoned
Waterford consented to march out after a faint show of
resistance : a few hours later the fort of Duncannon, which,
towering on a rocky promontory, commanded the entrance of
the harbour, surrendered; and William was master of the
whole of that secure and spacious basin which is formed by
the united waters of the Suir, the Nore, and the Barrow.
He then announced his intention of instantly returning to
England, and, having declared Count Solmes Commander
in Chief of the army of Ireland, set out for Dublin.*

But good news met him on the road. Tourville had
appeared on the coast of Devonshire, had put some troops on
shore, and had sacked Teignmouth : but the only effect of
this insult had been to raise the whole population of the
western counties in arms against the invaders. The enemy
had departed, after doing just mischief enough to make the
cause of James as odious for a time to Tories as to Whigs.
William therefore again changed his plans, and hastened
back to his army, which, during his absence, had moved
westward, and which he rejoined in the neighbourhood of
Cashel.†

About this time he received from Mary a letter requesting
him to decide an important question on which the Council of
Nine was divided. Marlborough was of opinion that all
danger of invasion was over for that year. The sea, he said,
was open : for the French ships had returned into port, and
were refitting. Now was the time to send an English fleet,
with five thousand troops on board, to the southern extremity of Ireland. Such a force might easily reduce Cork and
Kinsale, two of the most important strongholds still occupied
by the forces of James. Marlborough was strenuously sup-

---

* Story; London Gazette, Aug. 4.   † Story; William to Heinsius, $\frac{\text{July 31.}}{\text{Aug. 10.}}$
1690; Dumont MS.   1690; London Gazette, Aug. 11.

ported by Nottingham, and as strenuously opposed by the other members of the interior council with Caermathen at their head. The Queen referred the matter to her husband. He highly approved of the plan, and gave orders that it should be executed by the General who had formed it. Caermarthen submitted, though with a bad grace, and with some murmurs at the extraordinary partiality of His Majesty for Marlborough.*

William meanwhile was advancing towards Limerick. In that city the army which he had put to rout at the Boyne had taken refuge, discomfited, indeed, and disgraced, but very little diminished. He would not have had the trouble of besieging the place, if the advice of Lauzun and of Lauzun's countrymen had been followed. They laughed at the thought of defending such fortifications, and indeed would not admit that the name of fortifications could properly be given to heaps of dirt, which certainly bore little resemblance to the works of Valenciennes and Philipsburg. " It is unnecessary," said Lauzun, with an oath, " for the English to bring cannon against such a place as this. What you call your ramparts might be battered down with roasted apples." He therefore gave his voice for evacuating Limerick, and declared that, at all events, he was determined not to throw away, in a hopeless resistance, the lives of the brave men who had been entrusted to his care by his master.† The truth is, that the judgment of the brilliant and adventurous Frenchman was biassed by his inclinations. He and his companions were sick of Ireland. They were ready to face death with courage, nay, with gaiety, on a field of battle. But the dull, squalid, barbarous life, which they had now been leading during several months, was more than they could bear. They were as much out of the pale of the civilised world as if they had been banished to Dahomy or Spitzbergen. The climate affected their health and spirits. In that unhappy country, wasted by years of predatory war, hospitality could offer little more than a couch of straw, a trencher of meat half raw and half burned, and a draught of sour milk. A crust of bread, a pint of wine, could hardly be purchased for money. A year of such hardships seemed a century to men who had always been accustomed to carry with them to the camp the luxuries of Paris, soft bedding,

Marginal note: The Irish army collected at Limerick.

Marginal note: Lauzun pronounces that the place cannot be defended.

* Mary to William, Aug. $\frac{7}{17}$. $\frac{\text{Aug 22.}}{\text{Sept. 1.}}$ $\frac{\text{Aug. 26.}}{\text{Sept. 5.}}$ 1690.

† Macariæ Excidium; Mac Geoghegan; Life of James, ii. 420.; London Gazette, Aug. 14. 1690.

rich tapestry, sideboards of plate, hampers of Champagne, opera dancers, cooks, and musicians. Better to be a prisoner in the Bastille, better to be a recluse at La Trappe, than to be generalissimo of the half naked savages who burrowed in the dreary swamps of Munster. Any plea was welcome which would serve as an excuse for returning from that miserable exile to the land of cornfields and vineyards, of gilded coaches and laced cravats, of ballrooms and theatres.*

The Irish insist on defending Limerick.

Very different was the feeling of the children of the soil. The island, which to French courtiers was a disconsolate place of banishment, was the Irishman's home. There were collected all the objects of his love and of his ambition; and there he hoped that his dust would one day mingle with the dust of his fathers. To him even the heaven dark with the vapours of the ocean, the wildernesses of black rushes and stagnant water, the mud cabins where the peasants and the swine shared their meal of roots, had a charm which was wanting to the sunny skies, the cultured fields, and the stately mansions of the Seine. He could imagine no fairer spot than his country, if only his country could be freed from the tyranny of the Saxons; and all hope that his country would be freed from the tyranny of the Saxons must be abandoned if Limerick were surrendered.

The conduct of the Irish during the last two months had sunk their military reputation to the lowest point. They had, with the exception of some gallant regiments of cavalry, fled disgracefully at the Boyne, and had thus incurred the bitter contempt both of their enemies and of their allies. The English who were at Saint Germains never spoke of the Irish but as a people of dastards and traitors.† The French were so much exasperated against the unfortunate nation, that Irish merchants, who had been many years settled at Paris and Bordeaux, durst not walk the streets for fear of being insulted by the populace.‡ So strong was the preju-

---

* The impatience of Lauzun and his countrymen to get away from Ireland is mentioned in a letter of Oct. 21. 1690, quoted in the Memoirs of James, ii. 421. "Asimo," says Colonel Kelly, the author of the Macariæ Excidium, "diuturnam absentiam tam ægre molesteque ferebat ut bellum in Cypro protrahi continuarique ipso ei auditu acerbissimum esset. Nec incredibile est ducum in illius exercitu nonnullos, potissimum qui patrii cœli dulcedinem impatientius suspirabant, sibi persuasisse desperatas Cypri res nulla humana ope defendi sustenta-

rique posse." Asimo is Lauzun, and Cyprus Ireland.

† "Pauci illi ex Cilicibus aulicis, qui cum regina in Syria commorante remanserant, ... non cessabant universam nationem fœde traducere, et ingestis insuper convitiis lacerare, pavidos et malefidos proditores ac mortalium conscelaratissimos publice appellando."—Macariæ Excidium. The Cilicians are the English. Syria is France.

‡ "Tanta infamia tam operoso artificio et subtili commento in vulgus sparsa, tam constantibus de Cypriorum perfidia

dice, that absurd stories were invented to explain the intrepidity with which the horse had fought. It was said that the troopers were not men of Celtic blood, but descendants of the old English of the pale.* It was also said that they had been intoxicated with brandy just before the battle.† Yet nothing can be more certain than that they must have been generally of Irish race; nor did the steady valour which they displayed in a long and almost hopeless conflict against great odds bear any resemblance to the fury of a coward maddened by strong drink into momentary hardihood. Even in the infantry, undisciplined and disorganised as it was, there was much spirit, though little firmness. Fits of enthusiasm and fits of faintheartedness succeeded each other. The same battalion which at one time threw away its arms in a panic and shrieked for quarter, would on another occasion fight valiantly. On the day of the Boyne the courage of the ill trained and ill commanded kernes had ebbed to the lowest point. When they had rallied at Limerick, their blood was up. Patriotism, fanaticism, shame, revenge, despair, had raised them above themselves. With one voice officers and men insisted that the city should be defended to the last. At the head of those who were for resisting was the brave Sarsfield; and his exhortations diffused through all ranks a spirit resembling his own. To save his country was beyond his power. All that he could do was to prolong her last agony through one bloody and disastrous year.‡

Tyrconnel was altogether incompetent to decide the question on which the French and the Irish differed. The only military qualities that he had ever possessed were personal bravery and skill in the use of the sword. These qualities had once enabled him to frighten away rivals from the doors of his mistresses, and to play the Hector at cockpits and hazard tables. But more was necessary to enable him to form an opinion as to the possibility of defending Limerick. He would probably, had his temper been as hot as in the days when he diced with Grammont and threatened to cut the

Tyrconnel is against defending Limerick.

---

atque opprobrio rumoribus, totam qua lata est, Syriam ita pervasit, ut mercatores Cyprii, ... propter inustum genti dedecus, intra domorum septa clausi nunquam prodire auderent; tanto eorum odio populus in universum exarserat."—Macariæ Excidium.

* I have seen this assertion in a contemporary pamphlet of which I cannot recollect the title.

† Story; Dumont MS.

‡ Macariæ Excidium. Boisseleau remarked the ebb and flow of courage among the Irish. I have quoted one of his letters to his wife. It is but just to quote another. "Nos Irlandois n'avoient jamais vu le feu; et cela les a surpris. Presentement, ils sont si fâchés de n'avoir pas fait leur devoir que je suis bien persuadé qu'ils feront mieux pour l'avenir."

old Duke of Ormond's throat, have voted for running any
risk however desperate. But age, pain, and sickness had
left little of the ranting, bullying, fighting Dick Talbot of the
Restoration. He had sunk into deep despondency. He was
incapable of strenuous exertion. The French officers pronounced him utterly ignorant of the art of war. They had
observed that at the Boyne he had seemed to be stupified,
unable to give directions himself, unable even to make up
his mind about the suggestions which were offered by others.*
The disasters which had since followed one another in rapid
succession were not likely to restore the tone of a mind so
pitiably unnerved. His wife was already in France with the
little which remained of his once ample fortune : his own
wish was to follow her thither ; his voice was therefore given
for abandoning the city.

Limerick
defended
by the Irish
alone.

At last a compromise was made. Lauzun and Tyrconnel,
with the French troops, retired to Galway. The great body
of the native army, about twenty thousand strong, remained
at Limerick. The chief command there was entrusted to
Boisseleau, who understood the character of the Irish better,
and consequently judged them more favourably, than any of
his countrymen. In general, the French captains spoke of
their unfortunate allies with boundless contempt and abhorrence, and thus made themselves as hateful as the English.†

Lauzun and Tyrconnel had scarcely departed when the
advanced guard of William's army came in sight. Soon
the King himself, accompanied by Auverquerque and Ginkell,
and escorted by three hundred horse, rode forward to examine the fortifications. The city, then the second in Ireland, though less altered since that time than most large
cities in the British isles, has undergone a great change.
The new town did not then exist. The ground now covered
by those smooth and broad pavements, those neat gardens,
those stately shops flaming with red brick, and gay with
shawls and china, was then an open meadow lying without
the walls. The city consisted of two parts, which had been

---

* La Hoguette, writing to Louvois
from Limerick, $\frac{\text{July 31.}}{\text{Aug. 10.}}$ 1690, says of Tyrconnel : " Il a d'ailleurs trop peu de con-
noissance des choses de notre metier. Il
a perdu absolument la confiance des officiers du pays, surtout depuis le jour de
notre déroute ; et, en effet, Monseigneur,
je me crois obligé de vous dire que dès
le moment où les ennemis parurent sur
le bord de la rivière le premier jour, et

dans toute la journée du lendemain, il
parut à tout le monde dans une si grande
léthargie qu'il étoit incapable de prendre
aucun parti, quelque chose qu'on lui
proposât."
† Desgrigny says of the Irish : " Ils
sont toujours prêts de nous égorger par
l'antipathie qu'ils ont pour nous. C'est
la nation du monde la plus brutale, et
qui a le moins d'humanité." Aug. $\frac{12}{22}$.1690.

designated during several centuries as the English and the Irish town. The English town stands on an island surrounded by the Shannon, and consists of a knot of antique houses with gable ends, crowding thick round a venerable cathedral. The aspect of the streets is such that a traveller who wanders through them may easily fancy himself in Normandy or Flanders. Not far from the cathedral, an ancient castle overgrown with weeds and ivy looks down on the river. A narrow and rapid stream, over which, in 1690, there was only a single bridge, divides the English town from the quarter anciently occupied by the hovels of the native population. The view from the top of the cathedral now extends many miles over a level expanse of rich mould, through which the greatest of Irish rivers winds between artificial banks. But in the seventeenth century those banks had not been constructed; and that wide plain, of which the grass, verdant even beyond the verdure of Munster, now feeds some of the finest cattle in Europe, was then almost always a marsh and often a lake.*

When it was known that the French troops had quitted Limerick, and that the Irish only remained, the general expectation in the English camp was that the city would be an easy conquest.† Nor was that expectation unreasonable: for even Sarsfield desponded. One chance, in his opinion, there still was. William had brought with him none but small guns. Several large pieces of ordnance, a great quantity of provisions and ammunition, and a bridge of tin boats, which in the watery plain of the Shannon was frequently needed, were slowly following from Cashel. If the guns and gunpowder could be intercepted and destroyed, there might be some hope. If not, all was lost; and the best thing that a brave and high-spirited Irish gentleman could do was to forget the country which he had in vain tried to defend, and to seek in some foreign land a home or a grave.

A few hours, therefore, after the English tents had been pitched before Limerick, Sarsfield set forth, under cover of the night, with a strong body of horse and dragoons. He took the road to Killaloe, and crossed the Shannon there. During the day he lurked with his band in a wild mountain tract named from the silver mines which it contains. Those mines had many years before been worked by English pro-

Sarsfield surprised the English artillery.

---

* Story; Account of the Cities in Ireland that are still possessed by the Forces of King James, 1690. There are some curious old maps of Limerick in the British Museum.

† Story; Dumont MS.

prietors, with the help of engineers and labourers imported
from the Continent. But, in the rebellion of 1641, the aboriginal population had destroyed the works and massacred
the workmen; nor had the devastation then committed been
since repaired. In this desolate region Sarsfield found no
lack of scouts or of guides : for all the peasantry of Munster
were zealous on his side. He learned in the evening that the
detachment which guarded the English artillery had halted
for the night, seven miles from William's camp, on a pleasant
carpet of green turf, and under the ruined walls of an old
castle; that officers and men seemed to think themselves
perfectly secure; that the beasts had been turned loose to
graze, and that even the sentinels were dozing. When it was
dark the Irish horsemen quitted their hidingplace, and were
conducted by the people of the country to the spot where the
escort lay sleeping round the guns. The surprise was complete. Some of the English sprang to their arms and made
an attempt to resist, but in vain. About sixty fell. One only
was taken alive. The rest fled. The victorious Irish made
a huge pile of waggons and pieces of cannon. Every gun was
stuffed with powder, and fixed with its mouth in the ground;
and the whole mass was blown up. The solitary prisoner, a
lieutenant, was treated with great civility by Sarsfield. "If
I had failed in this attempt," said the gallant Irishman, "I
should have been off to France."*

Intelligence had been carried to William's headquarters
that Sarsfield had stolen out of Limerick and was ranging the
country. The King guessed the design of his brave enemy,
and sent five hundred horse to protect the guns. Unhappily
there was some delay, which the English, always disposed to
believe the worst of the Dutch courtiers, attributed to the
negligence or perverseness of Portland. At one in the morning the detachment set out, but had scarcely left the camp
when a blaze like lightning and a crash like thunder announced to the wide plain of the Shannon that all was over.†

Sarsfield had long been the favourite of his countrymen;
and this most seasonable exploit, judiciously planned and vigorously executed, raised him still higher in their estimation.
Their spirits rose; and the besiegers began to lose heart.
William did his best to repair his loss. Two of the guns
which had been blown up were found to be still serviceable.
Two more were sent for from Waterford. Batteries were con-

* Story; James, ii. 416.; Burnet, ii. 58.; Dumont MS.
† Story; Dumont MS.

structed of small field pieces, which, though they might have been useless against one of the fortresses of Hainault or Brabant, made some impression on the feeble defences of Limerick. Several outworks were carried by storm; and a breach in the rampart of the city began to appear.

During these operations, the English army was astonished and amused by an incident, which produced indeed no very important consequences, but which illustrates in the most striking manner the real nature of Irish Jacobitism. In the first rank of those great Celtic houses, which, down to the close of the reign of Elizabeth, bore rule in Ulster, were the O'Donnels. The head of that house had yielded to the skill and energy of Mountjoy, had kissed the hand of James the First, and had consented to exchange the rude independence of a petty prince for an eminently honourable place among British subjects. During a short time the vanquished chief held the rank of an Earl, and was the landlord of an immense domain of which he had once been the sovereign. But soon he began to suspect the government of plotting against him, and, in revenge or in selfdefence, plotted against the government. His schemes failed: he fled to the Continent: his title and his estates were forfeited; and an Anglosaxon colony was planted in the territory which he had governed. He meanwhile took refuge at the court of Spain. Between that court and the aboriginal Irish there had, during the long contest between Philip and Elizabeth, been a close connection. The exiled chieftain was welcomed at Madrid as a good Catholic flying from heretical persecutors. His illustrious descent and princely dignity, which to the English were subjects of ridicule, secured to him the respect of the Castilian grandees. His honours were inherited by a succession of banished men who lived and died far from the land where the memory of their family was fondly cherished by a rude peasantry, and was kept fresh by the songs of minstrels and the tales of begging friars. At length, in the eighty-third year of the exile of this ancient dynasty, it was known over all Europe that the Irish were again in arms for their independence. Baldearg O'Donnel, who called himself the O'Donnel, a title far prouder, in the estimation of his race, than any marquisate or dukedom, had been bred in Spain, and was in the service of the Spanish government. He requested the permission of that government to repair to Ireland; but the House of Austria was now closely leagued with England; and the permission was refused. The O'Donnel made his escape, and by

Arrival of Baldearg O'Donnel at Limerick.

a circuitous route, in the course of which he visited Turkey, arrived at Kinsale a few days after James had sailed thence for France. The effect produced on the native population by the arrival of this solitary wanderer was marvellous. Since Ulster had been reconquered by the Englishry, great multitudes of the Irish inhabitants of that province had migrated southward, and were now leading a vagrant life in Connaught and Munster. These men, accustomed from their infancy to hear of the good old times, when the O'Donnel, solemnly inaugurated on the rock of Kilmacrenan by the successor of Saint Columb, governed the mountains of Donegal in defiance of the strangers of the pale, flocked to the standard of the restored exile. He was soon at the head of seven or eight thousand Rapparees, or, to use the name peculiar to Ulster, Creaghts; and his followers adhered to him with a loyalty very different from the languid sentiment which the Saxon James had been able to inspire. Priests and even Bishops swelled the train of the adventurer. He was so much elated by his reception that he sent agents to France, who assured the ministers of Lewis that the O'Donnel would, if furnished with arms and ammunition, bring into the field thirty thousand Celts from Ulster, and that the Celts of Ulster would be found far superior in every military quality to those of Leinster, Munster, and Connaught. No expression used by Baldearg indicated that he considered himself as a subject. His notion evidently was that the House of O'Donnel was as truly and as indefeasibly royal as the House of Stuart; and not a few of his countrymen were of the same mind. He made a pompous entrance into Limerick; and his appearance there raised the hopes of the garrison to a strange pitch. Numerous prophecies were recollected or invented. An O'Donnel with a red mark was to be the deliverer of his country; and Baldearg meant a red mark. An O'Donnel was to gain a great battle over the English near Limerick; and at Limerick the O'Donnel and the English were now brought face to face.*

The besiegers suffer from the rains.

While these predictions were eagerly repeated by the defenders of the city, evil presages, grounded, not on barbarous oracles, but on grave military reasons, began to disturb

* See the account of the O'Donnels in Sir William Betham's Irish Antiquarian Researches. It is strange that he makes no mention of Baldearg, whose appearance in Ireland is the most extraordinary event in the whole history of the race.

See also Story's Impartial History; Macariæ Excidium, and Mr. O'Callaghan's note; Life of James, ii. 434.; the Letter of O'Donnel to Avaux, and the Memorial entitled, "Mémoire donnée par un homme du Comte O'Donnel à M. D'Avaux "

William and his most experienced officers. The blow struck by Sarsfield had told: the artillery had been long in doing its work: that work was even now very imperfectly done: the stock of powder had begun to run low: the autumnal rain had begun to fall. The soldiers in the trenches were up to their knees in mire. No precaution was neglected: but, though drains were dug to carry off the water, and though pewter basins of usquebaugh and brandy blazed all night in the tents, cases of fever had already occurred; and it might well be apprehended that, if the army remained but a few days longer on that swampy soil, there would be a pestilence more terrible than that which had raged twelve months before under the walls of Dundalk.† A council of war was held. It was determined to make one great effort, and, if that effort failed, to raise the siege.

On the twenty-seventh of August, at three in the afternoon, the signal was given. Five hundred grenadiers rushed from the English trenches to the counterscarp, fired their pieces and threw their grenades. The Irish fled into the town, and were followed by the assailants, who, in the excitement of victory, did not wait for orders. Then began a terrible street fight. The Irish, as soon as they had recovered from their surprise, stood resolutely to their arms; and the English grenadiers, overwhelmed by numbers, were, with great loss, driven back to the counterscarp. There the struggle was long and desperate. When indeed was the Roman Catholic Celt to fight if he did not fight on that day? The very women of Limerick mingled in the combat, stood firmly under the hottest fire, and flung stones and broken bottles at the enemy. In the moment when the conflict was fiercest a mine exploded, and hurled a fine German battalion into the air. During four hours the carnage and uproar continued. The thick cloud which rose from the breach streamed out on the wind for many miles, and disappeared behind the hills of Clare. Late in the evening the besiegers retired slowly and sullenly to their camp. Their hope was that a second attack would be made on the morrow; and the soldiers vowed to have the town or die. But the powder was now almost exhausted: the rain fell in torrents: the gloomy masses of cloud which came up from the south west threatened a havoc

margin note: Unsuccessful assault on Limerick. The siege raised.

---

* The reader will remember Corporal Trim's explanation of radical heat and radical moisture. Sterne is an authority not to be despised on these subjects. His boyhood was passed in barracks; he was constantly listening to the talk of old soldiers who had served under King William, and has used their stories like a man of true genius.

more terrible than that of the sword; and there was reason
to fear that the roads, which were already deep in mud,
would soon be in such a state that no wheeled carriage could
be dragged through them. The King determined to raise
the siege, and to move his troops to a healthier region. He
had in truth staid long enough : for it was with great difficulty that his guns and waggons were tugged away by long
teams of oxen.*

The history of the first siege of Limerick bears, in some
respects, a remarkable analogy to the history of the siege of
Londonderry. The southern city was, like the northern city,
the last asylum of a Church and of a nation. Both places
were crowded by fugitives from all parts of Ireland. Both
places appeared to men who had made a regular study of the
art of war incapable of resisting an enemy. Both were, in
the moment of extreme danger, abandoned by those commanders who should have defended them. Lauzun and
Tyrconnel deserted Limerick as Cunningham and Lundy had
deserted Londonderry. In both cases, religious and patriotic
enthusiasm struggled unassisted against great odds ; and, in
both cases, religious and patriotic enthusiasm did what veteran
warriors had pronounced it absurd to attempt.

Tyrcon-
nel and
Lauzun go
to France.
It was with no pleasurable emotions that Lauzun and
Tyrconnel learned at Galway the fortunate issue of the conflict in which they had refused to take a part. They were
weary of Ireland : they were apprehensive that their conduct
might be unfavourably represented in France : they therefore
determined to be beforehand with their accusers, and took
ship together for the Continent.

Tyrconnel, before he departed, delegated his civil authority
to one council, and his military authority to another. The
young Duke of Berwick was declared Commander in Chief :
but this dignity was merely nominal. Sarsfield, undoubtedly
the first of Irish soldiers, was placed last in the list of the

---

* Story; William to Waldeck, Sept.
22. 1690; London Gazette, Sept. 4.
Berwick asserts that when the siege
was raised not a drop of rain had fallen
during a month, that none fell during
the following three weeks, and that William pretended that the weather was wet
merely to hide the shame of his defeat.
Story, who was on the spot, says, "It
was cloudy all about, and rained very
fast, so that every body began to dread
the consequences of it;" and again,
"The rain which had already fallen had
softened the ways. . . . This was one
main reason for raising the siege: for,
if we had not, granting the weather to
continue bad, we must either have taken
the town, or of necessity have lost our
cannon." Dumont, another eyewitness,
says that before the siege was raised
the rains had been most violent; that
the Shannon was swollen; that the earth
was soaked; that the horses could not
keep their feet.

councillors to whom the conduct of the war was entrusted; and some believed that he would not have been in the list at all, had not the Viceroy feared that the omission of so popular a name might produce a mutiny.

William meanwhile proceeded to Waterford, and sailed thence for England. Before he embarked, he entrusted the government of Ireland to three Lords Justices. Henry Sidney, now Viscount Sidney, stood first in the commission; and with him were joined Coningsby and Sir Charles Porter. Porter had formerly held the Great Seal of the kingdom, had, merely because he was a Protestant, been deprived of it by James, and had now received it again from the hand of William. William returns to England.

On the sixth of September the King, after a voyage of twenty-four hours, landed at Bristol. Thence he travelled to London, stopping by the road at the mansions of some great lords; and it was remarked that all those who were thus honoured were Tories. He was entertained one day at Badminton by the Duke of Beaufort, who was supposed to have brought himself with great difficulty to take the oaths, and on a subsequent day at a large house near Marlborough, which, in our own time, before the great revolution produced by railways, was renowned as one of the best inns in England, but which, in the seventeenth century, was a seat of the Duke of Somerset. William was everywhere received with marks of respect and joy. His campaign indeed had not ended quite so prosperously as it had begun: but on the whole his success had been great beyond expectation, and had fully vindicated the wisdom of his resolution to command his army in person. The sack of Teignmouth too was fresh in the minds of Englishmen, and had for a time reconciled all but the most fanatical Jacobites to each other and to the throne. The magistracy and clergy of the capital repaired to Kensington with thanks and congratulations. The people rang bells and kindled bonfires. For the Pope, whom good Protestants had been accustomed to immolate, the French King was on this occasion substituted, probably by way of retaliation for the insults which had been offered to the effigy of William by the Parisian populace. A waxen figure, which was doubtless a hideous caricature of the most graceful and majestic of princes, was dragged about Westminster in a chariot. Above was inscribed, in large letters, "Lewis the greatest tyrant of fourteen." After the proces- Reception of William in England.

sion, the image was committed to the flames, amidst loud huzzas, in the middle of Covent Garden.*

Expedition to the South of Ireland. When William arrived in London, the expedition destined for Cork was ready to sale from Portsmouth; and Marlborough had been some time on board waiting for a fair wind. He was accompanied by Grafton. This young man had been, immediately after the departure of James, and while the throne was still vacant, named by William Colonel of the First Regiment of Foot Guards. The Revolution had scarcely been consummated, when signs of disaffection began to appear in that regiment, the most important, both because of its peculiar duties and because of its numerical strength, of all the regiments in the army. It was thought that the Colonel had not put this bad spirit down with a sufficiently firm hand. He was known not to be perfectly satisfied with the new arrangement; he had voted for a Regency; and it was rumoured, perhaps without reason, that he had dealings with Saint Germains. The honourable and lucrative command to which he had just been appointed was taken from him.† Though severely mortified, he behaved like a man of sense and spirit. Bent on proving that he had been wrongfully suspected, and animated by an honourable ambition to distinguish himself in his profession, he obtained permission to serve as a volunteer under Marlborough in Ireland.

At length, on the eighteenth of September, the wind changed. The fleet stood out to sea, and, on the twenty-first, appeared before the harbour of Cork. The troops landed, and were speedily joined by the Duke of Wurtemberg, with several regiments, Dutch, Danish, and French, detached from the army which had lately besieged Limerick. The Duke immediately put forward a claim which, if the English general had not been a man of excellent judgment and temper, might have been fatal to the expedition. His Highness contended that, as a prince of a sovereign house, he was entitled to command in chief. Marlborough calmly and politely showed that the pretence was unreasonable. A dispute followed, in which it is said that the German behaved with rudeness, and the Englishman with that gentle firmness to which, more perhaps than even to his great abilities, he owed his success in life. At length a Huguenot officer sug-

---

* London Gazette, September 11. 1690; Narcissus Luttrell's Diary. I have seen a contemporary engraving of Covent Garden as it appeared on this night.

† Van Citters to the States General, March 19/29. 1689.

gested a compromise. Marlborough consented to waive part of his rights, and to allow precedence to the Duke on the alternate days. The first morning on which Marlborough had the command, he gave the word "Wurtemberg." The Duke's heart was won by this compliment; and on the next day he gave the word "Marlborough."

But, whoever might give the word, genius asserted its indefeasible superiority. Marlborough was on every day the real general. Cork was vigorously attacked. Outwork after outwork was rapidly carried. In forty-eight hours all was over. The traces of the short struggle may still be seen. The old fort, where the Irish made the hardest fight, lies in ruins. The Doric Cathedral, so ungracefully joined to the ancient tower, stands on the site of a Gothic edifice which was shattered by the English cannon. In the neighbouring churchyard is still shown the spot where stood, during many ages, one of those round towers which have perplexed antiquaries. This venerable monument shared the fate of the neighbouring church. On another spot, which is now called the Mall, and is lined by the stately houses of banking companies, railway companies, and insurance companies, but which was then a bog known by the name of the Rape Marsh, four English regiments, up to the shoulders in water, advanced gallantly to the assault. Grafton, ever foremost in danger, while struggling through the quagmire, was struck by a shot from the ramparts, and was carried back dying. The place where he fell, then about a hundred yards without the City, but now situated in the very centre of business and population, is still called Grafton Street. The assailants had made their way through the swamp, and the close fighting was just about to begin, when a parley was beaten. Articles of capitulation were speedily adjusted. The garrison, between four and five thousand fighting men, became prisoners. Marlborough promised to intercede with the King both for them and for the inhabitants, and to prevent outrage and spoliation. His troops he succeeded in restraining: but crowds of sailors and camp followers came into the city through the breach; and the houses of many Roman Catholics were sacked before order was restored.

No commander has ever understood better than Marlborough how to improve a victory. A few hours after Cork had fallen, his cavalry were on the road to Kinsale. A trumpeter was sent to summon the place. The Irish threatened to hang him for bringing such a message, set fire

Marlborough takes Cork.

Marlborough takes Kinsale.

to the town, and retired into two forts called the Old and the New. The English horse arrived just in time to extinguish the flames. Marlborough speedily followed with his infantry. The Old Fort was scaled; and four hundred and fifty men who defended it were killed or taken. The New Fort it was necessary to attack in a more methodical way. Batteries were planted : trenches were opened : mines were sprung : in a few days the besiegers were masters of the counterscarp : and all was ready for storming, when the governor offered to capitulate. The garrison, twelve hundred strong, was suffered to retire to Limerick ; but the conquerors took possession of the stores, which were of considerable value. Of all the Irish ports Kinsale was the best situated for intercourse with France. Here, therefore, was a plenty unknown in any other part of Munster. At Limerick bread and wine were luxuries which generals and privy councillors were not always able to procure. But in the New Fort of Kinsale Marlborough found a thousand barrels of wheat and eighty pipes of claret.

His success had been complete and rapid : and indeed, had it not been rapid, it would not have been complete. His campaign, short as it was, had been long enough to allow time for the deadly work which, in that age, the moist earth and air of Ireland seldom failed, in the autumnal season, to perform on English soldiers. The malady which had thinned the ranks of Schomberg's army at Dundalk, and which had compelled William to make a hasty retreat from the estuary of the Shannon, had begun to appear at Kinsale. Quick and vigorous as Marlborough's operations were, he lost a much greater number of men by disease than by the fire of the enemy. He presented himself at Kensington only five weeks after he had sailed from Portsmouth, and was most graciously received. " No officer living," said William, " who has seen so little service as my Lord Marlborough, is so fit for great commands."*

Affairs of Scotland.

In Scotland, as in Ireland, the aspect of things had, during this memorable summer, changed greatly for the better. The Club of discontented Whigs which had, in the preceding year, ruled the Parliament, browbeaten the ministers, refused the supplies and stopped the signet, had sunk under general contempt, and had at length ceased to exist. There was har-

* As to Marlborough's expedition, see Story's Impartial History ; the Life of James, ii. 419, 420. ; London Gazette, Oct. 6. 13. 16. 27. 30. 1690.; Monthly Mercury for Nov. 1690 ; History of King William, 1702 ; Burnet, ii. 60. ; the Life of Joseph Pike, a Quaker of Cork.

mony between the Sovereign and the Estates; and the long contest between two forms ef ecclesiastical government had been terminated in the only way compatible with the peace and prosperity of the country.

This happy turn in affairs is to be chiefly ascribed to the errors of the perfidious, turbulent and revengeful Montgomery. Some weeks after the close of that session during which he had exercised a boundless authority over the Scottish Parliament, he went to London with his two principal confederates, the Earl of Annandale and the Lord Ross. The three had an audience of William, and presented to him a manifesto setting forth what they demanded for the public. They would very soon have changed their tone if he would have granted what they demanded for themselves. But he resented their conduct deeply, and was determined not to pay them for annoying him. The reception which he gave them convinced them that they had no favour to expect. Montgomery's passions were fierce: his wants were pressing: he was miserably poor; and, if he could not speedily force himself into a lucrative office, he would be in danger of rotting in a gaol. Since his services were not likely to be bought by William, they must be offered to James. A broker was easily found. Montgomery was an old acquaintance of Ferguson. The two traitors soon understood each other. They were kindred spirits, differing widely in intellectual power, but equally vain, restless, false, and malevolent. Montgomery was introduced to Neville Payne, one of the most adroit and resolute agents of the exiled family. Payne had been long well known about town as a dabbler in poetry and politics. He had been an intimate friend of the indiscreet and unfortunate Coleman, and had been committed to Newgate as an accomplice in the Popish plot. His moral character had not stood high: but he soon had an opportunity of proving that he possessed courage and fidelity worthy of a better cause than that of James, and of a better associate than Montgomery.

The negotiation speedily ended in a treaty of alliance. Payne confidently promised Montgomery, not merely pardon, but riches, power, and dignity. Montgomery as confidently undertook to induce the Parliament of Scotland to recall the rightful King. Ross and Annandale readily agreed to whatever their able and active colleague proposed. An adventurer, who was sometimes called Simpson and sometimes Jones, who was perfectly willing to serve or to betray any government for hire, and who received wages at once from

Intrigues of Montgomery with the Jacobites

Portland and from Neville Payne, undertook to carry the offers of the Club to James. Montgomery and his two noble accomplices returned to Edinburgh, and there proceeded to form a coalition with their old enemies, the defenders of prelacy and of arbitrary power.*

War in the Highlands. The two extreme Scottish factions, one hostile to all liberty, the other impatient of all government, flattered themselves during a short time with hopes that the civil war would break out in the Highlands with redoubled fury. But those hopes were disappointed. In the spring of 1690 an officer named Buchan arrived in Lochaber from Ireland. He bore a commission which appointed him general in chief of all the forces which were in arms for King James throughout the kingdom of Scotland. Cannon, who had, since the death of Dundee, held the first post, and had proved himself unfit for it, became second in command. Little however was gained by the change. It was no easy matter to induce the Gaelic princes to renew the war. Indeed, but for the influence and eloquence of Lochiel, not a sword would have been drawn in the cause of the House of Stuart. He, with some difficulty, persuaded the chieftains, who had, in the preceding year, fought at Killiecrankie, to come to a resolution that, before the end of the summer, they would muster all their followers and march into the Lowlands. In the meantime twelve hundred mountaineers of different tribes were placed under the orders of Buchan, who undertook, with this force, to keep the English garrison in constant alarm by feints and incursions, till the season for more important operations should arrive. He accordingly marched into Strathspey. But all his plans were speedily disconcerted by the boldness and dexterity of Sir Thomas Livingstone, who held Inverness for King William. Livingstone, guided and assisted by the Grants, who were firmly attached to the new government, came, with a strong body of cavalry and dragoons, by forced marches and through arduous defiles, to the place where the Jacobites had taken up their quarters. He reached the camp fires at dead of night. The first alarm was given by the rush of the horses over the terrified sentinels into the midst of the crowd of Celts who lay sleeping in their plaids. Buchan escaped bareheaded and without his sword. Cannon ran away in his shirt. The conquerors lost not a man. Four

---

* Balcarras; Annandale's Confession in the Leven and Melville Papers; Burnet, ii. 35. As to Payne, see the Second Modest Inquiry into the Cause of the present Disasters, 1690.

hundred Highlanders were killed or taken. The rest fled to their hills and mists.*

This event put an end to all thoughts of civil war. The gathering which had been planned for the summer never took place. Lochiel, even if he had been willing, was not able to sustain any longer the falling cause. He had been laid on his bed by a mishap which would alone suffice to show how little could be effected by a confederacy of the petty kings of the mountains. At a consultation of the Jacobite leaders, a gentleman from the Lowlands spoke with severity of those sycophants who had changed their religion to curry favour with King James. Glengarry was one of those people who think it dignified to suppose that everybody is always insulting them. He took it into his head that some allusion to himself was meant. "I am as good a Protestant as you;" he cried, and added a word not to be patiently borne by a man of spirit. In a moment both swords were out. Lochiel thrust himself between the combatants, and, while forcing them asunder, received a wound which was at first believed to be mortal.†

So effectually had the spirit of the disaffected clans been cowed that Mackay marched unresisted from Perth into Lochaber, fixed his headquarters at Inverlochy, and proceeded to execute his favourite design of erecting at that place a fortress which might overawe the mutinous Camerons and Macdonalds. In a few days the walls were raised: the ditches were sunk: the palisades were fixed: demiculverins from a ship of war were ranged along the parapets; and the general departed, leaving an officer named Hill in command of a sufficient garrison. Within the defences there was no want of oatmeal, red herrings, and beef; and there was rather a superabundance of brandy. The new stronghold, which, hastily and rudely as it had been constructed, seemed doubtless to the people of the neighbourhood the most stupendous work that power and science united had ever produced, was named Fort William in honour of the King.‡

Fort William built.

By this time the Scottish Parliament had reassembled at

Meeting of the Scottish Parliament.

---

* Balcarras; Mackay's Memoirs; History of the late Revolution in Scotland, 1690; Livingstone's Report, dated May 1.; London Gazette, May 12. 1690.
† History of the late Revolution in Scotland, 1690.
‡ Mackay's Memoirs and Letters to

Hamilton of June 20. and 24. 1690; Colonel Hill to Melville, July 10. 26.; London Gazette, July 17. 21. As to Inverlochy, see among the Culloden papers, a Plan for preserving the Peace of the Highlands, drawn up, at this time, by the father of President Forbes.

Edinburgh. William had found it no easy matter to decide what course should be taken with that capricious and unruly body. The English Commons had sometimes put him out of temper. Yet they had granted him millions, and had never asked from him such concessions as had been imperiously demanded by the Scottish legislature, which could give him little and had given him nothing. The English statesmen with whom he had to deal did not generally stand or deserve to stand high in his esteem. Yet few of them were so utterly false and shameless as the leading Scottish politicians. Hamilton was, in morality and honour, rather above than below his fellows; and even Hamilton was fickle, false, and greedy. "I wish to heaven," William was once provoked into exclaiming, "that Scotland were a thousand miles off, and that the Duke of Hamilton were King of it. Then I should be rid of them both."

Melville Lord High Commissioner. After much deliberation, William determined to send Melville down to Edinburgh as Lord High Commissioner. Melville was not a great statesman: he was not a great orator: he did not look or move like the representative of royalty: his character was not of more than standard purity: and the standard of purity among Scottish senators was not high: but he was by no means deficient in prudence or temper; and he succeeded, on the whole, better than a man of much higher qualities might have done.

The government obtains a majority. During the first days of the Session, the friends of the government desponded, and the chiefs of the opposition were sanguine. Montgomery's head, though by no means a weak one, had been turned by the triumphs of the preceding year. He believed that his intrigues and his rhetoric had completely subjugated the Estates. It seemed to him impossible that, having exercised a boundless empire in the Parliament House when the Jacobites were absent, he should be defeated when they were present, and ready to support whatever he proposed. He had not indeed found it easy to prevail on them to attend: for they could not take their seats without taking the oaths. A few of them had some slight scruple of conscience about forswearing themselves; and many, who did not know what a scruple of conscience meant, were apprehensive that they might offend the rightful King by vowing fealty to the actual King. Some Lords, however, who were supposed to be in the confidence of James, asserted that, to their knowledge, he wished his friends to perjure themselves; and this assertion induced most of the Jacobites, with Balcarras at their head, to be guilty of perfidy aggravated by impiety.*

It soon appeared, however, that Montgomery's faction, even with this reinforcement, was no longer a majority of the legislature. For every supporter that he had gained he had lost two. He had committed an error which has more than once, in British history, been fatal to great parliamentary leaders. He had imagined that, as soon as he chose to coalesce with those to whom he had recently been opposed, all his followers would imitate his example. He soon found that it was much easier to inflame animosities than to appease them. The great body of Whigs and Presbyterians shrank from the fellowship of the Jacobites. Some waverers were purchased by the government; nor was the purchase expensive; for a sum which would hardly be missed in the English treasury was immense in the estimation of the needy barons of the North.† Thus the scale was turned; and, in the Scottish Parliaments of that age, the turn of the scale was everything: the tendency of majorities was almost always to increase, the tendency of minorities to diminish.

The first question on which a vote was taken related to the election for a borough. The ministers carried their point by six voices.‡ In an instant everything was changed: the spell was broken: the Club, from being a bugbear, became a laughingstock: the timid and the venal passed over in crowds from the weaker to the stronger side. It was in vain that the opposition attempted to revive the disputes of the preceding year. The King had wisely authorised Melville to give up the Committee of Articles. The Estates, on the other hand, showed no disposition to pass another Act of Incapacitation, to censure the government for opening the Courts of Justice, or to question the right of the Sovereign to name the Judges. An extraordinary supply was voted, small, according to the notions of English financiers, but large for the means of Scotland. The sum granted was a hundred and sixty-two thousand pounds sterling, to be raised in the course of four years.§

The Jacobites, who found that they had forsworn themselves to no purpose, sate, bowed down by shame and writhing with vexation, while Montgomery, who had deceived himself and them, and who, in his rage, had utterly lost, not

* Balcarras.
† See the instructions to the Lord High Commissioner in the Leven and

Melville Papers.
‡ Balcarras.
§ Act. Parl. June 7. 1690,

indeed his parts and his fluency, but all decorum and self-command, scolded like a waterman on the Thames, and was answered with equal asperity and even more than equal ability by Sir John Dalrymple.*

Ecclesias-
tical legis-
lation. The most important Acts of this Session were those which fixed the ecclesiastical constitution of Scotland. By the Claim of Right it had been declared that the authority of Bishops was an insupportable grievance; and William, by accepting the Crown, had bound himself not to uphold an institution condemned by the very instrument on which his title to the Crown depended. But the claim of Right had not defined the form of Church government which was to be substituted for episcopacy; and, during the stormy Session held in the summer of 1689, the violence of the Club had made legislation impossible. During many months therefore everything had been in confusion. One polity had been pulled down; and no other polity had been set up. In the Western Lowlands, the beneficed clergy had been so effectually rabbled, that scarcely one of them had remained at his post. In Berwickshire, the three Lothians and Stirlingshire, most of the curates had been removed by the Privy Council for not obeying that vote of the Convention which had directed all ministers of parishes, on pain of deprivation, to proclaim William and Mary King and Queen of Scotland. Thus, throughout a great part of the realm, there was no public worship, except what was performed by Presbyterian divines, who sometimes officiated in tents, and sometimes, without any legal right, took possession of the churches. But there were large districts, especially on the north of the Tay, where the people had no strong feeling against episcopacy; and there were many priests who were not disposed to lose their manses and stipends for the sake of King James. Hundreds of the old curates, therefore, having been neither hunted by the populace nor deposed by the Council, still continued to exercise their spiritual functions. Every minister was, during this time of transition, free to conduct the service and to administer the sacraments as he thought fit. There was no controlling authority. The legislature had taken away the jurisdiction of Bishops, and had not established the jurisdiction of Synods.†

To put an end to this anarchy was one of the first duties of the Parliament. Melville had, with the powerful assist-

---

* Balcarras.
† Faithful Contendings Displayed;   Case of the present Afflicted Episcopal Clergy in Scotland, 1690.

ance of Carstairs, obtained from the King, in spite of the remonstrances of English statesmen and divines, authority to assent to such ecclesiastical arrangements as might satisfy the Scottish nation. One of the first laws which the Lord Commissioner touched with the sceptre repealed the Act of Supremacy. He next gave the royal assent to a law enacting that the Presbyterian divines who had been pastors of parishes in the days of the Covenant, and had, after the Restoration, been ejected for refusing to acknowledge episcopal authority, should be restored. The number of those pastors had originally been about three hundred and fifty : but not more than sixty were still living.*

The Estates then proceeded to fix the national creed. The Confession of Faith drawn up by the Assembly of Divines at Westminster, the Longer and Shorter Catechism, and the Directory, were considered by every good Presbyterian as the standards of orthodoxy ; and it was hoped that the legislature would recognise them as such.† This hope, however, was in part disappointed. The Confession was read at length, amidst much yawning, and adopted without alteration. But, when it was proposed that the Catechisms and the Directory should be taken into consideration, the ill humour of the audience broke forth into murmurs. For that love of long sermons which was strong in the Scottish commonalty was not shared by the Scottish aristocracy. The Parliament had already been listening during three hours to dry theology, and was not inclined to hear anything more about original sin and election. The Duke of Hamilton said that the Estates had already done all that was essential. They had given their sanction to a digest of the great principles of Christianity. The rest might well be left to the Church. The weary majority eagerly assented, in spite of the muttering of some zealous Presbyterian ministers who had been admitted to hear the debate, and who could sometimes hardly restrain themselves from taking part in it.‡

The memorable law which fixed the ecclesiastical constitution of Scotland was brought in by the Earl of Sutherland. By this law the synodical polity was reestablished. The rule of the Church was entrusted to the sixty ejected ministers

* Act. Parl. April 25. 1690.
† See the Humble Address of the Presbyterian Ministers and Professors of the Church of Scotland to His Grace His Majesty's High Commissioner and to the Right Honourable the Estates of Parliament.

‡ See the Account of the late Establishment of Presbyterian Government by the Parliament of Scotland, Anno 1690. This is an Episcopalian narrative. Act. Parl. May 26. 1690.

who had just been restored, and to such other persons, whether ministers or elders, as the Sixty should think fit to admit to a participation of power. The Sixty and their nominees were authorised to visit all the parishes in the kingdom, and to turn out all ministers who were deficient in abilities, scandalous in morals, or unsound in faith. Those parishes which had, during the interregnum, been deserted by their pastors, or, in plain words, those parishes of which the pastors had been rabbled, were declared vacant.*

To the clause which reestablished synodical government no serious opposition appears to have been made. But three days were spent in discussing the question whether the Sovereign should have power to convoke and to dissolve ecclesiastical assemblies; and the point was at last left in dangerous ambiguity. Some other clauses were long and vehemently debated. It was said that the immense power given to the Sixty was incompatible with the fundamental principle of the polity which the Estates were about to set up. That principle was that all presbyters were equal, and that there ought to be no order of ministers of religion superior to the order of presbyters. What did it matter whether the Sixty were called prelates or not, if they were to lord it with more than prelatical authority over God's heritage? To the argument that the proposed arrangement was, in the very peculiar circumstances of the Church, the most convenient that could be made, the objectors replied that such reasoning might suit the mouth of an Erastian, but that all orthodox Presbyterians held the parity of ministers to be ordained by Christ, and that, where Christ had spoken, Christians were not at liberty to consider what was convenient.†

With much greater warmth and much stronger reason, the minority attacked the clause which sanctioned the lawless acts of the Western fanatics. Surely, it was said, a rabbled curate might well be left to the severe scrutiny of the sixty Inquisitors. If he was deficient in parts or learning, if he was loose in life, if he was heterodox in doctrine, those stern judges would not fail to detect and to depose him. They would probably think a game at bowls, a prayer borrowed from the English Liturgy, or a sermon in which the slightest taint of Arminianism could be discovered, a sufficient reason

* Act. Parl. June 7. 1690.   Letter from a Person in Edinburgh to
† An Historical Relation of the late his Friend in London. London licensed
Presbyterian General Assembly in a April 20. 1691.

for pronouncing his benefice vacant. Was it not monstrous, after constituting a tribunal from which he could scarcely hope for bare justice, to condemn him without allowing him to appear even before that tribunal, to condemn him without a trial, to condemn him without an accusation? Did ever any grave senate, since the beginning of the world, treat a man as a criminal merely because he had been robbed, pelted, hustled, dragged through snow and mire, and threatened with death if he returned to the house which was his by law? The Duke of Hamilton, glad to have so good an opportunity of attacking the new Lord Commissioner, spoke with great vehemence against this odious clause. We are told that no attempt was made to answer him; and, though those who tell us so were zealous Episcopalians, we may believe their report: for what answer was it possible to return? Melville, on whom the chief responsibility lay, sate on the throne in profound silence through the whole of this tempestuous debate. It is probable that his conduct was determined by considerations which prudence and shame prevented him from explaining. The state of the southwestern shires was such that it would have been impossible to put the rabbled ministers in possession of their dwellings and churches without employing a military force, without garrisoning every manse, without placing guards round every pulpit, and without handing over some ferocious enthusiasts to the Provost Marshal; and it would be no easy task for the government to keep down by the sword at once the Jacobites of the Highlands and the Covenanters of the Lowlands. The majority, having, for reasons which could not well be produced, made up their minds, became clamorous for the question. "No more debate," was the cry: "We have heard enough: a vote! a vote!" The question was put according to the Scottish form, "Approve or not approve the article?" Hamilton insisted that the question should be, "Approve or not approve the rabbling?" After much altercation, he was overruled, and the clause passed. Only fifteen or sixteen members voted with him. He warmly and loudly exclaimed, amidst much angry interruption, that he was sorry to see a Scottish Parliament disgrace itself by such iniquity. He then left the house with several of his friends. It is impossible not to sympathise with the indignation which he expressed. Yet we ought to remember that it is the nature of injustice to generate injustice. There are wrongs which it is almost impossible to repair without committing other wrongs; and such a wrong had been done to the people of Scotland in the preceding generation. It was because the Parliament of the Restoration had legislated in insolent defiance of the sense of the nation that the Parliament of the Revolution had to abase itself before the mob.

When Hamilton and his adherents had retired, one of the preachers who had been admitted to the hall called out to the members who were near him; "Fie! Fie! Do not lose time. Make haste, and get all over before he comes back." This advice was taken. Four or five sturdy Prelatists staid to give a last vote against Presbytery. Four or five equally sturdy Covenanters staid to mark their dislike of what seemed to them a compromise between the Lord and Baal. But the Act was passed by an overwhelming majority.*

Two supplementary Acts speedily followed. One of them, now happily repealed, required every officebearer in every University of Scotland to sign the Confession of Faith and to give in his adhesion to the new form of Church government.† The other, long ago most unhappily repealed, settled the important and delicate question of patronage. Knox had, in the First Book of Discipline, asserted the right of every Christian congregation to choose its own pastor. Melville had not, in the Second Book of Discipline, gone quite so far; but he had declared that no pastor could lawfully be forced on an unwilling congregation. Patronage had been abolished by a Covenanted Parliament in 1649, and restored by a Royalist Parliament in 1661. What ought to be done in 1690 it was no easy matter to decide. Scarcely any question seems to have caused so much anxiety to William. He had, in his private instructions, given the Lord Commissioner authority to assent to the abolition of patronage, if nothing else would satisfy the Estates. But this authority was most unwillingly given; and the King hoped that it would not be used. "It is," he said, "the taking of men's property." Melville succeeded in effecting a compromise. Patronage was abolished: but it was enacted that every patron should receive six hundred marks Scots, equivalent to about thirty-five pounds sterling, as a compensation for his rights. The sum seems ludicrously small. Yet, when the nature of the property and the poverty of the country are considered, it may be doubted whether a patron would have made much more by going into the market. The largest sum that any member ventured to suggest was nine hundred marks, little more than fifty pounds

* Account of the late Establishment of the Presbyterian Government by the Parliament of Scotland, 1690.   † Act. Parl. July 4. 1690.

sterling. The right of proposing a minister was given to a parochial counsel consisting of the Protestant landowners and the elders. The congregation might object to the person proposed; and the Presbytery was to judge of the objections. This arrangement did not give to the people all the power to which even the Second Book of Discipline had declared that they were entitled. But the odious name of patronage was taken away; it was probably thought that the elders and landowners of a parish would seldom persist in nominating a person to whom the majority of the congregation had strong objections; and indeed it does not appear that, while the Act of 1690 continued in force, the peace of the Church was ever broken by disputes such as produced the schisms of 1732, of 1756, and of 1843.*

Montgomery had done all in his power to prevent the Estates from settling the ecclesiastical polity of the realm. He had incited the zealous Covenanters to demand what he knew that the government would never grant. He had protested against all Erastianism, against all compromise. Dutch Presbyterianism, he said, would not do for Scotland. She must have again the system of 1649. That system was deduced from the Word of God: it was the most powerful check that had ever been devised on the tyranny of wicked kings; and it ought to be restored without addition or diminution. His Jacobite allies could not conceal their disgust and mortification at hearing him hold such language, and were by no means satisfied with the explanations which he gave them in private. While they were wrangling with him on this subject, a messenger arrived at Edinburgh with important despatches from James and from Mary of Modena. These despatches had been written in the confident expectation that the large promises of Montgomery would be fulfilled, and that the Scottish Estates would, under his dexterous management, declare for the rightful Sovereign against the Usurper. James was so grateful for the unexpected support of his old enemies that he entirely forgot the services and disregarded the feelings of his old friends. The three chiefs of the Club, rebels and Puritans as they were, had become his favourites. Annandale was to be a Marquess, Governor of Edinburgh Castle, and Lord High Commissioner. Montgomery was to be Earl of Ayr and Secretary of State. Ross was to be an Earl and to command the guards. James Stewart, the most unprincipled of lawyers, who had been

The coalition between the Club and the Jacobites dissolved

* Act. Parl. July 19. 1690; Lockhart to Melville, April 29. 1690.

deeply concerned in Argyle's insurrection, who had changed sides and supported the dispensing power, who had then changed sides a second time and concurred in the Revolution, and who had now changed sides a third time and was scheming to bring about a Restoration, was to be Lord Advocate. The Privy Council, the Court of Session, the army, were to be filled with Whigs. A Council of Five was appointed, which all loyal subjects were to obey; and in this Council Annandale, Ross, and Montgomery formed the majority. Mary of Modena informed Montgomery that five thousand pounds sterling had been remitted to his order, and that five thousand more would soon follow. It was impossible that Balcarras and those who had acted with him should not bitterly resent the manner in which they were treated. Their names were not even mentioned. All that they had done and suffered seemed to have faded from their master's mind. He had now given them fair notice that, if they should, at the hazard of their lands and lives, succeed in restoring him, all that he had to give would be given to those who had deposed him. They too, when they read his letters, knew, what he did not know when the letters were written, that he had been duped by the confident boasts and promises of the apostate Whigs. He, when he despatched his messengers, imagined that the Club was omnipotent at Edinburgh; and, before the messengers reached Edinburgh, the Club had become a mere byword of contempt. The Tory Jacobites easily found pretexts for refusing to obey the Presbyterian Jacobites to whom the banished King had delegated his authority. They complained that Montgomery had not shown them all the despatches which he had received. They affected to suspect that he had tampered with the seals. He called God Almighty to witness that the suspicion was unfounded. But oaths were very naturally regarded as insufficient guarantees by men who had just been swearing allegiance to a King against whom they were conspiring. There was a violent outbreak of passion on both sides: the coalition was dissolved: the papers were flung into the fire; and, in a few days, the infamous triumvirs who had been, in the short space of a year, violent Williamites and violent Jacobites, became Williamites again, and attempted to make their peace with the government by accusing each other.*

The chiefs of the Club betray each other.   Ross was the first who turned informer. After the fashion of the school in which he had been bred, he committed this

---

* Balcarras; Confession of Annandale in the Leven and Melville papers.

base action with all the forms of sanctity. He pretended to be greatly troubled in mind, sent for a celebrated Presbyterian minister named Dunlop, and bemoaned himself piteously: "There is a load on my conscience: there is a secret which I know that I ought to disclose: but I cannot bring myself to do it." Dunlop prayed long and fervently: Ross groaned and wept: at last it seemed that heaven had been stormed by the violence of supplication: the truth came out, and many lies with it. The divine and the penitent then returned thanks together. Dunlop went with the news to Melville. Ross set off for England to make his peace at court, and performed his journey in safety, though some of his accomplices, who had heard of his repentance, but had been little edified by it, had laid plans for cutting his throat by the way. At London he protested, on his honour, and on the word of a gentleman, that he had been drawn in, that he had always disliked the plot, and that Montgomery and Ferguson were the real criminals.*

Dunlop was, in the meantime, magnifying, wherever he went, the divine goodness which had, by so humble an instrument as himself, brought a noble person back to the right path. Montgomery no sooner heard of this wonderful work of grace than he too began to experience compunction. He went to Melville, made a confession not exactly coinciding with Ross's, and obtained a pass for England. William was then in Ireland; and Mary was governing in his stead. At her feet Montgomery threw himself. He tried to move her pity by speaking of his broken fortunes, and to ingratiate himself with her by praising her sweet and affable manners. He gave up to her the names of his fellow plotters. He vowed to dedicate his whole life to her service, if she would obtain for him some place which might enable him to subsist with decency. She was so much touched by his supplications and flatteries that she recommended him to her husband's favour: but the just distrust and abhorrence with which William regarded Montgomery were not to be overcome.†

Before the traitor had been admitted to Mary's presence, he had obtained a promise that he should be allowed to depart in safety. The promise was kept. During some months, he lay hid in London, and contrived to carry on a negotiation with the government. He offered to be a witness against his

* Balcarras; Notes of Ross's Confession in the Leven and Melville Papers.
† Balcarras; Mary's account of her interview with Montgomery, printed among the Leven and Melville Papers.

accomplices on condition of having a good place. William would bid no higher than a pardon. At length the communications were broken off. Montgomery retired for a time to France. He soon returned to London and passed the miserable remnant of his life in forming plots which came to nothing, and in writing libels which are distinguished by the grace and vigour of their style from most of the productions of the Jacobite press.*

Annandale, when he learned that his two accomplices had turned approvers, retired to Bath, and pretended to drink the waters. Thence he was soon brought up to London by a warrant. He acknowledged that he had been seduced into treason : but he declared that he had only said Amen to the plans of others, and that his childlike simplicity had been imposed on by Montgomery, that worst, that falsest, that most unquiet of human beings. The noble penitent then proceeded to make atonement for his own crime by criminating other people, English and Scotch, Whig and Tory, guilty and innocent. Some he accused on his own knowledge, and some on mere hearsay. Among those whom he accused on his own knowledge was Neville Payne, who had not, it should seem, been mentioned either by Ross or by Montgomery.†

Payne, pursued by messengers and warrants, was so ill advised as to take refuge in Scotland. Had he remained in England he would have been safe : for, though the moral proofs of his guilt were complete, there was not such legal evidence as would have satisfied a jury that he had committed high treason : he could not be subjected to torture in order to force him to furnish evidence against himself; nor could he be long confined without being brought to trial. But the moment that he passed the border he was at the mercy of the government of which he was the deadly foe. The Claim of Right had recognised torture as, in cases like his, a legitimate mode of obtaining information; and no Habeas Corpus Act secured him against a long detention. The unhappy man was arrested, carried to Edinburgh, and brought before the Privy Council. The general notion was, that he was a knave and a coward, and that the first sight of the boots and thumbscrews would bring out all the guilty secrets with which he had been entrusted. But Payne had a far braver spirit than those highborn plotters with whom it was his misfortune to have

---

* Compare Balcarras with Burnet, ii. 62. The pamphlet entitled Great Britain's Just Complaint is a good specimen of Montgomery's manner.

† Balcarras ; Annandale's Confession.

been connected. Twice he was subjected to frightful torments; but not a word inculpating himself or any other person could be wrung out of him. Some councillors left the board in horror. But the pious Crawford presided. He was not much troubled with the weakness of compassion where an Amalekite was concerned, and forced the executioner to hammer in wedge after wedge between the knees of the prisoner till the pain was as great as the human frame can sustain without dissolution. Payne was then carried to the Castle of Edinburgh, where he long remained, utterly forgotten, as he touchingly complained, by those for whose sake he had endured more than the bitterness of death. Yet no ingratitude could damp the ardour of his fanatical loyalty; and he continued, year after year, in his cell, to plan insurrections and invasions.*

Before Payne's arrest the Estates had been adjourned after a Session as important as any that had ever been held in Scotland. The nation generally acquiesced in the new ecclesiastical constitution. The indifferent, a large portion of every society, were glad that the anarchy was over, and conformed to the Presbyterian Church as they had conformed to the Episcopal Church. To the moderate Presbyterians the settlement which had been made was on the whole satisfactory. Most of the strict Presbyterians brought themselves to accept it under protest, as a large instalment of what was due. They missed indeed what they considered as the perfect beauty and symmetry of that Church which had, forty years before, been the glory of Scotland. But, though the second temple was not equal to the first, the chosen people might well rejoice to think that they were, after a long captivity in Babylon, suffered to rebuild, though imperfectly, the House of God on the old foundations; nor could it misbecome them to feel for the latitudinarian William a grateful affection such as the restored Jews had felt for the heathen Cyrus.

General acquiescence in the new ecclesiastical polity.

There were however two parties which regarded the settlement of 1690 with implacable detestation. Those Scotchmen who were Episcopalians on conviction and with fervour appear to have been few: but among them were some persons superior, not perhaps in natural parts, but in learning, in taste, and in the art of composition, to the theologians

Complaints of the Episcopalians.

* Burnet, ii. 62.; Lockhart to Melville, Aug. 30. 1690; and Crawford to Melville, Dec. 11. 1690, in the Leven and Melville Papers; Neville Payne's letter of Dec. 3. 1692, printed in 1693.

of the sect which had now become dominant. It might not
have been safe for the ejected Curates and Professors to
give vent in their own country to the anger which they felt.
But the English press was open to them; and they were sure
of the approbation of a large part of the English people.
During several years they continued to torment their enemies
and to amuse the public with a succession of ingenious and
spirited pamphlets. In some of these works the hardships
suffered by the rabbled priests of the western shires are set
forth with a skill which irresistibly moves pity and indignation. In others, the cruelty with which the Covenanters
had been treated during the reigns of the last two kings of
the House of Stuart is extenuated by every artifice of sophistry. There is much joking on the bad Latin which some
Presbyterian teachers had uttered while seated in academic
chairs lately occupied by great scholars. Much was said
about the ignorant contempt which the victorious barbarians
professed for science and literature. They were accused of
anathematising the modern systems of natural philosophy
as damnable heresies, of condemning geometry as a soul-
destroying pursuit, of discouraging even the study of those
tongues in which the sacred books were written. Learning,
it was said, would soon be extinct in Scotland. The Universities, under their new rulers, were languishing, and must
soon perish. The booksellers had been half ruined: they
found that the whole profit of their business would not pay
the rent of their shops, and were preparing to emigrate to
some country where letters were held in esteem by those
whose office was to instruct the public. Among the ministers of religion no purchaser of books was left. The Episcopalian divine was glad to sell for a morsel of bread whatever
part of his library had not been torn to pieces or burned by
the Christmas mobs; and the only library of a Presbyterian
divine consisted of an explanation of the Apocalypse and a
commentary on the Song of Songs.* The pulpit oratory of
the triumphant party was an inexhaustible subject of mirth.
One little volume, entitled the Scotch Presbyterian Eloquence Displayed, had an immense success in the South
among both High Churchmen and scoffers, and is not yet
quite forgotten. It was indeed a book well fitted to lie on
the hall table of a Squire whose religion consisted in hating

* Historical Relation of the late lately practised against the Professors of
Presbyterian General Assembly, 1691; the College of Edinburgh, 1691.
The Presbyterian Inquisition as it was

extemporaneous prayer and nasal psalmody. On a rainy day, when it was impossible to hunt or shoot, neither the card table nor the backgammon board would have been, in the intervals of the flagon and the pasty, so agreeable a resource. Nowhere else, perhaps, can be found, in so small a compass, so large a collection of ludicrous quotations and anecdotes. Some grave men, however, who bore no love to the Calvinistic doctrine or discipline, shook their heads over this lively jest book, and hinted their opinion that the writer, while holding up to derision the absurd rhetoric by which coarseminded and ignorant men tried to illustrate dark questions of theology and to excite devotional feeling among the populace, had sometimes forgotten the reverence due to sacred things. The effect which tracts of this sort produced on the public mind of England could not be fully discerned while England and Scotland were independent of each other, but manifested itself, very soon after the union of the kingdoms, in a way which we still have reason, and which our posterity will probably long have reason, to lament.

The extreme Presbyterians were as much out of humour as the extreme Prelatists, and were as little inclined as the extreme Prelatists to take the oath of allegiance to William and Mary. Indeed, though the Jacobite nonjuror and the Cameronian nonjuror were diametrically opposed to each other in opinion, though they regarded each other with mortal aversion, though neither of them would have had any scruple about persecuting the other, they had much in common. They were perhaps the two most remarkable specimens that the world could show of perverse absurdity. Each of them considered his darling form of ecclesiastical polity, not as a means, but as an end, as the one thing needful, as the quintessence of the Christian religion. Each of them childishly fancied that he had found a theory of civil government in his Bible. Neither shrank from the frightful consequences to which his theory led. To all objections both had one answer,—Thus saith the Lord. Both agreed in boasting that the arguments which to atheistical politicians seemed irrefragable presented no difficulty to the Saint. It might be perfectly true that, by relaxing the rigour of his principles, he might save his country from slavery, anarchy, universal ruin. But his business was not to save his country, but to save his soul. He obeyed the commands of God, and left the event to God. One of the two fanatical sects held that, to the end of time, the nation would be bound to obey

The Presbyterian nonjurors.

the heir of the Stuarts : the other held that, to the end of time, the nation would be bound by the Solemn League and Covenant; and thus both agreed in regarding the new Sovereigns as usurpers.

The Presbyterian nonjurors have scarcely been heard of out of Scotland ; and perhaps it may not now be generally known, even in Scotland, that they still continue to form a distinct class. They maintained that their country was under a precontract to the Most High, and could never, while the world lasted, enter into any engagement inconsistent with that precontract. An Erastian, a latitudinarian, a man who knelt to receive the bread and wine from the hands of bishops, and who bore, though not very patiently, to hear anthems chaunted by choristers in white vestments, could not be King of a covenanted kingdom. William had moreover forfeited all claim to the crown by committing that sin for which, in the old time, a dynasty preternaturally appointed had been preternaturally deposed. He had connived at the escape of his father in law, that idolater, that murderer, that man of Belial, who ought to have been hewn in pieces before the Lord, like Agag. Nay, the crime of William had exceeded that of Saul. Saul had spared only one Amalekite, and had smitten the rest. What Amalekite had William smitten? The pure Church had been twenty-eight years under perse- cution. Her children had been imprisoned, transported, branded, shot, hanged, drowned, tortured. And yet he who called himself her deliverer had not suffered her to see her desire upon her enemies.* The bloody Claverhouse had been graciously received at St. James's. The bloody Mackenzie had found a secure and luxurious retreat among the malignants of Oxford. The younger Dalrymple who had prosecuted the Saints, the elder Dalrymple who had sate in judgment on the Saints, were great and powerful. It was said, by careless Gallios, that there was no choice but between William and James, and that it was wisdom to choose the less of two evils. Such was indeed the wisdom of this world. But the wisdom

---

* One of the most curious of the many curious papers written by the Co- venanters of that generation is entitled, "Nathaniel or the Dying Testimony of John Matthieson in Closeburn." Mat- thieson did not die till 1709, but his Testimony was written some years ear- lier, when he was in expectation of death. "And now," he says, "I, as a dying man, would in a few words tell you that are to live behind me my thoughts as to the times. When I saw, or rather heard, the Prince and Princess of Orange being set up as they were, and his par- doning all the murderers of the saints, and receiving all the bloody beasts, sol- diers, and others, all these officers of their state and army, and all the bloody counsellors, civil and ecclesiastic, and his letting slip that son of Belial, his father in law, who, both by all the laws of God and man, ought to have died, I knew he would do no good to the cause and work of God."

which was from above taught us that of two things, both of which were evil in the sight of God, we should choose neither. As soon as James was restored it would be a duty to disown and withstand him. The present duty was to disown and withstand his son in law. Nothing must be said, nothing must be done, that could be construed into a recognition of the authority of the man from Holland. The godly must pay no duties to him, must hold no offices under him, must receive no wages from him, must sign no instruments in which he was styled King. Anne succeeded William; and Anne was designated, by those who called themselves the Reformed Presbytery, and the remnant of the true Church, as the pretended Queen, the wicked woman, the Jezebel. George the first succeeded Anne; and George the First was the pretended King, the German Beast.* George the Second succeeded George the First. George the Second too was a pretended King; and he was accused of having outdone the wickedness of his wicked predecessors by passing a law in defiance of that divine law which ordains that no witch shall be suffered to live.† George the Third succeeded George the Second; and still these men continued, with unabated steadfastness, though in language less ferocious than before, to disclaim all allegiance to an uncovenanted Sovereign.‡ At length this schismatical body was subdivided by a new schism. The majority of the Reformed Presbyterians, though they still refused to swear fealty to the Sovereign or to hold office under him, thought themselves justified in praying for him, in paying tribute to him, and in accepting his protection. But there was a minority which would hear of no compromise. So late as the year 1806 a few persons were still bearing their public testimony against the sin of owning an Anti-

* See the Dying Testimony of Mr. Robert Smith, Student of Divinity, who lived in Douglas Town, in the Shire of Clydesdale, who died about two o'clock in the Sabbath morning, Dec. 13. 1724, aged 58 years; and the Dying Testimony of William Wilson, sometime Schoolmaster of Park in the Parish of Douglas, aged 68, who died May 7. 1757.

† See the Dying Testimony of William Wilson, mentioned in the last note. It ought to be remarked that, on the subject of witchcraft, the Divines of the Associate Presbytery were as absurd as this poor crazy Dominie. See their Act, Declaration, and Testimony, published in 1773 by Adam Gib.

‡ In the year 1791, Thomas Henderson of Paisley wrote, in defence of the Reformed Presbytery, against a writer who had charged them with "disowning the present excellent sovereign as the lawful King of Great Britain." "The Reformed Presbytery and their connections," says Mr. Henderson, "have not been much accustomed to give flattering titles to princes." . . . . "However, they entertain no resentment against the person of the present occupant, nor any of the good qualities which he possesses. They sincerely wish that he were more excellent than external royalty can make him, that he were adorned with the image of Christ," &c., &c., &c. "But they can by no means acknowledge him, nor any of the episcopal persuasion, to be a lawful king over these covenanted lands."

christian government by paying taxes, by taking out excise
licenses, or by labouring on public works.* The number of
these zealots went on diminishing till at length they were so
thinly scattered over Scotland that they were nowhere numerous enough to have a meeting house, and were known by
the name of the Nonhearers. They, however, still assembled
and prayed in private dwellings, and still persisted in considering themselves as the chosen generation, the royal
priesthood, the holy nation, the peculiar people, which,
amidst the common degeneracy, alone preserved the faith of
a better age. It is by no means improbable that this superstition, the most irrational and the most unsocial into which
Protestant Christianity has ever been corrupted by human
prejudices and passions may still linger in a few obscure
farmhouses.

William
dissatisfied
with the
ecclesias-
tical ar-
range-
ments in
Scotland.

The King was but half satisfied with the manner in which
the ecclesiastical polity of Scotland had been settled. He
thought that the Episcopalians had been hardly used; and
he apprehended that they might be still more hardly used
when the new system was fully organised. He had been
very desirous that the Act which established the Presbyterian
Church should be accompanied by an Act allowing persons
who were not members of that Church to hold their own
religious assemblies freely; and he had particularly directed
Melville to look to this.† But some popular preachers
harangued so vehemently at Edinburgh against liberty of
conscience, which they called the mystery of iniquity, that
Melville did not venture to obey his master's instructions.
A draught of a Toleration Act was offered to the Parliament

* An enthusiast, named George Cal-
derwood, in his preface to a Collection of
Dying Testimonies, published in 1806,
accuses the Reformed Presbytery of
scandalous compliances. "As for the
Reformed Presbytery," he says, "though
they profess to own the martyrs' testimony in hairs and hoofs, yet they have
now adopted so many new distinctions,
and given up their old ones, that they
have made it so evident that it is neither
the martyrs' testimony nor yet the one
that that Presbytery adopted at first that
they are now maintaining. When the
Reformed Presbytery was in its infancy,
and had some appearance of honesty
and faithfulness among them, they were
blamed by all the other parties for using
of distinctions that no man could justify,
i. e. they would not admit into their communion those that paid the land tax or

subscribed tacks to do so; but now they
can admit into their communions both
rulers and members who voluntarily pay
all taxes and subscribe tacks." . . . .
"It shall be only referred to government's books, since the commencement
of the French war, how many of their
own members have accepted of places of
trust, to be at government's call, such as
bearers of arms, driving of cattle, stopping of ways, &c.; and what is all their
license for trading by sea or land but a
serving under government?" The doctrines of those more moderate nonjurors
who call themselves the Reformed Presbyterian Church have been recently set
forth in a Prize Catechism by the Reverend Thomas Martin.

† The King to Melville, May 22. 1690,
in the Leven and Melville Papers.

by a private member, but was coldly received and suffered to drop.*

William, however, was fully determined to prevent the dominant sect from indulging in the luxury of persecution; and he took an early opportunity of announcing his determination. The first General Assembly of the newly established Church met soon after his return from Ireland. It was necessary that he should appoint a Commissioner and send a letter. Some zealous Presbyterians hoped that Crawford would be the Commissioner; and the ministers of Edinburgh drew up a paper in which they very intelligibly hinted that this was their wish. William, however, selected Lord Carmichael, a nobleman distinguished by good sense, humanity, and moderation.† The royal letter to the Assembly was eminently wise in substance and impressive in language. "We expect," the King wrote, "that your management shall be such that we may have no reason to repent of what we have done. We never could be of the mind that violence was suited to the advancing of true religion; nor do we intend that our authority shall ever be a tool to the irregular passions of any party. Moderation is what religion enjoins, what neighbouring Churches expect from you, and what we recommend to you." The Sixty and their associates would probably have been glad to reply in language resembling that which, as some of them could well remember, had been held by the clergy to Charles the Second during his residence in Scotland. But they had just been informed that there was in England a strong feeling in favour of the rabbled curates, and that it would, at such a conjuncture, be madness in the body which represented the Presbyterian Church to quarrel with the King.‡ The Assembly therefore returned a grateful and respectful answer to the royal letter, and assured His Majesty that they had suffered too much from oppression ever to be oppressors.§

Meanwhile the troops all over the Continent were going into

* Account of the Establishment of Presbyterian Government.

† Carmichael's good qualities are fully admitted by the Episcopalians. See the Historical Relation of the late Presbyterian General Assembly and the Presbyterian Inquisition.

‡ See, in the Leven and Melville Papers, Melville's Letters written from London at this time to Crawford, Rule, Williamson, and other vehement Presbyterians. He says: "The clergy that were putt out, and come up, make a great clamour: many here encourage and rejoyce at it. . . . . There is nothing now but the greatest sobrietie and moderation imaginable to be used, unless we will hazard the overturning of all: and take this as earnest, and not as imaginations and fears only."

§ Principal Acts of the General Assembly of the Church of Scotland held in and begun at Edinburgh the 16th day of October, 1690; Edinburgh, 1691.

winter quarters. The campaign had everywhere been indecisive. The victory gained by Luxemburg at Fleurus had produced no important effect. On the Upper Rhine great armies had eyed each other, month after month, without exchanging a blow. In Catalonia a few small forts had been taken. In the east of Europe the Turks had been successful on some points, the Christians on other points; and the termination of the contest seemed to be as remote as ever. The coalition had in the course of the year lost one valuable member, and gained another. The Duke of Lorraine, the ablest captain in the Imperial service, was no more. He had died, as he had lived, an exile and a wanderer, and had bequeathed to his children nothing but his name and his rights. It was popularly said that the confederacy could better have spared thirty thousand soldiers than such a general. But scarcely had the allied Courts gone into mourning for him when they were consoled by learning that another prince superior to him in power, and not inferior to him in capacity or courage, had joined the league against France.

The Duke of Savoy joins the coalition. This was Victor Amadeus, Duke of Savoy. He was a young man: but he was already versed in those arts for which the statesmen of Italy had, ever since the thirteenth century, been celebrated, those arts by which Castruccio Castracani and Francis Sforza rose to greatness, and which Machiavel reduced to a system. No sovereign in modern Europe has, with so small a principality, exercised so great an influence during so long a period. He had for a time submitted, with a show of cheerfulness, but with secret reluctance and resentment, to the French ascendency. When the war broke out, he professed neutrality, but entered into private negotiations with the House of Austria. He would probably have continued to dissemble till he found some opportunity of striking an unexpected blow, had not his crafty schemes been disconcerted by the decision and vigour of Lewis. A French army commanded by Catinat, an officer of great skill and valour, marched into Piedmont. The Duke was informed that his conduct had excited suspicions which he could remove only by admitting foreign garrisons into Turin and Vercelli. He found that he must be either the slave or the open enemy of his powerful and imperious neighbour. His choice was soon made; and a war began which, during seven years, found employment for some of the best generals and best troops of Lewis. An Envoy Extraordinary from Savoy went to the Hague, proceeded thence to London, presented his credentials in the Banqueting

State of affairs on the Continent.

House, and addressed to William a speech which was speedily translated into many languages and read in every part of Europe. The orator congratulated the King on the success of that great enterprise which had restored England to her ancient place among the nations, and had broken the chains of Europe. "That my master," he said, "can now at length venture to express feelings which have been long concealed in the recesses of his heart is part of the debt which he owes to Your Majesty. You have inspired him with the hope of freedom after so many years of bondage." *

It had been determined that, during the approaching winter, a Congress of all the powers hostile to France should be held at the Hague. William was impatient to proceed thither. But it was necessary that he should first hold a Session of Parliament. Early in October the Houses reassembled at Westminster. The members had generally come up in good humour. Those Tories whom it was possible to conciliate had been conciliated by the Act of Grace, and by the large share which they had obtained of the favours of the Crown. Those Whigs who were capable of learning had learned much from the lesson which William had given them, and had ceased to expect that he would descend from the rank of a King to that of a party leader. Both Whigs and Tories had, with few exceptions, been alarmed by the prospect of a French invasion, and cheered by the news of the victory of the Boyne. The Sovereign who had shed his blood for their nation and their religion stood at this moment higher in public estimation than at any time since his accession. His speech from the throne called forth the loud acclamations of Lords and Commons.† Thanks were unanimously voted by both Houses to the King for his achievements in Ireland, and to the Queen for the prudence with which she had, during his absence, governed England.‡ Thus commenced a Session distinguished among the Sessions of that reign by harmony and tranquillity. No report of the debates has been preserved, unless a long forgotten lampoon, in which some of the speeches made on the first day are burlesqued in doggrel rhymes, may be called a report.§ The time of the Commons appears to have been chiefly occupied in discussing questions arising out of the

* Monthly Mercuries; London Gazettes of November 3. and 6. 1690.

† Van Citters to the States General, Oct. ³⁄₁₃. 1690.

‡ Lords' Journals, Oct. 6. 1690 ; Commons' Journals, October 8.

§ I am not aware that this lampoon has ever been printed. I have seen it only in two contemporary manuscripts. It is entitled The Opening of the Session. 1690.

elections of the preceding spring. The supplies necessary for the war, though large, were granted with alacrity. The num-

ber of regular troops for the next year was fixed at seventy thousand, of whom twelve thousand were to be horse or dragoons. The charge of this army, the greatest that England had ever maintained, amounted to about two million three hundred thousand pounds ; the charge of the navy to about eighteen hundred thousand pounds. The charge of the ordnance was included in these sums, and was roughly estimated at one-eighth of the naval and one-fifth of the military expenditure.* The whole of the extraordinary aid granted to the King exceeded four millions.

The Commons justly thought that the extraordinary liberality with which they had provided for the public service entitled them to demand extraordinary securities against waste and peculation. A bill was brought in empowering nine Commissioners to examine and state the public accounts. The nine were named in the bill, and were all members of the Lower House. The Lords agreed to the bill without amendments ; and the King gave his assent.†

The debates on the Ways and Means occupied a considerable part of the Session. It was resolved that sixteen hundred and fifty thousand pounds should be raised by a direct monthly assessment on land. The excise duties on ale and beer were doubled ; and the import duties on raw silk, linen, timber, glass, and other articles, were increased.‡ Thus far there was little difference of opinion. But soon the smooth course of business was disturbed by a proposition which was much more popular than just or humane. Taxes of unprecedented severity had been imposed ; and yet it might well be doubted whether these taxes would be sufficient. Why, it was asked, should not the cost of the Irish war be borne by the Irish insurgents ? How those insurgents had acted in their mock Parliament all the world knew ; and nothing could be more reasonable than to mete to them from their own measure. They ought to be treated as they had treated the Saxon colony. Every acre which the Act of Settlement had left them ought to be seized by the state for the purpose of defraying that expense which their turbulence and perverseness had made necessary. It is not strange that a plan, which at once gratified national ani-

---

* Commons' Journals, Oct. 9, 10. 13, 14 1690.

† Commons' Journals of December,

1690, particularly of Dec. 26.; Stat. 2 W. & M. sess. 2. c. 11.

‡ Stat. 2 W. & M. sess. 2. c. 1. 3, 4.

mosity, and held out the hope of pecuniary relief, should have been welcomed with eager delight. A bill was brought in which bore but too much resemblance to some of the laws passed by the Jacobite legislators of Dublin. By this bill it was provided that the property of every person who had been in rebellion against the King and Queen since the day on which they were proclaimed should be confiscated, and that the proceeds should be applied to the support of the war. An exception was made in favour of such Protestants as had merely submitted to superior force: but to Papists no indulgence was shown. The royal prerogative of clemency was limited. The King might indeed, if such were his pleasure, spare the lives of his vanquished enemies: but he was not to be permitted to save any part of their estates from the general doom. He was not to have it in his power to grant a capitulation which should secure to Irish Roman Catholics the enjoyment of their hereditary lands. Nay, he was not to be allowed to keep faith with persons whom he had already received to mercy, who had kissed his hand, and had heard from his lips the promise of protection. An attempt was made to insert a proviso in favour of Lord Dover. Dover, who, with all his faults, was not without some English feelings, had, by defending the interests of his native country at Dublin, made himself odious to both the Irish and the French. After the battle of the Boyne his situation was deplorable. Neither at Limerick nor at Saint Germains could he hope to be welcomed. In his despair, he threw himself at William's feet, promised to live peaceably, and was graciously assured that he had nothing to fear. Though the royal word seemed to be pledged to this unfortunate man, the Commons resolved, by a hundred and nineteen votes to a hundred and twelve, that his property should not be exempted from the general confiscation.

The bill went up to the Peers: but the Peers were not inclined to pass it without considerable amendments; and such amendments there was not time to make. Numerous heirs at law, reversioners, and creditors implored the Upper House to introduce such provisoes as might secure the innocent against all danger of being involved in the punishment of the guilty. Some petitioners asked to be heard by counsel. The King had made all his arrangements for a voyage to the Hague; and the day beyond which he could not postpone his departure drew near. The bill was therefore, happily for the honour of English legislation, consigned to that dark repository in which the abortive statutes of many generations sleep a sleep rarely disturbed by the historian or the antiquary.*

Proceedings against Torrington.

Another question, which slightly, and but slightly, discomposed the tranquillity of this short session, arose out of the disastrous and disgraceful battle of Beachy Head. Torrington had, immediately after that battle, been sent to the Tower, and had ever since remained there. A technical difficulty had arisen about the mode of bringing him to trial. There was no Lord High Admiral: and whether the Commissioners of the Admiralty were competent to execute martial law was a point which to some jurists appeared not perfectly clear. The majority of the Judges held that the Commissioners were competent: but, for the purpose of removing all doubt, a bill was brought into the Upper House; and to this bill several Lords offered an opposition which seems to have been most unreasonable. The proposed law, they said, was a retrospective penal law, and therefore objectionable. If they used this argument in good faith, they were ignorant of the very rudiments of the science of legislation. To make a law for punishing that which, at the time when it was done, was not punishable, is contrary to all sound principle. But a law which merely alters the criminal procedure may with perfect propriety be made applicable to past as well as to future offences. It would have been the grossest injustice to give a retrospective operation to the law which made slavetrading felony. But there was not the smallest injustice in enacting that the Central Criminal Court should try felonies committed long before that Court was in being. In Torrington's case the substantive law continued to be what it had always been. The definition of the crime, the amount of the penalty, remained unaltered. The only change was in the form of procedure; and that change the legislature was perfectly justified in making retrospectively. It is indeed hardly possible to believe that some of those who opposed the bill were duped by the fallacy of which they condescended to make use. The truth probably is that the feeling of caste was strong among the Lords. That one of themselves should be tried for his life by a court composed of plebeians seemed to them a degradation of their whole order. If their noble brother had offended, articles of impeachment ought to be exhibited against him:

---

* Burnet, ii. 67. See the Journals of both Houses, particularly the Commons' Journals of the 19th of December and the Lords' Journals of the 30th of December and the 1st of January. The bill itself will be found in the archives of the House of Lords.

Westminster Hall ought to be fitted up: his peers ought to meet in their robes, and to give in their verdict on their honour: a Lord High Steward ought to pronounce the sentence, and to break the staff. There was an end of privilege if an Earl was to be doomed to death by tarpaulins seated round a table in the cabin of a ship. These feelings had so much influence that the bill passed the Upper House by a majority of only two.* In the Lower House, where the dignities and immunities of the nobility were regarded with no friendly feeling, there was little difference of opinion. Torrington requested to be heard at the bar, and spoke there at great length, but weakly and confusedly. He boasted of his services, of his sacrifices, and of his wounds. He abused the Dutch, the Board of Admiralty, and the Secretary of State. The bill, however, went through all its stages without a division.†

Early in December Torrington was sent under a guard down the river to Sheerness. There the Court Martial met on board of a frigate named the Kent. The investigation lasted three days; and during those days the ferment was great in London. Nothing was heard of on the exchange, in the coffeehouses, nay even at the church doors, but Torrington. Parties ran high: wagers to an immense amount were depending: rumours were hourly arriving by land and water; and every rumour was exaggerated and distorted by the way. From the day on which the news of the ignominious battle arrived, down to the very eve of the trial, public opinion had been very unfavourable to the prisoner. His name, we are told by contemporary pamphleteers, was hardly ever mentioned without a curse. But, when the crisis of his fate drew nigh, there was, as in our country there often is, a reaction. All his merits, his courage, his good nature, his firm adherence to the Protestant religion in the evil times, were remembered. It was impossible to deny that he was sunk in sloth and luxury, that he neglected the most important business for his pleasures, and that he could not say No to a boon companion or to a mistress: but for these faults excuses and soft names were found. His friends used without scruple all the arts which could raise a national feeling in his favour; and these arts were powerfully assisted by the intelligence

Torrington's trial and acquittal.

* Lords' Journals, Oct. 30. 1690. The numbers are never given in the Lords' Journals. That the majority was only two is asserted by Ralph, who had, I suppose, some authority which I have not been able to find.

† Van Citters to the States General, Nov. 14/24. 1690. The Earl of Torrington's speech to the House of Commons, 1710.

that the hatred which was felt towards him in Holland had
vented itself in indignities to some of his countrymen.   The
cry was that a bold, jolly, freehanded English gentleman, of
whom the worst that could be said was that he liked wine and
women, was to be shot in order to gratify the spite of the
Dutch.   What passed at the trial tended to confirm the populace in this notion.   Most of the witnesses against the prisoner were Dutch officers.   The Dutch rear admiral, who took
on himself the part of prosecutor, forgot himself so far as to
accuse the judges of partiality.   When at length, on the
evening of the third day, Torrington was pronounced not
guilty, many who had recently clamoured for his blood seemed
to be well pleased with his acquittal.   He returned to London
free, and with his sword by his side.   As his yacht went up
the Thames, every ship which he passed saluted him.   He took
his seat in the House of Lords, and even ventured to present
himself at court.   But most of the peers looked coldly on
him : William would not see him, and ordered him to be dismissed from the service.*

Animosity
of the
Whigs
against
Caermar-
then.   There was another subject about which no vote was passed
by either of the Houses, but about which there is reason to
believe that some acrimonious discussion took place in both.
The Whigs, though much less violent than in the preceding
year, could not patiently see Caermarthen as nearly prime
minister as any English subject could be under a prince of
William's character.   Though no man had taken a more
prominent part in the Revolution than the Lord President,
though no man had more to fear from a counterrevolution,
his old enemies would not believe that he had from his heart
renounced those arbitrary doctrines for which he had once
been zealous, or that he could bear true allegiance to a
government sprung from resistance.   Through the last six
months of 1690 he was mercilessly lampooned.   Sometimes
he was King Thomas, and sometimes Tom the Tyrant.†

---

* Burnet, ii., 67, 68. ; Van Citters to
the States General, $\frac{Nov. 20.}{Dec. 1.}$ Dec. $\frac{9}{19}$. $\frac{12}{22}$. $\frac{18}{28}$.
1690; An impartial Account of some
remarkable Passages in the Life of Arthur, Earl of Torrington, together with
some modest Remarks on the Trial and
Acquitment, 1691 ; Reasons for the
Trial of the Earl of Torrington by Impeachment, 1690; The Parable of the
Bearbaiting, 1690 ; The Earl of Torrington's Speech to the House of Commons,
1710.   That Torrington was coldly received by the peers I learned from an
Article in the Noticias Ordinarias of

February 6. 1691, Madrid.
    † In one Whig lampoon of this year
are these lines :

> "David, we thought, succeeded Saul,
>   When William rose on James's fall ;
>   But now King Thomas governs all."

In another are these lines :

> " When Charles did seem to fill the throne,
>   This tyrant Tom made England groan."

A third says :

> " Yorkshire Tom was raised to honour,
>   For what cause no creature knew ;
> He was false to the royal donor,
>   And will be the same to you."

William was adjured not to go to the Continent leaving his worst enemy close to the ear of the Queen. Halifax, who had, in the preceding year, been ungenerously and ungrate fully persecuted by the Whigs, was now mentioned by them with respect and regret: for he was the enemy of their enemy.* The face, the figure, the bodily infirmities of Caermarthen were ridiculed.† Those dealings with the French Court in which, twelve years before, he had, rather by his misfortune than by his fault, been implicated, were represented in the most odious colours. He was reproached with his impeachment and his imprisonment. Once, it was said, he had escaped: but vengeance might still overtake him; and London might enjoy the long deferred pleasure of seeing the old traitor flung off the ladder in the blue riband which he disgraced. All the members of his family, wife, son, daughters, were assailed with savage invective and contemptuous sarcasm.‡ All who were supposed to be closely connected with him by political ties came in for a portion of this abuse; and none had so large a portion as Lowther. The feeling indicated by these satires was strong among the Whigs in Parliament. Several of them deliberated on a plan of attack, and were in hopes that they should be able to raise such a storm as would make it impossible for Caermarthen to remain at the head of affairs. It should seem that, at this time, his influence in the royal closet was not quite what it had been. Godolphin, whom he did not love, and could not control, but whose financial skill had been greatly missed during the summer, was brought back to the Treasury, and made First Commissioner. Lowther, who was the Lord President's own man, still sate at the board, but no longer presided there. It is true that there was not then such a difference as there now is between the First Lord and his colleagues. Still the change was important and significant. Marlborough, whom Caermarthen disliked, was, in military affairs, not less trusted than Godolphin in financial affairs. The seals which Shrewsbury had resigned in the summer had ever since been lying in William's secret drawer. The Lord President probably expected that he should be consulted before they were given away; but he was disappointed. Sidney was sent for from

---

* A Whig poet compares the two Marquesses, as they were often called, and gives George the preference over Thomas:

"If a Marquess needs must steer us,
Take a better in his stead,
Who will in your absence cheer us,
And has far a wiser head."

† "A thin, illnatured ghost that haunts the King."

‡ "Let him with his blue riband be
Tied close up to the gallows tree;
For my lady a cart; and I'd contrive it,
Her dancing son and heir should drive it."

Ireland: and the seals were delivered to him. The first intimation which the Lord President received of this important appointment was not made in a manner likely to soothe his feelings. "Did you meet the new Secretary of State going out?" said William. "No, Sir," answered the Lord President; "I met nobody but my Lord Sidney." "He is the new Secretary," said William. "He will do till I find a fit man; and he will be quite willing to resign as soon as I find a fit man. Any other person that I could put in would think himself ill used if I were to put him out." If William had said all that was in his mind, he would probably have added that Sidney, though not a great orator or statesman, was one of the very few English politicians who could be as entirely trusted as Bentinck or Zulestein. Caermarthen listened with a bitter smile. It was new, he afterwards said, to see a nobleman placed in the Secretary's office, as a footman was placed in a box at the theatre, merely in order to keep a seat till his betters came.* But this jest was a cover for serious mortification and alarm. The situation of the prime minister was unpleasant and even perilous; and the duration of his power would probably have been short, had not fortune, just at this moment, enabled him to confound his adversaries by rendering a great service to the state.†

A Jacobite plot.

The Jacobites had seemed in August to be completely crushed. The victory of the Boyne, and the irresistible explosion of patriotic feeling produced by the appearance of Tourville's fleet on the coast of Devonshire, had cowed the boldest champions of hereditary right. Most of the chief plotters had passed some weeks in confinement or in concealment. But, widely as the ramifications of the conspiracy had extended, only one traitor had suffered the punishment of his crime. This was a man named Godfrey Cross, who kept an inn on the beach near Rye, and who, when the French fleet was on the coast of Sussex, had given information to Tourville. When it appeared that this solitary example was thought sufficient, when the danger of invasion was over, when the popular enthusiasm excited by that danger had subsided, when the lenity of the government had permitted some conspirators to leave their prisons and had encouraged others to venture out of

---

* See Lord Dartmouth's Note on Burnet, ii. 5.

† As to the designs of the Whigs against Caermarthen, see Burnet, ii. 68, 69., and a very significant protest in the Lords' Journals, October 30. 1690. As to the relations between Caermarthen and Godolphin, see Godolphin's letter to William dated March 20. 1691, in Dalrymple.

their hidingplaces, the faction which had been prostrated and stunned began to give signs of returning animation. The old traitors again mustered at the old haunts, exchanged significant looks and eager whispers, and drew from their pockets libels on the Court of Kensington, and letters in milk and lemon juice from the Court of Saint Germains. Preston, Dartmouth, Clarendon, Penn, were among the most busy. With them was leagued the nonjuring Bishop of Ely, who was still permitted by the government to reside in the palace, now no longer his own, and who had, but a short time before, called heaven to witness that he detested the thought of inviting foreigners to invade England. One good opportunity had been lost: but another was at hand, and must not be suffered to escape. The usurper would soon be again out of England. The administration would soon be again confided to a weak woman and a divided council. The year which was closing had certainly been unlucky; but that which was about to commence might be more auspicious.

In December a meeting of the leading Jacobites was held.* The sense of the assembly, which consisted exclusively of Protestants, was that something ought to be attempted, but that the difficulties were great. None ventured to recommend that James should come over unaccompanied by regular troops. Yet all, taught by the experience of the preceding summer, dreaded the effect which might be produced by the sight of French uniforms and standards on English ground. A paper was drawn up which would, it was hoped, convince both James and Lewis that a restoration could not be effected without the cordial concurrence of the nation. France,—such was the substance of this remarkable document,—might possibly make the island a heap of ruins, but never a subject province. It was hardly possible for any person, who had not had an opportunity of observing the temper of the public mind, to imagine the savage and dogged determination with which men of all classes, sects, and factions, were prepared to resist any foreign potentate who should attempt to conquer the kingdom by force of arms. Nor could England be governed as a Roman Catholic country. There were five millions of Protestants in the realm; there were not a hundred thousand Papists: that such a minority should keep down such a majority was physi-

Meeting of the leading conspirators.

---

* My account of this conspiracy is chiefly taken from the evidence, oral and documentary, which was produced on the trial of the conspirators. See also Burnet, ii. 69, 70., the Appendix to Dalrymple's Memoirs, Part II. Book vi., and the Life of James, ii. 441. Narcissus Luttrell remarks that no Roman Catholic appeared to have been admitted to the consultations of the conspirators.

cally impossible ; and to physical impossibility all other considerations must give way. James would therefore do well to take without delay such measures as might indicate his resolution to protect the established religion. Unhappily every letter which arrived from France contained something tending to irritate feelings which it was most desirable to soothe. Stories were everywhere current of slights offered at Saint Germains to Protestants who had given the highest proof of loyalty by following into banishment a master zealous for a faith which was not their own. The edicts which had been issued against the Huguenots might perhaps have been justified by the anarchical opinions and practices of those sectaries : but it was the height of injustice and of inhospitality to put those edicts in force against men who had been driven from their country solely on account of their attachment to a Roman Catholic King. Surely sons of the Anglican Church, who had, in obedience to her teaching, sacrificed all that they most prized on earth to the royal cause, ought not to be any longer interdicted from assembling in some modest edifice to celebrate her rites and to receive her consolations. An announcement that Lewis had, at the request of James, permitted the English exiles to worship God according to their national forms would be the best prelude to the great attempt. That attempt ought to be made early in the spring. A French force must undoubtedly accompany His Majesty. But he must declare that he brought that force only for the defence of his person and for the protection of his loving subjects, and that, as soon as the foreign oppressors had been expelled, the foreign deliverers should be dismissed. He must also promise to govern according to law, and must refer all the points which had been in dispute between him and his people to the decision of a Parliament.

The Conspirators determine to send Preston to Saint Germains.

It was determined that Preston should carry to Saint Germains the resolutions and suggestions of the conspirators. John Ashton, a person who had been clerk of the closet to Mary of Modena when she was on the throne, and who was entirely devoted to the interests of the exiled family, undertook to procure the means of conveyance, and for this purpose engaged the cooperation of a hotheaded young Jacobite named Elliot, who only knew in general that a service of some hazard was to be rendered to the good cause.

It was easy to find in the port of London a vessel the owner of which was not scrupulous about the use for which it might be wanted. Ashton and Elliot were introduced to the master of a smack named the James and Elizabeth. The Jacobite agents pretended to be smugglers, and talked of the thousands of pounds which might be got by a single lucky trip to France and back again. A bargain was struck: a sixpence was broken; and all the arrangements were made for the voyage.

Preston was charged by his friends with a packet containing several important papers. Among these was a list of the English fleet furnished by Dartmouth, who was in communication with some of his old companions in arms, a minute of the resolutions which had been adopted at the meeting of the conspirators, and the heads of a Declaration which it was thought desirable that James should publish at the moment of his landing. There were also six or seven letters from persons of note in the Jacobite party. Most of these letters were parables, but parables which it was not difficult to unriddle. One plotter used the cant of the law. There was hope that Mr. Jackson would soon recover his estate. The new landlord was a hard man, and had set the freeholders against him. A little matter would redeem the whole property. The opinions of the best counsel were in Mr. Jackson's favour. All that was necessary was that he should himself appear in Westminster Hall. The final hearing ought to be before the close of Easter Term. Other writers affected the style of the Royal Exchange. There was great demand for a cargo of the right sort. There was reason to hope that the old firm would soon form profitable connections with houses with which it had hitherto had no dealings. This was evidently an allusion to the discontented Whigs. But, it was added, the shipments must not be delayed. Nothing was so dangerous as to overstay the market. If the expected goods did not arrive by the tenth of March, the whole profit of the year would be lost. As to details entire reliance might be placed on the excellent factor who was going over. Clarendon assumed the character of a matchmaker. There was great hope that the business which he had been negotiating would be brought to bear, and that the marriage portion would be well secured. "Your relations," he wrote, in allusion to his recent confinement, "have been very hard on me this last summer. Yet, as soon as I could go safely abroad, I pursued the business." Catharine Sedley entrusted Preston with a letter in which, without allegory or circumlocution, she complained that her lover had left her a daughter to support, and begged very hard for money. But the two most important despatches were from Bishop Turner. They were

Papers entrusted to Preston.

directed to Mr. and Mrs. Redding: but the language was such
as it would be thought abject in any gentleman to hold except
to royalty. The Bishop assured Their Majesties that he was
devoted to their cause, that he earnestly wished for a great
occasion to prove his zeal, and that he would no more swerve
from his duty to them than renounce his hope of heaven. He
added, in phraseology metaphorical indeed, but perfectly intelligible, that he was the mouthpiece of several of the nonjuring prelates, and especially of Sancroft. "Sir, I speak in
the plural,"—these are the words of the letter to James,—
"because I write my elder brother's sentiments as well as my
own, and the rest of our family." The letter to Mary of Modena is to the same effect. "I say this in behalf of my elder
brother, and the rest of my nearest relations, as well as from
myself."*

All the letters with which Preston was charged referred the
Court of Saint Germains to him for fuller information. He
carried with him minutes in his own handwriting on the subjects on which he was to converse with his master and with
the ministers of Lewis. These minutes, though concise and
desultory, can for the most part be interpreted without difficulty. The vulnerable points of the coasts are mentioned.
Gosport is defended only by palisades. The garrison of Portsmouth is small. The French fleet ought to be out in April,
and to fight before the Dutch are in the Channel. There is a
memorandum which proves that Preston had been charged,—
by whom it is easy to guess,—with a commission relating to
Pennsylvania; and there are a few broken words clearly im-
porting that some at least of the nonjuring bishops, when they
declared, before God, that they abhorred the thought of inviting the French over, were dissembling.†

Information of the plot given to Caermarthen.

Everything was now ready for Preston's departure. But
the owner of the James and Elizabeth had conceived a suspicion that the expedition for which his smack had been

* The genuineness of these letters was
once contested on very frivolous grounds.
But the letter of Turner to Sancroft,
which is among the Tanner papers in the
Bodleian Library, and which will be
found in the Life of Ken by a Layman,
must convince the most incredulous.

† The memorandum relating to Pennsylvania ought to be quoted together
with the two sentences which precede it.
"A commission given to me from Mr.
P.—Fr. Fl. hinder Eng. and D. from
joining—two vessels of 150l. price for

Pensilvania for 13 or 14 months." I have
little doubt that the first and third of
these sentences are parts of one memorandum, and that the words which evidently relate to the fleets were jotted down
at a different time in the place left
vacant between two lines. The words
relating to the Bishops are these: "The
Modest Inquiry—The Bishops' Answer—
Not the chilling of them—But the satis-
fying of friends." The Modest Inquiry
was the pamphlet which hinted at De-
witting.

hired was rather of a political than of a commercial nature. It occurred to him that more might be made by informing against his passengers than by carrying them safely. Intelligence of what was passing was conveyed to the Lord President. No intelligence could be more welcome to him. He was delighted to find that it was in his power to give a signal proof of his attachment to the government which his enemies had accused him of betraying. He took his measures with his usual energy and dexterity. His eldest son, the Earl of Danby, a bold, volatile, and somewhat eccentric young man, was fond of the sea, lived much among sailors, and was the proprietor of a small yacht of marvellous speed. This vessel, well manned, was placed under the command of a trusty officer named Billop, and was sent down the river, as if for the purpose of pressing mariners.

At dead of night, the last night of the year 1690, Preston, Ashton, and Elliot went on board of their smack near the Tower. They were in great dread lest they should be stopped and searched, either by a frigate which lay off Woolwich, or by the guard posted at the blockhouse of Gravesend. But, when they had passed both frigate and blockhouse without being challenged, their spirits rose: their appetites became keen: they unpacked a hamper well stored with roast beef, mince pies, and bottles of wine, and were just sitting down to their Christmas cheer, when the alarm was given that a swift vessel from Tilbury was flying through the water after them. They had scarcely time to hide themselves in a dark hole among the gravel which was the ballast of their smack, when the chase was over, and Billop, at the head of an armed party, came on board. The hatches were taken up: the conspirators were arrested; and their clothes were strictly examined. Preston, in his agitation, had dropped on the gravel his official seal and the packet of which he was the bearer. The seal was discovered where it had fallen. Ashton, aware of the importance of the papers, snatched them up and tried to conceal them: but they were soon found in his bosom.

The prisoners then tried to cajole or to corrupt Billop. They called for wine, pledged him, praised his gentlemanlike demeanour, and assured him that if he would accompany them, nay, if he would only let that little roll of paper fall overboard into the Thames, his fortune would be made. The tide of affairs, they said, was on the turn: things could not go on for ever as they had gone on of late; and it was in the cap-

Arrest of Preston and his companions.

tain's power to be as great and as rich as he could desire. Billop, though courteous, was inflexible. The conspirators became sensible that their necks were in imminent danger. The emergency brought out strongly the true characters of all the three, characters which, but for such an emergency, might have remained for ever unknown. Preston had always been reputed a high spirited and gallant gentleman : but the near prospect of a dungeon and a gallows altogether unmanned him. Elliot stormed and blasphemed, vowed that, if he ever got free, he would be revenged, and, with horrible imprecations, called on the thunder to strike the yacht, and on London Bridge to fall in and crush her. Ashton alone behaved with manly firmness.

Late in the evening the yacht reached Whitehall Stairs ; and the prisoners, strongly guarded, were conducted to the Secretary's office. The papers which had been found in Ashton's bosom were inspected that night by Nottingham and Caermarthen, and were, on the following morning, put by Caermarthen into the hands of the King.

Soon it was known all over London that a plot had been detected, that the messengers whom the adherents of James had sent to solicit the help of an invading army from France had been arrested by the agents of the vigilant and energetic Lord President, and that documentary evidence, which might affect the lives of some great men, was in the possession of the government. The Jacobites were terrorstricken : the clamour of the Whigs against Caermarthen was suddenly hushed ; and the Session ended in perfect harmony. On the fifth of January the King thanked the Houses for their support, and assured them that he would not grant away any forfeited property in Ireland till they should reassemble. He alluded to the plot which had just been discovered, and expressed a hope that the friends of England would not, at such a moment, be less active or less firmly united than her enemies. He then signified his pleasure that the Parliament should adjourn. On the following day he set out, attended by a splendid train of nobles, for the Congress at the Hague *

* Lords' and Commons' Journals, Jan. 5. 169⁰⁄₁ ; London Gazette, Jan. 8.

CHAPTER XVII.

ON the eighteenth of January 1691, the King, having been detained some days by adverse winds, went on board at Gravesend. Four yachts had been fitted up for him and for his retinue. Among his attendants were Norfolk, Ormond, Devonshire, Dorset, Portland, Monmouth, Zulestein, and the Bishop of London. Two distinguished admirals, Cloudesley Shovel and George Rooke, commanded the men of war which formed the convoy. The passage was tedious and disagreeable. During many hours the fleet was becalmed off the Godwin Sands; and it was not till the fifth day that the soundings proved the coast of Holland to be near. The sea fog was so thick that no land could be seen; and it was not thought safe for the ships to proceed further in the darkness. William, tired out by the voyage, and impatient to be once more in his beloved country, determined to land in an open boat. The noblemen who were in his train tried to dissuade him from risking so valuable a life: but, when they found that his mind was made up, they insisted on sharing the danger. That danger proved more serious than they had expected. It had been supposed that in an hour the party would be on shore. But great masses of floating ice impeded the progress of the skiff: the night came on: the fog grew thicker: the waves broke over the King and the courtiers. Once the keel struck on a sand bank, and was with great difficulty got off. The hardiest mariners showed some signs of uneasiness. But William, through the whole night, was as composed as if he had been in the drawingroom at Kensington. "For shame," he said to one of the dismayed sailors: "are you afraid to die in my company?" A bold Dutch seaman ventured to spring out, and, with great difficulty, swam and scrambled through breakers, ice, and mud, to firm ground. Here he discharged a musket and lighted a fire as a signal that he was safe. None of his fellow passengers, however, thought it prudent to follow his example. They lay tossing in sight of the

flame which he had kindled, till the first pale light of a
January morning showed them that they were close to the
island of Goree. The King and his Lords, stiff with cold
and covered with icicles, gladly landed to warm and rest
themselves.*

After reposing some hours in the hut of a peasant, William
proceeded to the Hague. He was impatiently expected there:
for, though the fleet which brought him was not visible from
the shore, the royal salutes had been heard through the mist,
and had apprised the whole coast of his arrival. Thousands
had assembled at Honslaerdyk to welcome him with applause
which came from their hearts and which went to his heart.
That was one of the few white days of a life, beneficent
indeed and glorious, but far from happy. After more than
two years passed in a strange land, the exile had again set
foot on his native soil. He heard again the language of his
nursery. He saw again the scenery and the architecture
which were inseparably associated in his mind with the
recollections of childhood and the sacred feeling of home;
the dreary mounds of sand, shells, and weeds, on which the
waves of the German Ocean broke; the interminable meadows
intersected by trenches; the straight canals; the villas bright
with paint, and adorned with quaint images and inscriptions.
He had lived during many weary months among a people
who did not love him, who did not understand him, who
could never forget that he was a foreigner. Those Englishmen who served him most faithfully served him without
enthusiasm, without personal attachment, and merely from
a sense of public duty. In their hearts they were sorry that
they had no choice but between an English tyrant and a
Dutch deliverer. All was now changed. William was among
a population bv which he was adored, as Elizabeth had been
adored when she rode through her army at Tilbury, as
Charles the Second had been adored when he landed at
Dover. It is true that the old enemies of the House of
Orange had not been inactive during the absence of the
Stadtholder. There had been, not indeed clamours, but
mutterings against him. He had, it was said, neglected
his native land for his new kingdom. Whenever the dignity
of the English flag, whenever the prosperity of the English
trade was concerned, he forgot that he was a Hollander.

* Relation de la Voyage de Sa Majesté   London Gazette, Jan. 29. 169⅑; Burnet,
Britannique en Hollande, enrichie de   ii. 71.
planches très curieuses, 1692; Wagenaar;

But, as soon as his well remembered face was again seen, all jealousy, all coldness, was at an end. There was not a boor, not a fisherman, not an artisan, in the crowds which lined the road from Honslaerdyk to the Hague, whose heart did not swell with pride at the thought that the first minister of Holland had become a great King, had freed the English, and had conquered the Irish. It would have been madness in William to travel from Hampton Court to Westminster without a guard: but in his own land he needed no swords or carbines to defend him. "Do not keep the people off;" he cried: "let them come close to me: they are all my good friends." He soon learnt that sumptuous preparations were making for his entrance into the Hague. At first he murmured and objected. He detested, he said, noise and display. The necessary cost of the war was quite heavy enough. He hoped that his kind fellow townsmen would consider him as a neighbour, born and bred among them, and would not pay him so bad a compliment as to treat him ceremoniously. But all his expostulations were vain. The Hollanders, simple and parsimonious as their ordinary habits were, had set their hearts on giving their illustrious countryman a reception suited to his dignity and to his merit; and he found it necessary to yield. On the day of his triumph the concourse was immense. All the wheeled carriages and horses of the province were too few for the multitudes that flocked to the show. Many thousands came sliding or skating along the frozen canals from Amsterdam, Rotterdam, Leyden, Haarlem, Delft. At ten in the morning of the twenty-sixth of January, the great bell of the Town House gave the signal. Sixteen hundred substantial burghers, well armed, and clad in the finest dresses which were to be found in the recesses of their wardrobes, kept order in the crowded streets. Balconies and scaffolds, embowered in evergreens and hung with tapestry, hid the windows. The royal coach, escorted by an army of halberdiers and running footmen, and followed by a long train of splendid equipages, passed under numerous arches rich with carving and painting, amidst incessant shouts of "Long live the King our Stadtholder." The front of the Town House and the whole circuit of the marketplace were in a blaze with brilliant colours. Civic crowns, trophies, emblems of arts, of sciences, of commerce, and of agriculture, appeared everywhere. In one place William saw portrayed the glorious actions of his ancestors. There was the silent prince, the founder of the Batavian commonwealth, passing

William's entrance into the Hague

the Meuse with his warriors. There was the more impetuous Maurice leading the charge at Nieuport. A little further on, the hero might retrace the eventful story of his own life. He was a child at his widowed mother's knee. He was at the altar with Mary's hand in his. He was landing at Torbay. He was swimming through the Boyne. There, too, was a boat amidst the ice and the breakers; and above it was most appropriately inscribed, in the majestic language of Rome, the saying of the great Roman, "What dost thou fear? Thou hast Cæsar on board." The task of furnishing the Latin mottoes had been entrusted to two men, who, till Bentley appeared, held the highest place among the classical scholars of that age. Spanheim, whose knowledge of the Roman medals was unrivalled, imitated, not unsuccessfully, the noble conciseness of those ancient legends which he had assiduously studied; and he was assisted by Grævius, who then filled a chair at Utrecht, and whose just reputation had drawn to that University multitudes of students from every part of Protestant Europe.* When the night came, fireworks were exhibited on the great tank which washes the walls of the palace of the Federation. That tank was now as hard as marble; and the Dutch boasted that nothing had ever been seen, even on the terrace of Versailles, more brilliant than the effect produced by the innumerable cascades of flame which were reflected in the smooth mirror of ice.† The English Lords congratulated their master on his immense popularity. "Yes," said he: "but I am not the favourite. The shouting was nothing to what it would have been if Mary had been with me."

A few hours after the triumphal entry, the King attended a sitting of the States General. His last appearance among them had been on the day on which he embarked for England. He had then, amidst the broken words and loud weeping of those grave Senators, thanked them for the kindness with which they had watched over his childhood, trained his mind in youth, and supported his authority in his riper years;

---

* The names of these two great scholars are associated in a very interesting letter of Bentley to Grævius, dated April 29. 1698. " Sciunt omnes qui me norunt, et si vitam mihi Deus O. M. prorogaverit, scient etiam posteri, ut te et τὸν πάνυ Spanhemium, geminos hujus ævi Dioscuros, lucida literarum sidera, semper prædicaverim, semper veneratus sim."

† Relation de la Voyage de Sa Ma-

jesté Britannique en Hollande, 1692; London Gazette, Feb. 2. 169¾; Le Triomphe Royal où l'on voit descrits les Arcs de Triomphe, Pyramides, Tableaux et Devises au Nombre de 65, erigez à la Haye à l'honneur de Guillaume Trois, 1692; Le Carnaval de la Haye, 1691. This last work is a savage pasquinade on William.

and he had solemnly commended his beloved wife to their care. He now came back among them the King of three kingdoms, the head of the greatest coalition that Europe had seen since the League of Cambray; and nothing was heard in the hall but applause and congratulations.*

By this time the streets of the Hague were overflowing with the equipages and retinues of princes and ambassadors who came flocking to the great Congress. First appeared the ambitious and ostentatious Frederic, Elector of Brandenburg, who, a few years later, took the title of King of Prussia. Then arrived the young Elector of Bavaria, the Regent of Wurtemberg, the Landgraves of Hesse Cassel and Hesse Darmstadt, and a long train of sovereign princes, sprung from the illustrious houses of Brunswick, of Saxony, of Holstein, and of Nassau. The Marquess of Gastanaga, Governor of the Spanish Netherlands, repaired to the assembly from the viceregal Court of Brussels. Extraordinary ministers had been sent by the Emperor, by the Kings of Spain, Poland, Denmark, and Sweden, and by the Duke of Savoy. There was scarcely room in the town and the neighbourhood for the English Lords and gentlemen and the German Counts and Barons whom curiosity or official duty had brought to the place of meeting. The grave capital of the most thrifty and industrious of nations was as gay as Venice in the Carnival. The walks cut among those noble limes and elms in which the villa of the Princes of Orange is embosomed were gay with the plumes, the stars, the flowing wigs, the embroidered coats, and the gold hilted swords of gallants from London, Berlin, and Vienna. With the nobles were mingled sharpers not less gorgeously attired than they. At night the hazard tables were thronged; and the theatre was filled to the roof. Princely banquets followed one another in rapid succession. The meats were served in gold; and, according to that old Teutonic fashion with which Shakspeare had made his countrymen familiar, as often as any of the great princes proposed a health, the kettle drums and trumpets sounded. Some English Lords, particularly Devonshire, gave entertainments which vied with those of Sovereigns. It was remarked that the German potentates, though generally disposed to be litigious and punctilious about etiquette, associated, on this occasion, in an unceremonious manner,

Congress at the Hague.

* London Gazette, Feb. 5. 169⁰⁄₁; His Majesty's Speech to the Assembly of the States General of the United Provinces at the Hague, the 7th of February N.S., together with the Answer of their High and Mighty Lordships, as both are extracted out of the Register of the Resolutions of the States General, 1691.

and seemed to have forgotten their passion for heraldic controversy. The taste for wine, which was then characteristic of their nation, they had not forgotten. At the table of the Elector of Brandenburg much mirth was caused by the gravity of the statesmen of Holland, who, sober themselves, confuted out of Grotius and Puffendorf the nonsense stuttered by the tipsy nobles of the Empire. One of those nobles swallowed so many bumpers that he tumbled into the turf fire, and was not pulled out till his fine velvet suit had been burned.*

In the midst of all this revelry, business was not neglected. A formal meeting of the Congress was held at which William presided. In a short and dignified speech, which was speedily circulated throughout Europe, he set forth the necessity of firm union and strenuous exertion. The profound respect with which he was heard by that splendid assembly caused bitter mortification to his enemies both in England and in France. The German potentates were bitterly reviled for yielding precedence to an upstart. Indeed the most illustrious among them paid to him such marks of deference as they would scarcely have deigned to pay to the Imperial Majesty, mingled with the crowd in his antechamber, and at his table behaved as respectfully as any English lord in waiting. In one caricature the allied princes were represented as muzzled bears, some with crowns, some with caps of state. William had them all in a chain, and was teaching them to dance. In another caricature, he appeared taking his ease in an arm chair, with his feet on a cushion, and his hat on his head, while the Electors of Brandenburg and Bavaria, uncovered, occupied small stools on the right and left: the crowd of Landgraves and Sovereign dukes stood at humble distance; and Gastanaga, the unworthy successor of Alva, awaited the orders of the heretic tyrant on bended knee.†

It was soon announced by authority that, before the beginning of summer, two hundred and twenty thousand men would be in the field against France.‡ The contingent which each of the allied powers was to furnish was made known. Matters about which it would have been inexpe-

---

* Relation de la Voyage de Sa Majesté Britannique en Hollande; Burnet, ii. 72.; London Gazette, Feb. 12. 19. 23. 1692; Mémoires du Comte de Dohna; William Fuller's Memoirs.

† Wagenaar, lxii.; Le Carnaval de la Haye, Mars 1691; Le Tabouret des Electeurs, April 1691; Cérémonial de ce qui s'est passé à la Haye entre le Roi Guillaume et les Electeurs de Bavière et de Brandebourg. This last tract is a MS. presented to the British Museum by George IV.

‡ London Gazette, Feb. 23. 1692.

dient to put forth any declaration were privately discussed by the King of England with his allies. On this occasion, as on every other important occasion during his reign, he was his own minister for foreign affairs. It was necessary for the sake of form that he should be attended by a Secretary of State; and Nottingham had therefore followed him to Holland. But Nottingham, though, in matters relating to the internal government of England, he enjoyed a large share of his master's confidence, knew little more about the business of the Congress than what he saw in the Gazettes.

This mode of transacting business would now be thought most unconstitutional; and many writers, applying the standard of their own age to the transactions of a former age, have severely blamed William for acting without the advice of his ministers, and his ministers for submitting to be kept in ignorance of transactions which deeply concerned the honour of the Crown and the welfare of the nation. Yet surely the presumption is that what the most honest and honourable men of both parties, Nottingham, for example, among the Tories, and Somers among the Whigs, not only did, but avowed, cannot have been altogether inexcusable; and a very sufficient excuse will without difficulty be found.

William his own minister for foreign affairs.

The doctrine that the Sovereign is not responsible is doubtless as old as any part of our constitution. The doctrine that his ministers are responsible is also of immemorial antiquity. The doctrine that, where there is no responsibility, there can be no trustworthy security against maladministration, is one which, in our age and country, few people will be inclined to dispute. From these three propositions it plainly follows that the administration is likely to be best conducted when the Sovereign performs no public act without the concurrence and instrumentality of a minister. This argument is perfectly sound. But we must remember that arguments are constructed in one way, and governments in another. In logic, none but an idiot admits the premises and denies the legitimate conclusion. But, in practice, we see that great and enlightened communities often persist, generation after generation, in asserting principles, and refusing to act upon those principles. It may be doubted whether any real polity that ever existed has exactly corresponded to the pure idea of that polity. According to the pure idea of constitutional royalty, the prince reigns, and does not govern; and constitutional royalty, as it now exists in England, comes nearer than in any other country to the pure idea. Yet it would be a great error to imagine, even now, that our princes merely reign and never govern. In the seventeenth century, both Whigs and Tories thought it, not only the right, but the duty, of the first magistrate to govern. All parties agreed in blaming Charles the Second for not being his own Prime Minister: all parties agreed in praising James for being his own Lord High Admiral; and all parties thought it natural and reasonable that William should be his own Foreign Secretary.

It may be observed that the ablest and best informed of those who have censured the manner in which the negotiations of that time were conducted are scarcely consistent with themselves. For, while they blame William for being his own Ambassador Plenipotentiary at the Hague, they praise him for being his own Commander in Chief in Ireland. Yet where is the distinction in principle between the two cases? Surely every reason which can be brought to prove that he violated the constitution, when, by his own sole authority, he made compacts with the Emperor and the Elector of Brandenburg, will equally prove that he violated the constitution, when, by his own sole authority, he ordered one column to plunge into the water at Oldbridge and another to cross the bridge of Slane. If the constitution gave him the command of the forces of the State, the constitution gave him also the direction of the foreign relations of the State. On what principle then can it be maintained that he was at liberty to exercise the former power without consulting anybody, but that he was bound to exercise the latter power in conformity with the advice of a minister? Will it be said that an error in diplomacy is likely to be more injurious to the country than an error in strategy? Surely not. It is hardly conceivable that any blunder which William might have made at the Hague could have been more injurious to the public interests than a defeat at the Boyne. Or will it be said that there was greater reason for placing confidence in his military than in his diplomatic skill? Surely not. In war he showed some great moral and intellectual qualities: but, as a tactician, he did not rank high; and of his many campaigns only two were decidedly successful. In the talents of a negotiator, on the other hand, he has never been surpassed. Of the interests and the tempers of the continental courts he knew more than all his Privy Council together. Some of his ministers were doubtless men of great ability, excellent orators in the House of Lords, and versed in our insular politics. But, in the deliberations of the Congress, Caermarthen and Nottingham would have been found as far inferior to him as he would have been found inferior to them in a parliamentary debate on a question purely English. The coalition against France was his work. He alone had joined together the parts of that great whole; and he alone could keep them together. If he had trusted that vast and complicated machine in the hands of any of his subjects, it would instantly have fallen to pieces.

Some things indeed were to be done which none of his subjects would have ventured to do. Pope Alexander was really, though not in name, one of the allies: it was of the highest importance to have him for a friend: and yet such was the temper of the English nation that an English minister might well shrink from having any dealings, direct or indirect, with the Vatican. The Secretaries of State were glad to leave in the hands of their master a matter so delicate and so full of risk, and to be able to protest with truth that not a line to which the most intolerant Protestant could object had ever gone out of their offices.

It must not be supposed however that William ever forgot that his especial, his hereditary, mission was to protect the Reformed Faith. His influence with Roman Catholic princes was constantly and strenuously exerted for the benefit of their Protestant subjects. In the spring of 1691, the Waldensian shepherds, long and cruelly persecuted, and weary of their lives, were surprised by glad tidings. Those who had been in prison for heresy returned to their homes. Children, who had been taken from their parents to be educated by priests, were sent back. Congregations, which had hitherto met only by stealth and with extreme peril, now worshipped God without molestation in the face of day. Those simple mountaineers probably never knew that their fate had been a subject of discussion at the Hague, and that they owed the happiness of their firesides and the security of their humble temples to the ascendency which William exercised over the Duke of Savoy.*

William obtains a toleration for the Waldenses.

No coalition of which history has preserved the memory has had an abler chief than William. But even William often contended in vain against those vices which are inherent in the nature of all coalitions. No undertaking which requires the hearty and long continued cooperation of many

Vices inherent in the nature of coalitions.

* The secret article by which the Duke of Savoy bound himself to grant toleration to the Waldenses is in Dumont's collection. It was signed Feb. 8. 1691.

independent states is likely to prosper.   Jealousies inevitably
spring up.   Disputes engender disputes.   Every confederate
is tempted to throw on others some part of the burden which
he ought himself to bear.   Scarcely one honestly furnishes
the promised contingent.   Scarcely one exactly observes the
appointed day.   But perhaps no coalition that ever existed
was in such constant danger of dissolution as the coalition
which William had with infinite difficulty formed.   The long
list of potentates, who met in person or by their representatives at the Hague, looked well in the Gazettes.   The crowd
of princely equipages, attended by manycoloured guards and
lacqueys, looked well among the lime trees of the Voorhout.
But the very circumstances which made the Congress more
splendid than other congresses made the league weaker than
other leagues.   The more numerous the allies, the more
numerous were the dangers which threatened the alliance.
It was impossible that twenty governments, divided by quarrels about precedence, quarrels about territory, quarrels about
trade, quarrels about religion, could long act together in perfect harmony.   That they acted together during several years
in imperfect harmony is to be ascribed to the wisdom, patience,
and firmness of William.

The situation of his great enemy was very different.   The
resources of the French monarchy, though certainly not equal
to those of England, Holland, the House of Austria, and the
empire of Germany united, were yet very formidable : they
were all collected in a central position; and they were all
under the absolute direction of a single mind.   Lewis could
do with two words what William could hardly bring about by
two months of negotiation at Berlin, Munich, Brussels, Turin,
and Vienna.   Thus France was found equal in effective
strength to all the states which were combined against her.
For in the political, as in the natural world, there may be an
equality of momentum between unequal bodies, when the body
which is inferior in weight is superior in velocity.

This was soon signally proved.   In March the princes and
ambassadors who had been assembled at the Hague separated :
and scarcely had they separated when all their plans were
disconcerted by a bold and skilful move of the enemy.

Siege and
fall of
Mons.
Lewis was sensible that the meeting of the Congress
was likely to produce a great effect on the public mind of
Europe.   That effect he determined to counteract by striking
a sudden and terrible blow.   While his enemies were settling
how many troops each of them should furnish, he ordered

numerous divisions of his army to march from widely distant points towards Mons, one of the most important, if not the most important, of the fortresses which protected the Spanish Netherlands. His purpose was discovered only when it was all but accomplished. William, who had retired for a few days to Loo, learned with surprise and extreme vexation, that cavalry, infantry, artillery, bridges of boats, were fast approaching the fated city by many converging routes. A hundred thousand men had been brought together. All the implements of war had been largely provided by Louvois, the first of living administrators. The command was entrusted to Luxemburg, the first of living generals. The scientific operations were directed by Vauban, the first of living engineers. That nothing might be wanting which could kindle emulation through all the ranks of a gallant and loyal army, the magnificent King himself had set out from Versailles for the camp. Yet William had still some faint hope that it might be possible to raise the siege. He flew to the Hague, put all the forces of the States General in motion, and sent pressing messages to the German Princes. Within three weeks after he had received the first hint of the danger, he was in the neighbourhood of the besieged city, at the head of near fifty thousand troops of different nations. To attack a superior force commanded by such a captain as Luxemburg was a bold, almost a desperate enterprise. Yet William was so sensible that the loss of Mons would be an almost irreparable disaster and disgrace that he made up his mind to run the hazard. He was convinced that the event of the siege would determine the policy of the Courts of Stockholm and Copenhagen. Those Courts had lately seemed inclined to join the coalition. If Mons fell, they would certainly remain neutral; and they might possibly become hostile. " The risk," he wrote to Heinsius, " is great : yet I am not without hope. I will do what can be done. The issue is in the hands of God." On the very day on which this letter was written Mons fell. The siege had been vigorously pressed. Lewis himself, though suffering from the gout, had set the example of strenuous exertion. His household troops, the finest body of soldiers in Europe, had, under his eye, surpassed themselves. The young nobles of his court had tried to attract his notice by exposing themselves to the hottest fire with the same gay alacrity with which they were wont to exhibit their graceful figures at his balls. His wounded soldiers were charmed by the benignant courtesy with which he walked among their pallets, assisted while wounds were dressed by the hospital surgeons, and breakfasted on a porringer of the hospital broth. While all was obedience and enthusiasm among the besiegers, all was disunion and dismay among the besieged. The duty of the French lines was so well performed that no messenger sent by William was able to cross them. The garrison did not know that relief was close at hand. The burghers were appalled by the prospect of those horrible calamities which befall cities taken by storm. Showers of shells and redhot bullets were falling in the streets. The town was on fire in ten places at once. The peaceful inhabitants derived an unwonted courage from the excess of their fear, and rose on the soldiers. Thenceforth resistance was impossible ; and a capitulation was concluded. The armies then retired into quarters. Military operations were suspended during some weeks : Lewis returned in triumph to Versailles ; and William paid a short visit to England, where his presence was much needed.*

William returns to England.

He found the ministers still employed in tracing out the ramifications of the plot which had been discovered just before his departure. Early in January, Preston, Ashton, and

Trials of Preston and Ashton.

Elliot had been arraigned at the Old Bailey. They claimed the right of severing in their challenges. It was therefore necessary to try them separately. The audience was numerous and splendid. Many peers were present. The Lord President and the two Secretaries of State attended in order to prove that the papers produced in Court were the same which Billop had brought to Whitehall. A considerable number of Judges appeared on the bench ; and Holt presided. A full report of the proceedings has come down to us, and well deserves to be attentively studied, and to be compared with the reports of other trials which had not long before taken place under the same roof. The whole spirit of the tribunal had undergone in a few months a change so complete that it might seem to have been the work of ages. Twelve years earlier, unhappy Roman Catholics, accused of wickedness which had never entered into their thoughts, had stood in that dock. The witnesses for the Crown had repeated their hideous fictions amidst the applauding hums of the audience.

* London Gazette from March 26. to April 13. 1691 ; Monthly Mercuries of March and April ; William's Letters to Heinsius of March 18. and 29., April 7. 9. ; Dangeau's Memoirs ; the Siege of Mons, a tragi-comedy, 1691. In this drama the clergy, who are in the interest of France, persuade the burghers to deliver up the town. This treason calls forth an indignant exclamation :

" Oh priestcraft, shopcraft, how do ye effeminate The minds of men ! "

The judges had shared, or had pretended to share the stupid credulity and the savage passions of the populace, had exchanged smiles and compliments with the perjured informers, had roared down the arguments feebly stammered forth by the prisoners, and had not been ashamed, in passing the sentence of death, to make ribald jests on purgatory and the mass. As soon as the butchery of Papists was over, the butchery of Whigs had commenced; and the judges had applied themselves to their new work with even more than their old barbarity. To these scandals the Revolution had put an end. Whoever, after perusing the trials of Ireland and Pickering, of Grove and Berry, of Sidney, Cornish, and Alice Lisle, turns to the trials of Preston and Ashton, will be astonished by the contrast. The Solicitor General, Somers, conducted the prosecutions with a moderation and humanity of which his predecessors had left him no example. "I did never think," he said, "that it was the part of any who were of counsel for the King in cases of this nature to aggravate the crime of the prisoners, or to put false colours on the evidence."* Holt's conduct was faultless. Pollexfen, an older man than Holt or Somers, retained a little,—and a little was too much,—of the tone of that bad school in which he had been bred. But, though he once or twice forgot the austere decorum of his place, he cannot be accused of any violation of substantial justice. The prisoners themselves seem to have been surprised by the fairness and gentleness with which they were treated. "I would not mislead the jury, I'll assure you," said Holt to Preston, "nor do Your Lordship any manner of injury in the world." "No, my Lord;" said Preston; "I see it well enough that Your Lordship would not." "Whatever my fate may be," said Ashton, "I cannot but own that I have had a fair trial for my life."

The culprits gained nothing by the moderation of the Solicitor General or by the impartiality of the Court: for the evidence was irresistible. The meaning of the papers seized by Billop was so plain that the dullest juryman could not misunderstand it. Of those papers part was fully proved to be in Preston's handwriting. Part was in Ashton's hand-

* Trial of Preston in the Collection of State Trials. A person who was present gives the following account of Somers's opening speech: "In the opening the evidence, there was no affected exaggeration of matters, nor ostentation of a putid eloquence, one after another, as in former trials, like so many geese cackling in a row. Here was nothing besides fair matter of fact, or natural and just reflections from thence arising." The pamphlet from which I quote these words is entitled, An Account of the late horrid Conspiracy, by a Person who was present at the Trials, 1691.

writing : but this the counsel for the prosecution had not the
means of proving. They therefore rested the case against
Ashton on the indisputable facts that the treasonable packet
had been found in his bosom, and that he had used language
which was quite unintelligible except on the supposition that
he had a guilty knowledge of the contents.*

Execution of Ashton. Both Preston and Ashton were convicted and sentenced to
death. Ashton was speedily executed. He might have saved
his life by making disclosures. But, though he declared that,
if he were spared, he would always be a faithful subject of
Their Majesties, he was fully resolved not to give up the
names of his accomplices. In this resolution he was encouraged by the nonjuring divines who attended him in his
cell. It was probably by their influence that he was induced
to deliver to the Sheriffs on the scaffold a declaration which
he had transcribed and signed, but had not, it is to be hoped,
composed or attentively considered. In this paper he was
made to complain of the unfairness of a trial which he had
himself in public acknowledged to have been eminently fair.
He was also made to aver, on the word of a dying man, that
he knew nothing of the papers which had been found upon
him. Unfortunately his declaration, when inspected, proved
to be in the same handwriting with one of the most important of those papers. He died with manly fortitude.†

Preston's irresolution and confessions. Elliot was not brought to trial. The evidence against
him was not quite so clear as that on which his associates
had been convicted; and he was not worth the anger of the
ruling powers. The fate of Preston was long in suspense.
The Jacobites affected to be confident that the government
would not dare to shed his blood. He was, they said, a
favourite at Versailles, and his death would be followed by a
terrible retaliation. They scattered about the streets of London papers in which it was asserted that, if any harm befell
him, Mountjoy, and all the other Englishmen of quality who
were prisoners in France, would be broken on the wheel.‡
These absurd threats would not have deferred the execution
one day. But those who had Preston in their power were
not unwilling to spare him on certain conditions. He was
privy to all the counsels of the disaffected party, and could

---

* State Trials.
  † Paper delivered by Mr. Ashton, at
his execution, to Sir Francis Child, Sheriff of London ; Answer to the Paper
delivered by Mr. Ashton. The Answer
was written by Dr. Edward Fowler,

afterwards Bishop of Gloucester. Burnet,
ii. 70. ; Letter from Bishop Lloyd to
Dodwell, in the second volume of Gutch's
Collectanea Curiosa.
  ‡ Narcissus Luttrell's Diary.

furnish information of the highest value. He was informed
that his fate depended on himself. The struggle was long
and severe. Pride, conscience, party spirit, were on one side ;
the intense love of life on the other. He went during a time
irresolutely to and fro. He listened to his brother Jacobites ;
and his courage rose. He listened to the agents of the
government ; and his heart sank within him. In an evening,
when he had dined and drunk his claret, he feared nothing.
He would die like a man, rather than save his neck by an
act of baseness. But his temper was very different when he
woke the next morning, when the courage which he had
drawn from wine and company had evaporated, when he was
alone with the iron grates and stone walls, and when the
thought of the block, the axe, and the sawdust rose in his
mind. During some time he regularly wrote a confession
every forenoon, when he was sober, and burned it every night
when he was merry.* His nonjuring friends formed a plan
for bringing Sancroft to visit the Tower, in the hope, doubtless, that the exhortations of so great a prelate and so great
a saint would confirm the wavering virtue of the prisoner.†
Whether this plan would have been successful may be
doubted : it was not carried into effect : the fatal hour drew
near ; and the fortitude of Preston gave way. He confessed
his guilt, and named Clarendon, Dartmouth, the Bishop of
Ely, and William Penn, as his accomplices. He added a long
list of persons against whom he could not himself give evidence, but who, if he could trust to Penn's assurances, were
friendly to King James. Among these persons were Devonshire and Dorset.‡ There is not the slightest reason to believe
that either of these great noblemen ever had any dealings,
direct or indirect, with Saint Germains. It is not, however,
necessary to accuse Penn of deliberate falsehood. He was
credulous and garrulous. The Lord Steward and the Lord
Chamberlain had shared in the vexation with which their
party had observed the leaning of William towards the
Tories ; and they had probably expressed that vexation un-
guardedly. So weak a man as Penn, wishing to find Jacobites
everywhere, and prone to believe whatever he wished, might
easily put an erroneous construction on invectives such as the
naughty and irritable Devonshire was but too ready to utter,
and on sarcasms such as, in moments of spleen, dropped but

* Narcissus Luttrell's Diary ; Burnet,
ii. 71.
† Letter of Collier and Cook to Sancroft among the Tanner MSS.
‡ Caermarthen to William, February
3. 169 9/0 ; Life of James, ii. 443.

too easily from the lips of the keenwitted Dorset. Caermarthen, a Tory, and a Tory who had been mercilessly persecuted by the Whigs, was disposed to make the most of this idle hearsay. But he received no encouragement from his master, who, of all the great politicians mentioned in history, was the least prone to suspicion. When William returned to England, Preston was brought before him, and was commanded to repeat the confession which had already been made to the ministers. The King stood behind the Lord President's chair and listened gravely while Clarendon, Dartmouth, Turner, and Penn were named. But as soon as the prisoner, passing from what he could himself testify, began to repeat the stories which Penn had told him, William touched Caermarthen on the shoulder, and said, "My Lord, we have had too much of this."[*] The King's judicious magnanimity had its proper reward. Devonshire and Dorset became from that day more zealous than ever in the cause of the master who, in spite of calumny, for which their own indiscretion had perhaps furnished some ground, had continued to repose confidence in their loyalty.[†]

Lenity shown to the conspirators.

Even those who were undoubtedly criminal were generally treated with great lenity. Clarendon lay in the Tower about six months. His guilt was fully established; and a party among the Whigs called loudly and importunately for his head. But he was saved by the pathetic entreaties of his brother Rochester, by the good offices of the humane and generous Burnet, and by Mary's respect for the memory of her mother. The prisoner's confinement was not strict. He was allowed to entertain his friends at dinner. When at length his health began to suffer from restraint, he was permitted to go into the country under the care of a warder: the warder was soon removed; and Clarendon was informed that, while he led a quiet, rural life, he should not be molested.[‡]

Dartmouth.

The treason of Dartmouth was of no common dye. He

---

[*] That this account of what passed is true in substance is sufficiently proved by the Life of James, ii. 443. I have taken one or two slight circumstances from Dalrymple, who, I believe, took them from papers, now irrecoverably lost, which he had seen in the Scotch College at Paris.

[†] The wisdom of William's "seeming clemency" is admitted in the Life of James, ii. 443. The Prince of Orange's method, it is acknowledged, "succeeded

so well that, whatever sentiments those Lords which Mr. Penn had named might have had at that time, they proved in effect most bitter enemies to his Majesty's cause afterwards." It ought to be observed that this part of the Life of James was revised and corrected by his son.

[‡] See his Diary; Evelyn's Diary, Mar. 25., April 22., July 11. 1691; Burnet, ii. 71,; Letters of Rochester to Burnet, March 21. and April 2. 1691.

was an English seaman, and he had laid a plan for betraying Portsmouth to the French, and had offered to take the command of a French squadron against his country. It was a serious aggravation of his guilt that he had been one of the very first persons who took the oaths to William and Mary. He was arrested and brought to the Council Chamber. A narrative of what passed there, written by himself, has been preserved. In that narrative he admits that he was treated with great courtesy and delicacy. He vehemently asserted his innocence. He declared that he had never corresponded with Saint Germains, that he was no favourite there, and that Mary of Modena in particular owed him a grudge. "My Lords," he said, "I am an Englishman. I always, when the interest of the House of Bourbon was strongest here, shunned the French, both men and women. I would lose the last drop of my blood rather than see Portsmouth in the power of foreigners. I am not such a fool as to think that King Lewis will conquer us merely for the benefit of King James. I am certain that nothing can be truly imputed to me beyond some foolish talk over a bottle." His protestations seem to have produced some effect; for he was at first permitted to remain in the gentle custody of the Black Rod. On further enquiry, however, it was determined to send him to the Tower. After a confinement of a few weeks he died of apoplexy: but he lived long enough to complete his disgrace by offering his sword to the new government, and by expressing in fervent language his hope that he might, by the goodness of God and of Their Majesties, have an opportunity of showing how much he hated the French.[*]

Turner ran no serious risk: for the government was most unwilling to send to the scaffold one of the Seven who had signed the memorable petition. A warrant was however issued for his apprehension; and his friends had little hope that he would long remain undiscovered: for his nose was such as none who had seen it could forget; and it was to little purpose that he put on a flowing wig, and that he suffered his beard to grow. The pursuit was probably not very hot: for, after skulking a few weeks in England, he succeeded in crossing the Channel, and passed some time in France.[†]

Turner.

* Life of James, ii. 443. 450.; Legge Papers in the Mackintosh Collection.

† Burnet, ii. 71.; Evelyn's Diary, Jan. 4. and 18. 169⅖; Letter from Turner to Sancroft, Jan. 19. 169⅖; Letter from Sancroft to Lloyd of Norwich, April 2. 1692. These two letters are among the Tanner MSS. in the Bodleian Library, and are printed in the Life of Ken by a Layman. Turner's escape to France is

A warrant was issued against Penn; and he narrowly escaped the messengers. It chanced that, on the day on which they were sent in search of him, he was attending a remarkable ceremony at some distance from his home.   An event had taken place which a historian, whose object is to record the real life of a nation, ought not to pass unnoticed. While London was agitated by the news that a plot had been discovered, George Fox, the founder of the sect of Quakers, died.

Death of George Fox: his character.

More than forty years had elapsed since Fox had begun to see visions and to cast out devils.*   He was then a youth of pure morals and grave deportment, with a perverse temper, with the education of a labouring man, and with an intellect in the most unhappy of all states, that is to say, too much disordered for liberty, and not sufficiently disordered for Bedlam.   The circumstances in which he was placed were such as could scarcely fail to bring out in the strongest form the constitutional diseases of his mind.   At the time when his faculties were ripening, Episcopalians, Presbyterians, Independents, Baptists, were striving for mastery, and were, in every corner of the realm, refuting and reviling each other.   He wandered from congregation to congregation : he heard priests harangue against Puritans : he heard Puritans harangue against priests : and he in vain applied for spiritual direction and consolation to doctors of both parties. One jolly old clergyman of the Anglican communion told him to smoke tobacco and sing psalms : another counselled him to go and lose some blood.†   From these advisers the young enquirer turned in disgust to the Dissenters, and found them also blind guides.‡   After some time he came to the conclusion that no human being was competent to instruct him in divine things, and that the truth had been communicated to him by direct inspiration from heaven.   He argued that, as the division of languages began at Babel, and as the persecutors of Christ put on the cross an inscription in Latin, Greek, and Hebrew, the knowledge of languages, and more especially of Latin, Greek, and Hebrew, must be useless to a Christian Minister.§   Indeed, he was

mentioned in Narcissus Luttrell's Diary for February 1690.   See also a Dialogue between the Bishop of Ely and his Conscience, 16th February 169⅔.   The dialogue is interrupted by the sound of trumpets.   The Bishop hears himself proclaimed a traitor, and cries out,

" Come, brother Pen, 'tis time we both were gone."

* For a specimen of his visions, see his Journal, page 13.; for his casting out of devils, page 26.   I quote the folio edition of 1765.

† Journal, page 4.

‡ Ibid. page 7.

§ "What they know, they know naturally, who turn from the command and err from the spirit, whose fruit withers

so far from knowing many languages that he knew none : nor can the most corrupt passage in Hebrew be more unintelligible to the unlearned than his English often is to the most acute and attentive reader.* One of the precious truths which were divinely revealed to this new apostle was, that it was falsehood and adulation to use the second person plural instead of the second person singular. Another was, that to talk of the month of March was to worship the bloodthirsty god Mars, and that to talk of Monday was to pay idolatrous homage to the moon. To say Good morning or Good evening was highly reprehensible; for those phrases evidently imported that God had made bad days and bad nights.† A Christian was bound to face death itself rather than touch his hat to the greatest of mankind. When Fox was challenged to produce any Scriptural authority for this dogma, he cited the passage in which it is written that Shadrach, Meshach, and Abednego were thrown into the fiery furnace with their hats on ; and, if his own narrative may be trusted, the Chief Justice of England was altogether unable to answer this argument

who saith that Hebrew, Greek, and Latine is the original; before Babell was, the earth was of one language; and Nimrod the cunning hunter, before the Lord, which came out of cursed Ham's stock, the original and builder of Babell, whom God confounded with many languages. and this they say is the original who erred from the spirit and command; and Pilate had his original Hebrew, Greek, and Latine, which crucified Christ and set over him."—A message from the Lord to the Parliament of England, by G. Fox, 1654. The same argument will be found in the Journal, but has been put by the editor into a little better English. "Dost thou think to make ministers of Christ by these natural confused languages which sprung from Babell, are admired in Babell, and set atop of Christ, the Life, by a persecutor ?"—Page 64.

* His Journal, before it was published, was revised by men of more sense and knowledge than himself, and therefore, absurd as it is, gives no notion of his genuine style. The following is a fair specimen. It is the exordium of one of his manifestoes. "Them which the world who are without the fear of God calls Quakers in scorn do deny all opinions, and they do deny all conceivings, and they do deny all sects, and they do deny all imaginations, and notions, and judgments which riseth out of the will and

the thoughts, and do deny witchcraft and all oaths, and the world and the works of it, and their worships and their customs with the light, and do deny false ways and false worships, seducers and deceivers which are now seen to be in the world with the light, and with it they are condemned, which light leadeth to peace and life from death, which now thousands do witness the new teacher Christ, him by whom the world was made, who raigns among the children of light, and with the spirit and power of the living God, doth let them see and know the chaff from the wheat, and doth see that which must be shaken with that which cannot be shaken or moved, what gives to see that which is shaken and moved, such as live in the notions, opinions, conceivings, and thoughts, and fancies, these be all shaken and comes to be on heaps, which they who witness those things before mentioned shaken and removed walks in peace not seen and discerned by them who walks in those things unremoved and not shaken."—A Warning to the World that are Groping in the Dark, by G. Fox, 1655.

† See the piece entitled, Concerning Good morrow and Good even, the World's customs, but by the Light which into the World is come by it made manifest to all who be in the Darkness, by G. Fox, 1657.

except by crying out, "Take him away, gaoler."* Fox insisted much on the not less weighty argument that the Turks never show their bare heads to their superiors; and he asked, with great animation, whether those who bore the noble name of Christians ought not to surpass Turks in virtue.† Bowing he strictly prohibited, and, indeed, seemed to consider it as the effect of Satanical influence; for, as he observed, the woman in the Gospel, while she had a spirit of infirmity, was bowed together, and ceased to bow as soon as Divine power had liberated her from the tyranny of the Evil One.‡ His expositions of the sacred writings were of a very peculiar kind. Passages, which had been, in the apprehension of all the readers of the Gospels during sixteen centuries, figurative, he construed literally. Passages, which no human being before him had ever understood in any other than a literal sense, he construed figuratively. Thus, from those rhetorical expressions in which the duty of patience under injuries is enjoined he deduced the doctrine that selfdefence against pirates and assassins is unlawful. On the other hand, the plain commands to baptise with water, and to partake of bread and wine in commemoration of the redemption of mankind, he pronounced to be allegorical. He long wandered from place to place, teaching this strange theology, shaking like an aspen leaf in his paroxysms of fanatical excitement, forcing his way into churches, which he nicknamed steeple houses, interrupting prayers and sermons with clamour and scurrility,§ and pestering rectors and justices with epistles much resembling burlesques of those sublime odes in which the Hebrew prophets foretold the calamities of Babylon and Tyre.‖ He soon acquired great notoriety by these feats. His strange face, his strange chant, his immovable hat, and his leather breeches were known all over the country; and he boasts that, as soon as the rumour was heard, "The Man in Leather Breeches is coming," terror seized hypocritical professors, and hireling priests made haste to get out of his way.¶ He was repeatedly imprisoned and set in the stocks, sometimes justly, for disturbing the public worship of congregations, and sometimes unjustly, for

---

* Journal, page 166.

† Epistle from Harlingen, 11th of 6th month, 1677.

‡ Of Bowings, by G. Fox, 1657.

§ See, for example, the Journal, pages 24. 26. and 51.

‖ See, for example, the Epistle to Sawrey, a justice of the peace, in the Journal, page 86.; the Epistle to William Lampitt, a clergyman, which begins, "The word of the Lord to thee, oh Lampitt," page 88.; and the Epistle to another clergyman, whom he calls Priest Tatham, page 92.

¶ Journal, page 55.

merely talking nonsense. He soon gathered round him a body of disciples, some of whom went beyond himself in absurdity. He has told us that one of his friends walked naked through Skipton declaring the truth,* and that another was divinely moved to go naked during several years to marketplaces, and to the houses of gentlemen and clergymen. † Fox complains bitterly that these pious acts, prompted by the Holy Spirit, were requited by an untoward generation with hooting, pelting, coachwhipping, and horsewhipping. But, though he applauded the zeal of the sufferers, he did not go quite to their lengths. He sometimes, indeed, was impelled to strip himself partially. Thus he pulled off his shoes and walked barefoot through Lichfield, crying, " Woe to the bloody city."‡ But it does not appear that he ever thought it his duty to exhibit himself before the public without that decent garment from which his popular appellation was derived.

If we form our judgment of George Fox simply by looking at his own actions and writings, we shall see no reason for placing him, morally or intellectually, above Ludowick Muggleton or Joanna Southcote. But it would be most unjust to rank the sect which regards him as its founder with the Muggletonians or the Southcotians. It chanced that among the thousands whom his enthusiasm infected were a few persons whose abilities and attainments were of a very different order from his own. Robert Barclay was a man of considerable parts and learning. William Penn, though inferior to Barclay in both natural and acquired abilities, was a gentleman and a scholar. That such men should have become the followers of George Fox ought not to astonish any person who remembers what quick, vigorous, and highly cultivated intellects were in our own time duped by the unknown tongues. The truth is that no powers of mind constitute a security against errors of this description. Touching God and His ways with man, the highest human faculties can discover little more than the meanest. In theology the interval is small indeed between Aristotle and a child, between Archimedes and a naked savage. It is not strange, therefore, that wise men, weary of investigation, tormented by uncertainty, longing to believe something, and yet seeing objections to everything, should submit themselves absolutely to teachers who, with firm and undoubting faith, lay claim to a supernatural commission. Thus we frequently see inquisitive and restless spirits take refuge from

---

* Journal, page 300.   † Ibid. page 323.   ‡ Ibid. page 48.

their own scepticism in the bosom of a church which pretends to infallibility, and, after questioning the existence of a Deity, bring themselves to worship a wafer. And thus it was that Fox made some converts to whom he was immeasurably inferior in everything except the energy of his convictions. By these converts his rude doctrines were polished into a form somewhat less shocking to good sense and good taste. No proposition which he had laid down was retracted. No indecent or ridiculous act which he had done or approved was condemned: but what was most grossly absurd in his theories and practices was softened down, or at least not obtruded on the public: whatever could be made to appear specious was set in the fairest light: his gibberish was translated into English: meanings which he would have been quite unable to comprehend were put on his phrases; and his system, so much improved that he would not have known it again, was defended by numerous citations from Pagan philosophers and Christian fathers whose names he had never heard.* Still, however, those who had remodelled his theology continued to profess, and doubtless to feel, profound reverence for him; and his crazy epistles were to the last received and read with respect in Quaker meetings all over the country. His death produced a sensation which was not confined to his own disciples. On the morning of the funeral a great multitude assembled round the meeting house in Gracechurch Street. Thence the corpse was borne to the burial ground of the sect near Bunhill Fields. Several orators addressed the crowd which filled the cemetery. Penn was conspicuous among those disciples who committed the venerable corpse to the earth. The ceremony had scarcely been finished when he learned that warrants were out against him. He instantly took flight, and remained many months concealed from the public eye.†

---

* "Especially of late," says Leslie, the keenest of all the enemies of the sect, "some of them have made nearer advances towards Christianity than ever before; and among them the ingenious Mr. Penn has of late refined some of their gross notions, and brought them into some form, and has made them speak sense and English, of both which George Fox, their first and great apostle, was totally ignorant. . . . . They endeavour all they can to make it appear that their doctrine was uniform from the beginning, and that there has been no alteration; and therefore they take upon them to defend all the writings of George Fox, and others of the first Quakers,

and turn and wind them to make them (but it is impossible) agree with what they teach now at this day." (The Snake in the Grass, 3rd ed. 1698. Introduction.) Leslie was always more civil to his brother Jacobite Penn than to any other Quaker. Penn himself says of his master, "As abruptly and brokenly as sometimes his sentences would fall from him about divine things, it is well known they were often as texts to many fairer declarations." That is to say, George Fox talked nonsense, and some of his friends paraphrased it into sense.

† In the life of Penn which is prefixed to his works, we are told that the warrants were issued on the 16th of

A short time after his disappearance, Sidney received from him a strange communication. Penn begged for an interview, but insisted on a promise that he should be suffered to return unmolested to his hidingplace. Sidney obtained the royal permission to make an appointment on these terms. Penn came to the rendezvous, and spoke at length in his own defence. He declared that he was a faithful subject of King William and Queen Mary, and that, if he knew of any design against them, he would discover it. Departing from his Yea and Nay, he protested, as in the presence of God, that he knew of no plot, and that he did not believe that there was any plot, unless the ambitious projects of the French government might be called plots. Sidney, amazed probably by hearing a person, who had such an abhorrence of lies that he would not use the common forms of civility, and such an abhorrence of oaths that he would not kiss the book in a court of justice, tell something very like a lie, and confirm it by something very like an oath, asked how, if there were really no plot, the letters and minutes which had been found on Ashton were to be explained. This question Penn evaded. " If," he said, " I could only see the King, I would confess everything to him freely. I would tell him much that it would be important for him to know. It is only in that way that I can be of service to him. A witness for the Crown I cannot be : for my conscience will not suffer me to be sworn." He assured Sidney that the most formidable enemies of the government were the discontented Whigs. " The Jacobites are not dangerous. There is not a man among them who has common understanding. Some persons who came over from Holland with the King are much more to be dreaded." It does not appear that Penn mentioned any names. He was suffered to depart in safety. No active search was made for him. He lay hid in London during some months, and then stole down to the coast of Sussex and made his escape to France. After about three years of wandering and lurking he, by the mediation of some eminent men, who overlooked his faults for the sake of

January 169$\frac{0}{1}$, in consequence of an accusation backed by the oath of William Fuller, who is truly designated as a wretch, a cheat, and an impostor; and this story is repeated by Mr. Clarkson. It is, however, certainly false. Caermarthen, writing to William on the 3rd of February, says that there was then only one witness against Penn, and that Preston was that one witness. It is therefore evident that Fuller was not the informer on whose oath the warrant against Penn was issued. In fact Fuller appears, from his Life of Himself, to have been then at the Hague; nor is there any reason to believe that he ever pretended to know anything about Preston's plot. When Nottingham wrote to William on the 26th of June, a second witness against Penn had come forward.

his good qualities, made his peace with the government, and again ventured to resume his ministrations. The return which he made for the lenity with which he had been treated does not much raise his character. Scarcely had he again begun to harangue in public about the unlawfulness of war, when he sent a message earnestly exhorting James to make an immediate descent on England with thirty thousand men.*

Preston pardoned.

Some months passed before the fate of Preston was decided. After several respites, the government, convinced that, though he had told much, he could tell more, fixed a day for his execution, and ordered the sheriffs to have the machinery of death in readiness.† But he was again respited, and, after a delay of some weeks, obtained a pardon, which, however, extended only to his life, and left his property subject to all the consequences of his attainder. As soon as he was set at liberty he gave new cause of offence and suspicion, and was again arrested, examined, and sent to prison.‡ At length he was permitted to retire, pursued by the hisses and curses of both parties, to a lonely manor house in the North Riding of Yorkshire. There, at least, he had not to endure the scornful looks of old associates who had once thought him a man of dauntless courage and spotless honour, but who now pronounced that he was at best a meanspirited coward, and hinted their suspicions that he had been from the beginning a spy and a trepan.§ He employed the short and sad remains of his life in turning the Consolation of Boethius into English. The translation was published after the translator's death. It is remarkable chiefly on account of some very unsuccessful attempts to enrich our versification with new metres, and on account of the allusions with which the pre-

---

* Sidney to William, Feb. 27. 169$\frac{0}{1}$. The letter is in Dalrymple's Appendix, Part II. book vi. Narcissus Luttrell, in his Diary for September 1691, mentions Penn's escape from Shoreham to France. On the 5th of December 1693 Narcissus made the following entry: "William Penn the Quaker, having for some time absconded, and having compromised the matters against him, appears now in public, and, on Friday last, held forth at the Bull and Mouth, in Saint Martin's." On December $\frac{18}{28}$. 1693 was drawn up at Saint Germains, under Melfort's direction, a paper containing a passage of which the following is a translation: "Mr. Penn says that Your Majesty has had several occasions, but never any so favourable as the present; and he hopes

that Your Majesty will be earnest with the most Christian King not to neglect it: that a descent with thirty thousand men will not only reestablish Your Majesty, but, according to all appearance break the league." This paper is among the Nairne MSS., and was translated by Macpherson.

† Narcissus Luttrell's Diary, April 11. 1691.

‡ Narcissus Luttrell's Diary, August 1691; Letter from Vernon to Wharton, Oct. 17. 1691, in the Bodleian.

§ The opinion of the Jacobites appears from a letter which is among the archives of the French War Office. It was written in London on the 25th of June 1691.

face is filled.   Under a thin veil of figurative language,
Preston exhibited to the public compassion or contempt his
own blighted fame and broken heart.   He complained that
the tribunal which had sentenced him to death had dealt
with him more leniently than his former friends, and that
many, who had never been tried by temptations like his, had
very cheaply earned a reputation for courage by sneering at
his poltroonery, and by bidding defiance at a distance to horrors
which, when brought near, subdue even a constant mind.

The spirit of the Jacobites, which had been quelled for
a time by the detection of Preston's plot, was revived by the
fall of Mons.   The joy of the whole party was boundless.
The nonjuring priests ran backwards and forwards between
Sam's Coffee House and Westminster Hall, spreading the
praises of Lewis, and laughing at the miserable issue of the
deliberations of the great Congress.   In the Park the malecontents were in the habit of mustering daily, and one avenue
was called the Jacobite walk.   They now came to this rendezvous in crowds, wore their biggest looks, and talked
sedition in their loudest tones.   The most conspicuous among
these swaggerers was Sir John Fenwick, who had, in the
late reign, been high in royal favour and in military command, and was now an indefatigable agitator and conspirator.
In his exultation he forgot the courtesy which man owes to
woman.   He had more than once made himself conspicuous
by his incivility to the Queen.   He now ostentatiously put
himself in her way when she took her airing, and, while all
around him uncovered and bowed low, gave her a rude stare,
and cocked his hat in her face.   The affront was not only
brutal, but cowardly.   For the law had provided no punishment for mere impertinence, however gross ; and the King
was the only gentleman and soldier in the kingdom who could
not protect his wife from contumely with his sword.   All
that the Queen could do was to order the parkkeepers not to
admit Sir John again within the gates.   But, long after her
death, a day came when he had reason to wish that he had
restrained his insolence.   He found, by terrible proof, that
of all the Jacobites, the most desperate assassins not excepted, he was the only one for whom William felt an intense
personal aversion.*

Joy of the Jacobites at the fall of Mons.

* Welwood's Mercurius Reformatus,
April 11. 24. 1691 ; Narcissus Luttrell's
Diary, April 1691 ; L'Hermitage to the
States General, June $\frac{19}{29}$. 1696 ; Calamy's
Life.   The story of Fenwick's rudeness
to Mary is told in different ways.   I
have followed what seems to me the
most authentic, and what is certainly
the least disgraceful, version.

A few days after this event the rage of the malecontents began to flame more fiercely than ever. The detection of the conspiracy of which Preston was the chief had brought on a crisis in ecclesiastical affairs. The nonjuring bishops had, during the year which followed their deprivation, continued to reside in the official mansions which had once been their own. Burnet had, at Mary's request, laboured to effect a compromise. His direct interference would probably have done more harm than good. He therefore judiciously employed the agency of Rochester, who stood higher in the estimation of the nonjurors than any statesman who was not a nonjuror, and of Trevor, who, worthless as he was, had considerable influence with the High Church party. Sancroft and his brethren were informed that, if they would consent to perform their spiritual duty, to ordain, to institute, to confirm, and to watch over the faith and the morality of the priesthood, a bill should be brought into Parliament to excuse them from taking the oaths.* This offer was imprudently liberal: but those to whom it was made could not consistently accept it. For in the ordination service, and indeed in almost every service of the Church, William and Mary were designated as King and Queen. The only promise that could be obtained from the deprived prelates was that they would live quietly; and even this promise they had not all kept. One of them at least had been guilty of treason aggravated by impiety. He had, under the strong fear of being butchered by the populace, declared that he abhorred the thought of calling in the aid of France, and had invoked God to attest the sincerity of this declaration. Yet, a short time after, he had been detected in plotting to bring a French army into England; and he had written to assure the Court of Saint Germains that he was acting in concert with his brethren, and especially with Sancroft. The Whigs called loudly for severity. Even the Tory counsellors of William owned that indulgence had been carried to the extreme point. They made, however, a last attempt to mediate. "Will you and your brethren," said Trevor to Lloyd, the nonjuring Bishop of Norwich, "disown all connection with Doctor Turner and declare that what he has in his letters imputed to you is false?" Lloyd evaded the question. It was now evident that William's forbearance had only emboldened the adversaries whom he had hoped to conciliate. Even Caermarthen,

The vacant
sees filled.

* Burnet, ii. 71.

even Nottingham, declared that it was high time to fill the vacant sees.*

Tillotson was nominated to the Archbishopric, and was consecrated on Whitsunday, in the church of Saint Mary Le Bow. Compton, cruelly mortified, refused to bear any part in the ceremony. His place was supplied by Mew, Bishop of Winchester, who was assisted by Burnet, Stillingfleet, and Hough. The congregation was the most splendid that had been seen in any place of worship since the coronation. The Queen's drawingroom was, on that day, deserted. Most of the peers who were in town met in the morning at Bedford House, and went thence in procession to Cheapside. Norfolk, Caermarthen, and Dorset were conspicuous in the throng. Devonshire, who was impatient to see his woods at Chatsworth in their summer beauty, had deferred his departure in order to mark his respect for Tillotson. The crowd which lined the streets greeted the new primate warmly. For he had, during many years, preached in the City; and his eloquence, his probity, and the singular gentleness of his temper and manners, had made him the favourite of the Londoners.† But the congratulations and applauses of his friends could not drown the roar of execration which the Jacobites set up. According to them, he was a thief who had not entered by the door, but had climbed over the fences. He was a hireling whose own the sheep were not, who had usurped the crook of the good shepherd, and who might well be expected to leave the flock at the mercy of every wolf. He was an Arian, a Socinian, a Deist, an Atheist. He had cozened the world by fine phrases, and by a show of moral goodness: but he was in truth a far more dangerous enemy of the Church than he could have been if he had openly proclaimed himself a disciple of Hobbes, and had lived as loosely as Wilmot. He had taught the fine gentlemen and ladies who admired his style, and who were constantly seen round his pulpit, that they might be very good Christians, and yet might believe the account of the Fall in the Book of Genesis to be allegorical. Indeed they might easily be as good Christians as he: for he had never been christened: his parents were Anabaptists: he

Marginal note: Tillotson Archbishop of Canterbury.

---

* Lloyd to Sancroft, Jan. 24. 1691. The letter is among the Tanner MSS., and is printed in the Life of Ken by a Layman.

† London Gazette, June 1. 1691; Birch's Life of Tillotson; Congratulatory Poem to the Reverend Dr. Tillotson on his promotion, 1691; Vernon to Wharton, May 28. and 30. 1691. These letters to Wharton are in the Bodleian Library, and form part of a highly curious collection which was kindly pointed out to me by Dr. Bandinel.

had lost their religion when he was a boy; and he had never found another. In ribald lampoons he was nicknamed Undipped John. The parish register of his baptism was produced in vain. His enemies still continued to complain that they had lived to see fathers of the Church who never were her children. They made up a story that the Queen had felt bitter remorse for the great crime by which she had obtained a throne, that in her agony she had applied to Tillotson, and that he had comforted her by assuring her that the punishment of the wicked in a future state would not be eternal.[*] The Archbishop's mind was naturally of almost feminine delicacy, and had been rather softened than braced by the habits of a long life, during which contending sects and factions had agreed in speaking of his abilities with admiration and of his character with esteem. The storm of obloquy which he had to face for the first time at more than sixty years of age was too much for him. His spirits declined: his health gave way: yet he neither flinched from his duty nor attempted to revenge himself on his persecutors. A few days after his consecration, some persons were seized while dispersing libels in which he was reviled. The law officers of the Crown proposed to file informations; but he insisted that nobody should be punished on his account.[†]   Once, when he had company with him, a sealed packet was put into his hands: he opened it, and out fell a mask. His friends were shocked and incensed by this cowardly insult: but the Archbishop, trying to conceal his anguish by a smile, pointed to the pamphlets which covered his table, and said that the reproach which the emblem of the mask was intended to convey might be called gentle when compared with other reproaches which he daily had to endure. After his death a bundle of the savage lampoons which the nonjurors had circulated against him was found among his papers with this indorsement; "I pray God forgive them: I do."[‡]

---

[*] Birch's Life of Tillotson; Leslie's Charge of Socinianism against Dr. Tillotson considered by a True Son of the Church, 1695; Hickes's Discourses upon Dr. Burnet and Dr. Tillotson, 1695; Catalogue of Books, of the Newest Fashion, to be Sold by Auction at the Whig's Coffee House, evidently printed in 1693. More than sixty years later Johnson described a sturdy Jacobite as firmly convinced that Tillotson died an Atheist; Idler, No. 10. A Latin epitaph on the Church of England, written soon after Tillotson's consecration, ends thus:

"Oh Miseranda Ecclesia, cui Rex Batavus, et Patriarcha non baptizatus." In a poem called the Eucharisticon, which appeared in 1692, are these lines:
"Unblest and unbaptised this Church's son
   Hath all his Mother's children half undone."

[†] Tillotson to Lady Russell, June 23. 1691.

[‡] Birch's Life of Tillotson; Memorials of Tillotson by his pupil John Beardmore; Sherlock's Sermon preached in the Temple Church on the death of Queen Mary, 169⅘.

The deposed primate was of a less gentle nature. He seems to have been also under a complete delusion as to his own importance. The immense popularity which he had enjoyed three years before, the prayers and tears of the multitudes who had plunged into the Thames to implore his blessing, the enthusiasm with which the sentinels of the Tower had drunk his health under the windows of his prison, the mighty roar of joy which had risen from Palace Yard on the morning of his acquittal, the triumphant night when every window from Hyde Park to Mile End had exhibited seven candles, the midmost and tallest emblematical of him, were still fresh in his recollection; nor had he the wisdom to perceive that all this homage had been paid, not to his person, but to that religion and to those liberties of which he was, for a moment, the representative. The extreme tenderness with which the new government had long persisted in treating him had confirmed him in his error. That a succession of conciliatory messages was sent to him from Kensington; that he was offered terms so liberal as to be scarcely consistent with the dignity of the Crown and the welfare of the State; that his cold and uncourteous answers could not tire out the royal indulgence; that, in spite of the loud clamours of the Whigs, and of the provocations daily given by the Jacobites, he was residing, fifteen months after deprivation, in the metropolitan palace; these things seemed to him to indicate, not the lenity, but the timidity, of the ruling powers. He appears to have flattered himself that they would not dare to eject him. The news, therefore, that his see had been filled, threw him into a passion which lasted as long as his life, and which hurried him into many foolish and unseemly actions. Tillotson, as soon as he was appointed, went to Lambeth in the hope that he might be able, by courtesy and kindness, to soothe the irritation of which he was the innocent cause. He staid long in the antechamber, and sent in his name by several servants: but Sancroft would not even return an answer.* Three weeks passed; and still the deprived Archbishop showed no disposition to move. At length he received an order intimating to him the royal pleasure that he should quit the dwelling which had long ceased to be his own, and in which he was only a guest. He resented this order bitterly, and declared that he would not obey it. He would stay till he was pulled out by the Sheriff's officers. He would defend himself at law as long as he could do so without putting in any plea ac-

* Wharton's Collectanea, quoted in Birch's Life of Tillotson.

knowledging the authority of the usurpers.* The case was
so clear that he could not, by any artifice of chicanery, obtain
more than a short delay. When judgment had been given
against him, he left the palace, but directed his steward to
retain possession. The consequence was that the steward
was taken into custody and heavily fined. Tillotson sent a
kind message to assure his predecessor that the fine should
not be exacted. But Sancroft was determined to have a
grievance, and would pay the money.†

Difference
between
Sancroft
and Ken.

From that time the great object of the narrowminded and
peevish old man was to tear in pieces the Church of which he
had been the chief minister. It was in vain that some of
those nonjurors, whose virtue, ability, and learning were the
glory of their party, remonstrated against his design. "Our
deprivation,"—such was the reasoning of Ken,—"is, in the
sight of God, a nullity. We are, and shall be, till we die
or resign, the true Bishops of our sees. Those who assume
our titles and functions will incur the guilt of schism. But
with us, if we act as becomes us, the schism will die ; and in
the next generation the unity of the Church will be restored.
On the other hand, if we consecrate Bishops to succeed us,
the breach may last through ages ; and we shall be justly held
accountable, not indeed for its origin, but for its continuance.
These considerations ought, on Sancroft's own principles, to
have had decisive weight with him : but his angry passions
prevailed. Ken quietly retired from the venerable palace of
Wells. He had done, he said, with strife, and should henceforth vent his feelings, not in disputes, but in hymns. His
charities to the unhappy of all persuasions, especially to the
followers of Monmouth and to the persecuted Huguenots,
had been so large that his own private fortune consisted of
seven hundred pounds, and of a library which he could not
bear to sell. But Thomas Thynne, Viscount Weymouth,
though not a nonjuror, did himself honour by offering to the
most virtuous of the nonjurors a tranquil and dignified asylum in the princely mansion of Longleat. There Ken passed
a happy and honoured old age, during which he never regretted
the sacrifice which he had made to what he thought his duty,
and yet constantly became more and more indulgent to those
whose views of duty differed from his.‡

* Wharton's Collectanea, quoted in
D'Oyly's Life of Sancroft; Narcissus
Luttrell's Diary.
    † The Lambeth MS. quoted in
D'Oyly's Life of Sancroft; Narcissus
Luttrell's Diary; Vernon to Wharton,

June 9. 11. 1691.
    ‡ See a letter of R. Nelson, dated
Feb. 21. 17 99/10, in the appendix to N.
Marshall's Defence of our Constitution
in Church and State, 1717 ; Hawkins's
Life of Ken ; Life of Ken by a Layman.

Sancroft was of a very different temper. He had, indeed, as little to complain of as any man whom a revolution has ever hurled down from an exalted station. He had, at Fressingfield in Suffolk, a patrimonial estate, which, together with what he had saved during a primacy of twelve years, enabled him to live, not indeed as he had lived when he was the first peer of Parliament, but in the style of an opulent country gentleman. He retired to his hereditary abode; and there he passed the rest of his life in brooding over his wrongs. Aversion to the Established Church became as strong a feeling in him as it had been in Martin Marprelate. He considered all who remained in communion with her as heathens and publicans. He nicknamed Tillotson the Mufti. In the room which was used as a chapel at Fressingfield no person who had taken the oaths, or who attended the ministry of any divine who had taken the oaths, was suffered to partake of the sacred bread and wine. A distinction, however, was made between two classes of offenders. A layman who remained in communion with the Church was permitted to be present while prayers were read, and was excluded only from the highest of Christian mysteries. But with clergymen who had sworn allegiance to the Sovereigns in possession Sancroft would not even pray. He took care that the rule which he had laid down should be widely known, and, both by precept and by example, taught his followers to look on the most orthodox, the most devout, the most virtuous, of those who acknowledged William's authority with a feeling similar to that with which the Jew regarded the Samaritan.* Such intolerance would have been reprehensible, even in a man contending for a great principle. But Sancroft was contending for nothing more than a name. He was the author of the scheme of Regency. He was perfectly willing to transfer the whole kingly power from James to William. The question, which, to this smallest and sourest of minds, seemed important enough to justify the excommunicating of ten thousand priests and of five millions of laymen, was merely, whether the magistrate to whom the whole kingly power was transferred should assume the kingly title. Nor could Sancroft bear to think that the animosity which he had excited would die with himself. Having done all that he could to make the feud bitter, he determined to make it eternal. A list of the divines who had been ejected from their benefices was sent by him to Saint Germains with a request that James would

Hatred of Sancroft to the Established Church. He provides for the episcopal succession among the nonjurors.

---

* See a paper dictated by him on the 15th of Nov. 1693, in Wagstaffe's Letter from Suffolk.

nominate two who might keep up the episcopal succession.
James, well pleased, doubtless, to see another sect added to
that multitude of sects which he had been taught to consider
as the reproach of Protestantism, named two fierce and un-
compromising nonjurors, Hickes and Wagstaffe, the former
recommended by Sancroft, the latter recommended by Lloyd,
the ejected Bishop of Norwich.* Such was the origin of a
schismatical hierarchy, which, having, during a short time,
excited alarm, soon sank into obscurity and contempt, but
which, in obscurity and contempt, continued to drag on a
languid existence during several generations. The little
Church without temples, revenues, or dignities, was even
more distracted by internal disputes than the great Church,
which retained possession of cathedrals, tithes, and peerages.
Some nonjurors leaned towards the ceremonial of Rome:
others would not tolerate the slightest departure from the
Book of Common Prayer. Altar was set up against altar.
One phantom prelate pronounced the consecration of another
phantom prelate uncanonical. At length the pastors were
left absolutely without flocks. One of these Lords spiritual
very wisely turned surgeon: another deserted what he had
called his see, and settled in Ireland; and at length, in 1805,
the last Bishop of that society which had proudly claimed to
be the only true Church of England dropped unnoticed into
the grave.†

The new
Bishops.
The places of the bishops who had been ejected with Sancroft were filled in a manner creditable to the government.
Patrick succeeded the traitor Turner. Fowler went to Gloucester. Richard Cumberland, an aged divine, who had no
interest at Court, and whose only recommendations were his
piety and his erudition, was astonished by learning from a
newsletter which he found on the table of a coffeehouse
that he had been nominated to the see of Peterborough.‡
Beveridge was selected to succeed Ken: he consented:
and the appointment was actually announced in the London.
Gazette. But Beveridge, though an honest, was not a
strongminded man. Some Jacobites expostulated with him;
some reviled him: his heart failed him; and he retracted.
While the nonjurors were rejoicing in this victory, he
changed his mind again; but too late. He had by his
irresolution forfeited the favour of William, and never ob-

* Kettlewell's Life, iii. 59.
† See D'Oyly's Life of Sancroft, Hal-
lam's Constitutional History, and Mr.
Lathbury's History of the Nonjurors.

‡ See the autobiography of his descendant and namesake the dramatist.
See also Onslow's note on Burnet, ii. 76.

tained a mitre till Anne was on the throne.* The bishopric of Bath and Wells was bestowed on Richard Kidder, a man of considerable attainments and blameless character, but suspected of a leaning towards Presbyterianism. About the same time Sharp, the highest churchman that had been zealous for the Comprehension, and the lowest churchman that felt a scruple about succeeding a deprived prelate, accepted the Archbishopric of York, vacant by the death of Lamplugh.†

In consequence of the elevation of Tillotson to the See of Canterbury, the Deanery of Saint Paul's became vacant. As soon as the name of the new Dean was known, a clamour broke forth such as perhaps no ecclesiastical appointment has ever produced, a clamour made up of yells of hatred, of hisses of contempt, and of shouts of triumphant and half insulting welcome: for the new Dean was William Sherlock.

Sherlock, Dean of Saint Paul's.

The story of his conversion deserves to be fully told: for it throws great light on the character of the parties which then divided the Church and the State. Sherlock was, in influence and reputation, though not in rank, the foremost man among the nonjurors. His authority and example had induced some of his brethren, who had at first wavered, to resign their benefices. The day of suspension came: the day of deprivation came; and still he was firm. He seemed to have found, in the consciousness of rectitude, and in meditation on the invisible world, ample compensation for all his losses. While excluded from the pulpit where his eloquence had once delighted the learned and polite inmates of the Temple, he wrote that celebrated Treatise on Death which, during many years, stood next to the Whole Duty of Man in the bookcases of serious Arminians. Soon, however, it began to be suspected that his resolution was giving way. He declared that he would be no party to a schism: he advised those who sought his counsel not to leave their parish churches: nay, finding that the law which had ejected him from his cure did not interdict him from performing divine service, he officiated at Saint Dunstan's, and there prayed for King William and Queen Mary. The apostolical injunction, he said, was that prayers should be made for all in authority; and William

---

* A vindication of Their Majesties' authority to fill the sees of the deprived Bishops, May 20. 1691; London Gazette, April 27. and June 15. 1691; Narcissus Luttrell's Diary, May 1691. Among the Tanner MSS. are two letters from Jacobites to Beveridge, one mild and decent, the other scurrilous even beyond the ordinary scurrility of the nonjurors. The former will be found in the Life of Ken by a Layman.

† It is not quite clear whether Sharp's scruple about the deprived prelates was a scruple of conscience or merely a scruple of delicacy. See his Life by his Son.

and Mary were visibly in authority. His Jacobite friends
loudly blamed his inconsistency. How, they asked, if you
admit that the Apostle speaks in this passage of actual
authority, can you maintain that, in other passages of a
similar kind, he speaks only of legitimate authority? Or,
how can you, without sin, designate as King, in a solemn
address to God, one whom you cannot, without sin, promise
to obey as King? These reasonings were unanswerable; and
Sherlock soon began to think them so: but the conclusion
to which they led him was diametrically opposed to the conclusion to which they were meant to lead him. He hesitated,
however, till a new light flashed on his mind from a quarter
from which there was little reason to expect anything but
tenfold darkness. In the reign of James the First, Doctor
John Overall, Bishop of Exeter, had written an elaborate
treatise on the rights of civil and ecclesiastical governors.
This treatise had been solemnly approved by the Convocations
of Canterbury and York, and might therefore be considered
as an authoritative exposition of the doctrine of the Church
of England. A manuscript copy had come into Sancroft's
hands; and he, soon after the Revolution, sent it to the press.
He hoped, doubtless, that the publication would injure the
new government: but he was lamentably disappointed. The
book indeed condemned all resistance in terms as strong as
he could himself have used: but one passage, which had escaped his notice, was decisive against himself and his fellow
schismatics. Overall, and the two Convocations which had
given their sanction to Overall's teaching, pronounced that
a government, which had originated in rebellion, ought, when
thoroughly settled, to be considered as ordained by God, and
to be obeyed by Christian men.* Sherlock read, and was
convinced. His venerable mother the Church had spoken;

---

* See Overall's Convocation Book,
chapter 28. Nothing can be clearer or
more to the purpose than his language.

"When, having attained their ungodly
desires, whether ambitious kings by
bringing any country into their subjection, or disloyal subjects by rebellious
rising against their natural sovereigns,
they have established any of the said
degenerate governments among their
people, the authority either so unjustly
established, or wrung by force from the
true and lawful possessor, being always
God's authority, and therefore receiving
no impeachment by the wickedness of
those that have it, is ever, when such
alterations are thoroughly settled, to be
reverenced and obeyed; and the people
of all sorts, as well of the clergy as of
the laity, are to be subject unto it, not
only for fear, but likewise for conscience
sake."

Then follows the canon.

"If any man shall affirm that, when
any such new forms of government,
begun by rebellion, are after thoroughly
settled, the authority in them is not of
God, or that any who live within
the territories of any such new governments are not bound to be subject to
God's authority which is there executed,
but may rebel against the same, he doth
greatly err."

and he, with the docility of a child, accepted her decree. The government which had sprung from the Revolution might, at least since the battle of the Boyne and the flight of James from Ireland, be fairly called a settled government, and ought therefore to be passively obeyed till it should be subverted by another revolution and succeeded by another settled government.

Sherlock took the oaths, and speedily published in justification of his conduct, a pamphlet entitled The Case of Allegiance to Sovereign Powers stated. The sensation produced by this work was immense. Dryden's Hind and Panther had not raised so great an uproar. Halifax's Letter to a Dissenter had not called forth so many answers. The replies to the Doctor, the vindications of the Doctor, the pasquinades on the Doctor, would fill a library. The clamour redoubled when it was known that the convert had not only been reappointed Master of the Temple, but had accepted the Deanery of Saint Paul's, which had become vacant in consequence of the deprivation of Sancroft and the promotion of Tillotson. The rage of the nonjurors amounted almost to frenzy. Was it not enough, they asked, to desert the true and pure Church, in this her hour of sorrow and peril, without also slandering her? It was easy to understand why a greedy, cowardly, hypocrite should refuse to take the oaths to the usurper as long as it seemed probable that the rightful King would be restored, and should make haste to swear after the battle of the Boyne. Such tergiversation in times of civil discord was nothing new. What was new was that the turncoat should attempt to transfer his own guilt and shame to the Church of England, and should proclaim that she had taught him to lift his heel against the weak who were in the right, and to cringe to the powerful who were in the wrong. Had such indeed been her doctrine or her practice in evil days? Had she abandoned her Royal Martyr in the prison or on the scaffold? Had she enjoined her children to pay obedience to the Rump or to the Protector? Yet was the government of the Rump or of the Protector less entitled to be called a settled government than the government of William and Mary? Had not the battle of Worcester been as great a blow to the hopes of the House of Stuart as the battle of the Boyne? Had not the chances of a Restoration seemed as small in 1657 as they could seem to any judicious man in 1691? In spite of invectives and sarcasms, however, there was Overall's treatise: there were the approving votes of the two Convocations; and it was much easier to rail at Sherlock than to explain away either the treatise or the votes. One writer maintained that by a thoroughly settled government must have been meant a government of which the title was uncontested. Thus, he said, the government of the United Provinces became a settled government when it was recognised by Spain, and, but for that recognition, would never have been a settled government to the end of time. Another casuist, somewhat less austere, pronounced that a government, wrongful in its origin, might become a settled government after the lapse of a century. On the thirteenth of February 1789, therefore, and not a day earlier, Englishmen would be at liberty to swear allegiance to a government sprung from the Revolution. The history of the chosen people was ransacked for precedents. Was Eglon's a settled government when Ehud stabbed him? Was Joram's a settled government when Jehu shot him? But the leading case was that of Athaliah. It was indeed a case which furnished the malecontents with many happy and pungent allusions; a kingdom treacherously seized by an usurper near in blood to the throne; the rightful prince long dispossessed; a part of the sacerdotal order true, through many disastrous years, to the Royal House; a counterrevolution at length effected by the High Priest at the head of the Levites. Who, it was asked, would dare to blame the heroic pontiff who had restored the heir of David? Yet was not the government of Athaliah as firmly settled as that of the Prince of Orange? Hundreds of pages written at this time about the rights of Joash and the bold enterprise of Jehoiada are mouldering in the ancient bookcases of Oxford and Cambridge. While Sherlock was thus fiercely attacked by his old friends he was not left unmolested by his old enemies. Some vehement Whigs, among whom Julian Johnson was conspicuous, declared that Jacobitism itself was respectable when compared with the vile doctrine which had been discovered in the Convocation Book. That passive obedience was due to Kings was doubtless an absurd and pernicious notion. Yet it was impossible not to respect the consistency and fortitude of men who thought themselves bound to bear true allegiance, at all hazards, to an unfortunate, a deposed, an exiled oppressor. But the political creed which Sherlock had learned from Overall was unmixed baseness and wickedness. A cause was to be abandoned, not because it was unjust, but because it was unprosperous. Whether James had been a tyrant or had been the father of his people was, according to this theory, quite immaterial. If he had won the battle of the Boyne we should have been bound as Christians to be his slaves. He had lost it; and we were bound as Christians to be his foes. Other Whigs congratulated the proselyte on having come, by whatever road, to a right practical conclusion, but could not refrain from sneering at the history which he gave of his conversion. He was, they said, a man of eminent learning and abilities. He had studied the question of allegiance long and deeply. He had written much about it. Several months had been allowed him for reading, prayer, and reflection, before he incurred suspension, several months more before he incurred deprivation. He had formed an opinion for which he had declared himself ready to suffer martyrdom: he had taught that opinion to others; and he had then changed that opinion solely because he had discovered that it had been, not refuted, but dogmatically pronounced erroneous by the two Convocations more than eighty years before. Surely this was to renounce all liberty of private judgment, and to ascribe to the Synods of Canterbury and York an infallibility which the Church of England had declared that even Œcumenical Councils could not justly claim. If, it was sarcastically said, all our notions of right and wrong, in matters of vital importance to the wellbeing of society, are to be suddenly altered by a few lines of manuscript found in a corner of the library at Lambeth, it is surely much to be wished, for the peace of mind of humble Christians, that all the documents to which this sort of authority belongs may be rummaged out and sent to the press as soon as possible: for, unless this be done, we may all, like the Doctor when he refused the oaths last year, be committing sins in the full persuasion that we are discharging duties. In truth it is not easy to believe that the Convocation Book furnished Sherlock with anything more than a pretext for doing what he had made up his mind to do. The united force of reason and interest had doubtless convinced him that his passions and prejudices had led him into a great error. That error he determined to recant; and it cost him less to say that his opinion had been changed by newly discovered evidence, than that he had formed a wrong judgment with all the materials for the forming of a right judgment before him. The popular belief was that his retractation was the effect of the tears, expostulations, and reproaches of his wife. The lady's spirit was high: her authority in the family was great; and she cared much more about her house and her carriage, the plenty of her table and the prospects of her children, than about the patriarchal origin of government or the meaning of the word Abdication. She had, it was asserted, given her husband no peace by day or by night till he had got over his scruples. In letters, fables, songs, dialogues, without number, her powers of seduction and intimidation were malignantly extolled. She was Xanthippe pouring water on the head of Socrates. She was Dalilah shearing Samson. She was Eve forcing the forbidden fruit into Adam's mouth. She was Job's wife, imploring her ruined lord, who sate scraping himself among the ashes, not to curse and die, but to swear and live. While the balladmakers celebrated the victory of Mrs. Sherlock, another class of assailants fell on the theological reputation of her spouse. Till he took the oaths, he had always been considered as the most orthodox of divines. But the captious and malignant criticism to which his writings were now subjected would have found heresy in the Sermon on the Mount; and he, unfortunately, was rash enough to publish at the very moment when the outcry against his political tergiversation was loudest, his thoughts on the mystery of the Trinity. It is probable that, at another time, his work would have been hailed by good Churchmen as a triumphant answer to the Socinians and Sabellians. But unhappily, in his zeal against Socinians and Sabellians, he used expressions which might be construed into Tritheism. Candid judges would have remembered that the true path was closely pressed on the right and on the left by error, and that it was scarcely possible to keep far enough from danger on one side without going very close to danger on the other. But candid judges Sherlock was not likely to find among the Jacobites. His old allies affirmed that he had incurred all the fearful penalties denounced in the Athanasian Creed against those who divide the substance. Bulky quartos were written to prove that he held the existence of three distinct Deities; and some facetious malecontents, who troubled themselves very little about the Catholic verity, amused the town by lampoons in English and Latin on his heterodoxy. "We," said one of these jesters, "plight our faith to one King, and call one God to attest our promise. We cannot think it strange that there should be more than one King to whom the Doctor has sworn allegiance, when we consider that the Doctor has more Gods than one to swear by." *

Sherlock would, perhaps, have doubted whether the government to which he had submitted was entitled to be called a settled government, if he had known all the dangers by which it was threatened. Scarcely had Preston's plot been detected, when a new plot of a very different kind was formed in the camp, in the navy, in the treasury, in the very bedchamber of the King. This mystery of iniquity has, through five generations, been gradually unveiling, but is not yet entirely unveiled. Some parts which are still obscure may possibly, by the discovery of letters or diaries now reposing under the dust of a century and a half, be made clear to our posterity. The materials, however, which are at present accessible, are sufficient for the construction of a narrative not to be read without shame and loathing.†

We have seen that, in the spring of 1690, Shrewsbury, irritated by finding his counsels rejected, and those of his Tory rivals followed, suffered himself, in a fatal hour, to be drawn into a correspondence with the banished family. We have seen also by what cruel sufferings of body and mind he expiated his fault. Tortured by remorse, and by disease the

Marginal note: Treachery of some of William's servants.

* A list of all the pieces which I have read relating to Sherlock's apostasy would fatigue the reader. I will mention a few of different kinds; Parkinson's Examination of Dr. Sherlock's Case of Allegiance, 1691; Answer to Dr. Sherlock's Case of Allegiance, by a London Apprentice, 1691; the Reasons of the New Convert's taking the Oaths to the present Government, 1691; Utrum horum? or God's ways of disposing of Kingdoms, and some Clergymen's ways of disposing of them, 1691; Sherlock and Xanthippe, 1691; Saint Paul's Triumph in his sufferings for Christ, by Matthew Bryan, LL.D., dedicated Ecclesiæ sub cruce gementi; A Word to a wavering Levite; The Trimming Court Divine; Proteus Ecclesiasticus, or Observations on Dr. Sh—'s late Case of Allegiance; the Weasil Uncased; A Whip for the Weasil; the Anti-Weasils. Numerous allusions to Sherlock and his wife will be found in the ribald writings of Tom Brown, Tom Durfey, and Ned Ward. See the Life of James, ii. 318. Several curious letters about Sherlock's apostasy are among the Tanner MSS. I will give two or three specimens of the rhymes which the Case of Allegiance called forth:

" When Eve the fruit had tasted,
    She to her husband hasted,
        And chuck'd him on the chin-a.
    Dear Bud, quoth she, come taste this fruit;
    'Twill finely with your palate suit:
        To eat it is no sin-a."

" As moody Job, in shirtless case,
    With collyflowers all o'er his face,
        Did on the dunghill languish,
    His spouse thus whispers in his ear, .
    Swear, husband, as you love me, swear:
        'Twill ease you of your anguish."

" At first he had doubt, and therefore did pray
    That heaven would instruct him in the right way,
    Whether Jemmy or William he ought to obey,
        Which nobody can deny.

" The pass at the Boyne determin'd that case;
    And precept to Providence then did give place;
    To change his opinion he thought no disgrace ;
        Which nobody can deny.

" But this with the Scripture can never agree,
    As by Hosea the eighth and the fourth you may see ;
    ' They have set up kings, but yet not by me,'
        Which nobody can deny."

† The chief authority for this part of my history is the Life of James, particularly the highly important and interesting passage which begins at page 444. and ends at page 450. of the second volume. This passage was corrected by the Pretender with his own hand.

effect of remorse, he had quitted the Court : but he had left behind him men whose principles were not less lax than his, and whose hearts were far harder and colder.

Early in 1691, some of these men began to hold secret communications with Saint Germains. Wicked and base as their conduct was, there was in it nothing surprising. They did after their kind. The times were troubled. A thick cloud was upon the future. The most sagacious and experienced statesman could not see with any clearness three months before him. To a man of virtue and honour, indeed, this mattered little. His uncertainty as to what the morrow might bring forth might make him anxious, but could not make him perfidious. Though left in utter darkness as to what concerned his interests, he had the sure guidance of his principles. But, unhappily, men of virtue and honour were not numerous among the courtiers of that age. Whitehall had been, during thirty years, a seminary of every public and private vice, and swarmed with lowminded, doubledealing, selfseeking politicians. These politicians now acted as it was natural that men profoundly immoral should act at a crisis of which none could predict the issue. Some of them might have a slight predilection for William; others a slight predilection for James : but it was not by any such predilection that the conduct of any of the breed was guided. If it had seemed certain that William would stand, they would all have been for William. If it had seemed certain that James would be restored, they would all have been for James. But what was to be done when the chances appeared to be almost exactly balanced ? There were honest men of one party who would have answered, To stand by the true King and the true Church, and, if necessary, to die for them like Laud. There were honest men of the other party who would have answered, To stand by the liberties of England and the Protestant religion, and, if necessary, to die for them like Sidney. But such consistency was unintelligible to many of the noble and the powerful. Their object was to be safe in every event. They therefore openly took the oath of allegiance to one King, and secretly plighted their word to the other. They were indefatigable in obtaining commissions, patents of peerage, pensions, grants of crown land, under the great seal of William ; and they had in their secret drawers promises of pardon in the handwriting of James.

Among those who were guilty of this wickedness three

men stand preeminent, Russell, Godolphin, and Marlborough. No three men could be, in head and heart, more unlike to one another; and the peculiar qualities of each gave a peculiar character to his villany. The treason of Russell is to be attributed partly to fractiousness: the treason of Godolphin is to be attributed altogether to timidity: the treason of Marlborough was the treason of a man of great genius and boundless ambition.

It may be thought strange that Russell should have been out of humour. He had just accepted the command of the united naval forces of England and Holland with the rank of Admiral of the Fleet. He was Treasurer of the Navy. He had a pension of three thousand pounds a year. Crown property near Charing Cross, to the value of eighteen thousand pounds, had been bestowed on him. His indirect gains must have been immense. But he was still dissatisfied. In truth, with undaunted courage, with considerable talents both for war and for administration, and with a certain public spirit, which showed itself by glimpses even in the very worst parts of his life, he was emphatically a bad man, insolent, malignant, greedy, faithless. He conceived that the great services which he had performed at the time of the Revolution had not been adequately rewarded. Everything that was given to others seemed to him to be pillaged from himself. A letter is still extant which he wrote to William about this time. It is made up of boasts, reproaches, and sneers. The Admiral, with ironical professions of humility and loyalty, asks permission to put his wrongs on paper, because his bashfulness will not suffer him to explain himself by word of mouth. His grievances he represents as intolerable. Other people got large grants of royal domains: but he could get scarcely anything. Other people could provide for their dependants: but his recommendations were uniformly disregarded. The income which he derived from the royal favour might seem large: but he had poor relations; and the government, instead of doing its duty by them, had most unhandsomely left them to his care. He had a sister who ought to have a pension; for, without one, she could not give portions to her daughters. He had a brother who, for want of a place, had been reduced to the melancholy necessity of marrying an old woman for her money. Russell proceeded to complain bitterly that the Whigs were neglected, and that the Revolution had aggrandised and enriched men who had made the greatest efforts to avert it. There is

Russell.

reason to believe that this complaint came from his heart. For, next to his own interests, those of his party were dear to him; and, even when he was most inclined to become a Jacobite, he never had the smallest disposition to become a Tory. In the temper which this letter indicates, he readily listened to the suggestions of David Lloyd, one of the ablest and most active of the emissaries who at this time were constantly plying between France and England. Lloyd conveyed to James assurances that Russell would, when a favourable opportunity should present itself, try to effect by means of the fleet what Monk had effected in the preceding generation by means of the army.* To what extent these assurances were sincere was a question about which men who knew Russell well, and who were minutely informed as to his conduct, were in doubt. It seems probable that, during many months, he did not know his own mind. His interest was to stand well, as long as possible, with both Kings. His irritable and imperious nature was constantly impelling him to quarrel with both. His spleen was excited one week by a dry answer from William, and the next week by an absurd proclamation from James. Fortunately the most important day of his life, the day from which all his subsequent years took their colour, found him out of temper with the banished tyrant.

Godolphin.   Godolphin had not, and did not pretend to have, any cause of complaint against the government which he served. He was First Commissioner of the Treasury. He had been protected, trusted, caressed. Indeed the favour shown to him had excited many murmurs. Was it fitting, the Whigs had indignantly asked, that a man who had been high in office through the whole of the late reign, who had promised to vote for the Indulgence, who had sate in the Privy Council with a Jesuit, who had sate at the Board of Treasury with two Papists, who had attended an idolatress to her altar, should be among the chief ministers of a Prince whose title to the throne was derived from the Declaration of Right? But on William this clamour had produced no effect; and none of his English servants seems to have had at this time a larger share of his confidence than Godolphin.

Nevertheless, the Jacobites did not despair. One of the most zealous among them, a gentleman named Bulkeley, who had formerly been on terms of intimacy with Godolphin,

* Russell to William, May 10. 1691,   vii. See also the Memoirs of Sir John
in Dalrymple's Appendix, Part II. Book   Leake.

Lord Godolphin

undertook to see what could be done. He called at the Treasury, and tried to draw the First Lord into political talk. This was no easy matter: for Godolphin was not a man to put himself lightly into the power of others. His reserve was proverbial; and he was especially renowned for the dexterity with which he, through life, turned conversation away from matters of state to a main of cocks or the pedigree of a race horse. The visit ended without his uttering a word indicating that he remembered the existence of King James.

Bulkeley, however, was not to be so repulsed. He came again, and introduced the subject which was nearest his heart. Godolphin then asked after his old master and mistress in the mournful tone of a man who despaired of ever being reconciled to them. Bulkeley assured him that King James was ready to forgive all the past. "May I tell His Majesty that you will try to deserve his favour?" At this Godolphin rose, said something about the trammels of office and his wish to be released from them, and put an end to the interview.

Bulkeley soon made a third attempt. By this time Godolphin had learned some things which shook his confidence in the stability of the government which he served. He began to think, as he would himself have expressed it, that he had betted too deep on the Revolution, and that it was time to hedge. Evasions would no longer serve his turn. It was necessary to speak out. He spoke out, and declared himself a devoted servant of King James. " I shall take an early opportunity of resigning my place. But, till then, I am under a tie. I must not betray my trust." To enhance the value of the sacrifice which he proposed to make, he produced a most friendly and confidential letter which he had lately received from William. "You see how entirely the Prince of Orange trusts me. He tells me that he cannot do without me, and that there is no Englishman for whom he has so great a kindness: but all this weighs nothing with me in comparison of my duty to my lawful King."

If the First Lord of the Treasury really had scruples about betraying his trust, those scruples were soon so effectually removed that he very complacently continued, during six years, to eat the bread of one master, while secretly sending professions of attachment and promises of service to another.

The truth is that Godolphin was under the influence of a mind far more powerful and far more depraved than his own. His perplexities had been imparted to Marlborough, to whom he had long been bound by such friendship as two very unprincipled men are capable of feeling for each other, and to whom he was afterwards bound by close domestic ties.

Marlborough.

Marlborough was in a very different situation from that of William's other servants. Lloyd might make overtures to Russell, and Bulkeley to Godolphin. But all the agents of the banished Court stood aloof from the deserter of Salisbury. That shameful night seemed to have for ever separated the false friend from the Prince whom he had ruined. James had, even in the last extremity, when his army was in full retreat, when his whole kingdom had risen against him, declared that he would never pardon Churchill, never, never. By all the Jacobites the name of Churchill was held in peculiar abhorrence ; and, in the prose and verse which came forth daily from their secret presses, a precedence in infamy, among all the many traitors of the age, was assigned to him. In the order of things which had sprung from the Revolution, he was one of the great men of England, high in the state, high in the army. He had been created an Earl. He had a large share in the military administration. The emoluments, direct and indirect, of the places and commands which he held under the Crown were believed at the Dutch Embassy to amount to twelve thousand pounds a year. In the event of a counterrevolution it seemed that he had nothing in prospect but a garret in Holland or a scaffold on Tower Hill. It might therefore have been expected that he would serve his new master with fidelity ; not indeed with the fidelity of Nottingham, which was the fidelity of conscientiousness, not with the fidelity of Portland, which was the fidelity of affection, but with the not less stubborn fidelity of despair.

Those who thought thus knew but little of Marlborough. Confident in his own powers of deception, he resolved, since the Jacobite agents would not seek him, to seek them. He therefore sent to beg an interview with Colonel Edward Sackville.

Sackville was astonished and not much pleased by the message. He was a sturdy Cavalier of the old school. He had been persecuted in the days of the Popish plot for manfully saying what he thought, and what everybody now thinks, about Oates and Bedloe.* Since the Revolution he had repeatedly put his neck in peril for King James, had been chased by officers with warrants, and had been designated as a traitor in a proclamation to which Marlborough himself had been a party.† It was not without reluctance that the stanch royalist crossed the hated threshold of the deserter. He was repaid for his effort by the edifying spectacle of such an agony of repentance as he had never before seen. "Will you," said Marlborough, "be my intercessor with the King? Will you tell him what I suffer? My crimes now appear to me in their true light; and I shrink with horror from the contemplation. The thought of them is with me day and night. I sit down to table : but I cannot eat. I throw myself on my bed : but I cannot sleep. I am ready to sacrifice everything, to brave everything, to bring utter ruin on my fortunes, if only I may be free from the misery of a wounded spirit." If appearances could be trusted, this great offender was as true a penitent as David or as Peter. Sackville reported to his friends what had passed. They could not but acknowledge that, if the archtraitor, who had hitherto opposed to conscience and to public opinion the same cool and placid hardihood which distinguished him on fields of battle, had really begun to feel remorse, it would be absurd to reject, on account of his unworthiness, the inestimable services which it was in his power to render to the good cause. He sate in the interior council : he held high command in the army : he had been recently entrusted, and would doubtless again be entrusted, with the direction of important military operations. It was true that no man had incurred equal guilt : but it was true also that no man had it in his power to make equal reparation. If he was sincere, he might doubtless earn the pardon which he so much desired. But was he sincere? Had he not been just as loud in professions of loyalty on the very eve of his crime? It was necessary to put him to the test. Several tests were applied by Sackville and Lloyd. Marlborough was required to furnish full information touching the strength and the distribution of all the divisions of the English army; and he complied. He was required to disclose the whole plan of the approaching campaign; and he did so. The Jacobite leaders watched carefully for inaccuracies in his reports, but could find none. It was thought a still stronger proof of his fidelity that he

* Commons' Journals, Mar. 21. 24. 1679; Grey's Debates; Observator.
  † London Gazette, July 21. 1690.

gave valuable intelligence about what was doing in the office
of the Secretary of State. A deposition had been sworn
against one zealous royalist. A warrant was preparing
against another. These intimations saved several of the
malecontents from imprisonment, if not from the gallows;
and it was impossible for them not to feel some relenting
towards the awakened sinner to whom they owed so much.

He however, in his secret conversations with his new allies,
laid no claim to merit. He did not, he said, ask for confidence. How could he, after the villanies which he had
committed against the best of Kings, hope ever to be trusted
again? It was enough for a wretch like him to be permitted
to make, at the cost of his life, some poor atonement to the
gracious master, whom he had indeed basely injured, but
whom he had never ceased to love. It was not improbable
that, in the summer, he might command the English forces
in Flanders. Was it wished that he should bring them over
in a body to the French camp? If such were the royal pleasure, he would undertake that the thing should be done. But
on the whole he thought that it would be better to wait till
the next session of Parliament. And then he hinted at a
plan, which he afterwards more fully matured, for expelling
the usurper by means of the English legislature and the
English army. In the meantime he hoped that James
would command Godolphin not to quit the Treasury. A
private man could do little for the good cause. One who
was the director of the national finances, and the depository
of the gravest secrets of state, might render inestimable
services.

Marlborough's pretended repentance imposed so completely
on those who managed the affairs of James in London that
they sent Lloyd to France, with the cheering intelligence
that the most depraved of all rebels had been wonderfully
transformed into a loyal subject. The tidings filled James
with delight and hope. Had he been wise, they would have
excited in him only aversion and distrust. It was absurd to
imagine that a man really heartbroken by remorse and shame
for one act of perfidy would determine to lighten his conscience by committing a second act of perfidy as odious and
as disgraceful as the first. The promised atonement was so
wicked and base that it never could be made by any man
sincerely desirous to atone for past wickedness and baseness.
The truth was that, when Marlborough told the Jacobites
that his sense of guilt prevented him from swallowing his

food by day and taking his rest at night, he was laughing at them. The loss of half a guinea would have done more to spoil his appetite and to disturb his slumbers than all the terrors of an evil conscience. What his offers really proved was that his former crime had sprung, not from an ill regulated zeal for the interests of his country and his religion, but from a deep and incurable moral disease which had infected the whole man. James, however, partly from dulness and partly from selfishness, could never see any immorality in any action by which he was benefited. To conspire against him, to betray him, to violate an oath of allegiance sworn to him, were crimes for which no punishment here or hereafter could be too severe. But to be ungrateful to his enemies, to break faith with his enemies, was not only innocent but laudable. The desertion at Salisbury had been the worst of crimes: for it had ruined him. A similar desertion in Flanders would be an honourable exploit: for it might restore him.

The penitent was informed by his Jacobite friends that he was forgiven. The news was most welcome; but something more was necessary to restore his lost peace of mind. Might he hope to have, in the royal handwriting, two lines containing a promise of pardon? It was not, of course, for his own sake that he asked this. But he was confident that, with such a document in his hands, he could bring back to the right path some persons of great note who adhered to the usurper, only because they imagined that they had no mercy to expect from the legitimate King. They would return to their duty as soon as they saw that even the worst of all criminals had, on his repentance, been generously forgiven. The promise was written, sent, and carefully treasured up. Marlborough had now attained one object, an object which was common to him with Russell and Godolphin. But he had other objects which neither Russell nor Godolphin had ever contemplated. There is, as we shall hereafter see, strong reason to believe that this wise, brave, wicked man, was meditating a plan worthy of his fertile intellect and daring spirit, and not less worthy of his deeply corrupted heart, a plan which, if it had not been frustrated by strange means, would have ruined William without benefiting James, and would have made the successful traitor master of England and arbiter of Europe.

Thus things stood, when, in May 1690, William, after a short and busy sojourn in England, set out again for the

Continent, where the regular campaign was about to open. He took with him Marlborough, whose abilities he justly appreciated, and of whose recent negotiations with Saint Germains he had not the faintest suspicion. At the Hague several important military and political consultations were held; and, on every occasion, the superiority of the accomplished Englishman was felt by the most distinguished soldiers and statesmen of the United Provinces. Heinsius, long after, used to relate a conversation which took place at this time between William and the Prince of Vaudemont, one of the ablest commanders in the Dutch service. Vaudemont spoke well of several English officers, and among them of Talmash and Mackay, but pronounced Marlborough superior beyond comparison to the rest. "He has every quality of a general. His very look shows it. He cannot fail to achieve something great." "I really believe, cousin," answered the King, "that my Lord will make good everything that you have said of him."

William returns to the Continent.

There was still a short interval before the commencement of military operations. William passed that interval in his beloved park at Loo. Marlborough spent two or three days there, and was then despatched to Flanders, with orders to collect all the English forces, to form a camp in the neighbourhood of Brussels, and to have everything in readiness for the King's arrival.

And now Marlborough had an opportunity of proving the sincerity of those professions by which he had obtained from a heart, well described by himself as harder than a marble chimneypiece, the pardon of an offence such as might have moved even a gentle nature to deadly resentment. He received from Saint Germains a message claiming the instant performance of his promise to desert at the head of his troops. He was told that this was the greatest service which he could render to the Crown. His word was pledged; and the gracious master who had forgiven all past errors confidently expected that it would be redeemed. The hypocrite evaded the demand with characteristic dexterity. In the most respectful and affectionate language he excused himself for not immediately obeying the royal commands. The promise which he was required to fulfil had not been quite correctly understood. There had been some misapprehension on the part of the messengers. To carry over a regiment or two would do more harm than good. To carry over a whole army was a business which would require much time and management.* While James was murmuring over these apologies, and wishing that he had not been quite so placable, William arrived at the head quarters of the allied forces, and took the chief command.

The military operations in Flanders recommenced early in June and terminated at the close of September. No important action took place. The two armies marched and countermarched, drew near and receded. During some time they confronted each other with less than a league between them. But neither William nor Luxemburg would fight except at an advantage; and neither gave the other any advantage. Languid as the campaign was, it is on one account remarkable. During more than a century our country had sent no great force to make war by land out of the British isles. Our aristocracy had therefore long ceased to be a military class. The nobles of France, of Germany, of Holland, were generally soldiers. It would probably have been difficult to find in the brilliant circle which surrounded Lewis at Versailles a single Marquess or Viscount of forty who had not been at some battle or siege. But the immense majority of our peers, baronets, and opulent esquires had never served except in the trainbands, and had never borne a part in any military exploit more serious than that of putting down a riot or of keeping a street clear for a procession. The generation which had fought at Edgehill and Lansdowne had nearly passed away. The wars of Charles the Second had been almost entirely maritime. During his reign therefore the sea service had been decidedly more the mode than the land service; and, repeatedly, when our fleets sailed to encounter the Dutch, such multitudes of men of fashion had gone on board that the parks and the theatres had been left desolate. In 1691 at length, for the first time since Henry the Eighth laid siege to Boulogne, an English army appeared on the Continent under the command of an English King. A camp, which was also a court, was irresistibly attractive to many young patricians full of natural intrepidity, and ambitious of the favour which men of distinguished bravery have always found in the eyes of women. To volunteer for Flanders became the rage among the fine gentlemen who combed their flowing wigs and exchanged their richly perfumed snuffs at the Saint James's Coffeehouse. William's headquarters were enlivened by a crowd of splendid equipages and by a rapid

The campaign of 1691 in Flanders.

* Life of James, ii. 449.

succession of sumptuous banquets. For among the highborn and highspirited youths who repaired to his standard were some who, though quite willing to face a battery, were not at all disposed to deny themselves the luxuries with which they had been surrounded in Soho Square. In a few months Shadwell brought these valiant fops and epicures on the stage. The town was made merry with the character of a courageous but prodigal and effeminate coxcomb, who is impatient to cross swords with the best men in the French household troops, but who is much dejected by learning that he may find it difficult to have his Champagne iced daily during the summer. He carries with him cooks, confectioners, and laundresses, a waggonload of plate, a wardrobe of laced and embroidered suits, and much rich tent furniture, of which the patterns have been chosen by a committee of fine ladies.*

While the hostile armies watched each other in Flanders, hostilities were carried on with somewhat more vigour in other parts of Europe. The French gained some advantages in Catalonia and in Piedmont. Their Turkish allies, who in the east menaced the dominions of the Emperor, were defeated by Lewis of Baden in a great battle. But nowhere were the events of the summer so important as in Ireland.

The war in Ireland.

From October 1690 till May 1691, no military operation on a large scale was attempted in that kingdom. The area of the island was, during the winter and spring, not unequally divided between the contending races. The whole of Ulster, the greater part of Leinster, and about one third of Munster had submitted to the English. The whole of Connaught, the greater part of Munster, and two or three counties of Leinster were held by the Irish. The tortuous boundary formed by William's garrisons ran in a north eastern direction from the bay of Castlehaven to Mallow, and then, inclining still further eastward, proceeded to Cashel. From Cashel the line went to Mullingar, from Mullingar to Longford, and from Longford to Cavan, skirted Lough Erne on the west, and met the ocean again at Ballyshannon.†

State of the English part of Ireland.

On the English side of this pale there was a rude and imperfect order. Two Lords Justices, Coningsby and Porter, assisted by a Privy Council, represented King William at

---

* The description of this young hero in the list of the Dramatis Personæ is amusing: Sir Nicholas Dainty, A most conceited fantastic Beau, of drolling affected Speech; a very Coxcomb, but stout; a most luxurious effeminate Volunteer."

† Story's Continuation; Proclamation of February 21. 169 9/0 ; London Gazette of March 12.

Dublin Castle. Judges, Sheriffs, and Justices of the Peace had been appointed; and assizes were, after a long interval, held in several county towns. The colonists had meanwhile been formed into a strong militia, under the command of officers who had commissions from the Crown. The train-bands of the capital consisted of two thousand five hundred foot, two troops of horse, and two troops of dragoons, all Protestants, and all well armed and clad.* On the fourth of November, the anniversary of William's birth, and on the fifth, the anniversary of his landing at Torbay, the whole of this force appeared in all the pomp of war. The vanquished and disarmed natives assisted, with suppressed grief and anger, at the triumph of the caste which they had, five months before, oppressed and plundered with impunity. The Lords Justices went in state to Saint Patrick's Cathedral: bells were rung: bonfires were lighted: hogsheads of ale and claret were set abroach in the streets: fireworks were exhibited on College Green: a great company of nobles and public functionaries feasted at the Castle; and, as the second course came up, the trumpets sounded, and Ulster King at Arms proclaimed, in Latin, French, and English, William and Mary, by the grace of God, King and Queen of Great Britain, France, and Ireland.†

Within the territory where the Saxon race was dominant trade and industry had already begun to revive. The brazen counters which bore the image and superscription of James gave place to silver. The fugitives who had taken refuge in England came back in multitudes; and, by their intelligence, diligence, and thrift, the devastation caused by two years of confusion and robbery was soon in part repaired. Merchantmen heavily laden were constantly passing and repassing Saint George's Channel. The receipts of the custom houses on the eastern coast, from Cork to Londonderry, amounted in six months to sixty-seven thousand five hundred pounds, a sum such as would have been thought extraordinary even in the most prosperous times.‡

The Irish who remained within the English pale were, one and all, hostile to the English domination. They were therefore subjected to a rigorous system of police, the

* Story's Continuation.

† Story's Impartial History; London Gazette, Nov. 17. 1690.

‡ Story's Impartial History. The year 1684 had been considered as a time of remarkable prosperity, and the revenue from the Customs had been unusually large. But the receipt from all the ports of Ireland, during the whole year, was only a hundred and twenty-seven thousand pounds. See Clarendon's Memoirs.

natural though lamentable effect of extreme danger and extreme provocation. A Papist was not permitted to have a sword or a gun. He was not permitted to go more than three miles out of his parish except to the market town on the market day. Lest he should give information or assistance to his brethren who occupied the western half of the island, he was forbidden to live within ten miles of the frontier. Lest he should turn his house into a place of resort for malecontents, he was forbidden to sell liquor by retail. One proclamation announced that, if the property of any Protestant should be injured by marauders, his loss should be made good at the expense of his Popish neighbours. Another gave notice that, if any Papist who had not been at least three months domiciled in Dublin should be found there, he should be treated as a spy. Not more than five Papists were to assemble in the capital or its neighbourhood on any pretext. Without a protection from the government no member of the Church of Rome was safe; and the government would not grant a protection to any member of the Church of Rome who had a son in the Irish army.*

In spite of all precautions and severities, however, the Celt found many opportunities of taking a sly revenge. Houses and barns were frequently burned: soldiers were frequently murdered; and it was scarcely possible to obtain evidence against the malefactors, who had with them the sympathies of the whole population. On such occasions the government sometimes ventured on acts which seemed better suited to a Turkish than to an English administration. One of these acts became a favourite theme of Jacobite pamphleteers, and was the subject of a serious parliamentary enquiry at Westminster. Six musketeers were found butchered only a few miles from Dublin. The inhabitants of the village where the crime had been committed, men, women, and children, were driven like sheep into the Castle, where the Privy Council was sitting. The heart of one of the assassins, named Gafney, failed him. He consented to be a witness, was examined by the Board, acknowledged his guilt, and named some of his accomplices. He was then removed in custody: but a priest obtained access to him during a few minutes. What passed during those few minutes appeared when he was a second time brought before the Council. He

* Story's History and Continuation; London Gazettes of September 29. 1690 and Jan. 8. and Mar. 12. 169¾.

had the effrontery to deny that he had owned anything or accused anybody. His hearers, several of whom had taken down his confession in writing, were enraged at his impudence. The Lords Justices broke out; "You are a rogue: you are a villain: you shall be hanged: where is the Provost Marshal?" The Provost Marshal came. "Take that man," said Coningsby, pointing to Gafney; "take that man, and hang him." There was no gallows ready: but the carriage of a gun served the purpose; and the prisoner was instantly tied up, without a trial, without even a written order for the execution; and this though the courts of law were sitting at the distance of only a few hundred yards. The English House of Commons, some years later, after a long discussion, resolved, without a division, that the order for the execution of Gafney was arbitrary and illegal, but that Coningsby's fault was so much extenuated by the circumstances in which he was placed that it was not a proper subject for impeachment.[*]

It was not only by the implacable hostility of the Irish that the Saxon of the pale was at this time harassed. His allies caused him almost as much annoyance as his helots. The help of troops from abroad was indeed necessary to him: but it was dearly bought. Even William, in whom the whole civil and military authority was concentrated, had found it difficult to maintain discipline in an army collected from many lands, and composed in great part of mercenaries accustomed to live at free quarter. The powers which had been united in him were now divided and subdivided. The two Lords Justices considered the civil administration as their province, and left the army to the management of Ginkell, who was General in Chief. Ginkell kept excellent order among the auxiliaries from Holland, who were under his more immediate command. But his authority over the English and the Danes was less entire; and unfortunately their pay was, during part of the winter, in arrear. They indemnified themselves by excesses and exactions for the want of that which was their due; and it was hardly possible

---

[*] See the Lords' Journals of March 2. and 4. 169$\frac{2}{3}$, and the Commons' Journals of Dec. 16. 1693, and Jan. 29. 169$\frac{3}{4}$. The story, bad enough at best, was told by the personal and political enemies of the Lords Justices with additions which the House of Commons evidently considered as calumnious, and which I really believe to have been so. See the Gallienus Redivivus. The narrative which Colonel Robert Fitzgerald, a Privy Councillor and an eyewitness, delivered in writing to the House of Lords, under the sanction of an oath, seems to me perfectly trustworthy. It is strange that Story, though he mentions the murder of the soldiers, says nothing about Gafney.

to punish men with severity for not choosing to starve
with arms in their hands. At length in the spring large
supplies of money and stores arrived : arrears were paid up :
rations were plentiful; and a more rigid discipline was enforced. But too many traces of the bad habits which the
soldiers had contracted were discernible till the close of the
war.*

State of the part of Ireland which was subject to James.

In that part of Ireland, meanwhile, which still acknowledged James as King, there could hardly be said to be any
law, any property, or any government. The Roman Catholics
of Ulster and Leinster had fled westward by tens of thousands, driving before them a large part of the cattle which
had escaped the havoc of two terrible years. The influx of
food into the Celtic region, however, was far from keeping
pace with the influx of consumers. The necessaries of life
were scarce. Conveniences to which every plain farmer and
burgess in England was accustomed could hardly be procured
by nobles and generals. No coin was to be seen except
lumps of base metal which were called crowns and shillings.
Nominal prices were enormously high. A quart of ale cost
two and sixpence, a quart of brandy three pounds. The only
towns of any note on the western coast were Limerick and
Galway ; and the oppression which the shopkeepers of those
towns underwent was such that many of them stole away
with the remains of their stocks to the English territory,
where a Papist, though he had to endure much restraint and
much humiliation, was allowed to put his own price on his
goods, and received that price in silver. Those traders who
remained within the unhappy region were ruined. Every
warehouse that contained any valuable property was broken
open by ruffians who pretended that they were commissioned
to procure stores for the public service ; and the owner received in return for bales of cloth and hogsheads of sugar
some fragments of old kettles and saucepans which would
not in London or Paris have been taken by a beggar. As
soon as a merchant ship arrived in the bay of Galway or in
the Shannon, she was boarded by these robbers. The cargo
was carried away ; and the proprietor was forced to content
himself with such a quantity of cowhides, of wool, and of
tallow as the gang which had plundered him chose to give
him. The consequence was, that, while foreign commodities
were pouring fast into the harbours of Londonderry Carrick-

* Burnet, ii. 66.; Leslie's answer to King.

fergus, Dublin, Waterford, and Cork, every mariner avoided
Limerick and Galway as nests of pirates.*

The distinction between the Irish foot soldier and the Irish
Rapparee had never been very strongly marked. It now disappeared. Great part of the army was turned loose to live
by marauding. An incessant predatory war raged along the
line which separated the domain of William from that of
James. Every day companies of freebooters, sometimes
wrapped in twisted straw which served the purpose of armour,
stole into the English territory, burned, sacked, pillaged, and
hastened back to their own ground. To guard against these
incursions was not easy, for the peasantry of the plundered
country had a strong fellow feeling with the plunderers. To
empty the granary, to set fire to the dwelling, to drive away
the cows, of a heretic was regarded by every squalid inhabitant of a mud cabin as a good work. A troop engaged
in such a work might confidently expect to fall in, notwithstanding all the proclamations of the Lords Justices, with
some friend who would indicate the richest booty, the
shortest road, and the safest hidingplace. The English
complained that it was no easy matter to catch a Rapparee.
Sometimes, when he saw danger approaching, he lay down in
the long grass of the bog, and then it was as difficult to find
him as to find a hare sitting. Sometimes he sprang into a
stream, and lay there, like an otter, with only his mouth and
nostrils above the water. Nay, a whole gang of banditti would,
in the twinkling of an eye, transform itself into a crowd of
harmless labourers. Every man took his gun to pieces, hid
the lock in his clothes, stuck a cork in the muzzle, stopped
the touch hole with a quill, and threw the weapon into the
next pond. Nothing was to be seen but a train of poor
rustics, who had not so much as a cudgel among them, and
whose humble look and crouching walk seemed to show that
their spirit was thoroughly broken to slavery. When the
peril was over, when the signal was given, every man flew to
the place where he had hid his arms, and soon the robbers
were in full march towards some Protestant mansion. One
band penetrated to Clonmel, another to the vicinity of Mary-
borough : a third made its den in a woody islet of firm
ground, surrounded by the vast bog of Allen, harried the

---

* Macariæ Excidium; Fumeron to
Louvois, $\frac{\text{Jan. 31.}}{\text{Feb. 10.}}$ 1691. It is to be observed that Kelly, the author of the
Macariæ Excidium, and Fumeron, the
French intendant, are most unexcoption-
able witnesses. They were both at this
time within the walls of Limerick.
There is no reason to doubt the impartiality of the Frenchman ; and the Irishman was partial to his own countrymen.

county of Wicklow, and alarmed even the suburbs of Dublin. Such expeditions indeed were not always successful. Sometimes the plunderers fell in with parties of militia, or with detachments from the English garrisons, in situations in which disguise, flight, and resistance were alike impossible. When this happened, every kerne who was taken was hanged, without any ceremony, on the nearest tree.*

Dissensions among the Irish at Limerick.

At the headquarters of the Irish army there was, during the winter, no authority capable of exacting obedience even within a circle of a mile. Tyrconnel was absent at the Court of France. He had left the supreme government in the hands of a Council of Regency composed of twelve persons. The nominal command of the army he had confided to Berwick; but Berwick, though, as was afterwards proved, a man of no common courage and capacity, was young and inexperienced. His powers were unsuspected by the world and by himself†: and he submitted without reluctance to the tutelage of a Council of War nominated by the Lord Lieutenant. Neither the Council of Regency nor the Council of War was popular at Limerick. The Irish complained that men who were not Irish had been entrusted with a large share in the administration. The cry was loudest against an officer named Thomas Maxwell. For it was certain that he was a Scotchman: it was doubtful whether he was a Roman Catholic; and he had not concealed the dislike which he felt for that Celtic Parliament which had repealed the Act of Settlement and passed the Act of Attainder.‡ The discontent, fomented by the arts of intriguers, among whom the cunning and unprincipled Henry Luttrell seems to have been the most active, soon broke forth into open rebellion. A great meeting was held. Many officers of the army, some peers, some lawyers of high note, and some prelates of the Roman Catholic Church were present. It was resolved that the government set up by the Lord Lieutenant was unknown to the constitution. Ireland, it was said, could be legally governed, in the absence of the King, only by a Lord Lieutenant, by a Lord Deputy, or by Lords Justices. The King was absent. The Lord Lieutenant was absent. There was no Lord

* Story's Impartial History and Continuation, and the London Gazettes of December, January, February, and March 169⁰⁄₁.

† It is remarkable that Avaux, though a very shrewd judge of men, greatly underrated Berwick. In a letter to Louvois dated Oct. ¹⁵⁄₂₅. 1689, Avaux says:

"Je ne puis m'empescher de vous dire qu'il est brave de sa persone, à ce que l'on dit, mais que c'est un aussy mechant officier qu'il y en ayt, et qu'il n'a pas le sens commun."

‡ Leslie's answer to King; Macariæ Excidium.

Deputy. There were no Lords Justices. The edict by which Tyrconnel had delegated his authority to a junto composed of his creatures was a mere nullity. The nation was therefore left without any legitimate chief, and might, without violating the allegiance due to the Crown, make temporary provision for its own safety. A deputation was sent to inform Berwick that he had assumed a power to which he had no right, but that nevertheless the army and people of Ireland would willingly acknowledge him as their head if he would consent to govern by the advice of a council truly Irish. Berwick indignantly expressed his wonder that military men should presume to meet and deliberate without the permission of their general. The deputies answered that there was no general, and that, if His Grace did not choose to undertake the administration on the terms proposed, another leader would easily be found. Berwick very reluctantly yielded, and continued to be a puppet in a new set of hands.*

Those who had effected this revolution thought it prudent to send a deputation to France for the purpose of vindicating their proceedings. Of this deputation the Roman Catholic Bishop of Cork and the two Luttrells were members. In the ship which conveyed them from Limerick to Brest they found a fellow passenger whose presence was by no means agreeable to them, their enemy, Maxwell. They suspected, and not without reason, that he was going, like them, to Saint Germains, but on a very different errand. The truth was that Berwick had sent Maxwell to watch their motions and to traverse their designs. Henry Luttrell, the least scrupulous of men, proposed to settle the matter at once by tossing the Scotchman into the sea. But the Bishop, who was a man of conscience, and Simon Luttrell, who was a man of honour, objected to this expedient.†

Meanwhile at Limerick the supreme power was in abeyance. Berwick, finding that he had no real authority, altogether neglected business, and gave himself up to such pleasures as that dreary place of banishment afforded. There was among the Irish chiefs no man of sufficient weight and ability to control the rest. Sarsfield for a time took the lead. But Sarsfield, though eminently brave and active in the field, was little skilled in the administration of war, and still less skilled in civil business. Those who were most desirous to

* Macariæ Excidium.
† Macariæ Excidium; Life of James, ii. 422.; Memoirs of Berwick.

support his authority were forced to own that his nature was too unsuspicious and indulgent for a post in which it was hardly possible to be too distrustful or too severe. He believed whatever was told him. He signed whatever was set before him. The commissaries, encouraged by his lenity, robbed and embezzled more shamelessly than ever. They sallied forth daily, guarded by pikes and firelocks, to seize, nominally for the public service, but really for themselves, wool, linen, leather, tallow, domestic utensils, instruments of husbandry, searched every pantry, every wardrobe, every cellar, and even laid sacrilegious hands on the property of priests and prelates.*

Return of Tyrconnel to Ireland.

Early in the spring the government, if it is to be so called, of which Berwick was the ostensible head, was dissolved by the return of Tyrconnel. The Luttrells had, in the name of their countrymen, implored James not to subject so loyal a people to so odious and incapable a viceroy. Tyrconnel, they said, was old: he was infirm: he needed much sleep: he knew nothing of war: he was dilatory: he was partial: he was rapacious: he was distrusted and hated by the whole nation. The Irish, deserted by him, had made a gallant stand, and had compelled the victorious army of the Prince of Orange to retreat. They hoped soon to take the field again, thirty thousand strong; and they adjured their King to send them some captain worthy to command such a force. Tyrconnel and Maxwell, on the other hand, represented the delegates as mutineers, demagogues, traitors, and pressed James to send Henry Luttrell to keep Mountjoy company in the Bastille. James, bewildered by these criminations and recriminations, hesitated long, and at last, with characteristic wisdom, relieved himself from trouble by giving all the quarrellers fair words, and by sending them all back to have their fight out in Ireland. Berwick was at the same time recalled to France.†

Tyrconnel was received at Limerick, even by his enemies, with decent respect. Much as they hated him, they could not question the validity of his commission; and, though they still maintained that they had been perfectly justified in annulling, during his absence, the unconstitutional arrangements which he had made, they acknowledged that, when he was present, he was their lawful governor. He was not altogether unprovided with the means of conciliating them. He brought many gracious messages and promises, a patent

* Macariæ Excidium.
† Life of James, ii. 422, 423.; Mémoires de Berwick.

of peerage for Sarsfield, some money which was not of brass, and some clothing, which was even more acceptable than money. The new garments were not indeed very fine. But even the generals had long been out at elbows; and there were few of the common men whose habiliments would have been thought sufficient to dress a scarecrow in a more prosperous country. Now, at length, for the first time in many months, every private soldier could boast of a pair of breeches and a pair of brogues. The Lord Lieutenant had also been authorised to announce that he should soon be followed by several ships, laden with provisions and military stores. This announcement was most welcome to the troops, who had long been without bread, and who had nothing stronger than water to drink.*

During some weeks the supplies were impatiently expected. At last, Tyrconnel was forced to shut himself up: for, whenever he appeared in public, the soldiers ran after him clamouring for food. Even the beef and mutton, which, half raw, half burned, without vegetables, without salt, had hitherto supported the army, had become scarce; and the common men were on rations of horseflesh when the promised sails were seen in the mouth of the Shannon.†

A distinguished French general, named Saint Ruth, was on board with his staff. He brought a commission which appointed him commander in chief of the Irish army. The commission did not expressly declare that he was to be independent of the viceregal authority: but he had been assured by James that Tyrconnel should have secret instructions not to intermeddle in the conduct of the war. Saint Ruth was assisted by another general officer named D'Usson. The French ships brought some arms, some ammunition, and a plentiful supply of corn and flour. The spirits of the Irish rose; and the Te Deum was chaunted with fervent devotion in the cathedral of Limerick.‡

Tyrconnel had made no preparations for the approaching campaign. But Saint Ruth, as soon as he had landed, exerted himself strenuously to redeem the time which had been lost. He was a man of courage, activity, and resolution, but of a harsh and imperious nature. In his own country he was celebrated as the most merciless persecutor that had ever dragooned the Huguenots to mass. It was asserted by English

Marginal note: Arrival of a French fleet at Limerick: Saint Ruth.

* Life of James, ii. 433. 451.; Story's Continuation.
† Life of James, ii. 438.; Light to the Blind; Fumeron to Louvois, $\frac{\text{April 22.}}{\text{May 2.}}$ 1691.
‡ Macariæ Excidium; Mémoires de Berwick; Life of James, ii. 451, 452.

Whigs that he was known in France by the nickname of the
Hangman; that, at Rome, the very cardinals had shown their
abhorrence of his cruelty; and that even Queen Christina,
who had little right to be squeamish about bloodshed, had
turned away from him with loathing.   He had recently held a
command in Savoy.   The Irish regiments in the French service had formed part of his army, and had behaved extremely
well.   It was therefore supposed that he had a peculiar talent
for managing Irish troops.   But there was a wide difference
between the well clad, well armed, and well drilled Irish, with
whom he was familiar, and the ragged marauders whom he
found swarming in the alleys of Limerick.   Accustomed to the
splendour and to the discipline of French camps and garrisons,
he was disgusted by finding that, in the country to which he
had been sent, a regiment of infantry meant a mob of people
as naked, as dirty, and as disorderly as the beggars, whom he
had been accustomed to see on the Continent besieging the
door of a monastery or pursuing a diligence up hill.   With ill
concealed contempt, however, he addressed himself vigorously
to the task of disciplining these strange soldiers, and was day
and night in the saddle, galloping from post to post, from
Limerick to Athlone, from Athlone to the northern extremity
of Loughrea, and from Loughrea back to Limerick.*

The Eng-
lish take
the field.
It was indeed necessary that he should bestir himself: for,
a few days after his arrival, he learned that, on the other side
of the Pale, all was ready for action.   The greater part of the
English force was collected, before the close of May, in the
neighbourhood of Mullingar.   Ginkell commanded in chief.
He had under him the two best officers, after Marlborough,
of whom our island could then boast, Talmash and Mackay.
The Marquess of Ruvigny, the hereditary chief of the refugees,
and elder brother of that brave Caillemot who had fallen at
the Boyne, had joined the army with the rank of major general.   The Lord Justice Coningsby, though not by profession
a soldier, came down from Dublin, to animate the zeal of the
troops.   The appearance of the camp showed that the money
voted by the English Parliament had not been spared.   The
uniforms were new: the ranks were one blaze of scarlet; and
the train of artillery was such as had never before been
seen in Ireland.†

* Macariæ Excidium; Burnet, ii. 78;
Dangeau; The Mercurius Reformatus,
June 5. 1691.
      † An exact journal of the victorious

progress of Their Majesties' forces under
the command of General Ginckle this
summer in Ireland, 1691; Story's Continuation; Mackay's Memoirs.

On the sixth of June Ginkell moved his head quarters from Mullingar. On the seventh he reached Ballymore. At Ballymore, on a peninsula almost surrounded by something between a swamp and a lake, stood an ancient fortress, which had recently been fortified under Sarsfield's direction, and which was defended by above a thousand men. The English guns were instantly planted. In a few hours the besiegers had the satisfaction of seeing the besieged running like rabbits from one shelter to another. The governor, who had at first held high language, begged piteously for quarter, and obtained it. The whole garrison was marched off to Dublin. Only eight of the conquerors had fallen.*

Fall of Ballymore.

Ginkell passed some days in reconstructing the defences of Ballymore. This work had scarcely been performed when he was joined by the Danish auxiliaries under the command of the Duke of Wurtemberg. The whole army then moved westward, and, on the nineteenth of June, appeared before the walls of Athlone.†

Athlone was perhaps, in a military point of view, the most important place in the island. Rosen, who understood war well, had always maintained that it was there that the Irishry would, with most advantage, make a stand against the Englishry.‡ The town, which was surrounded by ramparts of earth, lay partly in Leinster and partly in Connaught. The English quarter, which was in Leinster, had once consisted of new and handsome houses, but had been burnt by the Irish some months before, and now lay in heaps of ruin. The Celtic quarter, which was in Connaught, was old and meanly built.§ The Shannon, which is the boundary of the two provinces, rushed through Athlone in a deep and rapid stream, and turned two large mills which rose on the arches of a stone bridge. Above the bridge, on the Connaught side, a castle, built, it was said, by King John, towered to the height of seventy feet, and extended two hundred feet along

Siege and fall of Athlone.

---

* London Gazette, June 18. 22. 1691; Story's Continuation ; Life of James, ii. 452. The author of the Life accuses the Governor of treachery or cowardice.

† London Gazette, June 22. 25., July 2. 1691 ; Story's Continuation ; Exact Journal.

‡ Life of James, ii. 373. 376, 377.

§ Macariæ Excidium. I may observe that this is one of the many passages which lead me to believe the Latin text to be the original. The Latin is, " Oppidum ad Salaminium amnis latus recenti-

bus ac sumptuosioribus ædificiis attollebatur ; antiquius et ipsa vetustate incultius quod in Paphiis finibus exstructum erat." The English version is, " The town on Salaminia side was better built than that in Paphia." Surely there is in the Latin the particularity which we might expect from a person who had known Athlone before the war. The English version is contemptibly bad. I need hardly say that the Paphian side is Connaught, and the Salaminian side Leinster.

the river. Fifty or sixty yards below the bridge was a narrow ford.*

During the night of the nineteenth the English placed their cannon. On the morning of the twentieth the firing began. At five in the afternoon an assault was made. A brave French refugee with a grenade in his hand was the first to climb the breach, and fell, cheering his countrymen to the onset with his latest breath. Such were the gallant spirits which the bigotry of Lewis had sent to recruit, in the time of his utmost need, the armies of his deadliest enemies. The example was not lost. The grenades fell thick. The assailants mounted by hundreds. The Irish gave way and ran towards the bridge. There the press was so great that some of the fugitives were crushed to death in the narrow passage, and others were forced over the parapets into the waters which roared among the mill wheels below. In a few hours Ginkell had made himself master of the English quarter of Athlone; and this success had cost him only twenty men killed and forty wounded.†

But his work was only begun. Between him and the Irish town the Shannon ran fiercely. The bridge was so narrow that a few resolute men might keep it against an army. The mills which stood on it were strongly guarded; and it was commanded by the guns of the castle. That part of the Connaught shore where the river was fordable was defended by works, which the Lord Lieutenant had, in spite of the murmurs of a powerful party, forced Saint Ruth to entrust to the care of Maxwell. Maxwell had come back from France a more unpopular man than he had been when he went thither. It was rumoured that he had, at Versailles, spoken opprobriously of the Irish nation; and he had, on this account, been, only a few days before, publicly affronted by Sarsfield.‡ On

---

* I have consulted several contemporary maps of Athlone. One will be found in Story's Continuation.

† Diary of the siege of Athlone, by an Engineer of the Army, a Witness of the Action, licensed July 11. 1691; Story's Continuation; London Gazette, July 2. 1691; Fumeron to Louvois, June 28. July 8. 1691. The account of this attack in the Life of James, ii. 453., is an absurd romance. It does not appear to have been taken from the King's original Memoirs, or to have been revised by his son.

‡ Macariæ Excidium. Here again I think that I see clear proof that the English version of this curious work is only a bad translation from the Latin. The English merely says: "Lysander," —Sarsfield,—" accused him, a few days before, in the general's presence," without intimating what the accusation was. The Latin original runs thus: "Acriter Lysander, paucos ante dies, coram præfecto copiarum illi exprobraverat nescio quid, quod in aula Syriaca in Cypriorum opprobrium effutivisse dicebatur." The English translator has by omitting the most important words, and by using the aorist instead of the preterpluperfect tense, made the whole passage unmeaning.

the twenty-first of June the English were busied in flinging up batteries along the Leinster bank. On the twenty-second, soon after dawn, the cannonade began. The firing continued all that day and all the following night. When morning broke again, one whole side of the castle had been beaten down : the thatched lanes of the Celtic town lay in ashes ; and one of the mills had been burned with sixty soldiers who had been posted in it.*

Still however the Irish defended the bridge resolutely. During several days there was sharp fighting hand to hand in the strait passage. The assailants gained ground, but gained it inch by inch. The courage of the garrison was sustained by the hope of speedy succour. Saint Ruth had at length completed his preparations ; and the tidings that Athlone was in danger had induced him to take the field in haste at the head of an army, superior in number, though inferior in more important elements of military strength, to the army of Ginkell. The French general seems to have thought that the bridge and the ford might easily be defended, till the autumnal rains, and the pestilence which ordinarily accompanied them, should compel the enemy to retire. He therefore contented himself with sending successive detachments to reinforce the garrison. The immediate conduct of the defence he entrusted to his second in command, D'Usson, and fixed his own headquarters two or three miles from the town. He expressed his astonishment that so experienced a commander as Ginkell should persist in a hopeless enterprise. " His master ought to hang him for trying to take Athlone ; and mine ought to hang me if I lose it." †

Saint Ruth, however, was by no means at ease. He had found, to his great mortification, that he had not the full authority which the promises made to him at Saint Germains had entitled him to expect. The Lord Lieutenant was in the camp. His bodily and mental infirmities had perceptibly increased within the last few weeks. The slow and uncertain step with which he, who had once been renowned for vigour and agility, now tottered from his easy chair to his couch, was no unapt type of the sluggish and wavering movement of that mind which had once pursued its objects with a vehemence restrained neither by fear nor by pity, neither by

---

* Story's Continuation ; Macariæ Excidium ; Daniel Macneal to Sir Arthur Rawdon, June 28. 1691, in the Rawdon Papers.

† London Gazette, July 6. 1691; Story's Continuation ; Macariæ Excidium ; Light to the Blind.

conscience nor by shame. Yet, with impaired strength, both physical and intellectual, the broken old man clung pertinaciously to power. If he had received private orders not to meddle with the conduct of the war, he disregarded them. He assumed all the authority of a sovereign, showed himself ostentatiously to the troops as their supreme chief, and affected to treat Saint Ruth as a lieutenant. Soon the interference of the Viceroy excited the vehement indignation of that powerful party in the army which had long hated him. Many officers signed an instrument by which they declared that they did not consider him as entitled to their obedience in the field. Some of them offered him gross personal insults. He was told to his face that, if he persisted in remaining where he was not wanted, the ropes of his pavilion should be cut. He, on the other hand, sent his emissaries to all the camp fires, and tried to make a party among the common soldiers against the French general.*

The only thing in which Tyrconnel and Saint Ruth agreed was in dreading and disliking Sarsfield. Not only was he popular with the great body of his countrymen; he was also surrounded by a knot of retainers whose devotion to him resembled the devotion of the Ismailite murderers to the Old Man of the Mountain. It was known that one of these fanatics, a colonel, had used language which, in the mouth of an officer so high in rank, might well cause uneasiness. "The King," this man had said, "is nothing to me. I obey Sarsfield. Let Sarsfield tell me to stab any man in the whole army; and I will do it." Sarsfield was, indeed, too honourable a gentleman to abuse his immense power over the minds of his worshippers. But the Viceroy and the Commander in Chief might not unnaturally be disturbed by the thought that Sarsfield's honour was their only guarantee against mutiny and assassination. The consequence was that, at the crisis of the fate of Ireland, the services of the first of Irish soldiers were not used, or were used with jealous caution, and that, if he ventured to offer a suggestion, it was received with a sneer or a frown.†

A great and unexpected disaster put an end to these disputes. On the thirtieth of June Ginkell called a council of war. Forage began to be scarce; and it was absolutely necessary that the besiegers should either force their way across the river or retreat. The difficulty of effecting a

---

* Macariæ Excidium; Light to the Blind.   † Life of James, ii. 460.; Life of William, 1702.

passage over the shattered remains of the bridge seemed almost insuperable. It was proposed to try the ford. The Duke of Wurtemberg, Talmash, and Ruvigny gave their voices in favour of this plan; and Ginkell, with some misgivings, consented.*

It was determined that the attempt should be made that very afternoon. The Irish, fancying that the English were about to retreat, kept guard carelessly. Part of the garrison was idling, part dozing. D'Usson was at table. Saint Ruth was in his tent, writing a letter to his master filled with charges against Tyrconnel. Meanwhile, fifteen hundred grenadiers, each wearing in his hat a green bough, were mustered on the Leinster bank of the Shannon. Many of them doubtless remembered that on that day year they had, at the command of King William, put green boughs in their hats on the banks of the Boyne. Guineas had been liberally scattered among these picked men: but their alacrity was such as gold cannot purchase. Six battalions were in readiness to support the attack. Mackay commanded. He did not approve of the plan: but he executed it as zealously and energetically as if he had himself been the author of it. The Duke of Wurtemberg, Talmash, and several other gallant officers, to whom no part in the enterprise had been assigned, insisted on serving that day as private volunteers; and their appearance in the ranks excited the fiercest enthusiasm among the soldiers.

It was six o'clock. A peal from the steeple of the church gave the signal. Prince George of Hesse Darmstadt, and a brave soldier named Hamilton, whose services were afterwards rewarded with the title of Lord Boyne, descended first into the Shannon. Then the grenadiers lifted the Duke of Wurtemberg on their shoulders, and, with a great shout, plunged twenty abreast up to their cravats in water. The stream ran deep and strong: but in a few minutes the head of the column reached dry land. Talmash was the fifth man that set foot on the Connaught shore. The Irish, taken unprepared, fired one confused volley and fled, leaving their commander, Maxwell, a prisoner. The conquerors clambered up the bank over the remains of walls shattered by a cannonade of ten days. Mackay heard his men cursing and swearing as they stumbled among the rubbish. "My lads," cried the stout

* Story's Continuation; Mackay's Memoirs; Exact Journal; Diary of the Siege of Athlone.

old Puritan in the midst of the uproar, "you are brave fellows : but do not swear. We have more reason to thank God for the goodness which He has shown us this day than to take His name in vain." The victory was complete. Planks were placed on the broken arches of the bridge, and pontoons laid on the river without any opposition on the part of the terrified garrison. With the loss of twelve men killed and about thirty wounded the English had, in a few minutes, forced their way into Connaught.*

Retreat of the Irish army.

At the first alarm D'Usson hastened towards the river ; but he was met, swept away, trampled down, and almost killed by the torrent of fugitives. He was carried to the camp in such a state that it was necessary to bleed him. "Taken !" cried Saint Ruth, in dismay. "It cannot be. A town taken, and I close by with an army to relieve it !" Cruelly mortified, he struck his tents under cover of the night, and retreated in the direction of Galway. At dawn the English saw far off, from the top of King John's ruined castle the Irish army moving through the dreary region which separates the Shannon from the Suck. Before noon the rearguard had disappeared.†

Even before the loss of Athlone the Celtic camp had been distracted by factions. It may easily be supposed, therefore, that, after so great a disaster, nothing was to be heard but crimination and recrimination. The enemies of the Lord Lieutenant were more clamorous than ever. He and his creatures had brought the kingdom to the verge of perdition. He would meddle with what he did not understand. He would overrule the plans of men who were real soldiers. He would entrust the most important of all posts to his tool, his spy, the wretched Maxwell, not a born Irishman, not a sincere Catholic, at best a blunderer, and too probably a traitor. Maxwell, it was affirmed, had left his men unprovided with ammunition. When they had applied to him for powder and ball, he had asked whether they wanted to shoot larks. Just before the attack he had told them to go to their supper and to take their rest, for that nothing more would be done that day. When he had delivered himself up a prisoner, he had uttered some words which seemed to indicate a previous understanding with the conquerors. The Lord Lieutenant's

---

* Story's Continuation ; Macariæ Excidium; Burnet, ii. 78, 79.; London Gazette, July 6. 13. 1689 ; Fumeron to Louvois, $\frac{\text{June 30.}}{\text{July 10.}}$ 1690 ; Diary of the

siege of Athlone ; Exact Account.

† Story's Continuation ; Life of James, ii. 455.; Fumeron to Louvois, $\frac{\text{June 30.}}{\text{July 10.}}$ 1691 ; London Gazette, July 13.

few friends told a very different story. According to them, Tyrconnel and Maxwell had suggested precautions which would have made a surprise impossible. The French General, impatient of all interference, had omitted to take those precautions. Maxwell had been rudely told that, if he was afraid, he had better resign his command. He had done his duty bravely. He had stood while his men had fled. He had consequently fallen into the hands of the enemy; and he was now, in his absence, slandered by those to whom his captivity was justly imputable.* On which side the truth lay it is not easy, at this distance of time, to pronounce. The cry against Tyrconnel was, at the moment, so loud, that he gave way and sullenly retired to Limerick. D'Usson, who had not yet recovered from the hurts inflicted by his own runaway troops, repaired to Galway.†

Saint Ruth, now left in undisputed possession of the supreme command, was bent on trying the chances of a battle. Most of the Irish officers, with Sarsfield at their head, were of a very different mind. It was, they said, not to be dissembled that, in discipline, the army of Ginkell was far superior to theirs. The wise course, therefore, evidently was to carry on the war in such a manner that the difference between the disciplined and the undisciplined soldier might be as small as possible. It was well known that raw recruits often played their part well in a foray, in a street fight, or in the defence of a rampart; but that, on a pitched field, they had little chance against veterans. "Let most of our foot be collected behind the walls of Limerick and Galway. Let the rest, together with our horse, get in the rear of the enemy, and cut off his supplies. If he advances into Connaught, let us overrun Leinster. If he sits down before Galway, which may well be defended, let us make a push for Dublin, which is altogether defenceless."‡ Saint Ruth might, perhaps, have thought this advice good, if his judgment had not been biassed by his passions. But he was smarting from the pain of a humiliating defeat. In sight of his tent, the English had passed a rapid river, and had stormed a strong town. He could not but feel that, though others might have been to

Saint Ruth determines to fight.

* The story, as told by the enemies of Tyrconnel, will be found in Macariæ Excidium, and in a letter written by Felix O'Neill to the Countess of Antrim on the 10th of July 1691. The letter was found on the corpse of Felix O'Neill after the battle of Aghrim. It is printed in the Rawdon Papers. The other story is told in Berwick's Memoirs and in the Light to the Blind.

† Macariæ Excidium; Life of James, ii. 456.; Light to the Blind.

‡ Macariæ Excidium.

blame, he was not himself blameless. He had, to say the least, taken things too easily. Lewis, accustomed to be served during many years by commanders who were not in the habit of leaving to chance anything which could be made secure by prudence, would hardly think it a sufficient excuse that his general had not expected the enemy to make so bold and sudden an attack. The Lord Lieutenant would, of course, represent what had passed in the most unfavourable manner; and whatever the Lord Lieutenant said James would echo. A sharp reprimand, a letter of recall, might be expected. To return to Versailles a culprit; to approach the great King in an agony of distress: to see him shrug his shoulders, knit his brow, and turn his back; to be sent, far from courts and camps, to languish at some dull country seat; this was too much to be borne; and yet this might well be apprehended. There was one escape; to fight, and to conquer or to perish.

In such a temper Saint Ruth pitched his camp about thirty miles from Athlone on the road to Galway, near the ruined castle of Aghrim, and determined to await the approach of the English army.

His whole deportment was changed. He had hitherto treated the Irish soldiers with contemptuous severity. But, now that he had resolved to stake life and fame on the valour of the despised race, he became another man. During the few days which remained to him, he exerted himself to win by indulgence and caresses the hearts of all who were under his command.* He, at the same time, administered to his troops moral stimulants of the most potent kind. He was a zealous Roman Catholic; and it is probable that the severity with which he had treated the Protestants of his own country ought to be partly ascribed to the hatred which he felt for their doctrines. He now tried to give to the war the character of a crusade. The clergy were the agents whom he employed to sustain the courage of his soldiers. The whole camp was in a ferment with religious excitement. In every regiment priests were praying, preaching, shriving, holding up the host and the cup. While the soldiers swore on the sacramental bread not to abandon their colours, the General addressed to the officers an appeal which might have moved the most languid and effeminate nature to heroic exertion. They were fighting, he said, for their religion, their liberty, and their honour. Unhappy events, too widely celebrated, had brought a reproach on the national character.

* Story's Continuation.

Irish soldiership was everywhere mentioned with a sneer. If they wished to retrieve the fame of their country, this was the time and this the place.*

The spot on which he had determined to bring the fate of Ireland to issue seems to have been chosen with great judgment. His army was drawn up on the slope of a hill, which was almost surrounded by red bog. In front, near the edge of the morass, were some fences out of which a breastwork was without difficulty constructed.

On the eleventh of July, Ginkell, having repaired the fortifications of Athlone, and left a garrison there, fixed his headquarters at Ballinasloe, about four miles from Aghrim, and rode forward to take a view of the Irish position. On his return he gave orders that ammunition should be served out, that every musket and bayonet should be got ready for action, and that early on the morrow every man should be under arms without beat of drum. Two regiments were to remain in charge of the camp : the rest, unincumbered by baggage, were to march against the enemy.

Soon after six, the next morning, the English were on the way to Aghrim. But some delay was occasioned by a thick fog which hung till noon over the moist valley of the Suck : a further delay was caused by the necessity of dislodging the Irish from some outposts ; and the afternoon was far advanced when the two armies at length confronted each other with nothing but the bog and the breastwork between them. The English and their allies were under twenty thousand ; the Irish above twenty-five thousand. *Battle of Aghrim.*

Ginkell held a short consultation with his principal officers. Should he attack instantly, or wait till the next morning ? Mackay was for attacking instantly ; and his opinion prevailed. At five the battle began. The English foot, in such order as they could keep on treacherous and uneven ground, made their way, sinking deep in mud at every step, to the Irish works. But those works were defended with a resolution such as extorted some words of ungracious eulogy even from men who entertained the strongest prejudices against the Celtic race.† Again and again the assailants were driven back. Again and again they returned to the struggle. Once they were broken, and chased across the

---

* Burnet, ii. 79.; Story's Continuation.

† "They maintained their ground much longer than they had been accustomed to do," says Burnet. "They behaved themselves like men of another nation," says Story. "The Irish were never known to fight with more resolution," says the London Gazette.

morass: but Talmash rallied them, and forced the pursuers
to retire. The fight had lasted two hours: the evening was
closing in; and still the advantage was on the side of the
Irish. Ginkell began to meditate a retreat. The hopes of
Saint Ruth rose high. "The day is ours, my boys," he
cried, waving his hat in the air. "We will drive them
before us to the walls of Dublin." But fortune was already
on the turn. Mackay and Ruvigny, with the English and
Huguenot cavalry, had succeeded in passing the bog at a
place where two horsemen could scarcely ride abreast. Saint
Ruth at first laughed when he saw the Blues, in single file,
struggling through the morass under a fire which every
moment laid some gallant hat and feather on the earth.
"What do they mean?" he asked; and then he swore
that it was pity to see such fine fellows rushing to certain
destruction. "Let them cross, however;" he said. "The
more they are, the more we shall kill." But soon he saw
them laying hurdles on the quagmire. A broader and safer
path was formed: squadron after squadron reached firm
ground: the flank of the Irish army was speedily turned.
The French general was hastening to the rescue when a
cannon ball carried off his head. Those who were about
him thought that it would be dangerous to make his fate
known. His corpse was wrapped in a cloak, carried from
the field, and laid, with all secresy, in the sacred ground
among the ruins of the ancient monastery of Loughrea.
Till the fight was over neither army was aware that he was
no more. The crisis of the battle had arrived; and there
was none to give direction. Sarsfield was in command of
the reserve. But he had been strictly enjoined by Saint
Ruth not to stir without orders; and no orders came.
Mackay and Ruvigny with their horse charged the Irish in
flank. Talmash and his foot returned to the attack in front
with dogged determination. The breastwork was carried.
The Irish, still fighting, retreated from enclosure to enclosure. But, as enclosure after enclosure was forced, their
efforts became fainter and fainter. At length they broke
and fled. Then followed a horrible carnage. The conquerors
were in a savage mood. For a report had been spread among
them that, during the early part of the battle, some English
captives who had been admitted to quarter had been put to
the sword. Only four hundred prisoners were taken. The
number of the slain was, in proportion to the number engaged,
greater than in any other battle of that age. But for the

:oming on of a moonless night, made darker by a misty rain, scarcely a man would have escaped. The obscurity enabled Sarsfield, with a few squadrons which still remained unbroken, to cover the retreat. Of the conquerors six hundred were killed, and about a thousand wounded.

The English slept that night on the ground which had been so desperately contested. On the following day they buried their companions in arms, and then marched westward. The vanquished were left unburied, a strange and ghastly spectacle. Four thousand Irish corpses were counted on the field of battle. A hundred and fifty lay in one small enclosure, a hundred and twenty in another. But the slaughter had not been confined to the field of battle. One who was there tells us that, from the top of the hill on which the Celtic camp had been pitched, he saw the country, to the distance of near four miles, white with the naked bodies of the slain. The plain looked, he said, like an immense pasture covered by flocks of sheep. As usual, different estimates were formed even by eyewitnesses. But it seems probable that the number of the Irish who fell was not less than seven thousand. Soon a multitude of dogs came to feast on the carnage. These beasts became so fierce, and acquired such a taste for human flesh, that it was long dangerous for men to travel that road otherwise than in companies.*

The beaten army had now lost all the appearance of an army, and resembled a rabble crowding home from a fair after a faction fight. One great stream of fugitives ran towards Galway, another towards Limerick. The roads to both cities were covered with weapons which had been flung away. Ginkell offered sixpence for every musket. In a short time so many waggon loads were collected that he reduced the price to twopence; and still great numbers of muskets came in.†

The conquerors marched first against Galway. D'Usson **Fall of** was there, and had under him seven regiments, thinned by **Galway.** the slaughter of Aghrim and utterly disorganised and disheartened. The last hope of the garrison and of the Roman

---

* Story's Continuation; London Gazette, July 20. 23. 1691; Mémoires de Berwick; Life of James, ii. 456; Burnet, ii. 79; Macariæ Excidium; Light to the Blind; Letter from the English camp to Sir Arthur Rawdon, in the Rawdon Papers; History of William the Third, 1702.

The narratives to which I have referred differ very widely from each other. Nor can the difference be ascribed solely or chiefly to partiality. For no two narratives differ more widely than that which will be found in the Life of James, and that which will be found in the memoirs of his son.

In consequence, I suppose, of the death of Saint Ruth, and of the absence of D'Usson, there is at the French War Office no despatch containing a detailed account of the battle.

† Story's Continuation.

Catholic inhabitants was that Baldearg O'Donnel, the promised deliverer of their race, would come to the rescue. But Baldearg O'Donnel was not duped by the superstitious veneration of which he was the object. While there had been any doubt about the issue of the conflict between the Englishry and the Irishry, he had stood aloof. On the day of the battle he had remained at a safe distance with his tumultuary army ; and, as soon as he had learned that his countrymen had been put to rout, he had fled, plundering and burning all the way, to the mountains of Mayo. Thence he sent to Ginkell offers of submission and service. Ginkell gladly seized the opportunity of breaking up a formidable band of marauders, and of turning to good account the influence which the name of a Celtic dynasty still exercised over the Celtic race. The negotiation, however, was not without difficulties. The wandering adventurer at first demanded nothing less than an earldom. After some haggling he consented to sell the love of a whole people, and his pretensions to regal dignity, for a pension of five hundred pounds a year. Yet the spell which bound his followers to him was not altogether broken. Some enthusiasts from Ulster were willing to fight under the O'Donnel against their own language and their own religion. With a small body of these devoted adherents, he joined a division of the English army, and on several occasions did useful service to William.*

When it was known that no succour was to be expected from the hero whose advent had been foretold by so many seers, the Irish who were shut up in Galway lost all heart. D'Usson had returned a stout answer to the first summons of the besiegers : but he soon saw that resistance was impossible, and made haste to capitulate. The garrison was suffered to retire to Limerick with the honours of war. A full amnesty for past offences was granted to the citizens ; and it was stipulated that, within the walls, the Roman Catholic priests should be allowed to perform in private the rites of their religion. On these terms the gates were thrown open. Ginkell was received with profound respect by the Mayor and Aldermen, and was complimented in a set speech by the Recorder. D'Usson, with about two thousand three hundred men, marched unmolested to Limerick.†

At Limerick, the last asylum of the vanquished race, the

---

* Story's Continuation ; Macariæ Excidium ; Life of James, ii. 464. ; London Gazette, July 30., Aug. 17. 1691 ; Light to the Blind.

† Story's Continuation ; Macariæ Excidium ; Life of James, ii. 459. ; London Gazette, July 30., Aug. 3. 1691.

authority of Tyrconnel was supreme. There was now no general who could pretend that his commission made him independent of the Lord Lieutenant; nor was the Lord Lieutenant now so unpopular as he had been for a fortnight earlier. Since the battle there had been a reflux of public feeling. No part of that great disaster could be imputed to the Viceroy. His opinion indeed had been against trying the chances of a pitched field, and he could with some plausibility assert that the neglect of his counsels had caused the ruin of Ireland.*

He made some preparations for defending Limerick, repaired the fortifications, and sent out parties to bring in provisions. The country, many miles round, was swept bare by these detachments, and a considerable quantity of cattle and fodder was collected within the walls. There was also a large stock of biscuit imported from France. The infantry assembled at Limerick were about fifteen thousand men. The Irish horse and dragoons, three or four thousand in number, were encamped on the Clare side of the Shannon. The communication between their camp and the city was maintained by means of a bridge called the Thomond Bridge, which was protected by a fort. These means of defence were not contemptible. But the fall of Athlone and the slaughter of Aghrim had broken the spirit of the army. A small party, at the head of which were Sarsfield and a brave Scotch officer named Wauchop, cherished a hope that the triumphant progress of Ginkell might be stopped by those walls from which William had, in the preceding year, been forced to retreat. But many of the Irish chiefs loudly declared that it was time to think of capitulating. Henry Luttrell, always fond of dark and crooked politics, opened a secret negotiation with the English. One of his letters was intercepted; and he was put under arrest: but many who blamed his perfidy agreed with him in thinking that it was idle to prolong the contest. Tyrconnel himself was convinced that all was lost. His only hope was that he might be able to prolong the struggle till he could receive from Saint Germains permission to treat. He wrote to request that permission, and prevailed, with some difficulty, on his desponding countrymen to bind themselves by an oath not to capitulate till an answer from James should arrive.†

A few days after the oath had been administered Tyrconnel

* He held this language in a letter to Lewis XIV., dated the $\frac{5}{15}$th of August. This letter, written in a hand which it is not easy to decipher, is in the French War Office. Macariæ Excidium; Light to the Blind.

† Macariæ Excidium; Life of James, ii. 461, 462.

was no more. On the eleventh of August he dined with
D'Usson. The party was gay. The Lord Lieutenant seemed

Death of Tyrconnel. to have thrown off the load which had bowed down his body
and mind: he drank: he jested: he was again the Dick
Talbot who had diced and revelled with Grammont. Soon
after he had risen from table, an apoplectic stroke deprived
him of speech and sensation. On the fourteenth he breathed
his last. The wasted remains of that form which had once
been a model for statuaries were laid under the pavement of
the Cathedral: but no inscription, no tradition, preserves the
memory of the spot.[*]

As soon as the Lord Lieutenant had expired, Plowden,
who had superintended the Irish finances while there were
any Irish finances to superintend, produced a commission
under the great seal of James. This commission appointed
Plowden himself, Fitton, and Nagle, Lords Justices in the
event of Tyrconnel's death. There was much murmuring
when the names were made known. For both Plowden and
Fitton were Saxons. The commission, however, proved to
be a mere nullity. For it was accompanied by instructions
which forbade the Lords Justices to interfere in the conduct
of the war; and, within the narrow space to which the
dominions of James were now reduced, war was the only
business. The government was, therefore, really in the hands
of D'Usson and Sarsfield.[†]

Second siege of Limerick. On the day on which Tyrconnel died, the advanced guard
of the English army came within sight of Limerick. Gin-
kell encamped on the same ground which William had occupied twelve months before. The batteries, on which were
planted guns and bombs, very different from those which
William had been forced to use, played day and night; and
soon roofs were blazing and walls crashing in every part of
the city. Whole streets were reduced to ashes. Meanwhile
several English ships of war came up the Shannon and
anchored about a mile below the city.[‡]

Still the place held out: the garrison was, in numerical
strength, little inferior to the besieging army; and it seemed
not impossible that the defence might be prolonged till the
equinoctial rains should a second time compel the English to

---

[*] Macariæ Excidium; Life of James,
ii. 459. 462.; London Gazette, Aug. 31.
1691 ; Light to the Blind; D'Usson and
Tessé to Barbesieux, Aug. $\frac{13}{23}$.

[†] Story's Continuation ; D'Usson and
Tessé to Barbesieux, Aug. $\frac{15}{25}$. 1691. An

unpublished letter from Nagle to Lord
Merion of Aug. 15. This letter is
quoted by Mr. O'Callaghan in a note on
the Macariæ Excidium.

[‡] Macariæ Excidium; Story's Continuation.

retire. Ginkell determined on striking a bold stroke. No
point in the whole circle of the fortifications was more
important, and no point seemed to be more secure, than the
Thomond Bridge, which joined the city to the camp of the
Irish horse on the Clare bank of the Shannon. The Dutch
General's plan was to separate the infantry within the ramparts from the cavalry without; and this plan he executed
with great skill, vigour, and success. He laid a bridge of
tin boats on the river, crossed it with a strong body of troops,
drove before him in confusion fifteen hundred dragoons who
made a faint show of resistance, and marched towards the
quarters of the Irish horse. The Irish horse sustained but
ill on this day the reputation which they had gained at the
Boyne. Indeed, that reputation had been purchased by the
almost entire destruction of the best regiments. Recruits
had been without much difficulty found. But the loss of
fifteen hundred excellent soldiers was not to be repaired.
The camp was abandoned without a blow. Some of the
cavalry fled into the city. The rest, driving before them as
many cattle as could be collected in that moment of panic,
retired to the hills. Much beef, brandy, and harness was
found in the magazines; and the marshy plain of the Shannon was covered with firelocks and grenades which the fugitives had thrown away.*

The conquerors returned in triumph to their camp. But
Ginkell was not content with the advantage which he had
gained. He was bent on cutting off all communication
between Limerick and the county of Clare. In a few days,
therefore, he again crossed the river at the head of several
regiments, and attacked the fort which protected the Thomond Bridge. In a short time the fort was stormed. The
soldiers who had garrisoned it fled in confusion to the city.
The Town Major, a French officer, who commanded at the
Thomond Gate, afraid that the pursuers would enter with
the fugitives, ordered that part of the bridge which was
nearest to the city to be drawn up. Many of the Irish went
headlong into the stream and perished there. Others cried
for quarter, and held up handkerchiefs in token of submission. But the conquerors were mad with rage: their cruelty
could not be immediately restrained: and no prisoners were

* Story's Continuation; London Gazette, Sept. 28. 1691; Life of James, ii.
463.; Diary of the Siege of Lymerick,
1692; Light to the Blind. In the account of the siege which is among the
archives of the French War Office, it
is said that the Irish cavalry behaved
worse than the infantry.

made till the heaps of corpses rose above the parapets. The garrison of the fort had consisted of about eight hundred men. Of these only a hundred and twenty escaped into Limerick.*

This disaster seemed likely to produce a general mutiny in the besieged city. The Irish clamoured for the blood of the Town Major who had ordered the bridge to be drawn up in the face of their flying countrymen His superiors were forced to promise that he should be brought before a court martial. Happily for him, he had received a mortal wound, in the act of closing the Thomond Gate, and was saved by a soldier's death from the fury of the multitude.†

The Irish desirous to capitulate. The cry for capitulation became so loud and importunate that the generals could not resist it. D'Usson informed his government that the fight at the bridge had so effectually cowed the spirit of the garrison that it was impossible to continue the struggle.‡ Some exception may perhaps be taken to the evidence of D'Usson: for undoubtedly he, like every other Frenchman who had held any command in the Irish army, was weary of his banishment, and impatient to see his country again. But it is certain that even Sarsfield had lost heart. Up to this time his voice had been for stubborn resistance. He was now not only willing, but impatient to treat.§ It seemed to him that the city was doomed. There was no hope of succour, domestic or foreign. In every part of Ireland the Saxons had set their feet on the necks of the natives. Sligo had fallen. Even those wild islands which intercept the huge waves of the Atlantic from the bay of Galway had acknowledged the authority of William. The men of Kerry, reputed the fiercest and most ungovernable part of the aboriginal population, had held out long, but had at length been routed, and chased to their woods and mountains.‖ A French fleet, if a French fleet were now to arrive

---

* Story's Continuation; Macariæ Excidium; R. Douglas to Sir A. Rawdon, Sept. 28. 1691, in the Rawdon Papers; London Gazette, Oct. 8.; Diary of the Siege of Lymerick; Light to the Blind; Account of the Siege of Limerick in the archives of the French War Office.

The account of this affair in the Life of James, ii. 464., deserves to be noticed merely for its preeminent absurdity. The writer tells us that seven hundred of the Irish held out some time against a much larger force, and warmly praises their heroism. He did not know, or did not choose to mention, one fact which is essential to the right understanding of the story; namely, that these seven hundred men were in a fort. That a garrison should defend a fort during a few hours against superior numbers is surely not strange. Forts are built because they can be defended by few against many.

† Account of the Siege of Limerick in the archives of the French War Office; Story's Continuation.

‡ D'Usson to Barbesieux, Oct. $\frac{4}{14}$. 1691.

§ Macariæ Excidium.

‖ Story's Continuation; Diary of the Siege of Limerick.

on the coast of Munster, would find the mouth of the Shannon guarded by English men of war. The stock of provisions within Limerick was already running low. If the siege were prolonged, the town would, in all human probability, be reduced either by force or by blockade. And, if Ginkell should enter through the breach, or should be implored by a multitude perishing with hunger to dictate his own terms, what could be expected but a tyranny more inexorably severe than that of Cromwell? Would it not then be wise to try what conditions could be obtained while the victors had still something to fear from the rage and despair of the vanquished; while the last Irish army could still make some show of resistance behind the walls of the last Irish fortress?

On the evening of the day which followed the fight at the Thomond Gate, the drums of Limerick beat a parley; and Wauchop, from one of the towers, hailed the besiegers, and requested Ruvigny to grant Sarsfield an interview. The brave Frenchman who was an exile on account of his attachment to one religion, and the brave Irishman who was about to become an exile on account of his attachment to another, met and conferred, doubtless with mutual sympathy and respect.* Ginkell, to whom Ruvigny reported what had passed, willingly consented to an armistice. For, constant as his success had been, it had not made him secure. The chances were greatly on his side. Yet it was possible that an attempt to storm the city might fail, as a similar attempt had failed twelve months before. If the siege should be turned into a blockade, it was probable that the pestilence which had been fatal to the army of Schomberg, which had compelled William to retreat, and which had all but prevailed even against the genius and energy of Marlborough, might soon avenge the carnage of Aghrim. The rains had lately been heavy. The whole plain might shortly be an immense pool of stagnant water. It might be necessary to move the troops to a healthier situation than the bank of the Shannon, and to provide for them a warmer shelter than that of tents. The enemy would be safe till the spring. In the spring a French army might land in Ireland: the natives might again rise in arms from Donegal to Kerry; and the war, which was now all but extinguished, might blaze forth fiercer than ever.

A negotiation was therefore opened with a sincere desire on both sides to put an end to the contest. The chiefs of the

Negotiations between the Irish chiefs and the besiegers.

---

* London Gazette, Oct. 8. 1691 ; Story's Continuation ; Diary of the Siege of Lymerick.

Irish army held several consultations at which some Roman
Catholic prelates and some eminent lawyers were invited to
assist. A preliminary question, which perplexed tender consciences, was submitted to the Bishops. The late Lord
Lieutenant had persuaded the officers of the garrison to swear
that they would not surrender Limerick till they should receive an answer to the letter in which their situation had
been explained to James. The Bishops thought that the oath
was no longer binding. It had been taken at a time when
the communications with France were open, and in the full
belief that the answer of James would arrive within three
weeks. More than twice that time had elapsed. Every
avenue leading to the city was strictly guarded by the enemy.
His Majesty's faithful subjects, by holding out till it had become impossible for him to signify his pleasure to them, had
acted up to the spirit of their promise.*

The next question was what terms should be demanded. A
paper, containing propositions which statesmen of our age will
think reasonable, but which to the most humane and liberal
English Protestants of the seventeenth century appeared extravagant, was sent to the camp of the besiegers. What was
asked was that all offences should be covered with oblivion,
that perfect freedom of worship should be allowed to the
native population, that every parish should have its Roman
Catholic priest, and that Irish Roman Catholics should be
capable of holding all offices, civil and military, and of enjoy-
ing all municipal privileges.†

Ginkell knew little of the laws and feelings of the English :
but he had about him persons who were competent to direct
him. They had a week before prevented him from breaking
a Rapparee on the wheel : and they now suggested an answer
to the propositions of the enemy. " I am a stranger here,"
said Ginkell : " I am ignorant of the constitution of these
kingdoms : but I am assured that what you ask is inconsistent
with that constitution ; and therefore I cannot with honour
consent." He immediately ordered a new battery to be
thrown up, and guns and mortars to be planted on it. But
his preparations were speedily interrupted by another message
from the city. The Irish begged that, since he could not
grant what they had demanded, he would tell them on what
terms he was willing to treat. He called his advisers round
him, and, after some consultation, sent back a paper containing the heads of a treaty, such as he had reason to believe

* Life of James, 464, 465.   † Story's Continuation.

that the government which he served would approve. What
he offered was indeed much less than what the Irish desired,
but was quite as much as, when they considered their situation and the temper of the English nation, they could expect.
They speedily notified their assent. It was agreed that there
should be a cessation of arms, not only by land, but in the
ports and bays of Munster, and that a fleet of French transports should be suffered to come up the Shannon in peace
and to depart in peace. The signing of the treaty was
deferred till the Lords Justices, who represented William at
Dublin, should arrive at Ginkell's quarters. But there was
during some days a relaxation of military vigilance on both
sides. Prisoners were set at liberty. The outposts of the
two armies chatted and messed together. The English
officers rambled into the town. The Irish officers dined in the
camp. Anecdotes of what passed at the friendly meetings of
these men, who had so lately been mortal enemies, were
widely circulated. One story, in particular, was repeated in
every part of Europe. "Has not this last campaign," said
Sarsfield to some English officers, "raised your opinion of
Irish soldiers?" "To tell you the truth," answered an Englishman, "we think of them much as we always did." "However meanly you may think of us," replied Sarsfield, "change
Kings with us, and we will willingly try our luck with you
again." He was doubtless thinking of the day on which he
had seen the two Sovereigns at the head of two great armies,
William foremost in the charge, and James foremost in the
flight.*

On the first of October, Coningsby and Porter arrived at the **The capitulation of
Limerick**
English headquarters. On the second the articles of capitulation were discussed at great length and definitely settled.
On the third they were signed. They were divided into two
parts, a military treaty and a civil treaty. The former was
subscribed only by the generals on both sides. The Lords
Justices set their names to the latter.†

By the military treaty it was agreed that such Irish officers
and soldiers as should declare that they wished to go to
France should be conveyed thither, and should, in the meantime, remain under the command of their own generals. Ginkell undertook to furnish a considerable number of transports.
French vessels were also to be permitted to pass and repass

---

* Story's Continuation; Diary of the
Siege of Lymerick; Burnet, ii. 81.; London Gazette, Oct. 12. 1691.

† Story's Continuation; Diary of the
Siege of Lymerick; London Gazette, Oct.
15. 1691.

freely between Britanny and Munster. Part of Limerick
was to be immediately delivered up to the English. But the
island on which the Cathedral and the Castle stand was to
remain, for the present, in the keeping of the Irish.

The terms of the civil treaty were very different from those
which Ginkell had sternly refused to grant. It was not stipulated that the Roman Catholics of Ireland should be competent to hold any political or military office, or that they
should be admitted into any corporation. But they obtained
a promise that they should enjoy such privileges in the exercise of their religion as were consistent with the law, or as
they had enjoyed in the reign of Charles the Second.

To all inhabitants of Limerick, and to all officers and
soldiers in the Jacobite army, who should submit to the
government and notify their submission by taking the oath
of allegiance, an entire amnesty was promised. They were
to retain their property : they were to be allowed to exercise
any profession which they had exercised before the troubles :
they were not to be punished for any treason, felony, or misdemeanour committed since the accession of the late King :
nay, they were not to be sued for damages on account of any
act of spoliation or outrage which they might have committed
during the three years of confusion. This was more than the
Lords Justices were constitutionally competent to grant. It
was therefore added that the government would use its
utmost endeavours to obtain a Parliamentary ratification of
the treaty.*

As soon as the two instruments had been signed, the English entered the city, and occupied one quarter of it. A
narrow but deep branch of the Shannon separated them from
the quarter which was still in the possession of the Irish.†

In a few hours a dispute arose which seemed likely to produce a renewal of hostilities. Sarsfield had resolved to seek his
fortune in the service of France, and was naturally desirous
to carry with him to the Continent such a body of troops as
would be an important addition to the army of Lewis.
Ginkell was as naturally unwilling to send thousands of men
to swell the forces of the enemy. Both generals appealed to
the treaty. Each construed it as suited his purpose, and each
complained that the other had violated it. Sarsfield was
accused of putting one of his officers under arrest for refusing
to go to the Continent. Ginkell, greatly excited, declared

---

* The articles of the civil treaty have   † Story's Continuation ; Diary of the
often been reprinted.   Siege of Lymerick.

that he would teach the Irish to play tricks with him, and began to make preparations for a cannonade. Sarsfield came to the English camp, and tried to justify what he had done. The altercation was sharp. "I submit," said Sarsfield, at last: "I am in your power." "Not at all in my power," said Ginkell: "go back and do your worst." The imprisoned officer was liberated: a sanguinary contest was averted; and the two commanders contented themselves with a war of words.* Ginkell put forth proclamations assuring the Irish that, if they would live quietly in their own land, they should be protected and favoured, and that, if they preferred a military life, they should be admitted into the service of King William. It was added that no man, who chose to reject this gracious invitation and to become a soldier of Lewis, must expect ever again to set foot on the island. Sarsfield and Wauchop exerted their eloquence on the other side. The present aspect of affairs, they said, was doubtless gloomy: but there was bright sky beyond the cloud. The banishment would be short. The return would be triumphant. Within a year the French would invade England. In such an invasion the Irish troops, if only they remained unbroken, would assuredly bear a chief part. In the meantime it was far better for them to live in a neighbouring and friendly country, under the parental care of their own rightful King, than to trust the Prince of Orange, who would probably send them to the other end of the world to fight for his ally the Emperor against the Janissaries.

The help of the Roman Catholic clergy was called in. On the day on which those who had made up their minds to go to France were required to announce their determination, the priests were indefatigable in exhorting. At the head of every regiment a sermon was preached on the duty of adhering to the cause of the Church, and on the sin and danger of consorting with unbelievers.* Whoever, it was said, should enter the service of the usurpers would do so at the peril of his soul. The heretics affirmed that, after the peroration, a plentiful allowance of brandy was served out to the audience, and that, when the brandy had been swallowed, a Bishop pronounced a benediction. Thus duly prepared by physical and moral stimulants, the garrison, consisting of about four-

The Irish troops required to make their election between their country and France.

* Story's Continuation; Diary of the Siege of Lymerick.

† Story's Continuation. His narrative is confirmed by the testimony which an Irish Captain who was present has left us in bad Latin. "Hic apud sacrum omnes advertizantur a capellanis ire potius in Galliam."

teen thousand infantry, was drawn up in the vast meadow which lay on the Clare bank of the Shannon. Here copies of Ginkell's proclamation were profusely scattered about; and English officers went through the ranks imploring the men not to ruin themselves, and explaining to them the advantages which the soldiers of King William enjoyed. At length the decisive moment came. The troops were ordered to pass in review. Those who wished to remain in Ireland were directed to file off at a particular spot. All who passed that spot were to be considered as having made their choice for France. Sarsfield and Wauchop on one side, Porter, Coningsby, and Ginkell on the other, looked on with painful anxiety. D'Usson and his countrymen, though not uninterested in the spectacle, found it hard to preserve their gravity. The confusion, the clamour, the grotesque appearance of an army in which there could scarcely be seen a shirt or a pair of pantaloons, a shoe or a stocking, presented so ludicrous a contrast to the orderly and brilliant appearance of their master's troops, that they amused themselves by wondering what the Parisians would say to see such a force mustered on the plain of Grenelle.*

Most of the Irish troops volunteer for France.

First marched what was called the Royal regiment, fourteen hundred strong. All but seven went beyond the fatal point. Ginkell's countenance showed that he was deeply mortified. He was consoled, however, by seeing the next regiment, which consisted of natives of Ulster, turn off to a man. There had arisen, notwithstanding the community of blood, language, and religion, an antipathy between the Celts of Ulster and those of the other three provinces; nor is it improbable that the example and influence of Baldearg O'Donnel may have had some effect on the people of the land which his forefathers had ruled.† In most of the regiments there was a division of opinion; but a great majority declared for France. Henry Luttrell was one of those who turned off. He was rewarded for his desertion, and perhaps for other services, with a grant of the large estate of his elder brother Simon, who firmly adhered to the cause of James, with a pension of five hundred pounds a year from the Crown, and with the abhorrence of the Roman Catholic population. After living in wealth, luxury, and infamy, during a quarter of a century, Henry Luttrell was murdered while going

* D'Usson and Tessé to Barbesieux, Oct. ⁷⁄₁₇ 1691.

† That there was little sympathy between the Celts of Ulster and those of

the Southern Provinces is evident from the curious memorial which the agent of Baldearg O'Donnel delivered to Avaux.

through Dublin in his sedan chair; and the Irish House of Commons declared that there was reason to suspect that he had fallen by the revenge of the Papists.* Eighty years after his death, his grave near Luttrellstown was violated by the descendants of those whom he had betrayed, and his skull was broken to pieces with a pickaxe.† The deadly hatred of which he was the object descended to his son and to his grandson; and, unhappily, nothing in the character either of his son or of his grandson tended to mitigate the feeling which the name of Luttrell excited.‡

When the long procession had closed, it was found that about a thousand men had agreed to enter into William's service. About two thousand accepted passes from Ginkell, and went quietly home. About eleven thousand returned with Sarsfield to the city. A few hours after the garrison had passed in review, the horse, who were encamped some miles from the town, were required to make their choice: and most of them volunteered for France.§

Sarsfield considered the troops who remained with him as under an irrevocable obligation to go abroad; and, lest they should be tempted to retract their consent, he confined them within the ramparts, and ordered the gates to be shut and strongly guarded. Ginkell, though in his vexation he muttered some threats, seems to have felt that he could not justifiably interfere. But the precautions of the Irish general were far from being completely successful. It was by no means strange that a superstitious and excitable kerne, with a sermon and a dram in his head, should be ready to promise whatever his priests required: neither was it strange that, when he had slept off his liquor, and when anathemas were no longer

Many of the Irish who had volunteered for France desert.

---

* Treasury Letter Book, June 19. 1696; Journals of the Irish House of Commons, Nov. 7. 1717.

† This I relate on Mr. O'Callaghan's authority. History of the Irish Brigades, Note 47.

‡ "There is," Junius wrote eighty years after the capitulation of Limerick, "a certain family in this country on which nature seems to have entailed a hereditary baseness of disposition. As far as their history has been known, the son has regularly improved upon the vices of the father, and has taken care to transmit them pure and undiminished into the bosom of his successors." Elsewhere he says of the member for Middlesex, "He has degraded even the name of Luttrell." He exclaims, in

allusion to the marriage of the Duke of Cumberland and Mrs. Horton, who was born a Luttrell, "Let Parliament look to it. A Luttrell shall never succeed to the Crown of England." It is certain that very few Englishmen can have sympathised with Junius's abhorrence of the Luttrells, or can even have understood it. Why then did he use expressions which to the great majority of his readers must have been unintelligible? My answer is that Philip Francis was born, and passed the first ten years of his life, within a walk of Luttrellstown.

§ Story's Continuation; London Gazette, Oct. 22. 1691; D'Usson and Tessé to Lewis, Oct. 4/14., and to Barbesieux, Oct. 7/17.; Light to the Blind.

ringing in his ears, he should feel painful misgivings. He had bound himself to go into exile, perhaps for life, beyond that dreary expanse of waters which impressed his rude mind with mysterious terror. His thoughts ran on all that he was to leave, on the well known peat stack and potatoe ground, and on the mud cabin, which, humble as it was, was still his home. He was never again to see the familiar faces round the turf fire, or to hear the familiar notes of the old Celtic songs. The ocean was to roll between him and the dwelling of his greyheaded parents and his blooming sweetheart. There were some who, unable to bear the misery of such a separation, and finding it impossible to pass the sentinels who watched the gates, sprang into the river and gained the opposite bank. The number of these daring swimmers, however, was not great; and the army would probably have been transported almost entire if it had remained at Limerick till the day of embarkation. But many of the vessels in which the voyage was to be performed lay at Cork; and it was necessary that Sarsfield should proceed thither with some of his best regiments. It was a march of not less than four days through a wild country. To prevent agile youths, familiar with all the shifts of a vagrant and predatory life, from stealing off to the bogs and woods under cover of the night, was impossible. Indeed many soldiers had the audacity to run away by broad daylight before they were out of sight of Limerick Cathedral. The Royal regiment, which had, on the day of the review, set so striking an example of fidelity to the cause of James, dwindled from fourteen hundred men to five hundred. Before the last ships departed, news came that those who had sailed by the first ships had been ungraciously received at Brest. They had been scantily fed: they had been able to obtain neither pay nor clothing: though winter was setting in, they slept in the fields with no covering but the hedges; and many had been heard to say that it would have been far better to die in old Ireland than to live in the inhospitable country to which they had been banished. The effect of these reports was that hundreds, who had long persisted in their intention of emigrating, refused at the last moment to go on board, threw down their arms, and returned to their native villages.*

The last division of the Irish army sails from Cork for France.

Sarsfield perceived that one chief cause of the desertion which was thinning his army was the natural unwillingness of the men to leave their families in a state of destitution.

Story's Continuation; London Gazette, Jan. 4. 169¼.

Cork and the neighbouring villages were filled with the kindred of those who were going abroad. Great numbers of women, many of them leading, carrying, suckling their infants, covered all the roads which led to the place of embarkation. The Irish general, apprehensive of the effect which the entreaties and lamentations of these poor creatures could not fail to produce, put forth a proclamation, in which he assured his soldiers that they should be permitted to carry their wives and children to France. It would be injurious to the memory of so brave and loyal a gentleman to suppose that when he made this promise he meant to break it. It is much more probable that he had formed an erroneous estimate of the number of those who would demand a passage, and that he found himself, when it was too late to alter his arrange-- ments, unable to keep his word. After the soldiers had embarked, room was found for the families of many. But still there remained on the waterside a great multitude clamouring piteously to be taken on board. As the last boats put off there was a rush into the surf. Some women caught hold of the ropes, were dragged out of their depth, clung till their fingers were cut through, and perished in the waves. The ships began to move. A wild and terrible wail rose from the shore, and excited unwonted compassion in hearts steeled by hatred of the Irish race and of the Romish faith. Even the stern Cromwellian, now at length, after a desperate struggle of three years, left the undisputed lord of the bloodstained and devastated island, could not hear unmoved that bitter cry, in which was poured forth all the rage and all the sorrow of a conquered nation.[*]

The sails disappeared. The emaciated and brokenhearted crowd of those whom a stroke more cruel than that of death had made widows and orphans dispersed, to beg their way home through a wasted land, or to lie down and die by the roadside of grief and hunger. The exiles departed, to learn in foreign camps that discipline without which natural courage is of small avail, and to retrieve on distant fields of battle the honour which had been lost by a long series of defeats at home. In Ireland there was peace. The domination of the colonists was absolute. The native population was tranquil with the ghastly tranquillity of exhaustion and of despair. There were indeed outrages, robberies, fireraisings, assassinations. But more than a century passed away with-

State of Ireland after the war.

[*] Story's Continuation; Macariæ Excidium, and Mr. O'Callaghan's note; London Gazette, Jan. 4. 169½.

out one general insurrection. During that century, two re-
bellions were raised in Great Britain by the adherents of the
House of Stuart. But neither when the elder Pretender
summoned his vassals to attend his coronation at Scone, nor
when the younger held his court at Holyrood, was the standard of that House set up in Connaught or Munster. In 1745,
indeed, when the Highlanders were marching towards London, the Roman Catholics of Ireland were so quiet that the
Lord Lieutenant could, without the smallest risk, send several
regiments across Saint George's Channel to reinforce the
army of the Duke of Cumberland. Nor was this submission
the effect of content, but of mere stupefaction and brokenness
of heart. The iron had entered into the soul. The memory
of past defeats, the habit of daily enduring insult and oppression, had cowed the spirit of the unhappy nation. There were
indeed Irish Roman Catholics of great ability, energy and
ambition : but they were to be found every where except in
Ireland, at Versailles and at Saint Ildefonso, in the armies of
Frederic and in the armies of Maria Theresa. One exile became a Marshal of France. Another became Prime Minister
of Spain. If he had staid in his native land, he would have
been regarded as an inferior by all the ignorant and worthless
squireens who had signed the Declaration against Transubstantiation. In his palace at Madrid he had the pleasure of
being assiduously courted by the ambassador of George the
Second, and of bidding defiance in high terms to the ambassador of George the Third.* Scattered over all Europe were
to be found brave Irish generals, dexterous Irish diplomatists,
Irish Counts, Irish Barons, Irish Knights of Saint Lewis and
of Saint Leopold, of the White Eagle and of the Golden
Fleece, who, if they had remained in the house of bondage,
could not have been ensigns of marching regiments or freemen
of petty corporations. These men, the natural chiefs of their
race, having been withdrawn, what remained was utterly
helpless and passive. A rising of the Irishry against the
Englishry was no more to be apprehended than a rising of
the women and children against the men.†

---

* Some interesting facts relating to
Wall, who was minister of Ferdinand
the Sixth and Charles the Third, will be
found in the letters of Sir Benjamin
Keene and Lord Bristol, published in
Coxe's Memoirs of Spain.

† This is Swift's language, language
held not once, but repeatedly and at
long intervals. In the Letter on the
Sacramental Test, written in 1708, he
says : "If we were under any real fear
of the Papists in this kingdom, it would
be hard to think us so stupid as not to
be equally apprehensive with others,
since we are likely to be the greater and
more immediate sufferers: but, on the
contrary, we look upon them to be altogether as inconsiderable as the women

There were indeed, in those days, fierce disputes between the mother country and the colony : but in such disputes the aboriginal population had no more interest than the Red Indians in the dispute between Old England and New England about the Stamp Act. The ruling few, even when in mutiny against the government, had no mercy for any thing that looked like mutiny on the part of the subject many. None of those Roman patriots, who poniarded Julius Cæsar for aspiring to be a king, would have had the smallest scruple about crucifying a whole school of gladiators for attempting to escape from the most odious and degrading of all kinds of servitude. None of those Virginian patriots, who vindicated their separation from the British empire by proclaiming it to be a selfevident truth that all men were endowed by the Creator with an unalienable right to liberty, would have had the smallest scruple about shooting any negro slave who had laid claim to that unalienable right. And, in the same manner, the Protestant masters of Ireland, while ostentatiously professing the political doctrines of Locke and Sidney, held that a people who spoke the Celtic tongue and heard mass could have no concern in those doctrines. Molyneux questioned the supremacy of the English legislature. Swift assailed, with the keenest ridicule and invective, every part of the system of government. Lucas disquieted the administration of Lord Harrington. Boyle overthrew the administration of the Duke of Dorset. But neither Molyneux nor Swift, neither Lucas nor Boyle, ever thought of appealing to the native population. They would as soon have thought of appealing to the swine.* At a later period Henry Flood excited

and children. . . . The common people, without leaders, without discipline or natural courage, being little better than hewers of wood and drawers of water, are out of all capacity of doing any mischief, if they were ever so well inclined." In the Drapier's Sixth Letter, written in 1724, he says : " As to the people of this kingdom, they consist either of Irish Papists, who are as inconsiderable, in point of power, as the women and children, or of English Protestants." Again, in the Presbyterians' Plea of Merit, written in 1731, he says : "The estates of Papists are very few, crumbling into small parcels, and daily diminishing; their common people are sunk in poverty, ignorance, and cowardice, and of as little consequence as women and children. Their nobility and gentry are at least one half ruined, banished or con-

verted. They all soundly feel the smart of what they suffered in the last Irish war. Some of them are already retired into foreign countries : others, as I am told, intend to follow them; and the rest, I believe to a man, who still possess any lands, are absolutely resolved never to hazard them again for the sake of establishing their superstition."

I may observe that, to the best of my belief, Swift never, in anything that he wrote, used the word Irishman to denote a person of Anglosaxon race born in Ireland. He no more considered himself as an Irishman than an Englishman born at Calcutta considers himself as a Hindoo.

* In 1749 Lucas was the idol of the democracy of his own caste. It is curious to see what was thought of him by those who were not of his own

the dominant class to demand a Parliamentary reform, and to use even revolutionary means for the purpose of obtaining that reform. But neither he, nor those who looked up to him as their chief, and who went close to the verge of treason at his bidding, would consent to admit the subject class to the smallest share of political power. The virtuous and accomplished Charlemont, a Whig of the Whigs, passed a long life in contending for what he called the freedom of his country. But he voted against the law which gave the elective franchise to Roman Catholic freeholders, and he died fixed in the opinion that the Parliament House ought to be kept pure from Roman Catholic members. Indeed, during the century which followed the Revolution, the inclination of an English Protestant to trample on the Irishry was generally proportioned to the zeal which he professed for political liberty in the abstract. If he uttered any expression of compassion for the majority oppressed by the minority, he might be safely set down as a bigoted Tory and High Churchman.[*]

All this time, hatred, kept down by fear, festered in the hearts of the children of the soil. They were still the same people that had sprung to arms in 1641 at the call of O'Neill, and in 1689 at the call of Tyrconnel. To them every festival instituted by the State was a day of mourning, and every trophy set up by the State was a memorial of shame. We have never known, and can but faintly conceive, the feelings of a nation doomed to see constantly in all its public places the monuments of its subjugation. Such monuments everywhere met the eye of the Irish Roman Catholic. In front of the Senate House of his country, he saw the statue which her conquerors had set up in honour of a memory, glorious indeed and immortal, but to him an object of mingled dread and abhorrence. If he entered, he saw the walls tapestried with the most ignominious defeats of his forefathers. At length, after a hundred years of servitude, endured without one struggle

caste. One of the chief Pariahs, Charles O'Connor, wrote thus: "I am by no means interested, nor is any of our unfortunate population, in this affair of Lucas. A true patriot would not have betrayed such malice to such unfortunate slaves as we." He adds, with too much truth, that those boasters the Whigs wished to have liberty all to themselves.

[*] On this subject Johnson was the most liberal politician of his time. "The

Irish," he said with great warmth, "are in a most unnatural state: for we see there the minority prevailing over the majority." I suspect that Alderman Beckford and Alderman Sawbridge would have been far from sympathising with him. Charles O'Connor, whose unfavourable opinion of the Whig Lucas I have quoted, pays, in the Preface to the Dissertations on Irish History, a high compliment to the liberality of the Tory Johnson.

for emancipation, the French revolution awakened a wild hope in the bosoms of the oppressed. Men who had inherited all the pretensions and all the passions of the Parliament which James had held at the King's Inns could not hear unmoved of the downfall of a wealthy established Church, of the flight of a splendid aristocracy, of the confiscation of an immense territory. Old antipathies, which had never slumbered, were excited to new and terrible energy by the combination of stimulants which, in any other society, would have counteracted each other. The spirit of Popery and the spirit of Jacobinism, irreconcilable antagonists every where else, were for once mingled in an unnatural and portentous union. Their joint influence produced the third and last rising up of the aboriginal population against the colony. The greatgrandsons of the soldiers of Galmoy and Sarsfield were opposed to the greatgrandsons of the soldiers of Wolseley and Mitchelburn. The Celt again looked impatiently for the sails which were to bring succour from Brest; and the Saxon was again backed by the whole power of England. Again the victory remained with the well educated and well organised minority. But, happily, the vanquished people found protection in a quarter from which they would once have had to expect nothing but implacable severity. By this time the philosophy of the eighteenth century had purified English Whiggism from that deep taint of intolerance which had been contracted during a long and close alliance with the Puritanism of the seventeenth century. Enlightened men had begun to feel that the arguments, by which Milton and Locke, Tillotson and Burnet, had vindicated the rights of conscience, might be urged with not less force in favour of the Roman Catholic than in favour of the Independent or the Baptist. The great party which traces its descent through the Exclusionists up to the Roundheads continued, during thirty years, in spite of royal frowns and popular clamours, to demand a share in all the benefits of our free constitution for those Irish Papists whom the Roundheads and the Exclusionists had considered merely as beasts of chase or as beasts of burden. But it will be for some other historian to relate the vicissitudes of that great conflict, and the late triumph of reason and humanity. Unhappily such a historian will have to relate that the victory won by such exertions and by such sacrifices was immediately followed by disappointment; that it proved far less easy to eradicate evil passions than to repeal evil laws; and that, long after every

trace of national and religious animosity had been obliterated
from the Statute Book, national and religious animosities
continued to rankle in the bosoms of millions. May he be
able also to relate that wisdom, justice, and time did in
Ireland what they had done in Scotland, and that all the
races which inhabit the British isles were at length in-
dissolubly blended into one people!

CHAPTER XVIII.

On the nineteenth of October 1691, William arrived at Kensington from the Netherlands.* Three days later he opened the Parliament. The aspect of affairs was, on the whole, cheering. By land there had been gains and losses: but the balance was in favour of England. Against the fall of Mons might well be set off the taking of Athlone, the victory of Aghrim, the surrender of Limerick, and the pacification of Ireland. At sea there had been no great victory: but there had been a great display of power and of activity; and, though many were dissatisfied because more had not been done, none could deny that there had been a change for the better. The ruin caused by the follies and vices of Torrington had been repaired: the fleet had been well equipped: the rations had been abundant and wholesome; and the health of the crews had consequently been, for that age, wonderfully good. Russell, who commanded the naval forces of the allies, had in vain offered battle to the French. The white flag, which, in the preceding year, had ranged the Channel unresisted from the Land's End to the Straits of Dover, now, as soon as our topmasts were descried, abandoned the open sea, and retired into the depths of the harbour of Brest. The appearance of an English squadron in the estuary of the Shannon had decided the fate of the last fortress which had held out for King James; and a fleet of merchantmen from the Levant, valued at four millions sterling, had, through dangers which had caused many sleepless nights to the underwriters of Lombard Street, been convoyed safe into the Thames.† The Lords and Commons listened with signs of satisfaction to a speech in which the King congratulated them on the event of the war in Ireland, and expressed his confidence that they would continue to support him in the war with France. He

Opening of the Parliament.

---

* London Gazette, Oct. 22. 1691.

† Burnet, ii. 78, 79.; Burchett's Memoirs of Transactions at Sea; Journal of the English and Dutch fleet, in a Letter from an Officer on board the Lennox, at Torbay, licensed Aug. 21. 1691. The writer says: "We attribute our health, under God, to the extraordinary care taken in the well ordering of our provisions, both meat and drink."

told them that a great naval armament would be necessary,
and that, in his opinion, the conflict by land could not be
effectually maintained with less than sixty-five thousand men.*

He was thanked in affectionate terms : the force which he
asked was voted ; and large supplies were granted with little
difficulty. But, when the Ways and Means were taken into
consideration, symptoms of discontent began to appear.
Eighteen months before, when the Commons had been employed in settling the Civil List, many members had shown a
very natural disposition to complain of the amount of the
salaries and fees received by official men. Keen speeches had
been made, and, what was much less usual, had been printed :
there had been much excitement out of doors : but nothing
had been done. The subject was now revived. A report
made by the Commissioners who had been appointed in the
preceding year to examine the public accounts disclosed some
facts which excited indignation, and others which raised
grave suspicion. The House seemed fully determined to make
an extensive reform ; and, in truth, nothing could have
averted such a reform except the folly and violence of the
reformers. That they should have been angry is indeed not
strange. The enormous gains, direct and indirect, of the
servants of the public went on increasing, while the gains of
everybody else were diminishing. Rents were falling : trade
was languishing : every man who lived either on what his
ancestors had left him or on the fruits of his own industry
was forced to retrench. The placeman alone throve amidst
the general distress. "Look," cried the incensed squires,
"at the Comptroller of the Customs. Ten years ago, he
walked, and we rode. Our incomes have been curtailed : his
salary has been doubled : we have sold our horses : he has
bought them ; and now we go on foot and are splashed by
his coach and six." Lowther vainly endeavoured to stand
up against the storm. He was heard with little favour by
those country gentlemen who had not long before looked up
to him as one of their leaders. He had left them : he had
become a courtier : he had two good places, one in the
Treasury, the other in the household. He had recently received from the King's own hand a gratuity of two thousand
guineas.† It seemed perfectly natural that he should defend
abuses by which he profited. The taunts and reproaches with

* Lords' and Commons' Journals, Oct. by Lowther, after he became Lord Lons-
22. 1691. dale, to his son. A copy of this letter is
† This appears from a letter written among the Mackintosh MSS.

which he was assailed were insupportable to his sensitive nature. He lost his head, almost fainted away on the floor of the House, and talked about righting himself in another place.* Unfortunately no member rose at this conjuncture to propose that the civil establishments of the kingdom should be carefully revised, that sinecures should be abolished, that exorbitant official incomes should be reduced, and that no servant of the State should be allowed to exact, under any pretence, anything beyond his known and lawful remuneration. In this way it would have been possible to diminish the public burdens, and at the same time to increase the efficiency of every public department. But, on this as on many other occasions, those who were loud in clamouring against the prevailing abuses were utterly destitute of the qualities necessary for the work of reform. On the twelfth of December, some foolish man, whose name has not come down to us, moved that no person employed in any civil office, the Speaker, Judges, and Ambassadors excepted, should receive more than five hundred pounds a year; and this motion was not only carried, but carried without one dissentient voice.† Those who were most interested in opposing it doubtless saw that opposition would, at that moment, only irritate the majority, and reserved themselves for a more favourable time. The more favourable time soon came. No man of common sense could, when his blood had cooled, remember without shame that he had voted for a resolution which made no distinction between sinecurists and laborious public servants, between clerks employed in copying letters and ministers on whose wisdom and integrity the fate of the nation might depend. The salary of the Doorkeeper of the Excise Office had been, by a scandalous job, raised to five hundred a year. It ought to have been reduced to fifty. On the other hand, the services of a Secretary of State who was well qualified for his post would have been cheap at five thousand. If the resolution of the Commons had been carried into effect, both the salary which ought not to have exceeded fifty pounds, and the salary which might without impropriety

---

* See Commons' Journals, Dec. 3. 1691; and Grey's Debates. It is to be regretted that the Report of the Commissioners of Accounts has not been preserved. Lowther, in his letter to his son, alludes to the badgering of this day with great bitterness. "What man," he asks, "that hath bread to eat, can endure, after having served with all the diligence and application mankind is capable of, and after having given satisfaction to the King, from whom all officers of state derive their authoritie, after acting rightly by all men, to be baited by men who do it to all people in authoritie?"

† Commons' Journals, Dec. 12. 1691.

have amounted to five thousand, would have been fixed at five hundred. Such absurdity must have shocked even the roughest and plainest foxhunter in the House. A reaction took place; and when, after an interval of a few weeks, it was proposed to insert in a bill of supply a clause in conformity with the resolution of the twelfth of December, the Noes were loud: the Speaker was of opinion that they had it: the Ayes did not venture to dispute his opinion: the senseless plan which had been approved without a division was rejected without a division; and the subject was not again mentioned. Thus a grievance so scandalous that none of those who profited by it dared to defend it was perpetuated merely by the imbecility and intemperance of those who attacked it.*

Act excluding Papists from public trust in Ireland.

Early in the Session the Treaty of Limerick became the subject of a grave and earnest discussion. The Commons, in the exercise of that supreme power which the English legislature possessed over all the dependencies of England, sent up to the Lords a bill providing that no person should sit in the Irish Parliament, should hold any Irish office, civil, military, or ecclesiastical, or should practise law or medicine in Ireland, till he had taken the Oaths of Allegiance and Supremacy, and subscribed the Declaration against Transubstantiation. The Lords were not more inclined than the Commons to favour the Irish. No peer was disposed to entrust Roman Catholics with political power. Nay, it seems that no peer objected to the principle of the absurd and cruel rule which excluded Roman Catholics from the liberal professions. But it was thought that this rule, though unobjectionable in principle, would, if adopted without some exceptions, be a breach of a positive compact. Their Lordships called for the Treaty of Limerick, ordered it to be read at the table, and proceeded to consider whether the law framed by the Lower House was consistent with the engagements into which the government had entered. One discrepancy was noticed. It was stipulated by the second civil article, that every person actually residing in any fortress occupied by an Irish garrison should be permitted, on taking the Oath of Allegiance, to resume

---

* Commons' Journals, Feb. 15. 169$\frac{1}{2}$; Baden to the States General, $\frac{\text{Jan. 26.}}{\text{Feb. 5.}}$. On the 8th of December 1797, Mr. John Nicholls, a reformer of much more zeal than wisdom, proposed, in the House of Commons, a resolution framed on the model of the resolution of the 12th of December 1691. Mr. Pitt justly remarked that the precedent on which Mr. Nicholls relied was of no value, for that the gentlemen who passed the resolution of the 12th of December 1691 had, in a very short time, discovered and acknowledged their error. The debate is much better given in the Morning Chronicle than in the Parliamentary History.

any calling which he had exercised before the Revolution. It would, beyond all doubt, have been a violation of this covenant to require that a lawyer or a physician, who had been within the walls of Limerick during the siege, and who was willing to take the Oath of Allegiance, should also take the Oath of Supremacy and subscribe the Declaration against Transubstantiation, before he could exercise his profession. Holt was consulted, and was directed to prepare clauses in conformity with the terms of the capitulation.

The bill, as amended by the Chief Justice, was sent back to the Commons. They at first rejected the amendment, and demanded a conference. The conference was granted. Rochester, in the Painted Chamber, delivered to the managers of the Lower House a copy of the Treaty of Limerick, and earnestly represented the importance of preserving the public faith inviolate. This appeal was one which no honest man, though inflamed by national and religious animosity, could resist. The Commons reconsidered the subject, and, after hearing the Treaty read, agreed, with some slight modifications, to what the Lords had proposed.*

The bill became a law. It attracted, at the time, little notice, but was, after the lapse of several generations, the subject of a very acrimonious controversy. Many of us can well remember how strongly the public mind was stirred, in the days of George the Third and George the Fourth, by the question whether Roman Catholics should be permitted to sit in Parliament. It may be doubted whether any dispute has produced stranger perversions of history. The whole past was falsified for the sake of the present. All the great events of three centuries long appeared to us distorted and discoloured by a mist sprung from our own theories and our own passions. Some friends of religious liberty, not content with the advantage which they possessed in the fair conflict of reason with reason, weakened their case by maintaining that the law which excluded Irish Roman Catholics from Parliament was inconsistent with the civil Treaty of Limerick. The first article of that Treaty, it was said, guaranteed to the Irish Roman Catholic such privileges in the exercise of his religion as he had enjoyed in the time of Charles the Second. In the time of Charles the Second no test excluded Roman Catholics from the Irish Parliament. Such a test could not therefore, it was argued, be imposed

* Stat. 3. W. & M. c. 2., Lords' Journals; Lords' Journals, 16 Nov. 1691; Commons' Journals, Dec. 1. 9 5.

without a breach of public faith. In the year 1828, especially, this argument was put forward in the House of Commons as if it had been the main strength of a cause which stood in need of no such support. The champions of Protestant ascendency were well pleased to see the debate diverted from a political question about which they were in the wrong, to a historical question about which they were in the right. They had no difficulty in proving that the first article, as understood by all the contracting parties, meant only that the Roman Catholic worship should be tolerated as in time past. That article was drawn up by Ginkell; and, just before he drew it up, he had declared that he would rather try the chance of arms than consent that Irish Papists should be capable of holding civil and military offices, of exercising liberal professions, and of becoming members of municipal corporations. How is it possible to believe that he would, of his own accord, have promised that the House of Lords and the House of Commons should be open to men to whom he would not open a guild of skinners or a guild of cordwainers? How, again, is it possible to believe that the English Peers would, while professing the most punctilious respect for public faith, while lecturing the Commons on the duty of observing public faith, while taking counsel with the most learned and upright jurist of the age as to the best mode of maintaining public faith, have committed a flagrant violation of public faith, and that not a single lord should have been so honest or so factious as to protest against an act of monstrous perfidy aggravated by hypocrisy? Or, if we could believe this, how can we believe that no voice would have been raised in any part of the world against such wickedness; that the Court of Saint Germains and the Court of Versailles would have remained profoundly silent; that no Irish exile, no English malecontent, would have uttered a murmur; that not a word of invective or sarcasm on so inviting a subject would have been found in the whole compass of the Jacobite literature; and that it would have been reserved for politicians of the nineteenth century to discover that a treaty made in the seventeenth century had, a few weeks after it had been signed, been outrageously violated in the sight of all Europe?*

* The Irish Roman Catholics complained, and with but too much reason, that, at a later period, the Treaty of Limerick was violated; but those very complaints are admissions that the Statute 3 W. & M. c. 2. was not a violation of the Treaty. Thus the author of A Light to the Blind, speaking of the first article, says, "This article, in seven years after, was broken by a Parliament

On the same day on which the Commons read for the first time the bill which subjected Ireland to the absolute dominion of the Protestant minority, they took into consideration another matter of high importance. Throughout the country, but especially in the capital, in the seaports, and in the manufacturing towns, the minds of men were greatly excited on the subject of the trade with the East Indies: a fierce paper war had during some time been raging; and several grave questions, both constitutional and commercial, had been raised, which the legislature only could decide. Debates on the East India trade.

It has often been repeated, and ought never to be forgotten, that our polity differs widely from those polities which have, during the last eighty years, been methodically constructed, digested into articles, and ratified by constituent assemblies. It grew up in a rude age. It is not to be found entire in any formal instrument. All along the line which separates the functions of the prince from those of the legislator there was long a disputed territory. Encroachments were perpetually committed, and, if not very outrageous, were often tolerated. Trespass, merely as trespass, was commonly suffered to pass unresented. It was only when the trespass produced some positive damage that the aggrieved party stood on his right, and demanded that the frontier should be set out by metes and bounds, and that the landmarks should thenceforward be punctiliously respected.

Many of the points which had occasioned the most violent disputes between our Sovereigns and their Parliaments had been finally decided by the Bill of Rights. But one question, scarcely less important than any of the questions which had been set at rest for ever, was still undetermined. Indeed, that question was never, as far as can now be ascertained, even mentioned in the Convention. The King had undoubtedly, by the ancient laws of the realm, large powers for the regulation of trade: but the ablest judge would have found it difficult to say what was the precise extent of those powers. It was universally acknowledged that it belonged to the King to prescribe weights and measures, and to coin money; that no fair or market could be held without autho-

---

in Ireland summoned by the Prince of Orange, wherein a law was passed for banishing the Catholic bishops, dignitaries, and regular clergy." Surely he never would have written thus, if the article really had, only two months after it was signed, been broken by the English Parliament. The Abbé Mac Geoghegan, too, complains that the Treaty was violated some years after it was made. But, by so complaining, he admits that it was not violated by Stat. 3. W. & M. c. 2.

rity from him; that no ship could unload in any bay or estuary which he had not declared to be a port. In addition to his undoubted right to grant special commercial privileges to particular places, he long claimed a right to grant special commercial privileges to particular societies and to particular individuals; and our ancestors, as usual, did not think it worth their while to dispute this claim, till it produced serious inconvenience. At length, in the reign of Elizabeth, the power of creating monopolies began to be grossly abused; and, as soon as it began to be grossly abused, it began to be questioned. The Queen wisely declined a conflict with a House of Commons backed by the whole nation. She frankly acknowledged that there was reason for complaint: she cancelled the patents which had excited the public clamours; and her people, delighted by this concession, and by the gracious manner in which it had been made, did not require from her an express renunciation of the disputed prerogative.

The discontents which her wisdom had appeased were revived by the dishonest and pusillanimous policy which her successor called kingcraft. He readily granted oppressive patents of monopoly. When he needed the help of his Parliament, he as readily annulled them. As soon as the Parliament had ceased to sit, his Great Seal was put to instruments more odious than those which he had recently cancelled. At length that excellent House of Commons which met in 1623 determined to apply a strong remedy to the evil. The King was forced to give his assent to a law which declared monopolies established by royal authority to be null and void. Some exceptions, however, were made, and, unfortunately, were not very clearly defined. It was especially provided that every Society of Merchants which had been instituted for the purpose of carrying on any trade should retain all legal privileges.* The question whether a monopoly granted by the Crown to such a society were or were not a legal privilege was left unsettled, and continued to exercise, during many years, the ingenuity of lawyers.†

* Stat. 21 Jac. I. c. 3.

† See particularly Two Letters by a Barrister concerning the East India Company (1676), and an Answer to the Two Letters published in the same year. See also the Judgment of Lord Jeffreys concerning the Great Case of Monopolies: This judgment was published in 1689, after the downfall of Jeffreys. It was thought necessary to apologise in the preface for printing anything that bore so odious a name. "To commend this argument," says the editor, "I'll not undertake, because of the author. But yet I may tell you what is told me, that it is worthy any gentleman's perusal." The language of Jeffreys is most offensive, sometimes scurrilous, sometimes basely adulatory: but his reasoning as to the mere point of law is certainly able, if not conclusive.

The nation, however, relieved at once from a multitude of impositions and vexations which were painfully felt every day at every fireside, was in no humour to dispute the validity of the charters under which a few companies in London traded with distant parts of the world.

Of these companies by far the most important was that which had been, on the last day of the sixteenth century, incorporated by Queen Elizabeth under the name of the Governor and Company of Merchants of London trading to the East Indies.* When this celebrated body began to exist, the Mogul monarchy was at the zenith of power and glory. Akbar, the ablest and the best of the princes of the House of Tamerlane, had just been borne, full of years and honours, to a mausoleum surpassing in magnificence any that Europe could show. He had bequeathed to his posterity an empire containing more than twenty times the population, and yielding more than twenty times the revenue, of the England which, under our great Queen, held a foremost place among European powers. It is curious and interesting to consider how little the two countries, destined to be one day so closely connected, were then known to each other. The most enlightened Englishmen looked on India with ignorant admiration. The most enlightened natives of India were scarcely aware that England existed. Our ancestors had a dim notion of endless bazaars, swarming with buyers and sellers, and blazing with cloth of gold, with variegated silks, and with precious stones; of treasuries where diamonds were piled in heaps, and sequins in mountains; of palaces, compared with which Whitehall and Hampton Court were hovels; of armies ten times as numerous as that which they had seen assembled at Tilbury to repel the Armada. On the other hand, it was probably not known to one of the statesmen in the Durbar of Agra that there was, near the setting sun, a great city of infidels called London, where a woman reigned, and that she had given to an association of Frank merchants the exclusive privilege of freighting ships from her dominions to the Indian seas. That this association would one day rule all India, from the ocean to the everlasting snow, would reduce to profound obedience great provinces which had never submitted to Akbar's authority, would send Lieutenant Governors to preside in his capital, and would dole out a monthly pension to

---

* I have left my account of the East India Company as it stood in 1855. It is unnecessary to say that it contains some expressions which would not have been used, if it had been written in 1858.

his heir, would have seemed to the wisest of European or of Oriental politicians as impossible as that inhabitants of our globe should found an empire in Venus or Jupiter.

Three generations passed away; and still nothing indicated that the East India Company would ever become a great Asiatic potentate. The Mogul empire, though undermined by internal causes of decay, and tottering to its fall, still presented to distant nations the appearance of undiminished prosperity and vigour. Aurengzebe, who, in the same month in which Oliver Cromwell died, assumed the magnificent title of Conqueror of the World, continued to reign till Anne had been long on the English throne. He was the sovereign of a larger territory than had obeyed any of his predecessors. His name was great in the farthest regions of the West. Here he had been made by Dryden the hero of a tragedy which would alone suffice to show how little the English of that age knew about the vast empire which their grandchildren were to conquer and to govern. The poet's Mussulman princes make love in the style of Amadis, preach about the death of Socrates, and embellish their discourse with allusions to the mythological stories of Ovid. The Brahminical metempsychosis is represented as an article of the Mussulman creed; and the Mussulman Sultanas burn themselves with their husbands after the Brahminical fashion. This drama, once rapturously applauded by crowded theatres, and known by heart to fine gentlemen and fine ladies, is now forgotten. But one noble passage still lives, and is repeated by thousands who know not whence it comes.*

Though nothing yet indicated the high political destiny of the East India Company, that body had a great sway in the City of London. The offices, built on a very small part of the ground which the present offices cover, had escaped the ravages of the fire. The India House of those days was an edifice of timber and plaster, rich with the quaint carving and latticework of the Elizabethan age. Above the windows was a painting which represented a fleet of merchantmen tossing on the waves. The whole was surmounted by a colossal wooden seaman, who, from between two dol-

---

* Addison's Clarinda, in the week of which she kept a journal, read nothing but Aurengzebe: Spectator, 323. She dreamed that Mr. Froth lay at her feet, and called her Indamora. Her friend Miss Kitty repeated, without book, the eight best lines of the play; those, no doubt, which begin, "Trust on, and think tomorrow will repay." There are not eight finer lines in Lucretius.

phins, looked down on the crowds of Leadenhall Street.* In this abode, narrow and humble indeed when compared with the vast labyrinth of passages and chambers which now bears the same name, the Company enjoyed, during the greater part of the reign of Charles the Second, a prosperity to which the history of trade scarcely furnishes any parallel, and which excited the wonder, the cupidity, and the envious animosity of the whole capital. Wealth and luxury were then rapidly increasing. The taste for the spices, the tissues, and the jewels of the East became stronger day by day. Tea, which, at the time when Monk brought the army of Scotland to London, had been handed round to be stared at and just touched with the lips, as a great rarity from China, was, eight years later, a regular article of import, and was soon consumed in such quantities that financiers began to consider it as an important source of revenue.† The progress which was making in the art of war had created an unprecedented demand for the ingredients of which gunpowder is compounded. It was calculated that all Europe would hardly produce in a year saltpetre enough for the siege of one town fortified on the principles of Vauban.‡ But for the supplies from India, it was said, the English government would be unable to equip a fleet without digging up the cellars of London in order to collect the nitrous particles from the walls.§ Before the Restoration scarcely one ship from the Thames had ever visited the Delta of the Ganges. But, during the twenty-three years which followed the Restoration, the value of the annual imports from that rich and populous district increased from eight thousand pounds to three hundred thousand.

The gains of the body which had the exclusive possession of this fast growing trade were almost incredible. The capital which had been actually paid up did not exceed three hundred and seventy thousand pounds : but the Company could, without difficulty, borrow money at six per cent, and the borrowed money, thrown into the trade, produced, it was

* A curious engraving of the India House of the seventeenth century will be found in the Gentleman's Magazine for December 1784.

† It is a curious fact, which I do not remember to have ever seen noticed, that tea came into fashion, and, after a short time, went out of fashion, at Paris, some years before the name appears to have been known in London.

Cardinal Mazarin and the Chancellor Seguier were great tea drinkers. See the letters of Gui Patin to Charles Spon, dated March 10. and 22. 1648, and April 1. 1657. Patin calls the taste for tea "l'impertinente nouveauté du siècle."

‡ See Davenant's Letter to Mulgrave.

§ Answer to Two Letters concerning the East India Company, 1676.

rumoured, thirty per cent. The profits were such that, in
1676, every proprietor received as a bonus a quantity of
stock equal to that which he held. On the capital, thus
doubled, were paid, during five years, dividends amounting
on an average to twenty per cent annually. There had been
a time when a hundred pounds of the stock could be purchased for sixty. Even in 1664 the price in the market was
only seventy. But in 1677 the price had risen to two hundred and forty-five: in 1681 it was three hundred: it subsequently rose to three hundred and sixty; and it is said that
some sales were effected at five hundred.*

The enormous gains of the Indian trade might perhaps
have excited little murmuring if they had been distributed
among numerous proprietors. But, while the value of the
stock went on increasing, the number of stockholders went
on diminishing. At the time when the prosperity of the
Company reached the highest point, the management was
entirely in the hands of a few merchants of enormous wealth.
A proprietor then had a vote for every five hundred pounds of
stock that stood in his name. It is asserted in the pamphlets
of that age that five persons had a sixth part, and fourteen
persons a third part of the votes.† More than one fortunate
speculator was said to derive an annual income of ten thousand pounds from the monopoly; and one great man was
pointed out on the Royal Exchange as having, by judicious
or lucky purchases of stock, created in no long time an estate
of twenty thousand a year. This commercial grandee, who
in wealth, and in the influence which attends wealth, vied
with the greatest nobles of his time, was Sir Josiah Child.
There were those who still remembered him an apprentice,
sweeping one of the counting houses of the City. But from
a humble position his abilities had raised him rapidly to
opulence, power, and fame. Before the Restoration he was
highly considered in the mercantile world. Soon after that
event he published his thoughts on the philosophy of trade.
His speculations were not always sound: but they were the
speculations of an ingenious and reflecting man. Into whatever errors he may occasionally have fallen as a theorist, it is
certain that, as a practical man of business, he had few
equals. Almost as soon as he became a member of the com-

* Anderson's Dictionary ; G. White's
Account of the Trade to the East Indies,
1691 ; Treatise on the East India Trade,
by Philopatris, 1681

† Reasons for constituting a New East
India Company in London, 1681 ; Some
Remarks upon the Present State of the
East India Company's Affairs, 1690.

mittee which directed the affairs of the Company, his ascendency was felt. Soon many of the most important posts, both in Leadenhall Street and in the factories of Bombay and Bengal, were filled by his kinsmen and creatures. His riches, though expended with ostentatious profusion, continued to increase and multiply. He obtained a baronetcy: he purchased a stately seat at Wanstead; and there he laid out immense sums in excavating fishponds, and in planting whole square miles of barren land with walnut trees. He married his daughter to the eldest son of the Duke of Beaufort, and paid down with her a portion of fifty thousand pounds.*

But this wonderful prosperity was not uninterrupted. Towards the close of the reign of Charles the Second the Company began to be fiercely attacked from without, and to be at the same time distracted by internal dissensions. The profits of the Indian trade were so tempting that private adventurers had sometimes, in defiance of the royal charter, fitted out ships for the Eastern seas. But the competition of these interlopers did not become really formidable till the year 1680. The nation was then violently agitated by the dispute about the Exclusion Bill. Timid men were anticipating another civil war. The two great parties, newly named Whigs and Tories, were fiercely contending in every county and town of England; and the feud soon spread to every corner of the civilised world where Englishmen were to be found.

The Company was popularly considered as a Whig body. Among the members of the directing committee were some of the most vehement Exclusionists in the City. Indeed two of them, Sir Samuel Barnardistone and Thomas Papillon, drew on themselves a severe persecution by their zeal against Popery and arbitrary power.† Child had been originally brought into the direction by these men: he had long acted in concert with them; and he was supposed to hold their political opinions. He had, during many years, stood high in the esteem of the chiefs of the parliamentary opposition, and had been especially obnoxious to the Duke of York.‡ The interlopers therefore determined to affect the character of loyal men, who were determined to stand by the throne against the insolent tribunes of the City. They spread, at all the factories in the East, reports that England was in con-

* Evelyn, March 16. 168⅔.
† See the State Trials.

‡ Pepys's Diary, April 2. and May 10. 1669.

fusion, that the sword had been drawn or would immediately be drawn, and that the Company was forward in the rebellion. These rumours, which, in truth, were not improbable, easily found credit among people separated from London by what was then a voyage of twelve months. Some servants of the Company who were in ill humour with their employers, and others who were zealous royalists, joined the private traders. At Bombay, the garrison and the great body of the English inhabitants declared that they would no longer obey a society which did not obey the King: they imprisoned the Deputy Governor; and they proclaimed that they held the island for the Crown. At Saint Helena there was a rising. The insurgents took the name of King's men, and displayed the royal standard. They were, not without difficulty, put down; and some of them were executed by martial law.*

If the Company had still been a Whig Company when the news of these commotions reached England, it is probable that the government would have approved of the conduct of the mutineers, and that the charter on which the monopoly depended would have had the fate which about the same time befell so many other charters. But while the interlopers were, at a distance of many thousands of miles, making war on the Company in the name of the King, the Company and the King had been reconciled. When the Oxford Parliament had been dissolved, when many signs indicated that a strong reaction in favour of prerogative was at hand, when all the corporations which had incurred the royal displeasure were beginning to tremble for their franchises, a rapid and complete revolution took place at the India House. Child, who was then Governor, or, in the modern phrase, Chairman, separated himself from his old friends, excluded them from the direction, and negotiated a treaty of peace and of close alliance with the Court.† It is not improbable that the near connection into which he had just entered with the great Tory house of Beaufort may have had something to do with this change in his politics. Papillon, Barnardistone, and other Whig shareholders, sold their stock: their places in the committee were supplied by persons devoted to Child; and he was henceforth the autocrat of the Company. The treasures of the Company were absolutely at his disposal. The most important papers of the Company were kept, not in the muniment room of the office in Leadenhall Street, but in his desk at

* Tench's Modest and Just Apology for the East India Company, 1690.
† Some Remarks on the Present State of the East India Company's Affairs, 1690; Hamilton's New Account of the East Indies.

Wanstead. The boundless power which he exercised at the India House enabled him to become a favourite at Whitehall; and the favour which he enjoyed at Whitehall confirmed his power at the India House. A present of ten thousand guineas was graciously received from him by Charles. Ten thousand more were accepted by James, who readily consented to become a holder of stock. All who could help or hurt at Court, ministers, mistresses, priests, were kept in good humour by presents of shawls and silks, birds' nests and atar of roses, bulses of diamonds, and bags of guineas.* Of what the Dictator expended no account was asked by his colleagues; and in truth he seems to have deserved the confidence which they reposed in him. His bribes distributed with judicious prodigality, speedily produced a large return. Just when the Court became all powerful in the State, he became all powerful at the Court. Jeffreys pronounced a decision in favour of the monopoly, and of the strongest acts which had been done in defence of the monopoly. James ordered his seal to be put to a new charter which confirmed and extended all the privileges bestowed on the Company by his predecessors. All captains of Indiamen received commissions from the Crown, and were permitted to hoist the royal ensigns.† John Child, brother of Sir Josiah, and Governor of Bombay, was created a baronet by the style of Sir John Child of Surat: he was declared General of all the English forces in the East; and he was authorised to assume the title of Excellency. The Company, on the other hand, distinguished itself among many servile corporations by obsequious homage to the throne, and set to all the merchants of the kingdom the example of readily and even eagerly paying those customs which James, at the commencement of his reign, exacted without the authority of Parliament.‡

It seemed that the private trade would now be utterly crushed, and that the monopoly, protected by the whole strength of the royal prerogative, would be more profitable than ever. But unfortunately just at this moment a quarrel arose between the agents of the Company in India and the Mogul Government. Where the fault lay is a question which was vehemently disputed at the time, and which it is now impossible to decide. The interlopers threw all the blame

---

* White's Account of the East India Trade, 1691; Pierce Butler's Tale, 1691.

† White's Account of the Trade to the East Indies, 1691; Hamilton's New Account of the East Indies; Sir John Wyborne to Pepys from Bombay, Jan. 7. 168⅞.

‡ London Gazette, Feb. ¹⁶⁄₂₆. 168⅘.

on the Company. The Governor of Bombay, they affirmed, had always been grasping and violent : but his baronetcy and his military commission had completely turned his head. The very natives who were employed about the factory had noticed the change, and had muttered in their broken English, that there must be some strange curse attending the word Excellency; for that, ever since the chief of the strangers was called Excellency, everything had gone to ruin. Meanwhile, it was said, the brother in England had sanctioned all the unjust and impolitic acts of the brother in India, till at length insolence and rapine, disgraceful to the English nation and to the Christian religion, had roused the just resentment of the native authorities. The Company warmly recriminated. The story told at the India House was that the quarrel was entirely the work of the interlopers, who were now designated not only as interlopers but as traitors. They had, it was alleged, by flattery, by presents, and by false accusations, induced the viceroys of the Mogul to oppress and persecute the body which in Asia represented the English Crown. And indeed this charge seems not to have been altogether without foundation. It is certain that one of the most pertinacious enemies of the Childs went up to the Court of Aurengzebe, took his station at the palace gate, stopped the Great King who was in the act of mounting on horseback, and, lifting a petition high in the air, demanded justice in the name of the common God of Christians and Mussulmans.* Whether Aurengzebe paid much attention to the charges brought by infidel Franks against each other may be doubted. But it is certain that a complete rupture took place between his deputies and the servants of the Company. On the sea the ships of his subjects were seized by the English. On land the English settlements were taken and plundered. The trade was suspended; and, though great annual dividends were still paid in London, they were no longer paid out of annual profits.

Just at this conjuncture, while every Indiaman that arrived in the Thames was bringing unwelcome news from the East, all the politics of Sir Josiah were utterly confounded by the revolution. He had flattered himself that he had secured the body of which he was the chief against the machinations of interlopers, by uniting it closely with the strongest government that had existed within his memory. That government had fallen ; and whatever had leaned on the ruined fabric began to totter. The bribes had been thrown away. The

* Hamilton's New Account of the East Indies.

connections which had been the strength and boast of the corporation were now its weakness and its shame. The King who had been one of its members was an exile. The Judge by whom all its most exorbitant pretensions had been pronounced legitimate was a prisoner. All the old enemies of the Company, reinforced by those great Whig merchants whom Child had expelled from the direction, demanded justice and vengeance from the Whig House of Commons which had just placed William and Mary on the throne. No voice was louder in accusation than that of Papillon, who had, some years before, been more zealous for the charter than any man in London.* The Commons censured in severe terms the persons who had inflicted death by martial law at Saint Helena, and even resolved that some of those offenders should be excluded from the Act of Indemnity.† The great question, how the trade with the East should for the future be carried on, was referred to a Committee. The report was to have been made on the twenty-seventh of January 1690; but on that very day the Parliament ceased to exist.

The first two sessions of the succeeding Parliament were so short and so busy that little was said about India in either House. But out of Parliament, all the arts both of controversy and of intrigue were employed on both sides. Almost as many pamphlets were published about the India trade as about the oaths. The despot of Leadenhall Street was libelled in prose and verse. Wretched puns were made on his name. He was compared to Cromwell, to the King of France, to Goliath of Gath, to the Devil. It was vehemently declared to be necessary that, in any Act which might be passed for the regulation of our traffic with the Eastern seas, Sir Josiah should be by name excluded from all trust.‡

There were, however, great differences of opinion among those who agreed in hating Child and the body of which he was the head. The manufacturers of Spitalfields, of Norwich, of Yorkshire, and of Wiltshire, considered the trade with the Eastern seas as rather injurious than beneficial to the king-

* Papillon was of course reproached with his inconsistency. Among the pamphlets of that time is one entitled, " A Treatise concerning the East India Trade, wrote at the Instance of Thomas Papillon, Esquire, and in his House, and printed in the year 1680, and now reprinted for the better Satisfaction of himself and others."

† Commons' Journals, June 8. 1689.

‡ Among the pamphlets in which Child is most fiercely attacked, are: Some Remarks on the Present State of the East India Company's Affairs, 1690; Pierce Butler's Tale, 1691; and White's Account of the Trade to the East Indies, 1691.

dom. The importation of Indian spices, indeed, was admitted to be harmless, and the importation of Indian saltpetre to be necessary. But the importation of silks and of Bengals, as shawls were then called, was pronounced to be a curse to the country. The effect of the growing taste for such frippery was that our gold and silver went abroad, and that much excellent English drapery lay in our warehouses till it was devoured by the moths. Those, it was said, were happy days for the inhabitants both of our pasture lands and of our manufacturing towns, when every gown, every waistcoat, every bed was made of materials which our own flocks had furnished to our own looms. Where were now the brave old hangings of arras which had adorned the walls of lordly mansions in the time of Elizabeth? And was it not a shame to see a gentleman, whose ancestors had worn nothing but stuffs made by English workmen out of English fleeces, flaunting in a calico shirt and a pair of silk stockings from Moorshedabad? Clamours such as these had, a few years before, extorted from Parliament the Act which required that the dead should be wrapped in woollen; and some sanguine clothiers hoped that the legislature would, by excluding all Indian textures from our ports, impose the same necessity on the living.*

But this feeling was confined to a minority. The public was, indeed, inclined rather to overrate than to underrate the benefits which might be derived by England from the Indian trade. What was the most effectual mode of extending that trade was a question which excited general interest, and which was answered in very different ways.

A small party, consisting chiefly of merchants resident at Bristol and other provincial seaports, maintained that the best way to extend trade was to leave it free. They urged the well known arguments which prove that monopoly is injurious to commerce; and, having fully established the general law, they asked why the commerce between England and India was to be considered as an exception to that law. Any trader ought, they said, to be permitted to send from any port in the kingdom a cargo to Surat or Canton as freely as he now sent a cargo to Hamburg or Lisbon.† In our

---

* Discourse concerning the East India Trade, showing it to be unprofitable to the Kingdom, by Mr. Cary; Pierce Butler's Tale, representing the State of the Wool Case, or the East India Trade truly stated, 1691. Several petitions to the same effect will be found in the Journals of the House of Commons.

† Reasons against establishing an East India Company with a Joint Stock, exclusive to all others, 1691.

time these doctrines may probably be considered, not only as sound, but as trite and obvious. In the seventeenth century, however, they were thought paradoxical. It was then generally held to be an almost selfevident truth, that our trade with the countries lying beyond the Cape of Good Hope could be advantageously carried on only by means of a great Joint Stock Company. There was no analogy, it was said, between our European trade and our Indian trade. Our government had diplomatic relations with the European States. If necessary, a maritime force could easily be sent from hence to the mouth of the Elbe or of the Tagus. But the English Kings had no envoy at the Court of Agra or Pekin. There was seldom a single English man of war within ten thousand miles of the Bay of Bengal or of the Gulf of Siam. As our merchants could not, in those remote seas, be protected by their Sovereign, they must protect themselves, and must, for that end, exercise some of the rights of sovereignty. They must have forts, garrisons, and armed ships. They must have power to send and receive embassies, to make a treaty of alliance with one Asiatic prince, to wage war on another. It was evidently impossible that every merchant should have this power independently of the rest. The merchants trading to India must therefore be joined together in a corporation which could act as one man. In support of these arguments the example of the Dutch was cited, and was generally considered as decisive. For in that age the immense prosperity of Holland was everywhere regarded with admiration, not the less earnest because it was largely mingled with envy and hatred. In all that related to trade, her statesmen were considered as oracles, and her institutions as models.

The great majority, therefore, of those who assailed the Company assailed it, not because it traded on joint funds and possessed exclusive privileges, but because it was ruled by one man, and because his rule had been mischievous to the public, and beneficial only to himself and his creatures. The obvious remedy, it was said, for the evils which his maladministration had produced was to transfer the monopoly to a new corporation so constituted as to be in no danger of falling under the dominion either of a despot or of a narrow oligarchy. Many persons who were desirous to be members of such a corporation formed themselves into a society, signed an engagement, and entrusted the care of their interests to a committee which contained some of the chief

traders of the City. This society, though it had, in the eye
of the law, no personality, was early designated, in popular
speech, as the New Company; and the hostilities between the
New Company and the Old Company soon caused almost as
much excitement and anxiety, at least in that busy hive of
which the Royal Exchange was the centre, as the hostilities
between the Allies and the French King. The headquarters of
the younger association were in Dowgate: the Skinners lent
their stately hall; and the meetings were held in a parlour
renowned for the fragrance which exhaled from a magnificent
wainscot of cedar.*

While the contention was hottest, important news arrived
from India, and was announced in the London Gazette as in
the highest degree satisfactory. Peace had been concluded
between the Great Mogul and the English. That mighty
potentate had not only withdrawn his troops from the
factories, but had bestowed on the Company privileges such
as it had never before enjoyed. Soon, however, appeared
a very different version of the story. The enemies of Child
had, before this time, accused him of systematically publish-
ing false intelligence. He had now, they said, outlied himself. They had obtained a true copy of the Firman which
had put an end to the war; and they printed a translation
of it. It appeared that Aurengzebe had contemptuously
granted to the English, in consideration of their penitence
and of a large tribute, his forgiveness for their past delinquency, had charged them to behave themselves better for the
future, and had, in the tone of a master, laid on them his
commands to remove the principal offender, Sir John Child,
from power and trust. The death of Sir John occurred so
seasonably that these commands could not be obeyed. But
it was only too evident that the pacification which the rulers
of the India House had represented as advantageous and
honourable had really been effected on terms disgraceful to
the English name.†

During the summer of 1691, the controversy which raged on
this subject between the Leadenhall Street Company and the
Dowgate Company kept the City in constant agitation. In
the autumn, the Parliament had no sooner met than both the
contending parties presented petitions to the House of Com-

---

* The engagement was printed, and   † London Gazette, May 11. 1691;
has been several times reprinted. As to White's Account of the East India
Skinner's Hall, see Seymour's History of Trade.
London, 1734.

mons.* The petitions were immediately taken into serious consideration, and resolutions of grave importance were passed. The first resolution was that the trade with the East Indies was beneficial to the kingdom: the second was that the trade with the East Indies would be best carried on by a joint stock company possessed of exclusive privileges.† It was plain, therefore, that neither those manufacturers who wished to prohibit the trade, nor those merchants at the outports who wished to throw it open, had the smallest chance of attaining their objects. The only question left was the question between the Old and the New Company. Seventeen years elapsed before that question ceased to disturb both political and commercial circles. It was fatal to the honour and power of one great minister, and to the peace and prosperity of many private families. The tracts which the rival bodies put forth against each other were innumerable. If the drama of that age may be trusted, the feud between the India House and Skinners' Hall was sometimes as serious an impediment to the course of true love in London as the feud of the Capulets and Montagues had been at Verona.‡ Which of the two contending parties was the stronger it is not easy to say. The New Company was supported by the Whigs, the Old Company by the Tories. The New Company was popular: for it promised largely, and could not yet be accused of having broken its promises: it made no dividends, and therefore was not envied: it had no power to oppress, and had therefore been guilty of no oppression. The Old Company, though generally regarded with little favour by the public, had the immense advantage of being in possession, and of having only to stand on the defensive. The burden of framing a plan for the regulation of the India Trade, and of proving that plan to be better than the plan hitherto followed, lay on the New Company. The Old Company had merely to find objections to every change that was proposed; and such objections there was little difficulty in finding. The members of the New Company were ill provided with the means of purchasing support at Court and in Parliament. They had no corporate existence, no common treasury. If any of them gave a bribe, he gave it out of his own pocket, with little chance of being reimbursed.

---

* Commons' Journals, Oct. 28. 1691.
† Ibid. Oct. 29. 1691.
‡ Rowe in the Biter, which was damned, and deserved to be so, introduced an old gentleman haranguing his daughter thus: "Thou hast been bred up like a virtuous and a sober maiden; and wouldest thou take the part of a profane wretch who sold his stock out of the Old East India Company?"

But the Old Company, though surrounded by dangers, still held its exclusive privileges, and still made its enormous profits. Its stock had indeed gone down greatly in value since the golden days of Charles the Second : but a hundred pounds still sold for a hundred and twenty-two.* After a large dividend had been paid to the proprietors, a surplus remained amply sufficient, in those days, to corrupt half a cabinet ; and this surplus was absolutely at the disposal of one able, determined, and unscrupulous man, who maintained the fight with wonderful art and pertinacity.

The majority of the Commons wished to effect a compromise, to retain the Old Company, but to remodel it, and to incorporate with it the members of the New Company. With this view it was, after long and vehement debates and close divisions, resolved that the capital should be increased to a million and a half. In order to prevent a single person or a small junto from domineering over the whole society, it was determined that five thousand pounds of stock should be the largest quantity that any single proprietor could hold, and that those who held more should be required to sell the overplus at any price not below par. In return for the exclusive privilege of trading to the Eastern seas, the Company was to be required to furnish annually five hundred tons of saltpetre to the Crown at a low price, and to export annually English manufactures to the value of two hundred thousand pounds.†

A bill founded on these resolutions was brought in, read twice, and committed, but was suffered to drop in consequence of the positive refusal of Child and his associates to accept the offered terms. He objected to every part of the plan ; and his objections are highly curious and amusing. The great monopolist took his stand on the principles of free trade. In a luminous and powerfully written paper he exposed the absurdity of the expedients which the House of Commons had devised. To limit the amount of stock which might stand in a single name would, he said, be most unreasonable. Surely a proprietor whose whole fortune was staked on the success of the Indian trade was far more likely to exert all his faculties vigorously for the promotion of that trade than a proprietor who had risked only what it would be no great disaster to lose. The demand that saltpetre should be furnished to the Crown for a fixed sum Child met

* Hop to the States General, $\frac{Oct. 30.}{Nov. 9.}$ 1691.

† Hop mentions the length and warmth of the debates ; Nov. $\frac{13.}{23.}$ 1691. See the Commons' Journals, Dec. 17. and 18.

by those arguments, familiar to our generation, which prove that prices should be left to settle themselves. To the demand that the Company should bind itself to export annually two hundred thousand pounds' worth of English manufactures he very properly replied that the Company would most gladly export two millions' worth if the market required such a supply, and that, if the market were overstocked, it would be mere folly to send good cloth half round the world to be eaten by white ants. It was never, he declared with much spirit, found politic to put trade into straitlaced bodices, which, instead of making it grow upright and thrive, must either kill it or force it awry.

The Commons, irritated by Child's obstinacy, presented an address requesting the King to dissolve the Old Company, and to grant a charter to a new Company on such terms as to His Majesty's wisdom might seem fit.* It is plainly implied in the terms of this address that the Commons thought the King constitutionally competent to grant an exclusive privilege of trading to the East Indies.

The King replied that the subject was most important, that he would consider it maturely, and that he would, at a future time, give the House a more precise answer.† In Parliament nothing more was said on the subject during that session: but out of Parliament the war was fiercer than ever; and the belligerents were by no means scrupulous about the means which they employed. The chief weapons of the New Company were libels: the chief weapons of the Old Company were bribes.

In the same week in which the bill for the regulation of the Indian trade was suffered to drop, another bill, which had produced great excitement and had called forth an almost unprecedented display of parliamentary ability, underwent the same fate.

During the eight years which preceded the Revolution, the Whigs had complained bitterly, and not more bitterly than justly, of the hard measure dealt out to persons accused of political offences. Was it not monstrous, they asked, that a culprit should be denied a sight of his indictment? Often an unhappy prisoner had not known of what he was accused till he had held up his hand at the bar. The crime imputed to him might be plotting to shoot the King: it might be plotting to poison the King. The more innocent the de-

Debates on the Bill for regulating trials in cases of high treason.

* Commons' Journals, Feb. 4. and 6. 1691. † Ibid. Feb. 11. 1691.

fendant was, the less likely he was to guess the nature of the
charge on which he was to be tried; and how could he have
evidence ready to rebut a charge the nature of which he could
not guess? The Crown had power to compel the attendance
of witnesses. The prisoner had no such power. If witnesses
voluntarily came forward to speak in his favour, they could
not be sworn. Their testimony therefore made less impression on a jury than the testimony of the witnesses for the
prosecution, whose veracity was guaranteed by the most
solemn sanctions of law and of religion. The juries, carefully selected by Sheriffs whom the government had named,
were men animated by the fiercest party spirit, men who had
as little tenderness for an Exclusionist or a Dissenter as for a
mad dog. The Crown was served by a band of able, experienced, and unprincipled lawyers, who could, by merely
glancing over a brief, distinguish every weak and every
strong point of a case, whose presence of mind never failed
them, whose flow of speech was inexhaustible, and who had
passed their lives in dressing up the worse reason so as to
make it appear the better. Was it not horrible to see three
or four of these shrewd, learned, and callous orators arrayed
against one poor wretch who had never in his life uttered a
word in public, who was ignorant of the legal definition of
treason and of the first principles of the law of evidence, and
whose intellect, unequal at best to a fencing match with professional gladiators, was confused by the near prospect of a
cruel and ignominious death? Such however was the rule;
and even for a man so much stupefied by sickness that he
could not hold up his hand or make his voice heard, even for
a poor old woman who understood nothing of what was passing except that she was going to be roasted alive for doing
an act of charity, no advocate was suffered to utter a word.
That a State trial so conducted was little better than a
judicial murder had been, during the proscription of the
Whig party, a fundamental article of the Whig creed. The
Tories, on the other hand, though they could not deny that
there had been some hard cases, maintained that, on the
whole, substantial justice had been done. Perhaps a few
seditious persons who had gone very near to the frontier of
treason, but had not actually passed that frontier, might have
suffered as traitors. But was that a sufficient reason for en-
abling the chiefs of the Rye House Plot and of the Western In
surrection to elude, by mere chicanery, the punishment of their
guilt? On what principle was the traitor to have chances of

escape which were not allowed to the felon? The culprit who was accused of larceny was subject to all the same disadvantages which, in the case of regicides and rebels, were thought so unjust: yet nobody pitied him. Nobody thought it monstrous that he should not have time to study a copy of his indictment, that his witnesses should be examined without being sworn, that he should be left to defend himself, without the help of counsel, against the most crafty veteran of the Old Bailey bar. The Whigs, it seemed, reserved all their compassion for those crimes which subvert government and dissolve the whole frame of human society. Guy Faux was to be treated with an indulgence which was not to be extended to a shoplifter. Bradshaw was to have privileges which were refused to a boy who had robbed a henroost.

The Revolution produced, as was natural, some change in the sentiments of both the great parties. In the days when none but Roundheads and Nonconformists were accused of treason, even the most humane and upright Cavaliers were disposed to think that the laws which were the safeguards of the throne could hardly be too severe. But, as soon as loyal Tory gentlemen and venerable fathers of the Church were in danger of being called in question for corresponding with Saint Germains, a new light flashed on many understandings which had been unable to discover the smallest injustice in the proceedings against Algernon Sidney and Alice Lisle. It was no longer thought utterly absurd to maintain that some advantages which were withheld from a man accused of felony might reasonably be allowed to a man accused of treason. What probability was there that any sheriff would pack a jury, that any barrister would employ all the arts of sophistry and rhetoric, that any judge would strain law and misrepresent evidence, in order to convict an innocent person of burglary or sheepstealing? But on a trial for high treason a verdict of acquittal must always be considered as a defeat of the government; and there was but too much reason to fear that many sheriffs, barristers, and judges might be impelled by party spirit, or by some baser motive, to do anything which might save the government from the inconvenience and shame of a defeat. The cry of the whole body of Tories now was that the lives of good Englishmen who happened to be obnoxious to the ruling powers were not sufficiently protected: and this cry was swelled by the voices of some lawyers who had distinguished themselves by the malignant zeal and dishonest ingenuity with which they had

conducted State prosecutions in the days of Charles and
James.

The feeling of the Whigs, though it had not, like the
feeling of the Tories, undergone a complete change, was yet
not quite what it had been. Some, who had thought it most
unjust that Russell should have no counsel and that Cornish
should have no copy of his indictment, now began to mutter
that the times had changed; that the dangers of the State
were extreme; that liberty, property, religion, national independence, were all at stake; that many Englishmen were
engaged in schemes of which the object was to make England
the slave of France and of Rome; and that it would be most
unwise to relax, at such a moment, the laws against political
offences. It was true that the injustice, with which, in the
late reigns, State trials had been conducted, had given great
scandal. But this injustice was to be ascribed to the bad
kings and bad judges with whom the nation had been cursed.
William was now on the throne: Holt was seated for life on
the bench; and William would never exact, nor would Holt
ever perform, services so shameful and wicked as those for
which the banished tyrant had rewarded Jeffreys with riches
and titles. This language however was at first held but by few.
The Whigs, as a party, seem to have felt that they could not
honourably defend, in the season of their prosperity, what, in
the time of their adversity, they had always designated as a
crying grievance. A bill for regulating trials in cases of high
treason was brought into the House of Commons, and was
received with general applause. Treby had the courage to
make some objections: but no division took place. The chief
enactments were that no person should be convicted of high
treason committed more than three years before the indictment was found; that every person indicted for high treason
should be allowed to avail himself of the assistance of counsel,
and should be furnished, ten days before the trial, with a copy
of the indictment, and with a list of the freeholders from
among whom the jury was to be taken; that his witnesses
should be sworn, and that they should be cited by the same
process by which the attendance of the witnesses against him
was secured.

The Bill went to the Upper House, and came back with an
important amendment. The Lords had long complained of
the anomalous and iniquitous constitution of that tribunal
which had jurisdiction over them in cases of life and death.
When a grand jury has found a bill of indictment against a
temporal peer for any offence higher than a misdemeanour,

the Crown appoints a Lord High Steward; and in the Lord
High Steward's Court the case is tried. This Court was
anciently composed in two very different ways. It consisted,
if Parliament happened to be sitting, of all the members of
the Upper House. When Parliament was not sitting, the
Lord High Steward summoned any twelve or more peers at
his discretion to form a jury. The consequence was that a
peer accused of high treason during a recess was tried by a
jury which his prosecutors had packed. The Lords now demanded that, during a recess as well as during a session,
every peer accused of high treason should be tried by the
whole body of the peerage.

The demand was resisted by the House of Commons with a
vehemence and obstinacy which men of the present generation may find it difficult to understand. The truth is that
some invidious privileges of peerage which have since been
abolished, and others which have since fallen into entire
desuetude, were then in full force and were daily used. No
gentleman who had had a dispute with a nobleman could
think, without indignation, of the advantages enjoyed by
the favoured caste. If His Lordship were sued at law, his
privilege enabled him to impede the course of justice. If a
rude word were spoken of him, such a word as he might himself utter with perfect impunity, he might vindicate his insulted dignity both by civil and criminal proceedings. If a
barrister, in the discharge of his duty to a client, spoke with
severity of the conduct of a noble seducer, if an honest squire
on the racecourse applied the proper epithets to the tricks of
a noble swindler, the affronted patrician had only to complain
to the proud and powerful body of which he was a member.
His brethren made his cause their own. The offender was
taken into custody by Black Rod, brought to the bar, flung
into prison, and kept there till he was glad to obtain forgiveness by the most degrading submissions. Nothing could
therefore be more natural than that an attempt of the Peers
to obtain any new advantage for their order should be regarded by the Commons with extreme jealousy. There is
strong reason to suspect that some able Whig politicians,
who thought it dangerous to relax, at that moment, the laws
against political offences, but who could not, without incurring the charge of inconsistency, declare themselves adverse to any relaxation, had conceived a hope that they might,
by fomenting the dispute about the Court of the Lord High
Steward, defer for at least a year the passing of a bill which
they disliked, and yet could not decently oppose. If this

really was their plan, it succeeded perfectly. The Lower House rejected the amendment: the Upper House persisted: a free conference was held; and the question was argued with great force and ingenuity on both sides.

The reasons in favour of the amendment are obvious, and indeed at first sight seem unanswerable. It was surely difficult to defend a system under which the Sovereign nominated a conclave of his own creatures to decide the fate of men whom he regarded as his mortal enemies. And could anything be more absurd than that a nobleman accused of high treason should be entitled to be tried by the whole body of his peers if his indictment happened to be brought into the House of Lords the minute before a prorogation, but that, if the indictment arrived a minute after the prorogation, he should be at the mercy of a small junto named by the very authority which prosecuted him? That anything could have been said on the other side seems strange: but those who managed the conference for the Commons were not ordinary men, and seem on this occasion to have put forth all their powers. Conspicuous among them was Charles Montague, who was rapidly rising to the highest rank among the orators of that age. To him the lead seems on this occasion to have been left; and to his pen we owe an account of the discussion, which gives an excellent notion of his talents for debate. "We have framed,"—such was in substance his reasoning,—"we have framed a law which has in it nothing exclusive, a law which will be a blessing to every class, from the highest to the lowest. The new securities, which we propose to give to innocence oppressed by power, are common between the premier peer and the humblest day labourer. The clause which establishes a time of limitation for prosecutions protects us all alike. To every Englishman accused of the highest crime against the state, whatever be his rank, we give the privilege of seeing his indictment, the privilege of being defended by counsel, the privilege of having his witnesses summoned by a writ of subpœna and sworn on the Holy Gospels. Such is the bill which we sent up to your Lordships, and you return it to us with a clause of which the effect is to give certain advantages to your noble order at the expense of the ancient prerogatives of the Crown. Surely before we consent to take away from the King any power which his predecessors have possessed for ages, and to give it to your Lordships, we ought to be satisfied that you are more likely to use it well than he. Something we must risk:

somebody we must trust; and since we are forced, much against our will, to institute what is necessarily an invidious comparison, we must own ourselves unable to discover any reason for believing that a prince is less to be trusted than an aristocracy. Is it reasonable, you ask, that you should be tried for your lives before a few members of your House, selected by the Crown? Is it reasonable, we ask in our turn, that you should have the privilege of being tried by all the members of your House, that is to say, by your brothers, your uncles, your first cousins, your second cousins, your fathers in law, your brothers in law, your most intimate friends? You marry so much into each other's families, you live so much in each other's society, that there is scarcely a nobleman who is not connected by consanguinity or affinity with several others, and who is not on terms of friendship with several more. There have been great men whose death put a third or fourth part of the baronage of England into mourning. Nor is there much danger that even those peers who may be unconnected with an accused lord will be disposed to send him to the block if they can with decency say ' Not Guilty, upon my honour.' For the ignominious death of a single member of a small aristocratical body necessarily leaves a stain on the reputation of his fellows. If, indeed, your Lordships proposed that every one of your body should be compelled to attend and vote, the Crown might have some chance of obtaining justice against a guilty peer, however strongly connected. But you propose that attendance shall be voluntary. Is it possible to doubt what the consequence will be? All the prisoner's relations and friends will be in their places to vote for him. Good nature and the fear of making powerful enemies will keep away many who, if they voted at all, would be forced by conscience and honour to vote against him. The new system which you propose would therefore evidently be unfair to the Crown; and you do not show any reason for believing that the old system has been found in practice unfair to yourselves. We may confidently affirm that, even under a government less just and merciful than that under which we have the happiness to live, an innocent peer has little to fear from any set of peers that can be brought together in Westminster Hall to try him. How stands the fact? In what single case has a guiltless head fallen by the verdict of this packed jury? It would be easy to make out a long list of squires, merchants, lawyers, surgeons, yeomen, artisans, ploughmen, whose blood, barbarously shed during the late evil times, cries for vengeance to heaven. But what single member of your House, in our days, or in the days of our fathers, or in the days of our grandfathers, suffered death unjustly by sentence of the Court of the Lord High Steward? Hundreds of the common people were sent to the gallows by common juries for the Rye House Plot and the Western Insurrection. One peer, and one alone, my Lord Delamere, was brought at that time before the Court of the Lord High Steward; and he was acquitted. You say that the evidence against him was legally insufficient. Be it so. But so was the evidence against Sidney, against Cornish, against Alice Lisle; yet it sufficed to destroy them. You say that the peers before whom my Lord Delamere was brought were selected with shameless unfairness by King James and by Jeffreys. Be it so. But this only proves that, under the worst possible King, and under the worst possible High Steward, a lord tried by lords has a better chance for life than a commoner who puts himself on his country. We cannot, therefore, under the mild government which we now possess, feel much apprehension for the safety of any innocent peer. Would that we felt as little apprehension for the safety of that government! But it is notorious that the settlement with which our liberties are inseparably bound up, is attacked at once by foreign and by domestic enemies. We cannot consent, at such a crisis, to relax the restraints which have, it may well be feared, already proved too feeble to prevent some men of high rank from plotting the ruin of their country. To sum up the whole, what is asked of us is that we will consent to transfer a certain power from their Majesties to your Lordships. Our answer is, that at this time, in our opinion, their Majesties have not too much power, and your Lordships have quite power enough."

These arguments, though eminently ingenious, and not without real force, failed to convince the Upper House. The Lords insisted that every peer should be entitled to be a Trier. The Commons were with difficulty induced to consent that the number of Triers should never be less than thirty-six, and positively refused to make any further concession. The bill was therefore suffered to drop.*

* The History of this bill is to be collected from the bill itself, which is among the archives of the Upper House, from the Journals of the two Houses during November and December 1690, and January 1691; particularly from the Commons' Journals of December 11. and January 13. and 25., and the Lords' Journals of January 20. and 28. See also Grey's Debates.

It is certain that those who in the conference on this bill represented the Commons did not exaggerate the dangers to which the government was exposed. While the constitution of the Court which was to try peers for treason was under discussion, a treason planned with rare skill by a peer was all but carried into execution.

Marlborough had never ceased to assure the Court of Saint Germains that the great crime which he had committed was constantly present to his thoughts, and that he lived only for the purpose of repentance and reparation. Not only had he been himself converted: he had also converted the Princess Anne. In 1688, the Churchills had, with little difficulty, induced her to fly from her father's palace. In 1691, they, with as little difficulty, induced her to copy out and sign a letter expressing her deep concern for his misfortunes and her earnest wish to atone for her breach of duty.* At the same time Marlborough held out hopes that it might be in his power to effect the restoration of his old master in the best possible way, without the help of a single foreign soldier or sailor, by the votes of the English Lords and Commons, and by the support of the English army. We are not fully informed as to all the details of his plan. But the outline is known to us from a most interesting paper written by James, of which one copy is in the Bodleian Library, and another among the archives of the French Foreign Office.

Plot formed by Marlborough against the government of William.

The jealousy with which the English regarded the Dutch was at this time intense. There had never been a hearty friendship between the nations. They were indeed near of kin to each other. They spoke two dialects of one widespread language. Both boasted of their political freedom. Both were attached to the reformed faith. Both were threatened by the same enemy, and could be safe only while they were united. Yet there was no cordial feeling between them. They would probably have loved each other more, if they had, in some respects, resembled each other less. They were the two great commercial nations, the two great maritime nations. In every sea their flags were found together, in the Baltic and in the Mediterranean, in the Gulf of Mexico and in the Straits of Malacca. Every where the merchant of London and the merchant of Amsterdam were trying to forestall each other and to undersell each other. In Europe the contest was not sanguinary. But too often in barbarous countries, where there was no law but force, the competitors had met, burning

* The letter, dated December 1. 1691, is in the Life of James, ii. 477.

with cupidity, burning with animosity, armed for battle, each suspecting the other of hostile designs, and each resolved to give the other no advantage. In such circumstances it is not strange that many violent and cruel acts should have been per-petrated. What had been done in those distant regions could seldom be exactly known in Europe. Everything was exagger-ated and distorted by vague report and by national prejudice. Here it was the popular belief that the English were always blameless, and that every quarrel was to be ascribed to the avarice and inhumanity of the Dutch. Lamentable events which had taken place in the Spice Islands were brought on our stage. The Englishmen were all saints and heroes; the Dutchmen all fiends in human shape, lying, robbing, ravish-ing, murdering, torturing. The angry passions indicated by these representations had more than once found vent in war. Thrice in the lifetime of one generation the two nations had contended, with equal courage and with various success, for the sovereignty of the Ocean. The tyranny of James, as it had reconciled Tories to Whigs, and Churchmen to Noncon-formists, had also reconciled the English to the Dutch. While our ancestors were looking to the Hague for deliverance, the massacre of Amboyna and the great humiliation of Chatham had seemed to be forgotten. But since the Revolution the old feeling had revived. Though England and Holland were now closely bound together by treaty, they were as far as ever from being bound together by affection. Once, just after the battle of Beachy Head, our countrymen had seemed disposed to be just: but a violent reaction had speedily followed. Tor-rington, who deserved to be shot, became a popular favourite; and the allies whom he had shamefully abandoned were ac-cused of persecuting him without a cause. The partiality shown by the King to the companions of his youth was the favourite theme of the sowers of sedition. The most lucrative posts in his household, it was said, were held by Dutchmen: the House of Lords was fast filling with Dutchmen: the finest manors of the Crown were given to Dutchmen: the army was commanded by Dutchmen. That it would have been wise in William to exhibit somewhat less obtrusively his laudable fondness for his native country, and to remunerate his early friends somewhat more sparingly is perfectly true. But it will not be easy to prove that, on any important occasion during his whole reign, he sacrificed the interests of our island to the interests of the United Provinces. The Eng-lish, however, were on this subject prone to fits of jealousy which made them quite incapable of listening to reason. One of the sharpest of those fits came on in the autumn of 1691. The antipathy to the Dutch was at that time strong in all classes, and no where stronger than in the Parliament and in the army.*

Of that antipathy Marlborough determined to avail himself for the purpose, as he assured James and James's adherents, of effecting a restoration. The temper of both Houses was such that they might not improbably be induced by skilful management to present a joint address requesting that all foreigners might be dismissed from the service of their Majesties. Marlborough undertook to move such an address in the the Lords; and there would have been no difficulty in finding some gentleman of great weight to make a similar motion in the Commons.

If the address should be carried, what could William do? Would he yield? Would he discard all his dearest, his oldest, his most trusty friends? It was hardly possible to believe that he would make so painful, so humiliating, a concession. If he did not yield, there would be a rupture between him and the Parliament; and the Parliament would be backed by the people. Even a King reigning by a hereditary title might well shrink from such a contest with the Estates of the Realm. But to a King whose title rested on a resolution of the Estates of the Realm such a contest must almost necessarily be fatal. The last hope of William would be in the army. The army Marlborough undertook to manage; and it is highly probable that what he undertook he could have performed. His courage, his abilities, his noble and winning manners, the splendid success which had attended him on every occasion on which he had been in command, had made him, in spite of his sordid vices, a favourite with his brethren in arms. They were proud of having one countryman who had shown that he wanted nothing but opportunity to vie with the ablest Marshal of France. The Dutch were even more disliked by the English troops than by the English nation generally. Had Marlborough, therefore, after securing the cooperation of some distinguished officers, presented himself at the critical moment

* Burnet, ii. 85.; and Burnet MS. Harl. 6584. See also a memoriaı signed by Holmes, but consisting of intelligence furnished by Ferguson, among the extracts from the Nairne Papers, printed by Macpherson. It bears date October 1691. "The Prince of Orange," says Holmes, "is mortally hated by the English. They see very fairly that he hath no love for them; neither doth he confide in them, but all in his Dutch. . . . . It's not doubted but the Parliament will not be for foreigners to ride them with a caveson."

to those regiments which he had led to victory in Flanders
and in Ireland, had he called on them to rally round him, to
protect the Parliament, and to drive out the aliens, there is
strong reason to think that the call would have been obeyed.
He would then have had it in his power to fulfil the promises
which he had so solemnly made to his old master.

Of all the schemes ever formed for the restoration of
James or of his descendants, this scheme promised the fairest.   That national pride, that hatred of arbitrary power,
which had hitherto been on William's side, would now be
turned against him.   Hundreds of thousands, who would
have put their lives in jeopardy to prevent a French army
from imposing a government on the English, would have
felt no disposition to prevent an English army from driving
out the Dutch.   Even the Whigs could scarcely, without
renouncing their old doctrines, support a prince who obstinately refused to comply with the general wish of his people
signified to him by his Parliament.   The plot looked well.
An active canvass was made.   Many members of the House
of Commons, who did not at all suspect that there was any
ulterior design, promised to vote against the foreigners.
Marlborough was indefatigable in inflaming the discontents
of the army.   His house was constantly filled with officers
who heated each other into fury by talking against the Dutch.
But, before the preparations were complete, a strange suspicion rose in the minds of some of the Jacobites.   That the
author of this bold and artful scheme wished to pull down
the existing government there could be little doubt.   But
was it quite certain what government he meant to set up?
Might he not depose William without restoring James?
Was it not possible that a man so wise, so aspiring, and so
wicked, might be meditating a double treason, such as would
have been thought a masterpiece of statecraft by the great
Italian politicians of the fifteenth century, such as Borgia
would have envied, such as Machiavel would have extolled to
the skies?   What if this consummate dissembler should
cheat both the rival kings?   What if, when he found himself commander of the army and protector of the Parliament, he should proclaim Queen Anne?   Was it not possible
that the weary and harassed nation might gladly acquiesce
in such a settlement?   James was unpopular because he was
a Papist influenced by Popish priests.   William was unpopular because he was a foreigner attached to foreign favourites.   Anne was at once a Protestant and an Englishwoman.

Under her government the country would be in no danger of being overrun either by Jesuits or by Dutchmen. That Marlborough had the strongest motives for placing her on the throne was evident. He could never, in the court of her father, be more than a repentant criminal, whose services were overpaid by a pardon. In her court the husband of her adored friend would be what Pepin Heristal and Charles Martel had been to the Chilperics and Childeberts. He would be the chief director of the civil and military government. He would wield the whole power of England. He would hold the balance of Europe. Great kings and commonwealths would bid against each other for his favour, and exhaust their treasuries in the vain hope of satiating his avarice. The presumption was, therefore, that, if he had the English crown in his hands, he would put it on the head of the Princess. What evidence there was to confirm this presumption is not known: but it is certain that something took place which convinced some of the most devoted friends of the exiled family that he was meditating a second perfidy, surpassing even the feat which he had performed at Salisbury. They were afraid that if, at that moment, they succeeded in getting rid of William, the situation of James would be more hopeless than ever. So fully were they persuaded of the duplicity of their accomplice, that they not only refused to proceed further in the execution of the plan which he had formed, but disclosed his whole scheme to Portland.

Marlborough's plot disclosed by the Jacobites.

William seems to have been alarmed and provoked by this intelligence to a degree very unusual with him. In general he was indulgent, nay, wilfully blind, to the baseness of the English statesmen whom he employed. He suspected, indeed he knew, that some of his servants were in correspondence with his competitor; and yet he did not punish them, did not disgrace them, did not even frown on them. He thought meanly, and he had but too good reason for thinking meanly, of the whole of that breed of public men which the Restoration had formed and had bequeathed to the Revolution. He knew them too well to complain because he did not find in them veracity, fidelity, consistency, disinterestedness. The very utmost that he expected from them was that they would serve him as far as they could serve him without serious danger to themselves. If he learned that, while sitting in his council and enriched by his bounty, they were trying to make for themselves at Saint Germains an interest which might be of use to them in the event of a counterrevolution, he was more inclined to bestow on them the contemptuous commendation which was bestowed of old on the worldly wisdom of the unjust steward than to call them to a severe account. But the crime of Marlborough was of a very different kind. His treason was not that of a fainthearted man desirous to keep a retreat open for himself in every event, but that of a man of dauntless courage, profound policy, and measureless ambition. William was not prone to fear; but, if there was any thing on earth that he feared, it was Marlborough. To treat the criminal as he deserved was indeed impossible: for those by whom his designs had been made known to the government would never have consented to appear against him in the witness box. But to permit him to retain high command in that army which he was then engaged in seducing would have been madness.

1692.
Disgrace
of Marlborough.

Late in the evening of the ninth of January the Queen had a painful explanation with the Princess Anne. Early the next morning Marlborough was informed that their Majesties had no further occasion for his services, and that he must not presume to appear in the royal presence. He had been loaded with honours, and with what he loved better, riches. All was at once taken away.

Various
reports
touching
the cause
of Marlborough's
disgrace.

The real history of these events was known to very few. Evelyn, who had in general excellent sources of information, believed that the corruption and extortion of which Marlborough was notoriously guilty had roused the royal indignation. The Dutch ministers could only tell the States General that six different stories were spread abroad by Marlborough's enemies. Some said that he had indiscreetly suffered an important military secret to escape him; some that he had spoken disrespectfully of their Majesties; some that he had done ill offices between the Queen and the Princess; some that he had been forming cabals in the army; some that he had carried on an unauthorised correspondence with the Danish government about the general politics of Europe; and some that he had been trafficking with the agents of the Court of Saint Germains.* His friends contradicted every one of these tales, and affirmed that his only crime was his dislike of the foreigners who were lording it over his countrymen, and that he had fallen a victim to the machinations of Portland, whom he was known to dislike, and whom he had not

* Evelyn's Diary, Jan. 24.; Hop to States General, $\frac{\text{Jan. 22.}}{\text{Feb. 1.}}$ 169½; Baden to States General, Feb. $\frac{16}{26}$.

very politely described as a wooden fellow. The mystery, which from the first overhung the story of Marlborough's disgrace, was darkened, after the lapse of fifty years, by the shameless mendacity of his widow. The concise narrative of James dispels that mystery, and makes it clear, not only why Marlborough was disgraced, but also how several of the reports about the cause of his disgrace originated.*

Though William assigned to the public no reason for exercising his undoubted prerogative by dismissing his servant, Anne had been informed of the truth; and it had been left

Rupture between Mary and Anne.

* The words of James are these; they were written in November 1692:—

"Mes amis, l'année passée, avoient dessein de me rappeler par le Parlement. La manière étoit concertée; et Milord Churchill devoit proposer dans le Parlement de chasser tous les étrangers tant des conseils et de l'armée que du royaume. Si le Prince d'Orange avoit consenti à cette proposition, ils l'auroient eu entre leurs mains. S'il l'avoit refusée, il auroit fait déclarer le Parlement contre lui; et en même temps Milord Churchill devoit se déclarer avec l'armée pour le Parlement; et la flotte devoit faire de même; et l'on devoit me rappeler. L'on avoit déjà commencé d'agir dans ce projet; et on avoit gagné un gros parti, quand quelques fidèles sujets indiscrets, croyant me servir, et s'imaginant que se que Milord Churchill faisoit n'étoit pas pour moi, mais pour la Princesse de Danemarck, eurent l'imprudence de découvrir le tout à Benthing, et détournèrent ainsi le coup."

A translation of this most remarkable passage, which at once solves many interesting and perplexing problems, was published eighty years ago by Macpherson. But, strange to say, it attracted no notice, and has never, as far as I know, been mentioned by any biographer of Marlborough.

The narrative of James requires no confirmation; but it is strongly confirmed by the Burnet MS. Harl. 6584. "Marleburrough," Burnet wrote in September 1693, "set himself to decry the King's conduct and to lessen him in all his discourses, and to possess the English with an aversion to the Dutch, who, as he pretended, had a much larger share of the King's favour and confidence than they,"—the English I suppose,—"had. This was a point on which the English, who are too apt to despise all other nations, and to overvalue themselves, were easily enough inflamed. So it grew to

be the universal subject of discourse, and was the constant entertainment at Marleburrough's, where there was a constant randivous of the English officers." About the dismission of Marlborough, Burnet wrote at the same time: "The King said to myself upon it that he had very good reason to believe that he had made his peace with King James, and was engaged in a correspondence with France. It is certain he was doing all he could to set on a faction in the army and the nation against the Dutch."

It is curious to compare this plain tale, told while the facts were recent, with the shuffling narrative which Burnet prepared for the public eye many years later, when Marlborough was closely united to the Whigs, and was rendering great and splendid services to the country. Burnet, ii. 90.

The Duchess of Marlborough, in her Vindication, had the effrontery to declare that she "could never learn what cause the King assigned for his displeasure." She suggests that Young's forgery may have been the cause. Now she must have known that Young's forgery was not committed till some months after her husband's disgrace. She was indeed lamentably deficient in memory, a faculty which is proverbially said to be necessary to persons of the class to which she belonged. Her own volume convicts her of falsehood. She gives a letter from Mary to Anne, in which Mary says, "I need not repeat the cause my Lord Marlborough has given the King to do what he has done." These words plainly imply that Anne had been apprised of the cause. If she had not been apprised of the cause, would she not have said so in her answer? But we have her answer: and it contains not a word on the subject. She was then apprised of the cause; and is it possible to believe that she kept it a secret from her adored Mrs. Freeman?

to her to judge whether an officer who had been guilty of a foul treason was a fit inmate of the palace. Three weeks passed. Lady Marlborough still retained her post and her apartments at Whitehall. Her husband still resided with her; and still the King and Queen gave no sign of displeasure. At length the haughty and vindictive Countess, emboldened by their patience, determined to brave them face to face, and accompanied her mistress one evening to the drawingroom at Kensington. This was too much even for the gentle Mary. She would indeed have expressed her indignation before the crowd which surrounded the card tables, had she not remembered that her sister was in a state which entitles women to peculiar indulgence. Nothing was said that night; but on the following day a letter from the Queen was delivered to the Princess. Mary declared that she was unwilling to give pain to a sister whom she loved, and in whom she could easily pass over any ordinary fault: but this was a serious matter. Lady Marlborough must be dismissed. While she lived at Whitehall her Lord would live there. Was it proper that a man in his situation should be suffered to make the palace of his injured master his home? Yet so unwilling was His Majesty to deal severely with the worst offenders, that even this had been borne, and might have been borne longer, had not Anne brought the Countess to defy the King and Queen in their own presence chamber. "It was unkind," Mary wrote, "in a sister: it would have been uncivil in an equal; and I need not say that I have more to claim." The Princess, in her answer, did not attempt to exculpate or excuse Marlborough, but expressed a firm conviction that his wife was innocent, and implored the Queen not to insist on so heartrending a separation. "There is no misery," Anne wrote, "that I cannot resolve to suffer rather than the thoughts of parting from her."

The Princess sent for her uncle Rochester, and implored him to carry her letter to Kensington and to be her advocate there. Rochester declined the office of messenger, and, though he tried to restore harmony between his kinswomen, was by no means disposed to plead the cause of the Churchills. He had indeed long seen with extreme uneasiness the absolute dominion exercised over his younger niece by that unprincipled pair. Anne's expostulation was sent to the Queen by a servant. The only reply was a message from the Lord Chamberlain, Dorset, commanding Lady Marlborough to leave the palace. Mrs. Morley would not be separated from Mrs. Freeman. As to Mr. Morley, all places where he could have his three courses and his three bottles were alike to him. The Princess and her whole family therefore retired to Sion House, a villa belonging to the Duke of Somerset, and situated on the margin of the Thames. In London she occupied Berkeley House, which stood in Piccadilly, on the site now covered by Devonshire House.* Her income was secured by Act of Parliament: but no punishment which it was in the power of the Crown to inflict on her was spared. Her guard of honour was taken away. The foreign ministers ceased to wait upon her. When she went to Bath, the Secretary of State wrote to request the Mayor of that city not to receive her with the ceremonial with which royal visitors were usually welcomed. When she attended divine service at St. James's Church, she found that the rector had been forbidden to show her the customary marks of respect, to bow to her from his pulpit, and to send a copy of his text to be laid on her cushion. Even the bell-man of Piccadilly, it was said, perhaps falsely, was ordered not to chant her praises in his doggrel verse under the windows of Berkeley House.†

That Anne was in the wrong is clear; but it is not equally clear that the King and Queen were in the right. They should have either dissembled their displeasure, or openly declared the true reasons for it. Unfortunately, they let everybody see the punishment, and they let scarcely any body know the provocation. They should have remembered that, in the absence of information about the cause of a quarrel, the public is naturally inclined to side with the weaker party, and that this inclination is likely to be peculiarly strong when a sister is, without any apparent reason, harshly treated by a sister. They should have remembered, too, that they were exposing to attack what was unfortunately the one vulnerable part of Mary's character. A cruel fate had put enmity between her and her father. Her detractors pronounced her utterly destitute of natural affection; and even her eulogists, when they spoke of the way in which she had discharged the duties of the filial relation, were forced

---

* My account of these transactions I have been forced to take from the narrative of the Duchess of Marlborough, a narrative which is to be read with constant suspicion, except when, as is often the case, she relates some instance of her own malignity and insolence.

† The Duchess of Marlborough's Vin-

dication; Dartmouth's Note on Burnet, ii. 92.; Verses of the Night Bellman of Piccadilly and my Lord Nottingham's Order thereupon, 1691. There is a bitter lampoon on Lady Marlborough of the same date, entitled the Universal Health, a true Union to the Queen and Princess.

to speak in a subdued and apologetic tone. Nothing therefore could be more unfortunate than that she should a second time appear unmindful of the ties of consanguinity. She was now at open war with both the two persons who were nearest to her in blood. Many, who thought that her conduct towards her parent was justified by the extreme danger which had threatened her country and her religion, were unable to defend her conduct towards her sister. While Mary, who was really guilty in this matter of nothing worse than imprudence, was regarded by the world as an oppressor, Anne, who was as culpable as her small faculties enabled her to be, assumed the interesting character of a meek, resigned, sufferer. In those private letters, indeed, to which the name of Morley was subscribed, the Princess expressed the sentiments of a fury in the style of a fishwoman, railed savagely at the whole Dutch nation, and called her brother in law sometimes the abortion, sometimes the monster, sometimes Caliban.* But the nation heard nothing of her language and saw nothing of her deportment but what was decorous and submissive. The truth seems to have been that the rancorous and coarseminded Countess gave the tone to her Highness's confidential correspondence, while the graceful, serene, and politic Earl was suffered to prescribe the course which was to be taken before the public eye. During a short time the Queen was generally blamed. But the charm of her temper and manners was irresistible; and in a few months she regained the popularity which she had lost.†

Fuller's plot.

It was a most fortunate circumstance for Marlborough that just at the very time when all London was talking about his disgrace, and trying to guess at the cause of the King's sudden anger against one who had always seemed to be a favourite, an accusation of treason was brought by William Fuller against many persons of high consideration, was strictly investigated, and was proved to be false and malicious. The consequence was that the public, which rarely discriminates nicely, could not, at that moment, be easily brought to believe in the reality of any Jacobite conspiracy.

That Fuller's plot is less celebrated than the Popish plot is the fault rather of the historians than of Fuller, who did all that man could do to secure an eminent place among villains.

---

* It must not be supposed that Anne was a reader of Shakspeare. She had, no doubt, often seen the Enchanted Island. That miserable *rifacimento* of the Tem-

pest was then a favourite with the town, on account of the machinery and the decorations,

† Burnet MS. Harl. 6584.

Every person well read in history must have observed that depravity has its temporary modes, which come in and go out like modes of dress and upholstery. It may be doubted whether, in our country, any man ever, before the year 1678, invented and related on oath a circumstantial history, altogether fictitious, of a treasonable plot, for the purpose of making himself important by destroying men who had given him no provocation. But in the year 1678 this execrable crime became the fashion, and continued to be so during the twenty years which followed. Preachers designated it as our peculiar national sin, and prophesied that it would draw on us some awful national judgment. Legislators proposed new punishments of terrible severity for this new atrocity.* It was not however found necessary to resort to those punishments. The fashion changed; and during the last century and a half there has perhaps not been a single instance of this particular kind of wickedness.

The explanation is simple. Oates was the founder of a school. His success proved that no romance is too wild to be received with faith by understandings which fear and hatred have disordered. His slanders were monstrous: but they were well timed: he spoke to a people made credulous by their passions; and thus, by impudent and cruel lying, he raised himself in a week from beggary and obscurity to luxury, renown, and power. He had once eked out the small tithes of a miserable vicarage by stealing the pigs and fowls of his parishioners.† He was now lodged in a palace: he was followed by admiring crowds: he had at his mercy the estates and lives of Howards and Herberts. A crowd of imitators instantly appeared. It seemed that much more might be got, and that much less was risked, by testifying to an imaginary conspiracy than by robbing on the highway or clipping the coin. Accordingly the Bedloes, Dangerfields, Dugdales, Turberviles, made haste to transfer their industry to an employment at once more profitable and less perilous than any to which they were accustomed. Till the dissolution of the Oxford Parliament, Popish plots were the chief manufacture. Then, during seven years, Whig plots were the only plots which paid. After the Revolution, Jacobite plots came in: but the public had become cautious; and, though the new false witnesses were in no respect less artful than their predecessors, they found much less encouragement. The history of the first great check given to

* The history of an abortive attempt to legislate on this subject will be found in the Commons' Journals of 169⅔. † North's Examen.

the practices of this abandoned race of men well deserves to
be circumstantially related.

In 1689, and in the beginning of 1690, William Fuller had
rendered to the government service such as the best governments sometimes require, and such as none but the worst men
ever perform. His useful treachery had been rewarded by his
employers, as was meet, with money and with contempt.
Their liberality enabled him to live during some months like
a fine gentleman. He called himself a Colonel, hired servants, clothed them in gorgeous liveries, bought fine horses,
lodged in Pall Mall, and showed his brazen forehead, over-
topped by a wig worth fifty guineas, in the antechambers of
the palace and in the stage box at the theatre. He even gave
himself the airs of a favourite of royalty, and, as if he thought
that William could not live without him, followed His Majesty
first to Ireland, and then to the Congress of Princes at the
Hague. The vagabond afterwards boasted that, at the Hague,
he appeared with a retinue fit for an ambassador, that he gave
ten guineas a week for an apartment, and that the worst waistcoat which he condescended to wear was of silver stuff at forty
shillings the yard. Such profusion, of course, brought him to
poverty. Soon after his return to England he took refuge
from the bailiffs in Axe Yard, a place lying within the verge
of Whitehall. His fortunes were desperate: he owed great
sums: on the government he had no claim: his past services
had been overpaid: no future service was to be expected from
him: having appeared in the witness box as evidence for the
Crown, he could no longer be of any use as a spy on the
Jacobites; and by all men of virtue and honour, to whatever
party they might belong, he was abhorred and shunned.

Just at this time, when he was in the frame of mind in
which men are open to the worst temptations, he fell in with
the worst of tempters, in truth, with the Devil in human
shape. Oates had obtained his liberty, his pardon, and a
pension which made him a much richer man than nineteen
twentieths of the members of that profession of which he was
the disgrace. But he was still unsatisfied. He complained
that he had now less than three hundred a year. In the
golden days of the Plot he had been allowed three times as
much, had been sumptuously lodged in the palace, had dined
on plate, and had been clothed in silk. He clamoured for an
increase of his stipend. Nay, he was even impudent enough
to aspire to ecclesiastical preferment, and thought it hard
that, while so many mitres were distributed, he could not get

a deanery, a prebend, or even a rectory. He missed no opportunity of urging his pretensions. He haunted the public offices and the lobbies of the Houses of Parliament. He might be seen and heard every day, hurrying as fast as his uneven legs would carry him, between Charing Cross and Westminster Hall, puffing with haste and self importance, chattering about what he had done for the good cause, and reviling, in the style of the boatmen on the river, all the statesmen and divines whom he suspected of doing him ill offices at Court, and keeping him back from a bishopric. When he found that there was no hope for him in the Established Church, he turned to the Baptists. They, at first, received him very coldly; but he gave such touching accounts of the wonderful work of grace which had been wrought in his soul, and vowed so solemnly, before Jehovah and the holy angels, to be thenceforth a burning and shining light, that it was difficult for simple and well meaning people to think him altogether insincere. He mourned, he said, like a turtle. On one Lord's day he thought he should have died of grief at being shut out from fellowship with the saints. He was at length admitted to communion: but, before he had been a year among his new friends, they discovered his true character, and solemnly cast him out as a hypocrite. Thenceforth he became the mortal enemy of the leading Baptists, and persecuted them with the same treachery, the same mendacity, the same effrontery, the same black malice, which had, many years before, wrought the destruction of more celebrated victims. Those who had lately been edified by his account of his blessed experiences stood aghast to hear him crying out that he would be revenged, that revenge was God's own sweet morsel, that the wretches who had excommunicated him should be ruined, that they should be forced to fly their country, that they should be stripped to the last shilling. His designs were at length frustrated by a righteous decree of the Court of Chancery, a decree which would have left a deep stain on the character of an ordinary man, but which makes no perceptible addition to the infamy of Titus Oates.* Through all changes, however, he was surrounded by a small knot of hotheaded and foulmouthed agitators, who, abhorred and despised by every respectable Whig, yet called themselves Whigs, and thought themselves injured because they were not rewarded for scurrility and slander with the best places under the Crown.

* North's Examen; Ward's London Spy; Crosby's English Baptists, vol. iii. chap. 2.

In 1691, Titus, in order to be near the focal point of political intrigue and faction, had taken a house within the precinct of Whitehall. To this house Fuller, who lived hard by, found admission. The evil work, which had been begun in him, when he was still a child, by the memoirs of Dangerfield, was now completed by the conversation of Oates. The Salamanca Doctor was, as a witness, no longer formidable; but he was impelled, partly by the savage malignity which he felt towards all whom he considered as his enemies, and partly by mere monkeylike restlessness and love of mischief, to do, through the instrumentality of others, what he could no longer do in person. In Fuller he had found the corrupt heart, the ready tongue, and the unabashed front, which are the first qualifications for the office of a false accuser. A friendship, if that word may be so used, sprang up between the pair. Oates opened his house and even his purse to Fuller. The veteran sinner, both directly and through the agency of his dependents, intimated to the novice that nothing made a man so important as the discovering of a plot, and that these were times when a young fellow who would stick at nothing and fear nobody might do wonders. The Revolution,—such was the language constantly held by Titus and his parasites,—had produced little good. The brisk boys of Shaftesbury had not been recompensed according to their merits. Even the Doctor,—such was the ingratitude of men,—was looked on coldly at the new Court. Tory rogues sate at the council board, and were admitted to the royal closet. It would be a noble feat to bring their necks to the block. Above all it would be delightful to see Nottingham's long solemn face on Tower Hill. For the hatred with which these bad men regarded Nottingham had no bounds, and was probably excited less by his political opinions, in which there was doubtless much to condemn, than by his moral character, in which the closest scrutiny will detect little that is not deserving of approbation. Oates, with the authority which experience and success entitle a preceptor to assume, read his pupil a lecture on the art of bearing false witness. "You ought," he said, with many oaths and curses, "to have made more, much more, out of what you heard and saw at Saint Germains. Never was there a finer foundation for a plot. But you are a fool: you are a coxcomb: I could beat you: I would not have done so. I used to go to Charles and tell him his own. I called Lauderdale names to his face. I made King, Ministers, Lords Commons, afraid of me. But you young men have no spirit.'

Fuller was greatly edified by these exhortations. It was, however, hinted to him by some of his associates that, if he meant to take up the trade of swearing away lives, he would do well not to show himself so often at coffeehouses in the company of Titus. "The Doctor," said one of the gang, "is an excellent person, and has done great things in his time: but many people are prejudiced against him; and, if you are really going to discover a plot, the less you are seen with him the better." Fuller accordingly ceased to appear in Oates's train at public places, but still continued to receive his great master's instructions in private.

To do Fuller justice, he seems not to have taken up the trade of a false witness till he could no longer support himself by begging or swindling. He lived for a time on the charity of the Queen. He then levied contributions by pretending to be one of the noble family of Sidney. He wheedled Tillotson out of some money, and requited the good Archbishop's kindness by passing himself off as His Grace's favourite nephew. But in the autumn of 1691 all these shifts were exhausted. After lying in several spunging houses, Fuller was at length lodged in the King's Bench prison, and he now thought it time to announce that he had discovered a plot.*

He addressed himself first to Tillotson and Portland: but both Tillotson and Portland soon perceived that he was lying. What he said was, however, reported to the King, who, as might have been expected, treated the information and the informer with cold contempt. All that remained was to try whether a flame could be raised in the Parliament.

Soon after the Houses met, Fuller petitioned the Commons to hear what he had to say, and promised to make wonderful disclosures. He was brought from his prison to the bar of the House; and he there repeated a long romance. James, he said, had delegated the regal authority to six commissioners, of whom Halifax was first. More than fifty lords and gentlemen had signed an address to the French King, imploring him to make a great effort for the restoration of the House of Stuart. Fuller declared that he had seen this address, and recounted many of the names appended to it. Some members made severe remarks on the improbability of the story and on the character of the witness. He is, it was said, one of the greatest rogues on the face of the earth; and he tells such things as could scarcely be credited if they were told by an angel from heaven. Fuller audaciously pledged himself to

* The history of this part of Fuller's life I have taken from his own narrative.

bring proofs which would satisfy the most incredulous. He was, he averred, in communication with some agents of James. Those persons were ready to make reparation to their country. Their testimony would be decisive; for they were in possession of documentary evidence which would confound the guilty. They held back only because they saw some of the traitors high in office and near the royal person, and were afraid of incurring the enmity of men so powerful and so wicked. Fuller ended by asking for a sum of money, and by assuring the Commons that he would lay it out to good account.* Had his impudent request been granted, he would probably have paid his debts, obtained his liberty, and absconded: but the House very wisely insisted on seeing his witnesses first. He then began to shuffle. The gentlemen were on the Continent, and could not come over without passports. Passports were delivered to him: but he complained that they were insufficient. At length the Commons, fully determined to get at the truth, presented an address requesting the King to send Fuller a blank safe conduct in the largest terms.† The safe conduct was sent. Six weeks passed, and nothing was heard of the witnesses. The friends of the lords and gentlemen who had been accused represented strongly that the House ought not to separate for the summer without coming to some decision on charges so grave. Fuller was ordered to attend. He pleaded sickness, and asserted, not for the first time, that the Jacobites had poisoned him. But all his plans were confounded by the laudable promptitude and vigour with which the Commons acted. A Committee was sent to his bedside, with orders to ascertain whether he really had any witnesses, and where those witnesses resided. The members who were deputed for this purpose went to the King's Bench prison, and found him suffering under a disorder, produced, in all probability, by some emetic which he had swallowed for the purpose of deceiving them. In answer to their questions, he said that two of his witnesses, Delaval and Hayes, were in England, and were lodged at the house of a Roman Catholic apothecary in Holborn. The Commons, as soon as the Committee had reported, sent some members to the house which he had indicated. That house and all the neighbouring houses were searched. Delaval and Hayes were not to be found; nor had anybody in the vicinity ever seen such men or heard of them. The House, therefore, on

* Commons' Journals, Dec. 2. and 9. 1691; Grey's Debates.   † Commons' Journals, Jan. 4. 169½ Grey's Debates.

the last day of the session, just before Black Rod knocked at the door, unanimously resolved that William Fuller was a cheat and a false accuser; that he had insulted the Government and the Parliament; that he had calumniated honourable men; and that an address should be carried up to the throne, requesting that he might be prosecuted for his villany.*
He was consequently tried, convicted, and sentenced to fine, imprisonment, and the pillory. The exposure, more terrible than death to a mind not lost to all sense of shame, he underwent with a hardihood worthy of his two favourite models, Dangerfield and Oates. He had the impudence to persist, year after year, in affirming that he had fallen a victim to the machinations of the late King, who had spent six thousand pounds in order to ruin him. Delaval and Hayes—so this fable ran—had been instructed by James in person. They had, in obedience to his orders, induced Fuller to pledge his word for their appearance, and had then absented themselves, and left him exposed to the resentment of the House of Commons.† The story had the reception which it deserved; and Fuller sank into an obscurity from which he twice or thrice, at long intervals, again emerged for a moment into infamy.

On the twenty-fourth of February 1692, about an hour after the Commons had voted Fuller an imposter, they were summoned to the chamber of the Lords. The King thanked the Houses for their loyalty and liberality, informed them that he must soon set out for the Continent, and commanded them to adjourn themselves. He gave his assent on that day to many bills, public and private; but when the title of one bill, which had passed the Lower House without a single division and the Upper House without a single protest, had been read by the Clerk of the Crown, the Clerk of the Parliaments answered, according to the ancient form, that the King and the Queen would consider of the matter. Those words had very rarely been pronounced before the accession of William. They have been pronounced only once since his death. But by him the power of putting a Veto on laws which had been passed by the Estates of the Realm was used on several important occasions. His detractors truly asserted that he rejected a greater number of important bills than all the Kings of the House of Stuart put together, and most absurdly inferred that the sense of the Estates of the Realm was much

Close of the session bill for ascertaining the salaries of the Judges rejected.

---

* Commons' Journals, Feb. 22., 23., and 24. 169$\frac{1}{2}$.

† Fuller's Original Letters of the late King James and others to his Greatest Friends in England.

less respected by him than by his uncles and his grandfather.
A judicious student of history will have no difficulty in discovering why William repeatedly exercised a prerogative to
which his predecessors very seldom had recourse, and which
his successors have suffered to fall into utter desuetude.

His predecessors passed laws easily because they broke
laws easily. Charles the First gave his assent to the Petition
of Right, and immediately violated every clause of that great
statute. Charles the Second gave his assent to an Act which
provided that a Parliament should be held at least once in
three years: but when he died the country had been near
four years without a Parliament. The laws which abolished
the Court of High Commission, the laws which instituted the
Sacramental Test, were passed without the smallest difficulty:
but they did not prevent James the Second from reestablishing
the Court of High Commission, and from filling the Privy
Council, the public offices, the courts of justice, and the municipal corporations with persons who had never taken the
Test. Nothing could be more natural than that a King
should not think it worth while to refuse his assent to a statute
with which he could dispense whenever he thought fit.

The situation of William was very different. He could
not, like those who had ruled before him, pass an Act in the
spring and violate it in the summer. He had, by assenting
to the Bill of Rights, solemnly renounced the dispensing
power; and he was restrained, by prudence as well as by
conscience and honour, from breaking the compact under
which he held his crown. A law might be personally offensive to him: it might appear to him to be pernicious to his
people: but, as soon as he had passed it, it was, in his eyes,
a sacred thing. He had therefore a motive, which preceding
Kings had not, for pausing before he passed such a law.
They gave their word readily, because they had no scruple
about breaking it. He gave his word slowly, because he
never failed to keep it.

But his situation, though it differed widely from that of
the princes of the House of Stuart, was not precisely that of
the princes of the House of Brunswick. A prince of the
House of Brunswick is guided, as to the use of every royal
prerogative, by the advice of a responsible ministry; and
this ministry must be taken from the party which pre-
dominates in the two Houses, or, at least, in the Lower
House. It is hardly possible to conceive circumstances in
which a Sovereign so situated can refuse to assent to a bill

which has been approved by both branches of the legislature. Such a refusal would necessarily imply one of two things, that the Sovereign acted in opposition to the advice of the ministry, or that the ministry was at issue, on a question of vital importance, with a majority both of the Commons and of the Lords. On either supposition the country would be in a most critical state, in a state which, if long continued, must end in a revolution. But in the earlier part of the reign of William there was no ministry. The heads of the executive departments had not been appointed exclusively from either party. Some were zealous Whigs, others zealous Tories. The most enlightened statesmen did not hold it to be unconstitutional that the King should exercise his highest prerogatives on the most important occasions without any other guidance than that of his own judgment. His refusal, therefore, to assent to a bill which had passed both Houses indicated, not, as a similar refusal would now indicate, that the whole machinery of government was in a state of fearful disorder, but merely that there was a difference of opinion between him and the two other branches of the legislature as to the expediency of a particular law. Such a difference of opinion might exist, and, as we shall hereafter see, actually did exist, at a time when he was, not merely on friendly, but on most affectionate terms with the Estates of the Realm.

The circumstances under which he used his Veto for the first time have never yet been correctly stated. A well meant but unskilful attempt had been made to complete a reform which the Bill of Rights had left imperfect. That great law had deprived the Crown of the power of arbitrarily removing the Judges, but had not made them entirely independent. They were remunerated partly by fees and partly by salaries. Over the fees the King had no control: but the salaries he had full power to reduce or to withhold. That William had ever abused this power was not pretended: but it was undoubtedly a power which no prince ought to possess; and this was the sense of both Houses. A bill was therefore brought in by which a salary of a thousand a year was strictly secured to each of the twelve Judges. Thus far all was well. But unfortunately the salaries were made a charge on the hereditary revenue. No such proposition would now be entertained by the House of Commons, without the royal consent previously signified by a Privy Councillor. But this wholesome rule had not then been established; and William could defend the proprietary rights of the Crown only by putting his negative on the bill. At the time there was, as far as can now be ascertained, no outcry. Even the Jacobite libellers were almost silent. It was not till the provisions of the bill had been forgotten, and till nothing but its title was remembered, that William was accused of having been influenced by a wish to keep the judges in a state of dependence.[*]

Ministerial changes in England.

The Houses broke up; and the King prepared to set out for the Continent. Before his departure he made some changes in his household and in several departments of the government, changes, however, which did not indicate a very decided preference for either of the great political parties. Rochester was sworn of the Council. It is probable that he had earned this mark of royal favour by taking the Queen's side in the unhappy dispute between her and her sister. Pembroke took charge of the Privy Seal, and was succeeded at the Board of Admiralty by Charles Lord Cornwallis, a moderate Tory: Lowther accepted a seat at the same board, and was succeeded at the Treasury by Sir Edward Seymour. Many Tory country gentlemen, who had looked on Seymour as their leader in the war against placemen and Dutchmen, were moved to indignation by learning that he had become a courtier. They remembered that he had voted for a Regency, that he had taken the oaths with no good grace, and that he had spoken with little respect of the Sovereign whom he was now ready to serve for the sake of emoluments hardly worthy

---

[*] Burnet (ii. 86.). Burnet had evidently forgotten what the bill contained. Ralph knew nothing about it but what he had learned from Burnet. I have scarcely seen any allusion to the subject in any of the numerous Jacobite lampoons of that day. But there is a remarkable passage in a pamphlet which appeared towards the close of William's reign, and which is entitled the Art of Governing by Parties. The writer says, "We still want an Act to ascertain some fund for the salaries of the judges; and there was a bill, since the Revolution, past both Houses of Parliament to this purpose: but whether it was for being any way defective or otherwise that His Majesty refused to assent to it, I cannot remember. But I know the reason satisfied me at that time. And I make no doubt but he'll consent to any good bill of this nature whenever 'tis offered." These words convinced me that the bill was open to some grave objection which did not appear in the title, and which no historian

had noticed. I found among the archives of the House of Lords the original parchment, endorsed with the words "Le Roy et la Royne s'aviseront;" and it was clear at the first glance what the objection was.

There is a hiatus in that part of Narcissus Luttrell's Diary which relates to this matter. "The King," he wrote, "passed ten public bills and thirty-four private ones, and rejected that of the ———"

As to the present practice of the House of Commons in such cases, see Hatsell's valuable work, ii. 356. I quote the edition of 1818. Hatsell says that many bills which affect the interest of the Crown may be brought in without any signification of the royal consent, and that it is enough if the consent be signified on the second reading, or even later; but that, in a proceeding which affects the hereditary revenue, the consent must be signified in the earliest stage.

of the acceptance of a man of his wealth and parliamentary interest. It was strange that the haughtiest of human beings should be the meanest, that one who seemed to reverence nothing on earth but himself should abase himself for the sake of quarter day. About such reflections he troubled himself very little. He found, however, that there was one disagreeable circumstance connected with his new office. At the Board of Treasury he must sit below the Chancellor of the Exchequer. The First Lord, Godolphin, was a peer of the realm; and his right to precedence, according to the rules of the heralds, could not be questioned. But everybody knew who was the first of English commoners. What was Richard Hampden that he should take place of a Seymour, of the head of the Seymours? With much difficulty, the dispute was compromised. Many concessions were made to Sir Edward's punctilious pride. He was sworn of the Council. He was appointed one of the Cabinet. The King took him by the hand and presented him to the Queen. "I bring you," said William, "a gentleman who will in my absence be a valuable friend." In this way Sir Edward was so much soothed and flattered that he ceased to insist on his right to thrust himself between the First Lord and the Chancellor of the Exchequer.

In the same Commission of Treasury in which the name of Seymour appeared, appeared also the name of a much younger politician, who had, during the late session, raised himself to high distinction in the House of Commons, Charles Montague. This appointment gave great satisfaction to the Whigs, in whose esteem Montague now stood higher than their veteran chiefs Sacheverell and Powle, and was indeed second to Somers alone.

Sidney delivered up the seals which he had held during more than a year, and was appointed Lord Lieutenant of Ireland. Some months elapsed before the place which he had quitted was filled up; and during this interval the whole business which had ordinarily been divided between two Secretaries of State was transacted by Nottingham.*

While these arrangements were in progress, events had taken place in a distant part of the island, which were not, till after the lapse of many months, known in the best in-

Ministerial changes in Scotland.

---

* The history of these ministerial arrangements I have taken chiefly from the London Gazette of March 3. and March 7. 169½, and from Narcissus Lut-trell's Diary for that month. Two or three slight touches are from contemporary pamphlets.

formed circles of London, but which gradually obtained a fearful notoriety, and which, after the lapse of more than a hundred and sixty years, are never mentioned without horror.

Soon after the Estates of Scotland had separated in the autumn of 1690, a change was made in the administration of that kingdom. William was not satisfied with the way in which he had been represented in the Parliament House. He thought that the rabbled curates had been hardly treated. He had very reluctantly suffered the law which abolished patronage to be touched with his sceptre. But what especially displeased him was that the Acts which established a new ecclesiastical polity had not been accompanied by an Act granting liberty of conscience to those who were attached to the old ecclesiastical polity. He had directed his Commissioner Melville to obtain for the Episcopalians of Scotland an indulgence similar to that which Dissenters enjoyed in England.* But the Presbyterian preachers were loud and vehement against lenity to Amalekites. Melville, with useful talents, and perhaps with fair intentions, had neither large views nor an intrepid spirit. He shrank from uttering a word so hateful to the theological demagogues of his country as Toleration. By obsequiously humouring their prejudices he quelled the clamour which was rising at Edinburgh; but the effect of his timid caution was that a far more formidable clamour soon rose in the south of the island against the bigotry of the schismatics who domineered in the north, and against the pusillanimity of the government which had not dared to withstand that bigotry. On this subject the High Churchman and the Low Churchman were of one mind, or rather the Low Churchman was the more angry of the two. A man like South, who had during many years been predicting that, if ever the Puritans ceased to be oppressed, they would become oppressors, was at heart not ill pleased to see his prophecy fulfilled. But in a man like Burnet, the great object of whose life had been to mitigate the animosity which the ministers of the Anglican Church felt towards the Presbyterians, the intolerant conduct of the Presbyterians could awaken no feeling but indignation, shame and grief. There was, therefore, at the English Court nobody to speak a good word for Melville. It was impossible that in such circumstances he should remain at the head of the Scottish administration. He was, however, gently let down from his high position. He continued during more than a year to be

* William to Melville, May 22. 1690.

Secretary of State : but another Secretary was appointed, who was to reside near the King, and to have the chief direction of affairs. The new Prime Minister for Scotland was the able, eloquent, and accomplished Sir John Dalrymple. His father, the Lord President of the Court of Session, had lately been raised to the peerage by the title of Viscount Stair; and Sir John Dalrymple was consequently, according to the ancient usage of Scotland, designated as the Master of Stair. In a few months Melville resigned his secretaryship, and accepted an office of some dignity and emolument, but of no political importance.*

The Lowlands of Scotland were, during the year which followed the parliamentary session of 1690, as quiet as they had ever been within the memory of man : but the state of the Highlands caused much anxiety to the government. The civil war in that wild region, after it had ceased to flame, had continued during some time to smoulder. At length, early in the year 1691, the rebel chiefs informed the Court of Saint Germains that, pressed as they were on every side, they could hold out no longer without succour from France. James had sent them a small quantity of meal, brandy, and tobacco, and had frankly told them that he could do nothing more. Money was so scarce among them that six hundred pounds sterling would have been a most acceptable addition to their funds : but even such a sum he was unable to spare. He could scarcely, in such circumstances, expect them to defend his cause against a government which had a regular army and a large revenue. He therefore informed them that he should not take it ill of them if they made their peace with the new dynasty, provided always that they were prepared to rise in insurrection as soon as he should call on them to do so.†

Meanwhile it had been determined at Kensington, in spite of the opposition of the Master of Stair, to try the plan which Tarbet had recommended two years before, and which, if it had been tried when he recommended it, would probably have prevented much bloodshed and confusion. It was resolved that twelve or fifteen thousand pounds should be laid

State of the High lands.

---

* See the preface to the Leven and Melville Papers. I have given what I believe to be a true explanation of Burnet's hostility to Melville. Melville's descendant, who has deserved well of all students of history by the diligence and fidelity with which he has performed his editorial duties, thinks that Burnet's judgment was blinded by zeal for Prelacy and hatred of Presbyterianism. This accusation will surprise and amuse English High Churchmen.

† Life of James, ii. 468, 469.

out in quieting the Highlands. This was a mass of treasure which to an inhabitant of Appin or Lochaber seemed almost fabulous, and which indeed bore a greater proportion to the income of Keppoch or Glengarry than fifteen hundred thousand pounds bore to the income of Lord Bedford or Lord Devonshire. The sum was ample; but the King was not fortunate in the choice of an agent.*

Breadal-
bane em-
ployed to
negotiate
with the
rebel clans. John Earl of Breadalbane, the head of a younger branch of the great house of Campbell, ranked high among the petty princes of the mountains. He could bring seventeen hundred claymores into the field; and, ten years before the Revolution, he had actually marched into the Lowlands with this great force for the purpose of supporting the prelatical tyranny.† In those days he had affected zeal for monarchy and episcopacy: but in truth he cared for no government and no religion. He seems to have united two different sets of vices, the growth of two different regions, and of two different stages in the progress of society. In his castle among the hills he had learned the barbarian pride and ferocity of a Highland chief. In the Council Chamber at Edinburgh he had contracted the deep taint of treachery and corruption. After the Revolution he had, like too many of his fellow nobles, joined and betrayed every party in turn, had sworn fealty to William and Mary, and had plotted against them. To trace all the turns and doublings of his course, during the year 1689 and the earlier part of 1690, would be wearisome.‡ That course became somewhat less tortuous when the battle of the Boyne had cowed the spirit of the Jacobites. It now seemed probable that the Earl would be a loyal subject of their Majesties, till some great disaster should befall them. Nobody who knew him could trust him: but few Scottish statesmen could then be trusted; and yet Scottish statesmen must be employed. His position and connections marked him out as a man who might, if he would, do much towards the work of quieting the Highlands; and his interest seemed to be a guarantee for his zeal. He had, as he declared with every appearance of truth, strong personal reasons for wishing to see tranquillity restored. His domains were so situated that, while the civil war lasted, his vassals could not tend their herds or sow their oats in peace. His lands were daily

* Burnet, ii. 88; Master of Stair to Breadalbane, Dec. 2. 1691.

† Burnet, i. 418.

‡ Crawford to Melville, July 23. 1689; The Master of Stair to Melville, Aug. 16. 1689; Cardross to Melville, Sept. 9. 1689; Balcarras's Memoirs; Annandale's Confession, Aug. 14. 1690.

Glencoe

ravaged : his cattle were daily driven away : one of his houses had been burnt down. It was probable, therefore, that he would do his best to put an end to hostilities.*

He was accordingly commissioned to treat with the Jacobite chiefs, and was entrusted with the money which was to be distributed among them. He invited them to a conference at his residence in Glenorchy. They came : but the treaty went on very slowly. Every head of a tribe asked for a larger share of the English gold than was to be obtained. Breadalbane was suspected of intending to cheat both the King and the clans. The dispute between the rebels and the government was complicated with another dispute still more embarrassing. The Camerons and Macdonalds were really at war, not with William, but with Mac Callum More; and no arrangement to which Mac Callum More was not a party could really produce tranquillity. A grave question therefore arose, whether the money entrusted to Breadalbane should be paid directly to the discontented chiefs, or should be employed to satisfy the claims which Argyle had upon them. The shrewdness of Lochiel and the arrogant pretensions of Glengarry contributed to protract the discussions. But no Celtic potentate was so impracticable as Macdonald of Glencoe, known among the mountains by the hereditary appellation of Mac Ian.†

Mac Ian dwelt in the mouth of a ravine situated not far Glencoe. from the southern shore of Lochleven, an arm of the sea which deeply indents the western coast of Scotland, and separates Argyleshire from Invernessshire. Near his house were two or three small hamlets inhabited by his tribe. The whole population which he governed was not supposed to exceed two hundred souls. In the neighbourhood of the little cluster of villages was some copsewood and some pasture land : but a little further up the defile no sign of population or of fruitfulness was to be seen. In the Gaelic tongue, Glencoe signifies the Glen of Weeping : and in truth that pass is the most dreary and melancholy of all the Scottish passes, the very Valley of the Shadow of Death. Mists and storms brood over it through the greater part of the finest summer; and even on those rare days when the sun is bright, and when there is no cloud in the sky, the impression made by the landscape is sad and awful. The path lies along a

* Breadalbane to Melville, Sept. 17. 1690.
† The Master of Stair to Hamilton, Aug. 17/27. 1691 ; Hill to Melville, June 26. 1691; The Master of Stair to Breadalbane, Aug. 24. 1690.

stream which issues from the most sullen and gloomy of mountain pools. Huge precipices of naked stone frown on both sides. Even in July the streaks of snow may often be discerned in the rifts near the summits. All down the sides of the crags heaps of ruin mark the headlong paths of the torrents. Mile after mile the traveller looks in vain for the smoke of one hut, or for one human form wrapped in a plaid, and listens in vain for the bark of a shepherd's dog, or the bleat of a lamb. Mile after mile the only sound that indicates life is the faint cry of a bird of prey from some storm beaten pinnacle of rock. The progress of civilisation, which has turned so many wastes into fields yellow with harvests or gay with apple blossoms, has only made Glencoe more desolate. All the science and industry of a peaceful age can extract nothing valuable from that wilderness : but, in an age of violence and rapine, the wilderness itself was valued on account of the shelter which it afforded to the plunderer and his plunder. Nothing could be more natural than that the clan to which this rugged desert belonged should have been noted for predatory habits. For, among the Highlanders generally, to rob was thought at least as honourable an employment as to cultivate the soil; and, of all the Highlanders, the Macdonalds of Glencoe had the least productive soil, and the most convenient and secure den of robbers. Successive governments had tried to punish this wild race : but no large force had ever been employed for that purpose ; and a small force was easily resisted or eluded by men familiar with every recess and every outlet of the natural fortress in which they had been born and bred. The people of Glencoe would probably have been less troublesome neighbours, if they had lived among their own kindred. But they were an outpost of the Clan Donald, separated from every other branch of their own family, and almost surrounded by the domains of the hostile race of Diarmid.* They were impelled by hereditary enmity, as well as by want, to live at the expense of the tribe of Campbell. Breadalbane's property had suffered greatly from their depredations ; and he

---

* "The real truth is, they were a branch of the Macdonalds (who were a brave courageous people always), seated among the Campbells, who (I mean the Glencoe men) are all Papists, if they have any religion, were always counted a people much given to rapine and plunder, or sorners as we call it, and much of a piece with your highway-men in England. Several governments desired to bring them to justice: but their country was inaccessible to small parties." See An impartial Account of some of the Transactions in Scotland concerning the Earl of Breadalbane, Viscount and Master of Stair, Glenco Men, &c., London, 1695.

was not of a temper to forgive such injuries. When, therefore, the Chief of Glencoe made his appearance at the congress in Glenorchy, he was ungraciously received. The Earl, who ordinarily bore himself with the solemn dignity of a Castilian grandee, forgot, in his resentment, his wonted gravity, forgot his public character, forgot the laws of hospitality, and, with angry reproaches and menaces, demanded reparation for the herds which had been driven from his lands by Mac Ian's followers. Mac Ian was seriously apprehensive of some personal outrage, and was glad to get safe back to his own glen.* His pride had been wounded; and the promptings of interest concurred with those of pride. As the head. of a people who lived by pillage, he had strong reasons for wishing that the country might continue to be in a perturbed state. He had little chance of receiving one guinea of the money which was to be distributed among the malecontents. For his share of that money would scarcely meet Breadalbane's demands for compensation; and there could be little doubt that, whoever might be unpaid, Breadalbane would take care to pay himself. Mac Ian therefore did his best to dissuade his allies from accepting terms from which he could himself expect no benefit; and his influence was not small. His own vassals, indeed, were few in number: but he came of the best blood of the Highlands: he kept up a close connection with his more powerful kinsmen; nor did they like him the less because he was a robber; for he never robbed them; and that robbery, merely as robbery, was a wicked and disgraceful act, had never entered into the mind of any Celtic chief. Mac Ian was therefore held in high esteem by the confederates. His age was venerable: his aspect was majestic; and he possessed in large measure those intellectual qualities which, in rude societies, give men an ascendency over their fellows. Breadalbane found himself, at every step of the negotiation, thwarted by the arts of his old enemy, and abhorred the name of Glencoe more and more every day.†

But the government did not trust solely to Breadalbane's diplomatic skill. The authorities at Edinburgh put forth a proclamation exhorting the clans to submit to King William and Queen Mary, and offering pardon to every rebel who, on or before the thirty-first of December 1691, should swear to live peaceably under the government of their Majesties. It

---

* Report of the Commissioners, signed at Holyrood, June 20. 1695.

† Gallienus Redivivus; Burnet, ii 88.; Report of the Commission of 1695

was announced that those who should hold out after that day would be treated as enemies and traitors.* Warlike preparations were made, which showed that the threat was meant in earnest. The Highlanders were alarmed, and, though the pecuniary terms had not been satisfactorily settled, thought it prudent to give the pledge which was demanded of them. No chief, indeed, was willing to set the example of submission. Glengarry blustered, and pretended to fortify his house.† "I will not," said Lochiel, "break the ice. That is a point of honour with me. But my tacksmen and people may use their freedom."‡ His tacksmen and people understood him, and repaired by hundreds to the Sheriff to take the oaths. The Macdonalds of Sleat, Clanronald, Keppoch, and even Glengarry, imitated the Camerons; and the chiefs, after trying to outstay each other as long as they durst, imitated their vassals.

The thirty-first of December arrived; and still the Macdonalds of Glencoe had not come in. The punctilious pride of Mac Ian was doubtless gratified by the thought that he had continued to defy the government after the boastful Glengarry, the ferocious Keppoch, the magnanimous Lochiel had yielded : but he bought his gratification dear.

At length, on the thirty-first of December, he repaired to Fort William, accompanied by his principal vassals, and offered to take the oaths. To his dismay, he found that there was in the fort no person competent to administer them. Colonel Hill, the Governor, was not a magistrate; nor was there any magistrate nearer than Inverary. Mac Ian, now fully sensible of the folly of which he had been guilty in postponing to the very last moment an act on which his life and his estate depended, set off for Inverary in great distress. He carried with him a letter from Hill to the Sheriff of Argyleshire, Sir Colin Campbell of Ardkinglass, a respectable gentleman, who, in the late reign, had suffered severely for his Whig principles. In this letter the Colonel expressed a good natured hope that, even out of season, a lost sheep, and so fine a lost sheep, would be gladly received. Mac Ian made all the haste in his power, and did not stop even at his own house, though it lay nigh to the road. But in that age a journey through Argyleshire in the depth of winter was necessarily slow. The old man's progress up steep mountains and along boggy valleys was obstructed by snow storms; and

* Report of the Glencoe Commission,   † Hill to Melville, May 15. 1691.
1895.   ‡ Ibid June 3. 1691.

it was not till the sixth of January that he presented himself before the Sheriff at Inverary. The Sheriff hesitated. His power, he said, was limited by the terms of the proclamation; and he did not see how he could swear a rebel who had not submitted within the prescribed time. Mac Ian begged earnestly and with tears that he might be sworn. His people, he said, would follow his example. If any of them proved refractory, he would himself send the recusant to prison, or ship him off for Flanders. His entreaties and Hill's letter overcame Sir Colin's scruples. The oath was administered; and a certificate was transmitted to the Council at Edinburgh, setting forth the special circumstances which had induced the Sheriff to do what he knew not to be strictly regular.*

The news that Mac Ian had not submitted within the prescribed time was received with cruel joy by three powerful Scotchmen who were then at the English Court. Breadalbane had gone up to London at Christmas in order to give an account of his stewardship. There he met his kinsman Argyle. Argyle was, in personal qualities, one of the most insignificant of the long line of nobles who have borne that great name. He was the descendant of eminent men, and the parent of eminent men. He was the grandson of one of the ablest of Scottish politicians; the son of one of the bravest and most true hearted of Scottish patriots; the father of one Mac Callum More renowned as a warrior and as an orator, as the model of every courtly grace, and as the judicious patron of arts and letters, and of another Mac Callum More distinguished by talents for business and command, and by skill in the exact sciences. Both of such an ancestry and of such a progeny Argyle was unworthy. He had even been guilty of the crime, common enough among Scottish politicians, but in him singularly disgraceful, of tampering with the agents of James while professing loyalty to William. Still Argyle had the importance inseparable from high rank, vast domains, extensive feudal rights, and almost boundless patriarchal authority. To him, as to his cousin Breadalbane, the intelligence that the tribe of Glencoe was out of the protection of the law was most gratifying; and the Master of Stair more than sympathised with them both.

The feeling of Argyle and Breadalbane is perfectly intelligible. They were the heads of a great clan; and they had

* Burnet, ii. 8, 9.; Report of the Glencoe Commission. The authorities quoted in this part of the Report were the depositions of Hill, of Campbell of Ardkinglass, and of Mac Ian's two sons.

an opportunity of destroying a neighbouring clan with which
they were at deadly feud. Breadalbane had received peculiar
provocation. His estate had been repeatedly devastated; and
he had just been thwarted in a negotiation of high moment.
Unhappily there was scarcely any excess of ferocity for
which a precedent could not be found in Celtic tradition.
Among all warlike barbarians revenge is esteemed the most
sacred of duties and the most exquisite of pleasures; and so
it had long been esteemed among the Highlanders. The
history of the clans abounds with frightful tales, some perhaps
fabulous or exaggerated, some certainly true, of vindictive
massacres and assassinations. The Macdonalds of Glengarry,
for example, having been affronted by the people of a parish
near Inverness, surrounded the parish church on a Sunday,
shut the doors, and burned the whole congregation alive.
While the flames were raging, the hereditary musician of the
murderers mocked the shrieks of the perishing crowd with
the notes of his bagpipe.* A band of Macgregors, having
cut off the head of an enemy, laid it, the mouth filled with
bread and cheese, on his sister's table, and had the satisfaction of seeing her go mad with horror at the sight. They
then carried the ghastly trophy in triumph to their chief.
The whole clan met under the roof of an ancient church.
Every one in turn laid his hand on the dead man's scalp, and
vowed to defend the slayers.† The inhabitants of Eigg seized
some Macleods, bound them hand and foot, and turned them
adrift in a boat to be swallowed up by the waves, or to perish
of hunger. The Macleods retaliated by driving the population
of Eigg into a cavern, lighting a fire at the entrance, and
suffocating the whole race, men, women, and children.‡ It
is much less strange that the two great Earls of the House
of Campbell, animated by the passions of Highland chieftains,
should have planned a Highland revenge, than that they
should have found an accomplice, and something more than
an accomplice, in the Master of Stair.

The Master of Stair was one of the first men of his time, a
jurist, a statesman, a fine scholar, an eloquent orator. His
polished manners and lively conversation were the delight of
aristocratical societies; and none who met him in such
societies would have thought it possible that he could bear

---

* Johnson's Tour to the Hebrides.
† Proclamation of the Privy Council
of Scotland, Feb. 4. 1589. I give this
reference on the authority of Sir Walter

Scott. See the preface to the Legend of
Montrose.
‡ Johnson's Tour to the Hebrides.

the chief part in any atrocious crime. His political principles were lax, yet not more lax than those of most Scotch politicians of that age. Cruelty had never been imputed to him. Those who most disliked him did him the justice to own that, where his schemes of policy were not concerned, he was a very goodnatured man.* There is not the slightest reason to believe that he gained a single pound Scots by the act which has covered his name with infamy. He had no personal reason to wish the Glencoe men any ill. There had been no feud between them and his family. His property lay in a district where their tartan was never seen. Yet he hated them with a hatred as fierce and implacable as if they had laid waste his fields, burned his mansion, murdered his child in the cradle.

To what cause are we to ascribe so strange an antipathy? This question perplexed the Master's contemporaries; and any answer which may now be offered ought to be offered with diffidence.† The most probable conjecture is that he was actuated by an inordinate, an unscrupulous, a remorseless zeal for what seemed to him to be the interest of the state. This explanation may startle those who have not considered how large a proportion of the blackest crimes recorded in history is to be ascribed to ill regulated public spirit. We daily see men do for their party, for their sect, for their country, for their favourite schemes of political and social reform, what they would not do to enrich or to avenge themselves. At a temptation directly addressed to our private cupidity or to our private animosity, whatever virtue we have takes the alarm. But virtue itself may contribute to the fall of him who imagines that it is in his power, by violating some general rule of morality, to confer an important benefit on a church, on a commonwealth, on mankind. He silences the remonstrances of conscience, and hardens his heart against the most touching spectacles of misery, by repeating to himself that his intentions are pure, that his objects are noble, that he is doing a little evil for the sake of a great good. By degrees he comes altogether to forget the turpitude of the means in the excellence of the end, and at length per-

* Lockhart's Memoirs.

† "What under heaven was the Master's byass in this matter? I can imagine none."—Impartial Account, 1695. "Nor can any man of candour and ingenuity imagine that the Earl of Stair, who had neither estate, friendship nor enmity in that country, nor so much as knowledge of these persons, and who was never noted for cruelty in his temper, should have thirsted after the blood of these wretches."—Complete History of Europe, 1707.

petrates without one internal twinge acts which would shock a buccaneer. There is no reason to believe that Dominic would, for the best archbishopric in Christendom, have incited ferocious marauders to plunder and slaughter a peaceful and industrious population, that Everard Digby would, for a dukedom, have blown a large assembly of people into the air, or that Robespierre would have murdered for hire one of the thousands whom he murdered from philanthropy.

The Master of Stair seems to have proposed to himself a truly great and good end, the pacification and civilisation of the Highlands. He was, by the acknowledgment of those who most hated him, a man of large views. He justly thought it monstrous that a third part of Scotland should be in a state scarcely less savage than New Guinea, that letters of fire and sword should, through a third part of Scotland, be, century after century, a species of legal process, and that no attempt should be made to apply a radical remedy to such evils. The independence affected by a crowd of petty sovereigns, the contumacious resistance which they were in the habit of offering to the authority of the Crown and of the Court of Session, their wars, their robberies, their fireraisings, their practice of exacting black mail from people more peaceable and more useful than themselves, naturally excited the disgust and indignation of an enlightened and politic gownsman, who was, both by the constitution of his mind and by the habits of his profession, a lover of law and order. His object was no less than a complete dissolution and reconstruction of society in the Highlands, such a dissolution and reconstruction as, two generations later, followed the battle of Culloden. In his view the clans, as they existed, were the plagues of the kingdom; and of all the clans the worst was that which inhabited Glencoe. He had, it is said, been particularly struck by a frightful instance of the lawlessness and ferocity of those marauders. One of them, who had been concerned in some act of violence or rapine, had given information against his companions. He had been bound to a tree and murdered. The old chief had given the first stab; and scores of dirks had then been plunged into the wretch's body.* By the mountaineers such an act was probably re-

---

* Dalrymple, in his Memoirs, relates this story, without referring to any authority. His authority probably was family tradition. That reports were current in 1692 of horrible crimes committed by the Macdonalds of Glencoe is certain from the Burnet MS. Harl. 6584. "They had indeed been guilty of many black murthers," were Burnet's words, written in 1693. He afterwards softened down this expression.

garded as a legitimate exercise of patriarchal jurisdiction. To the Master of Stair it seemed that people among whom such things were done and were approved ought to be treated like a pack of wolves, snared by any device, and slaughtered without mercy. He was well read in history, and doubtless knew how great rulers had, in his own and other countries, dealt with such banditti. He doubtless knew with what energy and what severity James the Fifth had put down the mosstroopers of the border, how the chief of Henderland had been hung over the gate of the castle in which he had prepared a banquet for the King; how John Armstrong and his thirty-six horsemen, when they came forth to welcome their sovereign, had scarcely been allowed time to say a single prayer before they were all tied up and turned off. Nor probably was the Secretary ignorant of the means by which Sixtus the Fifth had cleared the ecclesiastical state of outlaws. The eulogists of that great pontiff tell us that there was one formidable gang which could not be dislodged from a stronghold among the Apennines. Beasts of burden were therefore loaded with poisoned food and wine, and sent by a road which ran close to the fastness. The robbers sallied forth, seized the prey, feasted and died; and the pious old Pope exulted greatly when he heard that the corpses of thirty ruffians, who had been the terror of many peaceful villages, had been found lying among the mules and packages. The plans of the Master of Stair were conceived in the spirit of James and of Sixtus; and the rebellion of the mountaineers furnished what seemed to be an excellent opportunity for carrying those plans into effect. Mere rebellion, indeed, he could have easily pardoned. On Jacobites, as Jacobites, he never showed any inclination to bear hard. He hated the Highlanders, not as enemies of this or that dynasty, but as enemies of law, of industry, and of trade. In his private correspondence he applied to them the short and terrible form of words in which the implacable Roman pronounced the doom of Carthage. His project was no less than this, that the whole hill country from sea to sea, and the neighbouring islands, should be wasted with fire and sword, that the Camerons, the Macleans, and all the branches of the race of Macdonald, should be rooted out. He therefore looked with no friendly eye on schemes of reconciliation, and, while others were hoping that a little money would set everything right, hinted very intelligibly his opinion that whatever money was to be laid out on the clans would be best laid out in the form

of bullets and bayonets. To the last moment he continued
to flatter himself that the rebels would be obstinate, and
would thus furnish him with a plea for accomplishing that
great social revolution on which his heart was set.* - The
letter is still extant in which he directed the commander of
the forces in Scotland how to act if the Jacobite chiefs should
not come in before the end of December. There is something strangely terrible in the calmness and conciseness
with which the instructions are given. " Your troops will
destroy entirely the country of Lochaber, Lochiel's lands,
Keppoch's, Glengarry's and Glencoe's. Your power shall
be large enough. I hope the soldiers will not trouble the
government with prisoners." †

This despatch had scarcely been sent off when news arrived
in London that the rebel chiefs, after holding out long, had
at last appeared before the Sheriffs and taken the oaths.
Lochiel, the most eminent man among them, had not only
declared that he would live and die a true subject to King
William, but had announced his intention of visiting England, in the hope of being permitted to kiss His Majesty's
hand. In London it was announced exultingly that all the
clans had submitted; and the announcement was generally
thought most satisfactory.‡ But the Master of Stair was
bitterly disappointed. The Highlands were then to continue
to be what they had been, the shame and curse of Scotland.
A golden opportunity of subjecting them to the law had been
suffered to escape, and might never return. If only the Macdonalds would have stood out, nay, if an example could but
have been made of the two worst Macdonalds, Keppoch and
Glencoe, it would have been something. But it seemed that
even Keppoch and Glencoe, marauders who in any well
governed country would have been hanged thirty years before,
were safe. § While the Master was brooding over thoughts
like these, Argyle brought him some comfort. The report
that Mac Ian had taken the oaths within the prescribed time

---

* That the plan originally framed by
the Master of Stair was such as I have
represented it, is clear from parts of his
letters which are quoted in the Report
of 1695, and from his letters to Breadalbane of October 27., December 2., and
December 3. 1691. Of these letters to
Breadalbane, the last two are in Dalrymple's Appendix. The first is in the
Appendix to the first volume of Mr.
Burton's valuable History of Scotland,
"It appeared," says Burnet (ii. 157.),

" that a black design was laid, not only to
cut off the men of Glencoe, but a great
many more clans, reckoned to be in all
above six thousand persons."

† This letter is in the Report of 1695.

‡ London Gazette, Jan. 14. and 18. 169½.

§ " I could have wished the Macdonalds had not divided ; and I am sorry
that Keppoch and Mackian of Glenco are
safe."—Letter of the Master of Stair to
Levingstone, Jan. 9. 169½, quoted in the
Report of 1695.

was erroneous. The Secretary was consoled. One clan, then, was at the mercy of the government, and that clan the most lawless of all. One great act of justice, nay of charity, might be performed. One terrible and memorable example might be made.*

Yet there was a difficulty. Mac Ian had taken the oaths. He had taken them, indeed, too late to be entitled to plead the letter of the royal promise : but the fact that he had taken them was one which evidently ought to have been brought under consideration before his fate was decided. By a dark intrigue, of which the history is but imperfectly known, but which was, in all probability, directed by the Master of Stair, the evidence of Mac Ian's tardy submission was suppressed. The certificate which the Sheriff of Argyleshire had transmitted to the Council at Edinburgh was never laid before the Board, but was privately submitted to some persons high in office, and particularly to Lord President Stair, the father of the Secretary. These persons pronounced the certificate irregular, and, indeed, absolutely null ; and it was cancelled.

Meanwhile the Master of Stair was forming, in concert with Breadalbane and Argyle, a plan for the destruction of the people of Glencoe. It was necessary to take the King's pleasure, not, indeed, as to the details of what was to be done, but as to the question whether Mac Ian and his people should or should not be treated as rebels out of the pale of the ordinary law. The Master of Stair found no difficulty in the royal closet. William had, in all probability, never heard the Glencoe men mentioned except as banditti. He knew that they had not come in by the prescribed day. That they had come in after that day he did not know. If he paid any attention to the matter, he must have thought that so fair an opportunity of putting an end to the devastations and depredations from which a quiet and industrious population had suffered so much ought not to be lost.

An order was laid before him for signature. He signed it, but, if Burnet may be trusted, did not read it. Whoever has seen anything of public business knows that princes and ministers daily sign, and indeed must sign, documents which they have not read ; and of all documents a document relating to a small tribe of mountaineers, living in a wilderness not set down in any map, was least likely to interest a Sove-

* Letter of the Master of Stair to Levingstone, Jan. 11. 169½, quoted in the Report of 1695.

reign whose mind was full of schemes on which the fate of Europe might depend.* But, even on the supposition that he read the order to which he affixed his name, there seems to be no reason for blaming him. That order, directed to the Commander of the Forces in Scotland, runs thus: "As for Mac Ian of Glencoe and that tribe, if they can be well distinguished from the other Highlanders, it will be proper, for the vindication of public justice, to extirpate that set of thieves." These words naturally bear a sense perfectly innocent, and would, but for the horrible event which followed, have been universally understood in that sense. It is undoubtedly one of the first duties of every government to extirpate gangs of thieves. This does not mean that every thief ought to be treacherously assassinated in his sleep, or even that every thief ought to be put to death after a fair trial, but that every gang, as a gang, ought to be completely broken up, and that whatever severity is indispensably necessary for that end ought to be used. It is in this sense that we praise the Marquess of Hastings for extirpating the Pindarees, and Lord William Bentinck for extirpating the Thugs. If the King had read and weighed the words which were submitted to him by his Secretary, he would probably have understood them to mean that Glencoe was to be occupied by troops, that resistance, if resistance were attempted, was to be put down with a strong hand, that severe punishment was to be inflicted on those leading members of the clan who could be proved to have been guilty of great crimes, that some active young freebooters who were more used to handle the broad sword than the plough, and who did not seem likely to settle down into quiet labourers, were to be sent to the army in the Low Countries, that others were to be transported to the American plantations, and that those Macdonalds who were suffered to remain in their native valley were to be disarmed and required to give hostages for good behaviour. A plan very nearly resembling this had, we know, actually been the subject of much discussion in the political circles of Edinburgh.† There can be little doubt that William would have deserved well of his people if he had, in this manner, extirpated not only the tribe

* Burnet, ii. 89. Burnet, in 1693, wrote thus about William:—"He suffers matters to run till there is a great heap of papers; and then he signs them as much too fast as he was before too slow in despatching them." Burnet MS. Harl. 6584. There is no sign either of procrastination or of undue haste in William's correspondence with Heinsius. The truth is that the King understood Continental politics thoroughly, and gave his whole mind to them. To English business he attended less, and to Scotch business least of all.

† Impartial Account, 1695.

of Mac Ian, but every Highland tribe whose calling was to steal cattle and burn houses.

The extirpation planned by the Master of Stair was of a different kind. His design was to butcher the whole race of thieves, the whole damnable race. Such was the language in which his hatred vented itself. He studied the geography of the wild country which surrounded Glencoe, and made his arrangements with infernal skill. If possible the blow must be quick, and crushing, and altogether unexpected. But if Mac Ian should apprehend danger, and should attempt to take refuge in the territories of his neighbours, he must find every road barred. The pass of Rannoch must be secured. The Laird of Weem, who was powerful in Strath Tay, must be told that, if he harbours the outlaws, he does so at his peril. Breadalbane promised to cut off the retreat of the fugitives on one side, Mac Callum More on another. It was fortunate, the Secretary wrote, that it was winter. This was the time to maul the wretches. The nights were so long, the mountain tops so cold and stormy, that even the hardiest men could not long bear exposure to the open air without a roof or a spark of fire. That the women and the children could find shelter in the desert was quite impossible. While he wrote thus, no thought that he was committing a great wickedness crossed his mind. He was happy in the approbation of his own conscience. Duty, justice, nay charity and mercy, were the names under which he disguised his cruelty; nor is it by any means improbable that the disguise imposed upon himself.*

Hill, who commanded the forces assembled at Fort William, was not entrusted with the execution of the design. He seems to have been a humane man; he was much distressed when he learned that the government was determined on severity; and it was probably thought that his heart might fail him in the most critical moment. He was directed to put a strong detachment under the orders of his second in command, Lieutenant Colonel Hamilton. To Hamilton a significant hint was conveyed that he had now an excellent opportunity of establishing his character in the estimation of those who were at the head of affairs. Of the troops entrusted to him a large proportion were Campbells, and belonged to a regiment lately raised by Argyle, and called by Argyle's name. It was probably thought that, on such an occasion, humanity

* See his letters quoted in the Report of 1695, and in the Memoirs of the Massacre of Glencoe.

might prove too strong for the mere habit of military obedience, and that little reliance could be placed on hearts which had not been ulcerated by a feud such as had long raged between the people of Mac Ian and the people of Mac Callum More.

Had Hamilton marched openly against the Glencoe men and put them to the edge of the sword, the act would probably not have wanted apologists, and most certainly would not have wanted precedents. But the Master of Stair had strongly recommended a different mode of proceeding. If the least alarm were given, the nest of robbers would be found empty; and to hunt them down in so wild a region would, even with all the help that Breadalbane and Argyle could give, be a long and difficult business. "Better," he wrote, "not meddle with them than meddle to no purpose. When the thing is resolved let it be secret and sudden."* He was obeyed; and it was determined that the Glencoe men should perish, not by military execution, but by the most dastardly and perfidious form of assassination.

On the first of February a hundred and twenty soldiers of Argyle's regiment, commanded by a captain named Campbell and a lieutenant named Lindsay, marched to Glencoe. Captain Campbell was commonly called in Scotland Glenlyon, from the pass in which his property lay. He had every qualification for the service on which he was employed, an unblushing forehead, a smooth lying tongue, and a heart of adamant. He was also one of the few Campbells who were likely to be trusted and welcomed by the Macdonalds: for his niece was married to Alexander, the second son of Mac Ian.

The sight of the red coats approaching caused some anxiety among the population of the valley. John, the eldest son of the Chief, came, accompanied by twenty clansmen, to meet the strangers, and asked what this visit meant. Lieutenant Lindsay answered that the soldiers came as friends, and wanted nothing but quarters. They were kindly received, and were lodged under the thatched roofs of the little community. Glenlyon and several of his men were taken into the house of a tacksman who was named from the cluster of cabins over which he exercised authority, Inverriggen. Lindsay was accommodated nearer to the abode of the old chief. Auchintriater, one of the principal men of the clan, who governed the small hamlet of Auchnaion, found room there for a party commanded by a serjeant named Barbour. Provisions were liberally supplied. There was no want of beef, which had

* Report of 1695.

probably fattened in distant pastures: nor was any payment demanded: for in hospitality, as in thievery, the Gaelic marauders rivalled the Bedouins. During twelve days the soldiers lived familiarly with the people of the glen. Old Mac Ian, who had before felt many misgivings as to the relation in which he stood to the government, seems to have been pleased with the visit. The officers passed much of their time with him and his family. The long evenings were cheerfully spent by the peat fire with the help of some packs of cards which had found their way to that remote corner of the world, and of some French brandy which was probably part of James's farewell gift to his Highland supporters. Glenlyon appeared to be warmly attached to his niece and her husband Alexander. Every day he came to their house to take his morning draught. Meanwhile he observed with minute attention all the avenues by which, when the signal for the slaughter should be given, the Macdonalds might attempt to escape to the hills; and he reported the result of his observations to Hamilton.

Hamilton fixed five o'clock in the morning of the thirteenth of February for the deed. He hoped that, before that time, he should reach Glencoe with four hundred men, and should have stopped all the earths in which the old fox and his two cubs,—so Mac Ian and his sons were nicknamed by the murderers,—could take refuge. But, at five precisely, whether Hamilton had arrived or not, Glenlyon was to fall on, and to slay every Macdonald under seventy.

The night was rough. Hamilton and his troops made slow progress, and were long after their time. While they were contending with the wind and snow, Glenlyon was supping and playing at cards with those whom he meant to butcher before daybreak. He and Lieutenant Lindsay had engaged themselves to dine with the old Chief on the morrow.

Late in the evening a vague suspicion that some evil was intended crossed the mind of the Chief's eldest son. The soldiers were evidently in a restless state; and some of them uttered strange exclamations. Two men, it is said, were overheard whispering. "I do not like this job," one of them muttered: "I should be glad to fight the Macdonalds. But to kill men in their beds—" "We must do as we are bid," answered another voice. "If there is anything wrong, our officers must answer for it." John Macdonald was so uneasy that, soon after midnight, he went to Glenlyon's quarters. Glenlyon and his men were all up, and seemed to be getting their arms ready for action. John, much alarmed, asked what these preparations meant. Glenlyon was profuse of friendly assurances. "Some of Glengarry's people have been harrying the country. We are getting ready to march against them. You are quite safe. Do you think that, if you were in any danger, I should not have given a hint to your brother Sandy and his wife?" John's suspicions were quieted. He returned to his house, and lay down to rest.

It was five in the morning. Hamilton and his men were still some miles off; and the avenues which they were to have secured were open. But the orders which Glenlyon had received were precise; and he began to execute them at the little village where he was himself quartered. His host Inverrigen and nine other Macdonalds were dragged out of their beds, bound hand and foot, and murdered. A boy twelve years old clung round the Captain's legs, and begged hard for life. He would do anything: he would go any-where: he would follow Glenlyon round the world. Even Glenlyon, it is said, showed signs of relenting; but a ruffian named Drummond shot the child dead.

At Auchnaion the tacksman Auchintriater was up early that morning, and was sitting with eight of his family round the fire, when a volley of musketry laid him and seven of his companions dead or dying on the floor. His brother, who alone had escaped unhurt, called to Serjeant Barbour, who commanded the slayers, and asked as a favour to be allowed to die in the open air. "Well," said the Serjeant, "I will do you that favour for the sake of your meat which I have eaten." The mountaineer, bold, athletic, and favoured by the darkness, came forth, rushed on the soldiers who were about to level their pieces at him, flung his plaid over their faces, and was gone in a moment.

Meanwhile Lindsay had knocked at the door of the old Chief and had asked for admission in friendly language. The door was opened. Mac Ian, while putting on his clothes and calling to his servants to bring some refreshment for his visitors, was shot through the head. Two of his attendants were slain with him. His wife was already up and dressed in such finery as the princesses of the rude Highland glens were accustomed to wear. The assassins pulled off her clothes and trinkets. The rings were not easily taken from her fingers: but a soldier tore them away with his teeth. She died on the following day.

The statesman, to whom chiefly this great crime is to be ascribed, had planned it with consummate ability: but the execution was complete in nothing but in guilt and infamy. A succession of blunders saved three fourths of the Glencoe men from the fate of their chief. All the moral qualities which fit men to bear a part in a massacre Hamilton and Glenlyon possessed in perfection. But neither seems to have had much professional skill. Hamilton had arranged his plan without making allowance for bad weather, and this at a season when, in the Highlands, the weather was very likely to be bad. The consequence was that the fox earths, as he called them, were not stopped in time. Glenlyon and his men committed the error of despatching their hosts with firearms instead of using the cold steel. The peal and flash of gun after gun gave notice, from three different parts of the valley at once, that murder was doing. From fifty cottages the half naked peasantry fled under cover of the night to the recesses of their pathless glen. Even the sons of Mac Ian, who had been especially marked out for destruction, contrived to escape. They were roused from sleep by faithful servants. John, who, by the death of his father, had become the patriarch of the tribe, quitted his dwelling just as twenty soldiers with fixed bayonets marched up to it. It was broad day long before Hamilton arrived. He found the work not even half performed. About thirty corpses lay wallowing in blood on the dunghills before the doors. One or two women were seen among the number, and a yet more fearful and piteous sight, a little hand, which had been lopped in the tumult of the butchery from some infant. One aged Macdonald was found alive. He was probably too infirm to fly, and, as he was above seventy, was not included in the orders under which Glenlyon had acted. Hamilton murdered the old man in cold blood. The deserted hamlets were then set on fire; and the troops departed, driving away with them many sheep and goats, nine hundred kine, and two hundred of the small shaggy ponies of the Highlands.

It is said, and may but too easily be believed, that the sufferings of the fugitives were terrible. How many old men, how many women with babes in their arms, sank down and slept their last sleep in the snow; how many, having crawled, spent with toil and hunger, into nooks among the precipices, died in those dark holes, and were picked to the bone by the mountain ravens, can never be known. But it is probable that those who perished by cold, weariness, and want were not less numerous than those who were slain by the assassins. When the troops had retired, the Macdonalds crept out of the caverns of Glencoe, ventured back to the spot where the huts had formerly stood, collected the scorched corpses from among the smoking ruins, and performed some rude rites of sepulture. The tradition runs that the hereditary bard of the tribe took his seat on a rock which overhung the place of slaughter, and poured forth a long lament over his murdered brethren and his desolate home. Eighty years later that sad dirge was still repeated by the population of the valley.*

The survivors might well apprehend that they had escaped the shot and the sword only to perish by famine. The whole domain was a waste. Houses, barns, furniture, implements of husbandry, herds, flocks, horses, were gone. Many months must elapse before the clan would be able to raise on its own ground the means of supporting even the most miserable existence.†

It may be thought strange that these events should not have been instantly followed by a burst of execration from every part of the civilised world. The fact, however, is that years elapsed before the public indignation was thoroughly awakened, and that months elapsed before the blackest part of the story found credit even among the enemies of the government. That the massacre should not have been mentioned in the London Gazettes, in the Monthly Mercuries, which were scarcely less courtly than the Gazettes, or in pamphlets licensed by official censors, is perfectly intelligible. But that no allusion to it should be found in private journals and letters, written by persons free from all restraint, may seem extraordinary. There is not a word on the subject in Evelyn's Diary. In Narcissus Luttrell's Diary is a remarkable entry made five weeks after the butchery. The letters from Scotland, he says, described that kingdom as perfectly tranquil, except that there was still some grumbling about

---

* Deposition of Ronald Macdonald in the Report of 1695; Letters from the Mountains, May 17. 1773. I quote Mrs. Grant's authority only for what she herself heard and saw. Her account of the massacre was written apparently without the assistance of books, and is grossly incorrect. Indeed she makes a mistake of two years as to the date.

† I have taken the account of the Massacre of Glencoe chiefly from the Report of 1695, and from the Gallienus Redivivus. An unlearned, and indeed a learned, reader may be at a loss to guess why the Jacobites should have selected so strange a title for a pamphlet on the massacre of Glencoe. The explanation will be found in a letter of the Emperor Gallienus, preserved by Trebellius Pollio in the Life of Ingenuus. Ingenuus had raised a rebellion in Mœsia. He was defeated and killed. Gallienus ordered the whole province to be laid waste, and wrote to one of his lieutenants in language to which that of the Master of Stair bore but too much resemblance. "Non mihi satisfacies si tantum armatos occideris, quos et fors belli interimere potuisset. Perimendus est omnis sexus virilis. Occidendus est quicunque male dixit. Occidendus est quicunque male voluit. Lacera. Occide. Concide,"

ecclesiastical questions. The Dutch ministers regularly reported all the Scotch news to their government. They thought it worth while, about this time, to mention that a collier had been taken by a privateer near Berwick, that the Edinburgh mail had been robbed, that a whale, with a tongue seventeen feet long and seven feet broad, had been stranded near Aberdeen. But it is not hinted in any of their despatches that there was any rumour of any extraordinary occurrence in the Highlands. Reports that some of the Macdonalds had been slain did indeed, in about three weeks, travel through Edinburgh up to London. But these reports were vague and contradictory; and the very worst of them was far from coming up to the horrible truth. The Whig version of the story was that the old robber Mac Ian had laid an ambuscade for the soldiers, that he had been caught in his own snare, and that he and some of his clan had fallen sword in hand. The Jacobite version, written at Edinburgh on the twenty-third of March, appeared in the Paris Gazette of the seventh of April. Glenlyon, it was said, had been sent with a detachment from Argyle's regiment, under cover of darkness, to surprise the inhabitants of Glencoe, and had killed thirty-six men and boys and four women.* In this there was nothing very strange or shocking. A night attack on a gang of freebooters occupying a strong natural fortress may be a perfectly legitimate military operation; and, in the obscurity and confusion of such an attack, the most humane man may be so unfortunate as to shoot a woman or a child. The circumstances which give a peculiar character to the slaughter of Glencoe, the breach of faith, the breach of hospitality, the twelve days of feigned friendship and conviviality, of morning calls, of social meals, of healthdrinking, of cardplaying, were not mentioned by the Edinburgh correspondent of the Paris Gazette; and we may therefore confidently infer that those circumstances were as yet unknown even to inquisitive and busy malecontents residing in the Scottish capital within a hundred miles of the spot where the deed had been done. In the south of the island, the matter produced, as far as can now be judged, scarcely any sensation. To the Londoner of those days Appin was what Caffraria or Borneo is to us. He was not more moved by hearing that some Highland thieves had been surprised and killed than we are by hearing that a band of Amakosah cattle stealers

* What I have called the Whig version of the story is given, as well as the Jacobite version, in the Paris Gazette of April 7. 1692.

has been cut off, or that a bark full of Malay pirates has been sunk. He took it for granted that nothing had been done in Glencoe beyond what was doing in many other glens. There might have been violence; but it had been in a land of violence. There had been a night brawl, one of a hundred night brawls, between the Macdonalds and the Campbells; and the Campbells had knocked the Macdonalds on the head.

By slow degrees the whole came out. From a letter written at Edinburgh before the end of April, it appears that the true story was already current among the Jacobites of that city. In the summer Argyle's regiment was quartered in the south of England, and some of the men made strange confessions, over their ale, about what they had been forced to do in the preceding winter. The nonjurors soon got hold of the clue, and followed it resolutely: their secret presses went to work; and at length, near a year after the crime had been committed, it was published to the world.* But the world was long incredulous. The habitual mendacity of the Jacobite libellers had brought on them an appropriate punishment. Now, when, for the first time, they told the truth, they were supposed to be romancing. They complained bitterly that the story, though perfectly authentic, was regarded by the public as a factious lie.† So late as the year 1695, Hickes, in a tract in which he endeavoured to defend his darling tale of the Theban legion against the unanswerable argument drawn from the silence of historians, remarked that it might well be doubted whether any historian would make mention of the massacre of Glencoe. There were in England, he said, many thousands of well educated men who had never heard of that massacre, or who regarded it as a mere fable.‡

Nevertheless the punishment of some of the guilty began very early. Hill, who indeed can scarcely be called guilty, was much disturbed. Breadalbane, hardened as he was, felt the stings of conscience or the dread of retribution. A few days after the Macdonalds had returned to their old dwellingplace, his steward visited the ruins of the house of Glencoe, and endeavoured to persuade the sons of the murdered

---

* I believe that the circumstances which give so peculiar a character of atrocity to the Massacre of Glencoe were first published in print by Charles Leslie in the Appendix to his answer to King. The date of Leslie's answer is 1692. But it must be remembered that the date of 1692 was then used down to what we should call the 25th of March 1693. Leslie's book contains some remarks on a sermon by Tillotson which was not printed till November 1692. The Gallienus Redivivus speedily followed.

† Gallienus Redivivus.

‡ Hickes on Burnet and Tillotson, 1695.

chief to sign a paper declaring that they held the Earl guiltless of the blood which had been shed. They were assured that, if they would do this, all His Lordship's great influence should be employed to obtain for them from the Crown a free pardon and a remission of all forfeitures.[*] Glenlyon did his best to assume an air of unconcern. He made his appearance in the most fashionable coffeehouse at Edinburgh, and talked loudly and selfcomplacently about the important service in which he had been engaged among the mountains. Some of his soldiers, however, who observed him closely, whispered that all this bravery was put on. He was not the man that he had been before that night. The form of his countenance was changed. In all places, at all hours, whether he waked or slept, Glencoe was ever before him.[†]

But, whatever apprehensions might disturb Breadalbane, whatever spectres might haunt Glenlyon, the Master of Stair had neither fear nor remorse. He was indeed mortified: but he was mortified only by the blunders of Hamilton and by the escape of so many of the damnable breed. "Do right, and fear nobody;" such is the language of his letters. "Can there be a more sacred duty than to rid the country of thieving? The only thing that I regret is that any got away." [‡]

On the sixth of March, William, entirely ignorant, in all probability, of the details of the crime which has cast a dark shade over his glory, had set out for the Continent, leaving the Queen his vicegerent in England.[§] *William goes to the Continent.*

He would perhaps have postponed his departure if he had been aware that the French Government had, during some time, been making great preparations for a descent on our island.[||] An event had taken place which had changed the policy of the court of Versailles. Louvois was no more. He had been at the head of the military administration of his country during a quarter of a century; he had borne a chief part in the direction of two wars which had enlarged the French territory, and had filled the world with the renown of the *Death of Louvois.*

<hr/>

[*] Report of 1695.
[†] Gallienus Redivivus.
[‡] Report of 1695.
[§] London Gazette, Mar. 7. 169½.

[||] Burnet (ii. 93.) says that the King was not at this time informed of the intentions of the French Government. Ralph contradicts Burnet with great asperity. But that Burnet was in the right is proved beyond dispute by William's

correspondence with Heinsius. So late as $\frac{\text{April 24.}}{\text{May 4.}}$ William wrote thus: "Je ne puis vous dissimuler que je commence à apprehender une descente en Angleterre, quoique je n'aye pu le croire d'abord: mais les avis sont si multipliés de tous les côtés, et accompagnés de tant de particularités, qu'il n'est plus guère possible d'en douter." I quote from the French translation among the Mackintosh MSS.

French arms, and he had lived to see the beginning of a third war which tasked his great powers to the utmost. Between him and the celebrated captains who carried his plans into execution there was little harmony. His imperious temper and his confidence in himself impelled him to interfere too much with the conduct of troops in the field, even when those troops were commanded by Condé, by Turenne, or by Luxemburg. But he was the greatest Adjutant General, the greatest Quartermaster General, the greatest Commissary General, that Europe had seen. He may indeed be said to have made a revolution in the art of disciplining, distributing, equipping, and provisioning armies. In spite, however, of his abilities and of his services, he had become odious to Lewis and to her who governed Lewis. On the last occasion on which the King and the minister transacted business together, the ill humour on both sides broke violently forth. The servant, in his vexation, dashed his portfolio on the ground. The master, forgetting, what he seldom forgot, that a king should be a gentleman, lifted his cane. Fortunately his wife was present. She, with her usual prudence, caught his arm. She then got Louvois out of the room, and exhorted him to come back the next day as if nothing had happened. The next day he came, but with death in his face. The King, though full of resentment, was touched with pity, and advised Louvois to go home and take care of himself. That evening the great minister died.*

Louvois had constantly opposed all plans for the invasion of England. His death was therefore regarded at Saint Germains as a fortunate event.† It was however necessary to look sad, and to send a gentleman to Versailles with some words of condolence. The messenger found the gorgeous circle of courtiers assembled round their master on the terrace above the orangery. " Sir," said Lewis, in a tone so easy and cheerful that it filled all the bystanders with amazement, " present my compliments and thanks to the King and Queen of England, and tell them that neither my affairs nor theirs will go on the worse for what has happened." These words were doubtless meant to intimate that the influence of Louvois had not been exerted in favour of the House of Stuart.‡ One compliment, however, a compliment which

---

* Burnet, ii. 95. and Onslow's note ; Mémoires de Saint Simon ; Journal de Dangeau.

† Life of James, ii. 411, 412.

‡ Mémoires de Dangeau ; Mémoires de Saint Simon. Saint Simon was on the terrace, and, young as he was, observed this singular scene with an eye which nothing escaped.

cost France dear, Lewis thought it right to pay to the memory of his ablest servant. The Marquess of Barbesieux, son of Louvois, was placed, in his twenty-fifth year, at the head of the war department. The young man was by no means deficient in abilities, and had been, during some years, employed in business of grave importance. But his passions were strong: his judgment was not ripe; and his sudden elevation turned his head. His manners gave general disgust. Old officers complained that he kept them long in his antechamber while he was amusing himself with his spaniels and his flatterers. Those who were admitted to his presence went away disgusted by his rudeness and arrogance. As was natural at his age, he valued power chiefly as the means of procuring pleasure. Millions of crowns were expended on the luxurious villa where he loved to forget the cares of office in gay conversation, delicate cookery, and foaming Champagne. He often pleaded an attack of fever as an excuse for not making his appearance at the proper hour in the royal closet, when in truth he had been playing truant among his boon companions and mistresses. "The French King," said William, "has an odd taste. He chooses an old woman for his mistress, and a young man for his minister."*

There can be little doubt that Louvois, by pursuing that course which had made him odious to the inmates of Saint Germains, had deserved well of his country. He was not maddened by Jacobite enthusiasm. He well knew that exiles are the worst of all advisers. He had excellent information: he had excellent judgment: he calculated the chances; and he saw that a descent was likely to fail, and to fail disastrously and disgracefully. James might well be impatient to try the experiment, though the odds should be ten to one against him. He might gain; and he could not lose. His folly and obstinacy had left him nothing to risk. His food, his drink, his lodging, his clothes, he owed to charity. Nothing could be more natural than that, for the very smallest chance of recovering the three kingdoms which he had thrown away, he should be willing to stake what was not his own, the honour of the French arms, the grandeur and the safety of the French monarchy. To a French statesman such a wager might well appear in a different light. But Louvois was

* Mémoires de Saint Simon; Burnet, ii. 95.; Guardian, No. 48. See the excellent letter of Lewis to the Archbishop of Rheims, which is quoted by Voltaire in the Siècle de Louis XIV.

gone. His master yielded to the importunity of James, and
determined to send an expedition against England.*

The scheme was, in some respects, well concerted. It was
resolved that a camp should be formed on the coast of Normandy, and that in this camp all the Irish regiments which
were in the French service should be assembed under their
countryman Sarsfield. With them were to be joined about
ten thousand French troops. The whole army was to be
commanded by Marshal Bellefonds.

A noble fleet of about eighty ships of the line was to convoy this force to the shores of England. In the dockyards
both of Britanny and of Provence immense preparations were
made. Four and forty men of war, some of which were
among the finest that had ever been built, were assembled in
the harbour of Brest under Tourville. The Count of Estrees,
with thirty-five more, was to sail from Toulon. Ushant was
fixed for the place of rendezvous. The very day was named.
In order that there might be no want either of seamen or of
vessels for the intended expedition, all maritime trade, all
privateering was, for a time, interdicted by a royal mandate.†
Three hundred transports were collected near the spot where
the troops were to embark. It was hoped that all would be
ready early in the spring, before the English ships were half
rigged or half manned, and before a single Dutch man of war
was in the Channel.‡

James had indeed persuaded himself that, even if the
English fleet should fall in with him, it would not oppose
him. He imagined that he was personally a favourite with
the mariners of all ranks. His emissaries had been busy
among the naval officers, and had found some who remembered him with kindness, and others who were out of humour
with the men now in power. All the wild talk of a class
of people not distinguished by taciturnity or discretion was
reported to him with exaggeration, till he was deluded into a
belief that he had more friends than enemies on board of the
vessels which guarded our coasts. Yet he should have
known that a rough sailor, who thought himself ill used by
the Admiralty, might, after the third bottle, when drawn on
by artful companions, express his regret for the good old
time, curse the new government, and curse himself for being
such a fool as to fight for that government, and yet might be

---

* In the Nairne Papers printed by
Macpherson are two memorials from
James urging Lewis to invade England.
Both were written in January 1692.

† London Gazette, Feb. 15. 169½.
‡ Mémoires de Berwick, Burnet, ii. 92. ;
Life of James, ii. 478. 491.

by no means prepared to go over to the French on the day of battle. Of the malecontent officers, who, as James believed, were impatient to desert, the great majority had probably given no pledge of their attachment to him except an idle word hiccoughed out when they were drunk, and forgotten when they were sober. One of those from whom he expected support, Rear Admiral Carter, had indeed heard and perfectly understood what the Jacobite agents had to say, had given them fair words, and had reported the whole to the Queen and her ministers.*

But the chief dependence of James was on Russell. That false, arrogant, and wayward politician was to command the Channel Fleet. He had never ceased to assure the Jacobite emissaries that he was bent on effecting a Restoration. Those emissaries fully reckoned, if not on his entire cooperation, yet at least on his connivance; and there could be no doubt that, with his connivance, a French fleet might easily convey an army to our shores. James flattered himself that, as soon as he had landed, he should be master of the island. But in truth, when the voyage had ended the difficulties of his enterprise would have been only beginning. Two years before he had received a lesson by which he should have profited. He had then deceived himself and others into the belief that the English were regretting him, were pining for him, were eager to rise in arms by tens of thousands to welcome him. William was then, as now, at a distance. Then, as now, the administration was entrusted to a woman. There were then fewer regular troops in England than now. Torrington had then done as much to injure the government which he served as Russell could now do. The French fleet had then, after riding during several weeks, victorious and dominant in the Channel, landed some troops on the southern coast. The immediate effect had been that whole counties, without distinction of Tory or Whig, Churchman or Dissenter, had risen up, as one man, to repel the foreigners, and that the Jacobite party, which had, a few days before, seemed to be half the nation, had crouched down in silent terror, and had made itself so small that it had, during some time, been invisible. What reason was there for believing that the multitudes who had, in 1690, at the first lighting of the beacons, snatched up firelocks, pikes, scythes, to defend their native soil against the French, would now welcome the French as allies? And of the army by which James was

Conduct of Russell.

---

* History of the late Conspiracy, 1693.

now to be accompanied the French formed the least odious part. More than half of that army was to consist of Irish Papists; and the feeling, compounded of hatred and scorn, with which the Irish Papists had long been regarded by the English Protestants, had by recent events been stimulated to a vehemence before unknown. The hereditary slaves, it was said, had been for a moment free; and that moment had sufficed to prove that they knew neither how to use nor how to defend their freedom. During their short ascendency they had done nothing but slay, and burn, and pillage, and demolish, and attaint, and confiscate. In three years they had committed such waste on their native land as thirty years of English intelligence and industry would scarcely repair. They would have maintained their independence against the world, if they had been as ready to fight as they were to steal. But they had retreated ignominiously from the walls of Londonderry. They had fled like deer before the yeomanry of Enniskillen. The Prince whom they now presumed to think that they could place, by force of arms, on the English throne, had himself, on the morning after the rout of the Boyne, reproached them with their cowardice, and told them that he would never again trust to their soldiership. On tnis subject Englishmen were of one mind. Tories, Nonjurors, even Roman Catholics, were as loud as Whigs in reviling the ill-fated race. It is, therefore, not difficult to guess what effect would have been produced by the appearance on our soil of enemies whom, on their own soil, we had vanquished and trampled down.

James, however, in spite of the recent and severe teaching of experience, believed whatever his correspondents in England told him; and they told him that the whole nation was impatiently expecting him, that both the West and the North were ready to rise, that he would proceed from the place of landing to Whitehall with as little opposition as he had encountered when, in old times, he made a progress through his kingdom, escorted, by long cavalcades of gentlemen, from one lordly mansion to another. Ferguson distinguished himself by the confidence with which he predicted a complete and bloodless victory. He and his printer, he was absurd enough to write, would be the two first men in the realm to take horse for His Majesty. Many other agents were busy, up and down the country, during the winter and the early part of the spring. It does not appear that they had much success in the counties south of Trent. But in the north, particularly in Lancashire, where the Roman Catholics were more numerous and more powerful than in any other part of the kingdom, and where there seems to have been, even among the Protestant gentry, more than the ordinary proportion of bigoted Jacobites, some preparations for an insurrection were made. Arms were privately bought: officers were appointed: yeomen, small farmers, grooms, huntsmen, were induced to enlist. Those who gave in their names were distributed into eight regiments of cavalry and dragoons, and were directed to hold themselves in readiness to mount at the first signal.*

One of the circumstances which filled James, at this time, with vain hopes, was that his wife was pregnant and near her delivery. He flattered himself that malice itself would be ashamed to repeat any longer the story of the warming pan, and that multitudes whom that story had deceived would instantly return to their allegiance. He took, on this occasion, all those precautions which, four years before, he had foolishly and perversely forborne to take. He contrived to transmit to England letters summoning many Protestant women of quality to assist at the expected birth; and he promised, in the name of his dear brother the Most Christian King, that they should be free to come and go in safety. Had some of those witnesses been invited to Saint James's on the morning of the tenth of June 1688, the House of Stuart might, perhaps, now be reigning in our island. But it is easier to keep a crown than to regain one. It might be true that a calumnious fable had done much to bring about the Revolution. But it by no means followed that the most complete refutation of that fable would bring about a Restoration. Not a single lady crossed the sea in obedience to James's call. His Queen was safely delivered of a daughter; but this event produced no perceptible effect on the state of public feeling in England.† *(margin: A daughter born to James.)*

Meanwhile the preparations for his expedition were going on fast. He was on the point of setting out for the place of embarkation before the English government was at all aware of the danger which was impending. It had been long known indeed that many thousands of Irish were assembled in Normandy: but it was supposed that they had been assembled merely that they might be mustered and drilled before they were sent to Flanders, Piedmont, and Catalonia.‡ Now, however, intelligence, arriving from many quarters, left no doubt *(margin: Preparations made in England to repel invasion.)*

---

* Life of James, ii. 479. 524. Memorials furnished by Ferguson to Holmes in the Nairne Papers.

† Life of James, ii. 474.

‡ See the Monthly Mercuries of the spring of 1692.

that an invasion would be almost immediately attempted. Vigorous preparations for defence were made. The equipping and manning of the ships was urged forward with vigour. The regular troops were drawn together between London and the Channel. A great camp was formed on the down which overlooks Portsmouth. The militia all over the kingdom was called out. Two Westminster regiments and six City regiments, making up a force of thirteen thousand fighting men, were arrayed in Hyde Park, and passed in review before the Queen. The trainbands of Kent, Sussex, and Surrey marched down to the coast. Watchmen were posted by the beacons. Some nonjurors were imprisoned, some disarmed, some held to bail. The house of the Earl of Huntingdon, a noted Jacobite, was searched. He had had time to burn his papers and to hide his arms: but his stables presented a most suspicious appearance. Horses enough to mount a whole troop of cavalry were at the mangers; and this circumstance, though not legally sufficient to support a charge of treason, was thought sufficient, at such a conjuncture, to justify the Privy Council in sending him to the Tower.[*]

James goes down to his army at La Hogue. Meanwhile James had gone down to his army, which was encamped round the basin of La Hogue, on the northern coast of the peninsula known by the name of the Cotentin. Before he quitted Saint Germains, he held a Chapter of the Garter for the purpose of admitting his son into the order. Two noblemen were honoured with the same distinction, Powis, who, among his brother exiles, was now called a Duke, and Melfort, who had returned from Rome, and was again James's Prime Minister.[†] Even at this moment, when it was of the greatest importance to conciliate the sons of the Church of England, none but sons of the Church of Rome were thought worthy of any mark of royal favour. Powis indeed might be thought to have a fair claim to the Garter. He was an eminent member of the English aristocracy; and his countrymen disliked him as little as they disliked any conspicuous Papist. But Melfort was not even an Englishman: he had never held office in England: he had never sate in the English Parliament; and he had therefore no pretensions to a decoration peculiarly English. He was moreover hated by all the contending factions of all the three kingdoms. Royal letters countersigned by him had been sent both to the Convention at Westminster and to the Convention at Edinburgh; and

[*] Narcissus Luttrell's Diary for April and May 1692; London Gazette, May 9. and 12.   [†] Sheridan MS.; Life of James, ii. 492.

both at Westminster and at Edinburgh, the sight of his odious name and handwriting had made the most zealous friends of hereditary right hang down their heads in shame. It seems strange that even James should have chosen, at such a conjuncture, to proclaim to the world that the men whom his people most abhorred were the men whom he most delighted to honour.

Still more strange seems the Declaration in which he announced his intentions to his subjects. Of all the State papers which were put forth even by him it was the most elaborately and ostentatiously injudicious. When it had disgusted and exasperated all good Englishmen of all parties, the Papists at Saint Germains pretended that it had been drawn up by a stanch Protestant, Edward Herbert, who had been Chief Justice of the Common Pleas before the Revolution, and who now bore the empty title of Chancellor.* But it is certain that Herbert was never consulted about any matter of importance, and that the Declaration was the work of Melfort and of Melfort alone.† In truth, those qualities of head and heart which had made Melfort the favourite of his master shone forth in every sentence. Not a word was to be found indicating that three years of banishment had made the King wiser, that he had repented of a single error, that he took to himself even the smallest part of the blame of that revolution which had dethroned him, or that he purposed to follow a course in any respect differing from that which had already been fatal to him. All the charges which had been brought against him he pronounced to be utterly unfounded. Wicked men had put forth calumnies. Weak men had believed those calumnies. He alone had been faultless. He held out no hope that he would consent to any restriction of that vast dispensing power to which he had formerly laid claim, that he would not again, in defiance of the plainest statutes, fill the Privy Council, the bench of justice, the public offices, the army, the navy, with Papists, that he would not reestablish the High Commission, that he would not appoint a new set of regulators to remodel all the constituent bodies of the kingdom. He did indeed condescend to say that he would maintain the legal rights of the Church of England: but he had said this before; and all men knew what those words meant in his mouth. Instead of assuring his people of his forgiveness, he menaced them with a butchery more

James's Declaration.

* Life of James, ii. 488.
† James told Sheridan that the Declaration was written by Melfort. Sheridan MS.

terrible than any that our island had ever seen. He published a long list of persons who had no mercy to expect. Among these were Ormond, Caermarthen, Nottingham, Tillotson and Burnet. After the roll of those who were proscribed by name, came a series of categories. First stood all the crowd of rustics who had been rude to James when he was stopped at Sheerness in his flight. These poor ignorant wretches, some hundreds in number, were reserved for another bloody circuit. Then His Majesty, in open defiance of the law of the land, proceeded to doom to death a multitude of persons who were guilty only of having acted under William since William had been king in fact, and who were therefore under the protection of a well known statute of Henry the Seventh. But to James statutes were still what they had always been. He denounced vengeance against all persons who had in any manner borne a part in the punishment of any Jacobite conspirator, judges, counsel, witnesses, grand jurymen, petty jurymen, sheriffs and undersheriffs, constables and turnkeys, in short, all the ministers of justice from Holt down to Ketch. Then he threatened with the gallows all spies and all informers who had divulged to the usurpers the designs of the Court of Saint Germains. All justices of the peace who should not declare for their rightful Sovereign the moment they heard of his landing, all gaolers who should not instantly set political prisoners at liberty, were to be left to the extreme rigour of the law. No exception was made in favour of a justice or of a gaoler who might be within a hundred yards of one of William's regiments, and a hundred miles from the nearest place where there was a single Jacobite in arms.

It might have been expected that James, after thus declaring that he could hold out no hope of mercy to large classes of his subjects, would at least have offered a general pardon to the rest. But he pardoned nobody. He did indeed promise that any offender who was not in any of the categories of proscription, and who should by any eminent service merit indulgence, should have a special pardon passed under the Great Seal. But, with this exception, all the offenders, hundreds of thousands in number, were merely informed that, if they did no act or thing in opposition to the King's restoration, they might hope to be, at a convenient time, included in a general Act of Indemnity.

Effect produced by James's Declaration.

The agents of James speedily dispersed his Declaration over every part of the kingdom, and by doing so rendered a great service to William. The general cry was that the banished oppressor had at least given Englishmen fair warning, and that, if, after such a warning, they welcomed him home, they would have no pretence for complaining, though every county town should be polluted by an assize resembling that which Jeffreys had held at Taunton. That some hundreds of people,—the Jacobites put the number so low as five hundred,—were to be hanged without pity was certain ; and nobody who had concurred in the Revolution, nobody who had fought for the new government by sea or land, no soldier who had borne a part in the conquest of Ireland, no Devonshire ploughman or Cornish miner who had taken arms to defend his wife and children against Tourville, could be certain that he should not be hanged. It was easy to understand why James, instead of proclaiming a general amnesty, offered special pardons under his Great Seal. Every such pardon must be paid for. There was not a priest in the royal household who would not make his fortune. How abject too, how spiteful, must be the nature of a man who, engaged in the most momentous of all undertakings, and aspiring to the noblest of all prizes, could not refrain from proclaiming that he thirsted for the blood of a multitude of poor fishermen, because, more than three years before, they had pulled him about and called him Hatchetface ! * If, at the very moment when he had the strongest motives for trying to conciliate his people by the show of clemency, he could not bring himself to hold towards them any language but that of an implacable enemy, what was to be expected from him when he should be again their master ? So savage was his nature that, in a situation in which all other tyrants have resorted to blandishments and fair promises, he could utter nothing but reproaches and threats. The only words in his Declaration which had any show of graciousness were those in which he promised to send away the foreign troops as soon as his authority was reestablished; and many said that those words, when examined, would be found full of sinister meaning. He held out no hope that he would send away Popish troops who were his own subjects. His intentions were manifest. The French might go : but the Irish would remain. The people of England were to be kept down by these thrice

* That the Declaration made the impression which I have described, is acknowledged in the Life of James, ii. 489. "They thought," says the biographer, "His Majesty's resentment descended too low to except the Feversham Mob, that five hundred men were excluded, and no man realy pardon'd except he should merit it by some service, and then the Pardons being to pass the Seals look'd as if it were to bring money into the pocket of some favorits."

subjugated barbarians. No doubt a Rapparee who had run away at Newton Butler and the Boyne might find courage enough to guard the scaffolds on which his conquerors were to die, and to lay waste our country as he had laid waste his own.

The Queen and her ministers, instead of attempting to suppress James's manifesto, very wisely reprinted it, and sent it forth licensed by the Secretary of State, and interspersed with remarks by a shrewd and severe commentator. It was refuted in many keen pamphlets: it was turned into doggrel rhymes; and it was left undefended even by the boldest and most acrimonious libellers among the nonjurors.*

Indeed, some of the nonjurors were so much alarmed by observing the effect which this manifesto produced, that they affected to treat it as spurious, and published as their master's genuine Declaration a paper full of gracious professions and promises. They made him offer a free pardon to all his people with the exception of four great criminals. They made him hold out hopes of great remissions of taxation. They made him pledge his word that he would entrust the whole ecclesiastical administration to the nonjuring bishops. But this forgery imposed on nobody, and was important only as showing that even the Jacobites were ashamed of the prince whom they were labouring to restore.†

No man read the Declaration with more surprise and anger than Russell. Bad as he was, he was much under the influence of two feelings, which, though they cannot be called virtuous, have some affinity to virtue, and are respectable when compared with mere selfish cupidity. Professional spirit and party spirit were strong in him. He might be false to his sovereigns, but not to his flag; and, even in becoming a Jacobite, he had not ceased to be a Whig. In

---

* A Letter to a Friend concerning a French Invasion to restore the late King James to his Throne, and what may be expected from him should he be successful in it, 1692 ; A second Letter to a Friend concerning a French Invasion, in which the Declaration lately dispersed under the Title of His Majesty's most gracious Declaration to all his loving Subjects, commanding their Assistance against the P. of O. and his Adherents, is entirely and exactly published according to the Dispersed Copies, with some short Observations upon it, 1692 ; The Pretences of the French Invasion examined, 1692 ; Reflections on the late King James's Declaration. 1692. The

two Letters to a Friend were written, I believe, by Lloyd Bishop of St. Asaph. Sheridan says, " The King's Declaration pleas'd none, and was turn'd into ridicule burlesque lines in England." I do not believe that a defence of this unfortunate Declaration is to be found in any Jacobite tract. A virulent Jacobite writer, in a reply to Dr. Welwood, printed in 1693, says, "As for the Declaration that was printed last year, . . . I assure you that it was as much misliked by many, almost all, of the King's friends, as it can be exposed by his enemies."

† Narcissus Luttrell's Diary. April 1692.

truth, he was a Jacobite only because he was the most intolerant and acrimonious of Whigs. He thought himself and his faction ungratefully neglected by William, and was for a time too much blinded by resentment to perceive that it would be mere madness in the old Roundheads, the old Exclusionists, to punish William by recalling James. The near prospect of an invasion, and the Declaration in which Englishmen were plainly told what they had to expect if that invasion should be successful, produced, it should seem, a sudden change in Russell's feelings; and that change he distinctly avowed. "I wish," he said to Lloyd, "to serve King James. The thing might be done, if it were not his own fault. But he takes the wrong way with us. Let him forget all the past: let him grant a general pardon; and then I will see what I can do for him." Lloyd hinted something about the honours and rewards designed for Russell himself. But the Admiral, with a spirit worthy of a better man, cut him short. "I do not wish to hear anything on that subject. My solicitude is for the public. And do not think that I will let the French triumph over us in our own sea. Understand this, that if I meet them I fight them, aye, though His Majesty himself should be on board."

This conversation was truly reported to James: but it does not appear to have alarmed him. He was, indeed, possessed with a belief that Russell, even if willing, would not be able to induce the officers and sailors of the English navy to fight against their old King, who was also their old Admiral.

The hopes which James felt he and his favourite Melfort succeeded in imparting to Lewis and to Lewis's ministers.* But for those hopes, indeed, it is probable that all thoughts of invading England in the course of that year would have been laid aside. For the extensive plan which had been formed in the winter had, in the course of the spring, been disconcerted by a succession of accidents such as are beyond the control of human wisdom. The time fixed for the assembling of all the maritime forces of France at Ushant had long elapsed; and not a single sail had appeared at the place of rendezvous. The Atlantic squadron was still detained by bad weather in the port of Brest. The Mediterranean squadron, opposed by a strong west wind, was vainly struggling to pass the pillars of Hercules. Two fine vessels had gone to pieces on the rocks of Ceuta.† Meanwhile the

* Sheridan MS.; Mémoires de Dangeau.

† London Gazette, May 12. 16. 1692; Gazette de Paris, May $\frac{21}{31}$. 1692.

admiralties of the allied powers had been active. Before the end of April the English fleet was ready to sail. Three noble ships, just launched from our dockyards, appeared for the first time on the water.* William had been hastening the maritime preparations of the United Provinces; and his exertions had been successful. On the twenty-ninth of April a fine squadron from the Texel appeared in the Downs. Soon came the North Holland squadron, the Meuse squadron,

The English and Dutch fleets join. the Zealand squadron.† The whole force of the confederate powers was assembled at Saint Helen's in the second week of May, more than ninety sail of the line, manned by between thirty and forty thousand of the finest seamen of the two great maritime nations. Russell had the chief command. He was assisted by Sir Ralph Delaval, Sir John Ashby, Sir Cloudesley Shovel, Rear Admiral Carter, and Rear Admiral Rooke. Of the Dutch officers Van Almonde was highest in rank.

Temper of the English fleet. No mightier armament had ever appeared in the British Channel. There was little reason for apprehension that such a force could be defeated in a fair conflict. Nevertheless there was great uneasiness in London. It was known that there was a Jacobite party in the navy. Alarming rumours had worked their way round from France. It was said that the enemy reckoned on the co-operation of some of those officers on whose fidelity, in this crisis, the safety of the State might depend. Russell, as far as can now be discovered, was still unsuspected. But others, who were probably less criminal, had been more indiscreet. At all the coffee houses admirals and captains were mentioned by name as traitors who ought to be instantly cashiered, if not shot. It was even confidently affirmed that some of the guilty had been put under arrest, and others turned out of the service. The Queen and her counsellors were in a great strait. It was not easy to say whether the danger of trusting the suspected persons or the danger of removing them were the greater. Mary, with many painful misgivings, resolved,—and the event proved that she resolved wisely,— to treat the evil reports as calumnious, to make a solemn appeal to the honour of the accused gentlemen, and then to trust the safety of her kingdom to their national and professional spirit.

On the fifteenth of May a great assembly of officers was convoked at Saint Helen's on board of the Britannia, a fine threedecker, from which Russell's flag was flying. The

---

* London Gazette, April 28. 1692.　　† London Gazette, May 2. 5. 12. 16.

Admiral told them that he had received a despatch which he was charged to read to them. It was from Nottingham. The Queen, the Secretary wrote, had been informed that stories deeply affecting the character of the navy were in circulation. It had even been affirmed that she had found herself under the necessity of dismissing many officers. But Her Majesty was determined to believe nothing against those brave servants of the State. The gentlemen who had been so foully slandered might be assured that she placed entire reliance on them. This letter was admirably calculated to work on those to whom it was addressed. Very few of them probably had been guilty of any worse offence than rash and angry talk over their wine. They were as yet only grumblers. If they had fancied that they were marked men, they might in selfdefence have become traitors. They became enthusiastically loyal as soon as they were assured that the Queen reposed entire confidence in their loyalty. They eagerly signed an address in which they entreated her to believe that they would, with the utmost resolution and alacrity, venture their lives in defence of her rights, of English freedom, and of the Protestant religion, against all foreign and Popish invaders. " God," they added, " preserve your person, direct your counsels, and prosper your arms ; and let all your people say Amen." *

The sincerity of these professions was soon brought to the test. A few hours after the meeting on board of the Britannia the masts of Tourville's squadron were seen from the cliffs of Portland. One messenger galloped with the news from Weymouth to London, and roused Whitehall at three in the morning. Another took the coast road, and carried the intelligence to Russell. All was ready ; and on the morning of the seventeenth of May the allied fleet stood out to sea.†

Tourville had with him only his own squadron, consisting of forty-four ships of the line. But he had received positive orders to protect the descent on England, and not to decline a battle. Though these orders had been given before it was known at Versailles that the Dutch and English fleets had joined, he was not disposed to take on himself the responsibility of disobedience. He still remembered with bitterness the reprimand which his extreme caution had drawn upon him after the fight of Beachy Head. He would not again be

Battle of La Hogue.

* London Gazette, May 16. 1692; † Narcissus Luttrell's Diary ; London
Burchett.   Gazette, May 19. 1692.

told that he was a timid and unenterprising commander, that he had no courage but the vulgar courage of a common sailor. He was also persuaded that the odds against him were rather apparent than real. He believed, on the authority of James and Melfort, that the English seamen, from the flag officers down to the cabin boys, were Jacobites. Those who fought would fight with half a heart; and there would probably be numerous desertions at the most critical moment. Animated by such hopes he sailed from Brest, steered first towards the north east, came in sight of the coast of Dorsetshire, and then struck across the Channel towards La Hogue, where the army which he was to convoy to England had already begun to embark on board of the transports. He was within a few leagues of Barfleur when, before sunrise, on the morning of the nineteenth of May, he saw the great armament of the allies stretching along the eastern horizon. He determined to bear down on them. By eight the two lines of battle were formed; but it was eleven before the firing began. It soon became plain that the English, from the Admiral downwards, were resolved to do their duty. Russell had visited all his ships, and exhorted all his crews. "If your commanders play false," he said, "overboard with them, and with myself the first." There was no defection. There was no slackness. Carter was the first who broke the French line. He was struck by a splinter of one of his own yard-arms, and fell dying on the deck. He would not be carried below. He would not let go his sword. "Fight the ship," were his last words: "fight the ship as long as she can swim." The battle lasted till four in the afternoon. The roar of the guns was distinctly heard more than twenty miles off by the army which was encamped on the coast of Normandy. During the earlier part of the day the wind was favourable to the French: they were opposed to only half of the allied fleet; and against that half they maintained the conflict with their usual courage and with more than their usual seamanship. After a hard and doubtful fight of five hours, Tourville thought that enough had been done to maintain the honour of the white flag, and began to draw off. But by this time the wind had veered, and was with the allies. They were now able to avail themselves of their great superiority of force. They came on fast. The retreat of the French became a flight. Tourville fought his own ship desperately. She was named, in allusion to Lewis's favourite emblem, the Royal Sun, and was widely renowned as the finest vessel in the world. It was reported among the English sailors that she was adorned with an image of the Great King, and that he appeared there, as he appeared in the Place of Victories, with vanquished nations in chains beneath his feet. The gallant ship, surrounded by enemies, lay like a great fortress on the sea, scattering death on every side from her hundred and four portholes. She was so formidably manned that all attempts to board her failed. Long after sunset, she got clear of her assailants, and, with all her scuppers spouting blood, made for the coast of Normandy. She had suffered so much that Tourville hastily removed his flag to a ship of ninety guns which was named the Ambitious. By this time his fleet was scattered far over the sea. About twenty of his smallest ships made their escape by a road which was too perilous for any courage but the courage of despair. In the double darkness of night and of a thick sea fog, they ran, with all their sails spread, through the boiling waves and treacherous rocks of the Race of Alderney, and, by a strange good fortune, arrived without a single disaster at Saint Maloes. The pursuers did not venture to follow the fugitives into that terrible strait, the place of innumerable shipwrecks.*

Those French vessels which were too bulky to venture into the Race of Alderney fled to the havens of the Cotentin. The Royal Sun and two other threedeckers reached Cherburg in safety. The Ambitious, with twelve other ships, all firstrates or secondrates, took refuge in the Bay of La Hogue, close to the head quarters of the army of James.

The three ships which had fled to Cherburg were closely chased by an English squadron under the command of Delaval. He found them hauled up into shoal water where no large man of war could get at them. He therefore determined to attack them with his fireships and boats. The service was gallantly and successfully performed. In a short time the Royal Sun and her two consorts were burned to ashes. Part of the crews escaped to the shore; and part fell into the hands of the English.†

Meanwhile Russell with the greater part of his victorious

* Russell's Letter to Nottingham, May 20. 1692, in the London Gazette of May 23.; Particulars of Another Letter from the Fleet published by authority; Burchett; Burnet, ii. 93.; Life of James, ii. 493. 494.; Narcissus Luttrell's Diary; Mémoires de Berwick. See also the contemporary ballad on the battle, one of the best specimens of English street poetry, and the Advice to a Painter, 1692.

† See Delaval's Letter to Nottingham, dated Cherburg, May 22. 1692, in the London Gazette of May 26.

fleet had blockaded the Bay of La Hogue. Here, as at
Cherburg, the French men of war had been drawn up into
shallow water. They were close to the camp of the army
which was destined for the invasion of England. Six of
them were moored under a fort named Lisset. The rest lay
under the guns of another fort named Saint Vaast, where
James had fixed his head quarters, and where the British
flag, variegated by the crosses of Saint George and Saint
Andrew, hung by the side of the White flag of France. Marshal Bellefonds had planted several batteries which, it was
thought, would deter the boldest enemy from approaching
either Fort Lisset or Fort Saint Vaast. James, however,
who knew something of English seamen, was not perfectly at
ease, and proposed to send strong bodies of soldiers on board
of the ships. But Tourville would not consent to put such a
slur on his profession.

Russell meanwhile was preparing for an attack. On the
afternoon of the twenty-third of May all was ready. A
flotilla consisting of sloops, of fireships, and of two hundred
boats, was entrusted to the command of Rooke. The whole
armament was in the highest spirits. The rowers, flushed
by success, and animated by the thought that they were
going to fight under the eyes of the French and Irish troops
who had been assembled for the purpose of subjugating England, pulled manfully and with loud huzzas towards the six
huge wooden castles which lay close to Fort Lisset. The
French, though an eminently brave people, have always been
more liable to sudden panics than their phlegmatic neighbours the English and Germans. On this day there was a
panic both in the fleet and in the army. Tourville ordered
his sailors to man their boats, and would have led them to
encounter the enemy in the bay. But his example and his
exhortations were vain. His boats turned round and fled in
confusion. The ships were abandoned. The cannonade from
Fort Lisset was so feeble and ill directed that it did no execution. The regiments on the beach, after wasting a few
musket shots, drew off. The English boarded the men of
war, set them on fire, and having performed this great service without the loss of a single life, retreated at a late
hour with the retreating tide. The bay was in a blaze during
the night; and now and then a loud explosion announced
that the flames had reached a powder room or a tier of
loaded guns. At eight the next morning the tide came
back strong; and with the tide came back Rooke and his

two hundred boats. The enemy made a faint attempt to defend the vessels which were near Fort Saint Vaast. During a few minutes the batteries did some execution among the crews of our skiffs: but the struggle was soon over. The French poured fast out of their ships on one side: the English poured in as fast on the other, and, with loud shouts, turned the captured guns against the shore. The batteries were speedily silenced. James and Melfort, Bellefonds and Tourville, looked on in helpless despondency while the second conflagration proceeded. The conquerors, leaving the ships of war in flames, made their way into an inner basin where many transports lay. Eight of these vessels were set on fire. Several were taken in tow. The rest would have been either destroyed or carried off, had not the sea again begun to ebb. It was impossible to do more; and the victorious flotilla slowly retired, insulting the hostile camp with a thundering chant of " God save the King."

Thus ended, at noon on the twenty-fourth of May, the great conflict which had raged during five days over a wide extent of sea and shore. One English fireship had perished in its calling. Sixteen French men of war, all noble vessels, and eight of them threedeckers, had been sunk or burned down to the wateredge. The battle is called, from the place where it terminated, the battle of La Hogue.*

The news was received in London with boundless exulta-
tion. In the fight on the open sea, indeed, the numerical superiority of the allies had been so great that they had little reason to boast of their success. But the courage and skill with which the crews of the English boats had, in a French harbour, in sight of a French army, and under the fire of French batteries, destroyed a fine French fleet, amply justified the pride with which our fathers pronounced the name of La Hogue. That we may fully enter into their feelings, we must remember that this was the first great check that had ever been given to the arms of Lewis the Fourteenth, and the first great victory that the English had gained over the French since the day of Agincourt. The stain left on our

(margin note:) Rejoicings in England

---

* London Gaz. May 26. 1692; Burchett's Memoirs of Transactions at Sea; Baden to the States General, $\frac{May 24.}{June 3.}$; Life of James, ii. 494.; Russell's Letters in the Commons' Journals of Nov. 28. 1692; An Account of the Great Victory, 1692; Monthly Mercuries for June and July 1692; Paris Gazette, $\frac{May 28.}{June 7.}$; Van Almonde's despatch to the States General, dated $\frac{May 24.}{June 3.}$ 1692. The French official account will be found in the Monthly Mercury for July. A report drawn up by Foucault, Intendant of the province of Normandy, will be found in M. Capefigue's Louis XIV.

fame by the shameful defeat of Beachy Head was effaced. This time the glory was all our own. The Dutch had indeed done their duty, as they have always done it in maritime war, whether fighting on our side or against us, whether victorious or vanquished. But the English had borne the brunt of the fight. Russell who commanded in chief was an Englishman. Delaval who directed the attack on Cherburg was an Englishman. Rooke who led the flotilla into the Bay of La Hogue was an Englishman. The only two officers of note who had fallen, Admiral Carter and Captain Hastings of the Sandwich, were Englishmen. Yet the pleasure with which the good news was received here must not be ascribed solely or chiefly to national pride. The island was safe. The pleasant pastures, cornfields and commons of Hampshire and Surrey would not be the seat of war. The houses and gardens, the kitchens and dairies, the cellars and plate chests, the wives and daughters of our gentry and clergy would not be at the mercy of Irish Rapparees, who had sacked the dwellings and skinned the cattle of the Englishry of Leinster, or of French dragoons accustomed to live at free quarter on the Protestants of Auvergne. Whigs and Tories joined in thanking God for this great deliverance; and the most respectable nonjurors could not but be glad at heart that the rightful King was not to be brought back by an army of foreigners.

The public joy was therefore all but universal. During several days the bells of London pealed without ceasing. Flags were flying on all the steeples. Rows of candles were in all the windows. Bonfires were at all the corners of the streets.* The sense which the government entertained of the services of the navy was promptly, judiciously, and gracefully manifested. Sidney and Portland were sent to meet the fleet at Portsmouth, and were accompanied by Rochester, as the representative of the Tories. The three Lords took down with them thirty-seven thousand pounds in coin, which they were to distribute as a donative among the sailors.† Gold medals were given to the officers.‡ The remains of Hastings and Carter were brought on shore with every mark of honour. Carter was buried at Portsmouth, with a great display of military pomp.§ The corpse of Hastings was carried

---

* An Account of the late Great Victory, 1692; Monthly Mercury for June; Baden to the States General, $\frac{\text{May 24}}{\text{June 3}}$; Narcissus Luttrell's Diary.

† London Gazette, June 2. 1692; Monthly Mercury; Baden to the States

General, June $\frac{14}{24}$; Narcissus Luttrell's Diary.

‡ Narcissus Luttrell's Diary; Monthly Mercury.

§ London Gazette, June 9.; Baden to the States General, June $\frac{7}{17}$.

up to London, and laid, with unusual solemnity, under the pavement of Saint James's Church. The footguards with reversed arms escorted the hearse. Four royal state carriages, each drawn by six horses, were in the procession: a crowd of men of quality in mourning cloaks filled the pews, and the Bishop of Lincoln preached the funeral sermon.* While such marks of respect were paid to the slain, the wounded were not neglected. Fifty surgeons, plentifully supplied with instruments, bandages, and drugs, were sent down in all haste from London to Portsmouth.† It is not easy for us to form a notion of the difficulty which there then was in providing at short notice commodious shelter and skilful attendance for hundreds of maimed and lacerated men. At present every county, every large town, can boast of some spacious palace in which the poorest labourer who has fractured a limb may find an excellent bed, an able medical attendant, a careful nurse, medicines of the best quality, and nourishment such an invalid requires. But there was not then, in the whole realm, a single infirmary supported by voluntary contribution. Even in the capital the only edifices open to the wounded were the two ancient hospitals of Saint Thomas and Saint Bartholomew. The Queen gave orders that in both these hospitals arrangements should be made at the public charge for the reception of patients from the fleet.‡ At the same time it was announced that a noble and lasting memorial of the gratitude which England felt for the courage and patriotism of her sailors would soon rise on a site eminently appropriate. Among the suburban residences of our kings, that which stood at Greenwich had long held a distinguished place. Charles the Second liked the situation, and determined to rebuild the house and to improve the gardens. Soon after his Restoration, he began to erect, on a spot almost washed by the Thames at high tide, a mansion of vast extent and cost. Behind the palace were planted long avenues of trees which, when William reigned, were scarcely more than saplings, but which have now covered with their massy shade the summer rambles of several generations. On the slope which has long been the scene of the holiday sports of the Londoners, were constructed flights of terraces, of which the vestiges may still be discerned. The Queen now

* Baden to the States General, June $\frac{3}{13}$.   Narcissus Luttrell's Diary.

† Baden to the States General, $\frac{May 24.}{June 5.}$;   ‡ An Account of the late Great Victory, 1692; Narcissus Luttrell's Diary.

publicly declared, in her husband's name, that the building
commenced by Charles should be completed, and should be a
retreat for seamen disabled in the service of their country.*

One of the happiest effects produced by the good news was
the calming of the public mind. During about a month the
nation had been hourly expecting an invasion and a rising,
and had consequently been in an irritable and suspicious
mood. In many parts of England a nonjuror could not show
himself without great risk of being insulted. A report that
arms were hidden in a house sufficed to bring a furious mob
to the door. The mansion of one Jacobite gentleman in
Kent had been attacked, and, after a fight in which several
shots were fired, had been stormed and pulled down.† Yet
such riots were by no means the worst symptoms of the fever
which had inflamed the whole society. The exposure of
Fuller, in February, had, as it seemed, put an end to the
practices of that vile tribe of which Oates was the patriarch.
During some weeks, indeed, the world was disposed to be
unreasonably incredulous about plots. But in April there
was a reaction. The French and Irish were coming. There
was but too much reason to believe that there were traitors in
the island. Whoever pretended that he could point out
those traitors was sure to be heard with attention; and there
was not wanting a false witness to avail himself of the golden
opportunity.

Young's plot. This false witness was named Robert Young. His history
was in his own lifetime so fully investigated, and so much of
his correspondence has been preserved, that the whole man
is before us. His character is indeed a curious study. His
birthplace was a subject of dispute among three nations.
The English pronounced him Irish. The Irish, not being
ambitious of the honour of having him for a countryman,
affirmed that he was born in Scotland. Wherever he may
have been born, it is impossible to doubt where he was bred:
for his phraseology is precisely that of the Teagues, who were,
in his time, favourite characters on our stage. He called
himself a priest of the Established Church: but he was in
truth only a deacon; and his deacon's orders he had obtained
by producing forged certificates of his learning and moral
character. Long before the Revolution he held curacies in
various parts of Ireland; but he did not remain many days in
any spot. He was driven from one place by the scandal which

* Baden to the States General, June $\frac{7}{17}$. 1692.
† Narcissus Luttrell's Diary.

was the effect of his lawless amours. He rode away from another place on a borrowed horse, which he never returned. He settled in a third parish, and was taken up for bigamy. Some letters which he wrote on this occasion from the gaol of Cavan have been preserved. He assured each of his wives, with the most frightful imprecations, that she alone was the object of his love; and he thus succeeded in inducing one of them to support him in prison, and the other to save his life by forswearing herself at the assizes. The only specimens which remain to us of his method of imparting religious instruction are to be found in these epistles. He compares himself to David, the man after God's own heart, who had been guilty both of adultery and murder. He declares that he repents: he prays for the forgiveness of the Almighty, and then entreats his dear honey, for Christ's sake, to perjure herself. Having narrowly escaped the gallows, he wandered during several years about Ireland and England, begging, stealing, cheating, personating, forging, and lay in many prisons under many names. In 1684 he was convicted at Bury of having fraudulently counterfeited Sancroft's signature, and was sentenced to the pillory and to imprisonment. From his dungeon he wrote to implore the Primate's mercy. The letter may still be read with all the original bad grammar and bad spelling.* The writer acknowledged his guilt, wished that his eyes were a fountain of water, and declared that he should never know peace till he had received episcopal absolution. He very cunningly tried to ingratiate himself with the Archbishop, by professing a mortal hatred of Dissenters. But, as all this contrition and all this orthodoxy produced no effect, the penitent, after swearing bitterly to be revenged on Sancroft, betook himself to another device. The Western Insurrection had just broken out. The magistrates all over the country were but too ready to listen to any accusation that might be brought against Whigs and Nonconformists. Young declared on oath that, to his knowledge, a design had been formed in Suffolk against the life of King James, and named a peer, several gentlemen, and ten Presbyterian ministers, as parties to the plot. Some of the accused were brought to trial; and Young appeared in the witness box: but the story which he told was proved by overwhelming evidence to be false. Soon after the Revolution he was again convicted of forgery, pilloried for the fourth or fifth

* I give one short sentence as a specimen: " O fie that ever it should be said that a clergyman have committed such durty actions!"

time, and sent to Newgate. While he lay there, he determined
to try whether he should be more fortunate as an accuser of
Jacobites than he had been as an accuser of Puritans. He
first addressed himself to Tillotson. There was a horrible
plot against their Majesties, a plot as deep as hell; and some
of the first men in England were concerned in it. Tillotson,
though he placed little confidence in information coming from
such a source, thought that the oath which he had taken as
a Privy Councillor made it his duty to mention the subject to
William. William, after his fashion, treated the matter very
lightly. "I am confident," he said, "that this is a villany;
and I will have nobody disturbed on such grounds." After
this rebuff, Young remained some time quiet. But when
William was on the Continent, and when the nation was
agitated by the apprehension of a French invasion and of a
Jacobite insurrection, a false accuser might hope to obtain a
favourable audience. The mere oath of a man who was well
known to the turnkeys of twenty gaols was not likely to injure
any body. But Young was master of a weapon which is, of
all weapons, the most formidable to innocence. He had lived
during some years by counterfeiting hands, and had at length
attained such consummate skill in that bad art that even experienced clerks who were conversant with manuscript could
scarcely, after the most minute comparison, discover any difference between his imitations and the originals. He had
succeeded in making a collection of papers written by men of
note who were suspected of disaffection. Some autographs
he had stolen; and some he had obtained by writing in
feigned names to ask after the characters of servants or curates. He now drew up a paper purporting to be an Association for the Restoration of the banished King. This document
set forth that the subscribers bound themselves in the presence of God to take arms for His Majesty, and to seize on the
Prince of Orange, dead or alive. To the Association Young
appended the names of Marlborough, of Cornbury, of Salisbury, of Sancroft, and of Sprat, Bishop of Rochester and Dean
of Westminster.

The next thing to be done was to put the paper into some
hiding place in the house of one of the persons whose signatures had been counterfeited. As Young could not quit
Newgate, he was forced to employ a subordinate agent for
this pupose. He selected a wretch named Blackhead, who
had formerly been convicted of perjury, and sentenced to
have his ears clipped. The selection was not happy; for

Blackhead had none of the qualities which the trade of a false witness requires except wickedness. There was nothing plausible about him. His voice was harsh. Treachery was written in all the lines of his yellow face. He had no invention, no presence of mind, and could do little more than repeat by rote the lies taught him by others.

This man, instructed by his accomplice, repaired to Sprat's palace at Bromley, introduced himself there as the confidential servant of an imaginary Doctor of Divinity, delivered to the Bishop, on bended knee, a letter ingeniously manufactured by Young, and received, with the semblance of profound reverence, the episcopal benediction. The servants made the stranger welcome. He was taken to the cellar, drank their master's health, and entreated them to let him see the house. They could not venture to show any of the private apartments. Blackhead, therefore, after begging importunately, but in vain, to be suffered to have one look at the study, was forced to content himself with dropping the Association into a flowerpot which stood in a parlour near the kitchen.

Every thing having been thus prepared, Young informed the ministers that he could tell them something of the highest importance to the welfare of the State, and earnestly begged to be heard. His request reached them on perhaps the most anxious day of an anxious month. Tourville had just stood out to sea. The army of James was embarking. London was agitated by reports about the disaffection of the naval officers. The Queen was deliberating whether she should cashier those who were suspected, or try the effect of an appeal to their honour and patriotism. At such a moment the ministers could not refuse to listen to any person who professed himself able to give them valuable information. Young and his accomplice were brought before the Privy Council. They there accused Marlborough, Cornbury, Salisbury, Sancroft, and Sprat of high treason. These great men, Young said, had invited James to invade England, and had promised to join him. The eloquent and ingenious Bishop of Rochester had undertaken to draw up a Declaration which would inflame the nation against the government of King William. The conspirators were bound together by a written instrument. That instrument, signed by their own hands, would be found at Bromley if careful search was made. Young particularly requested that the messengers might be ordered to examine the Bishop's flowerpots.

The ministers were seriously alarmed. The story was circumstantial; and part of it was probable. Marlborough's dealings with Saint Germains were well known to Caermarthen, to Nottingham, and to Sidney. Cornbury was a tool of Marlborough, and was the son of a nonjuror and of a notorious plotter. Salisbury was a Papist. Sancroft had, not many months before, been, with too much show of reason, suspected of inviting the French to invade England. Of all the accused persons Sprat was the most unlikely to be concerned in any hazardous design. He had neither enthusiasm nor constancy. Both his ambition and his party spirit had always been effectually kept in order by his love of ease and his anxiety for his own safety. He had been guilty of some criminal compliances in the hope of gaining the favour of James, had sate in the High Commission, had concurred in several iniquitous decrees pronounced by that court, and had, with trembling hands and faltering voice, read the Declaration of Indulgence in the choir of the Abbey. But there he had stopped. As soon as it began to be whispered that the civil and religious constitution of England would speedily be vindicated by extraordinary means, he had resigned the powers which he had during two years exercised in defiance of law, and had hastened to make his peace with his clerical brethren. He had in the Convention voted for a Regency : but he had taken the oaths without hesitation : he had borne a conspicuous part in the coronation of the new Sovereigns ; and by his skilful hand had been added to the Form of Prayer used on the fifth of November those sentences in which the Church expresses her gratitude for the second great deliverance wrought on that day.* Such a man, possessed of a plentiful income, of a seat in the House of Lords, of one agreeable mansion among the elms of Bromley, and of another in the cloisters of Westminster, was very unlikely to run the risk of martyrdom. He was not, indeed, on perfectly good terms with the government. For the feeling, which, next to solicitude for his own comfort and repose, seems to have had the greatest influence on his public conduct, was his dislike of the Puritans, a dislike which sprang, not from bigotry, but from Epicureanism. Their austerity was a reproach to his slothful and luxurious life : their phraseology shocked his fastidious taste; and, where they were concerned, his ordinary good nature forsook him. Loathing the nonconformists as he did, he was not likely to be very zealous for a prince whom the nonconformists

* Gutch, Collectanea Curiosa.

regarded as their protector. But Sprat's faults afforded
ample security that he would never, from spleen against
William, engage in any plot to bring back James. Why
Young should have assigned the most perilous part in an
enterprise full of peril to a man singularly pliant, cautious,
and selfindulgent, it is difficult to say.

The first step which the ministers took was to send Marlborough to the Tower. He was by far the most formidable
of all the accused persons; and that he had held a traitorous
correspondence with Saint Germains was a fact which,
whether Young were perjured or not, the Queen and her
chief advisers knew to be true. One of the Clerks of the
Council and several messengers were sent down to Bromley
with a warrant from Nottingham. Sprat was taken into
custody. All the apartments in which it could reasonably
be supposed that he would have hidden an important document were searched, the library, the diningroom, the drawingroom, the bedchamber, and the adjacent closets. His
papers were strictly examined. Much good prose was found,
and probably some bad verse, but no treason. The messengers pried into every flowerpot that they could find, but to no
purpose. It never occurred to them to look into the room
in which Blackhead had hidden the Association: for that
room was near the offices occupied by the servants, and was
little used by the Bishop and his family. The officers returned to London with their prisoner, but without the document which, if it had been found, might have been fatal
to him.

Late at night he was brought to Westminster, and was
suffered to sleep at his deanery. All his bookcases and
drawers were examined; and sentinels were posted at the
door of his bedchamber, but with strict orders to behave
civilly and not to disturb the family.

On the following day he was brought before the Council.
The examination was conducted by Nottingham with great
humanity and courtesy. The Bishop, conscious of entire
innocence, behaved with temper and firmness. He made no
complaints. "I submit," he said, "to the necessities of
State at such a time of jealousy and danger as this." He
was asked whether he had drawn up a Declaration for King
James, whether he had held any correspondence with France,
whether he had signed any treasonable association, and
whether he knew of any such association. To all these
questions he, with perfect truth, answered in the negative,

on the word of a Christian and a Bishop. He was taken back to his deanery. He remained there in easy confinement during ten days, and then, as nothing tending to criminate him had been discovered, was suffered to return to Bromley.

Meanwhile the false accusers had been devising a new scheme. Blackhead paid another visit to Bromley, and contrived to take the forged Association out of the place in which he had hid it, and to bring it back to Young. One of Young's two wives then carried it to the Secretary's Office, and told a lie, invented by her husband, to explain how a paper of such importance had come into her hands. But it was not now so easy to frighten the ministers as it had been a few days before. The battle of La Hogue had put an end to all apprehensions of invasion. Nottingham, therefore, instead of sending down a warrant to Bromley, merely wrote to beg that Sprat would call on him at Whitehall. The summons was promptly obeyed, and the accused prelate was brought face to face with Blackhead before the Council. Then the truth came out fast. The Bishop remembered the villanous look and voice of the man who had knelt to ask the episcopal blessing. The Bishop's secretary confirmed his master's assertions. The false witness soon lost his presence of mind. His cheeks, always sallow, grew frightfully livid. His voice, generally loud and coarse, sank into a whisper. The Privy Councillors saw his confusion, and crossexamined him sharply. For a time he answered their questions by repeatedly stammering out his original lie in the original words. At last he found that he had no way of extricating himself but by owning his guilt. He acknowledged that he had given an untrue account of his visit to Bromley; and, after much prevarication, he related how he had hidden the Association, and how he had removed it from its hiding place, and confessed that he had been set on by Young.

The two accomplices were then confronted. Young, with unabashed forehead, denied every thing. He knew nothing about the flowerpots. " If so," cried Nottingham and Sidney together, "why did you give such particular directions that the flowerpots at Bromley should be searched?" "I never gave any directions about the flowerpots," said Young. Then the whole council broke forth. "How dare you say so? We all remember it." Still the knave stood up erect, and exclaimed, with an impudence which Oates might have envied, "This hiding is all a trick got up between the Bishop and Blackhead. The Bishop has taken Blackhead off; and they are both trying to stifle the plot." This was too much. There was a smile and a lifting up of hands all round the board. "Man," cried Caermarthen, "wouldst thou have us believe that the Bishop contrived to have this paper put where it was ten to one that our messengers had found it, and where, if they had found it, it might have hanged him?"

The false accusers were removed in custody. The Bishop, after warmly thanking the ministers for their fair and honourable conduct, took his leave of them. In the antechamber he found a crowd of people staring at Young, while Young sate, enduring the stare with the serene fortitude of a man who had looked down on far greater multitudes from half the pillories in England. "Young," said Sprat, "your conscience must tell you that you have cruelly wronged me. For your own sake I am sorry that you persist in denying what your associate has confessed." "Confessed!" cried Young: "no, all is not confessed yet; and that you shall find to your sorrow. There is such a thing as impeachment, my Lord. When Parliament sits you shall hear more of me." "God give you repentance," answered the Bishop. "For, depend upon it, you are in much more danger of being damned than I of being impeached."*

Forty-eight hours after the detection of this execrable fraud, Marlborough was admitted to bail. Young and Blackhead had done him an inestimable service. That he was concerned in a plot quite as criminal as that which they had falsely imputed to him, and that the government was in possession of moral proofs of his guilt, is now certain. But his contemporaries had not, as we have, the evidence of his perfidy before them. They knew that he had been accused of an offence of which he was innocent, that perjury and forgery had been employed to ruin him, and that, in consequence of these machinations, he had passed some weeks in the Tower. There was in the public mind a very natural confusion between his disgrace and his imprisonment. He had been imprisoned without sufficient cause. Might it not, in the absence of all information, be reasonably presumed that he had been disgraced without sufficient cause? It was certain that a vile calumny, destitute of all foundation, had caused him to be treated as a criminal in May. Was it not probable, then,

* My account of this plot is chiefly taken from Sprat's Relation of the late Wicked Contrivance of Stephen Black- head and Robert Young, 1692. There are very few better narratives in the language.

that calumny might have deprived him of his master's favour in January?

Young's resources were not yet exhausted. As soon as he had been carried back from Whitehall to Newgate, he set himself to construct a new plot, and to find a new accomplice. He addressed himself to a man named Holland, who was in the lowest state of poverty. Never, said Young, was there such a golden opportunity. A bold, shrewd, fellow might easily earn five hundred pounds. To Holland five hundred pounds seemed fabulous wealth. What, he asked, was he to do for it? Nothing, he was told, but to speak the truth, that was to say, substantial truth, a little disguised and coloured. There really was a plot; and this would have been proved if Blackhead had not been bought off. His desertion had made it necessary to call in the help of fiction. "You must swear that you and I were in a back room upstairs at the Lobster in Southwark. Some men came to meet us there. They gave a password before they were admitted. They were all in white camlet cloaks. They signed the Association in our presence. Then they paid each his shilling and went away. And you must be ready to identify my Lord Marlborough and the Bishop of Rochester as two of these men." "How can I identify them?" said Holland, "I never saw them." "You must contrive to see them," answered the tempter, "as soon as you can. The Bishop will be at the Abbey. Any body about the court will point out my Lord Marlborough." Holland immediately went to Whitehall, and repeated this conversation to Nottingham. The unlucky imitator of Oates was prosecuted, by order of the government, for perjury, subornation of perjury, and forgery. He was convicted and imprisoned, was again set in the pillory, and underwent, in addition to the exposure, about which he cared little, such a pelting as had seldom been known.* After his punishment, he was, during some years, lost in the crowd of pilferers, ringdroppers, and sharpers who infested the capital. At length, in the year 1700, he emerged from his obscurity, and excited a momentary interest. The newspapers announced that Robert Young, Clerk, once so famous, had been taken up for coining, then that he had been found guilty, then that the dead warrant had come down, and finally that the reverend gentleman had been hanged at Tyburn, and had greatly edified a large assembly of spectators by his penitence.†

---

* Baden to the States General, Feb. ⅓. 1693.

† Postman, April 13. and 20. 1700; Postboy, April 18.; Flying Post, April 20

CHAPTER XIX.

WHILE England was agitated, first by the dread of an invasion, and then by joy at the deliverance wrought for her by the valour of her seamen, important events were taking place on the Continent.   On the sixth of March the King had arrived at the Hague, and had proceeded to make his arrangements for the approaching campaign.*

Foreign policy of William.

The prospect which lay before him was gloomy.   The coalition of which he was the author and the chief had, during some months, been in constant danger of dissolution.   By what strenuous exertions, by what ingenious expedients, by what blandishments, by what bribes, he succeeded in preventing his allies from throwing themselves, one by one, at the feet of France, can be but imperfectly known.   The fullest and most authentic record of the labours and sacrifices by which he kept together, during eight years, a crowd of faint-hearted and treacherous potentates, negligent of the common interest and jealous of each other, is to be found in his correspondence with Heinsius.   In that correspondence William is all himself.   He had, in the course of his eventful life, to sustain some high parts for which he was not eminently qualified; and, in those parts, his success was imperfect.   As sovereign of England, he showed abilities and virtues which entitle him to honourable mention in history: but his deficiencies were great.   He was to the last a stranger among us, cold, reserved, never in good spirits, never at his ease.   His kingdom was a place of exile.   His finest palaces were prisons. He was always counting the days which must elapse before he should again see the land of his birth, the clipped trees, the wings of the innumerable windmills, the nests of the storks on the tall gables, and the long lines of painted villas reflected in the sleeping canals.   He took no pains to hide the preference which he felt for his native soil and for his early friends; and therefore, though he rendered great services to our country, he did not reign in our hearts.   As a general in

* London Gazette, March 14. 169$\frac{1}{2}$.

the field, again, he showed rare courage and capacity: but, from whatever cause, he was, as a tactician, inferior to some of his contemporaries, who, in general powers of mind, were far inferior to him.   The business for which he was preeminently fitted was diplomacy, in the highest sense of the word. It may be doubted whether he has ever had a superior in the art of conducting those great negotiations on which the welfare of the commonwealth of nations depends.   His skill in this department of politics was never more severely tasked or more signally proved than during the latter part of 1691 and the early part of 1692.

The Northern powers.

One of his chief difficulties was caused by the sullen and menacing demeanour of the Northern powers.   Denmark and Sweden had at one time seemed disposed to join the coalition : but they had early become cold, and were fast becoming hostile.   From France they flattered themselves that they had little to fear.   It was not very probable that her armies would cross the Elbe, or that her fleets would force a passage through the Sound.   But the naval strength of England and Holland united might well excite apprehension at Stockholm and Copenhagen.   Soon arose vexatious questions of maritime right, questions such as, in almost every extensive war of modern times, have arisen between belligerents and neutrals.   The Scandinavian princes complained that the legitimate trade between the Baltic and France was tyrannically interrupted. Though they had not in general been on very friendly terms with each other, they began to draw close together, intrigued at every petty German court, and tried to form what William called a Third Party in Europe.   The King of Sweden, who, as Duke of Pomerania, was bound to send three thousand men for the defence of the Empire, sent, instead of them, his advice that the allies would make peace on the best terms which they could get.*   The King of Denmark seized a great number of Dutch merchantships, and collected in Holstein an army which caused no small uneasiness to his neighbours.   " I fear," William wrote, in an hour of deep dejection, to Heinsius, " I fear that the object of this Third Party is a peace which will bring in its train the slavery of Europe.   The day will come when Sweden and her confederates will know too late how great an error they have committed.   They are farther, no doubt, than we from the danger ; and therefore it is that they are thus bent on working our ruin and their own.   That

* The Swedes came, it is true, but not till the campaign was over.   London Gazette, Sept. 10. 1691.

France will now consent to reasonable terms is not to be expected; and it were better to fall sword in hand than to submit to whatever she may dictate."*

While the King was thus disquieted by the conduct of the Northern powers, ominous signs began to appear in a very different quarter. It had, from the first, been no easy matter to induce sovereigns who hated, and who in their own dominions, persecuted, the Protestant religion, to countenance the revolution which had saved that religion from a great peril. But happily the example and the authority of the Vatican had overcome their scruples. Innocent the Eleventh and Alexander the Eighth had regarded William with ill concealed partiality. He was not indeed their friend; but he was their enemy's enemy; and James had been, and, if restored, must again be, their enemy's vassal. To the heretic nephew therefore they gave their effective support, to the orthodox uncle only compliments and benedictions. But Alexander the Eighth had occupied the papal throne little more than fifteen months. His successor, Antonio Pignatelli, who took the name of Innocent the Twelfth, was impatient to be reconciled to Lewis. Lewis was now sensible that he had committed a great error when he had roused against him at once the spirit of Protestantism and the spirit of Popery. He permitted the French Bishops to submit themselves to the Holy See. The dispute, which had, at one time, seemed likely to end in a great Gallican schism, was accommodated; and there was reason to believe that the influence of the head of the Church would be exerted for the purpose of severing the ties which bound so many Catholic princes to the Calvinist who had usurped the British throne.

Meanwhile the coalition, which the Third Party on one side and the Pope on the other were trying to dissolve, was in no small danger of falling to pieces from mere rottenness. Two of the allied powers, and two only, were hearty in the common cause; England, drawing after her the other British kingdoms, and Holland, drawing after her the other Batavian commonwealths. England and Holland were indeed torn by internal factions, and were separated from each other by mutual jealousies and antipathies: but both were fully resolved not to submit to French domination; and both were ready to bear their share, and more than their share, of the charges of the contest. Most of the members of the confederacy were not nations, but men, an Emperor, a King, Electors,

The Pope.

Conduct of the allies.

* William to Heinsius, March ¼⁴. 1692.

Dukes, Landgraves; and of these men there was scarcely one whose whole soul was in the struggle, scarcely one who did not hang back, who did not find some excuse for omitting to fulfil his engagements, who did not expect to be hired to defend his own rights and interests against the common enemy. But the war was the war of the people of England and of the people of Holland. Had it not been so, the burdens which it made necessary would not have been borne by either England or Holland during a single year. When William said that he would rather die sword in hand than humble himself before France, he expressed what was felt, not by himself alone, but by two great communities of which he was the first magistrate. With those two communities, unhappily, other states had little sympathy. Indeed those two communities were regarded by other states as rich, plaindealing, generous dupes are regarded by needy sharpers. England and Holland were wealthy; and they were zealous. Their wealth excited the cupidity of the whole alliance; and to that wealth their zeal was the key. They were persecuted with sordid importunity by all their confederates, from Cæsar, who, in the pride of his solitary dignity, would not honour King William with the title of Majesty, down to the smallest Margrave who could see his whole principality from the cracked windows of the mean and ruinous old house which he called his palace. It was not enough that England and Holland furnished much more than their contingents to the war by land, and bore unassisted the whole charge of the war by sea. They were beset by a crowd of illustrious mendicants, some rude, some obsequious, but all indefatigable and insatiable. One prince came mumping to them annually with a lamentable story about his distresses. A more sturdy beggar threatened to join the Third Party, and to make a separate peace with France, if his demands were not granted. Every Sovereign too had his ministers and favourites; and these ministers and favourites were perpetually hinting that France was willing to pay them for detaching their masters from the coalition, and that it would be prudent in England and Holland to outbid France.

Yet the embarrassment caused by the rapacity of the allied courts was scarcely greater than the embarrassment caused by their ambition and their pride. This prince had set his heart on some childish distinction, a title or a cross, and would do nothing for the common cause till his wishes were accomplished. That prince chose to fancy that he had been

slighted, and would not stir still reparation had been made
to him. The Duke of Brunswick Lunenburg would not
furnish a battalion for the defence of Germany unless he was
made an Elector.* The Elector of Brandenburg declared
that he was as hostile as he had ever been to France: but
he had been ill used by the Spanish government; and he
therefore would not suffer his soldiers to be employed in the
defence of the Spanish Netherlands. He was willing to bear
his share of the war: but it must be in his own way: he
must have the command of a distinct army; and he must
be stationed between the Rhine and the Meuse.† The Elector of Saxony complained that bad winter quarters had been
assigned to his troops: he therefore recalled them just when
they should have been preparing to take the field, but very
coolly offered to send them back if England and Holland
would give him four hundred thousand rixdollars.‡

It might have been expected that at least the two chiefs The Em-
of the House of Austria would have put forth, at this con- peror.
juncture, all their strength against the rival House of Bourbon. Unfortunately they could not be induced to exert themselves vigorously even for their own preservation. They
were deeply interested in keeping the French out of Italy.
Yet they could with difficulty be prevailed upon to lend the
smallest assistance to the Duke of Savoy. They seemed to
think it the business of England and Holland to defend the
passes of the Alps, and to prevent the armies of Lewis from
overflowing Lombardy. To the Emperor indeed the war
against France was a secondary object. His first object was
the war against Turkey. He was dull and bigoted. His
mind misgave him that the war against France was, in some
sense, a war against the Catholic religion; and the war
against Turkey was a crusade. His recent campaign on the
Danube had been successful. He might easily have concluded an honourable peace with the Porte, and have turned
his arms westward. But he had conceived the hope that he
might extend his hereditary dominions at the expense of the
Infidels. Visions of a triumphant entry into Constantinople
and of a Te Deum in Saint Sophia's had risen in his brain.
He not only employed in the East a force more than sufficient
to have defended Piedmont and reconquered Lorraine; but
he seemed to think that England and Holland were bound to

* William to Heinsius, Feb. ²⁄₁₂. 1692.   † William to Heinsius, Jan. ¹²⁄₂₂. 1692.
    ‡ William to Heinsius, Jan. ¹⁹⁄₂₉. 1692.

reward him largely for neglecting their interests and pursuing his own.*

Spain.

Spain already was what she has continued to be down to our own time. Of the Spain which had domineered over the land and the ocean, over the Old and the New World, of the Spain which had, in the short space of twelve years, led captive a Pope and a King of France, a Sovereign of Mexico and a Sovereign of Peru, of the Spain which had sent an army to the walls of Paris and had equipped a mighty fleet to invade England, nothing remained but an arrogance which had once excited terror and hatred, but which could now excite only derision. In extent, indeed, the dominions of the Catholic King exceeded those of Rome when Rome was at the zenith of power. But the huge mass lay torpid and helpless, and could be insulted or despoiled with impunity. The whole administration, military and, naval, financial and colonial, was utterly disorganized. Charles was a fit representative of his kingdom, impotent physically, intellectually, and morally, sunk in ignorance, listlessness, and superstition, yet swollen with a notion of his own dignity, and quick to imagine and to resent affronts. So wretched had his education been that, when he was told of the fall of Mons, the most important fortress in his vast empire, he asked whether Mons was in England.† Among the ministers who were raised up and pulled down by his sickly caprice, was none capable of applying a remedy to the distempers of the State. In truth to brace anew the nerves of that paralysed body would have been a hard task even for Ximenes. No servant of the Spanish Crown occupied a more important post, and none was more unfit for an important post, than the Marquess of Gastanaga. He was Governor of the Netherlands; and in the Netherlands it seemed probable that the fate of Christendom would be decided. He had discharged his trust as every public trust was then discharged in every part of that vast monarchy on which it was boastfully said that the sun never set. Fertile and rich as was the country which he ruled, he threw on England and Holland the whole charge of defending it. He expected that arms, ammunition, waggons, provisions, every thing, would be furnished by the heretics. It had never occurred to him that it was his business, and not theirs, to put Mons in a condition to stand a siege. The public voice loudly accused him of having sold that cele-

---

* Burnet, ii. 82, 83.; Correspondence of William and Heinsius, passim.
† Mémoires de Torcy.

*Lady Marlborough and the Princess Anne
at the Queen's Drawing-Room*

brated stronghold to France. But it is probable that he was guilty of nothing worse than the haughty apathy and sluggishness characteristic of his nation.

Such was the state of the coalition of which William was the head. There were moments when he felt himself overwhelmed, when his spirits sank, when his patience was wearied out, and when his constitutional irritability broke forth. "I cannot," he wrote, "offer a suggestion without being met by a demand for a subsidy."* "I have refused point blank," he wrote on another occasion, when he had been importuned for money: "it is impossible that the States General and England can bear the charge of the army on the Rhine, of the army in Piedmont, and of the whole defence of Flanders, to say nothing of the immense cost of the naval war. If our allies can do nothing for themselves, the sooner the alliance goes to pieces the better."† But, after every short fit of despondency and ill humour, he called up all the force of his mind, and put a strong curb on his temper. Weak, mean, false, selfish, as too many of the confederates were, it was only by their help that he could accomplish what he had from his youth up considered as his mission. If they abandoned him, France would be dominant without a rival in Europe. Well as they deserved to be punished, he would not, to punish them, acquiesce in the subjugation of the whole civilised world. He set himself therefore to surmount some difficulties and to evade others. The Scandinavian powers he conciliated by waiving, reluctantly indeed, and not without a hard internal struggle, some of his maritime rights.‡ At Rome his influence, though indirectly exercised, balanced that of the Pope himself. Lewis and James found that they had not a friend at the Vatican except Innocent; and Innocent, whose nature was gentle and irresolute, shrank from taking a course directly opposed to the sentiments of all who surrounded him. In private conversations with Jacobite agents he declared himself devoted to the interest of the House of Stuart: but in his public acts he observed a strict neutrality. He sent twenty thousand crowns to Saint Germains: but he excused himself to the enemies of France by protesting that this was not a subsidy for any political purpose, but merely an alms to be distributed among poor British Catholics. He permitted prayers for the good cause to be read in the English College at Rome: but he insisted that

margin note: William succeeds in preventing the dissolution of the coalition.

---

* William to Heinsius, $\frac{Oct. 28.}{Nov. 3.}$ 1691.
† Ibid. Jan. $\frac{19.}{49.}$ 1692.

‡ His letters to Heinsius are full of this subject.

those prayers should be drawn up in general terms, and that no name should be mentioned. It was in vain that the ministers of the Houses of Stuart and Bourbon adjured him to take a more decided course. " God knows," he exclaimed on one occasion, " that I would gladly shed my blood to restore the King of England. But what can I do ? If I stir, I am told that I am favouring the French, and helping them to set up an universal monarchy. I am not like the old Popes. Kings will not listen to me as they listened to my predecessors. There is no religion now, nothing but wicked, worldly, policy. The Prince of Orange is master. He governs us all. He has got such a hold on the Emperor and on the King of Spain that neither of them dares to displease him. God help us ! He alone can help us." And, as the old man spoke, he beat the table with his hand in an agony of impotent grief and indignation.*

To keep the German princes steady was no easy task : but it was accomplished. Money was distributed among them, much less indeed than they asked, but much more than they had any decent pretence for asking. With the Elector of Saxony a composition was made. He had, together with a strong appetite for subsidies, a great desire to be a member of the most select and illustrious orders of knighthood. It seems that, instead of the four hundred thousand rix dollars which he had demanded, he consented to accept one hundred thousand and the Garter.† His prime minister Schœning, the most covetous and perfidious of mankind, was secured, it was hoped, by a pension.‡ For the Duke of Brunswick Lunenburg, William, not without difficulty, procured the long desired title of Elector of Hanover. By such means as these the breaches which had divided the coalition were so skilfully repaired that it appeared still to present a firm front to the enemy.

William had complained bitterly to the Spanish Court of the incapacity and inertness of Gastanaga; and that government, helpless and drowsy as it was, could not be altogether

* See the Letters from Rome among the Nairne Papers. Those in 1692 are from Lytcott; those in 1693 from Cardinal Howard ; those in 1694 from Bishop Ellis; those in 1695 from Lord Perth. They all tell the same story.

† William's correspondence with Heinsius; London Gazette, Feb. 4. 1691. In a pasquinade published in 1693, and entitled "La Foire d'Ausbourg, Ballet Allégorique," the Elector of Saxony is introduced saying :

" Moy, je diray naïvement
Qu'une jartière d'Angleterre
Feroit tout mon empressement ;
Et je ne vois rien sur la terre
Ou je trouve plus d'agrément."

‡ William's correspondence with Heinsius. There is a curious account of Schœning in the Memoirs of Count Dohna.

insensible to the dangers which threatened Flanders and Brabant. Gastanaga was recalled; and William was invited to take upon himself the government of the Low Countries, with powers not less than regal. Philip the Second would not easily have believed that, within a century after his death, his greatgrandson would implore the greatgrandson of William the Silent to exercise the authority of a sovereign at Brussels.* New arrangements for the government of the Spanish Netherlands.

The offer was in one sense tempting: but William was too wise to accept it. He knew that the population of the Spanish Netherlands was firmly attached to the Church of Rome. Every act of a Protestant ruler was certain to be regarded with suspicion by the clergy and people of those countries. Already Gastanaga, mortified by his disgrace, had written to inform the Court of Rome that changes were in contemplation which would make Ghent and Antwerp as heretical as Amsterdam and London.† It had doubtless also occurred to William that if, by governing mildly and justly, and by showing a decent respect for the ceremonies and the ministers of the Roman Catholic religion, he should succeed in obtaining the confidence of the Belgians, he would inevitably raise against himself a storm of obloquy in our island. He knew by experience what it was to govern two nations strongly attached to two different Churches. A large party among the Episcopalians of England could not forgive him for having consented to the establishment of the presbyterian polity in Scotland. A large party among the Presbyterians of Scotland blamed him for maintaining the episcopal polity in England. If he now took under his protection masses, processions, graven images, friaries, nunneries, and, worst of all, Jesuit pulpits, Jesuit confessionals, and Jesuit colleges, what could he expect but that England and Scotland would join in one cry of reprobation? He therefore refused to accept the government of the Low Countries, and proposed that it should be entrusted to the Elector of Bavaria. The Elector of Bavaria was, after the Emperor, the most powerful of the Roman Catholic potentates of Germany. He was young, brave, and ambitious of military distinction. The Spanish Court was willing to appoint him; and he was desirous to be appointed: but much delay was caused by an absurd difficulty. The Elector thought it beneath him to ask for what he wished to have. The formalists of the Cabinet of Madrid thought it beneath the dignity of the Catholic King to give what had

* Burnet, ii. 84.   † Narcissus Luttrell's Diary.

not been asked. Mediation was necessary, and was at last
successful. But much time was lost; and the spring was far
advanced before the new Governor of the Netherlands entered
on his functions.*

William had saved the coalition from the danger of perishing by disunion. But by no remonstrance, by no entreaty,
by no bribe, could he prevail on his allies to be early in the
field. They ought to have profited by the severe lesson which
had been given them in the preceding year. But again every
one of them lingered, and wondered why the rest were lin-
gering; and again he who singly wielded the whole power of
France was found, as his haughty motto had long boasted, a
match for a multitude of adversaries.† His enemies, while
still unready, learned with dismay that he had taken the field
in person at the head of his nobility. On no occasion had
that gallant aristocracy appeared with more splendour in his
train. A single circumstance may suffice to give a notion of
the pomp and luxury of his camp. Among the musketeers
of his household rode, for the first time, a stripling of seventeen, who soon afterwards succeeded to the title of Duke of
Saint Simon, and to whom we owe those inestimable memoirs
which have preserved, for the delight and instruction of many
lands and of many generations, the vivid picture of a France
which has long passed away. Though the boy's family was at
that time very hard pressed for money, he travelled with thirty-
five horses and sumpter mules. The princesses of the blood,
each surrounded by a group of highborn and graceful ladies,
accompanied the King; and the smiles of so many charming
women inspired the throng of vain and voluptuous but high-
spirited gentlemen with more than common courage. In the
brilliant crowd which surrounded the French Augustus appeared the French Virgil, the graceful, the tender, the melodious Racine. He had, in conformity with the prevailing
fashion, become devout, and had given up writing for the
theatre. He now, having determined to apply himself vigorously to the discharge of the duties which belonged to him as
historiographer of France, came to see the great events which
it was his office to record.‡ In the neighbourhood of Mons,

---

* Monthly Mercuries of January and
April 1693; Burnet, ii. 84. In the
Burnet MS. Harl. 6584, is a warm
eulogy on the Elector of Bavaria. When
the MS. was written, he was allied with
England against France. In the History,
which was prepared for publication when
he was allied with France against England, the eulogy is omitted.

† "Nec pluribus impar."

‡ Mémoires de Saint Simon; Dangeau; Racine's Letters, and Narrative
entitled Relation de ce qui s'est passé
au Siège de Namur; Monthly Mercury,
May 1692.

Lewis entertained the ladies with the most magnificent review that had ever been seen in modern Europe. A hundred and twenty thousand of the finest troops in the world were drawn up in a line eight miles long. It may be doubted whether such an array was ever brought together under the Roman eagles. The show began early in the morning, and was not over when the long summer day closed. Racine left the ground, astonished, deafened, dazzled, and tired to death. In a private letter he ventured to give utterance to an amiable wish which he probably took good care not to whisper in the courtly circle : "Would to heaven that all these poor fellows were in their cottages again with their wives and their little ones!"*

After this superb pageant Lewis announced his intention of attacking Namur. In five days he was under the walls of that city, at the head of more than thirty thousand men. Twenty thousand peasants, pressed in those parts of the Netherlands which the French occupied, were compelled to act as pioneers. Luxemburg, with eighty thousand men, occupied a strong position on the road between Namur and Brussels, and was prepared to give battle to any force which might attempt to raise the siege.† This partition of duties excited no surprise. It had long been known that the Great Monarch loved sieges, and that he did not love battles. He professed to think that the real test of military skill was a siege. The event of an encounter between two armies on an open plain was, in his opinion, often determined by chance : but only science could prevail against ravelins and bastions which science had constructed. His detractors sneeringly pronounced it fortunate that the department of the military art which His Majesty considered as the noblest was one in which it was seldom necessary for him to expose to serious risk a life invaluable to his people.

Namur, situated at the confluence of the Sambre and the Meuse, was one of the great fortresses of Europe. The town lay in the plain, and had no strength except what was derived from art. But art and nature had combined to fortify that renowned citadel which, from the summit of a lofty rock, looks down on a boundless expanse of cornfields, woods and meadows, watered by two fine rivers. The people of the city and of the surrounding region were proud of their impregnable castle. Their boast was that never, in all the wars which had devastated the Netherlands, had skill or valour been able to

margin: Siege of Namur.

---

* Mémoires de Saint Simon; Racine to Boileau, May 21. 1692. † Monthly Mercury for June ; William to Heinsius, $\frac{May\ 26.}{June\ 5.}$ 1692.

penetrate those walls. The neighbouring fastnesses, famed throughout the world for their strength, Antwerp and Ostend, Ypres, Lisle and Tournay, Mons and Valenciennes, Cambray and Charleroy, Limburg and Luxemburg, had opened their gates to conquerors: but never once had the flag been pulled down from the battlements of Namur. That nothing might be wanting to the interest of the siege, the two great masters of the art of fortification were opposed to each other. Vauban had during many years been regarded as the first of engineers: but a formidable rival had lately arisen, Menno, Baron of Cohorn, the ablest officer in the service of the States General. The defences of Namur had been recently strengthened and repaired under Cohorn's superintendence; and he was now within the walls. Vauban was in the camp of Lewis. It might therefore be expected that both the attack and the defence would be conducted with consummate ability.

By this time the allied armies had assembled: but it was too late.* William hastened towards Namur. He menaced the French works, first from the west, then from the north, then from the east. But between him and the lines of circumvallation lay the army of Luxemburg, turning as he turned, and always so strongly posted that to attack it would have been the height of imprudence. Meanwhile the besiegers, directed by the skill of Vauban and animated by the presence of Lewis, made rapid progress. There were indeed many difficulties to be surmounted and many hardships to be endured. The weather was stormy; and, on the eighth of June, the feast of Saint Medard, who holds in the French Calendar the same inauspicious place which in our Calendar belongs to Saint Swithin, the rain fell in torrents. The Sambre rose and covered many square miles on which the harvest was green. The Mehaigne whirled down its bridges to the Meuse. All the roads became swamps. The trenches were so deep in water and mire that it was the business of three days to move a gun from one battery to another. The six thousand waggons which had accompanied the French army were useless. It was necessary that gunpowder, bullets, corn, hay, should be carried from place to place on the backs of the war horses. Nothing but the authority of Lewis could, in such circumstances, have maintained order and inspired cheerfulness. His soldiers, in truth, showed much more reverence for him than for what their religion had made sacred. They cursed Saint Medard heartily, and broke or burned every image of him

* William to Heinsius, $\frac{\text{May 26.}}{\text{June 5.}}$ 1692.

that could be found. But for their King there was nothing that they were not ready to do and to bear. In spite of every obstacle they constantly gained ground. Cohorn was severely wounded while defending with desperate resolution a fort which he had himself constructed, and of which he was proud. His place could not be supplied. The governor was a feeble man whom Gastanaga had appointed, and whom William had recently advised the Elector of Bavaria to remove. The spirit of the garrison gave way. The town surrendered on the eighth day of the siege, the citadel about three weeks later.*

The history of the fall of Namur in 1692 bears a close resemblance to the history of the fall of Mons in 1691. Both in 1691 and in 1692, Lewis, the sole and absolute master of the resources of his kingdom, was able to open the campaign, before William, the captain of a coalition, had brought together his dispersed forces. In both years the advantage of having the first move decided the event of the game. At Namur, as at Mons, Lewis, assisted by Vauban, conducted the siege: Luxemburg covered it: William vainly tried to raise it, and, with deep mortification, assisted as a spectator at the victory of his enemy.

In one respect however the fate of the two fortresses was very different. Mons was delivered up by its own inhabitants. Namur might perhaps have been saved if the garrison had been as zealous and determined as the population. Strange to say, in this place, so long subject to a foreign rule, there was found a patriotism resembling that of the little Greek commonwealths. There is no reason to believe that the burghers cared about the balance of power, or had any preference for James or for William, for the Most Christian King or for the Most Catholic King. But every citizen considered his own honour as bound up with the honour of the maiden fortress. It is true that the French did not abuse their victory. No outrage was committed: the privileges of the municipality were respected; the magistrates were not changed. Yet the people could not see a conqueror enter their hitherto unconquered castle without tears of rage and shame. Even the barefooted Carmelites, who had renounced all pleasures, all property, all society, all domestic affection,

* Monthly Mercuries of June and July 1692; London Gazettes of June; Gazette de Paris; Mémoires de Saint Simon; Journal de Dangeau; William to Heinsius. $\frac{\text{May 30.}}{\text{June 9.}}$, June $\frac{2}{12}$. June $\frac{11}{21}$.; Vernon's Letters to Colt, printed in Tindal's History; Racine's Narrative and Letters to Boileau of June 15. and 24.

whose days were all fast days, who passed month after month without uttering a word, were strangely moved. It was in vain that Lewis attempted to soothe them by marks of respect and by munificent bounty. Whenever they met a French uniform they turned their heads away with a look which showed that a life of prayer, of abstinence, and of silence had left one earthly feeling still unsubdued.*

This was perhaps the moment at which the arrogance of Lewis reached the highest point. He had achieved the last and the most splendid military exploit of his life. His confederated foes, English, Dutch and German, had, in their own despite, swelled his triumph, and had been witnesses of the glory which made their hearts sick. His exultation was boundless. The inscriptions on the medals which he struck, to commemorate his success, the letters by which he enjoined the prelates of his kingdom to sing the Te Deum, were boastful and sarcastic. His people, a people among whose many fine qualities moderation in prosperity cannot be reckoned, seemed for a time to be drunk with pride. Even Boileau, hurried along by the prevailing enthusiasm, forgot the good sense and good taste to which he owed his reputation. He fancied himself a lyric poet, and gave vent to his feelings in a hundred and sixty lines of frigid bombast about Alcides, Mars, Bacchus, Ceres, the lyre of Orpheus, the Thracian oaks, and the Permessian nymphs. He wondered whether Namur had, like Troy, been built by Apollo and Neptune. He asked what power could subdue a city stronger than that before which the Greeks lay ten years; and he returned answer to himself that such a miracle could be wrought only by Jupiter or by Lewis. The feather in the hat of Lewis was the loadstar of victory. To Lewis all things must yield, princes, nations, winds, waters. In conclusion the poet addressed himself to the banded enemies of France, and tauntingly bade them carry back to their homes the tidings that Namur had been taken in their sight. Before many months had elapsed both the boastful king and the boastful poet were taught that it is prudent as well as graceful to be modest in the hour of victory.

One mortification Lewis had suffered even in the midst of his prosperity. While he lay before Namur, he heard the sounds of rejoicing from the distant camp of the allies. Three peals of thunder from a hundred and forty pieces of cannon were answered by three volleys from sixty thousand

* Mémoires de Saint Simon.

muskets. It was soon known that these salutes were fired on account of the battle of La Hogue. The French King exerted himself to appear serene. "They make a strange noise," he said, "about the burning of a few ships." In truth he was much disturbed, and the more so because a report had reached the Low Countries that there had been a sea fight, and that his fleet had been victorious. His good humour however was soon restored by the brilliant success of those operations which were under his own immediate direction. When the siege was over, he left Luxemburg in command of the army, and returned to Versailles. At Versailles the unfortunate Tourville presented himself, and was graciously received. As soon as he appeared in the circle, the King welcomed him in a loud voice. "I am perfectly satisfied with you and with my sailors. We have been beaten, it is true: but your honour and that of the nation are unsullied." *

Lewis returns to Versailles.

Though Lewis had quitted the Netherlands, the eyes of all Europe were still fixed on that region. The armies there had been strengthened by reinforcements drawn from many quarters. Everywhere else the military operations of the year were languid and without interest. The Grand Vizier and Lewis of Baden did little more than watch each other on the Danube. Marshal Noailles and the Duke of Medina Sidonia did little more than watch each other under the Pyrenees. On the Upper Rhine, and along the frontier of Piedmont, an indecisive predatory war was carried on, by which the soldiers suffered little and the cultivators of the soil much. But all men looked, with anxious expectation of some great event, to the frontier of Brabant, where William was opposed to Luxemburg.

Luxemburg, now in his sixty-sixth year, had risen, by slow degrees, and by the deaths of several great men, to the first place among the generals of his time. He was of that noble house of Montmorency which united many mythical and many historical titles to glory, which boasted that it sprang from the first Frank who was baptised into the name of Christ in the fifth century, and which had, since the eleventh century, given to France a long and splendid succession of Constables and Marshals. In valour and abilities Luxemburg was not inferior to any of his illustrious race. But, highly descended and highly gifted as he was, he had with difficulty surmounted the obstacles which impeded him in the road to

Luxemburg.

* London Gazette, May 30. 1692; Dangeau; Boyer's History of William Mémoires de Saint Simon; Journal de III. 1702.

fame. If he owed much to the bounty of nature and fortune, he had suffered still more from their spite. His features were frightfully harsh : his stature was diminutive : a huge and pointed hump rose on his back. His constitution was feeble and sickly. Cruel imputations had been thrown on his morals. He had been accused of trafficking with sorcerers and with compounders of poison, had languished long in a dungeon, and had at length regained his liberty without entirely regaining his honour.* He had always been disliked both by Louvois and by Lewis. Yet the war against the European coalition had lasted but a very short time when both the minister and the King felt that the general who was personally odious to them was necessary to the state. Condé and Turenne were no more ; and Luxemburg was without dispute the first soldier that France still possessed. In vigilance, diligence, and perseverance he was deficient. He seemed to reserve his great qualities for great emergencies. It was on a pitched field of battle that he was all himself. His glance was rapid and unerring. His judgment was clearest and surest when responsibility pressed heaviest on him, and when difficulties gathered thickest around him. To his skill, energy, and presence of mind his country owed some glorious days. But, though eminently successful in battles, he was not eminently successful in campaigns. He gained immense renown at William's expense ; and yet there was, as respected the objects of the war, little to choose between the two commanders. Luxemburg was repeatedly victorious : but he had not the art of improving a victory. William was repeatedly defeated : but of all generals he was the best qualified to repair a defeat.

In the month of July William's headquarters were at Lambeque. About six miles off, at Steinkirk, Luxemburg had encamped with the main body of his army ; and about six miles further off lay a considerable force commanded by the Marquess of Boufflers, one of the best officers in the service of Lewis.

The country between Lambeque and Steinkirk was intersected by innumerable hedges and ditches ; and neither army

---

* Mémoires de Saint Simon ; Voltaire, Siècle de Louis XIV. Voltaire speaks with a contempt which is probably just of the account of this affair in the Causes Célèbres. See also the Letters of Madame de Sévigné during the months of January and February 1680. In several English lampoons Luxemburg is nicknamed Æsop, from his deformity, and called a wizard, in allusion to his dealings with La Voisin. In one Jacobite allegory he is the necromancer Grandorsio. In Narcissus Luttrell's Diary for June 1692 he is called a conjuror. I have seen two or three English caricatures of Luxemburg's figure.

could approach the other without passing through several long and narrow defiles. Luxemburg had therefore little reason to apprehend that he should be attacked in his entrenchments; and he felt assured that he should have ample notice before any attack was made: for he had succeeded in corrupting an adventurer named Millevoix, who was chief musician and private secretary of the Elector of Bavaria. This man regularly sent to the French headquarters authentic information touching the designs of the allies.

The Marshal, confident in the strength of his position, and in the accuracy of his intelligence, lived in his tent as he was accustomed to live in his hotel at Paris. He was at once a valetudinarian and a voluptuary; and, in both characters, he loved his ease. He scarcely ever mounted his horse. Light conversation and cards occupied most of his hours. His table was luxurious; and, when he had sate down to supper, it was a service of danger to disturb him. Some scoffers remarked that in his military dispositions he was not guided exclusively by military reasons, that he generally contrived to entrench himself in some place where the veal and the poultry were remarkably good, and that he was always solicitous to keep open such communications with the sea as might ensure him, from September to April, a regular supply of Sandwich oysters. If there were any agreeable women in the neighbourhood of his camp, they were generally to be found at his banquets. It may easily be supposed that, under such a commander, the young princes and nobles of France vied with one another in splendour and gallantry.*

While he was amusing himself after his wonted fashion, the confederate princes discovered that their counsels were betrayed. A peasant picked up a letter which had been dropped, and carried it to the Elector of Bavaria. It contained full proofs of the guilt of Millevoix. William conceived a hope that he might be able to take his enemies in the snare which they had laid for him. The perfidious secretary was summoned to the royal presence and taxed with his crime. A pen was put into his hand: a pistol was held to his breast; and he was commanded to write on pain of instant death. His letter, dictated by William, was conveyed to the French camp. It apprised Luxemburg that the allies meant to send out a strong foraging party on the next day. In order to protect this party from molestation, some battalions of

Battle of Steinkirk.

* Mémoires de Saint Simon; Mémoires de Villars; Racine to Boileau, May 21. 1692.

infantry, accompanied by artillery, would march by night to occupy the defiles which lay between the armies. The Marshal read, believed, and went to rest, while William urged forward the preparations for a general assault on the French lines.

The whole allied army was under arms while it was still dark. In the grey of the morning, Luxemburg was awakened by scouts, who brought tidings that the enemy was advancing in great force. He at first treated the news very lightly. His correspondent, it seemed, had been, as usual, diligent and exact. The Prince of Orange had sent out a detachment to protect his foragers, and this detachment had been magnified by fear into a great host. But one alarming report followed another fast. All the passes, it was said, were choked with multitudes of foot, horse, and artillery, under the banners of England and of Spain, of the United Provinces and of the Empire; and every column was moving towards Steinkirk. At length the Marshal rose, got on horseback, and rode out to see what was doing.

By this time the vanguard of the allies was close to his outposts. About half a mile in advance of his army was encamped a brigade named from the province of Bourbonnais. These troops had to bear the first brunt of the onset. Amazed and panickstricken, they were swept away in a moment, and ran for their lives, leaving their tents and seven pieces of cannon to the assailants.

Thus far William's plans had been completely successful: but now fortune began to turn against him. He had been misinformed as to the nature of the ground which lay between the station of the brigade of Bourbonnais and the main encampment of the enemy. He had expected that he should be able to push forward without a moment's pause, that he should find the French army in a state of wild disorder, and that his victory would be easy and complete. But his progress was obstructed by several fences and ditches: there was a short delay; and a short delay sufficed to frustrate his design. Luxemburg was the very man for such a conjuncture. He had committed great faults: he had kept careless guard: he had trusted implicitly to information which had proved false: he had neglected information which had proved true: one of his divisions was flying in confusion: the other divisions were unprepared for action. That crisis would have paralysed the faculties of an ordinary captain: it only braced and stimulated those of Luxemburg. His mind, nay his

sickly and distorted body, seemed to derive health and vigour
from disaster and dismay. In a short time he had disposed
every thing. The French army was in battle order. Conspicuous in that great array were the household troops of
Lewis, the most renowned body of fighting men in Europe ;
and at their head appeared, glittering in lace and embroidery
hastily thrown on and half fastened, a crowd of young princes
and lords who had just been roused by the trumpet from their
couches or their revels, and who had hastened to look death
in the face with the gay and festive intrepidity characteristic
of French gentlemen. Highest in rank among these highborn warriors was a lad of sixteen, Philip Duke of Chartres,
son of the Duke of Orleans, and nephew of the King of
France. It was with difficulty and by importunate solicitation that the gallant boy had extorted Luxemburg's permission to be where the fire was hottest. Two other youths of
royal blood, Lewis Duke of Bourbon, and Armand Prince of
Conti, showed a spirit worthy of their descent. With them
was a descendant of one of the bastards of Henry the Fourth,
Lewis Duke of Vendome, a man sunk in indolence and in the
foulest vice, yet capable of exhibiting on a great occasion the
qualities of a great soldier. Berwick, who was beginning to
earn for himself an honourable name in arms, was there ; and
at his side rode Sarsfield, whose courage and ability earned, on
that day, the esteem of the whole French army.* Meanwhile
Luxemburg had sent off a pressing message to summon
Boufflers. But the message was needless. Boufflers had heard
the firing, and, like a brave and intelligent captain, was already
hastening towards the point from which the sound came.

Though the assailants had lost all the advantage which
belongs to a surprise, they came on manfully. In front of
the battle were the British commanded by Count Solmes.
The division which was to lead the way was Mackay's. He
was to have been supported, according to William's plan, by
a strong body of foot and horse. Though most of Mackay's
men had never before been under fire, their behaviour gave
promise of Blenheim and Ramilies. They first encountered
the Swiss, who held a distinguished place in the French
army. The fight was so close and desperate that the muzzles
of the muskets crossed. The Swiss were driven back with
fearful slaughter. More than eighteen hundred of them
appear from the French returns to have been killed or
wounded. Luxemburg afterwards said that he had never in

* See the honourable mention of Sarsfield in Luxemburg's despatch.

his life seen so furious a struggle. He collected in haste the opinion of the generals who surrounded him. All thought that the emergency was one which could be met by no common means. The King's household must charge the English. The Marshal gave the word; and the household, headed by the princes of the blood, came on, flinging their muskets back on their shoulders. "Sword in hand," was the cry through all the ranks of that terrible brigade: "sword in hand. No firing. Do it with the cold steel." After a long and bloody contest, the English were borne down. They never ceased to repeat that, if Solmes had done his duty by them, they would have beaten even the household. But Solmes gave them no effective support. He pushed forward some cavalry which, from the nature of the ground, could do little or nothing. His infantry he would not suffer to stir. They could do no good, he said; and he would not send them to be slaughtered. Ormond was eager to hasten to the assistance of his countrymen, but was not permitted. Mackay sent a pressing message to represent that he and his men were left to certain destruction: but all was vain. "God's will be done," said the brave veteran. He died as he had lived, like a good Christian and a good soldier. With him fell Douglas and Lanier, two generals distinguished among the conquerors of Ireland. Mountjoy too was among the slain. After languishing three years in the Bastille, he had just been exchanged for Richard Hamilton, and, having been converted to Whiggism by wrongs more powerful than all the arguments of Locke and Sidney, had instantly hastened to join William's camp as a volunteer.* Five fine regiments were entirely cut to pieces. No part of this devoted band would have escaped but for the courage and conduct of Auverquerque, who came to the rescue in the moment of extremity with two fresh battalions. The gallant manner in which he brought off the remains of Mackay's division was long remembered and talked of with grateful admiration by the British camp fires. The ground where the conflict had raged was piled with corpses; and those who buried the slain remarked that almost all the wounds had been given in close fighting by the sword or the bayonet.

It was said that William so far forgot his wonted stoicism as to utter a passionate exclamation at the way in which the English regiments had been sacrificed. Soon, however, he recovered his equanimity, and determined to fall back. It

* Narcissus Luttrell, April 28. 1692.

was high time : for the French army was every moment becoming stronger, as the regiments commanded by Boufflers came up in rapid succession. The allied army returned to Lambeque unpursued and in unbroken order.*

The French owned that they had about seven thousand men killed and wounded. The loss of the allies had been little, if at all, greater. The relative strength of the armies was what it had been on the preceding day; and they continued to occupy their old positions. But the moral effect of the battle was great. The splendour of William's fame grew pale. Even his admirers were forced to own that, in the field, he was not a match for Luxemburg. In France the news was received with transports of joy and pride. The Court, the Capital, even the peasantry of the remotest provinces, gloried in the impetuous valour which had been displayed by so many youths, the heirs of illustrious names. It was exultingly and fondly repeated all over the kingdom that the young Duke of Chartres could not by any remonstrances be kept out of danger, that a ball had passed through his coat, that he had been wounded in the shoulder. The people lined the roads to see the princes and nobles who returned from Steinkirk. The jewellers devised Steinkirk buckles : the perfumers sold Steinkirk powder. But the name of the field of battle was peculiarly given to a new species of collar. Lace neckcloths were then worn by men of fashion; and it had been usual to arrange them with great care. But at the terrible moment when the brigade of Bourbonnais was flying

* London Gazette, Aug. 4. 8. 11. 1692 ; Gazette de Paris, Aug. 9. 16.; Voltaire, Siècle de Louis XIV.; Burnet, ii. 97 ; Mémoires de Berwick; Dykvelt's Letter to the States General, dated August 4. 1692. See also the very interesting debate which took place in the House of Commons on Nov. 21. 1692. An English translation of Luxemburg's elaborate and artful despatch will be found in the Monthly Mercury for September 1692. The original has recently been printed in the new edition of Dangeau. Lewis pronounced it the best despatch that he had ever seen. The editor of the Monthly Mercury maintains that it was manufactured at Paris. "To think otherwise," he says, " is mere folly: as if Luxemburg could be at so much leisure to write such a long letter, more like a pedant than a general, or rather the monitor of a school, giving an account to his master how the rest of the boys behaved themselves." In the Monthly Mercury will be found also the French official list of killed and wounded. Of all the accounts of the battle that which seems to me the best is in the Memoirs of Feuquières. It is illustrated by a map. Feuquières divides his praise and blame very fairly between the generals. The traditions of the English mess tables have been preserved by Sterne, who was brought up at the knees of old soldiers of William. " ' There was Cutts's,' continued the Corporal, clapping the forefinger of his right hand upon the thumb of his left, and counting round his hand; 'there was Cutts's, Mackay's, Angus's, Graham's and Leven's, all cut to pieces ; and so had the English Lifeguards too, had it not been for some regiments on the right, who marched up boldly to their relief, and received the enemy's fire in their faces, before any one of their own platoons discharged a musket. They'll go to heaven for it,' added Trim."

before the onset of the allies, there was no time for foppery; and the finest gentlemen of the Court came spurring to the front of the line of battle with their rich cravats in disorder. It therefore became a fashion among the beauties of Paris to wear round their necks kerchiefs of the finest lace studiously disarranged; and these kerchiefs were called Steinkirks.*

In the camp of the allies all was disunion and discontent. National jealousies and animosities raged without restraint or disguise. The resentment of the English was loudly expressed. Solmes, though he was said by those who knew him well to have some valuable qualities, was not a man likely to conciliate soldiers who were prejudiced against him as a foreigner. His demeanour was arrogant, his temper ungovernable. Even before the unfortunate day of Steinkirk the English officers did not willingly communicate with him, and the private men murmured at his harshness. But after the battle the outcry against him became furious. He was accused, perhaps unjustly, of having said with unfeeling levity, while the English regiments were contending desperately against great odds, that he was curious to see how the bulldogs would come off. Would anybody, it was asked, now pretend that it was on account of his superior skill and experience that he had been put over the heads of so many English officers? It was the fashion to say that those officers had never seen war on a large scale. But surely the merest novice was competent to do all that Solmes had done, to misunderstand orders, to send cavalry on duty which none but infantry could perform, and to look on at safe distance while brave men were cut to pieces. It was too much to be at once insulted and sacrificed, excluded from the honours of war, yet pushed on all its extreme dangers, sneered at as raw recruits, and then left to cope unsupported with the finest body of veterans in the world. Such were the complaints of the English army; and they were echoed by the English nation.

Fortunately about this time a discovery was made which furnished both the camp at Lambeque and the coffeehouses of London with a subject of conversation much less agreeable to the Jacobites than the disaster of Steinkirk.

Conspiracy of Grand- val.

A plot against the life of William had been, during some months, maturing in the French War Office. It should seem that Louvois had originally sketched the design, and had bequeathed it, still rude, to his son and successor Barbesieux.

* Voltaire, Siècle de Louis XIV.

By Barbesieux the plan was perfected. The execution was entrusted to an officer named Grandval. Grandval was undoubtedly brave, and full of zeal for his country and his religion. He was indeed flighty and half witted, but not on that account the less dangerous. Indeed a flighty and half witted man is the very instrument generally preferred by cunning politicians when very hazardous work is to be done. No shrewd calculator would, for any bribe, however enormous, have exposed himself to the fate of Chatel, of Ravaillac, or of Gerarts.*

Grandval secured, as he conceived, the assistance of two adventurers, Dumont, a Walloon, and Leefdale, a Dutchman. In April, soon after William had arrived in the Low Countries, the murderers were directed to repair to their posts. Dumont was then in Westphalia. Grandval and Leefdale were at Paris. Uden in North Brabant was fixed as the place where the three were to meet, and whence they were to proceed together to the headquarters of the allies. Before Grandval left Paris he paid a visit to Saint Germains, and was presented to James and to Mary of Modena. "I have been informed," said James, " of the business. If you and your companions do me this service, you shall never want."

After this audience Grandval set out on his journey. He had not the faintest suspicion that he had been betrayed both by the accomplice who accompanied him and by the accomplice whom he was going to meet. Dumont and Leefdale were not enthusiasts. They cared nothing for the restoration of James, the grandeur of Lewis, or the ascendency of the Church of Rome. It was plain to every man of common sense that, whether the design succeeded or failed, the reward of the assassins would probably be to be disowned, with affected abhorrence, by the Courts of Versailles and Saint Germains, and to be torn with redhot pincers, smeared with melted lead, and dismembered by horses. To vulgar natures the prospect of such a martyrdom was not alluring. Both these men, therefore, had, almost at the same time, though, as far as appears, without any concert, conveyed to William, through different channels, warnings that his life was in danger. Dumont had acknowledged every thing to the Duke of Zell, one of the Confederate Princes. Leefdale had transmitted full intelligence through his relations who resided in Holland. Meanwhile Morel, a Swiss Protestant of great

* Langhorne, the chief lay agent of the Jesuits in England, always, as he owned to Tillotson, selected tools on this principle. Burnet, i. 230.

learning who was then in France, wrote to inform Burnet that the weak and hotheaded Grandval had been heard to talk boastfully of the event which would soon astonish the world, and had confidently predicted that the Prince of Orange would not live to the end of the next month.

These cautions were not neglected. From the moment at which Grandval entered the Netherlands, his steps were among snares. His movements were watched : his words were noted : he was arrested, examined, confronted with his accomplices, and sent to the camp of the allies. About a week after the battle of Steinkirk he was brought before a Court Martial. Ginkell, who had been rewarded for his great services in Ireland with the title of Earl of Athlone, presided ; and Talmash was among the judges. Mackay and Lanier had been named members of the board : but they were no more ; and their places were filled by younger officers.

The duty of the Court Martial was very simple : for the prisoner attempted no defence. His conscience had, it should seem, been suddenly awakened. He admitted, with expressions of remorse, the truth of all the charges, made a minute, and apparently an ingenuous confession, and owned that he had deserved death. He was sentenced to be hanged, drawn, and quartered, and underwent his punishment with great fortitude and with a show of piety. He left behind him a few lines, in which he declared that he was about to lose his life for having too faithfully obeyed the injunctions of Barbesieux.

His confession was immediately published in several languages, and was read with very various and very strong emotions. That it was genuine could not be doubted : for it was warranted by the signatures of some of the most distinguished military men living. That it was prompted by the hope of pardon could hardly be supposed : for William had taken pains to discourage that hope. Still less could it be supposed that the prisoner had uttered untruths in order to avoid the torture. For, though it was the universal practice in the Netherlands to put convicted assassins to the rack in order to wring out from them the names of their employers and associates, William had given orders that, on this occasion, the rack should not be used or even named. It should be added, that the Court did not interrogate the prisoner closely, but suffered him to tell his story in his own way. It is therefore reasonable to believe that his narrative is substantially true ; and no part of it has a stronger air of truth than his account of the audience with which James had honoured him at Saint Germains.

In our island the sensation produced by the news was great. The Whigs loudly called both James and Lewis assassins. How, it was asked, was it possible, without outraging common sense, to put an innocent meaning on the words which Grandval declared that he had heard from the lips of the banished King of England? And who that knew the Court of Versailles would believe that Barbesieux, a youth, a mere novice in politics, and rather a clerk than a minister, would have dared to do what he had done without taking his master's pleasure? Very charitable and very ignorant persons might perhaps indulge a hope that Lewis had not been an accessory before the fact. But that he was an accessory after the fact no human being could doubt. He must have seen the proceedings of the Court Martial, the evidence, the confession. If he really abhorred assassination as honest men abhor it, would not Barbesieux have been driven with ignominy from the Royal presence, and flung into the Bastille? Yet Barbesieux was still at the War Office; and it was not pretended that he had been punished even by a word or a frown. It was plain, then, that both kings were partakers in the guilt of Grandval. And if it were asked how two princes who made a high profession of religion could have fallen into such wickedness, the answer was that they had learned their religion from the Jesuits. In reply to these reproaches the English Jacobites said very little: and the French Government said nothing at all.*

The campaign in the Netherlands ended without any other event deserving to be recorded. On the eighteenth of October William arrived in England. Late in the evening of the twentieth he reached Kensington, having traversed the whole length of the capital. His reception was cordial: the crowd was great: the acclamations were loud: and all the windows along his route, from Aldgate to Piccadilly, were lighted up.†

But, notwithstanding these favourable symptoms, the nation

Return of William to England.

---

* I have taken the history of Grandval's plot chiefly from Grandval's own confession. I have not mentioned Madame de Maintenon, because Grandval, in his confession, did not mention her. The accusation brought against her rests solely on the authority of Dumont. See also a True account of the horrid Conspiracy against the Life of His most Sacred Majesty William III. 1692; Reflections upon the late horrid Conspiracy contrived by some of the French Court to murder His Majesty in Flanders, 1692; Burnet, ii. 92.; Vernon's Letters from the camp to Colt, published by Tindal; the London Gazette, Aug. 11. The Paris Gazette contains not one word on the subject,—a most significant silence.

† London Gazette, Oct. 20. 24. 1692.

was disappointed and discontented. The war had been unsuccessful by land. By sea a great advantage had been
gained, but had not been improved. The general expectation had been that the victory of May would be followed by a
descent on the coast of France, that Saint Maloes would be
bombarded, that the last remains of Tourville's squadron
would be destroyed, and that the arsenals of Brest and Rochefort would be laid in ruins. This expectation was, no doubt,
unreasonable. It did not follow, because Rooke and his seamen had silenced the batteries hastily thrown up by Bellefonds,
that it would be safe to expose ships to the fire of regular
fortresses. The government, however, was not less sanguine
than the nation. Great preparations were made. The allied
fleet, having been speedily refitted at Portsmouth, stood out
again to sea. Rooke was sent to examine the soundings and
the currents along the shore of Britanny.* Transports were
collected at Saint Helen's. Fourteen thousand troops were
assembled at Portsdown under the command of Meinhart
Schomberg, who had been rewarded for his father's services
and his own with the highest rank in the Irish peerage, and
was now Duke of Leinster. Under him were Ruvigny, who,
for his good service at Aghrim, had been created Earl of Galway, La Melloniere and Cambon with their gallant bands of
refugees, and Argyle with the regiment which bore his name,
and which, as it began to be faintly rumoured, had last winter done something strange and horrible in a wild country of
rocks and snow, never yet explored by any Englishman.

On the twenty-sixth of July the troops were all on board.
The transports sailed and in a few hours joined the naval
armament in the neighbourhood of Portland. On the twenty-
eighth a general council of war was held. All the naval commanders, with Russell at their head, declared that it would be
madness to carry their ships within the range of the guns of
Saint Maloes, and that the town must be reduced to straits by
land before the men of war in the harbour could, with any
chance of success, be attacked from the sea. The military men
declared with equal unanimity that the land forces could effect
nothing against the town without the cooperation of the fleet.
It was then considered whether it would be advisable to make
an attempt on Brest or Rochefort. Russell and the other flag
officers, among whom were Rooke, Shovel, Van Almonde, and
Evertsen, pronounced that the summer was too far spent for

* See his report in Burchett.

either enterprise.* We must suppose that an opinion in which so many distinguished admirals, both English and Dutch, concurred, however strange it may seem to us, was in conformity with what were then the established principles of the art of maritime war. But why all these questions could not have been fully discussed a week earlier, why fourteen thousand troops should have been shipped and sent to sea, before it had been considered what they were to do, or whether it would be possible for them to do anything, we may reasonably wonder. The armament returned to Saint Helen's, to the astonishment and disgust of the whole nation.† The ministers blamed the commanders : the commanders blamed the ministers. The reproaches exchanged between Nottingham and Russell were loud and angry. Nottingham, upright, industrious, versed in civil business, and eloquent in parliamentary debate, was deficient in the qualities of a war minister, and was not at all aware of his deficiencies. Between him and the whole body of professional sailors there was a feud of long standing. He had, some time before the Revolution, been a Lord of the Admiralty ; and his own opinion was that he had then acquired a profound knowledge of maritime affairs. This opinion however he had very much to himself. Men who had passed half their lives on the waves, and who had been in battles, storms, and shipwrecks, were impatient of his somewhat pompous lectures and reprimands, and pronounced him a mere pedant, who, with all his book learning, was ignorant of what every cabin boy knew. Russell had always been froward, arrogant, and mutinous ; and now prosperity and glory brought out his vices in full strength. With the government which he had saved he took all the liberties of an insolent servant who believes himself to be necessary, treated the orders of his superiors with contemptuous levity, resented reproof, however gentle, as an outrage, furnished no plan of his own, and showed a sullen determination to execute no plan furnished by anybody else. To Nottingham he had a strong and very natural antipathy. They were indeed an ill matched pair. Nottingham was a Tory : Russell was a Whig. Nottingham was a speculative seaman, confident in his theories : Russell was a practical seaman, proud of his achievements. The strength of Nottingham lay in speech :

* London Gazette, July 28. 1692. See the resolutions of the Council of War in Burchett. In a letter to Nottingham, dated July 10., Russell says, "Six weeks will near conclude what we call summer." Lords' Journals, Dec. 19. 1692.

† Monthly Mercury, Aug. and Sept. 1692.

the strength of Russell lay in action. Nottingham's demeanour was decorous even to formality: Russell was passionate and rude. Lastly, Nottingham was an honest man; and Russell was a villain. They now became mortal enemies. The Admiral sneered at the Secretary's ignorance of naval affairs: the Secretary accused the Admiral of sacrificing the public interests to mere wayward humour; and both were in the right.[*]

While they were wrangling, the merchants of all the ports in the kingdom were clamouring against the naval administration. The victory of which the nation was so proud was, in the City, pronounced to have been a positive disaster. During some months before the battle all the maritime strength of the enemy had been collected in two great masses, one in the Mediterranean and one in the Atlantic. There had consequently been little privateering; and the voyage to New England or Jamaica had been almost as safe as in time of peace. Since the battle, the remains of the force which had lately been collected under Tourville were dispersed over the ocean. Even the passage from England to Ireland was insecure. Every week it was announced that twenty, thirty, fifty vessels belonging to London or Bristol had been taken by the French. More than a hundred prizes were carried during that autumn into Saint Maloes alone. It would have been far better, in the opinion of the shipowners and of the underwriters, that the Royal Sun had still been afloat with her thousand fighting men on board than that she should be lying a heap of ashes on the beach at Cherburg, while her crew, distributed among twenty brigantines, prowled for booty over the sea between Cape Finisterre and Cape Clear.[*]

The privateers of Dunkirk had long been celebrated; and among them, John Bart, humbly born, and scarcely able to sign his name, but eminently brave and active, had attained an undisputed preeminence. In the country of Anson and Hawke, of Howe and Rodney, of Duncan, Saint Vincent, and Nelson, the name of the most daring and skilful corsair would have little chance of being remembered. But France, among whose many unquestioned titles to glory very few are derived from naval war, still ranks Bart among her great

* Evelyn's Diary, July 25. 1692; Burnet, ii. 94, 95., and Lord Dartmouth's Note. The history of the quarrel between Russell and Nottingham will be best learned from the Parliamentary Journals and Debates of the Session of 169⅔.

† Commons' Journals, Nov. 19. 1692; Burnet, ii. 95.; Grey's Debates, Nov. 21. 1692; Paris Gazettes of August and September; Narcissus Luttrell's Diary

men. In the autumn of 1692 this enterprising freebooter was the terror of all the English and Dutch merchants who traded with the Baltic. He took and destroyed vessels close to the eastern coast of our island. He even ventured to land in Northumberland, and burned many houses before the trainbands could be collected to oppose him. The prizes which he carried back into his native port were estimated at about a hundred thousand pounds sterling.* About the same time a younger adventurer, destined to equal or surpass Bart, Du Guay Trouin, was entrusted with the command of a small armed vessel. The intrepid boy,—for he was not yet twenty years old, — entered the estuary of the Shannon, sacked a mansion in the county of Clare, and did not reimbark till a detachment from the garrison of Limerick marched against him.†

While our trade was interrupted and our shores menaced by these rovers, some calamities which no human prudence could have averted increased the public ill humour. An earthquake of terrible violence laid waste in less than three minutes the flourishing colony of Jamaica. Whole plantations changed their place. Whole villages were swallowed up. Port Royal, the fairest and wealthiest city which the English had yet built in the New World, renowned for its quays, for its warehouses, and for its stately streets, which were said to rival Cheapside, was turned into a mass of ruins. Fifteen hundred of the inhabitants were buried under their own dwellings. The effect of this disaster was severely felt by many of the great mercantile houses of London and Bristol.‡

Earthquake at Port Royal.

A still heavier calamity was the failure of the harvest. The summer had been wet all over Western Europe. Those heavy rains which had impeded the exertions of the French pioneers in the trenches of Namur had been fatal to the crops. Old men remembered no such year since 1648. No fruit ripened. The price of the quarter of wheat doubled. The evil was aggravated by the state of our silver coin, which had been clipped to such an extent that the words pound and shilling had ceased to have a fixed meaning. Compared with France indeed England might well be esteemed prosperous. Here the public burdens were heavy: there they were crush-

Distress in England.

---

* See Bart's Letters of Nobility, and the Paris Gazettes of the autumn of 1692.

† Mémoires de Du Guay Trouin.

‡ London Gazette, Aug. 11. 1692; Evelyn's Diary, Aug. 10.; Monthly Mercury for September; A Full Account of the late dreadful Earthquake at Port Royal in Jamaica, licensed Sept. 9. 1692.

ing. Here the labouring man was forced to husband his
coarse barley loaf: but there it not seldom happened that
the wretched peasant was found dead on the earth with half-
chewed grass in his mouth. Our ancestors found some consolation in thinking that they were gradually wearing out the
strength of their formidable enemy, and that his resources
were likely to be drained sooner than theirs. Still there was
much suffering and much repining. In some counties mobs
attacked the granaries. The necessity of retrenchment was
felt by families of every rank. An idle man of wit and pleasure, who little thought that his buffoonery would ever be
cited to illustrate the history of his times, complained that,
in this year, wine ceased to be put on many hospitable tables
where he had been accustomed to see it, and that its place
was supplied by punch.*

Increase of
crime.
A symptom of public distress much more alarming than
the substitution of brandy and lemons for claret was the
increase of crime. During the autumn of 1692 and the following winter, the capital was kept in constant terror by
housebreakers. One gang, thirteen strong, entered the
mansion of the Duke of Ormond in Saint James's Square,
and all but succeeded in carrying off his magnificent plate
and jewels. Another gang made an attempt on Lambeth
Palace.† When stately abodes, guarded by numerous servants, were in such danger, it may easily be believed that no
shopkeeper's till or stock could be safe. From Bow to Hyde
Park, from Thames Street to Bloomsbury, there was no
parish in which some quiet dwelling had not been sacked
by burglars.‡ Meanwhile the great roads were made almost
impassable by freebooters who formed themselves into troops
larger than had before been known. There was a sworn fra-
ternity of twenty footpads which met at an alehouse in Southwark.§ But the most formidable band of plunderers consisted
of two and twenty horsemen.‖ It should seem that, at this
time, a journey of fifty miles through the wealthiest and
most populous shires of England was as dangerous as a pil-
grimage across the deserts of Arabia. The Oxford stage coach
was pillaged in broad day after a bloody fight.¶ A waggon

* Evelyn's Diary, June 25., Oct. 1.
1690; Narcissus Luttrell's Diary, June
1692, May 1693; Monthly Mercury,
April, May, and June, 1693; Tom
Brown's Description of a Country Life,
1692.

† Narcissus Luttrell's Diary, Nov.

1692.

‡ See, for example, the London Gazette of Jan. 12. 169¾.

§ Narcissus Luttrell's Diary, Dec.
1692.

‖ Ibid. Jan. 1693.

¶ Ibid. July 1692.

laden with fifteen thousand pounds of public money was stopped and ransacked. As this operation took some time, all the travellers who came to the spot while the thieves were busy were seized and guarded. When the booty had been secured, the prisoners were suffered to depart on foot, but their horses, sixteen or eighteen in number, were shot or hamstringed, to prevent pursuit.* The Portsmouth mail was robbed twice in one week by men well armed and mounted.† Some jovial Essex squires, while riding after a hare, were themselves chased and run down by nine hunters of a different sort, and were heartily glad to find themselves at home again, though with empty pockets.‡

The friends of the government asserted that the marauders were all Jacobites; and indeed there were some appearances which gave colour to the assertion. For example, fifteen butchers, going on a market day to buy beasts at Thame, were stopped by a large gang, and compelled first to deliver their moneybags, and then to drink King James's health in brandy.§ The thieves, however, to do them justice, showed, in the exercise of their calling, no decided preference for any political party. Some of them fell in with Marlborough near Saint Albans, and, notwithstanding his known hostility to the Court and his recent imprisonment, compelled him to deliver up five hundred guineas, which he doubtless never ceased to regret to the last moment of his long career of prosperity and glory.‖

When William, on his return from the Continent, learned to what an extent these outrages had been carried, he expressed great indignation, and announced his resolution to put down the malefactors with a strong hand. A veteran robber was induced to turn informer, and to lay before the King a list of the chief highwaymen, and a full account of their habits and of their favourite haunts. It was said that this list contained not less than eighty names.¶ Strong parties of cavalry were sent out to protect the roads; and this precaution, which would, in ordinary circumstances, have caused much murmuring, seems to have been generally approved. A fine regiment, now called the Second Dragoon Guards,

---

* Evelyn's Diary, Nov. 20. 1692; Narcissus Luttrell's Diary; London Gazette, Nov. 24.; Hop to the Greffier of the States General, Nov. $\frac{13}{23}$.

† London Gazette, Dec. 19. 1692.

‡ Narcissus Luttrell's Diary, Dec. 1692.

§ Ibid. Nov. 1692.

‖ Ibid. August, 1692.

¶ Hop to the Greffier of the States General, $\frac{\text{Dec. 23.}}{\text{Jan. 2.}}$ 169$\frac{2}{3}$. The Dutch despatches of this year are filled with stories of robberies.

which had distinguished itself by activity and success in the
irregular war against the Irish Rapparees, was selected to
guard several of the great avenues of the capital. Blackheath, Barnet, Hounslow, became places of arms.* In a
few weeks the roads were as safe as usual. The executions
were numerous: for, till the evil had been suppressed, the
King resolutely refused to listen to any solicitations for
mercy.† Among those who suffered was James Whitney,
the most celebrated captain of banditti in the kingdom. He
had been, during some months, the terror of all who travelled
from London either northward or westward, and was at
length with difficulty secured after a desperate conflict in
which one soldier was killed and several wounded.‡ The
London Gazette announced that the famous highwayman had
been taken, and invited all persons who had been robbed by
him to repair to Newgate and to see whether they could
identify him. To identify him should have been easy; for
he had a wound in the face, and had lost a thumb.§ He,
however, in the hope of perplexing the witnesses for the
Crown, expended a hundred pounds in procuring a sumptuous embroidered suit against the day of trial. This ingenious
device was frustrated by his hardhearted keepers. He was
put to the bar in his ordinary clothes, convicted, and sentenced to death.‖ He had previously tried to ransom
himself by offering to raise a fine troop of cavalry, all highwaymen, for service in Flanders: but his offer had been
rejected.¶ He had one resource still left. He declared that
he was privy to a treasonable plot. Some Jacobite lords had
promised him immense rewards if he would, at the head of
his gang, fall upon the King at a stag hunt in Windsor
Forest. There was nothing intrinsically improbable in Whitney's story. Indeed a design very similar to that which he
imputed to the malecontents was, only three years later,
actually formed by some of them, and was all but carried
into execution. But it was far better that a few bad men
should go unpunished than that all honest men should live
in fear of being falsely accused by felons sentenced to the
gallows. Chief Justice Holt advised the King to let the law
take its course. William, never much inclined to give credit

* Hop, $\frac{Dec. 23.}{Jan. 2.}$ 169$\frac{2}{3}$; Historical Records of the Queen's Bays, published by
authority; Narcissus Luttrell's Diary,
Nov. 15.

† Narcissus Luttrell's Diary, Dec. 22.

‡ Ibid. Dec. 1692 ; Hop. Jan. $\frac{3}{13}$.

Hop calls Whitney, "den befaamsten
roover in Engelandt."

§ London Gazette, January 2. 169$\frac{2}{3}$.

‖ Narcissus Lutttell's Diary, Jan.
169$\frac{2}{3}$.

¶ Ibid. Dec. 1692.

to stories about conspiracies, assented. The Captain, as he was called, was hanged in Smithfield, and made a most penitent end.*

Meanwhile, in the midst of discontent, distress, and disorder, had begun a session of Parliament singularly eventful, a session from which dates a new era in the history of English finance, a session in which some grave constitutional questions, not yet entirely set at rest, were for the first time debated.

It is much to be lamented that any account of this session which can be framed out of the scanty and dispersed materials now accessible must leave many things obscure. The relations of the parliamentary factions were, during this year, in a singularly complicated state. Each of the two Houses was divided and subdivided by several lines. To omit minor distinctions, there was the great line which separated the Whig party from the Tory party; and there was the great line which separated the official men and their friends and dependents, who were sometimes called the Court party, from those who were sometimes nicknamed the Grumbletonians and sometimes honoured with the appellation of the Country party. And these two great lines were intersecting lines. For of the servants of the Crown and of their adherents about one half were Whigs and one half Tories. It is also to be remembered that there was, quite distinct from the feud between Whigs and Tories, quite distinct also from the feud between those who were in and those who were out, a feud between the Lords as Lords and the Commons as Commons. The spirit both of the hereditary and of the elective chamber had been thoroughly roused in the preceding session by the dispute about the Court of the Lord High Steward; and they met in a pugnacious mood.

The speech which the King made at the opening of the session was skilfully framed for the purpose of conciliating the Houses. He came, he told them, to ask for their advice and assistance. He congratulated them on the victory of La Hogue. He acknowledged with much concern that the operations of the allies had been less successful by land than by sea; but he warmly declared that, both by land and by sea, the valour of his English subjects had been preeminently conspicuous. The distress of his people, he said, was his

Meeting of Parliament.

State of parties,

The King's speech.

* Narcissus Luttrell's Diary, January and February; Hop, $\frac{\text{Jan. 31.}}{\text{Feb. 10.}}$ and Feb. $\frac{3}{13}$. 1693; Letter to Secretary Trenchard, 1694; New Court Contrivances, or More Sham Plots still, 1693.

own : his interest was inseparable from theirs : it was painful to him to call on them to make sacrifices : but from sacrifices which were necessary to the safety of the English nation and of the Protestant religion no good Englishman and no good Protestant would shrink.*

Question of privilege raised by the Lords.

The Commons thanked the King in cordial terms for his gracious speech.† But the Lords were in a bad humour. Two of their body, Marlborough and Huntingdon, had, during the recess, when an invasion and an insurrection were hourly expected, been sent to the Tower, and were still under recognisances. Had a country gentleman or a merchant been taken up and held to bail on even slighter grounds at so alarming a crisis, the Lords would assuredly not have interfered. But they were easily moved to anger by anything that looked like an indignity offered to their own order. They not only crossexamined with great severity Aaron Smith, the Solicitor of the Treasury, whose character, to say the truth, entitled him to little indulgence, but passed, by thirty-five votes to twenty-eight, a resolution implying a censure on the Judges of the King's Bench, men certainly not inferior in probity, and very far superior in legal learning, to any peer of the realm. The King thought it prudent to soothe the wounded pride of the nobility by ordering the recognisances to be cancelled ; and with this concession the House was satisfied, to the great vexation of the Jacobites, who had hoped that the quarrel would be prosecuted to some fatal issue, and who, finding themselves disappointed, vented their spleen by railing at the tameness of the degenerate barons of England.‡

Debates on the state of the nation.

Both Houses held long and earnest deliberations on the state of the nation. The King, when he requested their advice, had, perhaps, not foreseen that his words would be construed into an invitation to scrutinise every part of the administration, and to offer suggestions touching matters which parliaments have generally thought it expedient to leave entirely to the Crown. Some of the discontented peers proposed that a Committee, chosen partly by the Lords and partly by the Commons, should be authorised to enquire into the whole management of public affairs. But it was generally apprehended that such a Committee would become a second

* Lords' and Commons' Journals, Nov. 4., Jan. 1692.

† Commons' Journals, Nov. 10. 1692.

‡ See the Lords' Journals from Nov. to Nov. 18. 1692 ; Burnet, ii. 102.

Tindal's account of these proceedings was taken from letters addressed by Warre, Under Secretary of State, to Colt, Envoy at Hanover. Letter to Mr. Secretary Trenchard, 1694.

and more powerful Privy Council, independent of the Crown, and unknown to the constitution. The motion was therefore rejected by forty-eight votes to thirty-six. On this occasion the ministers, with scarcely an exception, voted in the majority. A protest was signed by eighteen of the minority, among whom were the bitterest Whigs and the bitterest Tories in the whole peerage.*

The Houses enquired, each for itself, into the causes of the public calamities. The Commons resolved themselves into a Grand Committee to consider of the advice to be given to the King. From the concise abstracts and fragments which have come down to us it seems that, in this Committee, which continued to sit many days, the debates wandered over a vast space. One member spoke of the prevalence of highway robbery: another deplored the quarrel between the Queen and the Princess, and proposed that two or three gentlemen should be deputed to wait on Her Majesty and try to make matters up. A third described the machinations of the Jacobites in the preceding spring. It was notorious, he said, that preparations had been made for a rising, and that arms and horses had been collected; yet not a single traitor had been brought to justice.†

The events of the war by land and sea furnished matter for several earnest debates. Many members complained of the preference given to aliens over Englishmen. The whole battle of Steinkirk was fought over again; and severe reflections were thrown on Solmes. "Let English soldiers be commanded by none but English generals," was the almost universal cry. Seymour, who had once been distinguished by his hatred of foreigners, but who, since he had been at the Board of Treasury, had reconsidered his opinions, asked where English generals were to be found. "I have no love for foreigners as foreigners: but we have no choice. Men are not born generals: nay, a man may be a very valuable captain or major, and not be equal to the conduct of an army. Nothing but experience will form great commanders: very few of our countrymen have that experience; and therefore we must for the present employ strangers." Lowther followed on the same side. "We have had a long peace; and the consequence is that we have not a sufficient supply of officers fit for high commands. The parks and the camp at Hounslow were very poor military schools, when compared with

<hr/>

* Lords' Journals, Dec. 7.; Tindal,   † Grey's Debates, Nov. 21. and **23.** from the Colt Papers; Burnet, ii. 105.   1692.

the fields of battle and the lines of contravallation in which
the great commanders of the continental nations have learned
their art." In reply to these arguments an orator on the other
side was so absurd as to declare that he could point out ten
Englishmen who, if they were in the French service, would
be made Marshals. Four or five colonels who had been at
Steinkirk took part in the debate. It was said of them that
they showed as much modesty in speech as they had shown
courage in action; and, from the very imperfect report which
has come down to us, the compliment seems to have been not
undeserved. They did not join in the vulgar cry against the
Dutch. They spoke well of the foreign officers generally,
and did full justice to the valour and conduct with which
Auverquerque had rescued the shattered remains of Mackay's
division from what seemed certain destruction. But in defence of Solmes not a word was said. His severity, his
haughty manners, and, above all, the indifference with which
he had looked on while the English, borne down by overwhelming numbers, were fighting hand to hand with the
French household troops, had made him so odious that many
members were prepared to vote for an address requesting
that he might be removed, and that his place might be filled
by Talmash, who, since the disgrace of Marlborough, was
universally allowed to be the best officer in the army. But
Talmash's friends judiciously interfered. "I have," said one
of them, "a true regard for that gentleman; and I implore
you not to do him an injury under the notion of doing him
a kindness. Consider that you are usurping what is peculiarly the King's prerogative. You are turning officers out
and putting officers in." The debate ended without any vote
of censure on Solmes. But a hope was expressed, in language not very parliamentry, that what had been said in the
Committee would be reported to the King, and that His
Majesty would not disregard the general wish of the representatives of his people.[*]

The Commons next proceeded to enquire into the naval
administration, and very soon came to a quarrel with the
Lords on that subject. That there had been mismanagement
somewhere was but too evident. It was hardly possible to
acquit both Russell and Nottingham; and each House stood
by its own member. The Commons had, at the opening of
the session, unanimously passed a vote of thanks to Russell
for his conduct at La Hogue. They now, in the Grand Com-

[*] Grey's Debates, Nov. 21. 1692; Colt Papers in Tindal.

mittee of Advice, took into consideration the miscarriages which had followed the battle. A motion was made so vaguely worded that it could hardly be said to mean any thing. It was understood however to imply a censure on Nottingham, and was therefore strongly opposed by his friends. On the division the Ayes were a hundred and sixty-five, the Noes a hundred and sixty-four.*

On the very next day Nottingham appealed to the Lords. He told his story with all the skill of a practised orator, and with all the authority which belongs to unblemished integrity. He then laid on the table a great mass of papers, which he requested the House to read and consider. The Peers seem to have examined the papers seriously and diligently. The result of the examination was by no means favourable to Russell. Yet it was thought unjust to condemn him unheard; and it was difficult to devise any way in which their Lordships could hear him. At last it was resolved to send the papers down to the Commons with a message which imported that, in the opinion of the Upper House, there was a case against the Admiral which he ought to be called upon to answer. With the papers was sent an abstract of the contents.†

The message was not very respectfully received. Russell had, at that moment, a popularity which he little deserved, but which will not seem strange to us when we remember that the public knew nothing of his treasons, and knew that he was the only living Englishman who had won a great battle. The abstract of the papers was read by the clerk. Russell then spoke with great applause; and his friends pressed for an immediate decision. Sir Christopher Musgrave very justly observed that it was impossible to pronounce judgment on such a pile of despatches without perusing them: but this objection was overruled. The Whigs regarded the accused member as one of themselves: many of the Tories were dazzled by the splendour of his recent victory; and neither Whigs nor Tories were disposed to show any deference for the authority of the Peers. The House, without reading the papers, passed an unanimous resolution expressing warm approbation of Russell's whole conduct. The temper of the assembly was such that some ardent Whigs thought that they might now venture to propose a vote of censure on Nottingham by name. But the attempt failed. " I am ready,"

* Tindal, Colt Papers; Commons' Journals, Jan. 11. 169⅔.
† Colt Papers in Tindal: Lords' Journals from Dec. 6. to Dec. 19. 1692, inclusive.

said Lowther,—and he doubtless expressed what many felt, —"I am ready to support any motion that may do honour to the Admiral : but I cannot join in an attack on the Secretary of State. For, to my knowledge, their Majesties have no more zealous, laborious, or faithful servant than my Lord Nottingham." Finch exerted all his mellifluous eloquence in defence of his brother, and contrived, without directly opposing himself to the prevailing sentiment, to insinuate that Russell's conduct had not been faultless. The vote of censure on Nottingham was not pressed. But the vote which pronounced Russell's conduct to have been deserving of all praise was communicated to the Lords ; and the papers which they sent down were very unceremoniously returned.* The Lords, much offended, demanded a free conference. It was granted ; and the managers of the two Houses met in the Painted Chamber. Rochester, in the name of his brethren, expressed a wish to be informed of the grounds on which the Admiral had been declared faultless. To this appeal the gentlemen who stood on the other side of the table answered only that they had not been authorised to give any explanation, but that they would report to those who had sent them what had been said.†

By this time the Commons were thoroughly tired of the enquiry into the conduct of the war. The members had got rid of much of the ill humour which they had brought up with them from their country seats by the simple process of talking it away. Burnet hints that those arts of which Caermarthen and Trevor were the great masters were employed for the purpose of averting votes which would have seriously embarrassed the government. But, though it is not improbable that a few noisy pretenders to patriotism may have been quieted with bags of guineas, it would be absurd to suppose that the House generally was influenced in this manner. Whoever has seen anything of such assemblies knows that the spirit with which they enter on long enquiries very soon flags, and that their resentment, if not kept alive by injudicious opposition, cools fast. In a short time every body was sick of the Grand Committee of Advice. The debates had been tedious and desultory. The resolutions which had been carried were for the most part merely childish. The King was to be humbly advised to employ men of ability

---

* As to the proceedings of this day in the House of Commons, see the Journals, Dec. 20., and the letter of Robert Wilmot, M.P. for Derby, to his colleague Anchitel Grey, in Grey's Debates.

† Commons' Journals, Jan. 4. 169⅔.

and integrity. He was to be humbly advised to employ men
who would stand by him against James. The patience of
the House was wearied out by long discussions ending in the
pompous promulgation of truisms like these. At last the
explosion came. One of the grumblers called the attention
of the Grand Committee to the alarming fact that two
Dutchmen were employed in the Ordnance department, and
moved that the King should be requested to dismiss them.
The motion was received with disdainful mockery. It was
remarked that the military men especially were loud in the
expression of contempt. "Do we seriously think of going to
the King and telling him that, as he has condescended to ask
our advice at this momentous crisis, we humbly advise him
to turn a Dutch storekeeper out of the Tower? Really, if
we have no more important suggestion to carry up to the
throne, we may as well go to our dinners." The members
generally were of the same mind. The chairman was voted
out of the chair, and was not directed to ask leave to sit
again. The Grand Committee ceased to exist. The resolutions which it had passed were formally reported to the
House. One of them was rejected : the others were suffered
to drop ; and the Commons, after considering during several
weeks what advice they should give to the King, ended by
giving him no advice at all.*

The temper of the Lords was different. From many circumstances it appears that there was no place where the
Dutch were, at this time, so much hated as in the Upper
House. The dislike with which an Englishman of the middle
class regarded the King's foreign friends was merely national.
The preferment which they had obtained was preferment
which he would have had no chance of obtaining if they had
never existed. But to an English peer they were objects of
personal jealousy. They stood between him and Majesty.
They intercepted from him the rays of royal favour. The
preference given to them wounded him both in his interests
and in his pride. His chance of a Garter or of a troop of
Life Guards was much smaller since they had become his
competitors. He might have been Master of the Horse but
for Auverquerque, Master of the Robes but for Zulestein,
Groom of the Stole but for Bentinck.† The ill humour of the

* Colt Papers in Tindal; Commons'
Journals, Dec. 16. 1692, Jan. 11. 169$\frac{2}{3}$;
Burnet, ii. 104.

† The peculiar antipathy of the English nobles to the Dutch favourites is
mentioned in a highly interesting note
written by Renaudot in 1698, and preserved among the archives of the French
Foreign Office.

aristocracy was inflamed by Marlborough, who, at this time, affected the character of a patriot persecuted for standing up against the Dutch in defence of the interests of his native land, and who did not foresee that a day would come when he would be accused of sacrificing the interests of his native land to gratify the Dutch. The Peers determined to present an address requesting William not to place his English troops under the command of a foreign general. They took up very seriously that question which had moved the House of Commons to laughter, and solemnly counselled their Sovereign not to employ foreigners in his magazines. At Marlborough's suggestion they urged the King to insist that the youngest English general should take precedence of the oldest general in the service of the States General. It was, they said, derogatory to the dignity of the Crown, that an officer who held a commission from His Majesty should ever be commanded by an officer who held a similar commission from a republic. To this advice, evidently dictated by an ignoble malevolence to Holland, William, who troubled himself little about votes of the Upper House which were not backed by the Lower, returned, as might have been expected, a very short and dry answer.*

Bill for the Regulation of Trials in cases of Treason.

While the enquiry into the conduct of the war was pending, the Commons resumed the consideration of an important subject which had occupied much of their attention in the preceding year. The Bill for the Regulation of Trials in cases of High Treason was again brought in, but was strongly opposed by the official men, both Whigs and Tories. Somers, now Attorney General, strongly recommended delay. That the law, as it stood, was open to grave objections, was not denied : but it was contended that the proposed reform would, at that moment, produce more harm than good. Nobody would assert that, under the existing government, the lives of innocent subjects were in any danger. Nobody would deny that the government itself was in great danger. Was it the part of wise men to increase the perils of that which was already in serious peril, for the purpose of giving new security to that which was already perfectly secure ? Those who held this language were twitted with their inconsistency, and asked why they had not ventured to oppose the bill in the preceding session. They answered very plausibly that the events which had taken place during the recess had

* Colt Papers in Tindal; Lords' Journals, Nov. 28. and 29. 1692, Feb. 18. and 24. 169⅔.

taught an important lesson to all who were capable of learning. The country had been threatened at once with invasion and insurrection. No rational man doubted that many traitors had made preparations for joining the French, and had collected arms, ammunition, and horses, for that purpose. Yet, though there was abundant moral evidence against these enemies of their country, it had not been possible to find legal evidence against a single one of them. The law of treason might, in theory, be harsh, and had undoubtedly, in times past, been grossly abused. But a statesman, who troubled himself less about theory than about practice, and less about times past than about the time present, would pronounce that law not too stringent but too lax, and would, while the commonwealth remained in extreme jeopardy, refuse to consent to any further relaxation. In spite of all opposition, however, the principle of the bill was approved by one hundred and seventy-one votes to one hundred and fifty-two. But in the committee it was moved and carried that the new rules of procedure should not come into operation till after the end of the war with France. When the report was brought up the House divided on this amendment, and ratified it by a hundred and forty-five votes to a hundred and twenty-five. The bill was consequently suffered to drop.* Had it gone up to the Peers it would in all probability have been lost after causing another quarrel between the Houses. For the Peers were fully determined that no such bill should pass, unless it contained a clause altering the constitution of the Lord High Steward's Court; and a clause altering the constitution of the Lord High Steward's Court would have been less likely than ever to find favour with the Commons. For in the course of this session an event took place which proved that the great were only too well protected by the law as it stood, and which well deserves to be recorded as a striking illustration of the state of manners and morals in that age.

Of all the actors who were then on the English stage the most graceful was William Mountford. He had every physical qualification for his calling, a noble figure, a handsome face, a melodious voice. It was not easy to say whether he succeeded better in heroic or in ludicrous parts. He was allowed to be both the best Alexander and the best Sir Courtly Nice that ever trod the boards. Queen Mary, whose

Case of Lord Mohun

* Grey's Debates, Nov. 18. 1692; Commons' Journals, Nov. 18., Dec. 1. 1692.

knowledge was very superficial, but who had naturally a quick perception of what was excellent in art, admired him greatly. He was a dramatist as well as a player, and has left us one comedy which is not contemptible.*

The most popular actress of the time was Anne Bracegirdle. There were on the stage many women of more faultless beauty, but none whose features and deportment had such power to fascinate the senses and the hearts of men. The sight of her bright black eyes and of her rich brown cheek sufficed to put the most turbulent audience into good humour. It was said of her that in the crowded theatre she had as many lovers as she had male spectators. Yet no lover, however rich, however high in rank, had prevailed on her to be his mistress. Those who are acquainted with the parts which she was in the habit of playing, and with the epilogues which it was her especial business to recite, will not easily give her credit for any extraordinary measure of virtue or of delicacy. She seems to have been a cold, vain, and interested coquette, who perfectly understood how much the influence of her charms was increased by the fame of a severity which cost her nothing, and who could venture to flirt with a succession of admirers, in the just confidence that no flame which she might kindle in them would thaw her own ice.* Among those who pursued her with an insane desire was a profligate captain in the army named Hill. With Hill was closely bound in a league of debauchery and violence Charles Lord Mohun, a young nobleman whose life was one long revel and brawl. Hill, finding that the beautiful brunette was invincible, took it into his head that he was rejected for a more favoured rival, and that this rival was the brilliant Mountford. The jealous lover swore over his wine at a tavern that he would stab the villain. "And I," said Mohun, "will stand by my friend." From the tavern the pair went, with some soldiers whose services Hill had secured, to Drury Lane, where the lady was to sup. They lay some time in wait for her. As soon as she appeared in the street she was seized and hurried to a coach. She screamed for help. Her mother clung round her: the whole neighbourhood rose; and she was rescued. Hill and Mohun went away vowing vengeance. They swaggered sword in hand during two hours about the streets near Mountford's dwelling. The

* See Cibber's Apology, and Mount-   Works, and indeed the works of every
ford's Greenwich Park.   man of wit and pleasure about town.
    † See Cibber's Apology, Tom Brown's

watch requested them to put up their weapons. But when the young lord announced that he was a peer, and bade the constables touch him if they dared, they let him pass. So strong was privilege then, and so weak was law. Messengers were sent to warn Mountford of his danger: but unhappily they missed him. He came. A short altercation took place between him and Mohun; and, while they were wrangling, Hill ran the unfortunate actor through the body, and fled.

The grand jury of Middlesex, consisting of gentlemen of note, found a bill of murder against Hill and Mohun. Hill escaped. Mohun was taken. His mother threw herself at William's feet, but in vain. "It was a cruel act," said the King: "I shall leave it to the law." The trial came on in the Court of the Lord High Steward: and as Parliament happened to be sitting, the culprit had the advantage of being judged by the whole body of the peerage. There was then no lawyer in the Upper House. It therefore became necessary, for the first time since Buckhurst had pronounced sentence on Essex and Southampton, that a peer who had never made jurisprudence his special study should preside over that grave tribunal. Caermarthen, who, as President of the Council, took precedence of all the nobility, was appointed Lord High Steward. A full report of the proceedings has come down to us. No person, who carefully examines that report, and attends to the opinion unanimously given by the Judges, in answer to a question which Nottingham drew up, and in which the facts established by the evidence are stated with perfect fairness, can doubt that the crime of murder was fully brought home to the prisoner. Such was the opinion of the King who was present during the trial; and such was the almost unanimous opinion of the public. Had the issue been tried by Holt and twelve plain men at the Old Bailey, there can be no doubt that a verdict of Guilty would have been returned. The Peers, however, by sixty-nine votes to fourteen, acquitted their accused brother. One great nobleman was so brutal and stupid as to say, "After all the fellow was but a player; and players are rogues." All the newsletters, all the coffeehouse orators, complained that the blood of the poor was shed with impunity by the great. Wits remarked that the only fair thing about the trial was the show of ladies in the galleries. Letters and journals are still extant in which men of all shades of opinion, Whigs, Tories, Nonjurors, condemn the partiality of the tribunal. It was not to be expected that, while the memory of this scandal was fresh in the public mind, the Commons would be induced to give any new advantage to accused peers.*

The Commons had, in the meantime, resumed the consideration of another highly important matter, the state of the trade with India. They had, towards the close of the preceding session, requested the King to dissolve the old Company and to constitute a new Company on such terms as he should think fit; and he had promised to take their request into his serious consideration. He now sent a messsage to inform them that it was out of his power to do what they had asked. He had referred the charter of the old Company to the Judges, and the Judges had pronounced that, under the provisions of that charter, the old Company could not be dissolved without three years' notice, and must retain during those three years the exclusive privilege of trading to the East Indies. He added that, being sincerely desirous to gratify the Commons, and finding himself unable to do so in the way which they had pointed out, he had tried to prevail on the old Company to agree to a compromise: but that body stood obstinately on its extreme rights; and his endeavours had been frustrated.†

This message reopened the whole question. The two factions which divided the City were instantly on the alert. The debates in the House were long and warm. Petitions against the old Company were laid on the table. Satirical handbills against the new Company were distributed in the lobby. At length, after much discussion, it was resolved to present an address requesting the King to give the notice which the Judges had pronounced necessary. He promised to bear the subject in mind, and to do his best to promote the welfare of the kingdom. With this answer the House was satisfied; and the subject was not again mentioned till the next session.‡

The debates of the Commons on the conduct of the war, on the law of treason, and on the trade with India, occupied much time, and produced no important result. But meanwhile real business was doing in the Committee of Supply

---

* The chief source of information about this case is the report of the trial, which will be found in the Collection of State Trials. See Evelyn's Diary, February 4. 169¾. I have taken some circumstances from Narcissus Luttrell's Diary, from a letter to Sancroft, which is among the Tanner MSS. in the Bodleian Library, and from two letters addressed by Brewer to Wharton, which are also in the Bodleian Library.

† Commons' Journals, Nov. 14. 1692.

‡ Commons' Journals of the Session, particularly of Nov. 17., Dec. 10., Feb. 25., March 3.; Colt Papers in Tindal.

and in the Committee of Ways and Means. In the Committee of Supply the estimates passed rapidly. A few members declared it to be their opinion that England ought to withdraw her troops from the Continent, to carry on the war with vigour by sea, and to keep up only such an army as might be sufficient to repel any invader who might elude the vigilance of her fleets. But this doctrine, which speedily became and long continued to be the badge of one of the great parties in the state, was as yet professed only by a small minority which did not venture to call for a division.*

In the Committee of Ways and Means, it was determined that a great part of the charge of the year should be defrayed by means of an impost, which, though old in substance, was new in form. From a very early period to the middle of the seventeenth century, our Parliaments had provided for the extraordinary necessities of the government chiefly by granting subsidies. A subsidy was raised by an impost on the people of the realm in respect of their reputed estates. Landed property was the chief subject of taxation, and was assessed nominally at four shillings in the pound. But the assessment was made in such a way that it not only did not rise in proportion to the rise in the value of land or to the fall in the value of the precious metals, but went on constantly sinking, till at length the rate was in truth less than twopence in the pound. In the time of Charles the First a real tax of four shillings in the pound on land would probably have yielded near a million and a half: but a subsidy amounted to little more than fifty thousand pounds.† *(margin: Ways and Means: Land Tax.)*

The financiers of the Long Parliament devised a more efficient mode of taxing estates. The sum which was to be raised was fixed. It was then distributed among the counties in proportion to their supposed wealth, and was levied within each county by a rate. The revenue derived from these assessments in the time of the Commonwealth varied from thirty-five thousand pounds to a hundred and twenty thousand pounds a month.

After the Restoration the legislature seemed for a time inclined to revert, in finance as in other things, to the ancient practice. Subsidies were once or twice granted to Charles the Second. But it soon appeared that the old system was

---

* Commons' Journals, Dec. 10. ; Tindal, Colt Papers.

† See Coke's Institutes, part iv. chapter 1. In 1566 a subsidy was 120,000*l.*; in 1598 78.000*l.* when Coke wrote his Institutes, about the end of the reign of James I., 70,000*l.* Clarendon tells us that, in 1640, twelve subsidies were estimated at about 600,000*l.*

much less convenient than the new system. The Cavaliers condescended to take a lesson in the art of taxation from the Roundheads; and, during the interval between the Restoration and the Revolution, extraordinary calls were occasionally met by assessments resembling the assessments of the Commonwealth. After the Revolution, the war with France made it necessary to have recourse annually to this abundant source of revenue. In 1689, in 1690, and in 1691, great sums had been raised on the land. At length, in 1692, it was determined to draw supplies from real property more largely than ever. The Commons resolved that a new and more accurate valuation of estates should be made over the whole realm, and that, on the rental thus ascertained, a pound rate should be paid to the government.

Such was the origin of the existing land tax. The valuation made in 1692 has remained unaltered down to our own time. According to that valuation, one shilling in the pound on the rental of the kingdom amounted, in round numbers, to half a million. During a hundred and six years, a land tax bill was annually presented to Parliament, and was annually passed, though not always without murmurs from the country gentlemen. The rate was, in time of war, four shillings in the pound. In time of peace, before the reign of George the Third, only two or three shillings were usually granted; and, during a short part of the prudent and gentle administration of Walpole, the government asked for only one shilling. But, after the disastrous year in which England drew the sword against her American colonies, the rate was never less than four shillings. At length, in the year 1798, the Parliament relieved itself from the trouble of passing a new Act every spring. The land tax, at four shillings in the pound, was made permanent; and those who were subject to it were permitted to redeem it. A great part has been redeemed; and at present little more than a fiftieth of the ordinary revenue required in time of peace is raised by that impost which was once regarded as the most productive of all the resources of the State.*

The land tax was fixed, for the year 1693, at four shillings in the pound, and consequently brought about two millions into the Treasury. That sum, small as it may seem to a generation which has expended a hundred and twenty millions in twelve months, was such as had never before been raised here in one year by direct taxation. It seemed im-

* See the old Land Tax Acts, and the debates on the Land Tax Redemption Bill of 1798.

mense both to Englishmen and to foreigners. Lewis, who found it almost impossible to wring by cruel exactions from the beggared peasantry of France the means of supporting the greatest army and the most gorgeous court that had existed in Europe since the downfall of the Roman empire, broke out, it is said, into an exclamation of angry surprise when he learned that the Commons of England had, from dread and hatred of his power, unanimously determined to lay on themselves, in a year of scarcity and of commercial embarrassment, a burden such as neither they nor their fathers had ever before borne. " My little cousin of Orange," he said, " seems to be firm in the saddle." He afterwards added, " No matter : the last piece of gold will win." This however was a consideration from which, if he had been well informed about the resources of England, he would not have derived much comfort. Kensington was certainly a mere hovel when compared to his superb Versailles. The display of jewels, plumes, and lace, led horses and gilded coaches, which daily surrounded him, far outshone the splendour which, even on great public occasions, our princes were in the habit of displaying. But the condition of the majority of the people of England was, beyond all doubt, such as the majority of the people of France might well have envied. In truth what was called severe distress here would have been called unexampled prosperity there.

The land tax was not imposed without a quarrel between the Houses. The Commons appointed commissioners to make the assessment. These commissioners were the principal gentlemen of every county, and were named in the bill. The Lords thought this arrangement inconsistent with the dignity of the peerage. They therefore inserted a clause providing that their estates should be valued by twenty of their own order. The Lower House indignantly rejected this amendment, and demanded an instant conference. After some delay, which increased the ill humour of the Commons, the conference took place. The bill was returned to the Peers with a very concise and haughty intimation that they must not presume to alter laws relating to money. A strong party among the Lords was obstinate. Mulgrave spoke at great length, and with great eloquence, against the pretensions of the plebeians. He told his brethren that, if they gave way, they would abdicate that authority which had belonged to the baronage of England ever since the foundation of the monarchy, and that they would have nothing left of their old

greatness except their coronets and ermines. Burnet says
that this speech was the finest that he ever heard in Parliament; and Burnet was undoubtedly a good judge of speaking,
and was neither partial to Mulgrave nor zealous for the
privileges of the aristocracy. The orator, however, though
he charmed his hearers, did not succeed in convincing them.
Most of them shrank from a conflict in which they would
have had against them the Commons united as one man, and
the King, who, in case of necessity, would undoubtedly have
created fifty peers rather than have suffered the land tax bill
to be lost. Two strong protests, however, signed, the first by
twenty-seven, the second by twenty-one dissentients, show
how obstinately many nobles were prepared to contend at all
hazards for the dignity of their caste. Another conference
was held; and Rochester announced that the Lords, for the
sake of the public interest, waived what they must nevertheless assert to be their clear right, and would not insist on
their amendment.* The bill passed, and was followed by
bills for laying additional duties on imports, and for taxing
the dividends of joint stock companies.

Still, however, the estimated revenue was not equal to the
estimated expenditure. The year 1692 had bequeathed a
large deficit to the year 1693; and it seemed probable that
the charge for 1693 would exceed by about five hundred
thousand pounds the charge for 1692. More than two
millions had been voted for the army and ordnance, near two
millions for the navy.† Only eight years before fourteen
hundred thousand pounds had defrayed the whole annual
charge of government. More than four times that sum was
now required. Taxation, both direct and indirect, had been
carried to an unprecedented point: yet the income of the
state still fell short of the outlay by about a million. It was
necessary to devise something. Something was devised,
something of which the effects are felt to this day in every
part of the globe.

There was indeed nothing strange or mysterious in the expedient to which the government had recourse. It was an
expedient familiar, during two centuries, to the financiers of

---

* Lords' Journals, Jan. 16, 17, 18,
19, 20.; Commons' Journals, Jan. 17,
18. 20. 1692; Tindal, from the Colt
Papers; Burnet, ii. 104, 105. Burnet
has used an incorrect expression, which
Tindal, Ralph, and others have copied.
He says that the question was whether
the Lords should tax themselves. The
Lords did not claim any right to alter
the amount of taxation laid on them by
the bill as it came up to them. They
only demanded that their estates should
be valued, not by the ordinary commissioners, but by special commissioners of
higher rank.

† Commons' Journals, Dec. $\frac{2}{12}$. 1692.

the Continent, and could hardly fail to occur to any English statesman who compared the void in the Exchequer with the overflow in the money market.

During the interval between the Restoration and the Revolution the riches of the nation had been rapidly increasing. Thousands of busy men found every Christmas that, after the expenses of the year's housekeeping had been defrayed out of the year's income, a surplus remained; and how that surplus was to be employed was a question of some difficulty. In our time, to invest such a surplus, at something more than three per cent, on the best security that has ever been known in the world, is the work of a few minutes. But, in the seventeenth century, a lawyer, a physician, a retired merchant, who had saved some thousands and who wished to place them safely and profitably, was often greatly embarrassed. Three generations earlier, a man who had accumulated wealth in a trade or a profession generally purchased real property or lent his savings on mortgage. But the number of acres in the kingdom had remained the same; and the value of those acres, though it had greatly increased, had by no means increased so fast as the quantity of capital which was seeking for employment. Many too wished to put their money where they could find it at an hour's notice, and looked about for some species of property which could be more readily transferred than a house or a field. A capitalist might lend on bottomry or on personal security: but, if he did so, he ran a great risk of losing interest and principal. There were a few joint stock companies, among which the East India Company held the foremost place: but the demand for the stock of such companies was far greater than the supply. Indeed the cry for a new East India Company was chiefly raised by persons who had found difficulty in placing their savings at interest on good security. So great was that difficulty that the practice of hoarding was common. We are told that the father of Pope the poet, who retired from business in the City about the time of the Revolution, carried to a retreat in the country a strong box containing near twenty thousand pounds, and took out from time to time what was required for household expenses; and it is highly probable that this was not a solitary case. At present the quantity of coin which is hoarded by private persons is so small that it would, if brought forth, make no perceptible addition to the circulation. But, in the earlier part of the reign of William the Third, all the greatest writers on currency were of opinion that a very considerable

Origin of the national debt.

mass of gold and silver was hidden in secret drawers and behind wainscots.

The natural effect of this state of things was that a crowd of projectors, ingenious and absurd, honest and knavish, employed themselves in devising new schemes for the employment of redundant capital. It was about the year 1688 that the word stockjobber was first heard in London. In the short space of four years a crowd of companies, every one of which confidently held out to subscribers the hope of immense gains, sprang into existence ; the Insurance Company, the Paper Company, the Lutestring Company, the Pearl Fishery Company, the Glass Bottle Company, the Alum Company, the Blythe Coal Company, the Swordblade Company. There was a Tapestry Company, which would soon furnish pretty hangings for all the parlours of the middle class and for all the bedchambers of the higher. There was a Copper Company, which proposed to explore the mines of England, and held out a hope that they would prove not less valuable than those of Potosi. There was a Diving Company, which undertook to bring up precious effects from shipwrecked vessels, and which announced that it had laid in a stock of wonderful machines resembling complete suits of armour. In front of the helmet was a huge glass eye like that of Polyphemus ; and out of the crest went a pipe through which the air was to be admitted. The whole process was exhibited on the Thames. Fine gentlemen and fine ladies were invited to the show, were hospitably regaled, and were delighted by seeing the divers in their panoply descend into the river, and return laden with old iron and ship's tackle. There was a Greenland Fishing Company, which could not fail to drive the Dutch whalers and herring busses out of the Northern Ocean. There was a Tanning Company, which promised to furnish leather superior to the best that was brought from Turkey or Russia. There was a society which undertook the office of giving gentlemen a liberal education on low terms, and which assumed the sounding name of the Royal Academies Company. In a pompous advertisement it was announced that the directors of the Royal Academies Company had engaged the best masters in every branch of knowledge, and were about to issue twenty thousand tickets at twenty shillings each. There was to be a lottery : two thousand prizes were to be drawn ; and the fortunate holders of the prizes were to be taught, at the charge of the Company, Latin, Greek, Hebrew, French, Spanish, conic sections, trigonometry, heraldry, japanning, fortification, book-keeping, and the art of playing the theorbo. Some of these companies took large mansions and printed their advertisements in gilded letters. Others, less ostentatious, were content with ink, and met at coffeehouses in the neighbourhood of the Royal Exchange. Jonathan's and Garraway's were in a constant ferment with brokers, buyers, sellers, meetings of directors, meetings of proprietors. Time bargains soon came into fashion. Extensive combinations were formed, and monstrous fables were circulated, for the purpose of raising or depressing the price of shares. Our country witnessed for the first time those phænomena with which a long experience has made us familiar. A mania of which the symptoms were essentially the same with those of the mania of 1720, of the mania of 1825, of the mania of 1845, seized the public mind. An impatience to be rich, a contempt for those slow but sure gains which are the proper reward of industry, patience, and thrift, spread through society. The spirit of the cogging dicers of Whitefriars took possession of the grave Senators of the City, Wardens of Trades, Deputies, Aldermen. It was much easier and much more lucrative to put forth a lying prospectus announcing a new stock, to persuade ignorant people that the dividends could not fall short of twenty per cent, and to part with five thousand pounds of this imaginary wealth for ten thousand solid guineas, than to load a ship with a well chosen cargo for Virginia or the Levant. Every day some new bubble was puffed into existence, rose buoyant, shone bright, burst, and was forgotten.*

The new form which covetousness had taken furnished the comic poets and satirists with an excellent subject; nor was that subject the less welcome to them because some of the most unscrupulous and most successful of the new race of gamesters were men in sad coloured clothes and lank hair, men who called cards the Devil's books, men who thought it a sin and a scandal to win or lose twopence over a backgammon board. It was in the last drama of Shadwell that the

* For this account of the origin of stockjobbing in the City of London I am chiefly indebted to a most curious periodical paper, entitled, "Collection for the Improvement of Husbandry and Trade, by J. Houghton, F.R.S." It is in fact a weekly history of the commercial speculations of that time. I have looked through the files of several years. In No. 33., March 17. 169$\frac{2}{3}$, Houghton says, "The buying and selling of Actions is one of the great trades now on foot. I find a great many do not understand the affair." On June 13. and June 22. 1694, he traces the whole progress of stockjobbing. On July 13. of the same year he makes the first mention of time bargains. Whoever is desirous to know more about the companies mentioned in the text may consult Houghton's Collection, and a pamphlet entitled Angliæ Tutamen, published in 1695.

hypocrisy and knavery of these speculators was, for the first time, exposed to public ridicule. He died in November 1692, just before his Stockjobbers came on the stage; and the epilogue was spoken by an actor dressed in deep mourning. The best scene is that in which four or five stern Nonconformists, clad in the full Puritan costume, after discussing the prospects of the Mousetrap Company and the Fleakilling Company, examine the question whether the godly may lawfully hold stock in a Company for bringing over Chinese ropedancers. "Considerable men have shares," says one unstere person in cropped hair and bands; "but verily I question whether it be lawful or not." These doubts are removed by a stout old Roundhead colonel who had fought at Marston Moor, and who reminds his weaker brother that the saints need not themselves see the ropedancing, and that, in all probability, there will be no ropedancing to see. "The thing," he says, "is like to take. The shares will sell well; and then we shall not care whether the dancers come over or no." It is important to observe that this scene was exhibited and applauded before one farthing of the national debt had been contracted. So ill informed were the numerous writers who, at a later period, ascribed to the national debt the existence of stockjobbing and of all the immoralities connected with stockjobbing. The truth is that society had, in the natural course of its growth, reached a point at which it was inevitable that there should be stockjobbing whether there were a national debt or not, and inevitable also that, if there were a long and costly war, there should be a national debt.

How indeed was it possible that a debt should not have been contracted, when one party was impelled by the strongest motives to borrow, and another was impelled by equally strong motives to lend? A moment had arrived at which the government found it impossible, without exciting the most formidable discontents, to raise by taxation the supplies necessary to defend the liberty and independence of the nation; and, at that very moment, numerous capitalists were looking round them in vain for some good mode of investing their savings, and, for want of such a mode, were keeping their wealth locked up, or were lavishing it on absurd projects. Riches sufficient to equip a navy which would sweep the German Ocean and the Atlantic of French privateers, riches sufficient to maintain an army which might retake Namur and avenge the disaster of Steinkirk, were lying idle, or were passing away from the owners into the hands of sharpers.

A statesman might well think that some part of the wealth which was daily buried or squandered might, with advantage to the proprietor, to the taxpayer, and to the State, be attracted into the Treasury. Why meet the extraordinary charge of a year of war by seizing the chairs, the tables, the beds of hardworking families, by compelling one country gentleman to cut down his trees before they were ready for the axe, another to let the cottages on his land fall to ruin, a third to take away his hopeful son from the University, when Change Alley was swarming with people who did not know what to do with their money and who were pressing everybody to borrow it?

It was often asserted at a later period by Tories, who hated the national debt most of all things, and who hated Burnet most of all men, that Burnet was the person who first advised the government to contract a national debt. But this assertion is proved by no trustworthy evidence, and seems to be disproved by the Bishop's silence. Of all men he was the least likely to conceal the fact that an important fiscal revolution had been his work. Nor was the Board of Treasury at that time one which much needed, or was likely much to regard, the counsels of a divine. At that Board sate Godolphin, the most prudent and experienced, and Montague, the most daring and inventive of financiers. Neither of these eminent men could be ignorant that it had long been the practice of the neighbouring states to spread over many years of peace the excessive taxation which was made necessary by one year of war. In Italy this practice had existed through several generations. France had, during the war which began in 1672 and ended in 1679, borrowed not less than thirty millions of our money. Sir William Temple, in his interesting work on the Batavian federation, had told his countrymen that, when he was ambassador at the Hague, the single province of Holland, then ruled by the frugal and prudent De Witt, owed about five millions sterling, for which interest at four per cent was always ready to the day, and that, when any part of the principal was paid off, the public creditor received his money with tears, well knowing that he could find no other investment equally secure. The wonder is not that England should have at length imitated the example both of her enemies and of her allies, but that the fourth year of her arduous and exhausting struggle against Lewis should have been drawing to a close before she resorted to an expedient so obvious.

On the fifteenth of December 1692 the House of Commons resolved itself into a Committee of Ways and Means. Somers took the chair. Montague proposed to raise a million by way of loan: the proposition was approved; and it was ordered that a bill should be brought in. The details of the scheme were much discussed and modified; but the principle appears to have been popular with all parties. The moneyed men were glad to have a good opportunity of investing what they had hoarded. The landed men, hard pressed by the load of taxation, were ready to consent to anything for the sake of present ease. No member ventured to divide the House. On the twentieth of January the bill was read a third time, carried up to the Lords by Somers, and passed by them without any amendment.*

By this memorable law new duties were imposed on beer and other liquors. These duties were to be kept in the Exchequer separate from all other receipts, and were to form a fund on the credit of which a million was to be raised by life annuities. As the annuitants dropped off, their annuities were to be divided among the survivors, till the number of survivors was reduced to seven. After that time, whatever fell in was to go to the public. It was therefore certain that the eighteenth century would be far advanced before the debt would be finally extinguished; and, in fact, long after King George the Third was on the throne, a few aged men were receiving large incomes from the State, in return for a little money which had been advanced to King William on their account when they were children.† The rate of interest was to be ten per cent till the year 1700, and after that year seven per cent. The advantages offered to the public creditor by this scheme may seem great, but were not more than sufficient to compensate him for the risk which he ran. It was not impossible that there might be a counterrevolution; and it was certain that if there were a counterrevolution, those who had lent money to William would lose both interest and principal.

Such was the origin of that debt which has since become the greatest prodigy that ever perplexed the sagacity and

---

* Commons' Journals; Stat. 4 W. & M. c. 3.

† William Duncombe, whose name is well known to curious students of literary history, and who, in conjunction with his son John, translated Horace's works, died in 1769, having been seventy-seven years an annuitant under the Act of 1692. A hundred pounds had been subscribed in William Duncombe's name when he was three years old; and, for this small sum, he received thousands upon thousands. Literary Anecdotes of the Eighteenth Century, viii. 265.

confounded the pride of statesmen and philosophers. At every stage in the growth of that debt the nation has set up the same cry of anguish and despair. At every stage in the growth of that debt it has been seriously asserted by wise men that bankruptcy and ruin were at hand. Yet still the debt went on growing; and still bankruptcy and ruin were as remote as ever. When the great contest with Lewis the Fourteenth was finally terminated by the Peace of Utrecht the nation owed about fifty millions; and that debt was considered, not merely by the rude multitude, not merely by foxhunting squires and coffeehouse orators, but by acute and profound thinkers, as an incumbrance which would permanently cripple the body politic. Nevertheless trade flourished: wealth increased: the nation became richer and richer. Then came the war of the Austrian Succession; and the debt rose to eighty millions. Pamphleteers, historians, and orators pronounced that now, at all events, our case was desperate.[*] Yet the signs of increasing prosperity, signs which could neither be counterfeited nor concealed, ought to have satisfied observant and reflecting men that a debt of eighty millions was less to the England which was governed by Pelham than a debt of fifty millions had been to the England which was governed by Oxford. Soon war again broke forth; and under the energetic and prodigal administration of the first William Pitt, the debt rapidly swelled to a hundred and forty millions. As soon as the first intoxication of victory was over, men of theory and men of business almost unanimously pronounced that the fatal day had now really arrived. The only statesman, indeed, active or speculative, who was too wise to share in the general delusion was Edmund Burke. David Hume, undoubtedly one of the most profound political economists of his time, declared that our madness had exceeded the madness of the Crusaders. Richard Cœur de Lion and Saint Lewis had not gone in the face of arithmetical demonstration. It was impossible to prove by figures that the road to Paradise did not lie through the Holy Land: but it was possible to prove by figures that the road to national ruin was through the national debt. It was idle, however, now to talk about the road: we had done with the road: we had

<hr>

[*] Smollett's Complete History of England from the Descent of Julius Cæsar to the Treaty of Aix la Chapelle, 1748, containing the Transactions of one thousand eight hundred and three years, was published at this time. The work ends with a vehement philippic against the government; and that philippic ends with the tremendous words, "the national debt accumulated to the enormous sum of eighty millions sterling."

reached the goal : all was over : all the revenues of the island
north of Trent and west of Reading were mortgaged. Better
for us to have been conquered by Prussia or Austria than to
be saddled with the interest of a hundred and forty millions.*
And yet this great philosopher,—for such he was,—had only
to open his eyes, and to see improvement all around him, cities
increasing, cultivation extending, marts too small for the
crowd of buyers and sellers, harbours insufficient to contain
the shipping, artificial rivers joining the chief inland seats of
industry to the chief seaports, streets better lighted, houses
better furnished, richer wares exposed to sale in statelier
shops, swifter carriages rolling along smoother roads. He
had, indeed, only to compare the Edinburgh of his boyhood
with the Edinburgh of his old age. His prediction remains
to posterity, a memorable instance of the weakness from
which the strongest minds are not exempt. Adam Smith
saw a little, and but a little further. He admitted that, immense as the pressure was, the nation did actually sustain it
and thrive under it in a way which nobody could have foreseen. But he warned his countrymen not to repeat so hazardous an experiment. The limit had been reached. Even a
small increase might be fatal.† Not less gloomy was the
view which George Grenville, a minister eminently diligent
and practical, took of our financial situation. The nation
must, he conceived, sink under a debt of a hundred and forty
millions, unless a portion of the load were borne by the American colonies. The attempt to lay a portion of the load on
the American colonies produced another war. That war left
us with an additional hundred millions of debt, and without
the colonies whose help had been represented as indispensable.
Again England was given over ; and again the strange patient
persisted in becoming stronger and more blooming in spite
of all the diagnostics and prognostics of State physicians.
As she had been visibly more prosperous with a debt of one
hundred and forty millions than with a debt of fifty millions,
so she was visibly more prosperous with a debt of two hundred
and forty millions than with a debt of one hundred and forty
millions. Soon however the wars which sprang from the
French Revolution, and which far exceeded in cost any that
the world had ever seen, tasked the powers of public credit to
the utmost. When the world was again at rest the funded
debt of England amounted to eight hundred millions. If the

---

* See a very remarkable note in Hume's History of England, Appendix III.
† Wealth of Nations, book v. chap. iii.

most enlightened man had been told, in 1792, that, in 1815, the interest on eight hundred millions would be duly paid to the day at the Bank, he would have been as hard of belief as if he had been told that the government would be in possession of the lamp of Aladdin or of the purse of Fortunatus. It was in truth a gigantic, a fabulous, debt; and we can hardly wonder that the cry of despair should have been louder than ever. But again that cry was found to have been as unreasonable as ever. After a few years of exhaustion, England recovered herself. Yet like Addison's valetudinarian, who continued to whimper that he was dying of consumption till he became so fat that he was shamed into silence, she went on complaining that she was sunk in poverty till her wealth showed itself by tokens which made her complaints ridiculous. The beggared, the bankrupt, society not only proved able to meet all its obligations, but, while meeting those obligations, grew richer and richer so fast that the growth could almost be discerned by the eye. In every county, we saw wastes recently turned into gardens : in every city, we saw new streets, and squares, and markets, more brilliant lamps, more abundant supplies of water : in the suburbs of every great seat of industry, we saw villas multiplying fast, each embosomed in its gay little paradise of lilacs and roses. While shallow politicians were repeating that the energies of the people were borne down by the weight of the public burdens, the first journey was performed by steam on a railway. Soon the island was intersected by railways. A sum exceeding the whole amount of the national debt at the end of the American war was, in a few years, voluntarily expended by this ruined people on viaducts, tunnels, embankments, bridges, stations, engines. Meanwhile taxation was almost constantly becoming lighter and lighter : yet still the Exchequer was full. It may be now affirmed without fear of contradiction that we find it as easy to pay the interest of eight hundred millions as our ancestors found it, a century ago, to pay the interest of eighty millions.

It can hardly be doubted that there must have been some great fallacy in the notions of those who uttered and of those who believed that long succession of confident predictions, so signally falsified by a long succession of indisputable facts. To point out that fallacy is the office rather of the political economist than of the historian. Here it is sufficient to say that the prophets of evil were under a double delusion. They erroneously imagined that there was an exact analogy between the case of an individual who is in debt to another individual and the case of a society which is in debt to a part of itself; and this analogy led them into endless mistakes about the effect of the system of funding. They were under an error not less serious touching the resources of the country. They made no allowance for the effect produced by the incessant progress of every experimental science, and by the incessant efforts of every man to get on in life. They saw that the debt grew; and they forgot that other things grew as well as the debt.

A long experience justifies us in believing that England may, in the twentieth century, be better able to pay a debt of sixteen hundred millions than she is at the present time to bear her present load. But be this as it may, those who so confidently predicted that she must sink, first under a debt of fifty millions, then under a debt of eighty millions, then under a debt of a hundred and forty millions, then under a debt of two hundred and forty millions, and lastly under a debt of eight hundred millions, were beyond all doubt under a twofold mistake. They greatly overrated the pressure of the burden: they greatly underrated the strength by which the burden was to be borne.*

It may be desirable to add a few words touching the way in which the system of funding has affected the interests of the great commonwealth of nations. If it be true that whatever gives to intelligence an advantage over brute force, and to honesty an advantage over dishonesty, has a tendency to promote the happiness and virtue of our race, it can scarcely be denied that, in the largest view, the effect of this system has been salutary. For it is manifest that all credit depends on two things, on the power of a debtor to pay debts, and on his inclination to pay them. The power of a society to pay debts is proportioned to the progress which that society has made in industry, in commerce, and in all the arts and sciences which flourish under the benignant influence of freedom and of equal law. The inclination of a society to pay debts is proportioned to the degreee in which that society respects the

---

* I have said that Burke alone among his contemporaries was superior to the vulgar error in which men so eminent as David Hume and Adam Smith shared. I will quote, in illustration of my meaning, a few weighty words from the Observations on the Late State of the Nation written by Burke in 1769. "An enlightened reader laughs at the inconsistent chimera of our author (George Grenville), of a people universally luxurious, and at the same time oppressed with taxes and declining in trade. For my part, I cannot look on these duties as the author does. He sees nothing but the burden. I can perceive the burden as well as he: but I cannot avoid contemplating also the strength that supports it. From thence I draw the most comfortable assurances of the future vigour and the ample resources of this great misrepresented country."

obligations of plighted faith. Of the strength which consists in extent of territory and in number of fighting men, a rude despot who knows no law but his own childish fancies and headstrong passions, or a convention of socialists which proclaims all property to be robbery, may have more than falls to the lot of the best and wisest government. But the strength which is derived from the confidence of capitalists such a despot, such a convention, never can possess. That strength,—and it is a strength which has decided the event of more than one great conflict,—flies, by the law of its nature, from barbarism and fraud, from tyranny and anarchy, to follow civilisation and virtue, liberty and order.

While the bill which first created the funded debt of England was passing, with general approbation, through the regular stages, the two Houses discussed, for the first time, the great question of Parliamentary Reform. *Parliamentary Reform.*

It is to be observed that the object of the reformers of that generation was merely to make the representative body a more faithful interpreter of the sense of the constituent body. It seems scarcely to have occurred to any of them that the constituent body might be an unfaithful interpreter of the sense of the nation. It is true that those disproportions in the structure of the constituent body, which, at length, in our own days, raised an irresistible storm of public indignation, were far less numerous and far less offensive in the seventeenth century than they had become in the nineteenth. Most of the boroughs which were disfranchised in 1832 were, if not positively, yet relatively, much more important places in the reign of William the Third than in the reign of William the Fourth. Of the populous and wealthy manufacturing towns, seaports, and watering places, to which the franchise was given in the reign of William the Fourth, some were, in the reign of William the Third, small hamlets, where a few ploughmen or fishermen lived under thatched roofs : some were fields covered with harvests, or moors abandoned to grouse. With the exception of Leeds and Manchester, there was not, at the time of the Revolution, a single town of five thousand inhabitants which did not send two representatives to the House of Commons. Even then, however, there was no want of startling anomalies. Looe, East and West, which contained not half the population or half the wealth of the smallest of the hundred parishes of London, returned as many members as London.* Old Sarum, a deserted ruin

* Wesley was struck with this anomaly in 1745. See his Journal.

which the traveller feared to enter at night lest he should
find robbers lurking there, had as much weight in the legislature as Devonshire or Yorkshire.* Some eminent individuals of both parties, Clarendon, for example, among the
Tories, and Pollexfen among the Whigs, condemned this
system. Yet both parties were, for very different reasons,
unwilling to alter it. It was protected by the prejudices of
one faction, and by the interests of the other. Nothing could
be more repugnant to the genius of Toryism than the thought
of destroying at a blow institutions which had stood through
ages, for the purpose of building something more symme-
trical out of the ruins. It was remembered too that Cromwell had tried to correct the deformities of the representative
system; and deformities which Cromwell had tried to correct were certain to be regarded as beauties by most of those
gentlemen who were zealous for the Church and the Crown.
The Whigs, on the other hand, could not but know that they
were much more likely to lose than to gain by a change in
this part of our polity. It would indeed be a great mistake
to imagine that a law transferring political power from small
to large constituent bodies would have operated in 1692 as
it operated in 1832. In 1832 the effect of the transfer was
to increase the power of the town population. In 1692 the
effect would have been to make the power of the rural population irresistible. Of the one hundred and forty-three members taken away in 1832 from small boroughs more than
half were given to large and flourishing towns. But in 1692
there was hardly one large and flourishing town which had
not already as many members as it could, with any show of
reason, claim. Almost all therefore that was taken from the
small boroughs must have been given to the counties; and
there can be no doubt that whatever tended to raise the
counties and to depress the towns must on the whole have
tended to raise the Tories and to depress the Whigs. From
the commencement of our civil troubles the towns had been
on the side of freedom and progress, the country gentlemen
and the country clergymen on the side of authority and pre-
scription. If therefore a reform bill, disfranchising many of
the smallest constituent bodies and giving additional members to many of the largest constituent bodies, had become
law soon after the Revolution, there can be little doubt that
a decided majority of the House of Commons would have
consisted of rustic baronets and squires, high Churchmen,

* Pepys, June 10. 1668.

high Tories, and half Jacobites. With such a House of Commons it is almost certain that there would have been a persecution of the Dissenters: it is not easy to understand how there could have been a peaceful union with Scotland; and it is not improbable that there would have been a restoration of the Stuarts. Those parts of our constitution, therefore which, in recent times, politicians of the liberal school have generally considered as blemishes, were, five generations ago, regarded with complacency by the men who were most zealous for civil and religious freedom.

But, while Whigs and Tories agreed in wishing to maintain the existing rights of election, both Whigs and Tories were forced to admit that the relation between the elector and the representative was not what it ought to be. Before the civil wars the House of Commons had enjoyed the fullest confidence of the nation. A House of Commons, distrusted, despised, hated by the Commons, was a thing unknown. The very words would, to Sir Peter Wentworth or Sir Edward Coke, have sounded like a contradiction in terms. But by degrees a change took place. The Parliament elected in 1661, during that fit of joy and fondness which followed the return of the royal family, represented, not the deliberate sense, but the momentary caprice of the nation. Many of the members were men who, a few months earlier or a few months later, would have had no chance of obtaining seats, men of broken fortunes and of dissolute habits, men whose only claim to public confidence was the ferocious hatred which they bore to rebels and Puritans. The people, as soon as they had become sober, saw with dismay, to what an assembly they had, during their intoxication, confided the care of their property, their liberty, and their religion. And the choice, made in a moment of frantic enthusiasm, might prove to be a choice for life. As the law then stood, it depended entirely on the King's pleasure whether, during his reign, the electors should have an opportunity of repairing their error. Eighteen years passed away. A new generation grew up. To the fervid loyalty with which Charles had been welcomed back from exile succeeded discontent and disaffection. The general cry was that the kingdom was misgoverned, degraded, given up as a prey to worthless men and more worthless women, that our navy had been found unequal to a contest with Holland, that our independence had been bartered for the gold of France, that our consciences were in danger of being again subjected to the yoke of Rome. The

people had become Roundheads: but the body which alone
was authorised to speak in the name of the people was still
a body of Cavaliers. It is true that the King occasionally
found even that House of Commons unmanageable. From
the first it had contained not a few true Englishmen: others
had been introduced into it as vacancies were made by death;
and even the majority, courtly as it was, could not but feel
some sympathy with the nation. A country party grew up
and became formidable. But that party constantly found its
exertions frustrated by systematic corruption. That some
members of the legislature received direct bribes was with
good reason suspected, but could not be proved. That the
patronage of the Crown was employed on an extensive scale
for the purpose of influencing votes was matter of notoriety.
A large proportion of those who gave away the public money
in supplies received part of that money back in salaries; and
thus was formed a mercenary band on which the Court might,
in almost any extremity, confidently rely.

The servility of this Parliament had left a deep impression
on the public mind. It was the general opinion that England ought to be protected against all risk of being ever
again represented, during a long course of years, by men who
had forfeited her confidence, and who were retained by a fee
to vote against her wishes and interests. The subject was
mentioned in the Convention; and some members wished to
deal with it while the throne was still vacant. The cry for
reform had ever since been becoming more and more importunate. The people, heavily pressed by taxes, were naturally
disposed to regard those who lived on the taxes with little
favour. The war, it was generally acknowledged, was just
and necessary; and war could not be carried on without large
expenditure. But the larger the expenditure which was
required for the defence of the nation, the more important it
was that nothing should be squandered. The immense gains
of official men moved envy and indignation. Here a gentleman was paid to do nothing. There many gentlemen were
paid to do what would be better done by one. The coach, the
liveries, the lace cravat, and the diamond buckles of the placeman were naturally seen with an evil eye by those who rose
up early and lay down late in order to furnish him with the
means of indulging in splendour and luxury. Such abuses
it was the especial business of a House of Commons to correct. What then had the existing House of Commons done
in the way of correction? Absolutely nothing. In 1690,

indeed, while the Civil List was settling, some sharp speeches had been made. In 1691, when the Ways and Means were under consideration, a resolution had been passed so absurdly framed that it had proved utterly abortive. The nuisance continued, and would continue while it was a source of profit to those whose duty was to abate it. Who could expect faithful and vigilant stewardship from stewards who had a direct interest in encouraging the waste which they were employed to check? The House swarmed with placemen of all kinds, Lords of the Treasury, Lords of the Admiralty, Commissioners of Customs, Commissioners of Excise, Commissioners of Prizes, Tellers, Auditors, Receivers, Paymasters, Officers of the Mint, Officers of the household, Colonels of regiments, Captains of men of war, Governors of forts. We send up to Westminster, it was said, one of our neighbours, an independent gentleman, in the full confidence that his feelings and interests are in perfect accordance with ours. We look to him to relieve us from every burden except those burdens without which the public service cannot be carried on, and which therefore, galling as they are, we patiently and resolutely bear. But, before he has been a session in Parliament, we learn that he is a Clerk of the Green Cloth or a Yeoman of the Removing Wardrobe, with a comfortable salary. Nay, we sometimes learn that he has obtained one of those places in the Exchequer of which the emoluments rise and fall with the taxes which we pay. It would be strange indeed if our interests were safe in the keeping of a man whose gains consist in a percentage on our losses. The evil would be greatly diminished, if we had frequent opportunities of considering whether the powers of our agent ought to be renewed or revoked. But, as the law stands, it is not impossible that he may hold those powers twenty or thirty years. While he lives, and while either the King or the Queen lives, it is not likely that we shall ever again exercise our elective franchise, unless there should be a dispute between the Court and the Parliament. The more profuse and obsequious a Parliament is, the less likely it is to give offence to the Court. The worse our representatives, therefore, the longer we are likely to be cursed with them.

The outcry was loud. Odious nicknames were given to the Parliament. Sometimes it was the Officers' Parliament: sometimes it was the Standing Parliament, and was pronounced to be a greater nuisance than even a standing army.

Two specifics for the distempers of the State were strongly

recommended, and divided the public favour.   One was a law
excluding placemen from the House of Commons.   The other
was a law limiting the duration of Parliaments to three years.
In general the Tory reformers preferred a Place Bill, and the
Whig reformers a Triennial Bill : but not a few zealous men
of both parties were for trying both remedies.

The Place
Bill.
Before Christmas a Place Bill was laid on the table of the
Commons.   That Bill has been vehemently praised by writers
who never saw it, and who merely guessed at what it contained.   But no person who takes the trouble to study the
original parchment, which, embrowned with the dust of a
hundred and sixty years, reposes among the archives of the
House of Lords, will find much matter for eulogy.

About the manner in which such a bill should have been
framed there will, in our time, be little difference of opinion
among enlightened Englishmen.   They will agree in thinking
that it would be most pernicious to open the House of Commons to all placemen, and not less pernicious to close that
House against all placemen.   To draw with precision the
line between those who ought to be admitted and those
who ought to be excluded would be a task requiring much
time, thought, and knowledge of details.   But the general
principles which ought to guide us are obvious.   The multitude of subordinate functionaries ought to be excluded.   A
few functionaries, who are at the head or near the head of the
great departments of the administration, ought to be admitted.

The subordinate functionaries ought to be excluded, because
their admission would at once lower the character of Parliament and destroy the efficiency of every public office.   They
are now excluded ; and the consequence is that the State
possesses a valuable body of servants who remain unchanged
while cabinet after cabinet is formed and dissolved, who
instruct minister after minister in his duties, and with whom
it is the most sacred point of honour to give true information,
sincere advice, and strenuous assistance to their superior for
the time being.   To the experience, the ability, and the
fidelity of this class of men is to be attributed the ease and
safety with which the direction of affairs has been many times,
within our own memory, transferred from Tories to Whigs
and from Whigs to Tories.   But no such class would have
existed if persons who received salaries from the Crown had
been suffered to sit without restriction in the House of Commons.   Those commissionerships, assistant secretaryships,
chief clerkships, which are now held for life by persons who

stand aloof from the strife of parties, would have been bestowed on members of Parliament who were serviceable to
the government as voluble speakers or steady voters. As
often as the ministry was changed, all this crowd of retainers
would have been ejected from office, and would have been
succeeded by another set of members of Parliament who
would probably have been ejected in their turn before they
had half learned their business. Servility and corruption in
the legislature, ignorance and incapacity in all the departments of the executive administration, would have been the
inevitable effects of such a system.

Still more noxious, if possible, would be the effects of a
system under which all the servants of the Crown, without
exception, should be excluded from the House of Commons.
Aristotle has, in that treatise on government which is perhaps
the most judicious and instructive of all his writings, left us
a warning against a class of laws artfully framed to delude
the vulgar, democratic in seeming, but the very opposite of
democratic in effect.* Had he had an opportunity of studying the history of the English constitution, he might easily
have enlarged his list of such laws. That men who are in
the service and pay of the Crown ought not to sit in an
assembly specially charged with the duty of guarding the
rights and interests of the community against all aggression
on the part of the Crown is a plausible and a popular doctrine.
Yet it is certain that if those who, five generations ago, held
that doctrine, had been able to mould the constitution according to their wishes, the effect would have been the depression
of that branch of the legislature which springs from the people,
and is accountable to the people, and the ascendency of the
monarchical and aristocratical elements of our polity. The
government would have been entirely in patrician hands. The
House of Lords, constantly drawing to itself the first abilities
in the realm, would have become the most august of senates,
while the House of Commons would have sunk almost to the
rank of a vestry. From time to time undoubtedly men of commanding genius and of aspiring temper would have made their
appearance among the representatives of the counties and
boroughs. But every such man would have considered the elective chamber merely as a lobby through which he must pass
to the hereditary chamber. The first object of his ambition
would have been that coronet without which he could not be
powerful in the state. As soon as he had shown that he could be

* See the Politics, iv. 13.

a formidable enemy and a valuable friend to the government, he would have made haste to quit what would then have been in every sense the Lower House for what would then have been in every sense the Upper. The conflict between Walpole and Pulteney, the conflict between Pitt and Fox, would have been transferred from the popular to the aristocratic part of the legislature. On every great question, foreign, domestic, or colonial, the debates of the nobles would have been impatiently expected and eagerly devoured. The report of the proceedings of an assembly containing no person empowered to speak in the name of the government, no person who had ever been in high political trust, would have been thrown aside with contempt. Even the control of the purse of the nation must have passed, not perhaps in form, but in substance, to that body in which would have been found every man who was qualified to bring forward a budget or explain an estimate. The country would have been governed by Peers; and the chief business of the Commons would have been to wrangle about bills for the inclosing of moors and the lighting of towns.

These considerations were altogether overlooked in 1692. Nobody thought of drawing a line between the few functionaries who ought to be allowed to sit in the House of Commons and the crowd of functionaries who ought to be shut out. The only line which the legislators of that day took pains to draw was between themselves and their successors. Their own interest they guarded with a care of which it seems strange that they should not have been ashamed. Every one of them was allowed to keep the places which he had got, and to get as many more places as he could before the next dissolution of Parliament, an event which might not happen for many years. But a member who should be chosen after the first of February 1693 was not to be permitted to accept any place whatever.*

In the House of Commons the bill went through all the stages rapidly and without a single division. But in the Lords the contest was sharp and obstinate. Several amendments were proposed in committee; but all were rejected. The motion that the bill should pass was supported by Mulgrave in a lively and poignant speech, which has been preserved, and which proves that his reputation for eloquence was not unmerited. The Lords who took the other side did not, it should seem, venture to deny that there was an evil

* The bill will be found among the archives of the House of Lords.

which required a remedy: but they maintained that the proposed remedy would only aggravate the evil. The patriotic representatives of the people had devised a reform which might perhaps benefit the next generation: but they had carefully reserved to themselves the privilege of plundering the present generation. If this bill passed, it was clear that, while the existing Parliament lasted, the number of placemen in the House of Commons would be little, if at all, diminished; and, if this bill passed, it was highly probable that the existing Parliament would last till both King William and Queen Mary were dead. For as, under this bill, Their Majesties would be able to exercise a much greater influence over the existing Parliament than over any future Parliament, they would naturally wish to put off a dissolution as long as possible. The complaint of the electors of England was that now, in 1692, they were unfairly represented. It was not redress, but mockery, to tell them that their children should be fairly represented in 1710 or 1720. The relief ought to be immediate; and the way to give immediate relief was to limit the duration of Parliaments, and to begin with that Parliament which, in the opinion of the country, had already held power too long.

The forces were so evenly balanced that a very slight accident might have turned the scale. When the question was put that the bill do pass, eighty-two peers were present. Of these forty-two were for the bill, and forty against it. Proxies were then called. There were only two proxies for the bill: there were seven against it: but of the seven three were questioned, and were with difficulty admitted. The result was that the bill was lost by three votes.

The majority appears to have been composed of moderate Whigs and moderate Tories. Twenty of the minority protested, and among them were the most violent and intolerant members of both parties, such as Warrington, who had narrowly escaped the block for conspiring against James, and Ailesbury, who afterwards narrowly escaped the block for conspiring against William. Marlborough, who since his imprisonment, had gone all lengths in opposition to the government, not only put his own name to the protest, but made the Prince of Denmark sign what it was altogether beyond the faculties of His Royal Highness to comprehend.*

It is a remarkable circumstance that neither Caermarthen, the first in power as well as in abilities of the Tory ministers,

* Lords' Journals, Jan. 3. 169².

nor Shrewsbury, the most distinguished of those Whigs who
were then on bad terms with the Court, was present on this
important occasion. Their absence was in all probability the
effect of design; for both of them were in the House no long
time before and no long time after the division.

The Trien-
nial Bill. A few days later Shrewsbury laid on the table of the Lords
a bill for limiting the duration of Parliaments. By this bill
it was provided that the Parliament then sitting should cease
to exist on the first of January 1694, and that no future Parliament should last longer than three years.

Among the Lords there seems to have been almost perfect
unanimity on this subject. William in vain endeavoured to
induce those peers in whom he placed the greatest confidence
to support his prerogative. Some of them thought the proposed change salutary: others hoped to quiet the public mind
by a liberal concession; and others had held such language
when they were opposing the Place Bill that they could not,
without gross inconsistency, oppose the Triennial Bill. The
whole House too bore a grudge to the other House, and had a
pleasure in putting the other House in a most disagreeable
dilemma. Burnet, Pembroke, nay, even Caermarthen, who was
very little in the habit of siding with the people against the
throne, supported Shrewsbury. "My Lord," said the King
to Caermarthen with bitter displeasure, "you will live to repent the part which you are taking in this matter." * The
warning was disregarded; and the bill, having passed the
Lords smoothly and rapidly, was carried with great solemnity
by two judges to the Commons.

1693. Of what took place in the Commons we have but very meagre
accounts: but from those accounts it is clear that the Whigs,
as a body, supported the bill, and that the opposition came
chiefly from Tories. Old Titus, who had been a politician in
the days of the Commonwealth, entertained the House with
a speech after the pattern which had been fashionable in those
days. Parliaments, he said, resembled the manna which God
bestowed on the chosen people. They were excellent while
they were fresh: but, if kept too long, they became noisome;
and foul worms were engendered by the corruption of that
which had been sweeter than honey. Several of the leading
Whigs spoke on the same side. Seymour, Finch, and Tre-
denham, all stanch Tories, were vehement against the bill;

---

* Introduction to the Copies and Ex-   Leeds, published by His Grace's Direc-
tracts of some Letters written to and   tion, 1710.
from the Earl of Danby, now Duke of

and even Sir John Lowther on this point dissented from his friend and patron Caermarthen. Some Tory orators appealed to a feeling which was strong in the House, and which had, since the Revolution, prevented many laws from passing. Whatever, they said, comes from the Peers is to be received with suspicion; and the present bill is of such a nature that, even if it were in itself good, it ought to be at once rejected merely because it has been brought down from them. If their Lordships were to send us the most judicious of all money bills, should we not kick it to the door? Yet to send us a money bill would hardly be a grosser affront than to send us such a bill as this. They have taken an initiative which, by every rule of parliamentary courtesy, ought to have been left to us. They have sate in judgment on us, convicted us, condemned us to dissolution, and fixed the first of January for the execution. Are we to submit patiently to so degrading a sentence, a sentence too passed by men who have not so conducted themselves as to have acquired any right to censure others? Have they ever made any sacrifice of their own interest, of their own dignity, to the general welfare? Have not excellent bills been lost because we would not consent to insert in them clauses conferring new privileges on the nobility? And, now that their Lordships are bent on obtaining popularity, do they propose to purchase it by relinquishing even the smallest of their own oppressive privileges? No: they seek to propitiate the multitude by a sacrifice which will cost themselves nothing, but which will cost us and will cost the Crown dear. In such circumstances it is our duty to repel the insult which has been offered to us, and, by doing so, to vindicate the lawful prerogative of the King.

Such topics as these were doubtless well qualified to inflame the passions of the House of Commons. The near prospect of a dissolution could not be very agreeable to a member whose election was likely to be contested. He must go through all the miseries of a canvass, must shake hands with crowds of freeholders or freemen, must ask after their wives and children, must hire conveyances for outvoters, must open alehouses, must provide mountains of beef, must set rivers of ale running, and might perhaps, after all the drudgery and all the expense, after being lampooned, hustled, pelted, find himself at the bottom of the poll, see his antagonists chaired, and sink half ruined into obscurity. All this evil he was now invited to bring on himself, and invited by men whose own seats in the legislature were permanent, who gave up neither dignity nor quiet, neither power nor money, but gained the praise of patriotism by forcing him to abdicate a high station, to undergo harassing labour and anxiety, to mortgage his cornfields and to hew down his woods. There was naturally much irritation, more probably than is indicated by the divisions. For the constituent bodies were generally delighted with the bill; and many members who disliked it were afraid to oppose it. The House yielded to the pressure of public opinion, but not without a pang and a struggle. The discussions in the committee seem to have been acrimonious. Such sharp words passed between Seymour and one of the Whig members that it was necessary to put the Speaker in the chair and the mace on the table for the purpose of restoring order. One amendment was made. The respite which the Lords had granted to the existing Parliament was extended from the first of January to Lady Day, in order that there might be time for another session. The third reading was carried by two hundred votes to a hundred and sixty-one. The Lords agreed to the bill as amended; and nothing was wanting but the royal assent. Whether that assent would or would not be given was a question which remained in suspense till the last day of the session.*

One strange inconsistency in the conduct of the reformers of that generation deserves notice. It never occurred to any one of those who were zealous for the Triennial Bill that every argument which could be urged in favour of that bill was an argument against the rules which had been framed in old times for the purpose of keeping parliamentary deliberations and divisions strictly secret. It is quite natural that a government which withholds political privileges from the commonalty should withhold also political information. But nothing can be more irrational than to give power, and not to give the knowledge without which there is the greatest risk that power will be abused. What could be more absurd than to call constituent bodies frequently together that they might decide whether their representative had done his duty by them, and yet strictly to interdict them from learning, on trustworthy authority, what he had said or how he had voted? The absurdity however appears to have passed altogether unchallenged. It is highly probable that among the two hundred members of the House of Commons who voted for the third reading of the Triennial Bill there was not one who

* Commons' Journals; Grey's Debates. The bill itself is among the archives of the House of Lords.

would have hesitated about sending to Newgate any person who had dared to publish a report of the debate on that bill, or a list of the Ayes and the Noes. The truth is that the secrecy of parliamentary debates, a secrecy which would now be thought a grievance more intolerable than the Shipmoney or the Star Chamber, was then inseparably associated, even in the most honest and intelligent minds, with constitutional freedom. A few old men still living could remember times when a gentleman who was known at Whitehall to have let fall a sharp word against a court favourite would have been brought before the Privy Council and sent to the Tower. Those times were gone, never to return. There was no longer any danger that the King would oppress the members of the legislature; and there was much danger that the members of the legislature might oppress the people. Nevertheless the words Privilege of Parliament, those words which the stern senators of the preceding generation had murmured when a tyrant filled their chamber with his guards, those words which a hundred thousand Londoners had shouted in his ears when he ventured for the last time within the walls of their city, still retained a magical influence over all who loved liberty. It was long before even the most enlightened men became sensible that the precautions which had been originally devised for the purpose of protecting patriots against the displeasure of the Court now served only to protect sycophants against the displeasure of the nation.

It is also to be observed that few of those who showed at this time the greatest desire to increase the political power of the people were as yet prepared to emancipate the press from the control of the government. The Licensing Act, which had passed, as a matter of course, in 1685, expired in 1693, and was renewed, not however without an opposition, which, though feeble when compared with the magnitude of the object in dispute, proved that the public mind was beginning dimly to perceive how closely civil freedom and freedom of conscience are connected with freedom of discussion. *The first parliamentary discussion on the liberty of the press.*

On the history of the Licensing Act no preceding writer has thought it worth while to expend any care or labour. Yet surely the events which led to the establishment of the liberty of the press in England, and in all the countries peopled by the English race, may be thought to have as much interest for the present generation as any of those battles and sieges of which the most minute details have been carefully recorded.

During the first three years of William's reign scarcely a voice seems to have been raised against the restrictions which the law imposed on literature. Those restrictions were in perfect harmony with the theory of government held by the Tories, and were not, in practice, galling to the Whigs. Sir Roger Lestrange, who had been licenser under the last two Kings of the House of Stuart, and who had shown as little tenderness to Exclusionists and Presbyterians in that character as in his other character of Observator, was turned out of office at the Revolution, and was succeeded by a Scotch gentleman, who, on account of his passion for rare books, and his habit of attending all sales of libraries, was known in the shops and coffeehouses near Saint Paul's by the name of Catalogue Fraser. Fraser was a zealous Whig. By Whig authors and publishers he was extolled as a most impartial and humane man. But the conduct which obtained their applause drew on him the abuse of the Tories, and was not altogether pleasing to his official superior Nottingham.* No serious difference however seems to have arisen till the year 1692. In that year an honest old clergyman named Walker, who had, in the time of the civil war, been intimately acquainted with Doctor John Gauden, wrote a book which convinced all sensible and dispassionate readers that Gauden, and not Charles the First, was the author of the Icon Basilike. This book Fraser suffered to be printed. If he had authorised the publication of a work in which the Gospel of Saint John or the Epistle to the Romans had been represented as spurious, the indignation of the High Church party could hardly have been greater. The question was not literary, but religious. Doubt was impiety. The Blessed Martyr was an inspired penman, his Icon a supplementary revelation. One grave divine indeed had gone so far as to propose that lessons taken out of the inestimable little volume should be read in the churches.† Fraser found it necessary to resign his place; and Nottingham appointed a gentleman of good blood and scanty fortune, named Edmund Bohun. This change of men produced an immediate and total change of system: for Bohun was as strong a Tory as a conscientious man who had taken the oaths could possibly be. He had been conspicuous as a persecutor of nonconformists and a champion of the doctrine of passive obedience. He had

---

* Dunton's Life and Errors; Autobiography of Edmund Bohun, privately printed in 1853. This autobiography is, in the highest degree, curious and interesting.

† Vox Cleri, 1689.

edited Filmer's absurd treatise on the origin of government, and had written an answer to the paper which Algernon Sidney had delivered to the Sheriffs on Tower Hill. Nor did Bohun admit that, in swearing allegiance to William and Mary, he had done anything inconsistent with his old creed. For he had succeeded in convincing himself that they reigned by right of conquest, and that it was the duty of an Englishman to serve them as faithfully as Daniel had served Darius, or as Nehemiah had served Artaxerxes. This doctrine, whatever peace it might bring to his own conscience, found little favour with any party. The Whigs loathed it as servile : the Jacobites loathed it as revolutionary. Great numbers of Tories had doubtless submitted to William on the ground that he was, rightfully or wrongfully, King in possession : but very few of them were disposed to allow that his possession had originated in conquest. Indeed the plea which had satisfied the weak and narrow mind of Bohun was a mere fiction, and, had it been a truth, would have been a truth not to be uttered by Englishmen without agonies of shame and mortification.* He however clung to his favourite whimsy with a tenacity which the general disapprobation only made more intense. His old friends, the steadfast adherents of indefeasible hereditary right, grew cold and reserved. He asked Sancroft's blessing, and got only a sharp word and a black look. He asked Ken's blessing; and Ken, though not much in the habit of transgressing the rules of Christian charity and courtesy, murmured something about a little scribbler. Thus cast out by one faction, Bohun was not received by any other. He formed indeed a class apart : for he was at once a zealous Filmerite and a zealous Williamite. He held that pure monarchy, not limited by any law or contract, was the form of government which had been divinely ordained. But he held that William was now the absolute monarch, who might annul the Great Charter, abolish trial by jury, or impose taxes by royal proclamation, without forfeiting the right to be implicitly obeyed by Christian men. As to the rest, Bohun was a man of some acuteness and learning, contracted understanding, and unpopular manners. He

---

* Bohun was the author of the History of the Desertion, published immediately after the Revolution. In that work he propounded his favourite theory. "For my part," he says, " I am amazed to see men scruple the submitting to the present King; for, if ever man had a just cause of war, he had ; and that creates a right to the thing gained by it. The King by withdrawing and disbanding his army yielded him the throne ; and if he had, without any more ceremony, ascended it, he had done no more than all other princes do on the like occasions."

had no sooner entered on his functions than all Paternoster Row and Little Britain were in a ferment. The Whigs had, under Fraser's administration, enjoyed almost as entire a liberty as if there had been no censorship. They were now as severely treated as in the days of Lestrange. A History of the Bloody Assizes was about to be published, and was expected to have as great a run as the Pilgrim's Progress. But the new licenser refused his Imprimatur. The book, he said, represented rebels and schismatics as heroes and martyrs: and he would not sanction it for its weight in gold. A charge delivered by Lord Warrington to the grand jury of Cheshire was not permitted to appear, because His Lordship had spoken contemptuously of divine right and passive obedience. Julian Johnson found that, if he wished to promulgate his notions of government, he must again have recourse, as in the evil times of King James, to a secret press.* Such restraint as this, coming after several years of unbounded freedom, naturally produced violent exasperation. Some Whigs began to think that the censorship itself was a grievance: all Whigs agreed in pronouncing the new censor unfit for his post, and were prepared to join in an effort to get rid of him.

Of the transactions which terminated in Bohun's dismission, and which produced the first parliamentary struggle for the liberty of unlicensed printing, we have accounts written by Bohun himself and by others: but there are strong reasons for believing that in none of those accounts is the whole truth to be found. It may perhaps not be impossible, even at this distance of time, to put together dispersed fragments of evidence in such a manner as to produce an authentic narrative which would have astonished the unfortunate licenser himself.

There was then about town a man of good family, of some reading, and of some small literary talent, named Charles Blount.† In politics he belonged to the extreme section of the Whig Party. In the days of the Exclusion Bill he had been one of Shaftesbury's brisk boys, and had, under the signature of Junius Brutus, magnified the virtues and public services of Titus Oates, and exhorted the Protestants to take signal vengeance on the Papists for the fire of London and

---

* Character of Edmund Bohun, 1692.
† Dryden, in his Life of Lucian, speaks in too high terms of Blount's abilities. But Dryden's judgment was biassed; for Blount's first work was a pamphlet in defence of the Conquest of Granada.

for the murder of Godfrey.* As to the theological questions which were in issue between Protestants and Papists, Blount was perfectly impartial. He was an infidel, and the head of a small school of infidels who were troubled with a morbid desire to make converts. He translated from the Latin translation part of the Life of Apollonius of Tyana, and appended to it notes of which the flippant profaneness called forth the severe censure of an unbeliever of a very different order, the illustrious Bayle.† Blount also attacked Christianity in several original treatises, or rather in several treatises purporting to be original; for he was the most audacious of literary thieves, and transcribed, without acknowledgment, whole pages from authors who had preceded him. His delight was to worry the priests by asking them how light existed before the sun was made, how Paradise could be bounded by Pison, Gihon, Hiddekel, and Euphrates, how serpents moved before they were condemned to crawl, and where Eve found thread to stitch her figleaves. To his speculations on these subjects he gave the lofty name of the Oracles of Reason; and indeed whatever he said or wrote was considered as oracular by his disciples. Of those disciples the most noted was a bad writer named Gildon, who lived to pester another generation with doggrel and slander, and whose memory is still preserved, not by his own voluminous works, but by two or three lines in which his stupidity and venality have been contemptuously mentioned by Pope.‡

Little as either the intellectual or the moral character of Blount may seem to deserve respect, it is in a great measure to him that we must attribute the emancipation of the English press. Between him and the licensers there was a feud of long standing. Before the Revolution one of his heterodox treatises had been grievously mutilated by Lestrange, and at last suppressed by orders from Lestrange's superior the Bishop of London.§ Bohun was a scarcely less severe critic than Lestrange. Blount therefore began to make war on the censorship and the censor. The hostilities were commenced by a tract which came forth without any license, and which was entitled A Just Vindication of Learning and of the

---

* See his Appeal from the Country to the City for the Preservation of His Majesty's Person, Liberty, Property, and the Protestant Religion.

† See the article on Apollonius in Bayle's Dictionary. I say that Blount made his translation from the Latin; for his works contain abundant proofs that

he was not competent to translate from the Greek.

‡ See Gildon's edition of Blount's Works, 1695.

§ Wood's Athenæ Oxonienses, under the name Henry Blount (Charles Blount's father); Lestrange's Observator No. 290.

Liberty of the Press, by Philopatris.* Whoever reads this piece, and is not aware that Blount was one of the most unscrupulous plagiaries that ever lived, will be surprised to find, mingled with the poor thoughts and poor words of a thirdrate pamphleteer, passages so elevated in sentiment and style that they would be worthy of the greatest name in letters. The truth is that the Just Vindication consists chiefly of garbled extracts from the Areopagitica of Milton. That noble discourse had been neglected by the generation to which it was addressed, had sunk into oblivion, and was at the mercy of every pilferer. The literary workmanship of Blount resembled the architectural workmanship of those barbarians who used the Coliseum and the Theatre of Pompey as quarries, built hovels out of Ionian friezes and propped cowhouses on pillars of lazulite. Blount concluded, as Milton had concluded, by recommending that the law should be so framed as to permit any book to be printed without a license, provided that the name of the author or publisher were registered.† The Just Vindication was well received. The blow was speedily followed up. There still remained in the Areopagitica many fine passages which Blount had not used in his first pamphlet. Out of these passages he constructed a second pamphlet entitled Reasons for the Liberty of Unlicensed Printing.‡ To these Reasons he appended a postscript entitled A Just and True Character of Edmund Bohun. This Character was written with extreme bitterness. Passages were quoted from the licenser's writings to prove that he held the doctrines of passive obedience and nonresistance. He was accused of using his power systematically for the purpose of favouring the enemies and silencing the friends of the Sovereigns whose bread he ate; and it was asserted that he was the friend and the pupil of his predecessor Sir Roger.

The Just and True Character of Bohun could not be pub-

---

* This piece was reprinted by Gildon in 1695 among Blount's Works.

† That the plagiarism of Blount should have been detected by few of his contemporaries is not wonderful. But it is wonderful that in the Biographia Britannica his Just Vindication should be warmly extolled, without the slightest hint that everything good in it is stolen. The Areopagitica is not the only work which he pillaged on this occasion. He took a splendid passage from Bacon without acknowledgment.

‡ I unhesitatingly attribute this pamphlet to Blount, though it was not reprinted among his works by Gildon. If Blount did not actually write it, he must certainly have superintended the writing. That two men of letters, acting without concert, should bring out within a very short time two treatises on the same subject, one made out of one half of the Areopagitica and the other made out of the other half is incredible. Why Gildon did not choose to reprint the second pamphlet will appear hereafter.

licly sold; but it was widely circulated. While it was passing from hand to hand, and while the Whigs were every where exclaiming against the new censor as a second Lestrange, he was requested to authorise the publication of an anonymous work entitled King William and Queen Mary Conquerors.* He readily and indeed eagerly complied. For there was between the doctrines which he had long professed and the doctrines which were propounded in this treatise a coincidence so exact that many suspected him of being the author; nor was this suspicion weakened by a passage in which a compliment was paid to his political writings. But the real author was that very Blount who was, at that very time, labouring to inflame the public both against the Licensing Act and the licenser. Blount's motives may easily be divined. His own opinions were diametrically opposed to those which, on this occasion, he put forward in the most offensive manner. It is therefore impossible to doubt that his object was to ensnare and to ruin Bohun. It was a base and wicked scheme. But it cannot be denied that the trap was laid and baited with much skill. The republican succeeded in personating a high Tory. The atheist succeeded in personating a high Churchman. The pamphlet concluded with a devout prayer that the God of light and love would open the understanding and govern the will of Englishmen, so that they might see the things which belonged to their peace. The censor was in raptures. In every page he found his own thoughts expressed more plainly than he had ever expressed them. Never before, in his opinion, had the true claim of their Majesties to obedience been so clearly stated. Every Jacobite who read this admirable tract must inevitably be converted. The nonjurors would flock to take the oaths. The nation, so long divided, would at length be united. From these pleasing dreams Bohun was awakened by learning, a few hours after the appearance of the discourse which had charmed him, that the titlepage had set all London in a flame, and that the odious words, King William and Queen Mary Conquerors, had moved the indignation of multitudes who had never read further. Only four days after the publication he heard that the House of Commons had taken the matter up, that the book had been called by some members a rascally book, and that, as the author was unknown, the Serjeant at Arms was in search of the licenser.† Bohun's mind had never been

* Bohun's Autobiography.
† Bohun's Autobiography; Commons' Journals, Jan. 20. 169$\frac{2}{3}$.

strong; and he was entirely unnerved and bewildered by the fury and suddenness of the storm which had burst upon him. He went to the House. Most of the members whom he met in the passages and lobbies frowned on him. When he was put to the bar, and, after three profound obeisances, ventured to lift his head and look round him, he could read his doom in the angry and contemptuous looks which were cast on him from every side. He hesitated, blundered, contradicted him-self, called the Speaker My Lord, and, by his confused way of speaking, raised a tempest of rude laughter which confused him still more. As soon as he had withdrawn, it was un-animously resolved that the obnoxious treatise should be burned in Palace Yard by the common hangman. It was also resolved, without a division, that the King should be requested to remove Bohun from the office of licenser. The poor man, ready to faint with grief and fear, was conducted by the officers of the House to a place of confinement.*

But scarcely was he in his prison when a large body of members clamorously demanded a more important victim. Burnet had, shortly after he became Bishop of Salisbury, addressed to the clergy of his diocese a Pastoral Letter, exhorting them to take the oaths. In one paragraph of this letter he had held language bearing some resemblance to that of the pamphlet which had just been sentenced to the flames. There were indeed distinctions which a judicious and im-partial tribunal would not have failed to notice. But the tribunal before which Burnet was arraigned was neither judi-cious nor impartial. His faults had made him many enemies, and his virtues many more. The discontented Whigs com-plained that he leaned towards the Court, the High Church-men that he leaned towards the Dissenters; nor can it be supposed that a man of so much boldness and so little tact, a man so indiscreetly frank and so restlessly active, had passed through life without crossing the schemes and wound-ing the feelings of some whose opinions agreed with his. He was regarded with peculiar malevolence by Howe. Howe had never, even while he was in office, been in the habit of re-straining his bitter and petulant tongue; and he had recently been turned out of office in a way which had made him un-governably ferocious. The history of his dismission is not accurately known: but there was no doubt that something had happened which had cruelly galled his temper. If rumour could be trusted, he had fancied that Mary was in love with

* Bohun's Autobiography; Commons' Journals, Jan 20, 21. 169$\frac{2}{3}$.

him, and had availed himself of an opportunity which offered itself while he was in attendance on her as Vice Chamberlain to make some advances which had justly moved her indignation. Soon after he was discarded, he was prosecuted for having, in a fit of passion, beaten one of his servants savagely within the verge of the palace. He had pleaded guilty, and had been pardoned: but from this time he showed, on every occasion, the most rancorous personal hatred of his royal mistress, of her husband, and of all who were favoured by either. It was known that the Queen frequently consulted Burnet; and Howe was possessed with the belief that her severity was to be imputed to Burnet's influence.* Now was the time to be revenged. In a long and elaborate speech the spiteful Whig,—for such he still affected to be,—represented Burnet as a Tory of the worst class. "There should be a law," he said, "making it penal for the clergy to introduce politics into their discourses. Formerly they sought to enslave us by crying up the divine and indefeasible right of the hereditary prince. Now they try to arrive at the same result by telling us that we are a conquered people." It was moved that the Bishop should be impeached. To this motion there was an unanswerable objection, which the Speaker pointed out. The Pastoral Letter had been written in 1689, and was therefore covered by the Act of Grace which had been passed in 1690. Yet a member was not ashamed to say, "No matter: impeach him; and force him to plead the Act." Few, however, were disposed to take a course so unworthy of a House of Commons. Some wag cried out, "Burn it; burn it;" and this bad pun ran along the benches, and was received with shouts of laughter. It was moved that the Pastoral Letter should be burned by the common hangman. A long and vehement debate followed. For Burnet was a man warmly loved as well as warmly hated. The great majority of the Whigs stood firmly by him; and his good nature and generosity had made him friends even among the Tories. The contest lasted two days. Montague and Finch, men of widely different opinions, appear to have been foremost among the Bishop's champions. An attempt to get rid of the subject by moving the previous question failed. At length the main question was put; and the Pastoral Letter was condemned to the flames by a small majority in a full house. The Ayes were a hundred and sixty-two; the Noes

* Oldmixon; Narcissus Luttrell's Diary, Nov. and Dec. 1692; Burnet, ii. 334.; Bohun's Autobiography.

a hundred and fifty-five.* The general opinion, at least of the capital, seems to have been that Burnet was cruelly treated.†

He was not naturally a man of fine feelings: and the life which he had led had not tended to make them finer. He had been during many years a mark for theological and political animosity. Grave doctors had anathematised him: ribald poets had lampooned him: princes and ministers had laid snares for his life: he had been long a wanderer and an exile, in constant peril of being kidnapped, struck in the boots, hanged, quartered. Yet none of these things had ever moved him. His selfconceit had been proof against ridicule, and his dauntless temper against danger. But on this occasion his fortitude seems to have failed him. To be stigmatized by the popular branch of the legislature as a teacher of doctrines so servile that they disgusted even Tories, to be joined in one sentence of condemnation with the editor of Filmer, was too much. How deeply Burnet was wounded appeared many years later, when, after his death, his History of his Life and Times was given to the world. In that work he is ordinarily garrulous even to minuteness about all that concerns himself, and sometimes relates with amusing ingenuousness his own mistakes and the censures which those mistakes brought upon him. But about the ignominious judgment passed by the House of Commons on his Pastoral Letter he has preserved a most significant silence.‡

The plot which ruined Bohun, though it did no honour to those who contrived it, produced important and salutary effects. Before the conduct of the unlucky licenser had been brought under the consideration of Parliament, the Commons had resolved, without any division, and, as far as appears, without any discussion, that the Act which subjected literature to a censorship should be continued. But the question had now assumed a new aspect; and the continuation of the Act was no longer regarded as a matter of course. A feeling

---

* Grey's Debates; Commons' Journals, Jan. 21. 23. 169⅔; Bohun's Autobiography; Kennet's Life and Reign of King William and Queen Mary.

† "Most men pitying the Bishop."— Bohun's Autobiography.

‡ The vote of the Commons is mentioned with much feeling in the memoirs which Burnet wrote at the time. "It look'd," he says, "somewhat extraordinary that I, who perhapps was the greatest assertor of publick liberty, from

my first setting out, of any writer of the age, should be soe severely treated as an enemy to it. But the truth was the Toryes never liked me, and the Whiggs hated me because I went not into their notions and passions. But even this, and worse things that may happen to me shall not, I hope, be able to make me depart from moderate principles and the just asserting the liberty of mankind."—Burnet MS. Harl. 6584.

in favour of the liberty of the press, a feeling not yet, it is true, of wide extent or formidable intensity, began to show itself. The existing system, it was said, was prejudicial both to commerce and to learning. Could it be expected that any capitalist would advance the funds necessary for a great literary undertaking, or that any scholar would expend years of toil and research on such an undertaking, while it was possible that, at the last moment, the caprice, the malice, the folly of one man might frustrate the whole design? And was it certain that the law which so grievously restricted both the freedom of trade and the freedom of thought had really added to the security of the State? Had not recent experience proved that the licenser might himself be an enemy of their Majesties, or, worse still, an absurd and perverse friend; that he might suppress a book of which it would be for their interest that every house in the country should have a copy, and that he might readily give his sanction to a libel which tended to make them hateful to their people, and which deserved to be torn and burned by the hand of Ketch? Had the government gained much by establishing a literary police which prevented Englishmen from having the History of the Bloody Circuit, and allowed them, by way of compensation, to read tracts which represented King William and Queen Mary as conquerors?

In that age persons who were not specially interested in a public bill very seldom petitioned Parliament against it or for it. The only petitions therefore which were at this conjuncture presented to the two Houses against the censorship came from booksellers, bookbinders, and printers.* But the opinion which these classes expressed was certainly not confined to them.

The law which was about to expire had lasted eight years. It was renewed for only two years. It appears, from an entry in the Journals of the Commons which unfortunately is defective, that a division took place on an amendment about the nature of which we are left entirely in the dark. The votes were ninety-nine to eighty. In the Lords it was proposed, according to the suggestion offered fifty years before by Milton and stolen from him by Blount, to exempt from the authority of the licenser every book which bore the name of an author or publisher. This amendment was rejected; and the bill passed, but not without a protest signed by eleven peers, who declared that they could not think it for

* Commons' Journals, Feb. 27. 169⅔; Lords' Journals, Mar. 4.

the public interest to subject all learning and true information to the arbitrary will and pleasure of a mercenary and
perhaps ignorant licenser. Among those who protested were
Halifax, Shrewsbury, and Mulgrave, three noblemen belonging to different political parties, but all distinguished by their
literary attainments. It is to be lamented that the signatures
of Tillotson and Burnet, who were both present on that day,
should be wanting. Dorset was absent.*

Blount, by whose exertions and machinations the opposition
to the censorship had been raised, did not live to see that
opposition successful. Though not a very young man, he
was possessed by an insane passion for the sister of his de-
ceased wife. Having long laboured in vain to convince the
object of his love that she might lawfully marry him, he at
last, whether from weariness of life, or in the hope of
touching her heart, inflicted on himself a wound of which,
after languishing long, he died. He has often been mentioned
as a blasphemer and selfmurderer. But the important service
which, by means doubtless most immoral and dishonourable,
he rendered to his country, has passed almost unnoticed.†

State of
Ireland.

Late in this busy and eventful session the attention of the
Houses was called to the condition of Ireland. The government of that kingdom had, during the six months which
followed the surrender of Limerick, been in an unsettled
state. It was not till those Irish troops who adhered to
Sarsfield had sailed for France, and till those who had made
their election to remain at home had been disbanded, that
William at length put forth a proclamation solemnly announcing the termination of the civil war. From the hostility of the aboriginal inhabitants, destitute as they now
were of chiefs, of arms, and of organisation, nothing was to
be apprehended beyond occasional robberies and murders.
But the warcry of the Irishry had scarcely died away when

---

* Lords' Journals, March 8. 169⅔.

† In the article on Blount in the
Biographia Britannica he is extolled as
having borne a principal share in the
emancipation of the press. But the
writer was very imperfectly informed
as to the facts.

It is strange that the circumstances of
Blount's death should be so uncertain.
That he died of a wound inflicted by his
own hand, and that he languished long,
are undisputed facts. The common story
was that he shot himself; and Narcissus
Luttrell, at the time, made an entry to
this effect in his Diary. On the other
hand, Pope, who had the very best op-

portunities of obtaining accurate information, asserts that Blount, " being in
love with a near kinswoman of his, and
rejected, gave himself a stab in the arm,
as pretending to kill himself, of the
consequence of which he really died."—
Note on the Epilogue to the Satires,
Dialogue I. Warburton, who had lived,
first with the heroes of the Dunciad, and
then with the most eminent men of
letters of his time, ought to have known
the truth ; and Warburton, by his silence,
confirms Pope's assertion. Gildon's rhap-
sody about the death of his friend will
suit either story equally.

the murmurs of the Englishry began to be heard. Coningsby was during some months at the head of the administration. He soon made himself in the highest degree odious to the dominant caste. He was an unprincipled man : he was insatiable of riches ; and he was in a situation in which riches were easily to be obtained by an unprincipled man. Immense sums of money, immense quantities of military stores, had been sent over from England. Immense confiscations were taking place in Ireland. The rapacious governor had daily opportunities of embezzling and extorting ; and of those opportunities he availed himself without scruple or shame. This however was not, in the estimation of the colonists, his greatest offence. They might have pardoned his covetousness : but they could not pardon the clemency which he showed to their vanquished and enslaved enemies. His clemency indeed amounted merely to this, that he loved money more than he hated Papists, and that he was not unwilling to sell for a high price a scanty measure of justice to some of the oppressed class. Unhappily, to the ruling minority, sore from recent conflict and drunk with recent victory, the subjugated majority was as a drove of cattle, or rather as a pack of wolves. Man acknowledges in the inferior animals no right inconsistent with his own convenience ; and as man deals with the inferior animals the Cromwellian thought himself at liberty to deal with the Roman Catholic. Coningsby therefore drew on himself a greater storm of obloquy by his few good acts than by his many bad acts. The clamour against him was so violent that he was removed ; and Sidney went over, with the full power and dignity of Lord Lieutenant, to hold a Parliament at Dublin.*

* The charges brought against Coningsby will be found in the Journals of the two Houses of the English Parliament. Those charges were, after the lapse of a quarter of a century, versified by Prior, whom Coningsby had treated with great insolence and harshness. I will quote a few stanzas. It will be seen that the poet condescended to imitate the style of the street ballads.

" Of Nero, tyrant, petty king,
     Who heretofore did reign
  In famed Hibernia, I will sing,
     And in a ditty plain.

" The articles recorded stand
     Against this peerless peer ;
  Search but the archives of the land,
     You'll find them written there."

The story of Gaffney is then related. Coningsby's peculations are described thus :

" Vast quantities of stores did he
     Embezzle and purloin ;
  Of the King's stores he kept a key,
     Converting them to coin.

" The forfeited estates also,
     Both real and personal,
  Did with the stores together go.
     Fierce Cerberus swallow'd all."

The last charge is the favour shown the Roman Catholics :

" Nero, without the least disguise,
     The Papists at all times
  Still favour'd, and their robberies
     Look'd on as trivial crimes.

" The Protestants whom they did rob
     During his government,
  Were forced with patience, like good Job,
     To rest themselves content.

" For he did basely them refuse
     All legal remedy ;
  The Romans still he well did use,
     Still screen'd their roguery."

But the easy temper and graceful manners of Sidney failed
to produce a conciliatory effect. He does not indeed appear
to have been greedy of unlawful gain. But he did not restrain
with a sufficiently firm hand the crowd of subordinate functionaries whom Coningsby's example and protection had encouraged to plunder the public and to sell their good offices
to suitors. Nor was the new Viceroy of a temper to bear
hard on the feeble remains of the native aristocracy. He
therefore speedily became an object of suspicion and aversion
to the Anglosaxon settlers. His first act was to send out the
writs for a general election. The Roman Catholics had been
excluded from every municipal corporation : but no law had
yet deprived them of the county franchise. It is probable
however that not a single Roman Catholic freeholder ventured
to approach the hustings. The members chosen were, with
scarcely an exception, men animated by the spirit of Enniskillen and Londonderry, a spirit eminently heroic in times of
distress and peril, but too often cruel and imperious in the
season of prosperity and power. They detested the civil
treaty of Limerick, and were indignant when they learned
that the Lord Lieutenant fully expected from them a parliamentary ratification of that odious contract, a contract
which gave a licence to the idolatry of the mass, and which
prevented good Protestants from ruining their Popish neighbours by bringing civil actions for injuries done during the
war.*

On the fifth of October 1692 the Parliament met at Dublin in Chichester House. It was very differently composed
from the assembly which had borne the same title in
1689. Scarcely one peer, not one member of the House of
Commons, who had sate at the King's Inn, was to be seen.
To the crowd of O's and Macs, descendants of the old
princes of the island, had succeeded men whose names indicated a Saxon origin. A single O, an apostate from the
faith of his fathers, and three Macs, evidently emigrants
from Scotland, and probably Presbyterians, had seats in
the assembly.

The Parliament, thus composed, had then less than the
powers of the Assembly of Jamaica or of the Assembly of
Virginia. Not only was the legislature which sate at Dublin
subject to the absolute control of the legislature which sate
at Westminster : but a law passed in the fifteenth century,

* An Account of the Sessions of Parliament in Ireland, 1692, London, 1693.

during the administration of the Lord Deputy Poynings, and called by his name, had provided that no bill which had not been considered and approved by the Privy Council of England should be brought into either House in Ireland, and that every bill so considered and approved should be either passed without amendment or rejected.*

The session opened with a solemn recognition of the paramount authority of the mother country. The Commons ordered their clerk to read to them the English Act which required them to take the Oath of Supremacy and to subscribe the Declaration against Transubstantiation. Having heard the Act read, they immediately proceeded to obey it. Addresses were then voted which expressed the warmest gratitude and attachment to the King. Two members, who had been untrue to the Protestant and English interest during the troubles, were expelled. Supplies, liberal when compared with the resources of a country devastated by years of predatory war, were voted with eagerness. But the bill for confirming the Act of Settlement was thought to be too favourable to the native gentry, and, as it could not be amended, was with little ceremony rejected. A Committee of the whole House resolved that the unjustifiable indulgence with which the Irish had been treated since the battle of the Boyne was one of the chief causes of the misery of the kingdom. A Committee of Grievances sate daily till eleven in the evening; and the proceedings of this inquest greatly alarmed the Castle. Many instances of gross venality and knavery on the part of men high in office were brought to light, and many instances also of what was then thought a criminal lenity towards the subject nation. This Papist had been allowed to enlist in the army: that Papist had been allowed to keep a gun: a third had too good a horse: a fourth had been protected against Protestants who wished to bring actions against him for wrongs committed during the years of confusion. The Lord Lieutenant, having obtained nearly as much money as he could expect, determined to put an end to these unpleasant inquiries. He knew, however, that if he quarrelled with the Parliament for treating either peculators or Papists with severity, he should have little support in England. He therefore looked out for a pretext, and was fortunate enough to find one. The Commons had passed a vote which might with some plausibility be represented as

* This Act is 10 H. 7. c. 4. It was explained by another Act, 3 & 4 P. & M. c. 4.

inconsistent with the Poynings statute. Any thing which looked like a violation of that great fundamental law was likely to excite strong disapprobation on the other side of Saint George's Channel. The Viceroy saw his advantage, and availed himself of it. He went to the chamber of the Lords at Chichester House, sent for the Commons, reprimanded them in strong language, charged them with undutifully and ungratefully encroaching on the rights of the mother country, and put an end to the session.*

Those whom he had lectured withdrew full of resentment. The imputation which he had thrown on them was unjust. They had a strong feeling of love and reverence for the land from which they sprang, and looked with confidence for redress to the supreme Parliament. Several of them went to London for the purpose of vindicating themselves and of accusing the Lord Lieutenant. They were favoured with a long and attentive audience, both by the Lords and by the Commons, and were requested to put the substance of what had been said into writing. The humble language of the petitioners, and their protestations that they had never intended to violate the Poynings statute, or to dispute the paramount authority of England, effaced the impression which Sidney's accusations had made. Both Houses addressed the King on the state of Ireland. They censured no delinquent by name: but they expressed an opinion that there had been gross maladministration, that the public had been plundered, and that the Roman Catholics had been treated with unjustifiable tenderness. William in reply promised that what was amiss should be corrected. His friend Sidney was soon recalled, and consoled for the loss of the viceregal dignity with the lucrative place of Master of the Ordnance. The government of Ireland was for a time entrusted to Lords Justices, among whom Sir Henry Capel, a zealous Whig, very little disposed to show indulgence to Papists, had the foremost place.

The prorogation drew nigh; and still the fate of the Tri-

---

* The history of this session I have taken from the Journals of the Irish Lords and Commons, from the narratives laid in writing before the English Lords and Commons by members of the Parliament of Ireland, and from a pamphlet entitled a Short Account of the Sessions of Parliament in Ireland, 1692, London, 1693. Burnet seems to me to have taken a correct view of the dispute; ii. 118. "The English in Ireland thought the government favoured the Irish too much: some said this was the effect of bribery, whereas others thought it was necessary to keep them safe from the prosecutions of the English, who hated them, and were much sharpened against them. . . . There were also great complaints of an ill administration, chiefly in the revenue, in the pay of the army, and in the embezzling of stores."

ennial Bill was uncertain. Some of the ablest ministers
thought the bill a good one; and, even had they thought it
a bad one, they would probably have tried to dissuade their
master from rejecting it. It was impossible, however, to
remove from his mind the impression that a concession on
this point would seriously impair his authority. Not relying
on the judgment of his ordinary advisers, he sent Portland to
ask the opinion of Sir William Temple. Temple had made a
retreat for himself at a place called Moor Park, in the neighbourhood of Farnham. The country round his dwelling was
almost a wilderness. His amusement during some years had
been to create in the waste what those Dutch burgomasters,
among whom he had passed some of the best years of his life,
would have considered as a paradise. His hermitage had
been occasionally honoured by the presence of the King, who
had from a boy known and esteemed the author of the Triple
Alliance, and who was well pleased to find among the heath
and furze of the wilds of Surrey, a spot which seemed to be
part of Holland, a straight canal, a terrace, rows of clipped
trees, and rectangular beds of flowers and potherbs.

The King
refuses to
pass the
Triennial
Bill.

Portland now repaired to this secluded abode and consulted
the oracle. Temple was decidedly of opinion that the bill
ought to pass. He was apprehensive that the reasons which
led him to form this opinion might not be fully and correctly
reported to the King by Portland, who was indeed as brave a
soldier and as trusty a friend as ever lived, whose natural
abilities were not inconsiderable, and who, in some departments of business, had great experience, but who was very
imperfectly acquainted with the history and constitution of
England. As the state of Sir William's health made it impossible for him to go himself to Kensington, he determined
to send his secretary thither. The secretary was a poor
scholar of four or five and twenty, under whose plain garb
and ungainly deportment were concealed some of the choicest
gifts that have ever been bestowed on any of the children of
men, rare powers of observation, brilliant wit, grotesque
invention, humour of the most austere flavour, yet exquisitely
delicious, eloquence singularly pure, manly, and perspicuous.
This young man was named Jonathan Swift. He was born
in Ireland, but would have thought himself insulted if he
had been called an Irishman. He was of unmixed English
blood, and, through life, regarded the aboriginal population
of the island in which he first drew breath as an alien and a
servile caste. He had in the late reign kept terms at the

University of Dublin, but had been distinguished there only by his irregularities, and had with difficulty obtained his degree. At the time of the Revolution, he had, with many thousands of his fellow colonists, taken refuge in the mother country from the violence of Tyrconnel, and had been so fortunate as to obtain shelter at Moor Park.[*] For that shelter, however, he had to pay a heavy price. He was thought to be sufficiently remunerated for his services with twenty pounds a year and his board. He dined at the second table. Sometimes, indeed, when better company was not to be had, he was honoured by being invited to play at cards with his patron; and, on such occasions, Sir William was so generous as to give his antagonist a little silver to begin with.[†] The humble student would not have dared to raise his eyes to a lady of family: but, when he had become a clergyman, he began, after the fashion of the clergymen of that generation, to make love to a pretty waitingmaid, who was the chief ornament of the servants' hall, and whose name is inseparably associated with his in a sad and mysterious history.

Swift many years later confessed some part of what he felt when he found himself on his way to Court. His spirit had been bowed down, and might seem to have been broken, by calamities and humiliations. The language which he was in the habit of holding to his patron, as far as we can judge from the specimens which still remain, was that of a lacquey, or rather of a beggar.[‡] A sharp word or a cold look of the master sufficed to make the servant miserable during several days.[§] But this tameness was merely the tameness with which a tiger, caught, caged, and starved, submits to the keeper who brings him food. The humble menial was at heart the haughtiest, the most aspiring, the most vindictive, the most despotic of men. And now at length a great, a boundless prospect was opening before him. To William he was already slightly known. At Moor Park the King had sometimes, when his host was confined by gout to an easy chair, been attended by the secretary about the grounds. His majesty had condescended to teach his companion the Dutch way of cutting and eating asparagus, and had graciously asked whether Mr. Swift would like to have a captain's commission in a cavalry regiment. But now for the first time the young man was to stand in the royal presence as a

---

[*] As to Swift's extraction and early life, see the Anecdotes written by himself.

[†] Journal to Stella, Letter liii.

[‡] See Swift's Letter to Temple of Oct. 6. 1694.

[§] Journal to Stella, Letter xix.

counsellor. He was admitted into the closet, delivered a letter from Temple, and explained and enforced the arguments which that letter contained, concisely, but doubtless with clearness and ability. There was, he said, no reason to think that short Parliaments would be more disposed than long Parliaments to encroach on the just prerogatives of the Crown. In fact the Parliament which had, in the preceding generation, waged war against a king, led him captive, sent him to prison, to the bar, to the scaffold, was known in our annals as emphatically the Long Parliament. Never would such disasters have befallen the monarchy but for the fatal law which secured that assembly from dissolution.* In this reasoning there was, it must be owned, a flaw which a man less shrewd than William might easily detect. That one restriction of the royal prerogative had been mischievous did not prove that another restriction would be salutary. It by no means followed, because one sovereign had been ruined by being unable to get rid of a hostile Parliament, that another sovereign might not be ruined by being forced to part with a friendly Parliament. To the great mortification of the ambassador, his arguments failed to shake the King's resolution. On the fourteenth of March the Commons were summoned to the Upper House : the title of the Triennial Bill was read ; and it was announced, after the ancient form, that the King and Queen would take the matter into their consideration. The Parliament was then prorogued.

Soon after the prorogation William set out for the Continent. It was necessary that, before his departure, he should make some important changes. He was resolved not to discard Nottingham, on whose integrity, a virtue rare among English statesmen, he placed a well founded reliance. Yet, if Nottingham remained Secretary of State, it was impossible to employ Russell at sea. Russell, though much mortified, was induced to accept a lucrative place in the household ; and two naval officers of great note in their profession, Killegrew and Delaval, were placed at the Board of Admiralty and entrusted with the command of the Channel Fleet.† These arrangements caused much murmuring among the Whigs : for Killegrew and Delaval were certainly Tories, and were by many suspected of being Jacobites. But other promotions which took place at the same time proved that the King wished to bear himself evenly between the hostile factions. Nottingham had, during a year, been the sole

Marginal note: Ministerial arrangements.

---

* Swift's Anecdotes.   † London Gazette, March 27. 1693.

Secretary of State. He was now joined with a colleague in whose society he must have felt himself very ill at ease, John Trenchard. Trenchard belonged to the extreme section of the Whig party. He was a Taunton man, animated by that spirit which had, during two generations, peculiarly distinguished Taunton. He had, in the days of Popeburnings and of Protestant flails, been one of the renowned Green Riband Club: he had been an active member of several stormy Parliaments: he had brought in the first Exclusion Bill: he had been deeply concerned in the plots formed by the chiefs of the opposition: he had fled to the Continent: he had been long an exile; and he had been excepted by name from the general pardon of 1686. Though his life had been passed in turmoil, his temper was naturally calm: but he was closely connected with a set of men whose passions were far fiercer than his own. He had married the sister of Hugh Speke, one of the falsest and most malignant of the libellers who brought disgrace on the cause of constitutional freedom. Aaron Smith, the solicitor of the Treasury, a man in whom the fanatic and the pettifogger were strangely united, possessed too much influence over the new Secretary, with whom he had, ten years before, discussed plans of rebellion at the Rose. Why Trenchard was selected in preference to many men of higher rank and greater ability for a post of the first dignity and importance, it is difficult to say. It seems however that, though he bore the title and drew the salary of Secretary of State, he was not trusted with any of the graver secrets of State, and that he was little more than a superintendent of police, charged to look after the printers of unlicensed books, the pastors of nonjuring congregations, and the haunters of treason taverns.*

Another Whig of far higher character was called at the same time to a far higher place in the administration. The Great Seal had now been four years in commission. Since Maynard's retirement, the constitution of the Court of Chancery had commanded little respect. Trevor, who was the First Commissioner, wanted neither parts nor learning: but his integrity was with good reason suspected; and the duties, which, as Speaker of the House of Commons, he had to perform during four or five months in the busiest part of every year, made it impossible for him to be an efficient judge in equity. The suitors complained that they had to wait a

* Burnet, ii. 108., and Speaker Onslow's Note; Sprat's True Account of the   Horrid Conspiracy; Letter to Trenchard, 1694.

most unreasonable time for judgment, and that, when, after long delay, a judgment had been pronounced, it was very likely to be reversed on appeal. Meanwhile there was no minister of justice, no great functionary to whom it especially belonged to advise the King as to the appointment of Judges, of Counsel for the Crown, of Justices of the Peace.* It was known that William was sensible of the inconvenience of this state of things; and, during several months, there had been flying rumours that a Lord Keeper or a Lord Chancellor would soon be appointed.† The name most frequently mentioned was that of Nottingham. But the reasons which had prevented him from accepting the Great Seal in 1689 had, since that year, rather gained than lost strength. William at length fixed his choice on Somers.

Somers was only in his forty-second year; and five years had not elapsed since, on the great day of the trial of the Bishops, his powers had first been made known to the world. From that time his fame had been steadily and rapidly rising. Neither in forensic nor in parliamentary eloquence had he any superior. The consistency of his public conduct had gained for him the entire confidence of the Whigs; and the urbanity of his manners had conciliated the Tories. It was not without great reluctance that he consented to quit an assembly over which he exercised an immense influence for an assembly where it would be necessary for him to sit in silence. He had been but a short time in great practice. His savings were small. Not having the means of supporting a hereditary title, he must, if he accepted the high dignity which was offered to him, preside during some years in the Upper House without taking part in the debates. The opinion of others, however, was that he would be more useful as head of the law than even as head of the Whig party in the Commons. He was sent for to Kensington, and called into the Council Chamber. Caermarthen spoke in the name of the King. "Sir John," he said, "it is necessary for the public service that you should take this charge upon you; and I have it in command from His Majesty to say that he can admit of no excuse." Somers submitted. The seal was delivered to him, with a patent which entitled him to a pension of two thousand a year from the day on which he should quit his office; and he was immediately sworn in a Privy Councillor and Lord Keeper.‡

* Burnet, ii. 107.
† These rumours are more than once mentioned in Narcissus Luttrell's Diary.
‡ London Gazette, March 27. 1693; Narcissus Luttrell's Diary.

The Gazette which announced these changes in the administration, announced also the King's departure. He set out for Holland on the twenty-fourth of March.

He left orders that the Estates of Scotland should, after a recess of more than two years and a half, be again called together. Hamilton, who had lived many months in retirement, had, since the fall of Melville, been reconciled to the Court, and now consented to quit his retreat, and to occupy Holyrood House as Lord High Commissioner. It was necessary that one of the Secretaries of State for Scotland should be in attendance on the King. The Master of Stair had therefore gone to the Continent. His colleague, Johnstone was chief manager for the Crown at Edinburgh, and was charged to correspond regularly with Carstairs, who never quitted William.*

It might naturally have been expected that the session would be turbulent. The Parliament was that very Parliament which had, in 1689, passed, by overwhelming majorities, all the most violent resolutions which Montgomery and his club could frame, which had refused supplies, which had proscribed the ministers of the Crown, which had closed the Courts of Justice, which had seemed bent on turning Scotland into an oligarchical republic. In 1690 the Estates had been in a better temper. Yet, even in 1690, they had, when the ecclesiastical polity of the realm was under consideration, paid little deference to what was well known to be the royal wish. They had abolished patronage : they had sanctioned the rabbling of the Episcopal clergy : they had refused to pass a Toleration Act. It seemed likely that they would still be found unmanageable when questions touching religion came before them ; and such questions it was unfortunately necessary to bring forward. William had, during the recess, attempted to persuade the General Assembly of the Church to receive into communion such of the old curates as should subscribe the Confession of Faith and should submit to the government of Synods. But the attempt had failed ; and the Assembly had consequently been dissolved by the representative of the King. Unhappily, the Act which established the Presbyterian polity had not defined the extent of the power which was to be exercised by the Sovereign over the Spiritual Courts. No sooner therefore had the dissolution been announced than the Moderator requested permission to

* Burnet, ii. 123. ; Carstairs Papers.

speak. He was told that he was now merely a private person. As a private person he requested a hearing, and protested, in the name of his brethren, against the royal mandate. The right, he said, of the officers of the Church to meet and deliberate touching her interests was derived from her Divine Head, and was not dependent on the pleasure of the temporal magistrate. His brethren stood up, and by an approving murmur signified their concurrence in what their President had said. Before they retired they fixed a day for their next meeting.* It was indeed a very distant day; and when it came neither minister nor elder attended: for even the boldest members shrank from a complete rupture with the civil power. But, though there was not open war between the Church and the Government, they were estranged from each other, jealous of each other, and afraid of each other. No progress had been made towards a reconciliation when the Estates met; and which side the Estates would take might well be doubted.

But the proceedings of this strange Parliament, in almost every one of its sessions, falsified all the predictions of politicians. It had once been the most unmanageable of senates. It was now the most obsequious. Yet the old men had again met in the old hall. There were all the most noisy agitators of the club, with the exception of Montgomery, who was dying of want and of a broken heart in a garret far from his native land. There were the canting Ross and the perfidious Annandale. There was Sir Patrick Hume, lately created a peer, and henceforth to be called Lord Polwarth, but still as eloquent as when his interminable declamations and dissertations ruined the expedition of Argyle. Nevertheless, the whole spirit of the Assembly had undergone a change. The members listened with profound respect to the royal letter, and returned an answer in reverential and affectionate language. An extraordinary aid of a hundred and fourteen thousand pounds sterling was granted to the Crown. Severe laws were enacted against the Jacobites. The legislation on ecclesiastical matters was as Erastian as William himself could have desired. An Act was passed requiring all ministers of the Established Church to swear fealty to their Majesties, and directing the General Assembly to receive

* Register of the Actings or Proceedings of the General Assembly of the Church of Scotland, held at Edinburgh, Jan. 15. 1692, collected and extracted from the Records by the Clerk thereof. This interesting record was printed for the first time in 1852.

into communion those Episcopalian ministers, not yet deprived, who should declare that they conformed to the Presbyterian doctrine and discipline.* Nay, the Estates carried adulation so far as to make it their humble request to the King that he would be pleased to confer a Scotch peerage on his favourite Portland. This was indeed their chief petition. They did not ask for redress of a single grievance. They contented themselves with hinting in general terms that there were abuses which required correction, and with referring the King for fuller information to his own Ministers, the Lord High Commissioner and the Secretary of State.†

There was one subject on which it may seem strange that even the most servile of Scottish Parliaments should have kept silence. More than a year had elapsed since the massacre of Glencoe; and it might have been expected that the whole assembly, peers, commissioners of shires, commissioners of burghs, would with one voice have demanded a strict investigation into that great crime. It is certain, however, that no motion for investigation was made. The state of the Gaelic clans was indeed taken into consideration. A law was passed for the more effectual suppressing of depredations and outrages beyond the Highland line; and in that law was inserted a special proviso reserving to Mac Callum More his hereditary jurisdiction. But it does not appear, either from the public records of the proceedings of the Estates, or from those private letters in which Johnstone regularly gave Carstairs an account of what had passed, that any speaker made any allusion to the fate of Mac Ian and Mac Ian's tribe.‡ The only explanation of this extraordinary silence seems to be that the public men who were assembled in the capital of Scotland knew little and cared little about the fate of a thieving tribe of Celts. The injured clan, bowed down by fear of the all powerful Campbells, and little

---

* Act. Parl. Scot., June 12. 1693.

† Act. Parl. Scot., June 15. 1693.

‡ The editor of the Carstairs Papers was evidently very desirous, from whatever motive, to disguise this most certain and obvious truth. He therefore, with gross dishonesty, prefixed to some of Johnstone's letters descriptions which may possibly impose on careless readers. For example, Johnstone wrote to Carstairs on the 18th of April, before it was known that the session would be a quiet one, " All arts have been used and will be used to embroil matters." The editor's account of the contents of this letter is as follows: " Arts used to embroil matters with reference to the affair of Glencoe." Again, Johnstone, in a letter written some weeks later, complained that the liberality and obsequiousness of the Estates had not been duly appreciated. " Nothing," he says, " is to be done to gratify the Parliament, I mean that they would have reckoned a gratification." The editor's account of the contents of this letter is as follows: " Complains that the Parliament is not to be gratified by an inquiry into the massacre of Glencoe."

accustomed to resort to the constituted authorities of the kingdom for protection or redress, presented no petition to the Estates. The story of the butchery had been told at coffeehouses, but had been told in different ways. Very recently, one or two books, in which the facts were but too truly related, had come forth from the secret presses of London. But those books were not publicly exposed to sale. They bore the name of no responsible author. The Jacobite writers were, as a class, savagely malignant and utterly regardless of truth. Since the Macdonalds did not complain, a prudent man might naturally be unwilling to incur the displeasure of the King, of the ministers, and of the most powerful family in Scotland, by bringing forward an accusation grounded on nothing but reports wandering from mouth to mouth, or pamphlets which no licenser had approved, to which no author had put his name, and which no bookseller ventured to place in his shopwindow. But whether this be or be not the true solution, it is certain that the Estates separated quietly after a session of two months, during which, as far as can now be discovered, the name of Glencoe was not once uttered in the Parliament House.

This book, designed by
Eric Tschumi,
is a production of
Heron Books, London

Printed in Switzerland